after nine years and took the children—but more particularly she took her son. As Yates wrote in *A Good School,* he and his father had an "unspoken agreement":

> I had been given over to my mother. There was pain in that assumption—for both of us, I would guess, though I can't speak for him—yet there was an uneasy justice in it too. Much as I might wish it otherwise, I did prefer my mother. I knew she was foolish and irresponsible, that she talked too much, that she made crazy emotional scenes over nothing and could be counted on to collapse in a crisis, but I had come to suspect, dismally, that my own personality might be built along much the same lines. In ways that were neither profitable nor especially pleasant, she and I were a comfort to one another.

By the time Yates wrote these lines he'd had fifty years to reflect on just how alike he and his mother were, indeed to be reminded of it again and again, and while he despised his mother's failings all the more for seeing them in himself, such an awareness certainly improved (and in some ways was limited to) his art. As a young man he discovered Flaubert, and Dookie became his foremost Emma; his sense of her, and hence humanity, proved vital to his bleakly deterministic worldview. As he explained in a 1972 interview, his characters "all rush around trying to do their best— trying to live well, within their known or unknown limitations, doing what they can't help doing, ultimately and inevitably failing because they can't help being the people they are. *That's* what brings on the calamity at the end." Yates's compassion for human weakness, for the flaws that make failure so inevitable, is everywhere in his work—with the occasional exception of certain characters based on his mother, which range from the rounded and essentially forgivable Alice Prentice in *A Special Providence* to Dickensian grotesques such as Pookie in *The Easter Parade* and Gloria Drake in *Cold Spring Harbor.* Tellingly or not, Yates also tended to be hard on characters based on himself. But all are worthy of our sympathy in at least one respect: They try to do their best but fail because of limitations over which they have no control. "After all, she was only human," Yates liked to say of his mother, having just relieved himself of some scathing diatribe on the subject.

For much of Yates's early life, though, he and Dookie were a comfort to one another. Daughter Ruth was something of a comfort as well, but she was more her father's child, and after the divorce she continued to visit him as much as possible; at one point she even pretended to need weekly (rather than monthly) orthodontia as a pretext for going into the city. But Richard had never really known his father and never really would; he preferred to stay home with Dookie, a kindred soul whom he resembled not only in temperament but appearance—from the great mournful eyes and dark pouches beneath them to the never-corrected overbite that made his plump upper lip protrude slightly—features he despised.

The first thing Dookie did after the divorce was take that trip to Paris. She'd been accepted by the Académie Julian to study under the eminent sculptor Paul Landowski, but also she wanted to expose her precocious three-year-old to the kind of high culture that only Paris could provide.* She left Ruth behind with her sister Elsa, a decision that was likely a mutual one. There was the expense of taking both children, and while it seems reasonable to take a sentient eight-year-old for company rather than a toddler, Ruth was probably only too happy to stay behind, knowing even then what a trip abroad with Dookie might entail.

What Dookie hoped to achieve was perhaps more complicated than she was willing to admit: On the one hand, she meant to learn her craft from a great master and perhaps achieve greatness herself; but the girl from Greenville might also observe Continental manners firsthand, and refine the kind of sophisticated persona that might enable her, along with her reputation as an artist, to be admitted into the highest social circles. "The art of sculpture and the idea of aristocracy had always appealed to her equally," Yates wrote in *A Good School*, a notion he explored further in "Oh, Joseph, I'm So Tired": "Her idea was that any number of rich

---

*Later Yates said that his mother's *excuse* for dragging him around Europe was to "broaden his horizons," but really it was just a matter of ensuring that his father would keep paying the bills. One suspects it was a little of both.

people, all of them gracious and aristocratic, would soon discover her: they would want her sculpture to decorate their landscaped gardens, and they would want to make her their friend for life." It's possible that Dookie's artistic aspirations were animated to some extent by petty snobbery; but it's also fair to point out—as many do—that she worked hard to realize such talent as she had, and often under circumstances that were far from aristocratic. And then, too, it's hard to blame her for hoping to make friends with the sort of people to whom it might never occur to collect *Saturday Evening Post* covers in bound volumes.

Whether Dookie found what she was looking for in Paris is impossible to say. What was meant to be a year of study was cut short after six months or so, when the stock market crashed and she had to come home. The toddler Richard remembered little or nothing of the whole expedition and rarely spoke of it, though he reported in his fiction that it had been "confused and unpleasant" for his mother—who could hardly pronounce, much less speak, French, and who was almost certainly broke most of the time (no matter how much she later milked the subject for conversational purposes). As for her work as a sculptor, it must have improved somewhat, since she began to have her first minor successes not long after her return, and certainly she liked to invoke Landowski as one of her mentors.

But perhaps the most significant impact was psychological: Dookie seems to have become even less conventional after Paris, a liberation that may have begun amid the studios and cafés of the Left Bank, or else was just the inevitable letting-go of a lonely divorcée at loose ends (in Depression-era Greenwich Village, no less). Somewhat paradoxically, though, she remained much concerned with matters of propriety: reluctant to speak of indelicate things, and always an elegant dresser—though also rather loud and crude at times, and her well-chosen clothes tended to be stained in some sadly obvious way. Perhaps all this was reconciled in the name of worldliness, or nobility at odds with circumstance, but one can't help wondering how it affected her son, who inherited the same contradictions to a remarkable degree. Also (as a young man anyway) he cherished the dream of Paris as a place where one might find oneself as an artist and a man, though in this respect his mother wasn't the only influence.

. . .

For a while after her return, Dookie and the children were all but alone in the world. Her family hadn't approved of the divorce, and later relished the chance to spell this out by refusing to come to Ruth's wedding. In the meantime they simply stayed away. Dookie's older sister Elsa was the one exception, and since she lived nearby and was willing to help (her ill-fated husband lay a few years in the future), she must have been a comfort—anyway up to a point. "Elsa was very sensible in contrast to Dook," Yates's first wife Sheila remembered. "But she rode it pretty hard." The woman appears as the "bossy and meddlesome and condescending" Eva in *A Special Providence,* who disapproves of her sister's marriage and then of her divorce; still, Elsa deserves a certain amount of credit just for sticking around, as she did for the duration of Yates's childhood and beyond, amid sporadic (and no doubt salutary) estrangements. Her grandnephew Peter described her as "a stable center" in the children's lives, suggesting the lack of that quality in every other respect. And while Yates would sometimes complain that it was his lot to live among women—a mother, sister, and maiden aunt; later two wives and three daughters—he seemed grateful to Elsa for propping his mother up through her many misadventures.

And Elsa had every reason to be exasperated, of course. A notable cause of Dookie's loneliness, then as later, was her singular lack of compunction where money was concerned. Her only income at the height of the Depression was whatever small amount Vincent could spare in the way of alimony and child support, and yet she insisted on a standard of gentility—large apartments in the Village or rented homes in "nice" suburban neighborhoods—that she couldn't remotely afford to maintain. When the money ran out, as it always did, she'd sponge off friends and neighbors until there was nobody left and it was time to move on. "Dook's fantastic schemes have a horribly dreamlike almost nightmarish quality when they begin to crash about her ears," Sheila Yates wrote her husband in the fifties, when such disasters had become a dreadful theme in their lives. But the whole "hysterical odyssey" had begun some twenty years before, as Dookie's determination to be an artist—to vindicate herself in the eyes of a patronizing, provincial family and ex-husband—distracted her almost entirely from the more practical aspects of motherhood.

And while the bills went unpaid and the family was evicted from one place after another, Dookie became all the more emotionally dependent on her children. She encouraged them to view their chaotic lives as an adventure—the three of them against the world. "She was a free spirit," Yates wrote in "Regards at Home." "*We* were free spirits, and only a world composed of creditors or of 'people like your father' could fail to appreciate the romance of our lives." As part of the romance Dookie would read aloud from *Great Expectations* when they were hungry or awaiting another eviction. The children could further identify with Dickens in terms of their seedy clothes, which made them conspicuous at whatever new school, in whatever "nice" neighborhood, they found themselves from one year to the next. At the time Yates adored what he perceived to be his mother's "gallantry and goodness," and since he made few friends—perpetually being "the only new boy and the only poor boy"—he became almost desperately attached to Dookie, and vice versa. For the rest of his life he was terrified of being left alone, and during childhood his shattered nerves were evidenced by (among other things) a bad stammer, which later seemed to return in the form of a chronic cough that became more pronounced when he was ill at ease.

And what about the art for which all these sacrifices were made? "She wasn't a very good sculptor," Yates put it bluntly in "Joseph," referring mostly (if not entirely) to the "stiff and amateurish" quality of her early work, circa 1932. Her specialty, after Paris, was modeled garden figures cast in lead—nymphs and geese and pipe-playing Pans that were meant to decorate the lawns of the wealthy but usually ended up as part of a growing clutter that followed the family into their next living space, however modest. But Dookie remained undaunted; a big sale or "one-man exhibition" was forever in the offing, and while occasional little coups did occur, they never brought much in the way of money or acclaim. Meanwhile Dookie's favorite model for her faunlets, often posed in the nude, was the small, obliging Richard; in *A Special Providence* the mortified four-year-old son of Alice Prentice hunches over to cover his genitals, "round-eyed with humiliation," while neighborhood children laugh at him from a studio window.*

Many years later Yates told his youngest daughter, Gina, that what he remembered best about his mother was her body odor—that she smelled bad, no matter how hard she tried to clean herself, doubtless the "rotten tomato" smell he attributes to Gloria Drake in *Cold Spring Harbor*. And body odor is one of many ignominious, nasty physical details that recur among Dookie's fictional personae: rotten teeth, lipstick smeared outside the mouth, stained clothing, sweat-darkened armpits, and so on—most of which work to suggest the essential instability of the woman, her sweaty incipient hysteria. In many cases Yates makes the matter explicit, as in "Regards at Home": "It had often occurred to me that she was crazy—there had been people who said she was crazy as long as I could remember." Gloria Drake is flatly described as "mentally ill," and everywhere in Yates's work there are scenes of screaming, writhing fits thrown by mother characters ("after she'd lost all control and gone on shouting anyway"). In short, it seems far from implausible that Dookie suffered from a degree of mental illness, possibly the manic depression that afflicted her son (a disorder that's almost entirely genetic in origin), or perhaps some other form of mood disorder. And even if there weren't such a hereditary link, the chaos she always engendered would have certainly taken a psychological toll. As it happened, Yates later complained of "cruel, bullying voices" in his head that made it hard to sleep and often horrific to dream—voices that evoked some bizarre tantrum or another that he'd overheard as a child.

After a couple of years in a rural Connecticut farmhouse (though it was far beyond Dookie's means, its chief virtue was a large barn where she could work on her sculpture), the family moved to its first and perhaps best Greenwich Village apartment—the place on Bedford Street so lovingly described in "Joseph": "There were six or eight old houses facing

---

*A childhood friend recalled seeing a Pan figurine for which the very young Yates had modeled. Dookie had altered the face, but the spindly upper body (above the goat legs) was recognizably Richard.

our side of the courtyard . . . and ours was probably the showplace of the row because the front room on its ground floor was two stories high." Dookie crowded the room with her garden figures and turned it into a "high, wide, light-flooded studio," while Ruth and Richard shared one of the two small bedrooms upstairs. When alone together, the children mostly spent their time either playing in the courtyard ("a few stunted city trees and a patch of grass" that Dookie always called "the garden") or listening to afternoon children's programs on their Majestic radio in the dining room. Toward the back of the ground floor was the least appealing part of this or any of their apartments: a "roach-infested kitchen" with "a stove and sink that were never clean" and "a brown wooden icebox with its dark, ever-melting block of ice." Apart from an instinct for rudimentary tidiness that she passed on to her son, Dookie had little apparent relish for detailed housework. Rather than wash the dirty dishes, she'd regularly send her children out to buy paper plates, and Yates mentions the odors of mildew and cat droppings and plasticene to evoke the basic bouquet of his childhood.

Most days Dookie worked hard at her craft, but it would be several years before she had any sort of gainful employment, and the leisure hours must have seemed long at times. Later she became active in a number of art organizations, but as long as her children were still at home there was less need for such distraction. The three of them were together constantly, and their principal way of killing time was going to the movies. As an adult Yates lost the habit entirely, and once when someone left him a television he never bothered to plug it in; but he often startled friends with detailed and rather emotional accounts of the movies he'd seen in the thirties. "I wasn't a bookish child," he wrote in a 1981 essay; "reading was such hard work for me that I avoided it whenever possible. But I wasn't exactly the rough-and-ready type either, and so the movies filled a double need: They gave me an awful lot of cheap story material and a good place to hide." Slight, frail, and morbidly shy, Yates felt intimidated by the tough Italian kids in the Village, and for a long time wasn't entirely at ease in any company other than his mother and sister's. Like the Drakes in *Cold Spring Harbor*, the three didn't bother to check show times, but simply wandered in off the street: "[M]uch of their pleasure came from waiting for a prolonged confusion to clarify itself on the screen"; then, after the movie had come full circle, they'd watch it again "to intensify the story they already knew." Such total insularity in their everyday routines might have led to rather esoteric behavior, not unlike the Drakes' "ritual-ized baby talk that no outsider could probably have followed." Little wonder Yates had trouble adjusting to the various institutions (prep school, the army, and so on) of the outside world.

Despite a lifelong dependence on her children, Dookie was not entirely without friends; in fact her new Village milieu afforded a number of con-genial people who seemed to appreciate her as an artist and hostess. One of her neighbors on Bedford Street was Howard Cushman, best known as E. B. White's roommate at Cornell. Dookie and "Cush" became friends, and at least once he brought the illustrious White around to meet the twelve-year-old Ruth, who'd started her own weekly courtyard newspa-per modeled somewhat after *The New Yorker* (Ruth's younger brother would also become a great fan of the magazine). Cushman's daughter from a previous marriage, Nancy, was Richard's age and a playmate of sorts. One of her father's gags was to drape her in his suit jacket and crouch behind her with his own arms in the sleeves—a routine Yates described in "Joseph" and later adopted with his own daughters: "the sight of a smiling little girl . . . waving and gesturing with huge, expres-sive hands, was enough to make everyone smile." Such parlor tricks formed the lighter side of Village domestic life.

Perhaps the most abiding friendship of Dookie's adult life was with Cushman's ex-wife Elisabeth, a journalist who'd met her former husband in the city room of a New Rochelle newspaper. On the surface she and Dookie had little in common: Elisabeth Cushman was a self-supporting socialist who (as Yates characterized her in "Trying Out for the Race") "liked to have it known that both her parents were illiterate Irish immi-grants"; while Dookie's ancestors were scarcely more distinguished, this was the sort of thing that chafed at her quasi-aristocratic Republican sen-sibilities. But happily each was rather bitter about life and appreciated the other's mordant wit—"they would get together and trash things," as one friend put it—beyond which lay an even deeper affinity. "Richard, we are growing old," Cushman wrote the nineteen-year-old Yates in the course of describing how she and Dookie had just celebrated VE-day. "You were too young to know the evenings when a pinch bottle, Haig and Haig, was but a drop in our bucket." Judging by his fiction, however, Yates had known such evenings all too vividly, as well as other evenings and other drinking companions—the various boozy, dilettantish divorcées whom Dookie cultivated in the Village, the Natalie Crawford and Sloane Cabot types who "liked to use words like 'simpatico' " and wrote unsalable radio scripts whose characters included "a sad-eyed, seven-year-old philosopher" with a comical stammer.

There was a lot of drinking, and the consequences were often unfortunate given the presence of small children. Yates never quite got over the shock, however often repeated, of seeing strange men at his mother's breakfast table, and made a point of never exposing his daughters to any woman who was not his wife. Indeed, Dookie's alcoholism and love affairs suggested a larger, more troubling theme to Yates's mind—what he referred to, reluctantly in so many words, as an improper closeness with his mother. One hastens to add that Yates despised psychological jargon and wasn't apt to invoke Oedipus complexes and the like, much less accuse his mother of sinister motives, conscious or otherwise. Which is not to say that he didn't blame her, and deeply, for the damage done. Such was his sense of helplessness as a child—reinforced in any number of ways by his mother—that he'd often throw panic-stricken, seizurelike tantrums when she'd leave him alone at night, and he never forgot what it was like to lie awake in the dark, wondering when or if she'd ever come home. And when she did, late, drunk, she had a tendency to comfort her son by getting into bed with him—at least once, as in "Joseph," she vomited on his pillow. "Yates felt enraged at his mother," said his psychiatrist Winthrop Burr, who recalled that Yates (usually circumspect to the point of brusqueness during their sessions) would often get "on the edge of tearful" when he discussed her. Her alcoholic inconstancy, along with the mutual dependence she always elicited, was a disastrous combination. "It was as if he were her only confidant," said Burr. "He gave a picture of the two of them alone in the world. The sister was a blank."

To a great extent the sister was overshadowed by the mother (Prentice's lack of a sibling in A Special Providence is telling), at least in terms of pathological impact. But Ruth, too, was much on Yates's mind, especially in light of later events. On the rare occasions that he'd mention her as an adult, he tended to say they had little in common, and in a way this was true; but it was also misleading, if only by omission, perhaps because Yates preferred to work out the deeper truth in his fiction. Ruth was characterized as "the most stable member of the family," the one like her father, and as such she was a good sister to Richard. "They were comrades in a difficult situation," said Martha Speer, Yates's second wife, who remembered stories of Ruth and her brother having to forage for food and generally look out for each other. But it was more than a matter of Ruth's being the (relatively) responsible, protective one—she was also the imaginative one, at least as a child, and almost as painfully sensitive as her brother. Like him she aspired to be a writer from a very early age: There were the weekly newspapers she devised, the plays she acted out with paper dolls, and at night she'd lull Richard to sleep with stories she made up in the various bedrooms they shared ("someone should probably have told my mother that a girl and boy of our ages ought to have separate rooms," Yates noted ruefully in "Joseph"). And all her life Ruth cried a lot, though the cause was liable to be emotional rather than physical. Like Sarah Grimes in *The Easter Parade*, the young Ruth split her head open on a steel pipe,* which left a small but permanent scar as well as the impression, which her brother never forgot, that she bore pain remarkably well.

But perhaps Ruth's most salient feature is suggested by Sarah's "look of trusting innocence that would never leave her." Such innocence, coupled with the awful insecurity she shared with her brother, would lead Ruth into a ruinous life-wrecking marriage—or so Yates believed, and characteristically he blamed his mother. "Even now, at nineteen," he wrote of the Ruth character, Rachel Drake, in *Cold Spring Harbor*, "she felt heavily handicapped by ignorance"; but Rachel's mother refuses to discuss indelicate things like the facts of life with her: "She could evade almost any question with her little shuddering laugh . . . and the troubling thing

---

*Martha Speer remembers it as a clothesline, which may be so; but Yates was fastidious about rendering such literal details as accurately as possible in his fiction, and the "horizontal steel pipe" in *The Easter Parade* almost certainly reflects a further effort of memory.

about this attitude was that it seemed always to come from carelessness, or laziness, rather than from any kind of principle." Pookie in *The Easter Parade* is similarly evasive, and when the fourteen-year-old Alice Towers in "Trying Out for the Race" asks her mother Lucy about a pregnant schoolmate, Lucy responds with "revulsion" and tells her daughter, in effect, to mind her own business: "And Alice looked wounded, an expression even more frequent on her face lately than on her mother's, or her brother's." Whether Dookie was guilty of such pernicious hypocrisy is hard to say, and may be little more than a tendentious attempt on Yates's part to make sense of his sister's tragedy. That Ruth was something of a naïf, though, and sadly desperate for love and assurance, is not in doubt. As a teenager she joined Frank Buchman's "Moral Rearmament" movement, which encouraged confessions and chaste "open love" among its members, and not long after that she would find a more final escape in marriage.

Dookie's first real success as an artist, at least in terms of exposure, came in 1933 when she was given the opportunity to sculpt a bust of President-elect Roosevelt. The whole episode is so superbly recounted in "Oh, Joseph, I'm So Tired," that it's difficult to do much more than speculate and summarize. Probably her friend Howard Cushman (called Howard Whitman in the story) did get her the entrée, as Dookie would have it, through an old newspaper friend who was part of Roosevelt's New York staff. And Dookie would certainly be apt to regale her friends with an account of irreverent banter at FDR's expense while she measured his head: "I said, 'I didn't vote for you, Mr. President.' I said, 'I'm a good Republican and I voted for President Hoover.' He said, 'Why are you here, then?' . . . and I said, 'Because you have a very interesting head . . . I like the bumps on it.' " And Yates's appraisal of the motive for such effrontery, indeed for the whole affair—namely, that the headlines would scream, GAL SCULPTOR TWITS FDR FOR "BUMPS" ON HEAD—pretty much puts the matter in a nutshell. The episode seems almost too pat in terms of the quintessential Yates story, what with its romantic-minded mother about to realize her dreams at last, only to be crushed by the cruel disparity between expectations and reality.

Of course such a précis hardly does justice to a story as subtly textured as "Joseph," though perhaps it does sum up the basic facts of the case. That Dookie's FDR head was laughably "too small" and "looked like a serviceable bank for loose change" is not just an ingenious objective correlative for the story's sake (though it's that too)—in fact the head was "about half life-size," according to the only real publicity the business attracted, about seventy-five words buried in section 2, page 3, column 8, of the *New York Times*:

BUST GIVEN ROOSEVELT. President Sat for Ruth Yates at January Press Conference. . . . A small bronze [lead] bust of President Roosevelt was presented to him today by Miss Ruth Yates, New York sculptor. The bust, which is about half life-size, was made during Mr. Roosevelt's press conference at his New York house, just before his trip to Warm Springs in January. This was the only time he could devote to sittings for the bust.

A further line mentioned that Miss Yates "studied under Paul Landowski in Paris," but said nothing about how (as Yates imagined the newsreel and feature articles Dookie might have hoped for) "she'd come from a small Ohio town, or of how she'd nurtured her talent through the brave, difficult, one-woman journey that had brought her to the attention of the world."

But it was a start, and meanwhile Dookie's life seemed to look up in other respects, since around this time she found her only enduring boyfriend after the divorce—the "tall and dignified and aristocratic" Englishman who appears as Eric Nicholson in "Joseph" and Sterling Nelson in *A Special Providence*. As with the FDR story, one can add little to the fiction; all that's known for sure, more or less, is that such a man existed and stuck around for a year or so before suddenly dropping out of sight to Dookie's and the children's regret—though in the children's case it was more a matter of longing for a conventional home life than any particular fondness for the man himself. As for the details, they're all but identical in both the novel and story: The man apparently worked in the New York office of a British export firm (specified as a "chain of foundries" in "Joseph") and "had a wife in England from whom he wasn't yet technically divorced"; at some point he seems to have persuaded Dookie and the children to share a house with him in Scarsdale, despite the stigma of living out of wedlock in such a community ("the question of whether or not she would find it awkward being called 'Mrs. Nelson' remained unsolved; nobody in Scarsdale called her anything at all"); and one day he escaped his creditors by returning to England and his wife, leaving a lot of shabby furniture and forged art as a kind of consolation prize for Dookie. The forged art (described as such in *A Special Providence*) may have been a flourish of poetic license on Yates's part, along with the three-year subscription to *Field & Stream* Nicholson gives the seven-year-old son in "Joseph" ("that impenetrable magazine was the least appropriate of all his gifts because it kept coming in the mail for such a long, long time after everything else had changed for us")—but one suspects such details are as true as the rest of it, further testimony to Yates's selective genius, his ability to shape life in the precise terms of his artistic vision.

The gentility of living in Scarsdale must have grown on Dookie, despite her neighbors' indifference or outright hostility toward the odd woman who spent her days sculpting in the garage. Because the Englishman's desertion left her unable to pay the rent, and because she was lonely, she coaxed her friend Elisabeth Cushman to move with her daughter Nancy into a somewhat cheaper house Dookie had found on the nearby Post Road. Together the two families could even afford a live-in maid, though that left them with only one bedroom per family.

The arrangement was probably not as volatile as it's depicted in the story "Trying Out for the Race," or rather there seems not to have been any (lasting) clash between the two mothers; but the respective dysfunctions of the families appear to be faithfully portrayed. "Some time let's have a little discussion about that sentiment-smothered thing called maternity," Elisabeth Cushman wrote Yates somewhat later, having referred to her daughter in the same letter as a "zombie child." From this one might safely assume the factual basis of the frenzied quarreling between Elizabeth Hogan Baker and her nine-year-old daughter in the story, culminating in such remarks as, "I wish that child were at the bottom of the sea." Bad mothers and a tendency to throw tantrums were things Nancy and Richard had in common as children, with a difference in the former's case that might have proved fortunate to the latter: "I know she'll come back,"

Nancy says calmly to Russell/Richard in the story,* after her mother abandons her for an assignation in the city. "She always does"—whereupon the boy reflects that "an attitude like that was exactly what he needed in his own life." Whether or not by Nancy's example, a somewhat greater maturity on Richard's part is suggested by the fact that, around the age of ten, he began to make a friend or two among boys his own age; and lest he seem a sissy in their eyes, he made a point of either ignoring or terrorizing his female housemate during their visits, as she remembers to this day.

The move in 1937 to Beechwood, the vast estate of Frank A. Vanderlip in Scarborough-on-Hudson, was the result of Dookie's work as a sculpting teacher. The Westchester Workshop in White Plains didn't pay much, but Dookie's loneliness and boredom must have been desperate enough by then to make her classes more than worthwhile, especially since her students (as Yates described them in *A Special Providence*) tended to be "women of her own age or older, prosperously married and vaguely dissatisfied." A few of these women befriended Dookie, and one of them arranged for her to meet the chatelaine of Beechwood, Mrs. Vanderlip herself, who seems to have been charmed: She not only agreed to rent Dookie one of the outbuildings but also gave her the use of a large studio space where she could teach private classes and thereby make enough money, in theory, to pay for the privilege of being in such rarefied surroundings.

And for a time they were happy. Beechwood was congenial in almost every respect: The fifty-acre estate was a well-manicured wilderness of elms and beeches and giant rhododendron bushes, in the midst of which ran a clear brook and many slate paths, past statuary and gardens transplanted whole from European castles. Above it all loomed the Vanderlip's five-story mansion, visible from every part of the estate, and a constant reminder

---

*The careful reader will note that Yates didn't bother to change either Nancy's or her mother's real first names (save one letter). In drafts of his later fiction, Yates would often write the actual name of the person on whom a given character was based, and then alter the name slightly in revision. Perhaps as a mnemonic device, he tended to retain actual first names as well as the cadence of his models' last names.

of the sort of aristocratic grace to which Dookie so wistfully aspired. Just as importantly, the Vanderlips themselves were no philistine tycoons but rather great patrons of education and the arts. On the property was the ultraprogressive Scarborough Country Day School, founded by Frank Vanderlip in 1913, a place where arts and crafts were emphasized almost as much as science and math. Creativity in general was much admired, and talented people were always welcome at Beechwood: Isadora Duncan had danced on the lawn, and another great chronicler of the American middle class would later occupy a house there. "The swimming pool is curbed with Italian marble," John Cheever wrote in a 1951 letter from Beechwood, at the beginning of his almost-ten-year tenancy, "lucent and shining like loaves of fine sugar."

The Yates family had recourse to the same pool, not far from the northeast corner of the estate, where they lived in a white stucco gatehouse. Formerly the school's kindergarten, it consisted of a single large room (about thirty feet square) plus a tiny bedroom, bathroom, and kitchen. The quarters were tight as ever—the children had to sleep in the main studio-cum-living-room—but at least now there was less reason for the timid Richard to hide inside with his mother and sister. Dookie had enrolled her children in Scarborough Country Day (needless to say she couldn't really afford the tuition), and the eleven-year-old Yates blossomed there. "He used to speak of it as the peak of his childhood popularity," said his daughter Sharon, "followed by a long, nasty descent into an unhappy puberty."

The school philosophy placed heavy emphasis on fostering "growth" and "uniqueness," and this allowed Yates to tap into a latent (at least where the outside world was concerned) silliness that stood him in good stead among children almost as quirky as he. He was much given to making droll and generally inoffensive fun of students and teachers alike. When the art teacher asked the class to paint a picture expressing their emotions, Yates submitted a blank sheet of paper titled "Gloom"—a work that belied his remarkable facility as a cartoonist. "He doodled on everything," his friend Stephen Benedict remembered, "papers at school, doilies, letters—images of cats, caricatures of teachers, Joe Louis, Adolf Hitler." Such doodling remained an abiding interest, but at the time Yates's fame as a poet was far greater. "The doggerel poured out of him,"

said Benedict, and the headmaster's daughter, Mary Jo McClusky (who
had a crush on Yates), wrote him a fan letter forty years later in which she
remarked, "I remember how you used to delight us all with your spur-of-
the-moment poems—guess you were destined to be a writer!" A writer of
prose anyway; a sample of Yates's output from this time suggests he was
unlikely to rival his beloved Keats:

> The only noise I hear all day,
> is the clanking of a can.
> I drive a dirty-smelly truck,
> for I am a garbage man.
>
> The city dumps its waste on me,
> to throw into the river.
> And I can't stand that gooey smell,
> it kinda turns my liver.

Yates was elected president of his class,* which must have seemed an
apotheosis of sorts after the morbidities of his early childhood.

Stephen Benedict and his older brother Russell were Yates's best friends
in Scarborough, and the youngsters' activities suggest the kind of off-
center precocity Yates may have had in mind when he described the
"interesting" products of progressive education in A Special Providence.
Stephen and Richard formed the Scarborough Jitterbugs, a two-man ocarina band that approximated such popular standards as the Andrews Sisters' "Bei Mir Bist Du Schoen" and "Oh, Johnny, Oh!" "We energetically
rehearsed, then tootled away on numerous occasions for anyone who'd
listen," Benedict recalled. "Almost every piece would be punctuated by
one of us with the sepulchral *moo* of an enormous bass ocarina, certain to
break up anyone in range. That sad yet comic sound will forever bring
Dick to mind." Perhaps encouraged by her son's ocarina prowess—or just
the general ambience of juvenile creativity—Dookie hired a Mr. Bostelman

---

*Or so he remembered. Others remember differently or not at all, though most agree Yates was
fairly popular.

to give Richard private violin lessons at the gatehouse; either the instrument didn't catch on or Dookie didn't pay the man or both, but Yates's musical career seems to have stalled with the Scarborough Jitterbugs. Meanwhile Russell Benedict (influenced by Yates's sister?) started a weekly newspaper in his basement, the *Scarborough News Sheet*—six pages of society items, gossip, cartoons and gags (Yates's contribution), and the odd subversive bit such as a photo Russell had taken, and pasted in all one hundred copies, of a drowned vagrant woman on a slab at the local morgue. Corpses withal, such a novel and nourishing world came at a crucial time for Yates, and had a lingering impact that went well beyond the obvious. He pondered this in a 1961 letter, written after a reunion with Stephen Benedict and two weeks before the publication of his first and most famous novel:

> Had dinner tonight with an old boyhood friend from the years 1937–39 when I lived in a town called Scarborough, whose amateur theatre group ("The Beechwood Players") served as the original for "The Laurel Players" in my book. He found it incredible, and I found it spooky, that I had completely failed to remember the name of a winding blacktop road in that town on which he and I and many of our schoolmates used to pass the most impressionable hours of our formative years: "Revolutionary Road." Pretty Freudian, buddy.

. . .

The "sad yet comic" *moo* of the bass ocarina (a strikingly apt leitmotiv for the life of Richard Yates) should be sounded at this point, as things began to fall apart in Scarborough. For one thing, Yates's relative popularity wasn't likely to last while his "long, nasty descent" into puberty gained momentum. By the age of thirteen he was already taller than most of his peers, but not much developed in other respects—if anything, the attenuation of his body seemed to make him weaker, and he could hardly have appeared more clumsy if he'd tried milking it for laughs (which he didn't). And despite the school's emphasis on creativity and so forth, it also lavished prestige on its student athletes, especially in the upper grades, and this universal fact of prep-school life boded ill for Yates. Even Stephen

Benedict—who was smaller and a year younger—always prevailed in their frequent wrestling matches, which seemed to bother Yates in a quiet way. For the rest of his life, in fact, he'd be haunted by a sense of physical inadequacy, which would manifest itself in a number of curious and not-so-curious ways.

And then of course there was the matter of Yates's poverty, for which his seedy, undernourished appearance served as a kind of advertisement. Most of his schoolmates came from wealthy or at least comfortably middle-class families, and Yates was made keenly and increasingly aware of their snobbery. Susan Cheever, who experienced the same paradox while living at Beechwood, wrote, "We had the luxuries of the very rich— rolling lawns, a swimming pool, gardeners who doffed their caps—but we were tenants, scraping to get by." And here was the dark side of Scarborough: Though creativity and personal charm were pluses, they were no substitute for money, and one learned the hard way how suddenly one's sense of belonging could evaporate when a few bills weren't paid. For her part Dookie worked hard to preserve her cherished foothold on the estate: She tried to recruit more students as well as improve her own work (in the hope of that elusive, lucrative "one-man exhibition") by dispensing with garden sculpture in favor of direct stone carving and abstract forms. But her progress as an artist brought little material reward, and the good life she'd come so close to grasping began to slip away.

It had to be a bitter business. Almost nightly the Vanderlips entertained in their downstairs parlor, and the elegant guests in their evening clothes could be seen through tall lighted windows. Dookie herself had attended the larger parties in the ballroom, amid grand pianos, liveried servants, and the great Van Dyck painting *Andromeda,* as such occasions tended to be open to the nicer and more creative part of the public—to all, that is, but the truly impecunious, as the Yateses would soon become. But then at least one member of the family definitely benefited (as an artist anyway) from such harsh reversals, since a lifelong sense of exclusion informed the best of Yates's work (a scene in *A Special Providence,* for example, has Alice arriving at "Boxwood" and attending the Vander Meers' lavish Christmas party; it pays homage to a similar scene in *Madame Bovary*).

From the practical viewpoint of which she was wholly incapable,

Dookie never had any business living at Beechwood, though she wasn't one to give up without a fight. No doubt she tried to get her children's scholarships increased at the school, and was denied on the basis of merit (or lack thereof).* And no doubt she got her exasperated ex-husband to agree, yet again, to exceed the terms of the divorce agreement and pay off the more immediate bills. Perhaps Dookie continued to hope that the larger situation could still be saved somehow (more students, a one-man show), even as she grew more "cranky," as Stephen Benedict recalled, "combined with a good deal of cynicism about life in general, which she clearly felt had not been good to her." Life would get a lot worse: Before long she was telling her children not to answer the door, and finally the Vanderlips took legal action to evict her and recover the many months of unpaid rent. There was no time to finish the school year when Dookie and her children fled an entire region of creditors in the spring of 1939. "All I remember is that you sort of disappeared overnight," the headmaster's daughter wrote Yates, "and no one would tell me why, and I was heartbroken!"

They found refuge of sorts in Austin, Texas, where Aunt Elsa had gone to live after her marriage to the math professor. This much we know, and if we trust *A Special Providence* (and perhaps we should at this point, at least in terms of the big picture), we can also assume that Elsa's semiretired husband was something of an anti-Semite who drank too much and liked to hold forth on such topics as "the menacing rise of the American Negro." What matters for our purpose is that he seems to have found Dookie distasteful and bullied her son, a mama's boy (he thought) who

---

*In *A Special Providence* the aptly named headmaster, Dr. Cool, produces Bobby Prentice's file and shares its contents with Alice: "[T]he record disclosed that [Bobby's IQ] had been assessed at slightly above average, and that he had done reasonably well in the fields of Social Adjustment and Personality Growth. But his Capacity for Self-Discipline had received the rating of Poor, and of the six Units of Study assigned to him during the academic year he had failed two." Finally he reads aloud one of the more biting teacher comments: " 'Robert may eventually turn out to be as precocious as he seems to think he is, but if he expects to prove it to me he will have to buckle down.' " All this rings true, and for what it's worth the actual headmaster recognized himself when he read the novel in 1977: "Dad has been running around calling himself Dr. Cool at every opportunity," his daughter wrote Yates.

should be back in school. "I *hate* him! I *hate* him!" Alice Prentice ends up screaming at her hapless sister. "Oh, I know you only married him because he was all you could get, but you're a fool! He's a *beast*!" Or words to that effect, which understandably might have led to both mother and children staggering through a sweltering construction site with their suitcases in hand and a total of seventy-five cents among them. What's interesting and pertinent about this scene, as rendered in the novel, is the way the "cheerful, heartening" son helps his mother overcome her exhaustion by encouraging her to imagine that the hot "caliche" dust is actually snow, a freezing blizzard from which they have to escape as quickly as possible. "For years, whenever they were faced with any ordeal, she would gain strength from saying 'Remember the Caliche Road?' "

Yates remembered the Caliche Road all right, in whatever form it took, but as time went on he became less inclined to collude in his mother's delusions. Indeed, his childhood tendency to be an accomplice to such folly, as well as its foremost victim, would forever rankle. As much as anything this was the goad that made him determined to expose the truth, no matter how depressing, that people like Dookie are apt to bury beneath layers of everyday self-deceit. For Yates it was a matter of good art, though it certainly applied to life as well—to friends, family, and (arguably with the poorest result) himself. "The most important thing," he liked to say, "is not to tell or live a lie." Pity and forgiveness were important too, however hard they came when one knew the worst about a person. Once, when Yates was responding to questions about his work, a young woman commented on how *awful* the mother was in *A Special Providence*—"so careless and thoughtless and self-centered"—and asked Yates what *he* thought of her. "Oh, I don't know," he said quietly. "I guess I sort of love her."

CHAPTER TWO

A Good School: 1939-1944

By the fall of 1939 they were back in the Village, and all was well again, at least as far as Dookie was concerned. She'd somehow wangled a commission to sculpt a bust of the boxer Joe Louis; in fact, a photograph of her doing so—with the great heavyweight posing in person and the artist's awestruck children looking on—appeared in the *New York Herald Tribune* and other newspapers around the country. "We're celeberaties [sic]," Yates wrote Stephen Benedict, amid doodles of the various photographic groupings sent out by the Associated Press. "And you had to see the lousy one. Roof [Ruth] looks ten times as big as [I do], mater looks like she was a 300 pounder, and I look like I was nine years old." For as long as his mother worked on the bust, Yates was one of Louis's biggest fans. He and Dookie were given ringside seats at the Louis–Arturo Godoy fight at Madison Square Garden, where Yates sat scribbling a "blow-by-slug" description of the "prolims" for Benedict: "I can't describe the Louis fight, cause I want to enjoy that without interruption. Do you blame me? If you never got this letter, you'll know Joe lost, and I died of heart-failure." He enclosed a peanut shell from the Garden, and later a "chip off the old block" from the completed Louis bust—which was eventually placed in the permanent collection of the Norfolk Museum of Arts and Sciences.* Meanwhile former champion Jack Dempsey was next; Dookie dubbed the incipient series her "Sports Hall of Fame."

---

*Or so Dookie reported in her *Who's Who* entry. However, the Norfolk (Virginia) Museum of Arts and Sciences became (in 1971) the Chrysler Museum, which has no record of this or any other work by Ruth Yates.

Around this time Yates wrote many letters to his best friend Stephen, whose family had moved to California for the year. Apart from a sort of sophisticated whimsy and an ear for colloquial language (as an example of both, he addresses Stephen as "T-bon" throughout, to mimic the pronunciation of a Japanese friend the latter had made), the thirteen- and fourteen-year-old Yates gave little indication in these letters of the grimly precise writer he'd soon set out to become: Spelling and punctuation are almost entirely random, the penmanship sprawls, and as for substance—well, the letters are mostly about cats, or *kahts* as Yates calls them. Even Joe Louis is "just like a big kaht," and Yates's own *kaht* has just run away, hence he doodles the pet bounding off in a whiff of smoke. Occasionally he makes some passing mention of his new school, or a movie he's just seen ("the Cowardly Lion was a giggle"), or Joe Louis of course, but he rarely strays altogether from the main theme:

> I really wrote you the verra nite what I gotcher letter. But the giggleiest thing happened! You see mine honorable sister took an excuse to her verra strict princepal [sic], and (oh-ho-ho-haw) she (this'll kill you) was about to depart from the principle's [sic] desk, and (haw-*haw*) she glanced out of the corner of her eye and saw that her "excuse" bore the picture of a *kaht,* and a "Dear T-bon." Laugh? I thought I'd die!!

The passage gives a fair idea of Yates's epistolary style, perhaps the kind of mock-refined patois affected by some of the more precocious wags at Scarborough Country Day. Certainly the letters suggest that he badly misses both Benedict and the school, more in what he omits than otherwise ("It will be peachy to see the T-bon this summer"). But the overall impression is one of flighty evasive boredom, rather like a child playing with his food; reading between the lines and doodles, it seems as if there was little in Yates's life except cats and Joe Louis that he much cared to write or even think about. In fact one is vividly reminded of the fourteen-year-old Phil Drake in *Cold Spring Harbor,* a boy who can "cut through a lot of confusion" with his occasional insight, "even if all he wanted to do was fool around with the cat or examine his face in the mirror, even if he lapsed into the kind of willfully exasperating childishness that suggested he would always be younger than his age." As for these will-fully childish letters to "T-bon," their subtext is suggested by Yates's reaction to them forty years later, when Benedict sent him copies in the hope he'd find them amusing. Yates was not amused: It was good to hear from Benedict again, he wrote back, but not so good to get the letters; he didn't like to think about that time in his life.

"My school is peachy (oh-so)," Yates wrote in October 1939, and for his friend's benefit drew caricatures of his new teachers; as a cartoonist Yates was adept at finding just the right physical detail (an effete way of folding the arms, an asymmetrical scowl) to reveal the essence of his subject. Yates may have found the all-male staff of Grace Church School to be a group of ludicrous grotesques, but at least the location was convenient (less than two blocks from the family's latest apartment on West Eleventh), and Dookie was no doubt pleased by the Episcopal affiliation ("the only aristocratic faith in America"). The school, however, was probably not as "peachy" as Yates made it out to be. In his novel *Uncertain Times,* Yates's alter ego William Grove casts back to his traumatic first day of school as a thirteen-year-old, "as the only new boy where everyone else had known each other all their lives":

> He was standing alone in the school yard when another boy came up to him with a look of lazy menace, said "Hey there, Bubbles" and turned away again. And there was no denying that his face at thirteen did have a sort of bubbly look: eyes so girlishly round they seemed incapable of squinting in a manly way; lips so plump that only an effort of will could compress them into dignity. Luckily, or mercifully, the name "Bubbles" had failed to catch on, and later in adolescence he had managed almost to come to terms with his face.

The key word is *almost.* Yates—a strikingly handsome man by any standard, at least in his youth—disliked the way he looked. With the same faculty that made him a decent amateur cartoonist and superb fiction writer, he fixed on his round eyes and plump lips as physiognomic signs of weakness; more to the point, he thought they made him look feminine, "bubbly," and he had a lifelong horror of being perceived as homosexual.

The beard he grew in his forties was by way of partially concealing his "Aubrey Beardsley mouth" (as one friend put it), and the gathering bags under his eyes helped take care of the roundness somewhat, though he never stopped squinting a little for formal portraits.

But there's really not much reason to think Yates was more than normally miserable that first year at Grace Church School, or rather that school life per se was more than a minor cause of whatever misery he felt. That the "Bubbles" tag (or its equivalent) did in fact "[fail] to catch on" is borne out somewhat by the lapel pin for "leadership" he was awarded in December, along with pins for "improvement" and "an average of above 80 for the last month." Yates's "actual size" doodles of these pins (smaller than a fingernail) also suggest that he was aware of just how dubious they were, though perhaps his giddiness in relating the news to "T-bon" is not entirely a matter of self-mockery: "You might be inerested [sic] in getting an ear*ful* of the glee*ful* fact that due to my duti*ful* studies . . . I, R. Walden Yates, was awarded 3 little bronze lapel-pins." But if this means that Yates was not quite a pariah, he doesn't seem to have been all that popular either. In the many letters he wrote that year, amid all the manic chatter about cats and movies and so on, there's only a single glancing reference to a potential new companion: "Me and another guy who swings a wicked harmonica, have a sort of an orchestra (not as good as the scarborough jitterbugs)." Clearly he missed Scarborough, and especially his friend Stephen, whose return in June at least gave him something to look forward to.

But it wasn't to be. Dookie had decided to rent a cottage that summer near Milton, Vermont, in the mountains around Lake Champlain. Yates tried hard to coax Benedict into joining them: "You're invited to a peachy joint in VT where there's a lake—a free rowboat a big mountain a bathing suit a rustic cabin and best of all Homer [the cat] will be there!!" At the bottom of the letter is a cartoon of Homer lugging his suitcase in the direction of a festive sign ("VERMONT!"), followed by a typical Yatesian witticism: "Remember: 'You can't get 'T.B.' in 'V.T.' " All for naught. Benedict couldn't come, and Yates was faced with the task of finding friends among fellow campers. "Bud Hoyt is getting to be quite chummy and stays late every nite at our cottage playing every kind of game from slap-jack to monopoly," he wrote enticingly to T-bon a few weeks later, but that was the only mention of Bud Hoyt or anybody else. In late July he wrote a last wan postcard—"You can still come, you know"—by which time he'd probably reverted to spending his days in the usual manner, à la Phil Drake, "fooling around on the floor with the cat . . . hearing his mother's relentless talk and longing for it to stop, dying a little when the alcohol began to thicken her tongue."

Along with the curative powers of fresh water and mountain air, another motive for the Vermont sojourn was to escape from creditors again; during their last days on Eleventh Street the family had been reduced to using the backstairs, the better to sneak in and out of their apartment without alerting the landlord. But Dookie had a flair: When the family came back in August she found a much better place at 62 Washington Square, one of four brownstones on the south side of the park known as "Genius Row," where writers such as Stephen Crane, O. Henry, and Frank Norris had lived around the turn of the century. The mystique appealed to Dookie, and besides, they had the entire ground floor to themselves. Soon the place was filled with students and statuary and the industrious odor of plasticene; life was back to normal again.

More or less. By then Ruth was nineteen, and college had never been in the picture; her flirtation with Buchmanism had long passed, and she'd begun dating a series of men whom Dookie found feckless and even a little sinister. The change in Ruth had been troublingly abrupt: Just a year before, she'd carried on a kind of calf-love courtship with Russell Benedict, who was almost two years younger than she; but when he returned from California he found that Ruth regarded him as little more than a boy. "I'd lost out to much older suitors," he remembered, "but she was nice about it—Ruth was always nice—and there were no hard feelings." She'd met some of these older men while working as a volunteer for the Associated Willkie Clubs of America, where Dookie had hoped she'd find some nice Republican boys from good families. And so she did, or rather they were Republican, but neither they nor certain others struck Dookie as remotely suitable. Happily the whole dilemma was solved on Easter Sunday 1941, shortly after a family of war refugees moved into the apartment upstairs.

Actually they were American, despite their faintly British accents. Frederick "Fritz" Rodgers, the father—perhaps *patriarch* is more apt—had been sent to London many years before by his employer, Cherry-Burrell, a company that designed dairy machinery. While the father traveled around Europe selling pasteurization units in countries with a high incidence of bacterial disease, his son Fred junior attended the exclusive Mr. Gibbs's School in London, along with Ambassador Joseph Kennedy's children and the future actor-playwright Peter Ustinov, who became Fred's good friend. During the Blitz the family was removed to rural Surrey, until the British government advised them as Americans to leave the country. And so they came in somewhat reduced circumstances to live in that upstairs apartment on Genius Row, obligingly vacated by a bohemian aunt who painted.

Dookie was rather smitten by the gentlemanly Fritz Rodgers, all the more so when her sociable inquiries revealed a family pedigree that must have made her swoon. Fritz's sickly wife Louise was a descendant of John Alden, who'd come over on the *Mayflower* with William Bradford, and her father was a Nantucket Gardner, no less, whose home on India Street would later become an historical landmark. Nor was such distinction limited (as in the case of Dookie's children) to one side of the family. In fact the name Rodgers is all but synonymous with American naval history: Fritz was the great-grandson of John Rodgers, the "Father of the American Navy," and was maternally linked with Matthew C. Perry, who forced Japan to reopen trade with the West, and Oliver Hazard Perry, who won the Battle of Lake Erie. All the Rodgers men had pursued naval careers as a matter of course—a tradition that, alas, came to an end with Fritz himself, who became legally blind during his third year at Annapolis after a boxing mishap. Since then he'd dabbled in a number of things—architecture, poetry, acting, scientific inventions—and such a wide range of cultivation, coupled with Old World manners and a liking for sherry, made him an almost ideal companion for Dookie. Theirs was a platonic bond, facilitated somewhat by the fact that Louise Rodgers spent most of her time in bed.

And then there was the man's only son and namesake, who not only had the blood of the Aldens and Gardners and Rodgers and Perrys running through his veins, but was the spitting image of Laurence Olivier. As a former student at one of England's best public schools, his accent was more pronounced than that of his parents or even his London-born sister, and his manners seemed impeccable. For all the surface polish, though, Fred was something of a mystery even to his own family. "Charming but opaque" is how his younger sister described him with the benefit of much hindsight; "I never did know what made him tick." Unlike the rest of the family, Fred had little interest in books or art or for that matter anything that smacked of learning or culture. Rather than attend university he'd served a few years of apprenticeship with an engineering firm in England, and when he returned to the States he found work as a machinist with Grumman Aviation in Long Island—a job he held, with very occasional promotion, for the rest of his life. "I'm a laborer," he liked to say in that elegant accent of his, and indeed he preferred the company of other laborers at the aircraft plant. At first blush this suave, handsome, well-born young man seemed to have little in common with the proletariat; his fine manners held him in check, though like Tony Wilson in *The Easter Parade* he had a good sense of humor and "seemed always to be laughing at some subtle private joke that he might tell you when you got to know him better." And then you got to know him better and he'd tell you: "Oh, I believe in humanity. Humanity's perf'ly all right with me. I like everyone but coons, kikes, and Catholics." That was the Fred his friends knew.

But all Dookie knew in 1941 was that Fred was the son of a gentleman and the descendant of many more, and probably she was being sly when she asked her daughter to take a basket of Easter eggs to the little girl who lived upstairs. By then Ruth (through her Willkie contacts) had found a paying job with United China Relief, and for publicity purposes her employer had loaned her an elaborate silk dress and Mandarin hat to wear to the Fifth Avenue Easter Parade. Thus attired, Ruth knocked on the Rodgers's door and was met by a young man in grease-stained overalls who appeared to be Laurence Olivier blithely impersonating a laborer. The rest of her life was decided in that moment.

. . .

In the months leading up to her marriage, Ruth was away much of the time on all-day drives with Fred, and the fifteen-year-old Richard was lonelier than ever. As the clouds of puberty gathered around him, he began to resent his life and covet his sister's imminent freedom. He was even getting a little tired of his adored and adoring Dookie—her constant talk, tipsy jokes, silliness about money, the magazines she always smeared with lipsticky fingers, the dusty, noisy mess of her sculpting, the whole dingy rigmarole of being "free spirits."

Nor was school any escape. The only subjects he tended to pass anymore were English and History ("and I only passed History because I could fake it"); such was his depression that he simply couldn't muster the effort to work at things that didn't interest him. And among the things that didn't interest him were math and science, foreign languages, any kind of athletics that required his own participation, and (perhaps above all) having to relate to boys with whom he felt nothing in common, so alien was his experience to theirs. He didn't even like to read much; rather he spent most of his time, as ever, hiding in movie theaters and imagining a different sort of life for himself, and by way of further escape he began to write about it. Such "movie-haunted" stories were consistently praised by his English teachers, even stories that the author considered "pretty awful."* At age fifteen he'd suddenly found a vocation, and no matter how much difficulty it caused him in the years ahead, he never seriously considered a different one.

Of course Dookie had never doubted that her son was special; if he failed in school it was because his needs were different from those of ordinary boys. Meanwhile it must have pained her deeply to see what an unhappy, brooding adolescent he'd become. More than anyone she knew how sensitive he was, how like herself, and clearly he needed more understanding than he was liable to get at a pedestrian little church school in the Village. Or so she might have thought when, early that summer, she

---

*By his own recollection the first story Yates ever wrote was about a condemned man who learned, en route to the electric chair, that the officer beside him was his long-lost brother. One wonders if Yates knew of his grandfather Horatio's ordeal with the unfortunate William Kemmler.

learned of a prep school in Connecticut that *believed in individuality*. As Yates described this pivotal moment in *A Good School*, she was at the lavish wedding of one of her sculpting students ("a rich girl [who] must have romanticized my mother as a struggling artist"), when an overbearing grande dame insisted that Dookie look into Avon Old Farms for her gifted, maladjusted son; that it was the "only school in the East that understands boys." After that it would have been quite in character for Avon's headmaster at the time—a zealous recruiter named Brooke Stabler—to respond to Dookie's letter of inquiry with a personal visit to Genius Row and, having come this far, to pitch the school as *precisely* the sort of place where the otherwise foundering son of a sculptor was likely to flourish, and moreover to offer her on the spot a scholarship for half the (rather exorbitant) tuition. And finally, of course, it was entirely like Dookie to insist that Vincent Yates see the need, whether he could afford it or not, to send their son to a proper New England boarding school—until the man relented, at last, as usual.

Avon Old Farms was the brainchild of Mrs. Theodate Pope Riddle, though the school might have seemed (as Yates put it) "conceived in the studios of Walt Disney." Mrs. Riddle herself might have been so conceived, for the figure she struck as a stout, glowering dowager lent itself to the cartoonist's art. Born Effie Pope, she adopted her maternal grandmother's name, Theodate, at the already formidable age of twelve, and from that point on led a life of exemplary activity and idealism. She was the very tissue of which legends (local ones, at least) are made: Though whacked on the head by a heavy beam and given up for dead, Theodate survived the sinking of the *Lusitania* and went on to become Connecticut's first female architect. She deplored cold rationalism, and thus was able to reconcile an ardent socialism with the enormous personal fortune she inherited as a young woman; and finally she combined all her assets—fortune, idealism, architectural prowess, and not least an iron will—in building what would be, both in design and principle, "an indestructible school for boys."

For this purpose she acquired three thousand acres of lush woodlands around the Farmington River near the town of Avon, about twelve miles from Hartford. She designed her school in the English Cotswold style, and insisted it be built using red sandstone from local quarries. She further insisted, with bizarre but rather endearing fanaticism, that the five hundred or so construction workers restrict themselves to the use of seventeenth-century tools (e.g., broad axes and old-style staples and wedges), and even to "work by rule of thumb and to judge all verticals by eye." When she discovered a worker using a modern level and plumb rule, Mrs. Riddle became furious and sacked the lot of them; she hired a smaller group of costly artisans and finally ended up spending more than five million 1926 dollars to complete the project to her exacting satisfaction. And for a while it may have seemed worth it: The campus was like a Cotswold Brigadoon buried in the woods of Connecticut, what with the "gabled slate roofs whose timbers had intentionally been installed when the wood was young so that in aging they would warp and sag in interesting ways," as Yates described it, noting also the flagstone paths, the wide lawns, the lead-casement windows, and so on.

But all this was only a part—arguably the lesser part—of Mrs. Riddle's vision. *Aspirando et perseverando* was and is the Avon motto, and to embody this Mrs. Riddle chose as her mascot a winged beaver, hence the central tenet of her philosophy: No matter how modest one's abilities, if one persevered like a certain tenacious long-toothed rodent, then there were no heights to which one could not aspire. And it was precisely the student of modest ability—or thwarted potential as the case may be—that intrigued Mrs. Riddle. "There were always those who were wealthy, who wanted to play polo in a relaxed atmosphere," said alumnus Reed Estabrook, describing a typical Avon student in those days. "But most of us had been in academic trouble for one reason or another (like myself), or social trouble, at a more traditional school." The intolerance for misfits so commonplace at such bastions as St. Paul's, Andover, and Exeter was anathema to the arch-progressive Avon, which was innovative in a number of ways. Seventy-five years ago there was an on-site psychologist to commiserate with some of the quirkier students, as well as a remedial reading program instituted by Harvard-trained specialists. Indeed, Avon's remarkable success with both the quirky and dyslexic was its greatest claim to fame, and nowadays on-site psychologists and remediation programs are de rigueur at all but the most benighted schools.

But the paramount issue for Mrs. Riddle was *breeding*—an elusive concept, to be sure. Though Avon was "founded for the sons of the gentry," the phrase is misleading; the socialist founder was stern in pointing out that "good breeding is not dependent on birth" but rather cultivated after a fashion that Mrs. Riddle, in her Deed of Trust, was at pains to prescribe in rather byzantine but not wholly unreasonable terms. The matter almost defies summary (though the Deed is an interesting and readable document) but goes something like this: Manners, character, *breeding* if you will, are far more important than any academic test, which is *not* to say that intellectual discipline isn't important, merely that it needs to be pursued in terms of one's individual abilities and interests, and in conjunction with some form of creative manual labor—hence the "community service" requirement for every Avon student. "The Founder believes that a boy who has never known the hardship of work on a farm, in a forest, or in shops . . . has been deprived of one of the most valuable experiences that life can offer for the development of character." But all this is moot if one doesn't maintain "smartness in attire," and to this end the founder insisted on an almost Wodehousian dress code: During the day students wore either a herringbone tweed jacket or the official Avon blazer (burgundy, brass buttons, a winged beaver on the pocket), and at night they dressed for dinner in Oxford gray pin-striped trousers, black double-breasted suit jackets, white shirts with stiff detachable collars and hand-tied bow ties. "A slovenly, slouching lad is pleasing to no one," wrote Mrs. Riddle, and added a quote from William James: " 'If a young man does not dress well before he is twenty, he will never dress well.' "

All very true, no doubt, and undeniably influential in the moral and sartorial development of one Richard Yates. "Given good-enough clothes and shoes," one of his characters reflects, "you could always look dignified whether you were or not, and almost everybody could be counted on to call you 'sir.' " Now is not the time to pause over how much Yates took all this to heart, except to note that it went well beyond clothing and is best summarized by the inscription above the entrance to Scarborough Country Day: *Manners Maketh Man.* Frank Vanderlip and Theodate Riddle were alike in that essential sentiment, which was much impressed on Yates before, during, and even after Avon.

Prior to the decadent reforms of Headmaster Stabler, Mrs. Riddle had directed her students to buy uniforms exclusively at Brooks Brothers, by far the most traditional American clothier. But in an effort to make Avon more accessible to its growing number of scholarship students, Stabler had defied the Deed of Trust and switched the school's exclusive franchise to the more downscale Franklin Simon.* Avon students were advised to buy at least two tweed jackets, two sets of evening clothes, and one (optional) Avon blazer—but even at Franklin Simon's moderate prices, Yates could only afford one of each (and no blazer), as well as a few pieces of "community service" attire such as dungarees, work shirts, and boots from an Army and Navy store.

Finally, before his departure, Yates spent a rare evening in his father's company. "His home was refreshingly clean and neat after the chaotic sculpture shop where I lived," Yates noted in *A Good School*. "When we'd stacked the dishes we sat around talking for a couple of hours—hesitantly and awkwardly, as always, but I remember thinking we'd done better than usual." Before long Yates would have reason to be glad about the relative success of this visit, and in the meantime his father—determined to be gracious despite the "preposterous" expense of Dookie's latest venture—presented him with an old heavy suitcase and a "fitted leather shaving kit, new-looking and stamped with his initials," which Yates managed to keep for several years until he lost it in Germany during the war.

"And in 1941, there arrived at the School a young man by the name of Richard W. Yates," wrote Gordon Ramsey in his history of Avon, "who combined shrewd powers of observation and even more vivid powers of guesswork to salt away reminiscences for a novel, patently about Avon Old Farms, which appeared in 1978 under the title *A Good School*." According to Ramsey, the reactions of Yates's former classmates and teachers to "this obvious *roman à clef*" ranged from "apoplectic" to "philosophic and amused." In fact the latter was far more the norm

---

*In one respect (and certain others) Mrs. Riddle would have been pleased with the adult Yates, who bought his clothes almost entirely at Brooks Brothers. As for the relative raffishness of Franklin Simon, Lothar Candels (Avon '43) remembered an occasion when students watched Hitchcock's *Saboteur* on Saturday Movie Night; during the most famous scene a man hangs from the Statue of Liberty and his jacketsleeve rips at the armpit. *"FRANKLIN SIMON!"* the students yelled in unison.

(among the few who actually read the book), and naturally such reactions depended on the reader's sense of humor as well as how lightly one got off. As for denying that a particular character was (essentially) oneself, Yates made that difficult by hardly bothering to change names or physical details, and most of the novel's key episodes are based memorably on life. "That's me, all right," said Harry Flynn of the character *Terry* Flynn, when told of the latter's crooked pinkie, and such a formula applies pretty much to the rest of the characters as well.* "What a flood of memories your top-notch cast brought back," Mason Beekley (Avon '44) wrote Yates after the book appeared, and his response was representative. "Aside from being just plain well-written and excellently crafted, your book—so close to being biographical—provided an immensely poignant experience for me, and I thank you for that." Most of Yates's classmates have a generally fond memory of the school, as well as a sense that their experience—as the last class of the old Avon, drafted almost entirely into the war—was extraordinary, a story that needed to be told, and those who read the book were (mostly) glad Yates had seen fit to tell it.

And unlike most of his stories, this one *began* unhappily and ended on a somewhat hopeful note. As with his characters Robert Prentice and Phil Drake and William Grove, Yates's first year at prep school "was almost unalloyed in its misery." Apart from being poor, unathletic, untidy, and immature in every respect, Yates fancied himself a *writer* of all things, and (whether he meant to or not) looked the part. What he had to endure is the sort of everyday hazing that, however silly and unfounded, the victim never quite forgets. At the time Yates internalized his rage, and later sublimated it into his work; in fact one of his most common themes is pertinent, what he described (in a note to his story "A Really Good Jazz Piano") as "the pain implicit in any form of condescension." Yates came to despise condescension and sensed it everywhere, at all times, and the cathartic power of art went only so far toward calming him. Those who knew him as an adult and wondered at his bizarre outbursts—not always explicable in terms of alcohol or mental illness—would do well to consider what he suffered as

---

*Yates used real names in his first draft of *A Good School* and altered them slightly in revision.

the poorest, weakest boy at a New England prep school (much less as the smothered son of an unstable, alcoholic sculptress).

But then it would have been worse at almost any other school. Not only were there a fair number of misfits to rival Yates—Avon students were known to refer to *themselves* as "Avon Old Queers"—but a state of economic democracy was enforced to a remarkable degree. By the founder's design it was all but impossible for students to spend money: Other than occasional snack sales there were no vendors on campus, and it was a mile and a half to the nearest entrance to the estate. The dress code, too, served its purpose, as everyone wore the same clothes and were therefore equally inclined to play the parts of proper gentlemen. Also, in what would seem a tremendous boon for weaklings, athletics were restricted to intramural competition between two teams, "Diogenes" and "Eagles," as Mrs. Riddle thought games with other schools were a waste of time and emotion, and that athletics in general were much too emphasized at that age.

The playing field could hardly be leveled enough in Yates's case. He later told a friend that he was "held together by safety pins" at Avon, and such a remark resonates beyond the literal. Yates, especially that first year, was the quintessential "slovenly, slouching lad" who pleases no one. "Thin, haggard, disheveled," was how one classmate described him, and his good friend Hugh Pratt elaborated: "Dick was obviously poorer than the other students. He had to wear the same thing over and over, and it affected his demeanor: He was *not* happy-go-lucky." But the most vivid description of the fifteen-year-old Yates is found, as usual, in his own words—that is, from the viewpoint of teacher Frenchy La Prade in *A Good School*, as he confronts the "gangly, dreary-looking" William Grove: "The kid was a mess. His tweed suit hung greasy with lack of cleaning, his necktie was a twisted rag, his long fingernails were blue, and he needed a haircut."

Worst of all, and despite Mrs. Riddle's good intentions, athletics were the absolute key to social success, and everybody had to participate in at least two sports a semester. Those who were relegated to what was called the "track and soccer scenario" were stigmatized as sissies, and Yates was perhaps the most representative figure. "He was fragile," said classmate Jim Stewart, "and that's a bad thing to be at that age." For most of that first year, then, Yates was goaded into fights he had no hope of winning, paddled by upperclassmen, and humiliated in a number of more intimate ways. "The shower room was the worst part of [his] day," Yates wrote of William Grove. "Not only was he absurdly thin and weak-looking, but he hadn't yet developed a full growth of pubic hair: all he had was some brown fuzz, and there was no hiding it." By all accounts the *queer* jokes were most prevalent during shower time: The group would shrink away from their victim, as if to avert sexual assault, and then lock him out of his dorm room, naked, when he was due to report to the refectory. And because of Yates's frailty and fatal lack of pubic hair, such high jinks were liable to get even more out of hand, as happened one night toward the end of that first semester.

Perhaps the most memorable scene in *A Good School* is when Grove is held down and molested by a group including Terry Flynn, Ret Lear, and Art Jennings. To be more exact, Grove's sparse pubic hair is shaved off; then a vigorous but unsuccessful attempt is made to bring him to climax while Grove, with pathetic bravado, begins "laughing artificially and shouting through his laughter: 'Yeah, yeah, keep trying, you sonofabitches, keep trying—wow, are *you* guys ever having yourselves a good time.'"

Did it really happen that way? Ret Hunter, in a letter he wrote Yates in 1979, seemed unable or unwilling to recall: "Most of my friends have said everything from, 'Sue the bastard,' to 'What a sad, unhappy boy he must have been.' Irv Jennings said, 'You must admit, Ret, we were a couple of bastards!' The truth is somewhere in the middle." Irv Jennings, when asked about the incident, denied any direct involvement—though he did admit to being a witness and offered a few clarifying details: Yates was not actually masturbated, he said; rather a bottle of hair tonic was poured on his genitals to make (so the joke went) his pubic hair grow. And really it seems as if the whole episode ended almost fortunately for Yates: That is, when his genitals began to swell painfully from the tonic, his tormentors became worried that he'd report them to the headmaster, with almost certain expulsion to follow. But he never did; the whole thing blew over, and Yates was left alone after that—though like Bill Grove, he might have spent a number of nights "wondering how he was going to live the rest of his life."*

On December 6, 1941, Yates's sister Ruth married Fred Rodgers in an Episcopal ceremony. The bride's side of the church was somewhat depleted by the calculated absence of Dookie's sisters, and Vincent Yates (whose family was something of a mystery to his children) also came alone; nor were there many contemporaries of the bride, since Ruth's life had been too chaotic and itinerant for her to make lasting friendships. But friends and relatives of the Rodgers family, who came in force from Long Island, Cape Cod, and beyond, made a more than respectable gathering, and along with Fred's pals from Grumman there were as many as a hundred guests at the reception in the St. Regis Hotel. Dancing to a live orchestra followed the sit-down dinner, and Dookie made the most of the Shocking Pink dress and hat she'd bought for the occasion. A study in contrast was her son Richard—on a weekend pass from Avon—who seemed to resent his mother's extroversion and wasn't inclined to celebrate. He moped around and said little, while his mother danced with Fritz Rodgers and otherwise carried on as if to compensate for her son's dreariness.

Ruth was happy. She adored her husband and was utterly devoted to him and the three children they would produce in the first four years of marriage. In those early days she relished every aspect of motherhood, even the act of giving birth, which she likened to an operatic experience à la Wagner, and she loved Wagner. During the war Fred continued to work at the Grumman plant as enlisted naval personnel, and Ruth would wash his uniforms in the bathtub while listening to the Metropolitan Opera on the radio. "She was smart and beautiful," said her sister-in-law Louise, who described Ruth as having "a Judy Garland personality and a Joan Crawford look." But really Ruth was hard to pigeonhole one way or the other; for all her gentle, seeming simplicity, she was a person of

---

*Yates told his daughter Monica that the masturbation scene was true as written. Harry Flynn, for his part, said he doesn't recall the incident.

considerable refinement. She read widely, wrote stories for her children, and became an expert gardener—and while some of her finer nuances may have been lost on her husband, he loved and appreciated her in his fashion. For a while it was a far better life than she'd known before. And to a seemly but increasing degree, Ruth tried to distance herself from Dookie in favor of her husband, children, and comparatively stable in-laws, though Dookie wasn't easily gotten rid of.

While away at his sister's wedding, Yates missed a memorable moment or two at Avon. That Sunday one of the administrators, Commander Hunter, disrupted activity on the polo field to announce, with tears in his eyes, that Pearl Harbor had been attacked. Then, as if to punctuate the matter, Mrs. Riddle's long-suffering husband—who'd always served as the voice of reason during her more imperious moods—died the very next day. The two events would have intricate consequences for Avon, not altogether unpleasant as far as Yates was concerned. In any event he came back to an already changing atmosphere—a mood of fatalism that became all the more palpable a few days later, with the death of poet-hero John Magee (Avon '40) in the Battle of Britain.*

By the spring semester Headmaster Stabler was trying to instill a spartan, martial spirit in the students with an ambitious new program of "wartime discipline" (air-raid drills, blackouts, more community service), one aspect of which had a distinct impact on Yates's life at Avon and beyond. A schoolwide essay contest was held on the theme of "America at War"—and the winner was Yates, whose reward was a place on the staff of the school newspaper, *The Avonian,* to which he'd end up devoting most of his time and energy for the next two and a half years. *The Avonian* was something to do, or rather something he *could* do, having failed at everything else. It wasn't, however, any great social coup; there was no real prestige in any nonathletic activity, but at least *The Avonian* gave him a pretext for mingling with other would-be writers, whose absence from the fields of glory was almost as conspicuous as his own.

---

*Magee gained a certain degree of posthumous fame for his poem "High Flight": "Oh! I have slipped the surly bonds of earth. . . . Put out my hand and touched the face of God."

The first real friends he made were older boys who sympathized with his loneliness. Davis Pratt,* a sixth former, was something of a role model—"an individualist, a pixie," as his teacher Clarence Derrick recalled, "the type of person the Avon educational philosophy was designed to enroll and foster." Pratt's teachers indulged his aversion to conventional studies and gave him the freedom to pursue his own interests: photography and ornithology. Thus he found both his vocation and avocation at Avon, and when he wasn't wandering around the woods with his binoculars and camera, he was a friendly reader of Yates's apprentice fiction, which he compared to the work of Thomas Wolfe (an unequivocal compliment in those days). The two corresponded during the war and died within a year of each other, though it's doubtful they stayed in touch in the meantime. Still, a look at Pratt's later career suggests a bond of sorts: He went on to become the first curator of photography at Harvard, where (according to his *New York Times* obituary) he'd started as an unpaid volunteer. Clarence Derrick expressed the "moral of Davis Pratt" as follows: "If no niche exists, create one for yourself through persistence, dedication and hard work." Such a process, in Yates's case, also began in earnest at Avon.

Lothar Candels, who wrote *The Avonian's* humor column ("The Beaver's Log"), formed what he called a "mutual admiration society" with Yates. Candels was the son of the school cook—a trained European chef who prepared excellent meals but was nonetheless regarded as "a menial"—and thus was no stranger to condescension and outright persecution. Both he and Yates were rather quirky young men with unconventional interests: Candels, in addition to being an occasional writer and photographer, was an avid butterfly collector; once, when he'd proudly mounted a rare moth, a cloddish classmate (whose fictional counterpart figures prominently in *A Good School*) leaned his elbow on the glass and deliberately damaged the specimen. But Candels was so good-natured that most of the students were fond of him, and like Davis Pratt he became a kind of "parent figure" (as he put it) to the unhappy Yates. "He was always stooped," Candels remembered, "as though he were carrying around a burden." Even then Yates was given to sudden brooding

---

*No relation to Hugh Pratt, one of Yates's later friends at Avon.

depressions—during which, if coaxed, he'd speak in a desultory way of his family, his poverty, his feelings of oddness and despair. Often he wondered aloud whether he should see the school psychiatrist. But his own melancholy seemed to embarrass him, much less talking about it, and he was willing to be kidded out of his funks by the kindly, waggish author of "The Beaver's Log." And no matter how fragile Yates seemed in other respects, Candels was impressed by the strength of character he showed as a writer, his precocious sense of total commitment—an enthusiasm he was generous in sharing. "Dick inspired me to write," said Candels, who later courted his wife by composing sonnets. "He was a sensitive and very touching young man."

"I suppose you know Ruth is married now, and not only that but she is going to have a baby about the first of October," Yates wrote Stephen Benedict in the summer of 1942.* "She and her husband, and Mother and I are all living here in Cold Spring Harbor which is a swell little town on the North Shore, about thirty-five miles from New York."

The ménage to which Yates came home that summer in Cold Spring Harbor—so gruesomely evoked in his novel of the same name—was almost certainly Dookie's idea. The elder Rodgerses, Fritz and Louise, had moved out of Genius Row and gone to live in Nantucket for a while; with Ruth married and Richard away at Avon, Dookie found herself alone in an apartment she could scarcely afford in the first place, and now her child-support payments were cut in half. Meanwhile Ruth and Fred had a baby on the way, but the best they could do on his modest salary was a tiny Long Island apartment where they lived for a few months after the wedding. Little doubt, then, that Dookie took it on herself to solve their problems with her usual flair: Combining their meager incomes, they could just afford to rent a dilapidated clapboard house on the fringe of one of the more affluent communities on the North Shore—the hilly beaches of

---

*The two had been out of touch since the summer Yates went to Vermont. Sixty years later Benedict wrote, "Rereading the Cold Spring Harbor letter, when Dick was 16, three years after the others, the change seems quite poignant. The wonderful silliness is gone and the adult has begun to emerge."

which had been immortalized in the stained-glass designs of Louis Comfort Tiffany, whose estate was one of the many fine old places overlooking Cold Spring Harbor.

That summer Dookie and Richard really got to know Ruth's husband for the first time, and both formed an enduring dislike of him (and vice versa). It must have been a shock for Dookie, who believed so wholly in the idea of aristocracy, to be confronted with this awful daily reminder that every advantage of breeding and education could, sometimes, result in such a consummate lout as her son-in-law. And then to be fair: A better man than Fred might have buckled under the strain of having to live with Dookie. What must have been a fatal incompatibility is nicely suggested by the family dinner scenes in *Cold Spring Harbor*: "Well," says Gloria Drake; "I've always thought the dinner hour was for conversation." Fred appears as the cretinous Evan, shorn of his accent but essentially intact: "Evan Shephard hardly looked up from his plate, even in response to murmured questions from his wife, and his stolid concentration seemed to suggest that eating, no less than the day's work of fathering children, was just another part of a man's job in the world." Nor was this laconic laborer likely to find much in common with his bumbling, bug-eyed brother-in-law, and perhaps their one attempt to bond was very like the abortive driving lesson Evan gives Phil in the book, though the latter's humiliation (that is, Yates's) probably made little difference in his overall view of Fred: "[He] knew there might not be much profit or future in hating your brother-in-law, but that didn't mean you couldn't figure him out and see him plain. . . . This ignorant, inarticulate, car-driving son of a bitch would never even be promoted to a halfway decent job. . . . Fuck him."

In desperate need of pocket money and escape, Yates looked all over the countryside for a summer job, but discovered that most places wouldn't hire anybody under the age of eighteen. Finally he found employment of sorts as a parking-lot attendant at a roadside restaurant called Costello's: "All I do is rush around in a chauffeur's cap and tell people where to park their jalopies," he wrote Benedict. The chauffeur's cap had been his own idea: Except for a token sum of five dollars a week he was paid entirely in tips, which began to pick up once he'd found an official-looking cap in an

Army and Navy store and thus ceased being a random kid wagging a flashlight. One hesitates to make too much of this episode, Yates's first paying job, though it's fair to say that it whetted his appetite for financial independence—within a few months he'd be more or less self-supporting for the rest of his life—and then, too, one can hardly imagine the relief he felt at having some excuse to work all night and sleep most of the day.

Avon, no doubt, seemed a waiting Arcadia when the time came for Yates to return in mid-September. The living experiment in Cold Spring Harbor had turned cold indeed, at least this particular trial, and a parting of the ways was imminent. The elder Rodgerses were planning at last to resume residence of their family estate in St. James, Long Island, as soon as the tenant's lease expired in the fall, and they'd invited Fred and Ruth to join them there with the newborn baby. Dookie, meanwhile, would return to New York, but for now she pouted around the house and, always sensitive about her age, openly rued the prospect of becoming a grandmother ("Can you imagine me as a grandmother?" says Pookie in *The Easter Parade*; "I can't even imagine you as a mother," her daughter reflects). And in the midst of it all was Richard, whose departure from the scene, for any number of reasons, was almost surely as frantic as Phil Drake's:

> [His] final moments of leaving Cold Spring Harbor would always be blurred in his memory. He knew he must have hauled his suitcase downstairs fast because a station taxicab was already honking for him in the driveway; he knew he must have made a stop in the kitchen to accept one last sloppy embrace from his mother; then he was on the train and the rotten little town was far behind him.

· · ·

Yates's last two years at Avon were far happier than his first. He would always be the butt of a certain amount of teasing, but it became more benign as he learned to handle it better. Rather than trying to swagger off insults with more of the same (and getting beaten up or paddled), Yates became a soft-spoken eccentric who rolled with the punches. "I guess I left the coat hanger in by mistake," he'd say, if a person made fun of his sometimes rigid posture, the way his shoulders tended to bunch and shudder around his ears when he was tense. But perhaps the best way of pre-empting attack was, after all, simple good manners, and around this time Yates apparently began to take Mrs. Riddle's precepts to heart. He may have had an apple-size hole in the elbow of his only tweed jacket, and hair that stuck out at an odd angle, but Yates was *courteous*—shy, formal—or so certain of his would-be enemies remember him.

Happily he didn't have to strain himself with everybody. That second year he was named editor in chief of *The Avonian* and art director of the *Winged Beaver* (the school yearbook), and hence became a campus figure of sorts. Best of all, he began to make a few friends his own age. Perhaps the first of these was Pierre Van Nordan, whose relative weirdness is evoked by the uncharitable "Van Loon" conferred on his alter ego in *A Good School*. According to the *Winged Beaver,* Van Nordan was a connoisseur of "guns, game, Omar Khayyam, women and beer," and *A Good School* suggests he also had a penchant for sitting on the toilet longer than necessary. Whatever the case, Van Nordan was in fact regarded as a bit of a curiosity, and probably Yates (like Grove vis-à-vis Van Loon) eventually kept him at a distance while at Avon; however, Yates was at Van Nordan's bedside when the latter died of Hodgkin's disease in his early thirties, as the friendship had deepened in later years.

A more improbable friendship, and one that perished of natural causes shortly after the war, was the one Yates pursued with the studious Hugh Pratt. Pratt's greatest appeal appears to have been his almost daunting respectability: Apart from his work as editor of the *Winged Beaver* and associate editor of *The Avonian*, he was one of the school's top scholars and a standout football player to boot. Above all he was serious, and demanded seriousness from his friends. At least one thing he and Yates had in common was a fondness for late-night bull sessions of the loftier sort; both were charter members of something called the "Midnight Oil League." Beyond that the attachment is harder to fathom. Like Hugh Britt in *A Good School*, Pratt was quick to reproach Yates for failures of taste and more obvious personal shortcomings: "You're always late for everything," says Britt when Grove asks to be his roommate; "you flunk courses and don't seem to care; you're sloppy; that kind of thing could make trouble if we roomed together." A mutual friend described Pratt as Yates's "opposite," and Pratt seemed to agree in every respect but one: "Dick was not frivolous about his writing. He'd scribble over *reams* of blank paper. Every Saturday we'd build a fire in the Senior Club, and Dick would just sit there and write all day."

The extent to which Yates was playing a role for his friend, whose stability and high-mindedness he clearly envied, is worth considering; for that matter such posing in general—and Yates was nothing if not self-conscious as a young man—was arguably essential to his becoming what he was so determined to be. When Grove is announced as the winner of the "America at War" essay contest, he finds that he's developed "a strange new ability to see himself whole, from the outside, as if through a movie camera twenty feet away"; and Grove maintains this perspective when he plays, with relish, "his role as sportswriter":

> He would shamble along the sidelines, carrying a clipboard and a chewed pencil to record each play; when a game was stalled he would squat and write, holding the clipboard on one tense thigh and very much aware that a number of smaller kids were peering over his shoulder; when the game broke open again he'd get up and run with it, almost as fast as the ball carrier, with the little kids racing in his wake.

Yates's devotion to such tasks was so conspicuous at Avon that he was ultimately regarded as the embodiment of writerly aspiration, and indeed his influence was pervasive: He wrote almost every word of the newspaper, much of the yearbook and literary magazine, and performed all community-service hours in the school's eighteenth-century printshop. "Dick ran everything of a literary nature," said classmate Gilman Ordway. "He might have been the only one of us who knew exactly what he wanted to do with his life—become a writer of fiction."

And finally, with the arrival of fellow fifth former Ernest Bicknell Wright, Yates's success might have seemed, in its limited way, more or less complete. "Bicky" Wright was the rebellious scion of an old-money family in Philadelphia (he later had his name removed from the Social Register), and Avon was a last resort after he'd been expelled from two previous prep schools. Like his counterpart "Bucky" Ward in *A Good School*, Wright immediately "earned an outlaw's celebrity" by smoking on campus before he was seventeen and cultivating a moody, slouching persona in general. The son of a bullying, alcoholic father who openly professed not to like his children much, Wright despised authority and was alternately witty and bitter about it.

He and Yates could hardly believe their luck: Both flunked courses and didn't care, both were sloppy, both were rather curious physical specimens (the diminutive Wright would grow six more inches after he left Avon), and both felt alienated from their surroundings (whatever those happened to be); above all, both coped by making fun of the world. Now each had a perfect audience in the other. As Yates characterized the friendship in *A Good School*: "It was almost like falling in love. Bucky Ward could make him laugh over and over again until he began to feel like a girl who might at any moment cry 'Oh, you keep me in *stitches*!'" Wright was noted in the *Winged Beaver* as "the possessor of the school's quickest comeback," but in this respect Yates became (somewhat to his own surprise) a worthy rival. They had a ritual: Whenever one came up with a particularly choice witticism, the other would pretend to preserve it forever in the top drawer of a Platonic cabinet, filing it away with a flourish of the wrist. Indeed the friendship might have been all but ideal, were it not for Wright's weakness for melodrama. *"Things!"* cries Bucky Ward in *A Good School*. "Christ, Grove, do you ever get so you can't stand *things*? . . . You oughta see my family's house. Oh, it's very nice and it's very big and it cost my father a hell of a lot of money, but I can never make him understand it's just another *thing*." And so on. For Yates, who preferred to keep his weltschmerz to himself, such displays made for uncomfortable moments. He liked Wright better when he was funny.*

---

*Wright's widow confirmed his aptitude for melodrama. As a minor example (a major one will follow in due course), she remembered how Wright used to lurch tragically against walls, in all apparent seriousness, if dinner was late. He did suffer from low blood sugar, she pointed out, but the lurching was a bit much.

Yates was almost in danger of becoming a reasonably happy young man when his fifty-six-year-old father died suddenly of pneumonia (and general exhaustion, one suspects) on December 14, 1942. Family lore has it that Vincent died on the very day his daughter's second son was conceived, and moreover that this son, Peter, grew up to be an almost exact replica of his maternal grandfather (not to mention a minister like his great-grandfather). Alas, little else is known of Vincent's death outside Yates's fiction, though fortunately ample explication is found there. In fact the episode is treated similarly and at length in *A Good School, The Easter Parade, A Special Providence,* and especially "Lament for a Tenor." The protagonist of "Tenor," Jack Warren, is having breakfast in the refectory when he's discreetly informed by the headmaster that he has an urgent message to call home. This he does, and though he feels nothing on hearing the sad news except "an automatic tightening in his chest," he's impressed by his mother's uncontrollable weeping, as if she were "a real widow." In both this story and *A Special Providence,* Yates's alter ego is just able to stop himself from saying, in effect, "What the hell, Mother, are we supposed to *cry* when he dies?" An uncomfortable session with the headmaster follows in "Tenor" (the man speaks vaguely of God's will and arranges for Warren to leave on an afternoon train), after which the young man heads back to his room to pack and decide how best to get through the next few hours at school: "it was oddly enjoyable to have a secret like this, and he mounted the rest of the stairs with theatrical gravity, an inscrutable, tragic young man." But he's troubled by how empty he feels. "You couldn't very well cry over a man you hardly knew," Warren reflects, casting back to their last few meetings, which lately "had spaced out to three or four a year, usually just a restaurant lunch and an awkward afternoon during one of Jack's holidays."

In "Tenor" and elsewhere, Yates made note of his father's obvious deterioration in recent years—that he looked "smaller and grayer," that he coughed and drank more—though the man always treated his son with alert solicitude, and seemed to accept that it was incumbent on himself to keep the conversation going. One thing that evidently disturbed Yates in retrospect was his failure to call his father "Dad." In *A Good School* Bill Grove finds it "all but impossible": "He remembered having no trouble with the more childish 'Daddy,' years ago, but 'Dad' eluded his tongue. He tried to avoid the problem, on the rare occasions when he saw the man, by arranging his remarks in such a way as to require calling him nothing at all." But both Grove and Jack Warren are able to relieve their consciences somewhat by remembering the relative success of that last paternal visit at school, when father and son went for a pleasant-enough stroll around campus and the latter managed, finally, to say "Dad."

For the most part, though, the whole event seems to have evoked very little in the way of conventional sentiment. "You know, my father's really a pretty boring guy," Jack Warren remarks to his roommate after that visit, and once he knows his father is dead he reads over the man's last (unanswered) letter, which is full of well-meaning banality: "Was sorry to see you're still having trouble with that mark in math. You know the way to improve your math, or anything else for that matter, is just say to yourself, 'Who's going to win? This math, or me?'" Little wonder Yates felt bound to admit that he was, after all, his mother's son, or that his most definite emotion when his father died was a kind of piquant self-pity. When Jack Warren manages a few cathartic sobs on the train home, it dawns on him that he's really crying "for himself—a boy bereaved," whereupon he begins to retch rather than cry. The same moment recurs in *The Easter Parade*, when Emily stops crying over her father as soon as she realizes her tears are "wholly for herself—for poor, sensitive Emily Grimes whom nobody understood, and who understood nothing."*

It could be that Dookie's far more elaborate grief indicated a greater awareness of certain grim consequences to follow, along with perhaps a genuine fondness for the man and a slight pang for having hastened his decline. Whether she really kissed his corpse on the mouth à la Pookie Grimes and Alice Prentice is impossible to say, though the image serves nicely to suggest the disgust she provoked in her son on that occasion, and ever more frequently afterward. "It was *her* fault," Robert Prentice reflects at the funeral. "She had robbed him of a father and robbed his

---

*As may be evident by now, *The Easter Parade* is one of Yates's most autobiographical novels, even though the "Me character"—as Yates liked to refer to the inevitable character(s) based on himself—is a woman. "Emily fucking Grimes is *me*," Yates told a friend, paraphrasing Flaubert.

father of a son, and now it was too late." For a number of reasons Yates's disenchantment with his mother would accelerate after Vincent's death, and that may have been the man's most impressive legacy, both in terms of his son's life and his son's work. But Vincent remained something of a two-dimensional figure in Yates's mind: a mild-mannered, well-meaning fellow who tried to make the best of a terrible mistake—though just *how* terrible Yates could scarcely appreciate until years later, when his father became a more haunting abstraction. "All I'm really qualified to remember is the sadness of his later life—the bad marriage that cost him so much, the drab little office from which he assisted in managing the sales of light bulbs for so many years, the tidy West Side apartment . . . where I can only hope he found love before his death."

Yates spent that Christmas vacation mastering the fine points of a habit that probably killed his father and would eventually kill him, too. But then Yates always loved to smoke, and perhaps it was worth it as far as he was concerned: It gave a shy, nervous person something to do with his hands; it made him alert; he liked the taste; and besides he didn't much care about his health anyway. But it all began (and to some extent persisted) as the purest form of adolescent affectation, a way of looking—at last—somewhat masculine and grown-up: "Cigarettes were a great help because any big-eyed, full-lipped boy could be made to look all right if he smoked all the time." With his friend Bick, Yates had begun smoking illicitly during his first semester as a fifth former, but others had made fun of his beginner's cough; now that he was about to turn seventeen, and eligible to light up at will in the Senior Club, he was determined to outsmoke the lot of them. As he described his self-training in *A Good School*:

> First he had to learn the physical side of it . . . how to will his senses to accept drugged dizziness as pleasure rather than incipient nausea. Then came the subtler lessons in aesthetics, aided by the use of the bathroom mirror: learning to handle a cigarette casually, even gesturing with it while talking, as if scarcely aware of having it in his fingers; deciding which part of his lips formed the spot where a cigarette might hang most attractively . . . and how

best to squint against the smoke. . . . The remarkable thing about cigarettes . . . was that they added years to the face that had always looked nakedly younger than his age.

For the rest of his time at Avon, Yates was rarely seen outside the class-room without a butt dangling off his lip, and clearly he looked forward to the day when he'd never have to abstain at all—never have to leave his round-eyed vulnerable face exposed without a smoke screen to squint behind.

Most students at Avon spent their free time, especially during week-ends, availing themselves one way or another of Mrs. Riddle's vast estate, her picturesque farms and woodlands, playing polo, perhaps, or venturing into Hartford for a meal and a movie. Yates—never one for the outdoors and too poor for polo or Hartford—was almost always (from 1943 on) to be found at either the *Avonian* office or the Senior Club, smoking and writing. The ambience of the Senior Club particularly appealed to him, what with its leather sofas and armchairs, its phonograph and pool table, its overall conduciveness to "learning how to behave in college" (the clos-est Yates would ever come to that milieu). Occasionally he'd bestir himself for a game of pool—at least one classmate remembered him (likely in error) as "quite good"—but mostly he sat, smoked, drank coffee, and wrote.

One of the stories he finished as a fifth former, "Forgive Our Foolish Ways," was featured in the 1943 *Winged Beaver*. It is Yates's earliest sur-viving fiction, and its thousand or so words describe the spiritual conver-sion of a dying soldier, hitherto a hard-boiled skeptic. A representative patch of prose: "He remembered running like a scared rabbit across the sand, hearing the machine guns spitting at him, and being half-crazed with horror and fear. He remembered feeling that his face must look like a frightened child's, mouth open and cheeks jogging loosely." That last phrase is promising, as are certain others ("writhing like a squashed bee-tle"), but otherwise the story is unremarkable: At first its wounded pro-tagonist boldly dismisses the "phony ideas" of those who believe in a "phony God," but while dying he's surrounded by "an immense, radiant, all-inclusive light" and hears "a great choir," and so on. For what it's worth, the story is somewhat better than the three or four others featured in that year's *Winged Beaver,* and seems to give a fair sense of what was on Yates's mind at the time.

But a far better forum for his ideas—and abilities, too, at least as they stood then—was *The Avonian,* and perhaps the best proof of this is the last issue of that school year, dated June 9, 1943. At the bottom center of the front page is a box headlined "In Memoriam":

> As we go to press, tragic news reaches us. It is with profound sorrow that we announce the death of David James Stanley, one of the finest men Avon has ever known. Dave was killed at sea, just three weeks after his departure from School to join the United States Merchant Marine. The loss to Avon is irreparable, his memory imperishable.

Nothing brought the reality of war closer to Avon than the death of David Stanley, the lovable young man who appears as Larry Gaines in *A Good School.* Handsome and sweet-natured, Stanley had just become engaged to Alice Sperry, the pretty seventeen-year-old daughter of Avon's biology teacher. Stanley had finished school early to join the merchant marine and thus avoid the regular draft, when—only a day or two before Avon's graduation ceremony—his ship collided with a munitions vessel and sank to the bottom of Hampton Bay. As recorded in *A Good School,* the last issue of the newspaper was minutes away from press (in fact a blackly ironic item remains on page four, listing David Stanley as "Most Likely To Succeed") when the news reached Avon; alone, amid a community stunned with grief, Yates had to keep his head and compose a brief but seemly tribute, then reconfigure the front page and see *The Avonian* into press. Not only did he succeed, but the editorial he'd written for that issue could hardly have been more appropriate under the circumstances. Addressed to the graduating class, it put into well-considered words what was surely on the mind of every Avon student in 1943, more than ever after the death of David Stanley:

> In times like these, when everyone's future is completely uncertain, those of us who are leaving cannot help but be thankful for the steady and secure

existence Avon has afforded us. A few of the boys graduating today may never come out of the war alive. All of them will undoubtedly experience more trying and dangerous times than have ever confronted a generation of young men since history began.

Yates won a special award that year for his work on *The Avonian,* and deservedly so: Under his editorship the newspaper was "larger in size and more inclusive in scope" (so noted the *Winged Beaver*), and such improvements were appreciated more widely than one might expect. "You publish a splendid newspaper," wrote an alumnus stationed at Fort Leavenworth, Kansas. "I cannot in any way find fault with it, and I admire the wit of the news articles, the frankness of the editorials . . . [and] congratulate you sincerely on a masterpiece among school papers." Lest one think this sort of thing caused Yates to take himself too seriously, consider a filler item on page two of that same *Avonian*: "If the writing in this issue seems rather bumpy in spots, please don't condemn it too much. Our beloved Editor (?) was in the infirmary with the measles and consequently every single article in this *Avonian* has contacted [*sic*] the frightful disease." Clearly the wag who used to jape about "*kahts*" and garbagemen and " 'T.B.' in 'V.T.' " was still alive, if not altogether well.

Among friends Yates still spoke of his mother admiringly, as a "struggling artist," while remaining entirely silent on the subject of his father's death. During the man's life, though, Yates never really grasped what was involved in the subsidy of a struggling artist such as Dookie, and may have wondered why his father had waxed so solemn, so deadly earnest, whenever he tried to explain that someday she'd be Richard's responsibility.

The day had come. Dookie was left with nothing after Vincent's death, and when Yates returned to New York that summer he found her living in a cheap hotel on East Thirty-ninth Street, all her sculpture and remaining furniture in storage. She was predictably far behind in both rent and storage payments, and eating her meals out of cans. At something called the Ultima Optical Company she'd found a job grinding lenses, though she longed for something more glamorous and remunerative. Some twenty years before, as a single "career gal" in Manhattan, she'd been a fashion illustrator, and to that line of work she devoutly wished to return. One assumes her son was at least as skeptical as Robert Prentice in *A Special Providence*: "Even he could see how still and labored and hopelessly unsaleable-looking her drawings were, though she explained it was all a question of making the right contacts."

While Dookie applied her native flair to making contacts and grinding lenses, Yates found work as a copyboy at the *New York Sun*. Though the *Sun* "[wasn't] really much of a paper" (as Walter Grimes explains to his daughters in *The Easter Parade*), Yates enjoyed the role of an honest workingman. At the time the extra income made it possible for him and Dookie to move to a larger furnished apartment only a block away from the Ultima Optical Company on West Fifty-fifth, if somewhat farther from the *Sun* on Chambers Street. Also, the job gave him good material for his next short story (more on that below), some of which was deftly recycled for his fourth novel more than thirty years later.

For a while Yates may have enjoyed being the breadwinner at the age of seventeen, but the romance soon began to pall. The combined salaries of a copyboy and a lens grinder didn't amount to much, but Dookie was utterly debonair about the future. Night after night she jabbered about the contacts she was making in the fashion world, as well as the lucrative "one-man show" that was right around the corner, while her son listened and the canned soup simmered. As for Richard's hard work to pay for groceries and most of the rent, Dookie pretended with friends that it was just "a little laboring job . . . *you* know the kind of thing boys do in the summertime." And then, as if there were no pressing question of how to pay fees at an expensive private school in the fall, Dookie blew much of their wages on a new wardrobe—this, of course, to establish herself in the fashion world. "You sound just like your father," she'd sigh, when he ventured to suggest that they be more thrifty. Finally he began to lose his temper. When thus cornered (especially about money), Dookie tended to throw a kind of stylized fit—partly a matter of genuine hysterics, no doubt, and partly a matter of enlightened self-interest. In one form or another the performance is given by all her fictional personae, though perhaps most vividly by Alice Prentice:

> And she burst into tears. As if shot, she then clutched her left breast and collapsed full length on the floor. . . . She lay facedown, quivering all over and making spastic little kicks with her feet, while he stood and watched. . . . It had happened often enough, in various crises, that he knew she wasn't really having a heart attack; all he had to do was wait until she began to feel foolish lying there.

As it turned out, Dookie never did generate enough contacts to break back into the fashion world, though shortly before her son returned to school she managed to find a job in a factory that made department-store mannequins. This was better suited to her talents than lens grinding, but all such work was "harsh and degrading," as Yates put it in "Regards at Home"—"pitifully wrong for a bewildered, rapidly aging, often hysterical woman who had always considered herself a sculptor with at least as much intensity as I brought to the notion of myself as a writer."

Were it not for his home life and the wartime possibility of imminent death, Yates's final year at Avon might have been idyllic. As noted in *A Good School,* his classmates were actually *nice* to one another—not only because they were seniors, but also because of a general wish to live and let live in what little time was left before being drafted. The mood was one of rather blithe pessimism. Rumor had it that Mrs. Riddle and Headmaster Stabler—never on the best of terms—had reached an impasse over the budget and other matters, and even the faculty seemed a bit tongue-in-cheek about bothering with one's work. Yates's favorite English teacher, Dr. Knowles, occasionally spent whole classes in self-absorbed silence, studying Japanese characters with a magnifying glass and chuckling at nothing in particular. And when the school warden—an amiable but over-serious sixth former named David Bigelow (who affected not to care when people called him "Shorty")—tried to enforce the headmaster's blackout regulations, he was met with such brazen ridicule that the memory angers him still.

Yates thrived. Because of his excellent record as editor he was given the unprecedented privilege of running *The Avonian* without the aid of a faculty adviser, and the newspaper became more influential than ever—not only was it sent to training camps around the country, but also to every theater of war where alumni served. It was an ideal time to be a lackadaisical student wholly committed to other, more glorious pursuits, and Yates relished his role as a kind of maverick litterateur. Witness his senior profile in the *Winged Beaver* (accompanied by a snapshot of Yates sneering, with a cigarette):

> As Editor during his last two years, Dick's familiar figure has been seen many a Tuesday afternoon, draped in a pair of gray trousers and wilted blue shirt as he strides about with a harassed look. At five fifteen he totters into the Avon Club, lights the usual cigarette, and falls on the most comfortable sofa. The crisis has passed and our next *Avonian* will come out after all.

Yates was also the school's most gifted cartoonist, and his caricatures of Stabler and staff were prized as keepsakes among the students. As art director of the *Winged Beaver* (and later associate editor), he provided the yearbook illustrations for two years, and his lead cartoon for the 1944 edition was apt: a hulking, ape-faced drill sergeant holding a uniform in one hand and crooking a fat finger at some unseen recruit with the other. It was precisely what awaited them all, and everything else seemed beside the point. The time was right for antiheroes, and Yates was eulogized as such in the *Winged Beaver*: "And then Dick Yates, Our Editor,/ Our Novelist divine/ Who burned his midnight oil so much/ He switched to turpentine."

Yates's picturesque fretting over his various *Avonian* duties was mostly reserved for daylight hours; at night he burned his oil to work on fiction, and lost no time pouring his impressions from the *New York Sun* into a short story, "Schedule," which he finished early that autumn. Yates was proud enough of this effort to send it to Thomas Wolfe's agent and biographer, the rather celebrated Elizabeth Nowell,* who responded with an almost three-page, single-space critique that was remarkable in its prescience. "I think you're pretty good," she began, and continued in the same tone of candid, qualified congratulation. Nowell didn't know how old Yates was, only that he was in school, but noted that his story was far better than many she'd read by amateur adults. "I don't mean by that that I think you are ready to be published, but . . . keep on writing and getting surer of yourself: cutting deeper in the groove. The main thing is that you have a fine quality to your writing: the kind of feel to it that really good stuff has. As long as you've got that you'll never lose it."

"Schedule," which appeared in the 1944 *Winged Beaver,* is an apprentice work of unmistakable promise, and perhaps worth dwelling on at some little length. "The best part of [the story is] the very fine background of it," Nowell rightly pointed out, "the way you make the reader really see and hear and smell the newspaper building and all the departments in it." The first quarter of the story, in fact, is given over to some five hundred words of wonderfully irrelevant atmosphere: "The cigarette smoke rose listlessly, curling toward the ceiling, until it met the draft from the open top-halves of the windows and was whirled sharply out into the morning sunlight"—and from there we move on to the makeup editor "gingerly" sipping his coffee, to the pressroom workers with their "jaunty square hats of folded newspaper" (readers of *The Easter Parade* take note), to the great press machines "turning out newspapers fifteen a second, pushing them out wet with ink and hot from the dryers," and so forth.

"It seemed to me you had known a newspaper like this and had wanted to write about it," Nowell observed, "but had had to have some sort of regular story to weave it around so had taken Al Shapiro as the center of it." Just so: The great wave of descriptive eloquence with which the story begins washes up, finally and rather randomly, at the feet of Al Shapiro, whose menial task is to bundle the newspapers in twine. Shapiro is a kind

---

*Both Nowell and Yates's favorite teacher, Richard Knowles, were from the small town of South Dartmouth, Massachusetts. It seems reasonable to assume, then, that Knowles had something to do with getting his protégé's work read by someone of Nowell's stature.

of ur-version of the typical Yatesian loser: He wants to be a writer, but his prole father makes him drop out of school to haul ice; later he tries to take a journalism class (where all the students are younger and better dressed than he), but is humiliated by a tweedy pedant who advises him to learn basic grammar first; and finally, fifteen years later, the now middle-aged Al's diminished dreams take him all the way back to high school, despite the ridicule of a vulgar wife (" 'Listen, Al, I don' want no high school boy for a husband' "). In the end a coworker named Moe makes the mistake of teasing Al in precisely the wrong terms—" 'Christ almighty, are you gonna be ignorant *all* your life?' "—whereupon Al goes berserk and attacks the man with his twine cutter.

But mere plot summary fails to do justice to the many fine things here, such as the nicely sustained *time* theme—the schedule of various newspaper editions posted throughout the narrative (even as time runs out on poor Al Shapiro), the "great living monster" of the press machine rolling inexorably on to make the newspaper (as the story ends) "on *time*." Clearly Yates had worked hard and learned a few things about craft over the past year, and indeed Elizabeth Nowell not only detected his talent but also his autodidactic tendency: "I think you have enough natural feeling for writing to teach yourself and do it far better than anyone else can do it." This borders on the prophetic, and may explain why Yates kept the letter all his life, perhaps for the purpose of occasional reassurance.

According to federal law a high school student in 1943 could be drafted in the middle of his senior year if his eighteenth birthday fell before January. This applied to three of Yates's classmates—who took summer school to prepare for winter graduation and subsequent induction—among them Bick Wright. That year Wright had served as associate editor of *The Avonian* and succeeded Candels as the wit behind "The Beaver's Log"; this meant that Yates was necessarily exposed to his friend's vagaries on a more or less constant basis, which seems to have frayed their old rapport. Still, Bick's departure was a potent reminder that things were coming to an end, and probably the two marked the

occasion in much the same way as Grove and Ward in *A Good School*—
that is, by staying up late in the newspaper office and sharing a pint of
smuggled whiskey ("it tasted so awful that Grove couldn't imagine the
source of its celebrated power to give pleasure, let alone enslave the
soul"). Nor is there much reason to doubt that Wright was just as "dramatically morose" as Ward, full of gloomy bravado in the wake of a
Dear John letter he'd just received: " 'I don't care anymore. . . . I don't
care what happens to me in the Army or anything else.' " In any case he
left that December; Pierre Van Nordan took over as associate editor,
Yates became the new dorm inspector of Building One, and things continued to end.

It was a bad Christmas. As Yates would tell it later (not for laughs), this
was the year he was "kidnapped" by Avon—forbidden to go home for the
holidays because his tuition hadn't been paid since his father's death.
Extreme measures were therefore indicated, though this one was no more
successful than others. Dookie temporized as usual, and Yates spent
Christmas with the Avon staff, who if anything were less happy about it
than he.

Of course the really remarkable thing is their indulgence in allowing
him to stay at all, even as a Yuletide hostage. It suggested the larger
problem: Headmaster Stabler, in his zeal to recruit less privileged but
otherwise well-suited students, had perhaps overlooked the possibility
that Mrs. Riddle would choose to cut her losses at some point. But Stabler had all but ensured this result by enacting a number of reforms
without the founder's consent: Not only did he switch the clothing franchise from Brooks Brothers to the plebeian Franklin Simon (and was
planning to abolish the dress code altogether), but also he changed the
name from Avon Old Farms to the Avon School, tinkered with curricu-
lum, insisted on a greater religious presence, and to that end erected a
hideous Hodgson Portable Chapel on the campus. This last touch, in
particular, seemed to gall Mrs. Riddle. She'd become increasingly bellicose since the death of her husband, and when Stabler presumed to mar
the architectural purity of her "indestructible school," she dropped the
bomb: Either abide by the letter of her Deed of Trust, she demanded, or
all support would be forever withdrawn. Stabler and the faculty resigned

en masse, perhaps in the hope of calling her bluff, but the widow Riddle was not a bluffer. In a letter to her mutinous underlings she noted that she'd spent "seven-ninths of [her] fortune in building and supporting the School," but now saw no alternative but to close at the end of the academic year. "A noble experiment had somehow gone wrong," wrote historian Gordon Ramsey.

At any other time the students might have taken the news in the same spirit with which they mocked themselves as "Avon Old Queers," but given the bleak immediate future it was a real blow, yet another of life's moorings giving way. "Our school is closed, and probably the future will record many a similar disillusionment," a student wrote in that year's *Winged Beaver*. As for Yates, the yearbook noted: "He does plan a college education and a career as a professional writer, but that must wait until peace." Something else that would have to wait was Yates's diploma, which was withheld pending the Godot-like prospect of his tuition payment.

No matter. Yates was a graduate in spirit and more or less in fact; and besides, the school was in the process of becoming a home for blinded veterans.* And then after a fashion he did find a way to pay his debt to Avon, and to his father too, really, perhaps in penance for having been so dismissive of both. On the one hand Yates would always remember Avon as a "dopey little school," but he also realized it had been almost perfect for the strange young man he was, and like Bill Grove he felt beholden to his father for paying his way—until the poor man died, that is, having given up his life in more than one respect so that his son could become the writer he was meant to be. Yates wished he could thank him for that:

I might even have told him—and this would have been only a slight exaggeration—that in ways still important to me it *was* a good school. It saw

---

*The school reopened in 1948, after Mrs. Riddle had been safely deceased for two years, and prospers unto this day. At one point, as a matter of pure coincidence, Yates's daughter Monica was a counselor at a camp for overweight children held at Avon Old Farms.

me through the worst of my adolescence, as few other schools would have done, and it taught me the rudiments of my trade. I learned to write by working on the [newspaper], making terrible mistakes in print that hardly anybody ever noticed. Couldn't that be called a lucky apprenticeship?

CHAPTER THREE

The Canal: 1944-1947

In later life Yates would become almost a parody of the self-destructive personality: He smoked constantly despite tuberculosis, emphysema, and repeated bouts of pneumonia; he was an alcoholic who, when unable to write, would sometimes start the day with martinis at breakfast; he rarely exercised (indeed could hardly walk without gasping), and ate red meat at every meal if he could help it. Such behavior seems to indicate a death wish, but it wasn't that simple in Yates's case. It was true he had a gloomy temperament and was sometimes all but immobilized by depression, though often enough he was capable of high delight, and as for smoking and drinking—well, he liked smoking and drinking. How to explain a man who by no means lacked a fear of pain and suffering (he dreaded cancer in particular) and sometimes rather enjoyed being alive, yet behaved almost as much as humanly possible to the contrary? A number of factors come to mind, but perhaps the most compelling was suggested by Yates's friend and fellow World War II veteran Kurt Vonnegut: "People don't recover from a war. There's a fatalism that he picked up as a soldier. Enlisted men are surprisingly indifferent to survival. Death doesn't matter much."

Certainly it's hard to imagine Yates as a soldier, and it must have been a jaded group of army examiners before whom this morbidly frail, morbidly self-conscious eighteen-year-old stood in his underwear on June 17, 1944. He was six foot three and weighed just over 160 pounds, but skinniness per se wasn't enough to disqualify him. Nor did the army psychiatrist find much amiss. The man asked him two questions, pro forma: "Do you like girls?" Yates said he did, and the man recorded this fact. "Do you ever get nervous?" Yates said he did, and the man paused. "Like when?" "Like when I'm standing in my underwear with a bunch of other guys getting asked a bunch of questions," Yates replied, and passed the exam.

It was downhill from there. In the weeks that followed, whatever self-confidence Yates had gained from his Avon success was decimated. First there was the IQ test that recruits took at the induction center. Yates alluded to this experience twice in his fiction—in *Disturbing the Peace* and the more explicitly autobiographical "Regards at Home"—and both times he gave the same IQ score: 109. Like many a great writer before him (Salinger and Cheever come to mind), Yates was a poor test taker—a slow, careful reader whose aversion to math bordered on the phobic.* This being the case, John Wilder's ordeal in *Disturbing the Peace* rings true: Wilder recounts for his psychiatrist how he scored 100 on his first attempt at the "Army General Classification test," which he retook in hope of scoring the 110 or better needed to qualify for officers' training; when he missed by a single point, he tried to remonstrate with the examiner, who said, " 'Curious thing; you didn't get a single question wrong, but you only did about half of them.' . . . 'Well, but, sir [Wilder replies], if I got them all right doesn't that indicate—' . . . 'It indicates a hundred and nine. You must be a very slow reader, that's all.' " Like Wilder, too, Yates's relatively poor performances on such tests would be a lifelong source of insecurity, though in person he hardly gave the impression of one whose IQ was barely above average (except perhaps in his almost obsessive vigilance against any form of intellectual pretension).

And so Yates had to make his way among enlisted men, almost all of whom were older, stronger, and more comfortable in their own skin. Under other circumstances he might have withdrawn into the shy, courteous persona that had served him well among bullies at Avon, but with his

---

*Nor should one forget the "slightly above average" score [109?] that twelve-year-old Prentice earns in *A Special Providence*. Psychologist Nancy Andreasen offered a clinical explanation for why creative writers generally fail to excel on IQ tests: "[They] tend to sort in large groups, change dimensions while in the process of sorting, arbitrarily change starting points, or use vague distantly related concepts as categorizing principles." Perhaps, though in Yates's case one suspects he was simply too slow and methodical.

ineptitude on constant display it was hard to maintain any sort of sangfroid, nor was the army a place for little gentlemen. After a "mild and pampered" month as an air corps recruit, Yates was transferred to Camp Pickett, Virginia, for basic training as an infantry rifleman—where (as he wrote of Bill Grove in *Uncertain Times*) "he'd been a fuckup, in the unforgiving idiom of the time." Later the term "fuckup" would invariably come to Yates's lips whenever he discussed his army days, which he endeavored to do in a lighthearted way. "Dick was hilarious about his war experiences," said his friend Pat Dubus. "The stories were always at his own expense, and he could really make you *see* it." The humor, the pathos too, mostly arose from a vast discrepancy between his desperate *effort* as a soldier, his pure intentions, and the results achieved by his clownishly incompetent body. For it can hardly be emphasized enough that Yates was clumsy on a legendary scale: All his life he bumbled and tripped and knocked things down, and not only was he clumsy but absentminded too—a bad combination in the army, as illustrated by the newly recruited Prentice in *A Special Providence*:

> On the very first morning, late for reveille and sleepily fumbling with his unfamiliar infantry leggings, he had put the damned things on backward, with the hood lacings on the inside rather than the outside of his calves; he had taken four running steps across the barracks floor before the lacing hooks of one legging caught the lace of the other, and down he came—all gangling, flailing six-foot-three of him—in a spectacular locklegged fall that left his audience weak with laughter the rest of the day.

And when one considers, finally, that at eighteen Yates was still a boy in almost every particular but height, it's a wonder he survived at all.

At Camp Pickett he was again a pariah, and this time there was almost nothing he could do about it. He couldn't find a niche among the surly, mostly working-class men, and there was no way to prove himself, or any fellow fuckup of quite the same magnitude with whom to commiserate. In moments of humiliating defeat he might try to vent his defiance (and perhaps bridge the social gap) by being as loud and foul-mouthed as the best of them, but this only made him seem more ridiculous; and if he tried to keep his own counsel he was mocked and left out just the same. The one thing he could do well was the one thing nobody seemed to notice: stay in step on parade, perform his manual of arms in crisp unison with his comrades—an aptitude made possible, perhaps, by the very fact that nobody was watching.

Later Yates would blend with the masses in a more essential way, as part of a personal (and artistic) ethic. "Dick cultivated an anti-intellectual manner," his friend and student DeWitt Henry observed,

> but there was nothing phony or affected about it. In places like the army and tuberculosis wards he was put in contact with unlettered people, who were just as sensitive as anybody else. Dick instinctively took it as his mission to articulate the complexity of people who didn't have the official badge of an education. It was a special quality of his writing. But in person, too, his manner was based on his army experiences—this need to bond with unlettered people. To Dick, speaking clearly and simply was good manners; pedantry was bad manners.

Pedantry was bad manners because it was a form of condescension, perhaps the form that made Yates most defensive in later years. While in the army, though, he didn't know that his own formal education was already over, and his empathy with "unlettered people" was in a latent phase at best. Still, the hardships he suffered as the nonpareil fuckup of Camp Pickett helped teach him the value of action rather than fine words, and perhaps increased his awareness of how certain people were likely to perceive his own behavior: "An all-around incompetent was bad enough," the narrator remarks of Robert Prentice; "but when he turned out to be a little wise guy too—when he swore not only in bad temper but in what sounded like the clipped, snotty accents of a spoiled rich kid—that was too much."

It does seem likely that Yates finally made a friend and mentor of sorts at Camp Pickett: a man represented by the well-spoken, irascible character of Quint in *A Special Providence*. The man seems to have taken pity on Yates, though his typical mood toward the forlorn fuckup was, apparently, exasperation. In any case what happened to "Quint" later, and Yates's possible part in it, would seem to lend further credibility to Vonnegut's thesis about the self-destructive tendencies of veterans.*

As a member of the 75th Division†—nicknamed the "Diaper Division" because it was the youngest to enter the war—Yates went overseas on January 8, 1945. By the time his ship arrived in England, the war in Europe was almost won: The Battle of the Ardennes, or the "Bulge," was in its final days, and with it the last German offensive had been routed. A hopeful rumor was spread among the replacements of the 75th that they were headed for a camp near Southampton, where they'd be trained to serve as occupation troops in Germany. When they got to Southampton, however, they were told to keep marching until they boarded a foul-smelling troopship bound for France.

From Normandy a train took them through snowy countryside until they came to the First Army replacement depot near a bombed-out, mostly abandoned Belgian village, where Yates lost no time living up to his Camp Pickett legend. Among the many "hilarious" war stories he liked to tell, perhaps the most characteristic is the one about how he was almost reported AWOL within days of arriving overseas. As told in *A Special Providence,* Yates accepted a soldier's invitation to join him and others in spending the night at a nearby civilian house, rather than the grain mill where the rest of the men were sleeping. After a jolly time with a hospitable Belgian family—who shared their wine and marveled at Yates's height (*"un grand soldat"*)—he woke up, late, to the mass shuffling sound of men on the march. He raced back to the grain mill to retrieve his lone

---

*In *Uncertain Times* Grove is writing (or rather *not* writing, since he's just as blocked as Yates was) a novel exactly like *A Special Providence*—so exactly, in fact, that he ruminates much over "his friend and mentor, called Quint in the book." Called Quint in *both* books, Grove's and Yates's, which gives one a sense of what can happen when an author runs out of material, but more on that later.

†Yates was in the 289th Infantry Regiment of the 75th Division. For Robert Prentice this becomes the 189th Regiment of the 57th Division.

duffel bag, then ran a great distance to catch up with the last of the marching men, and a great distance more before he was staggering alongside his
own company. To make matters worse, he'd missed his chance to draw
rations and had to watch with famished exhaustion while the others
wolfed theirs down. Nor was anyone inclined to share, least of all the
mentorly "Quint": "Half the guys in this company are sick," he rails at
Grove in *Uncertain Times* (and at Prentice—in so many words—in the
other book), "but we don't fuck up all the time like you. We don't keep
losing our stuff in the snow and forgetting to draw our rations and expect-
ing somebody to take *care* of us all the time."

Perhaps to make amends, Yates volunteered for dangerous "runner"
duty during the Colmar Pocket Battle that began on January 30. The
troops had been transported over the freezing Vosges Mountains, and by
the time they reached the Alsace region Yates was seriously ill. Though
dizzy and feverish and hoarse from coughing, he ran about the tiny shelled-
out village from which his battalion planned to launch an attack on the
town of Horbourg, three miles away. "He took pride in delivering his small
messages, even though the effort of speaking made him twist and rise on
tiptoe before any sound came out." As it happened Yates had pneumonia
complicated by pleurisy, and apparently he wasn't the only one. His friend
"Quint" was sick too, and both Bill Grove and Robert Prentice would later
"agonize" over the fact that they'd proudly refused to go to an aid station
when Quint made the suggestion. "I mean after this Horbourg business is
over maybe I'll go back," says Prentice, "but not before." Shamed, Quint
decides to stay in the action too, and is killed a few days later—or such is
the fate of that character in two of Yates's most autobiographical novels. If
such a man existed, and if he died in these or similar circumstances, then
certain psychological ramifications might at least be considered, and for
what they're worth, the reader is left to consider them.* That said, let it be
noted that the subject of "Quint"—whoever he was or wasn't—seems
rarely if ever to have been broached outside the novels.

---

*From the *Uncertain Times* manuscript: "Grove *had* agonized over [Quint's death], and the rest of
the book would suggest that nothing between March and the end of the war had served to provide
a cleansing atonement for his sense of guilt and *nothing ever would* [italics mine]—though in some

Yates's own delay in going to an aid station would, without a doubt, have lifelong consequences. Such was his eagerness to redeem himself as a soldier that he continued running messages amid the rubble of Horbourg, as mortar shells burst around him, until he was all but dead with exhaustion. And when he finally woke up to find himself, at last, in an aid station, it was with a dawning sense of embarrassment: He wasn't even wounded. A doctor dismissively made note of that fact and poked him in the chest, whereupon Yates fell back unconscious. It later transpired that his lungs had been permanently damaged, and for the rest of his life he'd be a semi-invalid. For the time being he was awarded the Combat Infantry Badge (as was everyone who participated in ground combat), but this crumb was only the beginning of a lifetime of restitution the U.S. government would make toward Yates, in various forms, for his valor.

For five weeks he was far away from the front. The hospital was an old Catholic girls' school that overlooked the Alsatian hills, and Yates spent his days watching the snow melt and writing grim letters to his Avon friends. One detail he never forgot was the peculiar stench of the pneumonia ward, and sometimes he'd put down his pen and lie wondering at its source.

By the time Yates was released in March, the Seventy-fifth Division had driven deep into Germany and was positioned along the west bank of the Rhine; the men were moving from town to town, sometimes under heavy mortar attack, and by his own account Yates ended up shooting a lot of trees. As he later put it, he'd never been so "shit-scared" in all his life, but soon learned—while advancing through eighty-eight fire or flushing Germans out of ruined buildings—that he could "shut off [his] mind and keep a tight asshole and [not] even think about fear" until the danger had passed. ("Keep a tight asshole" became a favorite motto in times of adversity.)

Eventually he was made to feel rather proud of his own bravery, thanks

---

dim way he still believed that writing it out as a story might help." In the margin Yates had scribbled, "Cut all this."

in part to the reassurances of one Frank Knorr, who later told FBI agents that Yates had been "fine" under fire, and then persuaded his incredulous friend that he was quite sincere in saying so. Knorr had been the B.A.R. (Browning Automatic Rifle) man in their squad—the kind of solid, competent mensch that Yates would admire, wistfully, all his life; they'd met after Yates's return from the hospital in Alsace, and Yates was rather amazed that someone like Knorr was willing to be his friend. Indeed, the two would keep in touch for most of their lives, and something of hero worship is suggested by the fact that Yates, when deranged or in his cups or both, would occasionally claim that he himself had been a B.A.R. man, though the heavy Browning Automatic was generally handled by the burliest, most flatfooted, and reliable member of a twelve-man squad—the antithesis of Yates, in short, and thus a kind of ideal in his eyes.

Yates's long-standing ambivalence about his performance in combat was partly due to what happened at the Dortmund-Ems Canal, his company's last major engagement of the war. The canal was Germany's second line of defense, and in the dark early-morning hours of April 4 the Americans attempted to cross it. While engineers rushed to construct a footbridge and get ladders up on the other side, the men waiting on the bank were subject to constant artillery barrage, and the crossing itself was chaotic: Amid enemy fire and screaming casualties, one terrified column after another went shoving and scrambling over the wet ramshackle bridge and up the ladders, each man laden with heavy equipment. As he wrote in his early story "The Canal"—whose combat scenes were cannibalized almost word for word into A Special Providence—Yates (aka "Lew Miller" and Prentice respectively) was carrying a fifty-pound spool of communication wire as he staggered through the dark and tried to keep his eyes on the man in front of him. But like any number of men that night, Yates lost track of his squad in the melee, and when he finally caught up he was castigated by his sergeant as being, in effect, "more goddamn trouble than [he was] worth."

In "The Canal" Lew Miller takes this in silence, and the moment is meant to be emblematic of all the humiliation he felt—and still feels five years later—as a fuckup soldier. Yates's main revision of the scene in A Special Providence is revealing: Prentice recognizes the unfairness of the reprimand and finally stands up for himself ("Don't be telling me I can't keep up"), which might reflect Yates's change of heart about his own soldierly conduct—at least somewhat assisted by the belated good report of Frank Knorr—in the decade-plus that passed between writing "The Canal" and transplanting it into his second novel. In fact the fundamental problem with early drafts of *A Special Providence* was the lack of growth, the *non*–coming of age, of its autobiographical protagonist (a *prentice* no less); but Knorr's insistence that Yates was, after all, a good soldier, is momentously evoked in *Uncertain Times* (where Knorr appears as "Frank Marr") as "something like what patients in psychotherapy call a breakthrough . . . [that] would strengthen the whole latter part of the book, strengthen the tone of the book itself, and now [Grove] felt he could attack the writing of it with new confidence." Thus the meekly self-loathing Lew Miller became the more resilient Robert Prentice, by far a more hopeful (and accurate) portrait of the artist as a young GI. And Yates too, though he generally remained "hilarious" on the subject, later came to speak of his war experience with a certain pride.

By the end of April the 75th Division was mostly distributed among a number of soggy foxholes near Braumbauer and Plettenberg, Germany, in what was said to be a blocking position. After a few weeks of this, Yates's company was removed to one of the towns and given drier accommodations, and amid such relative luxury the war in Europe abruptly came to an end. Yates—who over the past few months had learned to drink ("out of badly made shoes and boots," he liked to say)—celebrated the surrender as many did, by staying drunk all night and sleeping most of the day, and perhaps "fraternizing" to some degree with the many unattached German women. Soon his unit was moved to the pleasant town of Kierspe-Bahnhof, where their nominal duty was to guard a thousand newly liberated Russians. Meanwhile the festivities continued, and despite the odd pang (over "Quint" perhaps, or the Dortmund-Ems Canal), Yates seems to have enjoyed himself immensely.

Dookie, however, was having a hard time of it back in New York. While her son's induction had enabled her to quit the mannequin factory—as a "Class A Dependent" she received a small sum from the government—she was lonely, bored, and poor, and the letters she'd gotten from overseas left her sick with worry. She tried to distract herself with membership in various art organizations: She was recording secretary of something called Artists for Victory, and also active in Pen and Brush, the National Association of Women Artists, and others. But she was essentially alone in the world, and Richard's absence made that clearer than ever. Her daughter contrived to see less and less of her, and apart from tiresome old Elsa she had no other family to speak of.

She was halfheartedly working on a statuette of the flag raising at Iwo Jima (an Artists for Victory job) when news of the German surrender came over the radio; such was her ecstasy that she tore up the papier-mâché marines and hurled them out the window, as if with a flash of insight into their true artistic worth. With her one good friend, Elisabeth Cushman, she went to an Episcopal church and prayed for her son's safe return and constant company thereafter, and lit a candle to that effect, and then the two women retired with a bottle of rye. When the equally lonely Cushman—"after my 85th drink," she noted—suggested they live together again, Dookie replied with tipsy bitterness, "I wouldn't be a bit surprised . . . it will serve us right!" Happily for both it wouldn't be necessary: Dookie's prayers would soon be answered, and as for Cushman, she moved to California a few months later and stayed there.

Meanwhile Yates and his Avon friends were comparing notes and planning reunions. Bick Wright hadn't heard from Yates in so long that he was "seriously afraid something had happened to [him]." That noted, Wright called his friend "assinine" [sic] for writing the following bit of garbled bravado: "Combat doesn't seem so bad from what I've seen about it." "I've seen enough of this horror and death to last me a hundred lifetimes," Wright rejoined, and he meant it too. In fact his experience bore a bleak resemblance to Yates's: Wright had also been widely reviled as a feckless preppy wise-ass, and one sergeant had always made a point of assigning him first scout in hope that the Germans would shoot him.* Having survived all that, Wright gloomily predicted that now he'd be sent to the

---

*As Wright liked to point out, the sergeant had probably saved his life (inadvertently), since the Germans generally assumed they could pick off the first scout and aimed at the second and third

Pacific, but hoped Yates and he could someday "take a toot around the country, hitch-hiking and what-have-you." Davis Pratt's vision of postwar life was somewhat less picaresque: Together in New York, he wrote Yates, they'd "enjoy good food, women and our interests together gathering at odd hours over some oysters at out of the way places." As for that other, graver Pratt (Hugh), he was more concerned with the philosophical side of peace. When Yates suggested that his own war experiences were "meaningless," at least until properly digested, Pratt begged to differ—-or not, depending on how one interprets such dicta as, "Your knowledge of what has happened mayhap be used to illustrate an attitude toward life whose sources will lie somewhere else."

Whatever Yates's world-weary pronouncements, the rest of his time overseas was pleasant enough, if a bit uneventful. Like Colby in "A Compassionate Leave," his service in Germany with the Army of Occupation "had begun to give every promise of turning into the best time of [his life]," when suddenly that summer he was transferred to Camp Pittsburgh near Reims, one of several redeployment camps named after American cities and cigarette brands, whose postwar purpose was to process soldiers back to the States. Yates's duties there were mostly clerical—that is, he processed others as opposed to being processed himself, since he still had plenty of time to serve according to the point system. Camp Pittsburgh offered a lot less in the way of liquor and wenching, but on the whole there was something to be said for "the order and the idleness of life in these tents in the grass. There was nothing to prove here."

One of the things a young soldier had to prove is suggested by the rotary condom dispenser of which the character Colby avails himself (in vain) prior to a three-day pass in Paris: "He was very likely the only soldier in Europe ever to have spent three days in Paris without getting laid." Whether Yates had any better luck, either then or before with all those lonely nihilistic German women, merits a moment of consideration. Yates was almost certainly a virgin when he entered the army; an all but total

scouts instead. Still, Wright was seriously damaged by the war—if not quite to the extent he claimed later (see below)—such that his wife could never rouse him from sleep without risking some sort of somnolent assault.

lack of female company was a notorious liability of life at Avon, where the best one could do was an occasional tea or dance at Ethel Walker's or Miss Porter's (always well-chaperoned, and besides such girls tended to take a dim view of Avon "fairies"). As for fictional evidence, the luckless Colby is but one of several callow young soldiers who bear a resemblance to Yates: Prentice loses his virginity almost in spite of himself, toward the end of basic training, while Warren Mathews of "Liars in Love" remembers how ("as a boy on his first furlough from the Army after the war") he longed to buy time with one of the "Piccadilly Commandos" in London, but ended up "despis[ing] himself for letting the whole two weeks of his leave run out without doing so." As we shall see, Yates seems to have gotten over the worst of his squeamishness while in the army, with the help of alcohol perhaps, but to some extent sex would always be a problematic business.

Yates got a pleasant reprieve from the dullness of camp life in December, when as part of an army employment program he was sent to England to work for three weeks as an apprentice reporter on the *Halifax Courier and Guardian*. Life in Halifax was very peaceful, and Yates made a good impression on all. His editor, a kindly fiftyish fellow named Harwood, referred to Yates as "one of the brethren of the Press" and later thanked him for giving "color to our hard-working life." But Harwood was sheepish about how little there was for Yates to do in Halifax, where even at the liveliest of times one had to scrape for news (hence the "hard-working" part). At the time meat and money were scarce, and not a single cigarette was for sale, the latter fact perhaps the most newsworthy item where Yates was concerned. But he made out all right. He and three other "juniors" in the office loafed and joked all day, and on weekends went to the Empress Dance Hall—where Yates met what may have been his first actual girlfriend, a stenographer named Joan. For two years they corresponded, and such was their lingering intimacy that Joan never bothered to write her last name or, for that matter, say anything remotely of interest. "Connie says you went out with me for a plaything whilst you were in Halifax," she chides him with an almost audible northern twang, though such rakishness seems well beyond Yates at the time. Indeed, he gave her a bracelet and ring, the first of which she went on wearing but *not* (as she punctiliously noted) the second, suggesting a novice attempt at betrothal on Yates's part. This tendency to become deeply attached to unlikely people would remain one of his most poignant and self-destructive qualities.

Yates spent the rest of his leave and a bit more in London, and was technically AWOL when he made friends with Tony Vevers at the Red Cross Club. Vevers was an Englishman who'd joined the U.S. Army after his family had emigrated during the Blitz. As a fellow prep-school boy and aspiring painter, he and the Anglophilic Yates found much to discuss while happily staggering from one pub to the next. Still in the flush of his Halifax conquest, Yates managed to impress Vevers with his relative suavity toward the opposite sex: Already he was seeing a young woman from the American Embassy, and was able to wangle a date for Vevers as well. The four attended a Brahms recital, after which Yates (possibly fortified from a flask) dropped to one knee like Al Jolson and began to sing "Mammy." "He was full of a sort of guileless joie de vivre then," Vevers recalled many decades later, with a rueful emphasis on *then,* since in the meantime he'd found himself in one of Yates's novels. For a while, though, the friendship would give him little to regret.

Yates was demobilized on January 15, 1946, and the next five months seem to have been filled with little more than idle waiting at one of the tent cities in France, with an occasional bit of Parisian monkey business to dispel the boredom. "Yates, please tell me how one guy manages to get into as many scrapes as you, and then manages to worm his way out of it undamaged," a friend wrote in March, but no details of such scrapes follow. "You don't sound very keen on France," wrote Halifax Joan, perhaps giving a better sense of Yates's mood at the time. No doubt he was homesick by then, or at least ready for a change. Most of his Avon friends were already back in the States and getting on with their lives, albeit with a kind of dreary sameness that might have given Yates pause. Hugh Pratt and David "Shorty" Bigelow had already settled on their future wives and careers (medicine, business), while Pratt—after years of spieling about Schopenhauer et al.—had even found God. Yates was perhaps a little bemused by Pratt's revelation, to say nothing of the news that Bick Wright had resolved his own perplexities by deciding to become a clergyman.

"Your news is great news," wrote the good Mr. Harwood of Halifax on June 14, five days before Yates was discharged at Fort Dix with a Good Conduct Medal and the rank of private first class. "Now you will be able to stretch that long length of yours, and, craning up to the topmost skyscraper, exclaim, 'Now wot?'" *Now wot* indeed.

Yates's permanent address on his honorable discharge is "High Hedges, St. James L.I., New York," and it was there that he was welcomed back from the war by Dookie, Ruth, and the Rodgers clan. High Hedges was the eight-acre estate bought by Fritz Rodgers's parents in 1916 for their retirement, though at the time it had no such imposing name. In fact the former North Shore golf course was rather weedy and nondescript; Fritz himself had designed the sixteen-room, white clapboard main house as well as a three-bedroom cottage originally built for his mother's widow-hood (where Ruth and Fred had lived since the birth of their second child). For many years after he'd inherited the place, Fritz had rented it out while he and his family lived in England, and the name "High Hedges" is said to have been the whim of a tenant struck by the over-growth of Oriental vines planted years before by Fritz's green-thumbed mother. But *The Easter Parade* suggests another possibility: "Does it have a name?" Pookie asks Geoffrey Wilson. "You know, the way estates have names." "Overgrown Hedges," Wilson proposes as a joke, which Pookie earnestly refines into "Great Hedges": "That's what I'm going to call it, anyway. . . . 'Great Hedges,' St. Charles, Long Island, New York."

Be that as it may, Yates's homecoming at High Hedges seems to have been a rather dismal affair—though one can imagine (assisted by a similar scene in *A Special Providence*) Dookie's elation on being reunited with her cherished son and soul mate: "Her frizzled gray head scarcely came up to his breast-pocket flap and she was frail as a sparrow, but the force of her love was so great that he had to brace himself in a kind of boxer's stance to absorb it." The others were more restrained, but went out of their way to be nice, and indeed Richard seemed badly in need of their niceness. "He moped around the whole time," Ruth's sister-in-law Louise remembered. "He was very depressed—didn't know what to do with his life." That was undoubtedly true, though Yates's uncertain future wasn't the only thing likely to depress him. Dookie, now fifty-four and hunched with osteo-porosis, was again facing destitution now that her son was out of the army. For the time being she was dependent on the Rodgerses, a fact that might have led Yates to brood over the general ethos of High Hedges. His brother-in-law was, if anything, more loutish than ever, and the two men quietly despised each other; the walls of the cottage where Ruth and Fred lived were covered with illustrations of the navy Hellcats and Wildcats built by Fred's employer. Most nights the adults would gather at the main house, which stank of mildew, to get drunk together—even Fritz's valetu-dinarian wife, who liked her sherry well enough to leave bed during the cocktail hour until she delicately passed out and was carried upstairs. Lit-tle wonder Yates wanted to escape and figure things out, though it meant abandoning his poor mother again.

In later years when Yates met the odd person from York, Pennsylvania, he'd tell how his professional career actually began with a very brief stint at the *York Gazette and Daily*—one of the most radical newspapers in the country, then or now. The *Gazette and Daily* opposed the cold war, cham-pioned the causes of organized labor and racial equality, and was one of only two daily newspapers in the country to support Henry Wallace's Pro-gressive Party bid for president in 1948. Yates, who would always con-sider himself something of a leftist (though his politics were a highly individual affair, to put it mildly), later told the writer Ken Rosen that he thought the newspaper represented the "best of America" at that time. But so little. is known of Yates's tenure at the *Gazette and Daily* that one broaches the matter only in passing, in the hope of shedding a little light on the "half-assed romantic ideas" Yates professed to have in those days—ideas compounded, perhaps, of various novels and a growing need to rebel against the snobbish, half-assed conservatism and overall preten-sion of his mother.

Meanwhile Yates was deeply conflicted as to whether he should take advantage of the GI Bill and go to college as he'd always planned—as every one of his Avon friends had done or were about to do—or get on with his writing career without further delay. By the time he returned to New York he'd apparently decided to put things off another year while reading as much as possible and leading the life of a "knockabout intellectual," à la

Frank Wheeler in *Revolutionary Road*. As he later reminisced, "At twenty, fresh out of the Army and surfeited with Thomas Wolfe, I embarked on a long binge of Ernest Hemingway that entailed embarrassingly frequent attempts to talk and act like characters in the early Hemingway books. And I was hooked on T. S. Eliot at the same time, which made for an uncomfortable set of mannerisms." But Yates's brief spell as a would-be T. S. Hemingway was curtailed by a letter from his sister: Dookie's presence at High Hedges was putting a strain on her marriage, she wrote, and while she herself didn't mind the arrangement so much, Fred most emphatically did. Therefore she hoped Richard would agree to end his bachelor idyll, at least for a while, and do his part in caring for their indigent, difficult mother.

So much, then, for college and knockabout intellectualizing. In short order Yates got a job writing for a trade journal, *Food Field Reporter*, while he and Dookie moved into an apartment on Hudson Street. The arrangement gave Yates a ready excuse when people asked why he didn't go to college, but for the rest of his life he'd bitterly regret the decision as a "dumb, arrogant thing to do." It was "arrogant" because it was based on a romantic notion out of Hemingway that a *real* writer didn't need college—but there was more to it than that. "It was partly fear," he admitted (as Bill Grove) in "Regards at Home": "I'd done poorly in high school, the Army had assessed my IQ at 109, and I didn't want the risk of further failure." Whatever the case, Yates's lack of a college education would become a lifelong obsession, a lodestone to which he'd forever return when he felt inadequate—intellectually, socially, professionally. "God, you can't mean that!" he exploded when one of his students wished aloud that he'd skipped college. "Jesus Christ, I'd give anything to have gotten a college education—I feel the lack of it *all* the time." And to another ex-student he wrote how "delighted" he was that the young man had decided to go back and finish his degree—"not because of any vicarious sentimental horseshit about Wishing I'd Gone Myself," he wrote, a disclaimer he belied somewhat by adding "[college is] the healthiest possible climate in which a talented young man can hope to experience growth and development"; and even more to the point, "it's probably a hell of a lot more fun than . . . doing any of the other dreary, mechanical, bread-winning things you'd have to do instead."

Not that he found work altogether unpleasant, at least not at first; like Emily Grimes he rather enjoyed composing headlines "quickly and well, so that the spaces counted out right the first time"—and in fact he later told a friend that Emily's nice headline for *Food Field Observer* was one he'd actually written for a journal of (almost) the same name:

"HOTEL BAR" BUTTER
HITS SALES PEAK;
MARGARINES FADE.

On the other hand it was awfully insipid stuff, and the romantic young man who'd gorged himself on Wolfe, Hemingway, and Eliot must have felt a rather keen sense of desperation. Nor was he likely to meet many congenial people in the course of his daily beat on behalf of the grocery industry. But finally it just wasn't "real journalism," and had nothing to do with being a writer—the gist of Yates's advice to his son-in-law, many years later, when the latter wondered if working for a trade journal was a valid way to practice the craft.

On weekends Yates would walk the streets in search of freelance ideas—in theory a way to make extra money and build his journalistic credentials, but more definitely a further respite from his mother's company. His old Scarborough friend Russell Benedict had also moved to the Village, and offered to come along as Yates's photographer. Whether they ever collaborated on a salable idea is doubtful, though at least once they managed to pick up girls in their roles as roving reporters. Roz Wellman and Ginny Shafer were showing a couple of Argentine midshipmen around town on liberty night, when Yates and Benedict approached: Would the two young ladies be willing to submit to an interview about their ambassadorial endeavors? Names and numbers were exchanged, and within a few days the two couples were inseparable. Roz was Yates's girl, or rather the one he slept with at Benedict's apartment, but the darker, hard-drinking, spoken-for Ginny was the one he really loved, and (such is the world) vice versa. "No, I didn't know you were 'painfully in love' with me," she wrote Yates in 1961, "I was so damned depressed I was unaware of any 'pain' other than my own. I knew that I loved you a lot."* For several months anyway, amid such poignant confusion, the four shuttled between bed and Pete's Tavern, where they drank some sort of "pink swill" and commiserated about being young and poor and unfulfilled.

Occasionally Bick Wright would visit the city from Princeton, where he was a student in the theological seminary, and regale Yates with stories about the war and his subsequent conversion. As Yates wrote of Bucky Ward in *A Good School,* "He limped a lot, saying he'd been wounded and had refused a Purple Heart, but there were embarrassing times when he would walk the streets for miles, deep in conversation, without limping at all." Indeed Wright would limp sporadically for many years—he told his brother he'd refused the Purple Heart because he didn't want to worry their parents—partly because of his old weakness for melodrama and also, perhaps, because he needed some empirical rationale for the religious vocation that would peter out in less than two years and, in general, for a psychological malaise that never quite left him. At some point, though, he sat his wife down and solemnly confessed that his "war wound" was actually due to a childhood tricycle accident. ("Aptly enough," his widow wryly noted, "Bick's senior thesis at Princeton was about *mythology.*") Certainly Yates was bound to find his old friend ridiculous, which might explain why Wright was unable to persuade him to quit his job and go to college; Wright even went so far as to fill out most of the applications for him. And soon Yates would also choose to disregard his friend's advice about marriage—"Bick was right about that, too," he admitted in retrospect—which may have caused the final rift in their friendship, though Yates hadn't quite heard the last of Bick Wright.

The writing career for which Yates had avowedly forfeited his college education was not flourishing. As a compromise he took evening courses in

---

*A somber postscript to this postwar lark: Shafer, who'd married and moved to Japan, got back in touch with Yates after seeing advertisements for *Revolutionary Road* in American magazines. In her first letter she confided her problems with mental illness over the years, and Yates responded with similar candor and incidentally mentioned his old love for her. Her last couple of letters, following what she described as "a schizophrenic reaction," were written from a mental hospital.

creative writing at Columbia, though it's unclear what effect these had, if any. For much of his adult life Yates would support himself by teaching writing (or "teaching" writing as he liked to put it, in heavy quotes), which if anything convinced him all the more that writing couldn't be taught. No doubt he was more credulous during his apprentice years, or simply desperate enough to try anything. For what it's worth, he did write in the bio-blurb that accompanied his first published story in 1953 that his "unimpressive" postwar career was "brightened" by the evening courses he took at Columbia; and six years after that, at the end of his faculty profile in the New School bulletin, he was able to note "Studied, Columbia" in lieu of the various M.A.'s and Ph.D.'s which his fellow instructors boasted. But in 1946, in the very midst of that "unimpressive" career, he was desperate for some kind of validation, be it a published story or a decent job or any sign of progress whatsoever. "I am sorry to hear you have not got working with a newspaper yet, Richard," wrote Halifax Joan in November, asking to see some of those short stories he was writing; "I've been wondering what type they are—mysteries—romances—or adventures."

And then his luck seemed to change a bit. Early in 1947 he was hired as a rewrite man on the financial news desk of the United Press. For a salary of fifty-four dollars a week, he wrote the daily Wall Street bond- and curb-market leads, as well as general business and industrial news for the national wire. The good part of the job was being able to say he worked for the "UP" rather than *Food Field Reporter* (he also liked playing the part of the young, Hemingwayesque newspaperman in his rumpled trench coat and fedora). And then, too, the basic contours of his daily routine were appealing: At ten in the morning he'd report to the *Daily News* building in his hardboiled attire, listen to the racket of teletypes and Wall Street tickers for two hours or so, then adjourn to a bar on Forty-second Street where fat slabs of roast beef were free with dime beer, followed at last by a long afternoon of punching out leads until it was six-thirty and time to go home. The bad part was the job itself. As Yates described it in "Builders," he had only the vaguest idea of what he was supposed to be doing:

"Domestic corporate bonds moved irregularly higher in moderately active trading today. . . ." That was the kind of prose I wrote all day long for the UP wire, and "Rising oil shares paced a lively curb market," and "Directors of Timken Roller Bearing today declared"—hundreds on hundreds of words that I never really understood (What in the name of God are puts and calls, and what is a sinking fund debenture? I'm still damned if I know). . . .

And when he wasn't writing about puts and calls and debentures, or heading uptown to attend his evening classes, or rutting about with Russ and the girls, he was home with his mother, who was always glad to see him. What had started as a temporary arrangement was showing every sign of becoming permanent. Dookie made no effort to get a job—though she often said she'd be "back on [her] feet" in no time—and indeed seemed more than content to live on her son's modest income, as long as she could afford to pay dues at Pen and Brush on Tenth Street, where as "resident sculptor" she conducted what was left of her social life. At first Yates hadn't really minded the setup, as he and his mother were still rather compatible in those days, and after all it was only a matter of time. But he continued to toy with the idea of college, or just a reasonable degree of independence, and after a while his mother's almost mad complacency began to seem ominous. "This wasn't making any sense," he wrote in "Regards at Home":

I didn't want to listen to her torrential talk anymore or join in her laughter; I thought she was drinking too much; I found her childish and irresponsible— two of my father's words—and I didn't even want to look at her: small and hunched in tasteful clothes that were never quite clean, with sparse, wild, yellow-gray hair and a soft mouth set in the shape either of petulance or hilarity.

One thing that might have inhibited his mother from taking positive action were her rotten teeth, which made her self-conscious and were painful besides. Yates took her to a free dental clinic in the Village, the Northern Dispensary, where a nice young dentist offered to fit her for dentures at his private office in Queens for half his normal fee. Yates sat with his mother as the rest of her teeth were extracted one by one, and found her agony "oddly satisfying": "There, I thought as each tooth fell bloody on the tray. There . . . there . . . there. How could she make a romance out of this? Maybe now, at last, she would come to terms with reality."

And for a few days, perhaps, she did—seeming "utterly defeated" by her caved-in face; but as soon as she got her new dentures "she seemed to shed twenty years." And this was a mixed blessing for her son, since now she was all the more willing to laugh and smile and talk—and *talk*—though she worried that her false teeth made a telltale clacking noise, and she still seemed disinclined to find a means of supporting herself.

CHAPTER FOUR

Liars in Love: 1947-1951

That first year back from the war was a lonely time for Yates. Whether by choice or circumstance, he was drifting away from his old Avon friends. Hugh Pratt, about to be married in Rochester, came home from medical school one day to find that Yates had showed up out of nowhere, left a wedding gift with Pratt's mother, and departed. Pratt never heard from him again. As for Yates's other friends, they were mostly busy with college or career, or had become tiresome like Bick Wright. Russell Benedict, too, was beginning to pall; whatever Yates wanted out of bachelorhood wasn't to be found in Benedict's company. Yates longed to make new friends who were "young, poor, bright, humorous, very much alive and headed in the right direction"—a direction off the beaten track, to be sure, the sort of path taken by abstract beings whom he really did call "golden people." The long hours he spent in Village bars ("trying to figure out what was going on") had proved a fruitless guide, and pretty much always would.

At some point he renewed his acquaintance with one Jeff Macaulay, an Avon classmate known for having coined the word *plerb* ("a synonym for anything you need a synonym for"); Macaulay is also noteworthy for having introduced Yates to Sheila Bryant, who at the time was having a small party at her mother's apartment on East Sixty-first. Sheila was not quite nineteen at the time—a tall, severely pretty redhead who'd recently graduated from Katharine Gibbs Secretarial School and now had what she rather defensively called "a good job" at the Cavendish Trading Corporation, where she worked as a stenographer in the accounting department. Before that she'd done a bit of acting at Bronxville High School and was deemed to have talent, though she was far too sensible to pursue it as a career. After a while she and Yates left the party to continue their talk in private—a talk that convinced both they had a great deal in common, which in a way they did.

For one thing Sheila's childhood was, perhaps, even more luridly awful than Yates's. Her father was the British actor Charles Bryant, whose one claim to fame, or infamy, was his involvement with the great theater and silent-movie actress Alla Nazimova. For more than ten years, beginning in 1912, the two lived together and claimed to be married, though in fact the union was never legally or physically consummated. Nazimova was a lesbian insofar as she bothered, and hence the burly six-foot-three Bryant served as a credible beard and pleasant, undemanding companion who agreed to be her business manager as well. Nazimova's friend Patsy Ruth described Bryant as "very pompous, ultra-British, extremely good-looking, or so people thought at the time. He had a self-important managerial air, but did nothing for Madame except spend her money." When at last Nazimova decided to "divorce" the no-talent Chumps (as she fondly called him), he persuaded his Allikins (as he called her) to sign a phony document, dated 1918, in which she agreed to pay both her and Bryant's future income tax, lest the IRS discover the true nature of their arrangement and demand back taxes. In return he gave his word as a gentleman never to reveal their secret, but was forced to renege when he married Sheila's mother, Marjorie Gilhooley, in 1925; as far as the public knew, Bryant and Nazimova had never been divorced, and hence it behooved the wily Chumps to point out that indeed they'd never been married in the first place. The ensuing scandal all but destroyed Nazimova's career, while Bryant settled into what he hoped would be a pleasantly domestic state of semiretirement.

His wife Marjorie had a bit of money and even a fine pedigree, despite a surname that suggested Irish peasantry. In fact her father was Justice Gilhooley of the New Jersey Supreme Court, but it was her mother, a New York Kendrick no less, who conferred a degree of gentility on the family. Marjorie attended Vassar and had an interest in French literature, in light of which it seems odd that she should end up marrying a washed-up, not overbright, middle-aged actor such as Charles Bryant, whatever his looks and dashing British manner. Perhaps what attracted each to each, apart from similarly polished facades, was their essential vulgarity: Bryant had been a bank clerk from a lower-middle-class family before he turned to acting and blackmail, while Marjorie would go on to become a member of the John Birch Society—a zealous reactionary racist who was known to return letters if they had FDR's likeness on the stamps. But what this unsavory couple may have had most in common was that both were miserable parents.

Sheila and her older brother Charlie were raised by her mother's sister—at first because their parents claimed to have no time for them (Marjorie sold real-estate and Charles still took the occasional stage role), and then because they weren't getting along, and finally because they were divorced (in 1936) and had little interest in caring for children anyway. Also, Charles Bryant had run through their money with the same skill he'd shown as Nazimova's business manager, and most of whatever was left was lost in the Depression. The caretaking aunt was also somewhat reduced, but still owned property and was solvent enough to move to Miami Beach for her arthritis, or wherever else her fancy took her. In fact they moved so often that Sheila would eventually attend some twelve different schools, though her formal education didn't actually begin until third grade. At that time they were still living in New York, where she and Charlie were enrolled at the elite Dalton School. Sheila, however, was a poor student (having never been taught so much as the alphabet), and Charlie's disturbing behavior soon got him expelled.* After that, whenever possible, the aunt would send them away to second-rate boarding schools, where they were invariably the shabbiest and most neglected among their wealthier classmates. Indeed, "shabby-genteel" would later become a favorite epithet of Sheila's, one that struck a deep chord in Yates as well.

Such an upbringing took a grievous toll on Sheila's brother, a bright but increasingly bizarre young man, while Sheila herself seemed to emerge relatively unscathed. All her adult life she'd briskly admit that she disliked

---

*Sheila's brother Charlie would later serve as the model for the mentally disturbed John Givings in *Revolutionary Road*.

her parents as well as the aunt who'd grudgingly cared for her, but that didn't mean she wanted anybody to feel sorry for her—least of all Yates, some of whose early stories (as well as parts of *Revolutionary Road*) were attempts to make sense of Sheila's inner life as a child. "It was nothing like what he imagined," she insists. "He made it seem like I was torn apart by my father's absence, but that's what *he* felt as a child, not me." Which seems plausible up to a point, though evidence suggests that Sheila's wounds were deep and abiding, however adept she became at hiding them.

She never did catch up in school. At Hunter High she flunked almost everything but English, and ended up at Bronxville her senior year. Her peripatetic childhood had left her socially awkward—like Yates she constantly found herself the only kid in school who didn't know anybody—and she was desperate for acceptance. At Bronxville there was a clique of girls who called themselves "the Web," and Sheila's only ambition was to become a member. "She did all the wrong things," said her friend Ann Barker. "She tried to suck up and was very gauche about it. And of course she had to smoke, because that was the thing to do." More than fifty years later, Barker asked Sheila if it still bothered her that she hadn't been accepted by the Bronxville clique. "Oh, you mean the *Web*!" Sheila replied, and said she didn't know *why* she hadn't gotten in, since her aunt had written her a recommendation, and so on. "She still felt the hurt," said Barker, who'd long forgotten the name of the clique until Sheila reminded her.

But at the time she affected not to care, and took to cultivating a jadedly sophisticated manner. Barker had a brother at West Point, and Sheila urged her to get them invited to a dance so they could meet cadets and mingle with college girls; also she insisted they had to have fur coats—a muskrat imitation of mink in Sheila's case and a "rat paw or rabbit wrapper of sorts" in Barker's. But at the dance they were not mistaken for college girls. As Barker recalled, "Sheila lit and smoked her cigarettes with great aplomb, and I just shrank, not even knowing how to feign worldliness." By then Sheila had decided to become a thespian like her father (whom she professed to admire greatly, though she later called him "a silly man"), and certainly her protean personality would seem conducive. When she got the lead in the Bronxville senior play she persuaded both parents to attend, and afterward her father observed that she was "very good at acting the actress." Whereupon Sheila dropped acting and decided to attend secretarial school, rather abruptly changing her accent from a genteel Westchester drawl to that of a savvy New York working girl. As Yates noted in "Regards at Home":

> . . . some of her speech mannerisms made me wince. Instead of "yeah" she said "yaw," often while squinting against the smoke of a cigarette; she said "as per usual" too—an accounting department witticism, I think—and instead of saying "everything" she often said "the works." That was the way smart, no-nonsense New York secretaries talked, and a smart, no-nonsense New York secretary was all she had ever allowed herself to be.

Not quite "ever," nor did Sheila entirely relinquish her old persona. She always dressed smartly, with elegant understatement, never wearing patterned clothes because, as she put it, she herself was too "printed" (that is, with a redhead's freckles) to wear a pattern. Also she refused to refer to her future husband as "Dick," which was too coarse; for most of their married life he became "Rich," and for a while that caught on with family and friends as well.

They were together constantly for the first year of their courtship, and the more they fought, the more they worked to convince each other that they were in love, since "the movies had proved time and again that love was like that." An early impediment to intimacy was solved when Sheila moved out of her mother's place (a step she would have taken in any case) and found an apartment on the Upper West Side with two sisters, Mary and Doris Bialek, both of whom were "wowed" by their roommate's new boyfriend.* Not only was he tall and "terribly good-looking," as Doris

---

*The Bialek sisters, fresh out of Glen Burnie, Maryland, excited Sheila's condescension with their lack of sophistication and lowbrow boyfriends. The dynamic between the roommates gave Yates the idea for his story "The Best of Everything." Several years later, through a curious turn of events (see below), Sheila would be reunited with a more worldly Doris Bialek and the two would form a friendship that abides to this day.

recalled, but also charming in a quiet sort of way; he was somewhat less quiet when he drank ("a bit too much" even then), but still charming and a lot more funny, since he rarely joked when sober.

The couple were torn between the bourgeois white-collar world of their working lives and that of hip nonconformity to be found, they supposed, in certain recesses of the Village and elsewhere. But both were wary of unconventional behavior for its own sake, and felt rather alienated from the whole bohemian milieu—the "half-phoney art talk that [made] the rafters ring at the San Remo," as Yates put it a few years later. At the time, though, they both seemed to concede the romantic appeal of such a scene, at least in comparison with whatever passed for fun among the Bialek sisters and certain friends from the office. At night, then, they shed their quotidian shells and worked at becoming personages. Before long they were both so comfortable in their newfound freedom that they even managed to shock a few friends, one of whom found the two in bed together and not even embarrassed about it—Sheila picked a pair of panties off the floor, then curtsied and withdrew to the bathroom without so much as a blush. Meanwhile the couple spoke of moving to Europe someday, where perhaps they'd find not only themselves, but others who weren't mortified by matters such as premarital sex.

Things were going about as well as could be expected until it came time to meet the parents. On one side this wasn't a problem—Yates's introduction to the divided Bryants went more or less without a hitch: Marjorie would always regard him as a nice-enough young man (never suspecting how intensely he disliked her), while the impressively bulky and semifamous father rather awed his prospective son-in-law, such was the contrast between Charles Bryant and the diminutive, meekly deceased Vincent Yates. It's possible Bryant might have become a father of sorts to Yates (if not Sheila), but as it happened he died of liver cancer a few months after that first meeting.

Dookie was another matter. In her loneliness she bitterly resented the demands this girl was making on Richard's time, and her paradoxical sense of delicacy was affronted by the manner in which that time was spent. She hardly saw her son anymore, except when he breezed through in the morning to change clothes for work, and when she finally did meet

Sheila—if one accepts the account given in "Regards at Home"*—the dislike was immediate and mutual. "Well, she's a pleasant girl, dear" (says the mother in the story), "but I don't see how you can find her so attractive." As for Sheila, she thought Dookie ridiculous at best, dismissing her as an "art bum." Dookie apparently tipped her hand (during "one of her uncontrollable rages") when she referred to Sheila as "that cheap little Irish slut"; and finally, when Yates was hospitalized with pneumonia toward the end of 1947, the two women's bedside visits seem to have coincided with unfortunate results. Who knows whether Sheila actually made a ribald reference to Yates's healthy color ("The best part is, he's the same color all over"), but Dookie's reaction to some such remark was apt to be that of her fictional alter ego: "[She chose] to take it in silence, slightly lowering her eyelids and lifting her chin, like a dowager obliged to confront an impudent scullery maid."

Dookie, in short, was like a whiff of ammonia to Sheila, abruptly rousing her from a dream of romantic questing with this handsome but frail young man who wanted to be a writer. There was no future in it, she decided, reverting at once to the level-headed outlook of a no-nonsense New York secretary. Yates's salary at the UP was hardly enough for him and his mother, much less a wife, and as for his fiction—what was likely to come of that? In a later letter to Sheila, Yates characterized her attitude as follows: "[Y]ou had [my writing] figured as a pleasant but hopelessly unworldly knack which anyone in their right mind would gladly swap for a degree in Accountancy out of NYU." True enough, though it was only part of the whole dismal picture: Sheila was all of twenty; she wanted to meet other, more practical men; and finally Yates had an obligation to his mother, an aging "art bum" with no other hope of subsistence. Sheila wanted to make a clean break.

After Yates's latest bout with pneumonia, the doctor advised him that he was highly susceptible to tuberculosis (yet another reason for Sheila to

---

*"Dookie and I got along fine," Sheila claims, and certainly in later years this appears to have been the case (though a sensible ambivalence on Sheila's part persisted, as letters prove). Perhaps Sheila had little reason to suspect that Dookie disliked her at first, since each seems to have treated the other with elaborate civility most of the time. At any rate, since the details in "Regards at Home" are accurate in almost every knowable respect, the antipathy between the Dookie and Sheila characters offers at least a credible sense of how things were.

beg off), and for a while he imagined himself heading for an early grave like Keats, minus the literary immortality. Despondent, he tried calling Sheila on the phone, though usually one of the Bialek sisters would answer and say (as instructed) that she wasn't home; but sometimes Sheila was obliged to pick up and listen, and it eventually began to wear her down. She wasn't made of stone, after all, nor was she meeting other viable men, and such persistence was flattering in a baffling sort of way. "Dick had a terrible thing with loneliness," she later observed. "If he formed an attachment, he'd be half-destroyed if it ended. Really I think that's what did him in. He could never bear the thought of losing close people."

Meanwhile his evenings were free again, and that meant coming home and keeping his mother company. According to "Regards," she greeted him one night with a peculiar buoyancy, and Yates thought "for a moment of unreasoning hope" that she might have found a job. But no. As "resident sculptor" at Pen and Brush she'd been asked to contribute a bit of light entertainment to an upcoming party, and she was eager to give her son a preview ("with bright eyes and a brisk little hopping around on the floor of our wretched home"). It was a parody of the old Chiquita Banana jingle:

> *Oh, we are the sculptors and we've—come to say*
> *You have to treat the sculptors in a—certain way . . .*

Yates decided to get out: "I borrowed three hundred dollars from the bank, gave it to my mother . . . and told her, in so many words, that she was on her own." Almost immediately life began to improve. He moved to a dark apartment on Jones Street and advertised for a roommate, who proved to be a compatible young man named Blanchard "Jerry" Cain—a mechanical engineer with a rather lurid past. Back in San Francisco Cain had become involved with a married woman named Jessie, who had a young son; when her husband divorced her and sought custody, she'd fled to New York with the boy and gone underground. After a seemly interval, Jerry had changed his name from "Redner" to "Cain" and followed her. Like Yates he was shy and outwardly conventional—an engineer, after all—but with quirky restive depths. According to his adopted son, he was a superb jazz-pianist who occasionally played in "low piano bars of the

Village," which suggested a sort of latent "golden person" status; but what surely appealed to Yates most, at least at the outset, was Cain's kindred disdain for a "pretentious" and "totally inadequate mother" who fancied herself a poet.* Also the roommates had extreme poverty in common: Cain was new to the city and holding an ad hoc job, while a good part of Yates's meager wages went toward paying off the bank loan that had bought his freedom. Cain would later remark that his most emblematic memory of this time was when Yates brandished the entire contents of their fridge—a rotten orange—and muttered over and over, "What is to be done . . . ?"

Once Dookie was out of the picture, Yates and Sheila were reconciled. The couple spent a lot of time with their new friends Jerry and Jessie, and perhaps that quixotic love affair made an impression. In any event, shortly after the Cains themselves were married, Sheila capitulated to Yates. "I figured 'Oh well, what the hell . . . ' " she remembered a half century later, and laughed. "*God*, whatever made me marry that guy in the first place?"

The wedding took place on June 8, 1948. Mary Bialek was the maid of honor; there was no best man or any other witnesses (the Cains had to work during the day). Because Sheila was under twenty-one the law required a church wedding, so after some calls from City Hall they took their license uptown to a Presbyterian church on Park Avenue, where the minister and his wife were waiting for them. The ceremony was performed with sweetness and dispatch, and before long they were back on Jones Street, where Yates was still on the lam from Dookie. Sheila's mother stopped by and gave them a cooking pot, a few friends wished them well, and that was that.

With the Cains they soon found a picturesque place on West Twelfth Street near the river: a three-story apartment building with a tunnel leading through the ground floor to a courtyard, in the middle of which was a

---

*Blanchard "Jerry" Cain was almost certainly a partial model for Shepherd "Shep" Campbell in *Revolutionary Road*. As his son, Robin, pointed out, "Blanchard and Shepherd were both mechanical engineers. They both worked in Stamford for a while, they both made a sojourn to Arizona and they both returned to New York having failed to find there what they sought."

tiny "Hansel and Gretel cottage," as one friend described it. The couples flipped a coin for the cottage and the Yateses lost, taking instead a seedy but well-lighted room on the third floor of the outer building. A frequent visitor was Sheila's brother, Charlie, who'd managed to graduate from Harvard and was now working for a government agency in Washington. Charlie was strange as ever, emphatic and opinionated, but he and his brother-in-law were friendly in a rather combative way. The only person Charlie felt entirely at ease with was his sister, though he admired the fact that Yates wanted to be a writer and was eager to read his stories and help in whatever way he could, which might have caused Yates a ticklish moment or two.

As he'd later admit, Yates's early publicity and newspaper work (to say nothing of Dookie and other drains) had left him without much time or vitality for writing fiction. What little he did produce seemed barely good enough to keep him going, or rather not bad enough to make him quit. But then he was only twenty-two, and so far he'd managed to live like his idol Hemingway in almost every other respect—he'd gone to war, skipped college, worked for a newspaper, and married young. Now that he was married, though, there was a constant witness to that awkward apprenticeship of his, and perhaps for her sake he tried harder than ever to make good. Each night after dinner—no matter how exhausted after a long day at a job he despised—Yates would retire behind a folding screen, switch on his desk lamp, and impersonate Hemingway at his typewriter. "But it was here, of course," as he wrote in "Builders,"

under the white stare of that lamp, that the tenuous parallel between Hemingway and me endured its heaviest strain. Because it wasn't "Up in Michigan" that came out of my machine; it wasn't any "Three Day Blow," or "The Killers"; very often, in fact, it wasn't really anything at all, and even when it was something [my wife] called "marvelous," I knew deep down that it was always, always something bad.

Let it serve as some measure of his desperation that he really did answer an ad for an "Unusual free-lance opportunity" placed by a cabbie in the *Saturday Review of Literature*. Readers of "Builders" will know the rest, but the episode warrants a brief summary here. The cabbie proposed that

Yates ghostwrite a series of "autobiographical" stories about, of course, a heroic cabbie who changes the lives of his clients with bits of wise advice given in the nick of time. At first Yates took the job because he misunderstood the terms (the man had shown him a canceled check to a previous ghostwriter in the amount of twenty-five dollars, which turned out to be in payment for *five* stories rather than one), and then kept doing it because he was almost able to believe that the cabbie would sell the stories as planned to *Reader's Digest*. Yates also persisted because he took pride in the surprising craftsmanship of his own hackwork. Nothing came of the arrangement, needless to say, except for the boost it gave Yates's shaky self-confidence as a writer.

But for every boost there were letdowns—a lot of them, as his stories were rejected one after the other. The editors of *Harper's,* however, went too far when they attached a flyer for *The Art of Readable Writing,* by Rudolf Flesch ("author of *The Art of Plain Talk*"), to the latest in a long series of rejections, whereupon the wounded Yates reacted with a letter of protest. A sympathetic editor hastened to assure him that no offense was intended; it was common practice for mavens such as Flesch to circularize the *Harper's* slush pile. "Seriously," the editor inquired, "does this practice seem to you improper, or were you just having some fun with us?" Yates's response doesn't survive, though a second note from *Harper's* suggests that Yates had been "very courteous" and perhaps a bit humorous in his initial indignation.

This is reassuring, since Yates's sense of humor was certainly being tried at the time. Almost as soon as he'd reconciled with his mother, she began calling him up "in meekness and urgency" to ask for loans of ten or twenty dollars, until he and Sheila were afraid to answer the phone. Also, being on (relatively) good terms with Dookie meant having her over for dinner, during which she'd talk and drink and finally pass out on the couch.*

---

* "She'd drink a couple of beers and fall asleep," said Sheila. "I didn't think she was an alcoholic, she just couldn't hold it. I didn't understand the hullabaloo about her being a drunk." Yates told Sheila that his mother had been more of a drunk when he was a child, but that her alcoholism had assumed less lurid forms with age.

By then Yates had lost patience with her; at best there was a constant bickering simmer between them, often boiling over into screaming fights. "They were both 'yelly' type people," as Sheila put it, "and Dookie would give as much as she got. She'd burst into tears, but still yell." The tension was eased for a time when she finally found freelance work sculpting mannequin heads. But it wasn't long before the National Association of Women Artists offered her a public relations job that—however—required her to work on an indefinite voluntary basis before they put her on salary. "And if she had to spend several months working full-time there without pay"—muses the narrator of "Regards"—"how could she get her mannequin heads done? Wasn't it ironic how things never seemed to work out quite right? Yeah."

Meanwhile Yates was "sweating out the ax" at work, since the assistant financial editor had long ago discovered how little this particular rewrite man knew about puts and calls and debentures. A few weeks before Christmas the editor's hand fell on his shoulder ("right in the middle of a paragraph about domestic corporate bonds in moderately active trading"), and a few days later Yates found himself winding up toy kittens for a Fifth Avenue dimestore. As he wrote in "Builders," it was "along in there sometime . . . that [he] gave up whatever was left of the idea of building [his] life on the pattern of Ernest Hemingway's." Nor was his next job, at a labor newspaper called the *Trade Union Courier,* likely to restore his faith in life as a romantic affair. The biweekly tabloid served as the model for the *Labor Leader* in Yates's story "A Wrestler with Sharks"—a "badly printed" rag whose employees were either the dregs of the profession or young men marking time until something better came along. At that point Yates may have wondered which category he belonged to.

And then in April 1949 his luck seemed to change at last, as he began his long intermittent association with Remington Rand, the business machine company that would soon introduce the world's first commercially viable electronic computer, the UNIVAC. For the exorbitant sum of eighty dollars a week, Yates was hired to write copy for the company's external house organ, a dismal monthly magazine called *Systems*. With a man named Dan Woskoff, who designed and illustrated *Systems*, Yates shared a peaceful cubicle on the eleventh floor and conducted his day in much the same way as Frank Wheeler at Knox Business Machines—chatting, taking long coffee breaks, and writing sales-promotion prose ("Speaking of Production Control, dot, dot, dot"). The best part was that his new colleagues were almost as apathetic and cynical as he, which meant he could goof off with a relatively clear conscience.

It also meant he could go home at night with plenty of energy stored up for his own work, and the results were encouraging. "With Hemingway safely abandoned," he wrote in "Builders," "I had moved on to an F. Scott Fitzgerald phase; then, the best of all, I had begun to find what seemed to give every indication of being my own style." Yates would go on forging his own style, but to some extent he'd never entirely abandon his "F. Scott Fitzgerald phase"—as his friend Robert Lacy put it, Yates was an "unabashed worshiper" of Fitzgerald. And apart from his admiration of the work, Yates found startling biographical parallels with the man: Both he and Fitzgerald were children of eccentric, smothering mothers and ineffectual salesmen fathers, and both were preeminently "shabby-genteel"— poor boys with storied ancestors who often found themselves among the rich, most notably at boarding school, where both endured formative ordeals as the poorest, most unpopular boys on campus. That Fitzgerald had gone to Princeton made Yates even more wistful about missing all that, and his rather mawkish, lifelong sense of the Ivy League derived from the Spires and Gargoyles milieu of *This Side of Paradise*. Indeed, Yates was quite self-conscious in his cultivation of a Fitzgeraldian mystique, with all that implies of romantic self-destruction—of smoking and drinking and lung ailments and emotional tumult, as well as courtliness (when sober) and a Brooks Brothers wardrobe. Finally, while Yates was at least a head taller than his idol, as young men they resembled each other as closely as brothers.

But it was the work that ultimately mattered, and for Yates *The Great Gatsby* was holy writ. Encountering the novel for the first time was, quite simply, the definitive milestone of his apprenticeship, without which he might well have found something else to do with his life: *Gatsby*, Yates declared, was his "formal introduction to the craft." Both the lyricism of the prose (to his dying day, Yates could hardly read the last page without tears in his eyes) and the peripheral first-person narrator (who is both "enchanted and repelled" by the world of the very rich) were features Yates admired and refined in terms of his own approach. In two other respects, the book's influence was fundamental. "Every line of dialogue in *Gatsby* serves to reveal more about the speaker than the speaker might care to have revealed," Yates wrote in his essay "Some Very Good Masters," and offered as an example "the awful little party in Myrtle Wilson's apartment." But another formal feature was more important still, and arguably became the backbone of Yates's aesthetic—it would not only prove crucial in his learning how to distance himself from highly personal material, but also provide fodder for a lifetime of teaching spiels:

> I had never understood what Eliot meant by the curious phrase "objective correlative" until the scene in *Gatsby* where the almost comically sinister Meyer Wolfsheim, who has just been introduced, displays his cuff links and explains that they are "the finest specimens of human molars."
>
> Get it? Got it. *That's* what Eliot meant.

Around this time Yates also discovered a contemporary with similar debts—"to Fitzgerald and Lardner," he later noted, "but he'd settled those accounts honorably"—when the story "A Perfect Day for Bananafish" appeared in *The New Yorker*. Yates loved the subtle accumulation of meaningful details, the elliptical dialogue, and above all the revelation of character through action (for example, Muriel Glass's oblivious manicure as the phone rings, as her husband ponders suicide, which the delighted Yates called "the essence of aplomb"). After "Bananafish" Yates became an even more devoted reader of *The New Yorker*; each week he looked forward to the day it came out, when he'd rush to the newsstand to see if there was another story by his favorite new writer, J. D. Salinger. Echoes of Salingerian diction are especially audible in Yates's early work, and linger faintly in his mature style, the result of his reading over and over his five favorite stories in *Nine Stories.** "Here was a man who used language as if it were pure energy beautifully controlled," Yates wrote, "and who knew exactly what he was doing in every silence as well as in every word."

One thing that Yates's early idols had in common was their precocity: By the age of twenty-three Fitzgerald was the best-selling author of *This Side of Paradise,* the Voice of a Generation no less; at the same age Hemingway was the protégé of Ezra Pound and Gertrude Stein, and was on the verge of publishing perhaps the most influential volume of short stories by a twentieth-century American; and whether Yates knew it or not at the time, the Salinger who seemed to emerge fully fledged in the pages of *The New Yorker* at the age of twenty-nine had in fact been publishing forgettable but polished fiction for almost eight years. At twenty-three Yates himself remained unpublished, unmentored, and largely unencouraged as a fiction writer. Also worth noting: The young Fitzgerald and Hemingway were married to Zelda and Hadley respectively—one a zany, glamorous muse who was gifted in her own right, the other a tenderhearted servant of her husband's talent.

Yates had Sheila, who wished him well but "wasn't really interested." She was happy to type his stories for him, but when it came to giving an opinion—as he'd insist—she just didn't know quite what to say. Actually, her letters prove that she was a rather shrewd intuitive reader, but "not literary" as she'd protest over and over, and besides she couldn't win with the guy: If she gave him a glib compliment ("marvelous"), he'd press her to be more specific, and her efforts to oblige him almost always went awry—either she liked the wrong things or the right things for the wrong reasons, or maybe she even *disliked* something for right or wrong reasons, whereupon he'd usually explode. It was futile, and after a while she became reluctant to say anything but "don't bother me," which only made matters worse. Unsupported, plagued with doubt, cut adrift and

---

*Yates's favorite was "Uncle Wiggily in Connecticut," though he disliked the didacticism and implausibility of "Teddy," and deplored the self-indulgence of the later Glass-family stories.

blocked most of the time, Yates would lapse into what Sheila called "the broods"—an almost catatonic state of crystallized depression, during which he'd sometimes sit bunched in a chair for hours without so much as a flinch, staring glassily at nothing. It was disturbing at first, and then it became tiresome: self-indulgence, she decided. He should snap out of it.

Sheila was almost as miserable, and no wonder. Secretarial work was a bore, and when she came home there were any number of menial things to do before she even got dinner started—mainly the labor involved in keeping their dingy apartment habitable while her husband, a consummate "bubblehead," left cigarette ashes all over the floor, the furniture, everywhere, and could hardly do any cleaning himself without breaking something. And if she showed her exasperation or even tried to tease him about it, he'd lose his temper and the fight would be on, until finally Sheila would cover her ears and refuse to say or listen to another word. The worst part was the utter hopelessness of it all: When would the drudgery, the screaming, end? When he became a famous writer?

Things had looked up for a while that previous winter, when Sheila decided to use the money she got for her twenty-first birthday to take acting classes at the New School. As Yates wrote in "Regards": "She would come home breathless with what she was learning, eager to talk without any secretarial rhetoric at all; those were the best of our times together." And when her acting class gave a public performance at the end of the term, Sheila's monologue from *Dream Girl* was such a hit that the New School offered her a full scholarship. Yates was thrilled, but then, after a few days' thought, she decided to refuse it: The class had been "fun," she said, a nice break from her work at Botany Mills (where she was secretary to the market research director, her best job yet), but it was pointless to continue; to pursue acting seriously she'd have to study full-time, and of course that was impossible under the circumstances. "Well, Jesus," says the husband in "Regards." "You could quit that dumb little job tomorrow. *I* can take care of—" "Oh, you can take care of *what?*" snaps the wife.

I loved the girl who'd wanted to tell me all about "the theater," the girl who'd stood calm and shy in the thunderclap of applause that followed her scene from *Dream Girl*. I didn't much like the dependable typist at Botany Mills, or the grudging potato peeler, or the slow, tired woman who frowned over the ironing board to prove how poor we were. And I didn't want to be married to anyone, ever, who said things like "Oh, you can take care of *what?*"

It was almost certainly after the brawl that followed, or sometime very early that summer, that the couple separated and Yates attempted suicide. One can only speculate about what was going through his head when he decided to cut his wrists: His wife was back with the Bialek sisters and wanted a divorce; the "big, ambitious, tragic novel" he'd begun with such hope that spring was now permanently stalled, and of course nobody wanted his short stories; his health was poor, his job was mindless, and there was little promise of anything better, ever. Plus he was very, very tired all the time, and probably at that moment very drunk as well. So he did it, and woke up the next day having to cope with the mess. Perhaps this episode was what he had in mind twelve years later, when Yates wrote apropos of the critic Alfred Kazin's remark that *Revolutionary Road* "locates the new American tragedy squarely on the field of marriage": "Mr. Yates may understand things very well when it comes to writing fiction, and it's terribly nice for him that he can locate an American tragedy, but the awful part is that in real life he has come painfully close to participating in one . . . and being one himself, squarely on the field of marriage." Arguably he'd have better reason at various times in later life to take such drastic action—but apparently he never did, except in the slow and steady fashion of four packs a day. In fact, he rarely missed an apt moment to denounce suicide as "self-indulgent," especially when one had obligations to others. That summer Yates discovered he was about to have such obligations, whether he and his wife wanted them or not.

For better or worse, then, she came back to him and even quit her "dumb little job" at Botany Mills; the baby was due in March, and meanwhile Sheila sometimes wondered if she'd imagined what Yates had told her about that episode in her absence. But another glance at his wrists confirmed it all over again.*

Sharon Elizabeth Yates (aka "Mousemeat," "Mussy," or simply "the Meat") was born on March 22, 1950, and was mostly a cause for celebration. Yates was a doting, playful father, though he was awkward changing diapers and handling the baby in general and tended to stick her with pins. Also his writing (such as it was) had to be interrupted while they adjusted themselves to the baby's schedule, and the prospect of Europe seemed ever dimmer—which was sad, as the thought of quitting their old grind and pursuing the ghosts of Scott and Ernest amid the cafés of Montparnasse had become more appealing than ever. On the other hand, the most practical reason for going—to put an ocean between themselves and Dookie—had become less urgent, since the latter's tireless volunteerism had finally paid off: A few months before, Ruth Yates had begun a two-year term as president of the National Association of Women Artists, at a salary equal to what her son was making at Remington Rand. A rather startling turn of events while it lasted.

Soon a new and far graver concern rushed to fill the void. For several weeks Yates's health had been worse than usual: He coughed constantly and felt exhausted and out of breath; mornings he woke up dripping with sweat. His weight had dropped to 140 pounds. Sheila would stand and wait at the top of subway steps while her twenty-four-year-old husband wheezed behind her like an old man. Finally, a month or so after the baby was born, Yates got his chest X-rayed and learned he had advanced tuberculosis. That evening an official from Bellevue came to the apartment and took Yates away to the crowded TB ward, where he stayed for three weeks until space was found at Halloran, the veterans' hospital on Staten Island. "[A]ll I knew then," he wrote, "was how good it felt to be encouraged—even to be ordered, by a grim ex-Army nurse wearing a sterile mask—to lie down and stay there."

---

*Yates's daughters never noticed such scars, which suggests they were superficial and perhaps half-heartedly inflicted.

In some ways it would prove one of the best things that had ever happened to him. Halloran wasn't a bad place—with its remote manicured lawns, its reverie of hushed waiting within the separate, single-story TB building. The hundred or so shuffling or wheelchair-bound patients tended to be friendly with one another in a quiet, diffident way that suited Yates: He could talk and listen as much or as little as he liked, and for the most part he felt a genuine sense of solidarity with his fellow consumptives. As he noted in an early draft of "Regards": "I think death was on all of our minds in those drowsing, melancholy wards, where the bedside radios droned all day in the very sound of boredom; most of us were in no real danger of dying, but our existence seemed clearly to be something less than life." Every so often Yates would see a doctor for his pneumothorax treatment—a needle between the ribs to inject air into the lung and collapse it—but otherwise there was little to do but lie there.

He had plentiful means to distract himself from morbid thoughts: A group of his Remington Rand friends had chipped in and bought him a large box of Modern Library books; as his future publisher Seymour Lawrence put it, Halloran became Yates's "Harvard, Yale, and Princeton." What had hitherto inhibited him most as a writer was a dire sense of his own ignorance; since high school his life had been a hamster wheel of war and work and worry, with Dookie's demands scotching any hope of repose in between. And while Yates would forever remain a slow, insecure writer with a wildly inflated idea of what he'd missed by way of college, his eight months in the TB ward began a lifelong process of autodidactic recompense. Some of the writers he got around to reading there ("without whose work I might never have put together a halfway decent book of my own") included Dickens, Tolstoy, Dostoyevsky, E. M. Forster, Katherine Mansfield, Sinclair Lewis, and Dylan Thomas; particularly he read (and reread) Chekhov, Conrad, Joyce, Jane Austen, Ring Lardner, and Keats. And Flaubert too, though he wouldn't accord *Madame Bovary* the sort of scrutiny it deserved (for his own purposes) until several years later.

"I was very independent at the time," said Sheila, a bit of elliptical dialogue that would have made the authors of *Gatsby* and *Revolutionary Road* proud. With her husband indefinitely hospitalized on Staten Island, Sheila was for all purposes single again. She farmed the baby out to a kindly old couple in New Rochelle and found a job at the Dobeckmun Company on West Fifty-seventh, where she was secretary to a publicity director whose mission it was to promote the metallic yarn Lurex. Meanwhile a kindly coworker from Remington Rand, who was fond of Yates and fancied herself a photographer, offered to shoot a portrait of Sheila and the baby that would serve to keep Yates company during the lonely intervals between visits. "It was a strained time," Sheila concedes; what with visiting the baby and doing her job and whatnot, she wasn't able to make it out to Halloran ("quite a schlep") more than every week or so. And when she got there Yates was often reticent or surly or both, and always "smoking like a chimney," tuberculosis withal, which made her wonder even more what conceivable future there was in staying married to such a man.

Her old Bronxville friend Ann Barker came to live with her in the Twelfth Street apartment, and proved a far more congenial roommate than either of the Bialek sisters or for that matter Yates himself. The two young women were a few doors down from eligible bachelors, and whether by chance or design the women's cat had a way of wandering into the men's apartment. At first the men simply tossed it out, until a neighbor advised them of its provenance ("that cat belongs to two pretty ladies"); the next time they returned it in person. A propitious visit: Within three months Barker was engaged to one of the men, John Kowalsky, while Sheila flirted with his roommate and several of his friends—an assortment of NYU and Columbia graduates, not a would-be writer in the bunch. When Sheila was overheard remarking that she was a "grass widow," Barker reminded her that she wasn't divorced *yet*; "Oh, that doesn't matter!" Sheila hissed, as if it were just a bothersome formality.

When her husband was finally released as an outpatient in February 1951, Sheila decided to stay married on a "wait-and-see basis": As a bitter Yates later described the situation, she'd decided to be "brave," taking him back "as a partner in a sensible arrangement of joint parenthood." A bit on the unromantic side, perhaps, though one can hardly blame Sheila: At twenty-three she had little to look forward to but a life of caring for an infirm "writer" who seemed disinclined to care for himself. There was, however, a peculiar sweetness to Yates—a tolerant devotion (or dependency) that Sheila came to appreciate better over time: "You're the only person who's ever loved me," she wrote him later, "no matter how much I played outside the rules." Another incentive for sticking around was the $207 a month Yates had been awarded for his "service-connected disability," which was guaranteed for five years as long as his lungs were checked on a weekly basis at VA-approved clinics "anywhere in the world." And since ten months had passed since his illness was originally diagnosed, he was entitled to a retroactive lump sum of more than two thousand dollars.

To Sheila the next move was clear: Paris. "Because I mean if we don't do it now" (says the wife in "Regards"), "while we're young enough and brave enough, when are we ever going to do it at all?" As Sheila recalled, Yates was suddenly intimidated by the idea: Though he'd "talked constantly" about Europe before his illness, "[tuberculosis] had sapped his will" and now he seemed bent on returning to Remington Rand. But Sheila had enough willpower for both of them; the allure of helping her boss promote Lurex had palled—she was ready for a change, the more drastic the better. Like April Wheeler tuning out her weak-willed, equivocating husband, she pressed ahead with the arrangements.

It didn't take long. Within a week Yates had done his part by getting in touch with Stephen Benedict, who was then living in Paris. They needed an affordable two- or three-room apartment, Yates wrote, and hoped Benedict could help them "steer clear of the conventional Cook's-Tour-filthy-postcard set." Benedict replied that a friend's place would fall vacant within a month or so, and in the meantime they could live cheaply in one of the pensions. For the sake of economy, though, he advised them to settle in the provinces eventually, and Yates assured him they'd probably head south for the winter: "Our only plans are that we want to stay in Europe indefinitely and I want to do an awful lot of writing."

They sailed on April 14 aboard the *United States*, where a "cramped farewell party" was held in their tourist-class cabin. While Sheila changed the baby's diapers on the upper berth, a dapper-hatted Dookie sat below and regaled the guests (the Cains and Bialeks, plus friends from Botany Mills and Remington Rand) with odd bits of esoterica about the National Association of Women Artists. As she went on talking and drinking, her knees sagged apart until her underpants showed ("an old failing")—but such ghastliness would soon be in the past, and Yates could afford to feel magnanimous: "I had luck, time, opportunity, a young girl for a wife, and a child of my own."

CHAPTER FIVE

The Getaway: 1951-1953

They arrived in Paris on April 20 and checked into a cheap hotel called the Atlantic. Yates went to the U.S. Embassy and arranged for medical care, which consisted of the usual weekly injections of air to maintain a partial collapse of both lungs. Meanwhile they waited for Benedict's friend to clear out of his apartment on the Rue du Bac in St.-Germain-des-Prés, and Yates took Sheila and the baby on long strolls around the Left Bank—where as a young GI he'd "walked himself weak down its endless blue streets and all the people who knew how to live had kept their tantalizing secret to themselves." Five years later the secret was safe as ever, though they did find a café they liked, the Deux Magots, where at least they could be among a fair number of people who spoke English.

Yates was determined to "[grind] out short stories at the rate of about one a month," and as soon as they were settled he got down to work. While he spent his days writing, smoking, and coughing, Sheila was obliged to find ways of keeping herself and the baby out of the apartment as much as possible—a pleasant-enough occupation, most of the time: She did the marketing, went to museums, shopped, explored, and consoled herself that at least it wasn't New York. But there were bad days when she felt at loose ends, anonymous—"that awful feeling of not quite being there when people look at you," she later described it—and the baby served as a constant reminder (if a winsome one) that she'd committed herself to a man, a life, that didn't seem right no matter what the scenery.

She was free to do as she liked at night, when it was her husband's turn to look after "the Meat," and before long she was recruited to act in a "dreadful" play. So negligible was this enterprise that Sheila hardly remembers the rather famous man who wrote and directed (novelist Meyer Levin, who later won acclaim as the author of *Compulsion*),* and has quite forgotten such matters as title, plot, character, or even how she got involved in the first place (she suspects she was hired with a group of other American and Swedish expatriates who were spotted at certain cafés). It was something to do. The evening rehearsals went on for a longish while, and finally on opening night there was a fairly large audience—then a bit fewer the next night, and hardly anybody after that. The play closed in less than a week. Yates attended one of the more uncrowded performances and seemed rather bemused by the badness of it all.

Sheila's steadiest companion was a former prostitute named Chantal, who was kept as a mistress by one of Yates's Avon acquaintances, a dull rich person whom everyone avoided as much as possible, and whose name is lost to posterity. Neither Chantal nor Sheila spoke the other's language, though they were compatible in other ways and managed to communicate quite effectively after a fashion. Once the play was over and Sheila again found herself with too much time to think, Chantal enticed her to explore some of the more raffish aspects of Paris—particularly the *bals musettes* where poor people went to amuse themselves on weekends, and where Sheila occasionally found herself in "sticky situations" with tough-looking laborers who wanted more than a dance. But Chantal knew how to handle such fellows, and in general their nights made for an exhilarating change.

As for Yates, he felt tired and ill at the end of the day, and apart from the odd drink at the Deux Magots he wasn't up to doing much or asking questions about whatever his wife was doing. He was happy to stay home with the Meat and consider his progress as a writer, and at least in this

---

*At first she thought it was *Ira* Levin, of *Rosemary's Baby* fame ("*some* fairly famous writer named Levin"). I wrote Mr. Levin a letter, and he kindly left a message on my machine to the effect that he wasn't anywhere near Paris in 1951, though he thought *Meyer* Levin had been. ("Was it *Meyer* Levin, by any chance?" I asked Sheila; "Yes! Exactly!" she replied.) Ira Levin went on to say that, as a matter of interesting coincidence, he did have a "Yates connection" all his own—to wit, Yates's former mother-in-law, Marjorie Bryant, sold Levin a house in Wilton, Connecticut, in the mid-sixties. "She was a charming lady who was quite proud of [Yates]," said Ira Levin, without audible irony.

respect he must have felt gratified. Two stories he wrote in Paris, "A Last Fling, Like," and "The Canal," give a sense of his range and growth at this time.

The first is little more than a well-done pastiche of the Lardneresque monologue wherein a stock vulgarian reveals herself as such in some unwitting way. The "fling" in question is a trip to Europe the narrator takes prior to going ahead with her marriage to some nonentity named Marty. As she tells it to a girlfriend, she spent the vacation flirting with a number of lackluster men (evoked with Salingerian pathos: "[He] looked a little bit like Richard Widmark, but he was sort of on the plump side and his hands were always wet") and having random misadventures, until she feels nothing but relief to be back in her familiar office-girl routine. Europe, in short, is a bust, though it does afford her a delicious chance to put Marty in his place when he protests that *he* wouldn't have gone gadding off to Europe before their wedding; as the narrator gleefully reports her riposte to the girlfriend: " 'Listen, brother, don't kid yourself.' I says, 'You'd do it quick enough, if you had the money.' "

With "The Canal" Yates began to find his own voice, as well as a vision to go with it—indeed, the story is such an advance over "Fling" that one can hardly believe they were written within months of each other. That "Canal" is a far more personal story may explain its relative success, up to a point: That is, such an exercise served to steer Yates away from second-hand characters and situations, though it would be a long time before he got over the worst of his squeamishness toward what he feared was subjective, "unformed" work. Perhaps he was also uncomfortable casting such a cold eye on, say, his marriage and the sustaining illusions thereof—as when Lew Miller, in the frame-story of "Canal," imagines how his wife perceives him at an awful party where he waxes reticent while a more prosperous man boasts about the war:

> Miller realized uneasily that for Betty there was a special kind of women's-magazine romanticism in having a husband who never talked about the war—a faintly tragic, sensitive husband, perhaps, or at any rate a charmingly modest one—so that it really didn't matter if Nancy Brace's husband *was*

more handsome, more solid in his Brooks Brothers suit and, once, more dashing in his trim lieutenant's uniform.

But the wife's "women's-magazine romanticism" is not so pronounced that she's immune to exasperation with her "modest" husband's dull refusal to discuss his own wartime heroics: "Darling," she says after the party, "*why* do you let an ass like that eclipse you so in a conversation?" The answer, of course, is that Lew Miller is deeply ashamed of his relative failure as a soldier—a secret he's kept from his wife—and while he'd rather not admit as much, he refuses to tell self-aggrandizing lies about it either. Thus, while Miller's final outburst at his wife (" 'Will you shut up? Will you please for God's sake shut up?' ") is somewhat derived from similar moments in famous stories by Salinger and Hemingway,* it also faithfully represents the reality of Yates's life with Sheila, in a way that probably made both uneasy. He would have to find a way to distance himself from such material.

In October they moved to Juan-les-Pins, near Cap d'Antibes and Cannes on the Riviera—where the Fitzgeralds had frolicked with the Murphys and Hemingways, with Isadora Duncan and Picasso and Dorothy Parker (later a fan of Richard Yates); the very place where Scott had written much of *Gatsby,* and the place he evoked so elegiacally in *Tender Is the Night.*

It was a different story for Yates. By the time he arrived, *le beau monde* was long gone, and their shabby apartment at La Monada was a far cry from Gausse's Hotel in *Tender.* Nor were there any wacky waterskiing antics behind whooshing hydroplanes, or swimming in a "choppy little four-beat crawl," or lounging on a raft where laughing expats sat clinking martini glasses. There was none of that: Yates was too sick to swim and didn't like the outdoors anyway. He couldn't even do the few things he'd

---

*Namely the end of Salinger's "Pretty My Mouth and Green My Eyes" (published in *The New Yorker* not long before Yates wrote "The Canal"), and the woman's climactic outburst in Hemingway's "Hills Like White Elephants."

enjoyed in Paris—walking around city streets, talking to English-speaking people in cafés—since they were almost two miles from town, and he was damned if he'd ride a girl's bicycle (with a child seat fixed to the back) to get there, even if he had the stamina to do so, which he didn't.

Instead of becoming some lesser, latter-day version of Scott and Zelda, Rich and Sheila reverted to a pair of homely alter egos they dubbed "Pinner and Shirley": Pinner was a clinging, doe-eyed invalid who resented his wife's unabashed enjoyment of the beach, the countryside, the long bike rides into town with the baby in tow for a pleasant day's marketing; Shirley was the caustic scold who tended to return from these outings wondering why on earth a man on death's door should keep smoking like a chimney and leaving ashes all over the place and couldn't he at least go for a *walk* now and then and get a little fresh air? And Shirley it was who put her foot down, finally, refusing to fetch her husband's cigarettes from Cannes anymore, no matter how pathetically he begged or threatened in her pedaling wake ("[Pinner's] old broken espadrilles slapping the dust," as he recalled the scene). What made matters worse was that Sheila herself liked to have the odd smoke after dinner, and went right on having it ("*I* wasn't going to quit! There wasn't anything wrong with *me*!") while her husband sat glowering but quiet because of the baby. Later he'd root her butts out of the trash and smoke them down to the last spark, but resented having to do so. "This was the principal source of friction," Sheila recalled, with marvelous understatement.

Thankfully Yates had better luck with his art. Sheila's brother Charlie had sent a copy of Yates's latest story, "A Really Good Jazz Piano," to an old show-business friend of the family, the agent Monica McCall, and on January 15, 1952, she replied: "Yates is without question a writer. There is an old cliché: 'The ink is in the hair,' and he definitely has it." And with that Yates made the single most important contact of his career, a woman whose support—professional, moral, and otherwise—would never flag, no matter how rocky the road became.

Monica McCall was one of five sisters born of Scottish parents in Leicester. Often described as "a perfect English lady," sweet and devoted to her clients, she was also tough as nails and never to be trifled with. A grande dame who resembled "a pretty version of Margaret Rutherford" (as her

protégé Mitch Douglas put it), McCall inherited the same quirky, determined nature that had spurred one of her sisters to leap off London's
Waterloo Bridge after a failed love affair and another to become a nun who
vanished at a tender age into a vow of silence. But Monica was nothing if
not worldly, and her career is the stuff of legend in the publishing world.
She was born in 1899 but refused to reveal that fact to anybody, not even
to company insurance representatives, choosing rather to do without coverage. And when she and her longtime partner, the poet Muriel Rukeyser,
were arrested with a crowd for lying down in the Senate visitors gallery to
protest the Vietnam War, McCall insisted the police take her to jail along
with everybody else, no matter what her age. On the other hand, she wasn't
averse to acting enfeebled if it fit her purpose, as when she'd commandeer
wheelchairs at airports, the better to sail through the crowd to her flight.
She brought the same wily righteousness to her professional conduct—an
elusive quality indistinguishable from tenderness with regard to her clients'
interests. When *Esquire* wanted to put her at the "Red-Hot Center" of its
"Literary Universe," she declined, as she thought it beneath the dignity of
herself and her authors. It was this sort of integrity that commanded Yates's
respect and even love, such that he named his second daughter after her, a
gesture McCall never forgot. She often inquired after her namesake, and
once sent the child an antique brooch with "Monica" engraved on it.

Her curious mixture of warmth and savvy was evident from the start of
their relationship. Two weeks after she remarked to Charlie Bryant that
his brother-in-law had ink in his hair, she wrote to Yates directly and
asked if she might "please call [him] Dick": "Since I have known your fine
Sheila since she was two years old, I don't believe I can address you as
'Mr. Yates'!" That said, she then deflated the jubilant Dick by making it
clear she hadn't, in fact, told Charlie that she was willing to handle him
solely on the basis of "A Really Good Jazz Piano"—though in fact she
had: "I'm delighted to read any other stories that you care, or he cares to
send in," she'd written Charlie in that first letter, "and furthermore to represent him." (She later apologized for the error when Yates pointed it out
to her.) She was, however, "very interested" to read more of his work, and
would then decide whether or not to take him on as a client.

Yates sent his seven best stories in the order he'd written them, and a month later McCall responded with a thumbnail critique of each and a definite decision to offer at least two of the stories for sale, and hence become his agent. Manifest in her letter is an all but infallible sense of what sold in the so-called literary fiction market, and in the future when Yates chose to ignore her advice he'd generally come to regret it. McCall noted that Yates's work showed a "good build"—i.e., that his more recent stories were better than his early ones, a good augury, but for now most of them didn't pass muster. A brief anecdote titled "Bells in the Morning" was a "promising beginning but not saleable," and "A Last Fling, Like" lacked everything from a strong story to a "vivid or interesting or moving character." Two other stories Yates sent in the batch, "The Misfits" and "Shepherd's Pie on Payday," are no longer extant in any form—and no wonder, given the awful verdict McCall passed on each: The first was "out of focus," and the second was "nothing more nor less than two rather briefly etched characters having a conversation which leads nowhere" (to which she tactfully added, "Don't forget that every good writer has an occasional lapse, and forgive me for thinking this one of your lapses!"). The only stories she thought potentially saleable were "The Canal" and "No Pain Whatsoever"—and though she had little apparent hope for the former ("I will do my best to place it"), her estimate of the latter was prescient as ever ("best story of the lot . . . deeply touching, beautifully characterized").

Most telling was her ambivalence toward that early draft of "A Really Good Jazz Piano"; though she thought it a "great improvement" over most of Yates's other stories, its ending was "unprepared for and obscure"—that is, in this version the two protagonists, Carson and Ken, erupt in weird laughter over their cruelty toward Sid, the black jazz pianist, and on that note the story ends. "Do you want to think about the end at all," McCall inquired, "or let me know what you were trying to do, or is that too dreary for you?" Yates replied that he thought the ending "honest" and wanted to keep it, and McCall agreed to offer the story as is. It would take Yates six years to accept his error.

In April the Yateses moved into Stephen Benedict's former apartment at Palais Beau Site in Cannes, once the place had finally been vacated by a navy wife who'd lived there after Benedict (she later became fodder for Yates's story, "Evening on the Côte d'Azur," about which more below). Before the war Palais Beau Site had been a rather stately hotel and, whatever its subsequent decline, was a vast improvement over La Monada in Juan-les-Pins. The new apartment was a compact arrangement of two rooms plus kitchen and bath, with pleasant ceramic-tiled floors and a little balcony in back that afforded a stunning view of the Mediterranean. "At its best and sunniest," Benedict recalled, "it was paradise."

Yates would have agreed in at least one respect: Now that he was closer to town he could buy his own cigarettes, the procurement of which was about the only thing that coaxed him outside. Occasionally he'd walk on the beach, but mostly he was content to stick to his old routine of writing, smoking, and coughing. As for Sheila, she was sick of the whole business, and chose to go her own way as much as possible. A letter she wrote in 1962 alludes to their "semi-separation in Cannes," and one can only guess what this entailed, since she now remembers the time as "tranquil" relative to later years. True, she was tired of "fussing about cigarettes" and so forth, but as for the rest of it she'd come to accept (at least in retrospect) that her husband was simply a "city person"—and *city* meant New York, Paris, or London, and not some overheated tourist trap like Cannes, where he'd just as soon stay at his desk.

Meanwhile the news from Monica McCall suggested that Yates wasn't headed for overnight success. Within a month both "The Canal" and "No Pain Whatsoever" were turned down by the *Atlantic Monthly, Harper's, Esquire,* and *The New Yorker.* "Yates has a lot of talent," wrote *Esquire* (returning "Canal"), "but we just aren't using much fiction with a World War II angle." The *Atlantic* thought "No Pain Whatsoever" was "bogged down in the wasteful conversation which seemed to fill far too much of the first two-thirds of the story." And while *Harper's* was "impressed" and willing to see more—they did, and declined—*The New Yorker* dispatched both stories with a standard rejection slip.* A few months later "No Pain Whatsoever" was also rejected by a new literary magazine

---

*In the hope of evoking dramatic irony rather than suspense, I remind the reader that *The New Yorker* rejected every story Yates ever wrote (four or five of which are classics, or so a number of

called *Discovery*, whose editor would someday become a friend and colleague of Yates. As Vance Bourjaily wrote McCall, the story was "perfectly handled," with "only one thing missing . . . some feeling of why the author has chosen to write it"; as far as Bourjaily could tell, the narrator "never develops an attitude" toward Myra, the adulterous protagonist, and hence one doesn't know "whether tragedy's involved or simply animal pathos." An elaborate way of saying, perhaps, that the reader can't tell whether Myra's supposed to be good or bad.

That a fine writer and reader like Bourjaily could render such a judgment suggests something of what Yates was up against. Of course there was less tolerance for moral ambiguity in those days, but that goes only so far in explaining the discomfort and even outrage that Yates's work (throughout his career) aroused in certain readers: "*Why* does he have to write so unpleasantly that one feels there's just no good in anybody?" wrote a *Harper's* editor in rejecting "A Really Good Jazz Piano"—and really, the saga of that story alone (assuredly a classic; Yates's own favorite as late as 1974) might serve to encapsulate the kind of reception his early work, in particular, received. "What a good story this must be for us to be going on about it so!" wrote Monica McCall in April 1952, as she remonstrated with Yates over that problematic ending. A few months later "Jazz" was turned down by both *New American Writing* and *New World Writing,* and the next year *Argosy* followed suit: "[T]he playboy setting and depressing ending rule it out for us." In 1955 the writer Peter Matthiessen, then an editor at *Paris Review,* rejected the story for a familiar reason, which he saw fit to frame in aesthetic rather than moral terms: "The cruelty which forms its climax is incredible, not in itself, but in terms of these characters and this situation." When *Esquire* also called the ending a "let-down" in 1957, Yates finally got the point and revised the story into its present superlative form—whereupon *The New Yorker* promptly rejected it with what must by then have seemed an almost mocking refrain: "Hope you [McCall] will let us see other stories from him."

---

famous writers think), including "The Canal," which a later generation of *New Yorker* editors saw fit to publish in the January 15, 2001, issue, eight years too late for Yates to enjoy it.

Esquire agreed to have another look at the revised version, and this time accepted it—only to reject it again when they learned that Yates would be including the story in the 1958 Scribner's volume *Short Story 1* ("Rust Hills did have the grace to say that he was distressed and apologetic about the manner in which they handled 'the matter,'" McCall wrote bitterly). *The New Yorker* offered to reconsider yet again, but this time found it "too pat and neatly contrived" (as opposed to lacking believability, an earlier charge), and other rejections followed from *Harper's,* the *Atlantic,* and *Saturday Evening Post* ("for fairly obvious reasons"). Finally—almost a decade after Yates had finished that draft on the Riviera—the story made its magazine debut in Vance Bourjaily's *Discovery.* To this day Bourjaily feels proud of having published one of Yates's best and most representative stories: "I'm a jazz snob like Carson," he said, "and by the end of the story I understood his offense, and saw it in myself, even if Carson didn't." That Bourjaily and other good readers tend to *see themselves* in Yates's characters is perhaps a clue worth remembering.

Meanwhile back in Cannes, 1952, the waves shushed outside and the sunlight dazzled the tiles and Yates lit another cigarette and got on with his work. He now had a superb agent, and several magazine editors thought he was talented (if misanthropic) and wanted to see more. Given that on a good day the most he could write was maybe half a polished page, or just over a hundred words, there was no time to let up—though he still had a lot to learn, and the quality of his work wavered. "Foursome," the next story he finished after "A Really Good Jazz Piano," was rejected without fanfare and doesn't survive.

"Thieves" is interesting as an early variation on one of Yates's favorite themes: the depths to which people deceive themselves into thinking they're somehow special, set apart from the herd. Protagonist Robert Blaine is the abrasive sage of a TB sanatorium, and for much of the story he holds forth on the meaning of "talent" ("knowing how to handle yourself"), and offers himself as a good example—as when he swaggered into a swanky Madison Avenue clothing store and conned the clerk into thinking he was a bigshot. Well in advance of Blaine's bleak epiphany, though, the reader is given a nudge: "All the stories whose purpose was to show Robert Blaine as a seasoned man of the world were laid in 'thirty-nine or 'forty, when he had first come to New York, just as those intended to show him as an irrepressible youth took place in Chicago, 'back in the Depression.'" Finally Blaine tells how he "stole" a woman named Irene from her well-heeled husband, whose money they spent for six months: "'[She] thought I was going to be another Sherwood Anderson. Probably still does.'" The disparity between his past and present "promise" occurs all at once to Blaine, and his breathing becomes "shallow and irregular"; but when a concerned patient seeks help for Blaine's "nerves," the matter-of-fact nurse delivers a blunt coup de grace: "Oh, honestly, that Blaine. *Nerves,* for God's sake. Big baby, that's all he is." Monica McCall was kind in her estimate of "Thieves": "It is a good story, beautifully characterized, but I think not any better selling bet than the stories on which I am working"—a tactful way of saying that it was little more than a few characters having a conversation which leads *somewhere,* perhaps, but nowhere interesting enough to justify the overall lack of drama.

Yates's next story, "The Comptroller and the Wild Wind," is an even broader repository of the themes and tendencies that would reappear in his later work, as well as a few he'd subsequently discard—Joycean lyricism, for instance: "A long time ago, he had married a girl with splendid long legs and a face that was described as pert (in the blue half-light of dawn she whispered, 'darling, darling, darling,' and the legs were strong, the face was wild and lovely)." With a further nod to Joyce, the latter's poem "Watching the Needleboats at San Sabba" is quoted in full here, as it would be more than thirty years later as the epigraph to *Young Hearts Crying,* whose title it supplied. And that poem, with all it suggests of the lost illusions of youth, is very much to the point in "Comptroller" and elsewhere (less blatantly) in Yates's work. Another gambit that would become almost a signature is the opening line(s) that foreshadows doom: "The morning after his wife left him, George Pollock, comptroller of the American Bearing Company, had breakfast at a counter for the first time in twenty years. He destroyed three paper napkins trying to remove one, whole, from the tight grip of the dispenser, and nearly upset a glass of water in an effort to keep his briefcase from sliding off his lap." Hence the bungling Pollock—a dull man judging by his job description and surname—is left utterly helpless by the desertion of his wife, the "Wild Wind" of the title, who was not so wild that she was unwilling to fix him breakfast every morning for twenty years. But no more: " 'Oh, how can anyone hate you,' " she tells him on the eve of her departure with a man who shares her fondness for poetry; " 'you're not hateful—you're just a pompous, posturing *fussy* little man!' " Just so: The decent Pollock is a lot less hateful than, say, Frank Wheeler (to whom the same sentiment would be applied in *Revolutionary Road*), such that one wonders, really, what the man has done to deserve so many humiliations in a single narrative day. "Close, but no cigar—I'm not sure why," wrote an *Esquire* editor in rejecting the story. "I think it's because there doesn't seem to be any occasion for so much bitter handling, and just a little contempt for the nonintellectual." To be sure there was compassion as well as contempt, but in terms of basic effect other editors agreed in toto.

Monica McCall was patient and duly encouraging: "You are progressing well from the more anecdotal character sketch type of story into the fuller, more rounded story." And Yates continued to make progress with his next story, "Nuptials," an early draft of one of his masterpieces, "The Best of Everything." McCall responded that it was a "swell story" and submitted it for consideration as an *Atlantic* "First"—the magazine's prestigious showcase for previously unpublished authors. But the *Atlantic* declined without comment, as did *The New Yorker* and *Esquire* a few weeks later, and when McCall proposed sending it to the somewhat obscure *Botteghe Oscure,* a plainly frustrated Yates dismissed the magazine as "an esoteric little tea-party journal."

By now Yates was badly in need of a success, even if it meant some sort of artistic compromise. After all, his hero Fitzgerald had written any number of hokey, formulaic stories for the *Saturday Evening Post,* and gotten rich in the bargain; why not Richard Yates? The result of such professionalism was "A Convalescent Ego," a story that turned the raw material of his illness and shaky marriage into a wacky Walter Mitty–like farce. Those who wonder what it must have been like for Sheila when Yates returned from the TB ward (or just on a daily basis for that matter) need look no further than "Convalescent Ego":

The porcelain soap dish had given way under his brush, dropped from the wall and smashed, breaking the cup and saucer he'd just washed. . . . Things like this had been happening nearly every day since he came home from the hospital. First there had been the discovery that he'd left his silver fountain pen behind, in the locker beside his hospital bed, and [his wife] had to make a special trip back to get it from the nurses. Then on the second or third day, when he'd insisted on helping with the housework, he had shaken the dust mop out the window so hard that the head of the thing fell off, five stories down into the courtyard, and left him absurdly shaking the naked stick over the windowsill.

Let that image of Yates's alter ego "shaking the naked stick" linger as a kind of endearing emblem of his domestic life. As for the rest of the story, it offers a number of fine moments such as these, and reflects the kind of frustrated escapism into which the high-strung Yates may well have lapsed whenever Sheila's "elaborate kindliness" or "tight-lipped silence" had implied what a hopeless bungler he was (hence the protagonist daydreams of various ways in which to redeem himself—e.g., heroically going back to work despite his illness, buying champagne for a bravura celebration, and so on). But as a narrative it doesn't go anywhere in particular except an ending so sappy and artificial that Yates must have held his nose to write it: "Oh Bill, I *have* been awful since you came home, haven't I?" says the nagging but now miraculously reformed wife. "Oh Bill, you ought to break *all* the dishes, right over my dumb head."

Monica McCall, who knew what Yates was up to, wrote that she might be able to sell the story to the "slicks" if he'd revise it in order to dramatize the Mittyish reveries—"[they] should be more acted out, rather than imagined in his mind"—and appended a list of notes to that purpose. But as it turned out, the "slicks" were no more interested than *The New Yorker* et al., though *Collier's* found the story "readable and amusing" and commended the author's "remarkable ear for dialogue." Yates appreciated the compliment, though wondered that it should be made "on the basis of 'Convalescent Ego,' for God's sake."

Perhaps to get the taste of "Ego" out of his mouth, Yates returned to his former manner with a vengeance. "Evening on the Côte d'Azur" seems almost pitiless in its treatment of the meager resources, mental or otherwise, available to a middle-class Everywoman such as Betty Meyers, a navy wife living in Cannes. Betty's days pass in a nausea of boredom: Oblivious to the beauty of the sea and beach, she resents her children, her absentee husband, her faded looks, the snotty French, and longs to be back in Bayonne, New Jersey, of all places. Inevitably she allows herself to be seduced by an affable officer named Tom, whom she immediately imagines she loves; as she lies "at peace" in the afterglow, her husband all but forgotten, the narrative point of view switches to that of her departed lover, who cruelly ridicules her for the benefit of two young sailors. "Son, any man couldn't make that oughta turn in his uniform." Nor is there any danger of a contretemps with Betty's husband, as one of the sailors seems to expect: "Oh, Jesus Christ, Junior," the crafty old officer tells the kid. "When're you gonna grow up? Whaddya think—I told her my real name?"

"Evening on the Côte d'Azur" was turned down by *The New Yorker,* *Harper's,* the *Atlantic,* and *Esquire,* whose editor wrote that it "suffers from a confusion of styles. Sometimes the story is seen by its heroine— stupid and adolescent—sometimes by its author, in rather rich prose." This is unjust. The third-person narrator who mimics the diction of the viewpoint character ("Oh, she knew the Sixth Fleet was supposed to be a good deal, and everything") is a valid approach, and one that Yates would refine to more subtle effect in his later work; moreover, the quick objective bridge between Betty's and Tom's points of view is hardly written in "rather rich prose"—but no matter. While the story falls a bit short of Yates's mature outlook and voice, he was clearly on the brink of finding a way out of the wilderness, at least as a writer.

Palais Beau Site became rather expensive in high season, and late that summer Yates suggested that Sheila write to her English aunt, a woman she hardly knew, and inquire about lodgings in London. The aunt replied that her own apartment in South Kensington had a basement flat that she'd be happy to rent for a nominal sum, two pounds a week, as long as they didn't mind her using the bathtub each morning. They didn't mind at all, and in October they moved.

For the first time in Europe, Yates was relatively happy. He liked almost everything about London, including Sheila's aunt—a bluff seventy-year-old widow who'd changed her first name, sensibly enough, from Bevin to Mary (Fagin). The frail, gentlemanly Yates seemed to excite the woman's maternal instinct, and before long they were thick as thieves: Aunt Mary was full of stories about London show-business types (her husband had been a theatrical producer), and Yates loved to listen as a way of unwinding after the day's work. Also, with what they saved on rent they could afford a good nursery school for Mussy, who'd grown into a charming but noisy two-year-old. Not only did this make for a more tranquil writing environment, but left Yates with enough energy in the evening to play games like "Ready for a Girl" and "Dup-dup-dup." The first, as his daughter recalls, was "some sort of running-chasing game," and the second involved putting her on his lap and singing "Dup-*dup*-dup" to the tune of an English martial jingle until, with great hilarity, his knees would part and she'd splash to the floor. "What are you doing on the *floor?*" Yates would say mock sternly; "I asked you to sit in my lap!" Another benefit of nursery school (Mrs. Pierce's Academy) was that it left Sheila free during the day—and so, contrary to their Paris arrangement, she agreed to stay home at night with the toddler while Yates went off to the pubs, an activity he enjoyed and she didn't.

In fact she didn't enjoy much of anything by then, almost as if her and Yates's respective levels of contentment were inversely related. In a letter she wrote him a year later, Sheila wondered why she'd gotten so "snarky and sick" in London, even though life there had been "perfect . . . in all its outside aspects." This was mostly a matter of lonely, wishful revisionism on her part, as their life in London (or hers anyway) had been far from "perfect," on the outside or in. By the time they'd come to live in that cozy, claustrophobic basement flat, Sheila was sicker than ever of Yates's vagaries—his moody scribbling, fecklessness, and self-neglect—and what made it even more intolerable was her hatred of London per se. As Yates evoked her views in the story "Liars in Love":

[London] was big and drab and unwelcoming; you could walk or ride a bus for miles without seeing anything nice, and the coming of winter brought an evil-smelling sulphurous fog that stained everything yellow, that seeped through closed windows and doors to hang in your rooms and afflict your wincing, weeping eyes.

Sheila made a fine distinction between the lesser of two evils and decided to stay inside the flat all day, amid a pall of cigarette smoke and seeping fog. Occasionally her cousins Gemma or Barbara—sweet but conventional— would visit, but that was about it. And though it was true that she and her husband didn't quarrel much anymore ("quarreling had belonged to an earlier phase of their marriage"), the thick awkward silences were hardly an improvement.

At least Yates had his writing to keep him busy, and on that score he was more hopeful than ever: The story he'd finished just before leaving Cannes, "Jody Rolled the Bones"—his fifteenth since moving to Europe ("Number 15 off the production line," as he put it)—had been gleefully received by Monica McCall. "Oh the new one is an absolute beauty," she wrote on September 16, "I think it quite the best piece you have done." A month later it was declined "by the narrowest margin" for an *Atlantic* "First," as the editors thought it was "simply a shade too predictable." But the next day a follow-up letter came from the new twenty-six-year-old assistant editor at the magazine, Seymour Lawrence, who wanted to hold the story for one more week pending the return of his celebrated mentor, Edward Weeks, who was just then wrapping up a lecture tour. Weeks returned and promptly read the story—"far and away superior to the general run of Army material," he glossed—and on October 21, 1952, Yates received a cable: ATLANTIC BUYING JODY FOR A "FIRST" AT TWO HUNDRED AND FIFTY MANY CONGRATULATIONS MONICA.

He was on his way at last. The first thing he did was write friends and family,* and naturally he expressed his rather solemn gratitude to Miss McCall, apologizing for the meagerness of her commission—twenty-five

---

*His sweet-natured sister Ruth was especially happy for him—her own stories had met with rejection for many years—such that her oldest son Fred vividly remembers her jubilation at the news.

dollars after all that hard work—a matter much on his mind, evidently. "Sweet of you to be concerned," she replied. "The pleasure and excitement in getting a young writer started is far greater than the interest financially, and believe me I never would have taken you on unless I believed that through the years we would all be making plenty of money to pay the rent."

A heady time, as one thing really did seem to lead to another. Within days of publication in the February 1953 issue, Yates received a promising overture from Frances Phillips of William Morrow: "That was one grand story in the Atlantic. . . . It would be a great pleasure to hear that you have a novel and that it is free. . . . If you have an agent, please tell him/her of my interest." Even more promptly he'd heard from Jacques Chambrun, who represented Somerset Maugham no less, and was known to be a roguish poacher of other people's clients: "I should like to have the opportunity to handle some, at least, of your future work." But no agent or editor would prove more persistent than Yates's young discoverer at the *Atlantic,* Seymour Lawrence, who even then was scheming to do bigger things in his own career: "I want to tell you how much I enjoyed Jody," he wrote. "I'm very much interested in your work, and I wonder if you are planning to do a novel. If you are, I should be very glad to offer you any help and editorial assistance I can." For now, though, Yates had no novel to discuss with him or anybody else, nor the remotest idea for one; he'd exhausted himself on those "big, ambitious, tragic" efforts of his earlier years, and preferred to perfect his craft in the shorter form.

His progress is everywhere apparent in "Jody Rolled the Bones," a story that fulfills one of the highest criteria of literary excellence: It's even more rewarding to read the second or third time than the first, as its nuances reveal themselves one after another. "If you're going to do something," Yates would later tell his students, "do it well. Stand in the stream and work down through the soft mulch to the rock bottom." "Jody" is perhaps the first story in which Yates managed to work all the way down to the bottom, beyond the rather easy pessimism that mars his earlier work.

At first "Jody" seems to conform to a conventional formula: the hardboiled sergeant who turns out to have, if not quite a heart of gold, then many lovable qualities. Yates even describes his protagonist, Sergeant

Reece, as "typical—almost a prototype," which prepares the reader all the more for that kind of story. But as a character Reece defies the formula. On the one hand he's a rather despicable, simple-minded bigot who affects to be incapable of pronouncing foreign names, calls foreigners "gorillas," and has few human skills apart from those required by the job. On the other hand he's a superb soldier whose approach to leadership is "classically simple: he led by being excellent"—as when he demonstrates the proper use of a bayonet: "At the instructor's commands [Reece] whipped smartly into each of the positions, freezing into a slim statue while the officer . . . [pointed out] the distribution of his weight and the angles of his limbs, explaining that this was how it should be done." And Yates strikes just the right note of fairness, of benign detachment, in dividing blame between Reece and his recruits: "But if excellence is easy to admire it is hard to like, and Reece refused to make himself likable. It was his only failing, but it was a big one, for respect without affection can't last long—not, at least, where the sentimentality of adolescent minds is involved."

One is tempted to go on exploring the craft of this story, from the nicely sustained metaphor of the title (derived from the chant that not only serves to unify the men but suggests the unfairness of army life and life in general) to the resonant ending in which the recruits revert to "a bunch of shameless little wise guys" in Reece's absence—a collective mediocrity that will haunt them, Yates implies, for the rest of their lives. "You've done it with 'Jody,' " an *Atlantic* reader from Hico, Texas, wrote Yates. "Better, I think, than Hemingway ever did it, better than you will do it again. But in doing it you have broken the code. A soldier does not write; he soldiers. (Kipling was a genius; you probably are not.)" Yates kept that letter, and twelve years later he got another from Colonel Roger Little of the Office of Military Psychology and Leadership: "Jody," wrote Little, had long been used "as a reference . . . because it is such a sensitive portrayal of the basic trainee's perception of the noncommissioned officer." Thus Yates had written about a "typical" sergeant after all, in itself something of a novelty.

Yates's brother-in-law Charlie had been strange all his life, but as a young man he seemed to pull himself together and even show signs of brilliance:

He prepped at Andover, earned a bachelor's degree in physics at Harvard and a master's in math at the University of Maryland. Later he held a job at the Bureau of Standards and then at Hughes Aircraft, where he was employed while the Yateses were abroad. For about a year after their departure, Charlie wrote long articulate letters signed with love, full of advice and encouragement about his brother-in-law's writing career. But one day Yates got a different kind of letter, written in a childish scrawl: "Dear Dick, This is you: a prick with ears!"—and there was an illustration to that effect. One such letter might easily be laughed off, but the ones that followed were even more bizarre: almost totally incoherent, and decorated with all sorts of obscene doodling. From time to time a more normal letter would appear that made little or no reference to the others, which hardly diminished the oddness of it all.

Then, over Christmas, Charlie had a breakdown so severe that he was committed to Fairfield Hospital in Connecticut. What exactly happened is unclear, though apparently Charlie had frightened his mother in some way, and she in turn wrote frantic letters to Sheila begging her to come home.* It would later transpire that Charlie had developed a kind of mania where his mother was concerned, such that he became enraged in her presence—loudly forcing her to sit down and listen to "the Truth" (a word he tended to capitalize all his life). He hadn't resorted to violence yet, but there was no telling what the future would bring. "If he were free today," Sheila observed shortly after the breakdown, "it might be only a matter of time before he went for mother. . . . He might, for instance, only burn [her] house down, but he just might kill or maim her."

The news came as a mixed blessing to Sheila, but a blessing nonetheless: Naturally she was worried about her brother (less so about her mother) and quite eager to return for his sake alone, but for a long time

---

*As Sheila's old friend Ann Barker tells it, Charlie tried to bludgeon the aunt who raised him. Sheila, however, dismisses the story with amused disdain: "Charlie didn't bludgeon *anybody*. We never even saw our aunt after we were children." As for what actually did happen, Sheila seemed disinclined to go into details, apart from pointing out that (*a*) it was purely between Charlie and their mother, and (*b*) there was no physical violence involved. "My mother was a very nervous person and Charlie yelled and frightened her, that's all."

she'd wanted to leave London on any pretext whatsoever, and this one was pretty well incontestable. To anyone who asked, then, the Yateses explained that Sheila had been "called back to attend to a Bryant family emergency," and this was true enough; what was less true was that Yates intended to follow "in a month or so," as soon as he could afford to book his own passage. In fact he and Sheila had agreed to an indefinite "trial separation"—and so matters stood on March 25, 1953, when Yates stood on a Southampton dock and watched his wife and daughter dwindle into the mist aboard the *Ile de France*. After a while he trained back to London and their basement flat, hauntingly deserted except for a surly Angora cat named Sweetheart.

The next day Yates wrote a loving letter to Sheila, in which he tried to strike a balance between muted desperation ("Talk about *missing* a person!") and brave self-sufficiency. Charlie was the most important person for now, he said, and their own problems would have to wait: "Don't worry about money, because I'm going to make it by the bushel-basket now that I've got these long empty days to work with. . . . Don't worry even for a minute about my taking care of myself. I'm eating enormous, beautifully planned meals and drinking absurd quantities of milk." The letter marked the launch of a long campaign to win his wife back, and if that meant contriving an absurdly idealized image of himself—as a conscientious breadwinner who worries about big balanced meals and drinking his milk—then so be it. At the same time Yates couldn't resist a dig at his wife's sentimentality and the awful failings implied thereby; when he mentioned that he'd gone to see the movie *Come Back, Little Sheba* and found it "excellent," he added that *she* would have called it "depressing": "You'd have been shattered by some of the grislier scenes (like a ward for violent alcoholics) and would have dissolved in tears over the 'happy' ending." That said, Yates ended the letter on a properly desolate, needy note: "I still have a tendency to buy vegetables for three, and tiptoe through Mussy's room at night, and heart-rending crap like that, but Sweetheart sets me a good example by not giving a damn."

Sheila found that she was lonely too, despite having wanted nothing so much as escape for the past six months. As she watched the forlorn Yates waving good-bye from that dock, it may have dawned rather heavily on her that, apart from her husband and daughter, there was virtually nobody in her life but a mother she couldn't stand and a brother who'd gone crazy. "Dear Rich," she wrote from the ship, "I felt so sad when you faded into the distance," and she added that Mussy "gets heartrending on the subject of her Daddy at bedtime every night." She went on to describe a "gala soirée" on the boat as being "the masses in action."

When they docked in Hoboken, she and Mussy were greeted by the curious threesome of Marjorie, Dookie, and Aunt Elsa, who described the scene in a letter she wrote her nephew a few weeks later: "Sheila and Ruth and Sheila's mother talked in the lounge while waiting for luggage. . . . How very unfortunate that Mrs. Bryant could not have had at least *one* of Ruth's attributes as a mother." (She was referring, of course, to Dookie's *positive* attributes, such as a loving heart.) "[Mrs. Bryant] has nothing to give, and everything to take. She was cordial enough to me at the pier, but I know her type of personality so well." One imagines a lightbulb flashing over Yates's head as he read that suggestive phrase, "nothing to give, and everything to take"—at least a subliminal origin, perhaps, of one of his all-time favorite character names, "Mrs. *Givings*," the ungiving mother of the mad John in *Revolutionary Road.*

Sheila, too, was repulsed as ever by her "knick-knacky and scatter-ruggy" mother ("a mental case, to be sure"), but had to be civil as long as she was living in the woman's house in Danbury ("like one of those spreads in *Better Homes and Gardens*"). This, however, was easily done, as Sheila had long ago conquered the worst of her aversion to Marjorie; she only wished her brother could cultivate the same detachment. "Charlie's hate is making him sick because he loves her, or did," she wrote Yates in April. "Mother, on the other hand, hates him but it doesn't violate anything because she has no feeling for him. . . . She doesn't feel anything for me either and the fact that she doesn't has long since stopped affecting me at all. And until Charlie feels as I do about her he'll be very sick in all departments of his life." Little wonder that Sheila, in such company, should discover a renewed fondness for her husband.

Yates was determined to make the most of his "Jody" success, and now he had the further incentive of seeming a worthy provider in Sheila's eyes. He

asked Monica McCall if there was any chance his "more shopworn stories"—terminal cases such as "Foursome," "Comptroller," and something
called "Stay Away from Liquids"—would sell on the English market.
McCall suggested he show them to her colleague Dorothy Daly at the
Curtis Brown agency in London, and a month later Daly reported that
Yates's work was "well-written" but "far, far too American in outlook to
find a home here." Yates continued to cast about. He even briefly revived
his cartooning career, with particular emphasis on his old specialty, *kahts,*
a portfolio of which he sent to Sheila with instructions to pass it on to
McCall. Mussy was delighted by her Daddy's drawings—"[she] showed
everybody the pictures of Sweetheart," Sheila wrote—but McCall was less
so: "I know nothing about placing of pictures," she tersely replied.

Meanwhile Yates realized his best career move by far would be to write
a novel—he might never again have such a bonus of time, money, and
freedom. But quite simply he didn't know how to proceed: "[M]ost of my
ideas so far seem better suited to short stories," he wrote Stephen Benedict, "and before I start a novel I want to be very damn sure I've got a grip
on a novel-sized theme. But I may take the plunge any day, and the notion
of a possible advance from Morrow makes it particularly tempting."
Instead he wrote "Lament for a Tenor," the sort of exercise in explicit
autobiography that always made him uneasy, no matter how well the
actual writing seemed to go. In fact he thought the story might turn out to
be his best yet in terms of the market, and he found himself envisaging
future scholars "trying to explain the streak of sentimentality that spoiled
all my work." With that in mind, his smile may have been a bit on the wry
side when he read McCall's ecstatic response: "Oh that is a *wonderful*
story! If *The New Yorker* made any sense they would buy it, but if they
don't I swear by everything I know that I will sell it." As usual, her
instincts would prove sound. ,

Yates's busy careerism was partly by way of distracting himself from an
awful loneliness. Apart from the pubs he had no social life to speak of,
and even the pubs were beginning to pall. As he wrote Sheila, none of the
regulars "ever seems to *talk* about anything—never, I mean, say anything
worth listening to. . . . None of them seems to like one another, either—
when they get hold of an outsider, like me, they all take turns backing him

into a corner and giving him the straight low-down on all the others present." He also remarked on the gratingly repetitive Anglicisms to which he was subjected: "[T]he favorite adverb for everything is 'madly' (This pub's getting madly smart, you know; I'm feeling madly hungover today) . . . [and] any sort of neurosis, real or suspected, is 'really quite mental.' " Nor did he have Aunt Mary to keep him company anymore, since she'd left in April to spend the season at her cottage in Sussex. When he got desperate enough he'd go visit her daughter Gemma, whom he found rather dull and abrasive but well-meaning, and a decent cook besides. It was Gemma who suggested he find a roommate, since Yates had qualms now about paying so little rent but doubted he could afford more. That he thought the roommate idea "pretty good," rent question or no, says volumes about his state of mind: "[I]t'll be nice to have someone to share the cleaning and shopping chores," he wrote, "and once the warm weather is here we won't necessarily have to be big buddies, because this place is really two separate rooms." In the same letter he was also at pains to point out that he'd sold their bicycle to Gemma for the lavish sum of thirty shillings ("how's *that* for the opposite of kick-me-again?"), that he'd managed to gain weight ("high testimony to my conscientiousness"), and that he was "efficiency personified about the housework." A changed man, in short, albeit a rather despondent one: "It's a wrench passing other meats [babies] on the street, and listening to them chatter on busses."

Whether Yates's loneliness led all the way to a disastrous affair with a Piccadilly prostitute, à la "Liars in Love," will have to remain a matter of conjecture. His daughter Monica doesn't recall his ever admitting as much, and as she points out, "[H]e wouldn't have *not* admitted it," since he was nothing if not candid with her. But as readers familiar with "Liars" will have realized by now, most of its details about Yates's life in London are almost scrupulously accurate, from the chronology ("It was March of 1953, and he was twenty-seven years old") to the exact location of the basement flat at 2 Neville Terrace ("where Chelsea met South Kensington along the Fulham Road") to the English aunt who comes down to use the bathtub every morning, and so on. At any rate, something decidedly fishy appears to be lurking amid the pitiful braggadocio of a letter Yates wrote Sheila in June:

In the past three months. . . . I've learned that women—not just a particular kind of woman (and it's remarkable how few kinds there really are), but women in general—find me attractive as all get-out. They don't need any special indoctrination or any apologies, they just *like* me, and this has come as an enormous surprise. (It will also, I'm sure, give you a badly distorted idea of the way I've been spending my time, but never mind that for now.) The value of this is that it has enabled me to relax in a certain fundamental way for the first time in my life. It will make me a much more relaxed, less neurotic and less demanding kind of husband, I can assure you.

One could go on deconstructing this passage, but suffice to say that if the "women in general" who found Yates "attractive as all get-out" were anything like the devious, aggressive whore Christine in "Liars," then he was probably more eager than ever to return to the relative calm of domesticity. Though perhaps, too, he looked forward to a distant day when he could recollect the "subtler pleasure in considering all the pathetic things about [Christine]—the humorless ignorance, the cheap, drooping underwear, the drunken crying."

Sheila appears to have enjoyed less exotic diversions, though apart from her family problems she did feel a great relief at being home again. The United States was like "a beautiful sunlit garden" to her, "where it's even lovely to die or be sick." Lest her husband take this the wrong way, she added that she wasn't worrying so much about their separation anymore because "we both miss each other very much [and] know it's a good idea." Meanwhile an old childhood friend named Fess was teaching her how to drive (a skill she'd eventually attempt to pass on to Yates with curious results), and poor Charlie was disturbed as ever. The psychiatrist at Fairfield had told Sheila her brother was "completely recessed"—in other words, "acting like a very small child," as when he caused a brawl on the ward by pulling a chair out from under another patient. Nor did the shock treatments seem to help, and for a while they were stopped in favor of psychotherapy per se, though Charlie was a reluctant analysand at best. He had a way of saying *Why?* or *Prove it,* when he bothered to say anything at all.

Oddly enough, Mussy adored her deranged uncle and vice versa; she also proved an excellent go-between in Sheila's relations with Marjorie and Dookie. The first was "genuinely fascinated" by the child: Once when Mussy passed her grandmother a cookie during tea and topped this with a pack of cigarettes and a polite, "Haf a chicherette, gramer," the poor woman was stunned. "Did you teach her that?" she asked Sheila, who replied, "No. She does it because she likes to." Whereupon Marjorie tried to pay Sheila a rare compliment: "I guess I never saw a child that had been handled right." But no sooner were the words out that she got a "frantic" look and said, "But I couldn't, I just couldn't with you two," and fled the room. As for Dookie, she was quite comfortable as a grandmother, which didn't require her to be either a role model or a provider. At the time she was supporting herself by sculpting souvenir bunnies and turkeys for the holidays (this while hoping for more dignified employment at the City Center art complex), and by far her favorite audience for that sort of thing was little Mussy, who liked to wear Dookie's smocks and play with her plasticene animals. Nor was Dookie a bad companion to Sheila, especially now that the nervous old woman was out from under the scrutiny of her exasperated son. In fact she was often amusing and shrewd on subjects other than herself: After a rare gathering of the Maurer family (Ida's husband had died), Dookie remarked with cold satisfaction that her sisters were "in their second childhoods"; and on the subject of her son's work, she astutely observed that there were "innumerable things" he didn't write about because of her. For a while Sheila considered it a "terrific bulwark" to know she could always move in with Dookie if life became intolerable with Marjorie.

As the weather changed, Yates took long solitary walks and thought what a shame it was that his wife and daughter had never experienced London like this—"a far cry from the drab and grimy town we saw all winter," he wrote Sheila. Watching other parents with their "meats" was a torment, but one he couldn't help indulging in; he kept thinking of things he might have done with Mussy, such as taking her out on a rowboat in Hyde Park, and now perhaps he never would. He observed, too, the springtime tradition of "interesting-looking" people who congregated on the terrace of his favorite pub on Sunday afternoons, "like a big outdoor cocktail party," but he felt less and less inclined to join them. "My euphoria over the pleasures of bachelor life [has] pretty well palled," he wrote with doleful understatement—though reminders of married life were hardly an unadulterated pleasure: When a doctor at the "air clinic" remarked that he'd once examined Sheila, Yates was at first pleased and then dour as the man seemed to remember the occasion all too vividly ("I got the distinct impression that he wanted to compliment me on the firmness of your breasts").

The brooding monotony of his days was broken somewhat by the arrival of a roommate, a fortyish fellow named Bill Bray, who introduced himself as a stage director and theatrical business manager "between jobs." Yates noted with relief that the man was "decidedly not queer," but thought it a bad sign that he "seem[ed] to spend most of his time drifting around trying to borrow money while he waits for the big job." His roommate's picaresque lifestyle did, however, provide Yates with new material for his letters: He wrote how Bray had applied for National Assistance, but when a state welfare inspector came around to their flat, he found Bray passed out amid a litter of beer bottles; the inspector took a dim view and left, while Bray "spent the rest of the day muttering about the limitations of the bureaucratic mind." Then Bray had a scheme to get himself hired as an extra in a big American movie about King Arthur being filmed in Epping Forest; he thought that Yates, with his height, would make a perfect stand-in for the actor James Stewart and clear a thousand dollars for nine weeks' work. Alas, it didn't pan out, and finally Bray took what he called a "*very* temporary job" at an ice-cream parlor in Kensington, offering to "work [Yates] in as a counter-man or bus-boy."

When Yates wasn't waxing witty or wise or pitiful in his letters, he had a tendency to become bitter—the result of many hours of dark rumination. "Here's this month's alimony, with all my love," he wrote. "And I'll be damned if that isn't a masterpiece of a sentence, which could serve as an epigrammatic definition of our marriage." And such was their odd dynamic that Sheila's most loving letters tended to provoke the most biting replies. After she received (for the purpose of typing and feedback) the manuscript of "Lament for a Tenor," she wrote how "proud" she was: "I sort of forgot about being proud of you . . . and not just because of your work or because you're good-looking—because you have good taste in life . . . your coming home now could be nothing but good for me"; Charlie had even offered to loan them money for a boat ticket. For Yates this was surely the answer to his fondest prayer—but the more he thought about it, the more agitated and even enraged he became, or so the crescendo of his response suggests:

> Charlie's offer of the $165 is awfully damn nice, and very touching. Maybe I'll take him up on it, but let's give Tenor a chance to sell first, okay? Because I'd rather come home that way if I can. And don't you think, anyway, that we ought to let a little more time elapse? . . . When I come home it will probably be our absolutely last damn chance for a good life together, and I want to be sure we're both ready. . . . When you are [ready], . . . you won't *think* my coming home might be good for you, as you say you do now—you'll know damn well it would be . . . because you'll be ready to god damn it be my girl, and no crap about it. . . . I guess I'm the most naive son of a bitch in the world. But there isn't anything so terrible about being naive, is there? It's a far more appropriate trait for people our age, and a more fruitful one too . . . than the kind of sickly, emotion-starved world-weariness you find in the Chelsea pubs. Or to put it another way, I *like* being "born yesterday," because it gives me a pretty good chance of being alive tomorrow, when everybody else is dead.

By then Yates was all too familiar with Sheila's capriciousness and/or ambivalence where he was concerned. He knew that her loving, April Wheeler–like exaltations were temporary at best, and liable to be followed by some squelching matter-of-fact Shirleyism. "God damn it I love you, Sheila," he wrote, followed by the preemptive appraisal "I have now laid myself wide open for you to say coolly, in your next letter, that you see what I mean and it's very touching, but that you really don't feel equal to looking into the future at this point and can't make any promises, so I must not get my hopes up." And while he tried to end this letter on a somewhat positive note, with a bit of neutral humor about Bill Bray, it only spurred him on to a last caustic snipe: "You'd probably flirt outrageously with him if you were here."

Sheila's response was mollifying: "Everything you say about us is quite right and perfect, Rich"—and with that she pretty much let it go. This was partly an honest concession ("it's one thing to know where the trouble lies and another to get out of it") and partly an aversion to argument, even epistolary, with such a tenacious foe as Yates. Besides, she had other things to worry about. As it happened she'd gone ahead and moved in with Dookie, only to find her "still living on the usual financial cliff": Dookie's rent (shockingly high to begin with, as she felt she needed extra studio space and never mind how to pay for it) was so badly in arrears that eviction was imminent. And while Dookie spoke of "income just over the horizon" (the City Center job), her older sisters Elsa and Margaret, whose dotage she ridiculed, did their best to provide her with eating money.* But otherwise everything was fine: "Dookie is not bitter about any of it," Sheila noted, "[and] right now she is busy fixing herself an outfit to wear to a big glamorous affair tomorrow evening." Nor had Dookie changed in other fundamental respects, bad or good: "She still does a hell of a lot of talking but I've learned to tune out tactfully . . . and she is wonderful with Sharon." But the bottom line was this: "You should think very seriously about what you might feel to be living again in the same city with Dookie's finances."

Yates's reply reflected his eagerness to make amends for his previous outburst. He assured her that he was equal to coping with Dookie's periodic duns, however much he used to protest about the "strain" they put on him, which he now dismissed as a "pretty childish attitude": "If I can't help her, I can't—and until I can it certainly shouldn't matter much how close to her I live." In the meantime he was glad to know that Dookie's spirits were high withal, which of course was "the most important thing."

With Dookie facing another eviction, Sheila went about trying to solve her own living situation. Briefly she considered buying a house amid the

---

*That same month Elsa wrote her nephew and asked that he "pray that the time comes soon" when Dookie was less dependent on her—"for her sake certainly," the good woman added, "and to permit me to go forward in another direction." Hope springeth eternal.

dystopian sprawl of Levittown, near their friends the Cains, who admitted the place was a "wasteland." But then one could hardly beat the
price—a GI loan paid for the house, with carrying charges of sixty-three
dollars a month—so Sheila figured it wouldn't hurt to look. She was not
impressed: "The Levittown houses are clean and modern and very tempting but the people are simply awful and once the joy of the Bendix had
worn off, we'd all go crazy"; besides, she added, the nursery schools in
the area were full of "strident Jewish supervisors" and overcrowded to
boot. For the time being, then, she decided to find an apartment in the
city and get a job, though the idea of buying a place in the suburbs was
something she wanted her husband to bear in mind ("if we become a
family again").

Meanwhile Yates awaited news of "Tenor," and found himself in a
"creative slump": He was still without a good idea for a novel, and was
sick of writing short stories and living hand-to-mouth with a "completely
aimless, pointless, useless bastard" like Bill Bray for company. Two pieces
of bad news had deflated him further: His six best stories were returned in
a batch by the English magazine *Argosy,* whose editor remarked on their
"Americanness" and "bitter astringency of tone" ("You certainly shoot to
kill, don't you?"); and the next day he learned that *Collier's* had declined
"Tenor," since they "[didn't] have room for another story about the emotional problems of a young boy." Monica McCall remained confident,
though by then her mood wasn't contagious.

Yates tried to cheer himself up by observing the coronation of Queen
Elizabeth—a "terrific show" whose vast cheering crowds only served to
remind him of his loneliness, which in turn suggested how much worse
things might have been if Sheila were there: "I know perfectly well," he
wrote her, "that your cop-fear would have kept us home all day in a great
family snit, with you redundantly insisting that if I wanted to go there was
nothing to stop me, and me bellowing the whole *point* of the thing would
be lost unless you came too. I guess there are certain advantages in bachelorhood after all." One such advantage was decidedly *not* his roommate
Bill Bray, who got loudly drunk every night and brought home a "grubby,
homely Village type who not only Does It but talks about it in clarion
tones, almost entirely four-letter words," Yates wrote. "The sad thing

about old Bill is that he has absolutely nothing to show for his forty-odd years, despite what would seem to be all the advantages of breeding, native intelligence and good looks." If nothing else, the man acted as an impetus for Yates's getting out of the flat more often. He was even willing to accompany his cousin-in-law Barbara to a quaint choral concert at her club, which involved "about a million print-dress biddies" and other solid citizens singing to her majesty's health, a spectacle that moved Yates strangely: "It was so painful and so heartbreakingly nice that it was enough to make you fall in love with this country forever." A couple weeks later he took a four-hour bus trip to visit Aunt Mary in Sussex, and then rode all the way back the same afternoon to catch a "wolloping good party" at the flat of Mrs. Pierce (the nursery school proprietor), where Bill Bray turned up and "got blind, fall-down drunk as usual."

With such a cautionary figure in mind, Yates proposed that he end his expatriation forthwith and get on with supporting his family in the manner to which they wished to become accustomed. Mussy was soon to be put in a seedy, city-subsidized nursery where "there mightn't be anyone for [her] to have extra-curricular activities with," or so Sheila worried (though the situation was saved by the presence of two other "true blue shabby-genteel" parents and their daughters), and that was but a small aspect of the whole intolerable situation. "We're never going to get rich out of short stories," Yates wrote. The only "real dough" to be made was in the novel he'd sooner or later write, but until then it was time to face facts: "Don't you think it might be a healthier idea . . . if I *quit* writing stories, come home and get a really good job of the sort that Monica might be able to help me get, or that I might get myself on the strength of my *Atlantic* story, and mark time *that* way until the novel idea comes along?" Yates was desperately ready to "start living a decent upper-middle-class life—car, clothes, house, etc." And by a "really good job" he didn't mean Remington Rand: "a moral defeat [that] might put me back in the hospital (Fairfield, if not Halloran)." Nor did he wish for any kind of "physically grueling" newspaper work, but rather some kind of "well-paid" job on the staff of a magazine or publishing firm. And lest this seem a headlong retreat into respectability, Yates reminded Sheila of all the things he'd gained from his two years in Europe: "Monica, the *Atlantic*, the nibble from Morrow, and a great deal of practical writing experience without which I'd probably never have the guts to tackle a novel, let alone to write a good one."

Sheila professed to be appalled by the idea: "If you had a job that would be the end and in your heart you know it. . . . What would our crazy marriage be if you came here and made us comfortable with a 9–5 job? . . . I can find a man easily who can give me that kind of life and be a lot better company than you'd be doing it." Perhaps, but such shrill insistence that he remain abroad and follow his dream ("Stay in England," she ordered him; "write and forget about us all") suggested a rather unflattering subtext—namely, that her husband's company wasn't much desired either as a writer *or* a nine-to-five drone.

Yates agreed to table the matter for the time being, though not before venting his wounded feelings: Her "violent opposition," he wrote, was rife with the sort of "childishly arbitrary" overstatements that they'd "both have to outgrow" if they were "ever going to be adults, together *or* separately." He pointed out that the "social and economic limbo" of their lives was just as inhibiting to creative endeavor as a regular job would be, and the latter was less likely to involve "inadequate housing, illness, family strife, neurotic brooding and frenetic moves around the world." And really, he wondered, wherefore this sudden precious concern for his writing, which she'd once regarded as little more than a "knack" that distracted him from more worldly pursuits? "You *do* seem to have funny ideas as to what my talent is all about . . . now it's become a sacred flame which must be hovered over and protected at all cost while the world is held perilously at bay." He assured her that he had no intention of coming home and "demand[ing] restitution of [his] conjugal rights," though if he *did* decide to return it would be "altogether [his] business." He repeated his basic position: "I love you and would like to live with you and Mussy again more than anything, but I will not be Pinner again . . . and now make it clear again, that the only way you'll get me back is by wanting me." He then enumerated, at greater length than ever, the many ways in which he was making himself "a more desirable package than the bundle of raw nerve-tissue" she'd known in the bygone past:

I've discovered I am as competent as anybody at dealing with the small-change of practical life. . . . I can "pull my weight," "look out for myself," "stay on the ball" and "cope" as well if not better than the most banal bore in the world, and I can now afford a benign pity—strictly non-violent—for all the millions of people, bless their hearts, who enjoy that sort of thing. . . . I've [also] discovered at long last what you knew from the beginning—that my "broods" do not stem from any dark, Hamlet-like neurosis, incurable and tragic, but from plain laziness. . . . I have snapped out of countless minor broods, since you left, by suddenly remembering it was time to put the potatoes on, or that the laundromat was about to close, or that there was something good on the radio. And I've pulled myself out of several really major ones by the more painful but no less effective method of telling myself to shut up and get back to the typewriter. I'm not saying I've overcome them—I had a bad one just the other day—but I'm holding my own against the bastards. They don't immobilize me any more, and I'm confident it won't be long before I'll be able to brush them off like flies. I hope this shrill recital of my little triumphs doesn't bore you or sound like an old-fashioned "drone."

Yates appears here as an almost perfect character out of his own imagination—one of those deterministic victims who "rush around trying to do their best . . . doing what they can't help doing, ultimately and inevitably failing because they can't help being the people they are." Certainly Yates couldn't help being a practical bungler any more than he could snap out of his "broods" by putting the potatoes on or running off to the laundromat. Indeed, the only durable way of coping with the awful burden of being himself would always be the "more painful" method of "get[ting] back to the typewriter," though its effect on his marriages would prove neutral at best.

While Yates was bitterly converting himself into an ideal life-mate, things took a turn for the better on both sides of the Atlantic and tension began to ease somewhat. For one thing, the indomitable Dookie had managed to pry some part-time wages out of the City Center and thus get a "stay of execution" at her beloved apartment-cum-studio. This was a great relief for all, particularly Sheila, who'd had to cope with a sudden drop in Dookie's high spirits: "She was so low before—we had the real gamut of emotions daily," she wrote Yates. "Very wearing for the spectator, and impossible to comfort. She is really a person without shading." But with the promise of a salaried position in September—as director of the new City Center art gallery, no less—Dookie was not only planning to keep her old place in the West Fifties, but also to fix up the garage apartment at High Hedges as a country getaway, courtesy of Fritz Rodgers. "I am praying that it works out," wrote Sheila, "but the one snag is the Rodgers, Jr., who I gather feel as they always did about having her so near."

And Sheila knew just how they felt. Another month *chez* Dookie was simply out of the question, and in late June she moved to an apartment on King Street in the Village, where she and Mussy lived with a widow and her nine-year-old son. The rent was only fifty a month, and Sheila found her housemate pleasant enough. "She'd never stimulate me but there'd be no clashes, I think, and she's no Bialek. When she has time, she writes stories for the Confession magazines and she gets *The New Yorker*—I *think* she knows the difference." Yates was unthrilled by the arrangement ("If I do come home before August I guess I'll have to plan on living at the Y"), though he was somewhat appeased by the Mussy angle: That is, the three-year-old was thriving at the subsidized Village nursery they'd thought would be so Dickensian, and even tended to "[kick] up an awful row" when Sheila came to take her home in the afternoon. When informed of such naughtiness, Yates advised his wife to "feed [Mussy] lots of ice cream and let her run around in her [diapers] and that should take care of it."

Meanwhile Yates had managed to shut up and get back to the typewriter, which made it somewhat easier for him to stop coveting the life of a stable wage earner. In fact his latest story, "The Game of Ambush," had begun as an attempt to fictionalize the dilemma in some objectified form, and toward this purpose he'd tried (abortively) to adopt a Gatsbyesque first-person peripheral narrator. An early draft begins with the sentence, "For a while when I was nine years old, my friends and I thought falling dead was the very zenith of romance," and from there the narrator "Al" goes on to tell the story of his friend Walt Henderson, who ends up sacrificing his musical talent to take some idiot job selling plywood and thereby pay for his ex-wife's psychiatrists. Perhaps this version struck too close to home; in subsequent drafts, anyway, Yates dispensed with Al and wrote in the third person about Walt, developing an entirely different plot from the same nominal premise. Finally, after much exhaustive tinkering, he had a finished story that he could only describe to Sheila as a "pretty good B-plus effort," though he was proud of his tenacity in reworking it: "[I]t's *technically* as good as I can make it, however 'uninteresting' the essential idea of the thing may be, and I'm pretty sure it will get by." A fair assessment: The story was now about a compulsive failure who copes with being fired, and within certain intrinsic limits Yates had succeeded in an admirably B-plus way. And already he'd put it behind him to write another that he thought would be "very damn good indeed": "So I've been pretty happy these last few days, very un-neurotic and in love with all mankind including myself, the way I always am when I'm full of a new story."

Sheila thought the B-plus effort was "as good or perhaps better in its way than Tenor," and mentioned that Charlie had also read it while on a weekend pass from Fairfield: "He liked the story very much . . . though his comments are sometimes a bit over my head. He *did* say he wondered if his trouble wasn't the same as Walt in the story." Yates was pleased that both seemed to like his new title, "A Glutton for Punishment," and happily explained its origin: "It came to me in a flash one night when I had quit work rather guiltily to listen to the Turpin-Humez fight on the radio—the announcer said Humez was a glutton for punishment and I sprang for the typewriter like a madman."* Actually he typed less like a madman than a hard-nosed reporter of the old school—in the rapid two-finger method he used all his life—and Sheila retyped his work with secretarial precision; in the case of "Glutton" (and presumably others), she also took it upon herself to make minor changes of grammar and punctuation

---

*Note the Salingerian "like a madman." For the past two years Yates had often cheered himself up by reading *Catcher in the Rye,* and it showed in his everyday locutions. He also liked to say that things "killed" him.

which Yates retained in the published version.* However, he chose *not* to accept her rather astute criticism of the story's ending, which she reluctantly offered when pressed: "I remember thinking that particular cliché was overdoing the parallel a bit," she observed of Walt's last remark, " 'They got me,' " which alludes (tritely?) to the cops-and-robbers games of his youth.

Monica McCall had reacted much the same way—"I love the story and absolutely loathe the ending"—though in her case such objections were made with an eye on the market. McCall wanted the hapless Walt to make a "new stand" as she put it, or whatever it took to give the story "a twist, or a fulfillment and a satisfaction." She wanted a happy ending, in short, or if nothing else a bit of normal character development—but of course nothing could be more inimical to Yates's basic view of humanity and Walt in particular, and after a bit of brooding he decided to be "stubborn as a mule" about it: "I'm not going to let her turn me into that kind of a writer," he wrote Sheila. "If I'm going to start switching endings to suit markets I might as well be back at Remington Rand; and I really think there's a hell of a lot more future in writing my own way." Whether Yates was right about the "future" depends, perhaps, on how one views the vagaries of posterity. In any case McCall enjoyed the "funny and nice letter" he wrote declining her suggestions, and within a month the story was returned by the *Atlantic, Charm,* and *The New Yorker* (the last of which "continue[d] to be interested in Mr. Yates's work").

Yates's social life was hardly a draining distraction, though at the end of the day there was always Bill Bray ("drearier and drearier"), whose "headquarters" were across the street at the Anglesea Pub; thither Yates was dragged when either his roommate or loneliness got the better of him. The clientele tended to be "slightly more rewarding" than Bray, but of course that wasn't a lavish compliment. The only person who seemed to interest him at all was "a young journalist and writer named Douglas

---

*E.g., in the first paragraph of the story, Sheila changed "('pretty good') or ('too stiff')"—etc.—into one parenthetical statement and capitalized each separate remark, thus: "('Pretty good,' or 'Too stiff,' or 'It didn't look natural')." A small point, perhaps, but Yates was a stickler for such points and clearly valued her input.

something," with whom he could talk about books. ("Remarkable how few writers I've known," Yates reflected, and in fact five more years would pass before he'd meet his first "real" writer, a distinction he made only in retrospect.) Douglas-something was about Yates's age and had lived in New York as an evacuee during the early part of the war ("at the Sherry Netherlands, which gives you an idea of his class," Yates noted for Sheila's benefit); but the writing life hadn't paid off for the once-posh young man, and now he looked "even broker than Bill." Indeed there was a kind of striving-yet-aimless quality about the whole Anglesea crowd that rather intrigued Yates: Their "established routine" was to turn up at the pub each night, then "shift en masse" to a club on the Fulham Road, and then to coffee shops and diners and so on, looking for a party that generally failed to materialize. "I'm damned if I know how they can stick it night after night and not end up with faintly suicidal tendencies," Yates mused. Little did he know that he was about to become the darling of that set.

It began on July 14, when he got his first really good news in nine months—as before, from Monica McCall: COSMOPOLITAN BUYING TENOR EIGHT HUNDRED FIFTY MANY CONGRATULATIONS. "How much money can we *stand*?" the ecstatic Yates wrote Sheila, and reported that he'd "been wandering around in a haze for two days." His haze was abetted by the inevitable Bill Bray and all the manqué rowdies at the Anglesea, who got "deliriously drunk" in his honor and seemed to regard him "as an authentic and indisputed genius." Yates's roommate was particularly disposed to press this claim, and for the soundest possible reason: "[Bray has] figured out that I have earned fourteen cents a word, and can't get over it. It sounds like a hell of a lot over here, where short story writers traditionally think in terms of twenty-five pounds a story instead of three hundred." Thus while the two staggered about the neighborhood with red carnations in their buttonholes, Bray roared of his friend's triumph in terms of three-hundred-quid-a-pop.

But leave it to Yates to seize on what he called the "depressing aspect of the thing": namely, that *Cosmopolitan* was a "dead-loss prestigewise." In those days the magazine pandered to sentimental hausfraus, and Yates worried that the editors would butcher his story beyond recognition. If nothing else he expected them to tone down his dialogue—"make my 'bastards' into 'buzzards' and stuff like that" (in fact they substituted the only slightly less excruciating "jerks" and "stinkers"). But there was a more troubling problem: "[I]f I've got to appear among the cookie recipes I sure would rather have it be with a less personal story than this one. This will sort of be like taking off all your clothes for the amusement of several million Bialeks."* Such an issue would loom larger in Yates's later career, as his fiction became more baldly autobiographical (and his mental health more precarious), and whether or not there were cookie recipes or Bialeks in the picture would never matter to his shattered peace of mind. For the present, though, Bill Bray acted as a voice of reason: "Really, old boy," he told the fretful Yates, "one can't have *jam* on it." Bray planned to spend some of the proceeds on a big party for the "madly smart," and had little patience for such quibbling.

Yates agreed that a celebration was in order. Misgivings aside, the sale of "Tenor" was a milestone: positive proof that he could actually make a living as a writer. But such a métier was fraught with hazards, the most common of which would bedevil Yates from the outset: "[McCall] has left me in a real jam by failing to send the damn check," he wrote Sheila ten days after the sale. "I'd already invited about a million people to a party tomorrow night . . . and it's been pretty grim hounding the mailbox every day and picturing all the Madly Smart guests arriving with nothing at all to drink." For the moment he'd been able to persuade Mrs. Capon at the dairy ("who loves me so dearly") to cash a postdated check, but things were already spiraling out of control: Bill Bray had borrowed five pounds, the party would cost ten, and the phone and gas bills were due. Suddenly Yates found himself eighty dollars in the red rather than eight hundred in the black—"a lousy, painful, Dook-style mess," he gloomily concluded.

But he was somewhat cheered by the party itself, which turned out to be "a really first-rate job." With a bar set up in front and a phonograph

---

*In the same letter, Yates wrote of "screw[ing] up all his tact and courage" to tell his mother what it was about—and this for a story that didn't even directly concern her! As for his decision not to collect "Tenor" in book form, he almost surely considered it too sentimental, no matter how well it played as competent commercial fiction. And finally it's possible, too, that even then he was planning to put the same material—a crucial episode in his life, after all—to better use later, post-Dookie, as of course he did.

for dancing in back, the basement flat was converted into a tiny *bal musette* for the Madly Smart. Along with the wastrels of the Anglesea, Yates reported the attendance of "a bigtime theatrical producer, a French ballet dancer, a bunch of actors and newspaper men, two architects . . . and about seven beautiful girls." Also present was the *Argosy* editor who'd rejected so many of Yates's stories; eager to make amends, she called him a "terrific writer" ("bitter astringency" aside) and left with his carbon of "Tenor," which she promised to press on her colleagues. And finally the party peaked when the place was besieged by a pack of less-than-madly-smart Chelsea types, whom Bill Bray (of all people) had sworn to keep out:

> The local bohemians got in at last, but only . . . after their ringleader had floored Bill in the doorway with a right to the nose and held him down in absurdly drunken combat while his followers climbed in over their writhing bodies. Everybody seemed to feel that the brawl was just what was needed to give the party a fine old pre-war flavor, and it ended in a great deal of sentimental handshaking.

Thus was Yates's launch as a successful author celebrated, and for the moment anything seemed possible—perhaps he'd prove to be a writer like Fitzgerald who could have his cake and eat it too, money *and* prestige, and be something of a bon vivant in the bargain. "So I am now a famous host," he merrily noted.

The *Cosmopolitan* sale worked wonders for Yates's marital problems, which seemed to vanish overnight. Both he and Sheila wished the other were present so each could celebrate with the one person who really understood what it meant—a further reminder that, for better or worse, there was nobody else who mattered much in their lives. Nor was there any question about Yates's coming home now as soon as possible, since Sheila's long-held ambivalence toward him had suddenly been turned against herself: She conceded "what an odd view of the world and its people" she'd always had, and now it was she, not Yates, who spoke of all the ingenious "little tricks" she was practicing for becoming a better person—

such as "hugging Mussy (much against her will) when there are 'a million things to do,'" and cultivating an easier, more tolerant nature in general. "I do love you so much, Rich," she declared. "I won't kid myself about that anymore." Yates was gratified, if a bit leery of that exalted tone he knew so well: "Absence sure does seem to have made your heart grow fonder," he wrote; "presence will make it cool off somewhat." Meanwhile he warned her against turning their marriage into an "intellectual project," adding that if she just relaxed and loved him, "all the little tricks . . . will learn themselves."

For the most part, though, they were too happy to bicker anymore, as they busily prepared to become a family again. After a month of frustrated searching, Sheila had found a "quaint and Villagy" three-room apartment at 96 Perry Street, between Bleecker and Hudson (Dookie had helped close the deal "by throwing her weight around in a realty office when she noticed some very *bad* paintings on the wall"). By mid-August she and Mussy had moved in, and a week later Yates reported to the American Express that he was ready to return to the States as soon as possible. He was told that a cancellation would probably make a berth available within two or three weeks, which wasn't soon enough for Yates. At first he considered inventing "some heart-rending emergency" to persuade the American Welfare Service to book a more immediate passage, but on second thought decided "it might be a bit awkward if they got wise."

While he waited Yates got a good start on a story he called "The Ordeal of Vincent Sabella" ("all about meats in the fourth grade") and spent leisure hours mulling the future with unwonted optimism. Now that he was making good as a writer, he could even allow himself to consider taking the odd freelance job from Remington Rand; in fact an old coworker had just inquired ("with some temerity," said Sheila, "in light of your success") whether they should prepare an account for him. For the moment Yates could afford to make them wait. He was almost a shoo-in to win the *Atlantic* "First" Award in December—so far there was only one other "First" in competition for that year—and that would mean another $750.

Indeed the only thing that cast a shadow was the prospect of what *Cosmopolitan* might do to his story: "The main illustration will probably be something very corny with the tenor in full song and the little boy sniveling in the corner," he wrote. "Shudder to think about it. My next twelve stories are going to be so damn unsentimental that *Cosmopolitan* wouldn't touch them with a ten-foot pole." Sheila noted reassuringly that she'd gone through a whole stack of *Cosmopolitan*s in the ladies' room at work—the stories were "good," the illustrations "quite tasteful"—but Yates was not comforted. He even considered running the story under a pseudonym.

Fortunately he was distracted by any number of cheerful errands to run while he waited for a berth. There was the question of how best to transport Sweetheart, the crotchety Angora, whose return Mussy had demanded. Yates solemnly inquired at the American Express about traveling with cats, and was told the law required a proper "basket": "So I looked into cat-baskets at Selfridge's and found they are very elaborate damn things costing two pounds five." He bought one. Also, Sheila sent him a list of toys to bring back for Mussy—"a coloring book with *water* paints; a little sailboat for the tub; a whistle; a gun (honest to God! but no caps, please)"—as well as "those lovely smelly English soaps" for herself and either a black or "nice antiquey red" pocketbook. Most pressing and intricate by far was the matter of Yates's new suit, about which he sent almost daily dispatches from Savile Row.* Early in August he'd settled on Oxford gray flannel ("this may not sound very imaginative, but it's the most useful and best-looking kind of suit I know"), but vacillated as to the right tailor, until at last tradition in its hoariest form won the day: Gieves and Hawkes at Number One Savile Row, he wrote, was "sort of the English version of Brooks Brothers" and the sign outside assured one that "[they'd] been in business since 1066 or something."

Yates's giddiness waxed as his departure approached, such that even a bitter end to his friendship with Bill Bray couldn't dampen his spirits. "Old Bill" had been in a "pout" since Yates refused to loan him more money, and left his debt unpaid when he cleared out of the flat in late

---

*Though the opposite of a materialist (particularly later in life), Yates would always have a weakness for "smart attire," as Mrs. Riddle would have it: "Just buy clothes," he'd say, when asked what he'd do with a lot of money.

August. It was the end of something, to be sure, but Yates felt marvelous: "I don't think I've ever been *less* depressed about life in general," he wrote Sheila. "I just don't see how we can fail to have a damn good time together when I come home, Pretty.* The setup on Perry Street sounds ideal, and the idea of having you and the Meat under the same roof again is staggeringly nice." By the time his passage was cleared on the *Maasdam* in mid-September, Yates had wrapped up his affairs with admirable efficiency: He'd obtained a clean bill of health and complete X-ray records from the hospital, run a vacuum over the rug at Neville Terrace, taken his leave of Aunt Mary, and gotten himself and Sweetheart aboard the ship in good time. And in the midst of a pleasant crossing (the food was "wonderful" and little girls were stroking the cat "at regular intervals"), he received a telegram from Sheila: *Cosmopolitan* had bought "A Glutton for Punishment"—unhappy ending and all—for another $850.

The *Maasdam* docked at Hoboken on September 19, 1953, and the chipper Yates disembarked with a scowling cat in his arms. This was his daughter Sharon's first definite memory of her father.

---

* "Pretty" was Yates's primary term of endearment for Sheila.

CHAPTER SIX

A Cry of Prisoners: 1953-1959

Yates and Sheila had planned "a sort of honeymoon" after his return, and perhaps this came to pass in one form or another; but it wasn't long before Remington Rand had lured him back on a rather feverish "freelance" basis. Yates began to report twice a month to a man named Andy Borno (the physical model for the squat, balding Laurel Players director in *Revolutionary Road*), who gave him new assignments in the form of so-called case histories, to wit: Yates would visit companies that had purchased Remington Rand products and interview the relevant engineers, systems analysts, and salespeople, then ghostwrite articles under the name of whatever executive made the purchase. Such puff pieces were placed in business magazines by Remington Rand, which paid Yates $125 (plus expenses) per job. "All this was very boring stuff," Yates said in 1981, "but it occupied only about half of my working time and so financed the whole of my first novel." For the next seven years, then, Yates devoted the first half of each month to PR work and the second to fiction (it was necessary to segregate the tasks as much as possible)—a routine that resulted in one novel, a handful of stories, at least five hundred ghostwritten articles, many executive speeches, and almost every word of Remington Rand's internal house organ, perhaps the only writing Yates ever did drunk.

His particular beat was the UNIVAC, to which Remington Rand had recently acquired exclusive rights. The first electronic computer designed for business use, the UNIVAC had made a splash in 1951, when it predicted an Eisenhower landslide based on less than 1 percent of the vote.* But talk of an impending "computer revolution" continued to leave most people cold, and the UNIVAC, at eight tons per unit, was hardly an easy sell. That Yates was entrusted with much of its promotion attests to the quality of his work. Not only was he able to translate esoteric technological jargon into chatty Babbittese for the layman, but his articles were also effective in soothing worries over "the broad economic and social implications of what was then the new and controversial phenomenon of 'automation,'" as Yates noted in a later résumé. Such was his known expertise on the subject that he was hired to write the UNIVAC entry for Funk & Wagnall's *Encyclopedia*. Nor were the rich "implications" of automation (economic, social, metaphorical) lost on Yates as a fiction writer—hence Frank Wheeler explains to his wife, on the morning of her suicide, how an electronic computer works: "'Only instead of mechanical parts, you see, it's got thousands of little individual vacuum tubes . . .' And in a minute he was drawing for her, on a paper napkin, a diagram representing the passage of binary digit pulses through circuitry." Flaubert himself might have coveted those "vacuum tubes" and "binary digit pulses"; as for Yates, he thought it the best scene he ever wrote.

Now that Yates was making $850 a story, he and Sheila thought it high time to distance themselves from the Cains and Bialeks of the world, the better to meet some of those "young, poor, bright, humorous" golden people they'd always dreamed of knowing. They made a start when Yates renewed his acquaintance with Tony Vevers, the English painter he'd met during that roisterous furlough in London eight years before. Vevers and his wife Elspeth had recently moved to New York, where they led a life of romantic squalor in a Lower East Side loft. Yates was impressed by the painter's sincere indifference to his own poverty: Vevers, who supported himself with a number of menial odd jobs, seemed the very embodiment of the idea that one's art was what mattered most and wages were simply

---

*An episode that provided the McGuffin for Yates's 1989 film treatment, *The World on Fire*. Yates's version of the event was historically inaccurate, to put it mildly, for reasons I look forward to exploring later.

a means to that end. That both he and his wife came from posh families made it all the more impressive.

Yates also became friends with Robert Riche, who was dating Vevers's sister at the time. In a letter he wrote Yates many years later, Riche described himself as "no different than I ever was: somewhat naive, somewhat boisterous if encouraged, occasionally funny, generally a bit apprehensive about my position in life, but holding to a basically decent value system, I think." By the time he wrote those words, Riche had been portrayed in *Young Hearts Crying* as the naive, boisterous, occasionally funny, basically decent, and utterly preposterous Bill Brock; that Riche was aware of (and angered by) this lampoon, but could still write Yates with such candor, attests to the verisimilitude of his fictional counterpart's more amiable traits.

The two had met at a gallery opening a few weeks after Yates's return from Europe. Yates was wearing his tailored English suit, and Riche thought he resembled a young T. S. Eliot (perhaps the desired effect; years later, at any rate, in the midst of a typical round of banter between the two, Riche told Yates he looked like an "English fag" in that suit). They were the same age and seemed to have a lot in common. Both had left-wing sympathies, and Riche went so far as to call himself a "revolutionary" (he'd worked in a factory and served as a labor organizer). Also, Riche had gone to Yale (as had Tony Vevers), and Yates wished he'd gone there. Above all Riche vaguely aspired to be a writer and both were involved in what they wryly called the "PR dodge"; such mutual disdain for their bread and butter was itself the basis for immediate camaraderie. Or so it seemed to Riche when he was invited, on the spot, to a big Halloween party on Perry Street—though in retrospect he realized both Yateses were more taken by his date, the attractive young Pamela Vevers.*

---

*Nobody seems to remember much about that Halloween party on Perry Street, except that at some point the Yateses presented a sleepy but well-groomed Mussy to their guests. As for Bob Riche's then-girlfriend Pamela Vevers, she vaguely remembers seeing the Yateses on that occasion and perhaps two or three others. Thirty years later she was bemused, to say the least, when it was called to her attention that she'd appeared in *Young Hearts Crying* as Diana Maitland, Michael Davenport's ideal love object. As Pamela Vevers will assure anyone who asks, there was no flirtation (imagined

As for Tony Vevers, he found Yates much changed from the rambunctious, "Mammy"-singing nineteen-year-old he'd known in London. For one thing the older Yates drank more, minus the boyish joie de vivre: "He'd become sharp-tongued and bitter," Vevers recalled. "One got the impression he wasn't as successful as he wanted to be." Bob Riche, who hadn't known Yates as a younger man, simply found him a good drinking companion—a "riot," even—though Yates's abrasive side was hardly lost on him. In fact, both he and Vevers remarked on what struck them as Yates's peculiar attitude toward women: "He expected them to drink a lot and be beautiful all the time," as Vevers put it. Riche remembered a typical outing to his father's cottage in the country, when he and Yates and a man named Larry Fleischer stayed up drinking and telling dirty jokes long after their wives had gone to bed. Fleischer's wife got fed up with all the laughing, shouting, and coughing, and more than once stuck her head in the door and asked her husband to call it a night. Yates waved her off with increasing contempt, and when the weekend was over the two were no longer speaking. As for Sheila, she seemed to defer to her husband as a matter of choice on social occasions, though sometimes she'd silence him with a frown or a nudge, especially if he got to singing too much.

More than ever Yates's greatest scorn was reserved for his mother, about whom he was almost compulsively disparaging—and this, ironically, at a time when she was most deserving of his esteem. "You know where my mother works?" he asked a friend while in his cups. "She's the fucking *cloakroom lady* at the City Center gallery." A more jaundiced view of Dookie's employment would be hard to imagine. She may obligingly have offered to stow the wraps of certain theatergoers who stood in her gallery during intermission, and the long corridor that comprised the gallery (actually the emergency exit from the Fifty-fifth Street auditorium) might easily have been taken as a lounge of sorts, but Dookie was no cloakroom lady. In fact, as the gallery's director, she was a colleague of George Balanchine and Jean Dalrymple, who headed the ballet and theater

---

or otherwise) between her and Yates or any other Davenport-like person; that said, she does concede a superficial resemblance on her part to Diana Maitland, and thinks certain other real-life people (e.g., Bob Riche) were very accurately portrayed.

companies at what was then called New York's "temple for the performing arts." It was through Dookie's efforts that painters such as Robert
Motherwell, Larry Rivers, and Franz Kline served as jurors for the traditional, centrist, and avant-garde shows that alternated at the center, and it
was Dookie who raised money for her impoverished gallery by helping to
organize the annual Easter Bonnet Tea Dance in the main ballroom of the
Plaza Hotel, where such celebrity judges as Celeste Holm and Helen
Hayes gave prizes for "Prettiest Bonnet," "Best Dancers," and "Grandmother with the Loveliest Outfit." (This event was later abolished in the
wake of criticism that it was "too society" for the "people's theater.")
Dookie not only knew such luminaries as Holm and Hayes et al., she had
lunch with them and called them Celeste and Helen, to say nothing of
Bob, Larry, and Franz. Indeed, the gala opening of the gallery on September 29, 1953, was less than two weeks after Yates's return from Europe;
perhaps his mother's curious ascendancy was a bit too much to digest, as
well as a bit too good to be true.

To this day, anyhow, Dookie has her defenders and deserves them to
some extent, though it's necessary to point out that such people knew her
best during her redemptive City Center phase: Thus they perceived her as
"amusing," "outspoken," and even "heroic," while Yates (vis-à-vis his
mother at least) was "sarcastic," "impatient," and "spiteful."* Tony Vevers has a number of reasons for taking Dookie's side, not the least being
that she gave him a job soon after he moved to New York. "I said, 'I know
your son,' " Vevers recalled, "and she said, 'You're hired.' Just like that."
And not only was Vevers hired, but so was his wife Elspeth, who was put
to work as Dookie's secretary despite the fact that she couldn't type. In
short, Dookie took them under her wing, all because they were friends of
her beloved son. She gave them theater tickets and got them into
rehearsals to watch Balanchine and his company; she took them to lunch,
where they drank martinis and met famous artists, and City Center paid

---

*Let it not pass without comment that such Dookie partisans tend to have axes to grind against
Yates: e.g., Riche and Vevers because of *Young Hearts Crying,* and Louise Rodgers because of *The
Easter Parade* (wherein the house designed by her beloved father appears as the hideous mildewy
wreck "Great Hedges").

for it all. "Ruth Yates was an extraordinary person," said Louise Rodgers, who as a young woman helped Dookie in the gallery. "She was temperamental, yes, and I suppose she drank a lot, but she worked hard, and *everybody* drank a lot."

By the time he returned from Europe, though, Yates had seen enough of his mother's drinking. In fact he could hardly bear her company, especially when friends were present: If she got tipsy and began to talk too much, Yates would roll his eyes and make faces at her while she wasn't looking, until finally he'd get so agitated that sometimes he'd have to leave the room. Even Sheila—who could understand better than most—thought her husband's attitude a bit much, though she herself could only take Dookie in moderate doses.

Happily for Dookie's sake, she had less need of their company or philanthropy. City Center kept her busy and paid her a living wage, and during weekends at High Hedges her grandchildren saved her from the worst of her loneliness. On Saturdays they'd visit her cozy, overgrown garage apartment on the estate (she stored her sculpture below), and Dookie would make them a treat of fried bananas in sugar. Even Yates gave her credit for being a good enough grandmother (despite her old complaint that she couldn't *imagine* herself as such), and would leave Mussy in her care for days at a time during the summer. But otherwise Dookie kept mostly to herself at High Hedges, though she still liked to visit Fritz and Louise for sherry in the evening. As for relations with her daughter, they were civil but strained: Ruth, out of loyalty to her husband (as well as grievances known only to herself), had made it clear at the outset that Dookie was not wanted by the younger Rodgerses at High Hedges; she relented when Dookie appealed to Fritz, but both women would nurse the hurt for the rest of their lives.

Ruth's life was as full as it would ever be: Her children were all at home and she was a happily attentive mother. Twice a week she worked at WGSM in Huntington, where she wrote scripts for radio programs on gardening and local history, and sometimes served as announcer as well. And whatever her differences with Dookie, they were kindred spirits in at least one respect—Ruth's early involvement with the Willkie campaign had led to a lifelong interest in Republican politics: Ruth was one of the first Republican committeewomen on Long Island, and wrote speeches for Nelson Rockefeller's gubernatorial campaign. But like her brother— who in time would write a number of political speeches himself (though not at gunpoint would he ever have written for a Republican)—she wanted to be a fiction writer most of all. So great was her ambition to "crack *The New Yorker*" with one of her "humorous sketches about family life," that she papered her powder room with the magazine's covers as a form of hopeful tribute. Fred's position on the subject of his wife's diversions was this: They were fine as long as they didn't distract her from motherhood or cause any confusion as to who the real breadwinner was.

It was understood that Yates didn't visit High Hedges very often because of the enmity between him and Fred—or rather Fred served as a convenient excuse. The fact was, Yates loved and cared for his sister and would always feel a bond, but found her frankly dull and depressing. He made the trip to Long Island as a matter of duty, and tended to be cordial but distant while there. His niece Ruth (called Dodo by the family) remembers him as "a mellow sort of man" who smiled a lot, but often looked grave when he and his sister sat talking together, particularly in later years. Sometimes he'd spend time clearing brush on the property (hardly a characteristic activity otherwise), and though he was always kind to Ruth's children, he was rarely attentive or playful. Once he went on a squirrel-shooting expedition with six-year-old Peter (who can't remember whether "Uncle Dick" was delighted or horrified by the idea) and once he let thirteen-year-old Fred drive his new Chevy around the grounds, but that was about it. No matter how rare and tense his visits, though, Ruth was not a whit resentful: She adored her talented little brother, and always spoke of him with tender pride.

As anticipated, Yates won the *Atlantic* "First" award of $750 in December, and a few days later Seymour Lawrence came to New York and invited him to dinner at the Harvard Club. It was the beginning of a long and peculiar friendship. To be sure, things were less complicated in their salad days, when the two got along more or less famously—a bond assisted by their being exact contemporaries (Yates was eight days older) with similar tastes and tendencies. "We would order several Jack Daniel's on the rocks followed by sirloin steaks, rare please," Lawrence recalled forty years later. "We would gossip, tell stories, talk about life and letters, who were the good guys and who were the shits." At the time such meetings were particularly bracing for Yates, who liked being courted at the Harvard Club ("a big deal for me") and by his own reckoning had no other "literary" friends to speak of.

And Sam Lawrence was almost as monomaniacal and quirky; if he hadn't existed it might have been necessary to make him up, at least for the sake of Yates and certain other worthy if problematic writers. "The first time I met Sam Lawrence," a colleague remembered, "he was making an argument on behalf of one of his authors. The last time I spoke with him . . . he was doing the same thing." Quite simply, Lawrence's life and work were indistinguishable. A man with a bad stammer who drank to overcome shyness, Lawrence had gravitated to writers from the beginning—without, it seems, ever seriously wishing to be a writer himself. As a freshman at Columbia he fell in with a "bad crowd" that included Kerouac and Ginsberg, until his mother made him transfer to Harvard, where he founded the magazine *Wake* and coaxed submissions from the likes of T. S. Eliot and Tennessee Williams. By the time he met Yates he'd been at the Atlantic Monthly Press in Boston for just over a year. By 1955 he was director of the firm, and thereafter would insist "I'm a publisher, *not* an editor"—that is, while he had sovereign faith in his editorial judgment (whose dictates he was always willing to follow in defiance of conventional wisdom), he wasn't remotely interested in the hands-on task of editing books. For a hands-off perfectionist such as Yates, this turned out to be an almost ideal arrangement, but most writers were less autonomous. In the latter case Lawrence had a solution—he simply farmed out the editing chores to his own stable of writers: Thus Kurt Vonnegut edited Dan Wakefield, Wakefield edited Tim O'Brien, and so on.* "Lawrence's writers were a happy little family," said DeWitt Henry, who made the intriguing point that most of these writers were not only

---

*Yates excused himself from this incestuous arrangement, though he was happy to offer input when solicited.

friends but tended to have drinking and realism in common—or, to put a finer point on it, that "alcohol and its vision" informed their themes to a remarkable degree: "the harrowing experience of reality without illusions that drives the pathology," as Henry put it.

Be that as it may, in 1953 Yates and Lawrence were just a couple of boozy young men swapping gossip and dividing the good guys from the shits. Also there was the matter of mutual self-interest: Yates was a talented new writer whose inevitable novel Lawrence wanted to publish, but in the meantime Yates needed to sell his other work. At their first meeting, then, Lawrence agreed to reconsider a few stories that had been previously rejected by the *Atlantic*—among them the story of Vincent Sabella, the alienated welfare child, which Yates had retitled "Doctor Jack-o'-Lantern." Yates thought the story one of his best, but Lawrence demurred: "The psychology did not ring wholly true," he wrote Monica McCall, though he reiterated that "Dick Yates is a writer whom we respect and want to publish frequently." That said, he rejected Yates's other stories a second time too, and his judgment of "Doctor Jack-o'-Lantern" would be validated by every magazine from *The New Yorker* to *Discovery* to the *Yale Review*—until a year later it was finally sent back to Yates by a "heartbroken" and "frankly stumped" Monica McCall.

In early 1954 Yates started a novel that failed to "jell," and so returned to writing stories. In that genre the level of his work was now consistently excellent, but if anything less saleable than ever. With soul-killing monotony the consensus opinion was expressed by the formula *Extremely well-written, but* . . . "Fun with a Stranger" was well-written but inconsequential in terms of its payoff. "Out with the Old" was "a little masterpiece" according to McCall, but a doubtful sell because of the protagonist's pregnant teenage daughter. "The B.A.R. Man," she thought, "belongs in *The New Yorker*, who won't buy it." And a story called "Sobel" (later retitled "A Wrestler with Sharks") was "a beauty as usual, though subject-wise not too easy a one." Finally in August a rewrite of the two-year-old "Nuptials"—now called "I'll Be All in Clover" and soon to be called "The Best of Everything"—was bought by the magazine *Charm*, whose editors also reconsidered in favor of "Fun with a Stranger." The two stories were Yates's only sales in 1954.

• • •

After less than a year on Perry Street, the world and Dookie were too much with the Yateses, and they decided to move to the country. Elspeth Vevers's mother owned a converted barn in northern Westchester, where the Yateses lived for most of that summer in an awkward communal arrangement with the Veverses and two other couples. The house was big, dark, and hot—a bit *too* much like a barn, converted or otherwise—and Sheila appealed to her mother to find them a better place. Marjorie Bryant was now one of the region's most successful real estate brokers, as well as an indefatigable fixer-upper in what spare time she allowed herself; as such, she was almost ominously eager to be of use to her daughter and son-in-law. In no time she found them a lovely A-frame carriage house in Salem, Westchester, on the estate of an affable Cossack named Guirey—a great horseman and drinker who'd known Tony Vevers at Yale. He and Yates hit it off, and for a while the place was almost perfect.

One of their first visitors was Bob Riche, who'd been invited to come out with his then-girlfriend Pamela Vevers. By the time Yates met Riche at the train station, though, the couple had broken up and Pamela was already dating theater director Ed Sherin.* Riche was devastated, and by his own admission had a hard time getting off the subject. Yates tried to console his tearful friend by making fun of the notoriously charming Sherin, whom he described as an "actor type." But Sheila was less sympathetic. She went out of her way to talk about a delightful recent visit with Sherin and Pamela, and when Riche persisted in licking his wounds, she casually remarked, "Oh Bob, but he's *much* better-looking than you." It began to seem an almost systematic attempt to demoralize Riche, culminating in an episode that haunts him still. As he tried to sleep in an open loft directly over his hosts' bed, he was disturbed by what struck him as an outrageous act of conjugal derision: "She was giggling and carrying on like a mad sex fiend," he recalled, "and I always felt it was at the least a

---

*Whom she married and eventually divorced. Sherin's second wife was the actress Jane Alexander, and he went on to a very successful career in television, as producer of such hits as *Law and Order*. He served as the model for Ralph Morin in *Young Hearts Crying*.

bit inappropriate, and more likely deliberate cruelty." "More likely"
indeed, as the Yateses had already turned Riche into something of a private joke; as Sheila later explained, "Bob was the sort of person who gets
analysis year in year out," and her husband (while fond of Riche) found
him every bit as ridiculous.* But it is Sheila's glee that stuck in Riche's
mind: "She had a laugh that snapped out like a whip," he said.

Unfortunately the Yateses weren't able to entertain at the carriage house
as much as they might have liked; the place wasn't heated, and by winter
it was time to move on again. At this point the transience of their lives was
getting them down again: They wanted their own home in a nice community, where Mussy could be raised in a proper middle-class environment,
though Yates wondered if he could handle a mortgage on his rather unstable income. Re-enter Marjorie Bryant, absentee mother turned ubiquitous
benefactor: She'd found a lovely little house in the suburban town of Redding, Connecticut, and what's more she was willing to make the down
payment and hold the mortgage herself. Yates loathed the idea of being
beholden to his mother-in-law—or anyone, ever—but it was a difficult
offer to refuse. Redding provided a pastoral but convenient setting right
off Route Seven: The schools in the area were excellent, and the house
itself, though not exactly *lovely,* was suitable—a newish one-story ranch
in a broken L-shape, with two bedrooms, a living room, and a big picture
window. The latter was a bit of a fright, but on balance they liked the way
the cellar had doors on the outside like an old-fashioned farmhouse, and
all things considered they decided to take it. Meanwhile Yates arranged to
do extra PR work for a firm called Lester Rossin Associates, the better not
to miss a single mortgage payment to Marjorie Bryant.

Sheila's old friend Ann Barker Kowalsky lived in nearby Brewster, and
she and her husband became frequent guests. John "Crash" Kowalsky
was a discontented engineer who worked for a microwave electronics
company in Pleasantville, and drinking was perhaps the one thing he and
Yates had in common. For a while it was a formidable bond. Their nights

---

*One will recall the "favorite subject" of the widowed Frank Wheeler: " 'my analyst this'; 'my ana-
lyst that.' " In his notes to *Revolutionary Road,* Yates described this composite character as being
like "Bob [Riche] without humor and me without talent."

followed a predictable pattern: The two couples would drink and chat for as long as pleasantly possible before the men became unruly—arguing or bellowing army songs while the women receded into an icy silence. Sometimes, too, Yates would lapse into grumpy, drunken boredom and tell Kowalsky to "get the hell out," whenever the man's stories about his proletarian childhood began to pall. One night Yates announced that "Crash" was the model for the "engineering square" in his novel-in-progress,* a characterization that made Kowalsky bridle at the time, though he never did get around to reading the book in question.

The odd *Walpurgisnacht* aside, the overall domestic scene on Old Redding Road was tranquil enough. Sheila (whether happily or not) had always been an excellent housewife, and now at last she had a proper venue for her talents. She kept the little house tidy despite Yates's presence in it, and the family sat down twice a day to tasty, well-balanced meals—especially on holidays, when Sheila would prepare an Anglophilic feast of juicy rare rib roast of beef, mashed potatoes, and Yorkshire pudding. And no matter how much the couple occasionally chafed in each other's company, they were at pains to be on good behavior for Mussy, who was calming down into a gentle, ladylike child. When she indulged in occasional naughtiness, the worst Yates would do was send her to her room, and only that after a long series of jocular admonishments: "Stop this clownlike behavior," he'd order the giggling girl, "or I'll have to get the stick with the nail in it!"

A drawback of living in the hinterland was that it convinced Yates that he needed to drive a car, and this would become a fresh and fertile source of marital strife. Yates's lifelong wish to seem "competent as anybody at dealing with the small-change of practical life" was coupled with a terrible awareness that he *wasn't* competent, and this made him frustrated and defensive and all but hopeless as a student driver. As he wrote of Bill Grove in *Uncertain Times*, "He was too nervous and easily rattled ever to handle a car well, and his stubbornness in hating to admit it only made it

---

*Namely, Shepherd "Shep" Campbell in *Revolutionary Road*. As noted, Blanchard "Jerry" Cain was perhaps the main model for this composite.

worse." Just so. But as Yates would prove time and again, the capacity for knowing thyself in art rarely translates into everyday life. In any event Sheila soon decided she had better things to do than teach her husband how to drive, and so delegated the job to her brother Charlie—a bad choice, not only because Charlie was a long-term mental patient but because Charlie was Charlie: possessed of "an uncannily keen and very articulate insight into other people's weaknesses," as Yates put it.*

One can only imagine the extent to which Charlie brought such insight to his driving instruction, but it wasn't long before a fistfight erupted between teacher and pupil. Sheila, who witnessed the incident and called it "pretty horrible," is almost certain it was the direct result of a driving lesson. In later years, though, Yates would tell a different story, which perhaps conflated a number of similar episodes, and anyway seems to shed light on certain aspects of his family life at the time. According to his version, it all began with a typical phone call from his mother-in-law: Charlie was harassing her, she said; would they come right away and take him back to the hospital? As ever the Yateses tried to oblige, but this time Charlie refused to go. "You're just pushing me around because I'm a mental patient," he said. "In Connecticut you can put the cops on me, but in New York I could fight back." The only way he'd go quietly was if they agreed to drive him to the state line and let him "fight back," so off they went. When they came to New York the men got out of the car and scuffled a bit in the headlight beams, but both were heavy smokers and soon gasping for breath. "*God*—" said Charlie as they slumped against the car, "can you believe some guys do this for a living?"

Whatever the circumstances, no lingering rift resulted. The same can't be said for Yates's marriage once he learned how to drive, as the car proved an apt battlefield for the pair. "When he was really being dopey," Sheila recalled, "he had this big thing about how *he* had to drive the car, no *woman* could help him." One may recall how Michael Davenport in *Young Hearts Crying* feels "humiliated—even emasculated" when his wife

---

*The quote is taken from the 1972 *Ploughshares* interview. Yates was explaining how his brother-in-law's personality was similar to that of John Givings in *Revolutionary Road*.

makes him ride on the passenger's side. Yates felt the same way, and for that matter aspired to a rather cartoonish stereotype of masculinity in general, forever threatened on all sides and particularly so when he was behind the wheel of a car. And this, in turn, gave Sheila the irresistible opportunity to get her own back for any number of pent-up grievances. As Bob Riche observed, "Dick bumbled around Sheila, especially in the car. I think it was a self-fulfilling prophecy. That is, she reinforced his feelings of inadequacy, and he played into it unconsciously." According to Riche, it was a "nightmare" being in the same car with the couple, and the cycle was always the same: Yates would struggle to remain calm while Sheila needled him ("Oh, be careful! You don't know what you're doing!" and so on), until finally Yates would snap and the fight would be on. Nor was their daughter exempt from such scenes. Once she watched them bicker over how to run the car heater; when Sheila turned out to be right, Yates exploded *"Well, cut my penis off!"* and lapsed into a long brooding silence.

Sheila's tendency to emphasize her husband's ineptitude was more than idle perversity, as she came to understand better in retrospect. "I hate the thought of mentally calculating the added amount of cooking, cleaning and wash you add up to," she later wrote Yates, as they considered another reconciliation; "but I think you know from the Remington Rand years . . . that doing something you hate for someone you love makes for a cancerous kind of grudge." Which suggests, too, the insidiously reciprocal nature of that grudge, insofar as each resented the other for putting them in a situation they hated—housework and Remington Rand respectively. Because of Yates's awful efforts to pay the bills, he might have expected his domestic failings to be pardoned; beyond a certain point, though, even an attitude of weary acceptance on Sheila's part was liable to be taken (accurately enough) as dire reproach. The mounting tension made for some curious scenes, particularly in the eyes of a five-year-old child. One time, Sharon recalls, her parents sat quietly chatting in the living room, when suddenly Yates hurled his glass into the fireplace and stormed bellowing out of the house.

He wanted to be a proper country husband, a productive member of his household and community. He wanted to show he could "pull his weight," "stay on the ball," and "cope" as well or better than the most banal bore in Redding, but his efforts had a way of ending badly. One morning while his wife was fixing breakfast he went outside to burn some trash. A few minutes later he let loose an aria of obscenities, but the jaded Sheila simply assumed he'd stubbed his toe and went on with her business. Finally she glanced outside: There was a brushfire in the backyard, on the edges of which Yates gamboled ineffectually. The volunteer fire department arrived in time to save their house, and a penitent Yates agreed to become a member, faithfully attending meetings every Saturday night. According to Bob Riche, he was just lonely: "Dick yearned to have friends. Sheila kept telling him to get out and become a part of the community. So he tried, the poor bastard, and joined the volunteer fire department . . . and sat around at meetings with local farm types trying to fit in, and crushing beer cans with one hand."

At last he gave up. His marriage was on the rocks again, everything was wrong, and he blamed it largely on Redding. Or rather: Because he'd accepted the charity of a woman he despised, he was forced into a wholly false and self-defeating position; not only was he obliged to be pleasant to Marjorie (as he was in any case), but also *grateful*—to visit her and be visited, to mediate between her and Charlie, and above all to work harder than ever at the "PR dodge" to pay off a mortgage and avoid the necessity of even *more* gratitude, all for the privilege of living in a place where he was lonely and miserable and couldn't get any decent work done. Sheila tried to remonstrate: They had a nice house in Connecticut where Mussy was likely to get a good education; everything would be fine (or tolerable) if he could just get over his resentment toward Marjorie and accept her good turn.

Yates referred to the whole arrangement as "Gethsemane" and wanted out, period. "He claimed all his problems in every way were caused by Remington Rand and my mother," Sheila said. "Finally I stopped arguing with him. I thought maybe that *was* true. I didn't realize this was an ongoing situation that would go on no matter where we lived or what happened." They'd lived in Redding for just over a year.

Yates would always say that when the work is going well, the rest follows. The work was going poorly. For the past three years Monica McCall and Sam Lawrence and everybody else had urged him to write a novel, but what with one thing and another he seemed no closer to getting started in early 1955 than he'd ever been. Meanwhile his other work was not only drying up but in danger of regressing, if one judges by the quality of "The End of the Great Depression"—as it happened, the last short story Yates would write for another six years.

"Depression" is mostly comprised of Walter Mittyish daydreams, much like the earlier "Convalescent Ego"—an ominous similarity. The story, set in 1937, is about a solitary twelve-year-old boy who assumes that the Depression will last well into the future, and hence fantasizes about becoming a hero to the downtrodden and ultimately the president who ends the crisis sometime in the fifties. For a while the boy's fantasy adheres to the same reassuring narrative, which at one point has him chastely kissing a generic dream-girl.* Eventually, however, the boy's naive idealism is eclipsed by puberty, and the fantasy is altered when the girl abruptly reveals her breasts and metamorphoses into "Gretchen Sondergaard, at school": "And he didn't know it then . . . but the nature of his dreams was changed forever." The young George Plimpton at the *Paris Review* rejected "Depression" with a lengthy critique advising, in effect, that Yates flesh out the frame story lest the reader "get so involved in the text of the daydreams that we forget it is a boy dreaming them and take them at face value." This Yates dutifully did, adding some dialogue between the boy's parents wherein they discuss his welfare in terms that are alternately gruff (father) and fretful (mother). It wasn't much of an improvement, and when Plimpton rejected the revised version he pointed to a more intrinsic flaw: "The Walter Mitty scenes [are] supposed to be ludicrous clichés, but they turn out as slapstick, with little subtlety worked in which might have given them originality." In other words, *neither* part of this strangely amateurish story worked, and one can only wonder why Yates ever allowed it to be published at all.†

---

*"He kissed her, and this, though one of the best parts of the story, was always a little uncertain. He wasn't sure how they would keep their noses from colliding." I'd wager this bit was inspired by the five-year-old boy's question to Sergeant X in Salinger's "For Esmé—with Love and Squalor": " 'Why do people in films kiss sideways?' " A bad sign that Yates seemed to be falling back on an old influence in so obvious a fashion.

†In the Winter 1962 issue of *Transatlantic Review*.

Clearly he was exhausted, and perhaps the banalities of PR work were beginning to infiltrate his imagination. The only hope of escape was to write a successful novel—the raw material of which, he already sensed, would be the stuff of his own predicament. But he wanted to transcend the merely personal, to avoid the pitfalls of sentiment and self-pity. And before he wrote a word he wanted above all to purge the stale residue of PR work from his brain; what better antidote than the great hater of the bourgeoisie and their cant, Flaubert, whose impersonal masterpiece proved the perfect goad at the time. "That was when *Madame Bovary* took command," Yates wrote in "Some Very Good Masters":

> I had read it before but hadn't studied it the way I'd studied *Gatsby* and other
> books; now it seemed ideally suited to serve as a guide, if not a model, for the
> novel that was taking shape in my mind. I wanted *that* kind of balance and
> quiet resonance on every page, that kind of foreboding mixed with comedy,
> that kind of inexorable destiny in the heart of a lonely, romantic girl. And all
> of it, of course, would have to be done with an F. Scott Fitzgerald kind of
> freshness and grace.

Flaubert offered a further tutorial on the proper use of the "objective correlative"—the telling detail that transmits meaning and emotion without laboring the point. In "Masters" Yates cited the green silk cigar case that Charles Bovary finds in the road after the ball, a fetish his wife uses "as a source of voluptuous daydreams"; Yates then referred to a later scene of exquisitely nuanced foreboding: "When the pharmacist's young apprentice Justin, who is hopelessly in love with Emma, is cruelly reprimanded by his employer, in her presence, for possessing an illustrated marriage manual *and* for messing around with the jar of arsenic. Wow." Flaubert also influenced what is known as Yates's "determinism"—though this was mostly a matter of innate sensibility and life experience.* " 'Fate is to

---

*Yates has been called a "naturalistic" (or "neonaturalistic") writer, though he had little affinity for
(or familiarity with) naturalism as a literary tradition. "Are you aware—you must be—that [*Revolutionary Road*] is just what Zola felt the naturalistic novel ought to be?" a reader wrote Yates,
who replied in part: "I was very flattered by your comparison of my book to Zola's work, but must

blame,' " says Charles Bovary in forgiving his dead wife's lover Rodolphe, and Yates had a lively subjective view of what "fate" entailed. "Another thing I have always liked about both *Gatsby* and *Bovary*," he wrote, "is that there are no villains in either one. The force of evil is felt in these novels but is never personified—neither novel is willing to let us off that easily." Yates's student Tim Parrish remembered discussing *The Easter Parade* with its author, who wistfully referred to Emily's fateful decision not to connect with her sister. When Parrish asked him what might have happened if she *had* made the connection, Yates replied, "I never thought of that"—meaning that the contingency wasn't available given who Emily was. Yates's determinism, like Flaubert's, was a matter of knowing his characters well enough to know their fates, and making the reader see this, too. Just as one never expects Emma to repent of her infidelity and embrace provincial life, one also figures the Wheelers won't move to Europe and live happily ever after. Their weaknesses, well defined at the outset, mark them for a bad end.

Flaubert was the catalyst for what became *Revolutionary Road,* but meanwhile other developments conspired to spur Yates on to the task. Hiram Haydn at Random House—"that absolutely supreme fiction editor," as Monica McCall described him—was impressed by Yates's work, and in April 1955 the two met over lunch to discuss the possibility of a book contract. "Like all publishers," McCall advised Yates prior to the meeting, "I must warn you that [Haydn] is allergic to publishing a book of short stories as an author's first work." This posed a problem, since Yates's "novel" at the time was little more than a notion, though he seems to have persuaded Haydn that something substantial would soon be ready. At any rate he and McCall gave Random House right of first refusal—a rather pointed snub of Sam Lawrence, whose eagerness to publish Yates's novel had begun to look a bit like complacency in light of his multiple rejections of the stories. But then, McCall would always be wary of Lawrence, and anyway Random House was a more prestigious publisher.

---

confess my ignorance of what he said the 'naturalistic novel ought to be'—or, for that matter, of the idea that my book was 'naturalistic' at all."

By late summer Yates was finally under way on a book that gave every appearance of jelling, such that in late October McCall was "daily watching the mails hoping for the beginnings." Three months later McCall was still waiting: "I hope your silence does not mean that you have been having trouble." It was generally safe to assume Yates was having trouble of one sort or another, but this time his silence was mostly a matter of keeping his head down and moving forward at his own glacial speed—until, almost a year after that lunch with Haydn, Yates was ready to submit the first 134-page section of a novel titled *The Getaway*. To this he appended a 7-page synopsis of the second half.

Haydn was persuaded of Yates's "real ability and the book's real worth," though more than a little taken aback by the author's express intention to end his novel with a fatal, self-inflicted abortion; stated in the pat terms of a synopsis, it seemed a bit much. "I express to you my doubts about his plan for the rest," Haydn wrote McCall, "and even though he and I have talked it over and he is certainly willing to tone down his tragic plan . . . there still remains much doubt on our part." Their "doubt" was hardly misplaced as to the ending, which Yates had no intention of changing. In fact, as he later pointed out, the main theme of the book was abortion in various forms, and the story itself had evolved around April's literal, climactic act: "I thought of the girl dying in that way, and then the whole problem was to construct a book that would justify that ending." Yates's reassurance to Haydn that he would "tone down his tragic plan" was deliberately ambiguous; what he actually hoped was that the completed novel would justify the tragedy in such a way as to make it seem inevitable—and cathartic—an effect that could hardly be conveyed by a simple summary, or indeed by the story and characters as they stood at the time.

Sam Lawrence had a similar response: "*Very* much impressed with the manuscript," he wrote McCall in June, "but the synopsis itself seemed to be a disappointment." Nevertheless he was willing to offer an option payment of three hundred dollars "as a vote of our confidence in his ability and as a way of urging him to go forward with the completion of his novel." McCall austerely insisted on a proper advance of fifteen hundred dollars, and the rather doubtful Lawrence agreed to recommend a contract to his associates at Atlantic–Little, Brown, who rejected the manuscript as "one of the many imitators of *The Man in the Gray Flannel Suit.*" Lawrence, on sober consideration, seemed to accept this verdict as perfectly valid, and his subsequent letter to McCall reflected little of his initial enthusiasm: Yates's "narrative competence" was not in doubt, he wrote, but the theme was "somewhat hackneyed" and the minor characters were "not sufficiently developed"—in sum, the author had yet to find "the most suitable subject and material for his talents," though Lawrence asked to be kept apprised of any further progress.

McCall reassured Yates that this was "no great blow," that he should simply finish the book as he saw fit, and in fact Yates was undaunted to a surprising degree. A few months later he reported to McCall that he was making good progress, and instructed her to destroy the previous version. Being compared with Sloan Wilson, it turned out, had proved the sort of strong medicine that cures the patient in the course of almost killing him. As Yates later explained:

> Most of my first drafts read like soap opera. I have to go over and over a scene before I get deep enough into it to bring it off. I think I'd be a slick, superficial writer if I didn't revise all the time. The first draft of *Revolutionary Road* was very thin, very sentimental. . . . I made the Wheelers sort of nice young folks with whom any careless reader could identify. Everything they said was exactly what they meant, and they talked very earnestly together even when they were quarreling, like people in a Sloan Wilson novel. It took me a long time to figure out what a mistake that was—that the best way to handle it was to have them nearly always miss each other's points, to have them talk around and through and *at* each other. There's a great deal of dialogue between them in the finished book . . . but there's almost no communication.

In other words Yates had remembered the lesson of his first great master, Fitzgerald—namely, that people rarely say what they mean, and good dialogue is a matter of catching one's characters "in the very act of giving themselves away." Now more than ever Yates was eager to lose himself in the almost archaeological labor of revision, while Sam Lawrence—whose "vote of confidence" had come full circle—was delighted to learn that such a promising writer remained undiscouraged.

In the summer of 1956 the Yateses moved to the rural town of Mahopac in Putnam County, New York, where they lived on a private estate called Babaril.* The pink stucco cottage they rented was arguably a step or two down from their sturdy little ranch house in Redding, but the new home possessed a sort of forlorn charm. The ground floor consisted of a low-ceilinged living room, dining room, and kitchen (Yates could hardly stand up straight), with two small bedrooms upstairs, the larger of which opened onto a narrow balcony with a spiral staircase leading to the flagstones below. The balcony was a picturesque feature (the French doors beneath it were another), though it was liable to collapse if anyone actually stood on it. It gave the impression of being held up by vines, as did the rest of the place, which resembled a kind of dilapidated Hollywood dollhouse; the Lilliputian perspective was enhanced by an adjacent hut where drunken guests could, in a pinch, spend the night. The hut had a tiny fireplace that couldn't be used without igniting the willow tree just above its tiny chimney.

Their landlady was an aging actress named Jill Miller, who with her vanished husband had founded the Putnam County Playhouse, a once-prestigious summer stock theater in the last stages of desuetude. Near the main house was a largely abandoned dormitory for actors, an annex of which was occupied by a local family named Jones. Around the hundred-acre estate were overgrown gardens and crumbling cottages and a weedy old tennis court, but the feature that most appealed to Yates—the clincher, in fact—was a five-by-eight wellhouse at the end of a long winding path. With his landlady's blessing, Yates installed a table, chair, typewriter, and kerosene stove, and wrote most of *Revolutionary Road* there.

In keeping with their old dynamic, Yates relished his quirky new venue

---

* "Donarann" in *Young Hearts Crying*, wherein the estate and its various tenants are depicted with almost absolute fidelity. Mahopac is called "Tonapac" in the novel.

almost as much as Sheila despised it. "It was the antithesis of Redding," she said, "so Dick thought it was great. But everything had gone to seed. It was a sad place owned by a sad lady." Naturally Sheila tried to make the best of things, and perhaps it was fortunate that she could rarely be idle, as her hands were full keeping their cottage in some sort of habitable order. In the summer the cellar flooded regularly, and the roof seemed to leak even when the sun was out. Sheila attended to the caulking and draining and other proprietary chores, while Yates tended to lie low in the well-house.

Winters were ghastly cold and the cottage was poorly heated, caulking or no, but at least the bizarre, shifting crowd of summer colonists thinned. The writer Edward Hoagland, who befriended the Yateses around this time, described Babaril as "a place for people at loose ends"—offhand he recalled such tenants as a reclusive Hallmark artist and a man in the middle of a bitter divorce who worked out his anger by firing a pistol. "You never knew *who* you were going to run into," Sheila complained, though she noted that some tenants were more permanent than others. There were the Joneses, of course, whose five children became playmates of Yates's daughters; the father George, a dull but amiable man with a white-collar job in the city, was recruited along with Sheila to perform in the Putnam Playhouse production of *A Midsummer Night's Dream*. By then Sheila had "lost interest in that sort of thing," but gamely went through the motions as Titania, while George Jones proved a remarkably able clown. A far more illustrious cast member was Will Geer, then a well-known character actor who later became famous as Grandpa Walton. For most of the fifties Geer was blacklisted, and worked as a gardener on the estate. He strolled about in cowboy boots and an undershirt and mostly kept to himself, though occasionally Sharon and the Jones children would stop by his hut at dusk and listen to ghost stories: "Who's got my arm . . . ?" Geer would intone. "*You do!*"—and the children would flee screaming to their cottages. Yates, who couldn't abide homosexuals, took a dim view of the folksy actor.*

---

*Geer was the model for Ben Duane in *Young Hearts Crying*. Michael Davenport's views on Duane's sexual orientation are pretty much those of his creator, a matter worthy of later discussion.

Much of this was made bearable for Sheila by the fact that she was pregnant again. It gave her something to look forward to, creaky marriage withal. Sharon had long wanted a sibling, and now that her only immediate playmates were the rowdy Jones children, the matter could no longer wait. And Yates was happy to oblige; Mahopac was a hick town—little more than a laundromat, bank, and ice-cream parlor—and he too wanted Mussy to have company other than the Joneses or whatever urchins she met at school. Besides, he was hoping to add a boy to the family (for the sake of novelty and moral support, perhaps), but it wasn't to be. Monica Jane was born on April 10, 1957, and when the nurse told Yates he had another daughter, he was surprised to find that he "felt like a million dollars" (as he later wrote a friend): "You can pick girls up and hug and kiss them anytime you feel like it, until they get too heavy to lift—that's one advantage; another is that they never expect you to teach them how to throw."

Among the first to congratulate him was Sam Lawrence; that done, Lawrence briskly reaffirmed his great confidence in Yates's novel-in-progress: "[Y]our best [work has] always indicated the gifts of a natural writer. There are so many writers today who don't have that unmistakable quality." Yates needed the encouragement. When he wasn't gouging away at his novel between long despondent fortnights lost to PR work, he was trying to stay in the public eye as a fiction writer by reworking a few of his more promising stories. The revised "B.A.R. Man" was now being tried on such magazines as *Swank, Bachelor, Gentry,* and *Nugget,* none of whose editors chose to introduce Yates to their special readership. *Esquire* sniffed that they'd "gotten away a bit from woman-hating stories like the BAR Man one," and also rejected (again) "A Really Good Jazz Piano" and "Evening on the Côte d'Azur." Meanwhile Sam Lawrence's latest sop was vitiated somewhat when he returned the revised "Out with the Old" with yet another perfunctory note along the lines of *extremely well-written, but.* A year later the same story was accepted by the *Western Review,* which on further consideration rejected it, as did the *Dial* ("encouragingly").

Yates was taking things hard. Two years had passed since he'd started his novel, and a satisfactory draft was nowhere in sight; at this rate he'd never be able to support himself as a fiction writer, yet he could hardly bear the thought of indefinite hacking for Remington Rand. The future looked grim, and Yates behaved accordingly. For most of his adult life he'd been a beer drinker who limited himself to the occasional binge, but now he routinely drank almost a fifth of bourbon a day. At his worst Yates was like one of his own characters facing the terrible truth of his limitations: He'd bemoan his lack of progress to anybody who cared to listen, or else lapse into loud opinionated rants on some elusive general theme, or simply fall over the furniture. He also began vomiting in the morning. At first Sheila assumed the obvious, but in fact drinking was only a general factor. For most of his life from Mahopac on, even in times of relative sobriety, Yates's pulmonary health was such that he'd never again know what it was like to feel good when he started the day. Sometimes the hacking and vomiting would go on for hours before his lungs were clear enough to light a cigarette and get on with his work.

"From the time Monica was born," said Sheila, "I knew the marriage was going down the tubes." When work had gone poorly at the wellhouse, Yates would stalk back to the cottage in a foul mood and spend the night soaking under his wife's censorious or indifferent gaze. Sometimes they'd have dreary repetitive arguments once the children were in bed, but once again (as in Europe) these became rare. Sheila didn't have the heart to bother anymore. It wasn't that Yates was a mean drunk, just noisy and stubborn and self-absorbed, and she decided to find better uses for her time. Beyond a point, she began to consider her life as mostly separate from that of her husband, who was fast becoming a rather ghostly presence. After dinner he'd go back to the wellhouse to drink in peace, while Sheila took evening classes at Danbury State College.

The time came when Yates could no longer juggle fiction with drinking and Remington Rand. The deeper he got into his novel, the more of its intricate design he had to keep in his head, and the forced return to hackwork every couple of weeks became a hideous distraction. This of course led to more despair, drinking, and exhaustion, until something had to give. Perhaps the most loathsomely mechanical aspect of his Remington Rand work was writing the internal house organ—sifting through a bulging monthly envelope full of scraps, which had to be converted into

sprightly items about regional sales meetings, or companies that had purchased certain products and why, or who had been promoted to what and
so on. Yates couldn't do it anymore. It was all too close to the quiet desperation at the heart of his novel, the sort of thing that taxed his Flaubertian detachment to the utmost. Sheila, however, flatly refused to give up
the three hundred dollars a month brought in by the newsletter alone, and
so began to write the thing herself. The subterfuge went on for years
without a hitch. If anything, the newsletter might have improved somewhat, as it's hard to imagine Yates putting much thought into a playlet
about the invention of the typewriter, as Sheila was glad to do for a special
centennial issue.

They socialized more than ever, as company seemed to relieve the strain,
and generally they were adept at acting the happy couple. Amid such seeming conjugal peace, their friend Ann Kowalsky was impressed by the
vaguely dissonant note struck by the Yateses' dinner table, a tasteful old
refectory piece in the Spanish style: "It was the support for Sheila's marvelous meals *and* the numerous bottles—beer, wines, Old Grand Dad and
Old Crow." At the time Yates, too, was a curious compound of courtesy
and boorishness, gloom and hilarity—one or the other with rather little in
between, all aspects of the same restive temperament. An essential sweetness was in evidence when Kowalsky was about to give birth to twins in
1957; the couples agreed she'd call Yates as soon as she went into labor, as
he was bound to be home and could drive her to the hospital in Mount
Kisco. When the time came, Yates rushed over at once and waited in jittery,
chain-smoking misery while Kowalsky got some last-minute chores done.
By the time they pulled onto the Merritt Parkway he was barely capable of
speech, and sped obliviously past the Mount Kisco exit. This shattered his
nerves further, and when they finally arrived at the hospital he was attracting almost as much attention as his hugely pregnant companion. "Please
try to calm down," an orderly said to the trembling, pacing, deathly pale
man whom everyone assumed to be the father. "These must be your first
twins." Yates hastened to deny it, and when Kowalsky began teasing him—
"Dick, how can you *say* that at this point! I'm in *labor*" etc.—he became
even more painfully distraught. Such tortured solicitude was touching, and
Kowalsky bore it in mind when Yates later made a drunken pass at her.

Perhaps the best times were with their friends Bob and Dot Parker, whom they met shortly after moving to Mahopac. Robert Andrew Parker was a rising young artist who combined a pawky sense of humor with a pokerfaced fondness for toy soldiers and military clothing.* He was especially receptive to Yates's rather caustic wit, and the two tended to bring out the best in each other. "I used to get a headache behind my eyes from laughing so hard," Parker said of their times together. Before long he and Yates were embarking on all sorts of improbable outings around Putnam County and points beyond. Once they rose before dawn so they could stake out a good place on the first day of pheasant-hunting season, which officially began at 8:04 A.M. A few minutes before eight, a cock pheasant alighted some twenty yards away, and the excited Yates couldn't resist blasting it to pieces. *"Who shot that bird?"* shouted Parker's angry neighbor. *"Was that you, Bob? You should know better than that!"* Another time they spent a tipsy afternoon cruising the suburbs of western Connecticut, laughing at street names; Yates needed to find a title for his novel, and this seemed a good place to start.

One of Parker's friends, Peter Kane Dufault, seemed to interest Yates from afar. Dufault was a poet who'd gone to Harvard, lost early in the Golden Gloves, and married the wealthy heiress of the Spalding Sporting Goods fortune. Like Parker he was a toy soldier enthusiast, and the two would spend whole days planning elaborate campaigns and photographing the smoky aftermath. Yates hardly knew Dufault, though both were part of a loose, somewhat arty social circle that also included Tony Vevers and Bob Riche, and everyone tended to go to the same parties. Yates would eventually appropriate certain details of Dufault's life in creating his character Michael Davenport in *Young Hearts Crying*—due in part, perhaps, to Dufault's central role in an incident that inspired two linchpin scenes in the novel.

The bare facts are these: Dufault and Tony Vevers agreed to exchange punches at a drunken party; Dufault went first and landed a blow to

---

*Just like Tom Nelson in *Young Hearts Crying*. Parker would later have much to say about this novel and his part in it, as we shall see.

Vevers's solar plexus; the latter congratulated him, stepped back to return the punch, and fell over unconscious. There are, however, any number of *Rashomon* nuances, depending on who tells the story. Parker says the party in question took place at his house in Croton Falls; Riche thinks it was at the converted barn owned by Elspeth Vevers's mother; the still-bitter Tony Vevers insists it was at Yates's cottage in Mahopac. For Vevers the episode serves as an almost perfect narrative catalogue of Yates's more repellent qualities: First, Yates tended to pressure his guests to get so drunk they couldn't drive, and those who tried to do so on that particular snowy night ended up in a ditch; second, Yates was ignoring Vevers's wife, Elspeth, at the party because she was pregnant ("Dick had no use for pregnant women—you had to be skinny and cute"); third, Yates's overall "mean streak" was peculiarly manifest on this occasion—that is, when Vevers finally came-to after the punch, his wife hysterical, the party *and* its host had moved on "as though nothing had happened." Others point out that the muscular Vevers was roaring drunk that night, and in fact had belligerently challenged the affable, reluctant Dufault to punch him in the stomach as hard as he could—also, that chaos, *not* indifference, had ensued. In any case the memory of this event (colored further by its treatment in *Young Hearts Crying*) left Tony and Elspeth Vevers with a very dim view of Yates: "Other people were just a source of entertainment to him," they both insist.

But many considered Yates a capital source of entertainment himself, and perhaps his most appreciative audience was Sheila. The everyday grind of their marriage might have been wretched beyond words, but when it wasn't just the two of them, and Yates was on a roll, nobody could make his wife laugh harder. In fact—at least while they were married—she came to share his worldview in almost every objective particular. "They seemed to connect very well," said Dot Parker. "One could start a thought and the other could finish it." Sheila was even amused (or acted that way) when she herself was the target of her husband's barbs, as with a routine of his that involved dancing a jig and singing a ribald ditty that began, "Oh my name is Gilhooley . . ."—nobody remembers the rest, but the gist of it was that Sheila's Irish background was more shabby than genteel, which (as Yates knew better than anyone) struck at the heart of some rather tenacious pretensions. By then, however, Sheila seemed to know better than to engage Yates in a battle of wit, and was more inclined to sit back and enjoy the show as best she could. "Ever since I first met you," she later wrote him,

> I've been so awed by your intellectual and aesthetic *quality*, that I've been dogged by a feeling of never being quite able to make it. Your critical faculties are *never* suspended, and it never seems to require any effort on your part to keep this going—your taste and judgment seem to operate unerringly and inexhaustibly. . . . I know you'll say "Well, hell, I need to collapse, too," but when you do you go right on thinking and say more witty and observant things about Felix the Cat (or whatever it happens to be) than I could think of in a million years.

One might bear this *"quality"* in mind when trying to comprehend why Sheila persevered so long in the marriage, and also why it ultimately wore her out: That is, her husband's acuity—whether witty or vindictive or both, drunk or sober—was *"never"* suspended."

The lighter side of this quality is nicely illustrated by the Conrad Jones affair. In 1958 Bob Parker was named one of the "Bright Young Men in the Arts" by *Esquire,* and subsequently received a letter from one of the "Bright Young Men in Business," Conrad Jones: "Greetings! I feel a little pale in this select company and obliged to explain . . . that my inclusion is based probably on being the youngest partner (33) of the largest management consulting firm. . . . Maybe we 'bright young men' should know each other. This, then, is a standing invitation for you to stop in and get acquainted when you are in Chicago." Parker couldn't resist showing this exuberant letter to Yates, whose response was startlingly heated: A ruthless reprisal was in order, he insisted; long and bitter experience with such people (and their prose) convinced Yates that Jones was simply trying to wangle a business contact. Thus, while Sheila and the Parkers stood by with the odd suggestion, Yates found a blunt pencil and composed a response on his friend's behalf: "I surely do say 'yes' to finding common interests in our different lines. You say you feel pale Mr. Conrad, well you could of 'knocked me over with a feather' when I heard they were going to have me in the esquire [*sic*] magazine." As for Jones's invitation to visit, "it just so happen[ed]" (Yates wrote) that Parker and his wife would soon be in the Chicago area: "Therefore, please write me you're [*sic*] home street address number and telephone number (home) in case we get there after the close of business." He added a postscript: "Say! Do you bowl I could give you a pretty good game if you do!" They crumbled half a cookie into the envelope, addressed it in crayon (marked VERY PER-SONAL), and dropped it in the mail.

Jones didn't reply. "I guess some people think their [*sic*] better than others," began Yates's second note, and went on from there. Apparently Jones couldn't bear such a charge, and wrote back with the sort of civility and lack of irony that had led to his becoming the youngest partner (at thirty-three) of Booz, Allen and Hamilton. Jones pointed out that he and his family would be on vacation for three weeks in December, and suggested the Parkers visit either before or after; he gave his home phone number in Winnetka. Yates was delighted, and labored over his third and final letter with the kind of loving care he accorded his best fiction; the manuscript is heavily scored with strike-outs, subtle emendations, and long marginal second thoughts. "My dear Jones," began the flawlessly typed final draft,

> How nice to have your second note. And how distressing, alas, to find my cal-endar so filled with a sudden profusion of commitments here that I'm afraid our plans for a jaunt across the Great Plains must be set aside for a time. I may say that Mrs. Parker's disappointment is as keen as my own, and that nothing would have given us greater pleasure than to accept your hospitality at Winnetka (such a charming place-name—evokes visions of frosty pump-kins and so on, straight out of Whitcomb Riley).

The letter goes on for two more pages. "I've taken the liberty of passing your address to several friends," Yates wrote, "all of whom do plan west-ern junkets of one sort or another in the next few weeks." These "friends" included Bertrand Meubles, the lutanist; Bart Pardee, the beat novelist ("One can't altogether dismiss the charge of incoherence in his early 'Burn All Your Cities'* and 'Go, Man, Go!' "); Aubrey Creavey Ewing, the poet ("author of 'Trembling Shadows' [Nuance Press, 1956] in which the critic E. E. Toste found 'some of the most delicately tentative imagery in contemporary verse' "); P. Loomis Llewellyn ("who could be capable of unusual achievement . . . if his all-but-crippling emotional problem could be transcended"); and Max Klopp, the political scientist (author of "Marx, Man, and the Tyranny of the Middle Class"). One can only imagine what effect this had on Conrad Jones, who perhaps lost some of his innocence along the way.

Of course it's one thing to bait some faceless Babbitt in Winnetka, another to mock more or less inoffensive people—chiefly female—about matters over which they have no control. One of the more curious paradoxes of Yates's nature was his almost archaic courtliness toward women on the one hand, and his lifelong tendency to emphasize their physical defects and/or dubious upbringing on the other. "Margaret Truman" was how he referred to a tall, skinny woman whom a friend briefly dated, while another became "the druggist's daughter" because of her humble background in the Bronx. And once, when Yates was introduced to a young woman who exposed her upper gums when she smiled, he turned around and mimicked her with a precise ugly grimace. "In those days," said Bob Riche, "he reminded me of F. Scott Fitzgerald on the Côte d'Azur: an awful pain in the ass, but fun to be around."

More so than most, Yates was at his best among people he admired—generally those who combined talent with integrity, particularly other writers—and one explanation for his abrasiveness in the mid-fifties was that he knew very few people who fitted that description. Nor was he quite the sickly, uncertain, and mostly sober young man who'd gone to Europe to teach himself how to write; since then Yates had grown more

---

*Also the title of Chester Pratt's first novel in *Disturbing the Peace*—which suggests that, fifteen years later, Yates continued to reflect fondly on his Conrad Jones correspondence.

sure of his own essential talent, and this (plus alcohol) made him less patient with people he regarded as pretentious and self-deluding—who reminded him of Dookie, in short. But in 1958 Yates had the good fortune of meeting a few peers, and all the better that this should come about as the result of breakthroughs in his career.

Esquire had decided to buy "The B.A.R. Man" after all, whereupon fiction editor Rust Hills and his assistant took Yates out to lunch. As he later described the occasion, Yates listened with bored annoyance while the two editors "kept cracking each other up at the table with inside jokes and references that [Yates] couldn't follow." At one point, though, they mentioned R. V. Cassill, a name Yates recognized (barely, since he thought it was pronounced "*Cassill*") as the author of such excellent stories as "The Prize" and "The Biggest Band." When Yates expressed his admiration, Hills told him that *Cass*ill and his wife were living in New York and about to give a party, to which an extra invitation could easily be obtained. Yates was delighted, and his subsequent meeting with Verlin Cassill at the man's "ramshackle" Village apartment was (almost) an unqualified success:

> He was the first real writer I had ever met [Yates wrote], though I'd known plenty of the other kind, and he made an excellent first impression: an intense, black-haired man of thirty-eight or so, tired-looking and very courteous, with a voice so deep you had to lean a little forward in the party noise for fear of missing something. And even before that party was over, though his courtesy never flagged, I had found out something instructive about him. When Verlin says "Ah" in a certain way it means you have just said something dumb. It means he has decided to let you get away with it for now, but that if you don't start watching your mouth, in about a minute he may tear you apart—verbally, of course.

A long time would pass before Yates experienced the full effect of failing to heed that monitory "Ah," and in the meantime he benefited greatly from Cassill's many kindnesses. From the beginning, though, there were awkward moments, as when Cassill and his wife spent a weekend in Mahopac shortly after that first encounter: "There was a lot of drinking,"

Yates wrote, "and Verlin held forth at some length on 'marriage' as an abstract idea, which didn't go over very well with my wife and me because our own marriage was about to collapse, though we knew he couldn't possibly have known that." The visit improved when Cassill presented Sharon and Monica with toy airplanes he'd made out of balsa wood and rice paper, which flew for impressive distances with the help of a windup propeller. It seemed to Yates, then as later, that Cassill constructed such planes with the same craft and care he brought to his (and others') fiction: "He has always understood fine structure and firm surface, the coiling and release of power, and the necessary illusion of weightlessness. . . . Verlin understands wreckage, too."

The privilege of meeting his first "real writer" coincided with another encouraging development: Yates and three others were picked out of 250 candidates to be featured in Scribner's forthcoming *Short Story 1,* the first volume in a series meant to showcase promising new writers. Four of Yates's stories were selected for the collection: "Jody Rolled the Bones," "The Best of Everything," "Fun with a Stranger," and (at last) "A Really Good Jazz Piano." Moreover, Scribner's contract included an option on his next book—"a happy and peaceful solution to the long drawn-out Sam Lawrence flirtation," as Monica McCall put it, though Lawrence was not so easily put off. Like a fickle lover whose flame returns with jealousy, he tried to woo Yates back with honeyed words ("I have absolute faith in you as an author"), as well as a proposed two-book contract that would involve the novel-in-progress and a collection of short stories. For the moment, however, all he was really offering was an option of five hundred dollars, and McCall squelched him with the sort of acerbic curtness she reserved for Lawrence alone: "I fully appreciate your longtime interest in Dick Yates, but he does feel that he wants to make no commitments on the novel until the manuscript is finished to his satisfaction."

Short Story 1 was published in September 1958, and included stories by Yates, Gina Berriault, B. L. Barrett, and Seymour Epstein. Under the headline "Gifted Quartet," the *New York Times* commended Yates for his "skill and insight" as well as the "admirable variety" of his stories, but Epstein's work was more favorably noted, and the reviewer generally deplored an "emphasis on characterization at the expense of plot" and "the preponderance of unlikable character types." Granville Hicks in the *Saturday Review* called the four writers "talented and serious" but thought none was "quite first-rate," and the *New York Herald Tribune* was similarly equivocal: "Despite several small drawbacks, it is only fair to say that the trial is off to a distinguished start." The *San Francisco Chronicle*, however, picked Yates out of the lineup for a particularly nasty slur: "Yates presents the outward appearances of a bright new talent, but a close inspection of his four stories reveals that his stylistic graces are imitative, in the bad sense, of Scott Fitzgerald and other writers."

Yates's own favorite of the four was Gina Berriault, in whose exquisitely gloomy work he recognized a soul mate; he wrote her a fan letter that launched a lifelong mutual admiration. "I can't remember when I've enjoyed a letter as much as I did yours," she replied, adding that she had to accept his compliments because she had such respect for *his* work: "[Y]ou're a subtle, painstaking, warmhearted writer and so it follows that I believe what you say." Berriault was the same kind of writer, and in Yatesian terms an almost ideal human being: She approached her work with such humility that she was often incapable of doing it, yet cared about little else; unapologetically private, she professed not to know any critics, belong to any societies, or have any unusual anecdotes about herself. Berriault and Yates, a month apart in age, would not actually meet face to face for another eleven years, and rarely thereafter, but kept in touch and forever championed each other as writers and human beings. "Richard Yates is my guardian angel," she wrote, "one of the few or many who each of us has close by, even though they're continents away and centuries away. . . . They look after our conscience as we write just as they looked after their own." Yates looked after Berriault in more practical ways as well, helping her to get hired at the Iowa Workshop even though, like him, she had no college degree. He also named his third daughter after her, which gives one a sense of what Berriault ultimately meant to Yates, as well as what human qualities mattered in general.

He also became friends with Seymour Epstein, whom he met one day at the old Scribner's Building on Fifth Avenue. For the next few years they were frequent companions, though it was hardly a matter of deep calling to deep. "Dick was like a Janus head," said Epstein. "Two different people." One of these people, he concedes, was "charming and honorable" ("if somebody needed help in the world of writing, Dick would immediately put himself forward"), while the other was an "emotional parasite" who drank too much and went around "bleed[ing] on people." As for Yates's view of Epstein, one needn't look much further than *Disturbing the Peace,* in which the latter appears (through a jaundiced lens) as Paul Borg, a pharisaic bore.

As Yates entered his fourth year of obsessively precise labor—as the form of his novel gradually prevailed over chaos—his life deteriorated. Outside the wellhouse he was a sullen, coughing drunk, and Sheila steered clear as much as possible. About the only times he'd pull himself together were his biweekly trips to the Remington Rand offices, from which he generally returned sober. But one night he called home from Grand Central in a state of curious disorientation. "I can't get home," he said in a panic. "I don't know how to get home." Sheila wasn't sure what to make of this: He didn't sound drunk, though he'd been so "saturated with booze" the day before that it seemed plausible he was still affected by it; but that would hardly explain his frantic inability to negotiate a commute he'd made hundreds of times. Sheila finally got him to calm down and listen to careful instructions, and promised to meet him at the train. He was still "not right in the head" when he arrived, and clearly he hadn't been drinking.

By the beginning of 1959 Yates was a mental and physical wreck. In January he was hospitalized with an inguinal hernia—a congenital defect, made all the more painful by constant coughing fits. As for his being "not right in the head," it was some measure of how out of touch he'd become that he seemed amazed to learn that his marriage was not only troubled but moribund. Things came to a head when he was offered (through Cassill's good offices) a part-time teaching position at the Iowa Workshop. As he'd never ceased to believe that Remington Rand was at the bottom of his woes, Yates figured this was at least one solution, however temporary, though in fact he didn't much like the idea of leaving New York—and neither, to put it mildly, did Sheila.

When she couldn't find an elegant way to explain why she objected to moving out to the sticks with an unstable alcoholic, Yates accused her of not loving him anymore. Sheila wasn't inclined to deny it, and Yates decided she was insane. Very much in the manner of Frank Wheeler lecturing April on the definition of insanity, he took the position that her childhood had warped her as surely as Charlie—that she was, in effect, incapable of love. Sheila admitted she'd never been entirely sure what "love" was, but also pointed out that it didn't really matter in the present case. She was fed up, period. Mostly she was tired of all the roaring, repetitive arguments, eleven years' worth, and when Yates persisted she finally fell silent and refused to respond. "I wasn't as glib as he was," she said. "He could talk rings around me and everyone else, drunk or sober." In the end he wore her down sufficiently to persuade her that, as a last resort, they should see a marriage counselor.*

These sessions didn't work out the way Yates seemed to expect. Before long the counselor suggested that his drinking, not Sheila's emotionally deprived childhood, was the main problem. Yates in turn accused the woman of taking his wife's side against him, and finally became so belligerent that the counselor refused to see him anymore; she was only a psychiatric social worker, she said, and Yates's "serious disorders" were beyond her scope. Sheila, however, was welcome to continue and did, though the woman's advice was simple enough: Unless her husband agreed to stop drinking and get help, the marriage had to end. As for

---

*Yates retroactively incorporated these disputes into *Revolutionary Road*, as witnessed by Sheila's remark in a 1962 letter comparing the published novel with an earlier draft: "It seems to me now that both Frank's idea that [April] should be psychoanalyzed and her recognition of lack of love for him are new to the book, am I right?" Curiously enough Sheila later insisted that she'd never read *Revolutionary Road* in its entirety: "Our relations were such that last year he was working on it that I didn't *want* to read it. It was too uncomfortable. . . . I couldn't take the constant agonizing over every word of it. I had other interests by then." She also claims she had no idea the novel was dedicated to her until very recently, when her daughter Monica showed her the 2000 Vintage edition ("It came as a complete surprise," said Sheila, "though it makes sense"). But of course she *did* read the novel. According to the letter quoted above, she found it "a great creation, and the writing extraordinarily fine," and went on to make a number of more specific observations. For what it's worth, I myself am convinced that Sheila—whose memory is clear as a bell in most respects—has sincerely persuaded herself over the past forty years that she never read the published novel. Yates once mentioned to his psychiatrist that Sheila, a few years after the divorce, told him the book had hurt her feelings and that she'd never read his work since. Yates was crushed.

Yates, he was only too happy to discuss the matter further at home: that is, to explain that his drinking was *not* a relevant issue. "By then," said Sheila, "I just wanted a good night's sleep."

They decided to separate, neither of them in any particular rush to go through the "needless expense" of divorce unless one or the other found somebody else to marry. As for Yates's immediate plans, he couldn't bear the thought of being in a strange place without his children; later that summer, then, he wired Paul Engle at the Iowa Workshop that "other commitments" had come up, though he hoped a "similar opportunity may exist at some future date." Verlin Cassill, who was moving to Iowa in the fall, had arranged for Yates to take over his writing class at the New School for Social Research. In August, Yates moved back to the city.

CHAPTER SEVEN

A Glutton for Punishment: 1959-1961

For a week or so Yates floated among his few friends in the city, sober only for such intervals required to skim the classifieds and look at the odd apartment. For a couple of nights he stayed with Bob Riche on Jones Street, where he ended up vomiting on the rug. In later years the unfading stain never failed to remind Riche of Yates, who for his part would occasionally refer to "the time [he] ruined Bob's rug" in a doleful voice, as though it had been a very dark time indeed.

The basement apartment Yates rented near Sheridan Square on the corner of Seventh Avenue South and Bedford Street was a prototype for the various places he'd inhabit as a bachelor in the years ahead. It was cramped, dark, bare, roach-infested, nicotine-stained, and deeply depressing to his friends and children. Yates came to accept their perception of his new apartment as accurate (though he'd go on living there, on and off, for five years), but when he first discovered the place he could hardly believe his luck: It was dirt cheap and conveniently located near the New School and his old haunts. There was even a small street-level window where he could relieve his claustrophobia by watching the feet of fellow Villagers pass to and fro. All he had to do was move in a few wan belongings—bed, sling chairs, bookcase (small), desk, typewriter, gooseneck lamp, map of London—and get back to writing his novel. Visitors were struck by certain awful details to which Yates himself seemed oblivious: the bloodstains on his deskchair cushion (from piles), the calm roaches in plain sight, nothing but bourbon and instant coffee in the tiny kitchen. Peter Najarian, one of Yates's New School students, was haunted by the memory of 27 Seventh Avenue South; later, when he learned of Yates's death, he thought of "thirty-three years ago when Richard lived in that basement studio"—as he wrote in *The Great American Loneliness*: " 'Love Genius,' Blake said, 'it is the face of God.' But why the cigarettes and bourbon . . . why the misery for the sake of a line, what kind of love was it that shoved a man into a basement and made him want to escape through art?"

Escape of one sort or another was much on Yates's mind. He had deep misgivings about being a teacher, given his furtive conviction that writing couldn't be taught, or at any rate that he wasn't the person to teach it. Within days of moving into the basement he was clearly panicking at the prospect; he asked Cassill and Sam Lawrence to recommend him for an immediate place at the Yaddo and MacDowell colonies respectively, where perhaps he could finish his novel that very fall and forgo the trauma of teaching altogether. Yates would later make a practice of escaping to such places (particularly Yaddo) at troubled times in his life—but not now. Though Cassill and Lawrence were happy to oblige with glowing letters in his behalf, no spots were available on short notice, and Yates had little alternative but to report to the classroom as planned. "My New School class began yesterday," he wrote a friend, "after a semi-sleepless night of certainty that I'd make a Hopeless Fool out of myself"—this in regard to his first class of the Fall 1960 semester; one can only imagine how he'd felt the year before.

But Yates was desperate enough to put aside his anxiety and give teaching a try. He could think of no more demoralizing prospect, after all, than an indefinite future of PR work—insipid, time-consuming, exhausting, and damaging to one's talent, not to mention sanity. To be sure, the New School per se (where he was paid all of $450 per class a semester) wasn't going to liberate him from Remington Rand, but graduate writing programs were becoming a kind of cottage industry, and Yates knew he'd have to build his credentials in order to get a secure footing at places that paid real money (e.g., Iowa). The New School, then, was the ground floor, but even at that humble level Yates was daunted—indeed, could hardly believe a man with only a high school education had any business teaching at all. Whatever else he lacked, it wasn't humility.

For a number of reasons, the New School was perhaps the ideal place to start. The program, founded by editor Hiram Haydn (who continued to watch Yates's career with interest), managed to attract a number of good writers who happened to be down on their luck. "If you were teaching at the New School, you acknowledged you weren't making it," said Sidney Offit, one of Yates's colleagues along with Marguerite Young, Anatole Broyard, and Seymour Epstein. The upside of such tacit failure was that very few demands were made—no lesson plans, no meetings, no scrutiny. The head of the program, Hayes Jacobs, was a witty, easygoing man whose own writing had been almost entirely forfeited to the exigencies of teaching and hackwork (including Remington Rand); far from insisting that others follow his lead, Jacobs had become all the more laissez-faire toward his betters on the faculty. He and Yates got along famously.

New School teachers were on their own to the extent of having to compete for students, and this involved writing eye-catching course descriptions, lest a class be canceled for lack of interest. "Write it like a billboard," Broyard advised Sidney Offit. "Yours is too understated." The course description Yates wrote for *his* class ("Writing the Short Story. Thursdays, 10:30 A.M.–12:10 P.M.") was nothing if not understated, though it managed to convey exactly the type of student Yates wanted, inasmuch as he wanted students at all: "Emphasis is on the craft and art of the short story as a serious fictional form, rather than on its commercial possibilities." This was meant to warn away what Yates came to call the "dunces," "clowns," and "nice-biddy hobbyists" who expected to launch a lucrative sideline writing potboilers for the *Saturday Evening Post*.

The later Yates who taught at the Iowa Workshop and sometimes liked to end sessions by, say, tossing a copy of *All the King's Men* into a trashcan (and kicking it for emphasis) was little in evidence at the New School. "Melancholy" is the first word that occurs to Lucy Davenport when she encounters the Yatesian teacher Carl Traynor in *Young Hearts Crying*, and the same word came to Peter Najarian's lips when he recalled his own New School class with Yates. "He didn't seem into teaching," said Najarian. "People would read their work and Dick would comment on it. He was intelligent, gentle, but reticent and a little unprepared. He seemed very unsure of himself. It was clear that this was the first time he'd taught." At the New School, Yates tended to be conciliatory to a fault—like Carl Traynor he'd "try to appease every difference of opinion in the room"—largely because he didn't think it his business to disparage the dunces, clowns, and nice-biddy hobbyists who populated most of his classes. But even then, students who were serious about writing and sought Yates's opinion in private could always expect consideration and total candor.

Najarian was perhaps the most noteworthy example of such a student from Yates's first year. In a letter to Cassill, Yates referred to Najarian as "a nineteen-year-old ex–juvenile delinquent (male) who's so loaded with talent it's almost a crime in itself." As with all students who ever struck him as such, Yates took great pains with the young man: He recommended Najarian's work for inclusion in Hayes Jacobs's anthology *New Voices*, and responded to his stories with typed critiques that were blunt, funny, and generous:

> "Theodore Schwertheim" was the only one of these [stories] that really interested me, because it's the one in which I sense the clearest detachment between writer and material. Theodore is truly poignant because you have taken the trouble to see him in the round; the others tend to be flat—quick illustrations of assorted human traits rather than real people. Your wisecrack about Sherwood Anderson at the end spares me the job of telling you who it derives from, but I'm not sure if I'd have bothered pointing that out anyway. The only way to get over being derivative is to go on writing until your own style evolves, and you've got plenty of time and ability for that.

He was also willing to meet informally with Najarian outside class, as it didn't occur to Yates then (and never would) that as a teacher he should make a distinction between students and drinking companions. An intense young man who desperately wanted to be a writer, Najarian took it upon himself to track Yates down to his subterranean lair, whereupon the latter poured him a tumbler of bourbon and listened gravely to whatever he had to say. Later, when they got hungry, they went to Chumley's restaurant and bar. "You are worth a thousand professors even though you do not know Latin, German, French, and why T. S. Eliot is god," Najarian wrote Yates once the class was over.

Yates's own attitude toward his teaching remained skeptical at best, though at the end of that first year he waxed enthusiastic for Cassill's benefit: "I've had a real ball at the New School and can't thank you enough for the job," he wrote with courteous hyperbole, and went on to say that while he hoped to teach the class again next year, he'd been advised that "some clown named Don M. Wolfe might be returning from Europe" to take over the job: "I'm quite prepared for your taking over again in the fall, but I would resent the hell out of being squeezed out by this Wolfe character (and who but a shithead would bill himself as 'Don M.' anyway?)." Happily neither Wolfe nor Cassill returned, and the job remained Yates's for as long as he wanted it.

Next to finishing his novel, Yates's most urgent priority was to find a steady female companion. Night was a time of peculiar dread when he was alone, scarcely less so as a grown man than as a child sitting in the dark waiting for his mother to come home. He drank to get to sleep, and also to control a nervous desperation that threatened to overwhelm him since his marriage had ended. Such instability was hardly conducive to attracting even the most motherly, well meaning, or for that matter unconventional young woman—at least two of whom vividly remember, more than forty years later, their disquieting one-night encounters with the newly single Yates. Betty Rollin was a recent Sarah Lawrence graduate when Bob Riche introduced the two at a Village party.* Yates seemed charming and well spoken (if a bit too old), and Rollin allowed herself to be coaxed back to his apartment for a drink. But the ambience of the basement unnerved her, and she suddenly sensed that all was not well with her host: "There was something broken about the man," she recalled, "as if he'd *been* through something. His talk was breezy and he had a good sense of humor, but I got the impression he was covering up a lot of darkness." Rollin had no further contact with Yates, nor did Gail Richards

---

*Rollin went on to become a celebrity of sorts as a writer and NBC news correspondent. She's perhaps best known for the book *First You Cry,* about her mastectomy.

after a single dinner at the Blue Mill. Richards was twenty-one when she met Yates through Rust Hills at *Esquire*. At first she was rather attracted by his brooding quality—but something more unsettling emerged at the Blue Mill: "I thought I was witnessing the beginning of a breakdown," she said. "I wasn't easily scared off in those days—a certain amount of angst was interesting—but this was outside my comprehension. He had a kind of fractured intensity: distraught, jumpy, anxious, with these very busy gesticulating hands." And no matter what Yates's terrible need at the time, neither episode was simply a matter of first-date jitters; the unanimous impression among his acquaintances, male or female, was that he was fighting a losing battle to hold himself together. "It was exhausting to be in his company," said Warren Owens, who'd met Yates shortly after his separation. "He showed constant signs of strain—smoking, fidgeting, knocking over glasses. I was always happy to see Dick, but just as happy to leave him."

Yates's quest for a mate sometimes took him far afield. In November 1959 he and Bob Parker went on a road trip to a Montreal television studio to watch a live performance of "The Best of Everything," adapted for the Canadian Broadcasting Company. The excursion was the basis for a memorable scene in *Young Hearts Crying,* in which Tom Nelson remarks to Davenport, "You figure there'll be some nice girl in the show, and she'll come up to you with big eyes and say 'You mean you're the *author?*' "— and Davenport takes offense, since that was exactly what he (and Yates) *had* figured. Bob Parker points out that the fictional version of this incident is "accurate in almost every respect," except for the "insidious motives" attributed to himself in the person of Tom Nelson. Indeed, Parker remembers a rather pleasant outing, quite devoid of friction as far as he could tell at the time. The only abrasive teasing took place at the Canadian border, where Parker made fun of a Mountie's hat, but the rest of the drive was a cheerful wintry idyll. And then in Montreal, just as the lonely Yates had hoped, there *was* "some nice girl in the show" who thought highly of his story and writers in general, and she *did* invite both men back to her house and, yes, it *was* a little awkward. But as Parker wrote in his essay "A Clef"—a barbed rebuttal to *Young Hearts Crying*— there was no question of his refusing, à la Tom Nelson, to take the hint and leave Yates alone with an actress ripe for seduction: "Yates was so preoccupied with the whiskey that he didn't notice the glazed look in her eyes. She finally said to me, 'I'm going to bed. Tell him to leave some of Daddy's liquor.'"*

Yates's ongoing funk may have discouraged romance, but it was rarely without its lighter side. Once, when he and Riche were having a diner breakfast after a long night, Yates wandered off to get cigarettes out of a machine and inadvertently put his quarter into the jukebox instead (after a puzzled moment he selected "Love Me Tender"). And sometimes he'd channel his "fractured intensity" into madcap improvisational shticks, such as the blocked songwriter at the piano: "Baked Alaska! Baked Alaska!" he'd sing to the tune of "K-K-K-Katie," then scratch his head and mutter, "No no, that's not it." Or else he'd invent wacky variations on clichéd movie scenarios, his favorite being *A Star Is Born*; Yates adored the idea of the washed-up husband dying for the sake of an ascendant, noble wife, and liked to ponder the many diverting ways such a situation might come to pass.

In some respects Yates's "second bachelorhood" (as he called it) began to look up when he befriended his New School colleague, Anatole Broyard. For a decade or so, Broyard's stories had appeared in prestigious little magazines, and Yates had lasting respect for him not only as the author of "some of the finest autobiographical fiction [he'd] ever read," but also as a wit whose various *mots* Yates quoted for many years. In the early days, though, the larger part of Broyard's reputation rested on his being— as the writer Anne Bernays (a former girlfriend) put it—"the greatest cocksman in New York for a decade"; she also called him "a mean man," and was not alone in thinking so, particularly among women. Cassill, who lived around the corner from Broyard in the late fifties, would often step

---

*"A Clef" was accepted by *Grand Street* in 1985 but never published, perhaps out of consideration for Yates's feelings or (more likely) because of concerns that it was libelous. Parker's version of the Montreal story is mostly true, no doubt, but subjective: In fact the young actress was impressed enough by Yates to write him a few letters afterward, in the first of which she apologized for the awful CBC adaptation of his story: "I felt we deserved all the indifference, contempt, and, what was worse, your tired acceptance, as if one could expect no more from provincial actors." One will return to such matters as this actress and Parker's "A Clef" by and by.

out to get a morning newspaper and spot his illustrious neighbor escorting a young woman home or to school. As for Broyard's friendship with Yates, it puzzled Cassill for a while, and then it didn't: "Dick was forthright, honest, a bit unsophisticated at times. Broyard was the opposite: mendacious, crafty, disingenuous. But he had a success formula with women, and Dick envied that. He'd come to New York to lead a bolder life, and Broyard was a model for this life."

Certainly Yates needed all the laughs he could get, and Broyard had a nice way of working ribaldry into even the most elevated discourse. Of a writer well-known to both, Broyard told Yates, "Reading him is like the guy trying to fuck his girlfriend on the beach, but his dick keeps falling in the sand. Finally he gets it in and the girl says, 'Put it back in the sand.'" Broyard was perhaps Yates's first writer friend for whom literature was a digression rather than the main theme. Some twenty years later, when another of Yates's friends was wondering whether to circumcise his first son, Yates remarked how Broyard used to brag about the way women liked to play with his foreskin during fellatio. At the time Yates was mostly amused, but also a little appalled: "Anatole goes up to the Museum of Modern Art on Friday afternoons," he told Cassill, "picks up a nice girl from a good college, takes her home for the weekend—then kicks her out. And they *love* him for this. I go to bed with *one* of them and they want to marry me!" But then Yates was grateful for whatever odd success came his way, and Broyard's example was something of an inspiration.

A month or so after Yates's marriage ended, Sam Lawrence had come to New York and commiserated with Yates at the Harvard Club ("one of the most fruitful non-literary discussions we have had in a long time," Lawrence noted a few days later). Yates, perhaps touched by the man's sympathy, agreed at last to accept an option payment of one thousand dollars giving Atlantic Monthly Press first consideration of his novel, then titled *Contemporary Life on the Eastern Seaboard*. Such an option, however, was already held by Scribner's via the *Short Story 1* contract, until a disgruntled Charles Scribner agreed to release Yates with the epistolary equivalent of scraping something nasty off his shoe: "This option was very important in our agreeing to publish [your] stories . . . and we thought this was a commitment in good faith on your part. On the other hand, our Firm does not like to bring out the work of anyone wishing to change publishers."

In mid-March 1960, after five years of labor that had wreaked havoc on his health and personal life, Yates informed Sam Lawrence that he'd finished his novel. Or rather, almost: On second thought he decided to take another six weeks in order to get "every sentence right, every comma and semicolon in place"—until, on May 5, he was able to write Cassill, "My book is finally done, as of last Monday, and is now being typed by a lovely blonde named Suzanne Schwertley who was a student in your New School class two years ago and says she found it (or you; it's hard to tell which) 'fascinating.' Nice girl, too."* A week later the freshly typed manuscript was mailed to Lawrence, who in the meantime had recommended Yates for a scholarship to the Bread Loaf Writers' Conference later that summer: "Although you may not learn too much there," he wrote Yates, "it should be a pleasant break from the New York treadmill." Lawrence of all people appreciated how badly his friend needed a break.

For Yates, of course, it remained to be seen whether the past five years had been well or ill spent—at least according to the judgment of Sam Lawrence, whose treatment of his work had tended to be capricious at best. But this time there was no room for doubt, nor did Lawrence keep him in suspense: "I spent the entire weekend reading *Revolutionary Road*," he wrote Yates on May 17, "and I was impressed and struck with its dramatic force, the dimensions of its themes, and the mature professional control of your narrative." It was, in short, an "extraordinary

---

*Suzanne Schwertley's place in literary history must be reduced to a footnote—that is, as the woman who typed the final draft of *Revolutionary Road*. According to Bob Riche, she was also romantically involved with Yates, who "dropped her like a hotcake" as soon as she finished the typing job. Riche described her as a "nice but rather sad woman" in her late thirties whom Yates "kept under wraps." After the couple parted, Riche distinctly remembers her describing Yates as "a thug." Whether Yates's cavalier thuggishness was the bitter exaggeration of a woman scorned, or perhaps a passing effect of Broyard's Svengalian influence, or pure invention, will have to remain a mystery, as Schwertley could not be traced for an interview.

performance," as Lawrence wrote in his two-page editorial report, which emphasized the novel's universality (as opposed to its derivative Sloan Wilsonish triteness) and recommended immediate acceptance:

> Yates is dealing with very real problems of the mid-century American. . . . Frank Wheeler is the prototype of thousands of young Americans who have been in the war, got married too early, began a family by mistake, taken a job which they are indifferent to, and then try to make their lives and marriages work. Frank is intelligent enough to know he is trapped, but he doesn't have anything he really believes in or wants instead. . . . There are a few minor changes to be made—an over-emphasis on what it means to be "a man" and the harangues on what is wrong with American life. But these *are* minor, and I would be glad to see the book published exactly as it is. . . . Richard Yates is speaking for his generation, and he is speaking forcefully, and truly, and alas, tragically.

One notes with a cocked eyebrow that little mention is made of April Wheeler—that she too is "trapped," say, and for that matter the main victim of the tragedy—though Lawrence tags her in passing as "spirited, defiant"; one assumes there were few if any women on the Atlantic–Little, Brown editorial board. As for changing Frank's "harangues" against America, Yates may have pointed out that these were intended to be somewhat ironic, ditto that stuff about being "a man," since the book was indeed published almost "exactly as it is."

For years Yates's life had seemed a pretty hapless affair, but suddenly he began to get one good break after another. Little, Brown not only concurred with Lawrence's opinion of *Revolutionary Road,* they agreed to increase the author's advance to $2,500 (in exchange for 10 percent of the radio, movie, and television sales). A few days later Lawrence wrote Yates, "Congratulations on your Bread Loaf scholarship! Everything seems to be coming your way, and I hope this establishes a pattern. Now all that's left is Marilyn Monroe." The next week Yates traveled to Boston to sign the novel contract as well as a separate contract for a book of short stories, after which he and Lawrence had a "funny evening" on the town that eventually petered out because the latter couldn't show Yates "more of the night life, [because] there wasn't any to show." One matter they seemed to have discussed over bourbon and sirloins was the clinical accuracy of April Wheeler's abortion technique, as Lawrence followed up by suggesting Yates consult *Babies by Choice or Chance* by Alan F. Cuttmacher.

All this was good for morale, but the problem of sustenance remained. The advance from Little, Brown was in payment for five years of work, during which Yates's literary income had been next to nothing—a bit of math that boded ill for a man paying alimony and child support each month. Bob Parker suggested he try for a Guggenheim Fellowship; Yates had invited the artist to the city to discuss the possibility of illustrating his novel's jacket (in terms of its latest title, *An Outrage in Toyland*), and when Parker saw the "ugly, damp" basement on Seventh Avenue, he began casting about for ways to extricate Yates. Sam Lawrence was skeptical— "[I]t's practically impossible for a young writer to win a Guggenheim if he has not already published a book"—but he was also keenly aware of Yates's bottom line, and urged him to go ahead and apply. For his part Lawrence tried to recruit such eminent sponsors as the critic Alfred Kazin, who doubted he could oblige but agreed to serve as an advance reader of *Revolutionary Road*. Meanwhile Yates began to draft a Guggenheim statement concerning a novel he wanted to write about World War II: "Owing to its autobiographical nature I was reluctant to start work on it until I had first learned to write a more objective novel. That book is now finished."

That book was now finished except for a title. After *An Outrage in Toyland* was scrapped, Yates was tempted to return to *Revolutionary Road,* but his publisher was adamantly opposed; such a title, thought Lawrence, made the book seem "a work of history and not a contemporary novel." Lawrence continued: "Several of us did like *The Players,* but there was no overriding enthusiasm for it. Someone did suggest that perhaps you could keep the word 'Road,' but simply substitute another one for 'Revolutionary.' " Lawrence thought *Morningside Road* had a nice ring to it, but on second thought liked *Generation of Strangers* even better. The writer Dan Wakefield remembers visiting Atlantic Monthly Press and being told by Lawrence's associate, Peter Davison, "We have a terrific novel with a lousy title"; he then showed Wakefield a list of ten alternative titles and asked his opinion.* By August, Lawrence was leaning toward *A Connecticut Tragedy,* while Yates was reverting back to *Revolutionary Road.*

What seemed fairly certain at the time, snappy title or no, was that Yates was on the brink of becoming a somewhat famous writer—perhaps even a Voice of His Generation—and this made him a little less insecure about meeting other famous writers. "He used to stand around at parties of mine, looking sad and wondering what William Styron and William Humphrey were doing," said Bob Parker twenty-five years later, as he tried to remind a mutual friend who Richard Yates was. This is a bit much, but not without a kind of glancing malicious insight—that is, Yates (at least as a younger man) did seem to harbor a wistful desire to know the writers he admired, and to be admired in turn. But as long as he was little more than the obscure author of a few promising stories, he felt painfully unworthy in the presence of those who'd made it. Kay Cassill remembers that his early "awe" of her husband often bordered on the uncomfortable, and when Yates met the charismatic founder of the Iowa Workshop, Paul Engle, he seemed "shaken by the experience." Naturally he might have preferred for this sort of thing to work the other way around. Though modest about his work to an almost detrimental degree, Yates didn't lack a certain Fitzgeraldian zest for fame—for meeting other writers (intellectuals too) on an equal or superior footing. As Orwell pointed out, one of the "four great motives for writing" (indeed the paramount motive) is "sheer egoism": "Writing a book is a horrible, exhausting struggle, like a long bout of some painful illness. One should never undertake such a thing if one were not driven on by some demon whom one can neither resist nor understand." Yates had any number of demons,

---

*Such titles included *A Cry of Prisoners, Losers, Nectar in a Sieve, The Fiasco, The Big Nothing, Oak Hill, A House in the Country, A Rampage in Cellophane, The Acid Soil,* and (Yates's "working title" according to a friend) *The Bullshit Artist.*

one of the more benign of which was a longing to be taken seriously by people who counted.

He was therefore elated on learning that William Styron had read galleys of *Revolutionary Road* and declared it "A deft, ironic, beautiful novel that deserves to be a classic." Styron was akin to being the ultimate golden person in Yates's eyes: Though the same age, he'd already published three books, including *Lie Down in Darkness,* which Yates considered one of the best American novels of the postwar era. Not only that, but Styron was rich, charming, and accessible, a friend to the famous and less-than-famous in all walks of life, a man who'd never been reduced to the kind of "grubby little writing for hire" that had left Yates so exhausted at the age of thirty-four. In short—to paraphrase *Uncertain Times* (in which Styron appears as "Paul Cameron")—he would have made Yates weak with envy if it hadn't been clear from the start that he considered Yates a good writer too. "I smoke too much" was the first line out of Yates's mouth on meeting Styron ("that might have been his *last* line as well," Styron remarked at Yates's memorial service); he then launched into a detailed encomium of *Lie Down in Darkness.* Styron responded in kind: He had not only read Yates's novel but several short stories as well, and admired them all. And since both men liked to drink ("Dick was always lubricating his thoughts with alcohol," said Styron), it was an auspicious meeting. "He's a great guy," Yates later wrote a friend, "the least pretentious celebrity I've ever met." Nor would he ever find cause to change that opinion, a rare enough phenomenon in itself.

That summer he also met the poet Marianne Moore at an exhibition of Bob Parker's work at a posh Madison Avenue gallery. Their chat was engrossing enough for Parker's mother to feel left out; on the other hand, Moore didn't have much use for contemporary fiction, and Yates's interest in poetry was roughly limited to Keats, so there it was. Still, Yates's tipsy-but-dignified poise in the great woman's presence was such that it stuck in Parker's mind, as did a subsequent exchange on a train. Calling Yates's attention to a tall, bug-eyed conductor, Parker said, "If he took his hat off, he'd look just like you." Yates was not amused. "I don't look at *all* like that guy!" he exploded. Parker was startled: Such ragging was typical of the friendship, and Yates had always taken it (and returned it) in stride. But no more, apparently, and Parker wasn't alone in noticing this. As Bob Riche remarked, "A self-effacing, insecure, self-denigrating guy suddenly saw himself as different than before. His life changed dramatically (for the worse, I think) from that point on."

Yates's coming out as a soon-to-be-celebrated author took place at the Bread Loaf Writers' Conference that August. The two-week gathering was in part a pastoral alcoholic boondoggle, particularly so for the designated "scholars" such as Yates, whose optional duties included critiquing the odd apprentice manuscript and attending to their own work amid the rustle and birdsong of the Vermont woods. For Yates it was a long-deferred and richly deserved vacation, and he made the most of it.

Bob Riche also went to Bread Loaf that year, as did a couple of Yates's fellow teachers at the New School, Edward Lewis Wallant and Arthur Roth. All were about the same age and believed themselves on the verge of greatness, and together they rode the bus to Vermont. Yates set the tone by approaching the prettiest, most dauntingly well-groomed girl and asking if she, too, was bound for Bread Loaf; she gave him a nodding smile, and Yates returned to his seat with an anticipatory swagger. On arrival, however, the young woman fell in with a Dartmouth man, and for the next few days Yates would bellow *"Booo, Dartmouth!"* whenever the two passed by.

Some ten scholars roomed in the same cottage, resulting in a "drunken and frantic" atmosphere, in Yates's words. Nobody got much writing done. When they weren't swapping stories or holding profane literary arguments, Yates would loudly croon his repertoire of Broadway standards one after the other, word for word, verse and refrain. Nor was he any more decorous in public, particularly where Bob Riche was concerned. A lot of good-natured, foul-mouthed banter had passed between the two over the years, but now Yates seemed frankly contemptuous of his old friend. "Others were still dunces," Riche said, "but he himself was no longer that." As ever, Riche tried to give as well as he got, but lacked Yates's "authority of success"—as Fitzgerald would have it—and sometimes came across as petulant and ridiculous. One night in a local restaurant the two regaled their fellow scholars by roaring insults at each other; when a waiter asked them to lower their voices, a defensive Riche turned on a tablemate and asked why *he* was being so quiet. The man stood up and offered to fight Riche, who left the restaurant in a huff. By then Yates appeared to feel sorry for his friend and patiently coaxed him back inside, but when Riche learned the kitchen had since closed, he burst into tears.

When Yates's antic behavior wasn't mingled with contempt, he got along fine with staff and scholars alike. He felt a particular rapport with the black writer John A. Williams, who called the frail Yates "Dreadnought Dick" and lured him into a drunken touch-football game. To Yates's enduring amazement, he managed to catch Williams's pass and run for a touchdown (perhaps the last instance of athletic exertion in Yates's life).* Every other morning the two would walk to the state liquor store and stock up for their ongoing symposia on jazz, writing, and race in the scholars' cottage. Both were war veterans, and Yates was curious about the discrimination Williams had suffered as a black soldier relegated to rear-echelon service. A related subject was the dilemma of being a black writer in 1960: "I well remember," Williams wrote Yates ten years later, "even then how much of an outsider I felt, not racially, but professionally. The world belonged to you, Wallant . . . and others."

Ed Wallant and Yates did, in fact, seem to have a lot in common. For many years Wallant had supported his family in the suburbs by working for an advertising agency; he'd become the firm's art director by the time he began to write seriously at the age of thirty, and within four years he'd published one novel and finished another. "And speaking of incredible," Yates noted a month after Bread Loaf, "Ed Wallant has practically

---

*Williams appears as Arnold Clark in *Uncertain Times*: "Grove had met Arnold Clark at a summer writers' conference where a cheerful kind of touch football had been played on idle afternoons; and Clark, playing quarterback, had helped him briefly to overcome a chronic aversion to sports by saying 'Sure you can' when Grove said he didn't think he could go out and catch a long forward pass. Grove went out, the pass came high and fast, and he not only picked it out of the air like a real player but carried it thirty dizzy yards for a touchdown, to the beer-bloated cheers of at least a hundred people."

sold his *second* novel, this one having taken him a whole seven months to write (his first one took him all of five, the little bastard)." Wallant's just-completed second novel was *The Pawnbroker,* a minor classic of Holocaust fiction that was nominated with *Revolutionary Road* for the 1962 National Book Award. Not surprisingly, Yates was galled by Wallant's facility (he referred to the latter's third novel as a "premature ejaculation"), both as a matter of jovial envy and because he sincerely believed the man's work suffered as a result. Yates even tried to argue with Wallant about it, rather in the manner of Fitzgerald's telling Thomas Wolfe to be more like Flaubert than Zola, and with roughly the same effect. As it turned out, Wallant and Wolfe seem to have been driven by the same weird awareness, conscious or otherwise, that time was short.

Meanwhile, amid the boozy disputes and touch football, love was in the air. Bob Riche met his future wife that year at Bread Loaf, a happy occasion dampened only slightly by the fact that Yates didn't approve—this, Riche opined, because the woman was only five foot one ("Dick wasn't crazy about short people"), blind in one eye, and had been abandoned at birth—the last a detail Yates found peculiarly telling. "[She's] the greatest thing that ever happened to me," Riche reflected forty years later. "But it was not helpful having a guy who was pretty much my best friend at the time calling her 'the orphan.' "

Perhaps Yates was too besotted, in every sense, to be tactful. One day in the dining hall he spotted a pretty blond waitress struggling with a heavy tray. He rushed over to help her carry it, then shyly offered her a flower from his table. Ed Kessler, a Rutgers graduate student at Bread Loaf that year, observed that Yates's "Lost Soul quality" was apt to be found attractive by the kind of women who went to writers' conferences. Barbara Singleton Beury, the scholarship waitress in question, was decidedly one of these: A student at Sweet Briar (just like Peyton Loftis), she'd come to Bread Loaf in order to meet some real writers and, if possible, to become one herself. Yates was a real writer, all right, while in his eyes Beury was that Gatsbyesque abstraction, a genteel Southern girl with sensibility. Yates dubbed her his "Sweet Briar Sweetie" and could hardly believe his luck—was it all, he wondered later, some kind of hallucination? "Because that's exactly what I often think it was," he wrote Beury, "the whole magical business of meeting a golden girl in an alcoholic mist on a mountain."

The chaste courtship that began at Bread Loaf was to be resumed immediately in New York. Beury's roommate and best friend at the conference, Maria Sebastiani, was sailing back to Rome the following weekend, and Beury came to the city to see the girl off and visit her new suitor. As it happened, the two young women would have done better to say good-bye in Vermont.

For a full year now Yates had been skirting the abyss: He missed his wife and daughters to the point of desperation, and the frantic labor he'd poured into the final stretch of his novel, combined with teaching and Remington Rand, had left him ripe for a crisis. "A massive lethargy set in as soon as the novel was out of my hands," he wrote Cassill; "I've been feeling empty and lazy as hell ever since." Such moods of postpartum depression, as it were, began to alternate with overwhelming waves of elation or panic that only massive amounts of alcohol could allay. As another manic-depressive (who knew Yates well) explained, "We feel so *off* all the time, like a thermostat is forty degrees off. Alcohol is a way to medicate that uneasiness."* Yates's own uneasiness had risen steadily over the past few years, until at last—at the relatively tardy age of thirty-four—he could no longer stave off a full-blown breakdown.†

The first night of Barbara Beury's visit—Thursday, September 1— appears to have been merely hilarious. Yates drank the usual stupendous amount, but his twenty-year-old date figured "that's what writers did." They spent the evening with his friends Arthur and Ruth Roth, who

---

*An NIMH study found that almost half (46 percent) of those diagnosed with bipolar, or manic-depressive, disorder are also dependent on alcohol or drugs. As Kay Jamison points out, "Alcohol and drug abuse often worsens the overall course of manic-depressive illness, occasionally precipitates the disease in vulnerable individuals, and frequently undermines the effects of treatment." This was preeminently so in Yates's case.

†Onset of the illness usually occurs in late adolescence, though Yates's experience is not uncommon. Initial episodes tend to be triggered by unusual stress or personal losses; later episodes occur more or less spontaneously.

fawned over Yates's young lady and called the couple "Zelda and F. Scott FitzYates." Beury's thick Southern accent was West Virginian rather than Alabaman in origin, but like Zelda she was a bit fey and fancied herself a writer, and while Yates had never read her stuff (being, as he put it, too "drunk and self-absorbed" at Bread Loaf), he assumed it was the work of a rare soul, and persisted in calling her his "golden girl." Finally, slumped over the Roths' table, he mumbled something about marriage.

The next evening Beury and her friend Maria Sebastiani were supposed to meet Yates at his apartment and go out to dinner. Just prior to their arrival, Yates made a raving phone call to Sheila; whatever he was trying to say remained wholly unintelligible, and finally she told him to stay put while she called their only mutual friend in the city, Seymour Epstein. Beury and Maria got there first. "He was crying, hysterical, babbling," Beury recalled. "He'd laugh uncontrollably, and then burst into tears. He'd been drinking a lot. I didn't know what to do." This was overstepping the bounds of writerly eccentricity to be sure, and Yates would hasten to lend perspective in a subsequent letter to Beury:

> The worst possible way for a young lady to be introduced to her suitor is for him to have a nervous breakdown in her lap, and nobody is more painfully aware of that fact than me. But I also know . . . that there are certain happenings which nobody on earth can help. (This is the secret of tragedy in writing, by the way, and it's also the secret of comedy.) Please understand that I have never been as "crazy" (i.e. disorderly, irrational, out of control) as when you saw me last. . . .

The quotes around *crazy* are a nice touch, as they suggest that one is *crazy* only in a kind of transitory, ironical sense, the tragicomic victim of ineluctable cause and effect. The latter part of the equation was true, with or without the quotes.

When Seymour Epstein arrived, he assumed his hard-drinking friend was in the throes of delirium tremens (though the empty bottles scattered all over the apartment hardly indicated alcoholic withdrawal), and with Beury's help he managed to coax Yates into a taxi. What followed was reproduced with remarkable clarity in the opening pages of *Distur-bing the Peace*.* When they arrived at St. Vincent's Hospital, Yates was put in a wooden wheelchair and pushed into the emergency room, where his raving became louder and more abusive (insofar as he made sense at all). Finally a doctor told him to behave himself—"You're in line with everyone else"—and Yates exploded, *"Tell this dumb son of a bitch he doesn't know anything about writing!"* (a terrible indictment coming from Yates), then stamped on the footrest of the wheelchair and broke it. The doctor had seen enough. "This guy isn't coming into the hospi-tal," he told Epstein. "He just damaged hospital property." An orderly wheeled Yates back outside, where he was forced into a police car and taken to Bellevue. Epstein followed in a taxi, but was told in the psychi-atric wing that his friend would not be eligible for release until next Wednesday at the earliest, since the doctors were gone for the Labor Day weekend.

Yates awoke in a collapsible metal bunk in the Men's Violence Ward, and was made to walk the floor with the other patients—a milieu evoked in *Disturbing the Peace*:

> Steel-mesh panels were being drawn across the folded bunks to prevent anyone from using them: this was indeed the corridor, the place for walking. It was yellow and green and brown and black; it was neither very long nor very wide, but it was immensely crowded with men of all ages from adoles-cence to senility, whites and Negroes and Puerto Ricans, half of them walking one way and half in the other. . . . Then he saw that the black floor ahead was scattered with gobs of phlegm.

After a breakfast of oatmeal and canned milk, the patients were given doses of peraldehyde. This made them sleepy, until even the dirty sweat-soaked mattresses in a dark alcove at the end of the corridor became

---

*According to Yates's daughter Monica, the novel's entire opening sequence (St. Vincent's, Belle-vue, etc.) is a "totally true" rendering of the episode. It always amazed her—and anybody else who ever saw Yates in the midst of a breakdown—that he could remember any part of it later, much less in such lucid detail.

tempting. Yates would often tell of his horror on discovering (as does John Wilder) that the men lying on either side of him were masturbating. And it seems probable that Yates, enraged at finding himself in such a squalid place, made a disturbance à la Wilder and Michael Davenport that resulted in his being "shot out"—forcibly given an injection and locked in a padded cell to sleep it off.

On Tuesday or Wednesday of the following week, Yates was interviewed by a group of doctors and deemed competent enough for removal to the Rehabilitation Ward on a separate floor, where he was pleased to find "real beds, chrome-and-leatherette armchairs, good showers with soap and a kind of shampoo guaranteed to remove lice." Soon he was ready for his exit interview. A social worker sternly advised him to quit drinking and arrange for regular psychiatric care, while Yates affected to appreciate the probational nature of his release. "I have given the Belle-vue authorities my solemn promise," he wrote Beury, "to avail myself of what they call 'voluntary psychiatric assistance' whenever too many good *or* bad things start crowding in on me in bunches in the future." On September 8, after almost a week of incarceration, Yates was signed out by Seymour Epstein. "When he saw me in the waiting room," Epstein recalled with lingering pique, "he scurried off into a corner indicating he didn't want to see me—whether in shame or what, I don't know. I signed him out, but I didn't *take* him out. He never said a word to me."

In fact Yates blamed his friend for the whole horrific episode—for Epstein's failure of imagination, that is, in being unable to distinguish between "crazy" and crazy. Thus, when Yates would later tell people that "Bellevue was an epiphany," he was rarely if ever referring to his own condition, but rather to Seymour Epstein; everything that had ever struck Yates as faintly distasteful about the man was suddenly woven into a single explanatory pattern—he was "close-minded," "conventional," "unadventurous." He was a *square,* in other words, and when Epstein and his wife Miriam insisted on helping Yates find a good therapist, and when the latter turned out to be the kind of "quack" who made his patients stop drinking as a condition of treatment—well, it only proved Yates's "epiphany" all the more. As a later psychiatrist put it, "Yates was always the smart one; everyone else was stupid. As far as he was concerned, *none* of his hospitalizations was justified. They came about because other people were stupid or didn't understand what he was going through. He felt this way even when he was sane."

The "quack" who'd objected to Yates's drinking, a Dr. Wiedeman, recommended another therapist to the Epsteins ("You should get help for that man," he told them, "but you might lose a friend"), and for a while Yates was shaken enough to cooperate. Though he blithely assured Barbara Beury that "the chances are about 108 to one" that another breakdown would ever occur, he was terrified about the future. "There was always a fearfulness about Dick," a friend noted, "as if he were apprehensive that something bad was about to happen." On the other hand, Yates never quite saw the point in confiding as much to a "therapist" (another word he entombed in quotes)—a man in a bad suit who rarely bothered to take notes and whose remarks were either banal or fatuous, or so Yates thought. It wouldn't be long, then, before he decided to go his own way, finding guidance as ever in the precepts of literary sages, primarily Flaubert, who was echoed in a piece of advice he gave Peter Najarian two weeks after Bellevue. "For God's sake, take it easy," he wrote the young man, who'd favored his teacher with a self-loathing diatribe about his failures as an artist. Yates continued:

> All you ought to be worrying about now is order (not about how to impose it on chaos, which is the opposite of art, but about how to bring it out of chaos, which is art itself). And your worrying about this ought not to be a tortured thing—God knows there's enough torture growing wild in everybody's life so that nobody in his right mind needs to cultivate it—but a serene thing. Don't, in other words, jazz yourself up into a nervous wreck. Be quiet, be as sane as you can, and let the work come out of you. If it's going to come, it will; if it's not, no amount of self-induced frenzy is going to help it along.
>
> One final piece of solemn, teacherly advice, and I do mean this: Try to like yourself a little better.

This may be read as pure soliloquy, of course: Hamlet advising himself to be less indecisive, Lear warning himself away from madness, and fate remaining aloof.

. . .

Though Yates had known Beury less than three weeks, including the week spent in Bellevue, he was certain he wanted to marry her—all the more so since receiving, the day after his release, a letter of tender concern which he found not only "beautiful" but "very, very well-written." Beury, now back at Sweet Briar, had decided to leave the door ajar where Yates was concerned. She figured the meltdown she'd witnessed was perhaps (as Yates assured her) a once-in-a-lifetime aberration. Meanwhile, only two things were preventing Yates from packing his bags and moving to Virginia: "1. I have to set up new ways of making money, because my biggest ghost-writing contact (Remington Rand) dissolved under me in July." This was true, and a further source of prebreakdown stress: After more than a decade as Yates's bête noire and stalwart source of income, Remington Rand had sacked his contact, Andy Borno, and killed the magazine *Systems*. Having lost the devil he knew, Yates at least had "two excellent leads on new and painless ghost-writing opportunities" but would have to stay in New York to pursue them. Also: "2. At the present time I need, or rather want, to be geographically as close to my children as possible." He was, however, willing to get the ball rolling by asking his wife for a divorce as early as the following week. That said, he closed his letter to Beury with a poem he'd written for her at Bellevue ("with a borrowed pencil on a very, very small piece of paper"):

POPULAR SONG

I love you in the lips
And I love you in the nerves
And I love you in the head;
Which rhymes with dead.

And now do you know what I guess I'll do?
In the hope you'll help me to see it through?
I guess I'll love you in the heart;
Which rhymes with art.

The Bard of Scarborough Country Day hadn't lost his lyric touch, and Beury was sufficiently moved to suggest he visit her at Sweet Briar the weekend after next. She balanced this with a wary quip about how she might be better off with an "air-conditioning salesman" (an oblique response to his marital overtures?), and continued to express a lot of pointed concern for his well-being. "I wish you wouldn't 'worry' about me," Yates retorted, and made the familiar case that he was "boringly well-adjusted most of the time, and as able to look after [him]self as any other solid citizen." As for her invitation to Virginia, he'd like nothing better but was simply too strapped at the moment—however: "Could you come here? If so I'd arrange for you to stay at the Evangeline (Maria's hangout) or some other equally blameless sanctuary for young ladies, and I'd solemnly promise not to keep you up past your bedtime." Beury wrote back that it might be fun to come up with her roommate, especially if Yates could arrange to get the latter a date with one Jim Shokoff, a Rutgers student they'd met at Bread Loaf. "I think it's a very swell and interesting idea," Yates dryly replied; "but oh, how earnestly and prayerfully I would like to suggest that you contrive to do it some other weekend." In short, he wanted to see her alone, and to this end he wrote an elaborately polished satire of the various "Frightful Visions" such a visit seemed to conjure in Beury's "exquisitely close-cropped head." The first of these was a bit of stock humor about drugged drinks and seduction—this, perhaps, in hope that the next two scenarios would smack of the same breezy absurdity:

Or, Worse Still:

Barbara . . . twists one slightly soiled white glove in the other as she stands beneath the Biltmore clock, an hour and forty-five minutes past the carefully appointed time of her date. Peering down the carpeted stairway, she sees a sudden moil of confusion near the revolving door. The doorman, three cab drivers, seven bellhops and a Bellevue attendant are engaged in some frantic grappling activity; and somehow, out of this muddle, wobbles a man. Almost unrecognizable, his clothing caked with filth and bristling with the snouts of bourbon bottles, his face swollen and streaked with maudlin tears, he reels and fumbles his way upstairs. There he topples, falls headlong, grasps Barbara around the knees and says: "Help."

And finally, the Worst and Most Frightful Vision of All:

Gay as a day in May . . . Barbara bounces up the Biltmore steps and finds a hollow-eyed, tragically haggard apparition under the clock. . . . [He takes her to] the bleakest, dimmest, and most fourth-rate of all Tenth Avenue saloons. And there, surrounded by sawdust and urine puddles and tired prostitutes and lurching longshoremen, he begins a droning recital of all his Problems. . . . He starts telling her all over again—ever and ever more boringly—about his unhappy childhood and his unhappy marriage and his unhappy love affairs and his grinding, soul-wrenching, general all-around unhappiness; and this goes on for two nights and two days until it's time for Barbara to sink gratefully into the sports car and turn back toward sunnier climes and sweeter briars.

Give or take a Tenth Avenue saloon and a bellhop or two, it was perhaps a bit too plausible to get the really big laughs, and Yates sensed as much. "All this was supposed to be funny," he added, "but I've just read it over, and it doesn't give me any chuckles. Forced humor, you see." He abruptly turned to other matters, and mentioned in passing that a trip to Virginia might be feasible later that fall, as he wanted "to soak up a little of the landscape and foldways" for the opening Camp Pickett chapters of his novel-in-progress.

This novel existed only in the abstract, and the fact that Yates was in no hurry to start soaking up atmosphere suggests how little disposed he was to write. Most of the time he brooded nervously over the reception of *Revolutionary Road*, and no wonder: The news was so relentlessly good that it bordered on the portentous, and it was all Yates could do to maintain a tenuous grip on his equilibrium. The advance comment from Alfred Kazin, for example: "This excellent novel is a powerful commentary on the way we live now. It locates the new American tragedy squarely on the field of marriage. No other people has made of marriage quite what we have, has taught itself to invest so much in what is essentially a romantic idea. Mr. Yates understands this very well, but never points." Now that Kazin had actually read the novel, he was not only willing to endorse Yates's Guggenheim application, but also he persuaded Sam Lawrence to accept, at last, the title *Revolutionary Road*. "After Little, Brown got that letter from Kazin, I stopped being another chancy first novelist and became something of a celebrity up there," Yates wrote Beury. "[The advertising manager] and his public-relations lady came barreling down here this week, bought me triple bourbons and asked any number of discreet, respectful questions as to whether I'd mind being interviewed on the Dave Garroway show, etc. etc."

Also around this time—and not a moment too soon for Yates's finances—*Esquire* bought the opening chapters, to be published a month before the novel as a self-sustained excerpt titled "After the Laurel Players." And already Hollywood was interested: Saul David of Columbia Pictures wrote Monica McCall that he'd be "delighted to work with [Yates] . . . though I'd hope that *Revolutionary Road* will swiftly make him so rich that he wouldn't dream of working with me," while a bona fide mogul, Sam Goldwyn Jr., announced that he'd "never read a more brilliant first novel"—an impulsive bit of hype that, as Yates put it, "[came] drearily to naught, because cooler heads in his organization decided that the moviegoing public 'is not ready for a story of such unrelieved tragedy, for so relentless a probing of the sources of pain.' Sic transit the hell Gloria." This was far from the last time cooler heads in the industry would prevail where Yates was concerned.

Sam Lawrence and his associates realized they had a potentially hot property on their hands, but the book's packaging and promotion were problematic. Now that the title was definitely *Revolutionary Road,* they felt obliged to make it as obvious as possible that the book was in fact about the failure of contemporary marriage, *not* a work of historical fiction. Yates had balked at the original jacket design—a sepia photograph of a man and woman standing forlornly back to back, over a pithy snippet of the Kazin quote—but he was finally overwhelmed by the star treatment. As he wrote Beury:

The Presentation today came off with maximum glory: everybody solemnly sitting in silence around an enormous leather chair containing me, while the advertising manager read his script and flipped the frames of a visual-aid demonstrator, just like Madison Avenue. Their new jacket copy is overpoweringly reverent—starts out "Rarely does a publisher introduce a first novel filled with such devastating power and compassion that it seems destined to become an enduring comment and influence upon our very way of life, etc, etc, etc,—and I was so overpowered by the reverence that I allowed them to seduce me into accepting a somewhat modified version of the dreary photographic jacket design.

Yates would bitterly regret letting that "dreary" jacket pass, though in fairness there could be little doubt that Lawrence et al. were doing their best to market a very depressing novel by a virtually unknown writer. The advertising budget was based on an anticipated sale of twenty thousand copies, or roughly four times as many as most first novels; the paperback rights were already sold, and Yates would receive a first installment of $2,500 in January. High hopes abounded, hideous jacket or no: "The meeting broke up with many high-powered handshakes and floods of drink," Yates wrote of the sales presentation, "after which Sam Lawrence (editor) fed the hell out of me on about seven pounds of roast beef at the Algonquin; then he took me to a criminally expensive nightclub featuring giant Negress strip tease artists." How many first novelists could say as much?

For a man who seemed about to become the toast of two coasts, Yates continued to live on a grindingly humble scale. Earlier that fall he'd resumed teaching at the New School, a deadly business cheered only slightly by the fact that he now felt able to befriend his eminent colleague there, Alfred Kazin, who proved to be "very nice and un-awesome." Meanwhile as the weather got colder Yates moped about the basement "wearing forty-three sweaters" because the building's ancient furnace had died. He wrote no fiction, though he stayed busy doing freelance PR work. Johnson & Johnson's national sales conference in New Brunswick was coming up, and Yates had to write speeches for all the corporate and sales executives. He also tried his hand at ghostwriting an article for *Scientific American*—"a gruesome failure," as he put it, that left him in the gloomy position of having to "wrangle with the editor" in order to "rescue the lousy 300 bucks they promised." He implored Monica McCall to find him some kind of steady job in publishing, but it didn't pan out.

He consoled himself with thoughts of his "golden girl," whom he managed to coax back to New York in late October and again a few weeks later. Both visits were something of a bust. Yates's clothing wasn't quite "bristling with the snouts of bourbon bottles," nor did he dissolve into "maudlin tears" en route to Bellevue—but close enough. "Dick was *always* drinking," said Beury, "and sometimes he'd be slobbering drunk by the end of the evening." For Yates it was a matter of impossibly high expectations and poor health; he wanted to seem vibrant and charming but didn't have the energy or impulse. He drank to compensate. Also he was loath to be eclipsed by his friend Broyard, who (though five years older) was dating any number of college "popsies" as Yates called them; predictably the man's ears pricked up when Yates told him about Beury: "[Anatole] has expressed a keen desire to have dinner with us during your visit," Yates wrote her, "and I said okay, maybe. (But he'd better watch his God damn step, or there'll be Bad Trouble.)" As it happened Broyard indulged in a few suavely told tales about past conquests (e.g., the one about the woman whose "ass exploded like an inflatable raft" when she doffed her girdle*), but appears to have been on passably good behavior, and certainly a bit of comic relief was welcome at that point.

Otherwise there was little to remember about these visits except for telltale signs of instability on the part of Beury's host, whose October postmortem was duly bleak: "The whole three days went by so fast, and I spent so much of it being tired or half drunk or asleep, that I don't quite believe it happened and I'm full of regrets. . . . [You're likely] to write me off as the terribly nice but hopelessly sad young man whom no girl in her right mind could ever consider a permanent type." Beury was in her right

---

*This story was a staple of Broyard's repertoire, and appears in his posthumous memoir *Kafka Was All the Rage,* wherein the woman's expandable ass is described with a slightly different simile than Beury remembers.

mind, more or less, but still remained interested in Yates—or rather in the brilliant, sensitive man who'd written those stories in *Short Story 1* (her copy was inscribed, "If ever any beauty I did see/Which I desired, and got, 'twas but a dream of thee"—Dick [and John Donne]"), not to mention a novel that just might make him a household name. *That* man deserved a lot of patience.

His wife Sheila might have begged to differ. Back in September, Yates had reported to Beury that his "formal divorce talk" with his wife had been "friendly and pleasant, maximum cooperation guaranteed"—which implied that Sheila was now graciously willing to let him go since he'd found another, and so she was. Yates, however, was *not* cooperating to a maximum extent. "He drove the lawyers nuts," said Sheila. "He knew [a reconciliation] wasn't going to happen, but he was making trouble for the sake of making trouble." This was a bit reductive, perhaps; in fact Sheila's observation that Yates "could never bear losing close people" was nearer the mark, as she knew well enough at the time: "I thought I had explained my reasons for wanting an immediate settlement," she wrote him on November 2.

> Either you didn't listen, or I didn't make myself clear, or both, and I am willing to try again. They are quite simple: When we separated, I hoped for some time that a radical change in one or both of us would make possible a rebuilt marriage. I no longer have any such hope. . . . As to my seeing you any more or being friends, this is totally out of the question from now on. I don't hate or feel bitter towards you, but I soon would if I continued to see you. . . . Some things simply come to an end—I have relinquished two close friendships in my life, and so I am ready to accept this. It will be much easier for everyone if you accept it too. Once you have, I believe you will be relieved, as I am, to let Mr. Golditch [the lawyer] make arrangements that are comfortable for me, the children, and yourself.

The "radical change" for which Sheila had hoped was, of course, that Yates would curb his drinking and get help for whatever else was ailing him, but after Bellevue she knew better. As for Yates, neither then nor later would he be able to accept rejection on the basis of his drinking and/or mental health—hence Sheila's exasperated but not unkind "Some things simply come to an end."

Yates became all the more desperate to make things work with Beury. "The only nice thing in my life right now," he wrote her, a week after that letter from Sheila, "is that you've promised to come up here next Wednesday." But with so much emotionally at stake, Yates was too overwrought in Beury's presence to stay sober, and besides he always had a ready excuse: "He said he was irrational because *Revolutionary Road* was about to be published," said Beury, "and he'd worked so hard to finish it— etcetera—as if it were only a passing phase. It seemed plausible at the time, but it didn't change." There were moments, though, when he was at least somewhat sober (that is, on the way to getting drunk) and thus charming, courteous, and funny—in other words the very man Beury hoped he'd be whenever he got "well" again.

This alternating pattern was suggested by Yates's visit to Virginia a week or so before Christmas. All went well at first: Beury was touched by her gift—a pair of monogrammed gold cufflinks that Yates said was the most valuable thing he owned—and while they drove about the countryside they came upon a big plantation house with a For Sale sign in front. Yates spoke seriously about buying the place, and for the moment he made Beury see the "glamour" of it—the genteel literary life they'd lead there, writing all day and having drinks on the veranda "like Dash and Lillian Hellman." Full of the idea, Yates got excitably drunker than usual and was miserably hungover the next morning, when they'd planned to drive back to New York via Charlottesville, where the writer Nancy Hale was giving a cocktail party in Yates's honor. Hale, a very admiring advance reader of *Revolutionary Road,* had done a number of kind things for Yates, who was grateful enough to remain on good behavior during her party. Afterward he fell apart. Every few miles on the road he'd pull over and buy beer to "calm his nerves," and by the time they got to Washington he was a tipsy wreck. He tried to mollify his traveling companion by insisting they stop in a posh hotel—same room but separate beds, as Beury (with Yates's approval) was still a virgin—where he ordered a bottle of bourbon and drank himself to sleep.

. . .

The two months leading up to the publication of *Revolutionary Road*
were an eventful time for Yates, who bobbed about in the maelstrom
without quite going under. He coped as well as possible with such obligations as a "big Celebrity Interview" with a South American journalist—a
typically "boozy business," wrote Yates: "[I] feel bottomless chagrin at
having been a garrulous clown, and wonder how many of my ill-
considered pronouncements on literature and life got scribbled down for
the edification of fifty trillion South Americans, and am busy thanking
God that nobody I know can read Spanish." Perhaps the most important
advance publicity was the excerpt scheduled for the February issue of
Esquire. Yates had agonized over editing his work to the magazine's spec-
ifications, and was perturbed to learn that his own rather drastic cuts were
insufficient. On January 11 he and Rust Hills spent two hours going over
the proofs, line by line, until they'd reached a compromise of sorts, or so
Yates thought. "The author, the publishers, and I, are deeply shocked and
disappointed by the treatment given to this excerpt," Monica McCall
wrote *Esquire* editor Arnold Gingrich on January 20. "Not only has the
[published] text been cut and changed, after the very careful editing and
cutting which the author himself completed . . . but the illustration presents the characters as two vastly unattractive *middle-aged* people, in fact
the heroine looks something like Sophie Tucker." Gingrich, stiffly indignant, called the complaints "shocking." He conceded that he didn't much
like the illustration either, but denied that any further changes had been
made to the text without Yates's consent; he also pointed out that he'd
been so certain the excerpt was a credit to its author that he'd appended
proofs to his recommendation for Yates's Guggenheim.

Sam Lawrence was also dismayed by the *Esquire* treatment, but
remained optimistic on the whole: "I think we have a best-seller," he
wrote on January 25, calling Yates's attention to the current *Publisher's
Weekly,* which reflected "the kind of advance enthusiasm and exceptional
interest *Revolutionary Road* is creating." The book's sizable advertising
budget was being put to good use: A thousand promotional copies with
special jackets had been distributed among the various pundits in the trade

and media, while sales reps were instructed to attach personal cards to copies sent to all major booksellers in their territories. A big quote ad was planned for the *New York Times Book Review* just prior to publication. On the basis of the advance notice alone, Yates had every reason to feel jubilant.

What he felt was "semi-hysteria," as he put it, kept somewhat in abeyance by the steady, all-but-lethal flow of bourbon. At times in his life when he wasn't able to get on with his writing, for whatever reason, Yates would let himself go to a degree unusual even for him. This was one of those times. Things were happening and he let them happen. On February 3, Yates's thirty-fifth birthday, Sheila took a one-day trip to Alabama and got a no-fault divorce; the lawyer Golditch subsequently informed Yates that there was a sixty-day waiting period before he could remarry: "You are free to remarry at any place and at any time after April 3, 1961." By now Yates seemed rather to doubt the prospect, and informed Beury of the development with a single unembellished line: "Got my final divorce decree in the mail last Friday." Somewhat better news (though by no means unequivocally so) was that he'd been offered a part-time position by the Columbia School of General Studies, the adult education branch of the university. This in addition to his New School duties and freelance work.

Yates did not lack company during this time. Bread Loaf had widened his circle of acquaintance, and nowadays he was nothing if not socially available. The Irishman Arthur Roth was a good companion, as Yates not only admired him as a writer, but as a drinker almost as heedless as he. Yates and Roth enjoyed baiting each other while in their cups, and one night during a party at Bob Riche's apartment the two got in a violent, careening, "kidding" wrestling match that culminated amid broken glass in an empty bathtub, where Riche doused them both with a bucket of water.

At Bread Loaf there was also a group of writerly Rutgers students (the poet John Ciardi, then the director of the conference, was on the Rutgers faculty), who looked up to the hard-drinking Yates as a rather romantic role model. Alan Cheuse, editor of the undergraduate literary magazine, remembered the invariable routine involved in a visit to Yates's apartment:

"Dick would hand you a tumbler of bourbon as soon as you arrived. It'd be five or six in the evening and he'd be drunk already. You'd drink and talk, then have dinner at the Blue Mill and drink some more. After that Dick would go back to his apartment and pass out. He was always kind— he took a real interest in you—but clearly he didn't like sober people." Perhaps closest among the Rutgers crowd was Ed Kessler, who joined Yates for such anomalous outings as a Robert Lowell reading at Colum- bia, after which they adjourned downtown until, several blurred hours later, a groggy Kessler woke up on a cot in Yates's basement. Both Kessler and Cheuse arranged for Yates to give paid readings and lectures at Rut- gers, an ordeal that was new to him then: "For God's sake if you have any ideas about what I ought to say in my lecture," he wrote Kessler, "please don't keep them to yourself. Should I take the Beatniks over the jumps? . . . Or discuss Eliot's objective correlative as exemplified in Looney Tunes ('That's all, Folks')? Or do a double buck and wing soft- shoe routine and recite Kipling's 'If' for an encore? I mean like HELP me in this thing, Kessler." The lecture went without a hitch, but the party after- ward ended badly. The young writer Maureen Howard was there (her hus- band was on the faculty), and to everybody's surprise the drunken Yates had a bone to pick with her. He'd read her stories in the best-of-the-year anthologies, and didn't like the way she stylized her characters in terms of their tastes—what they wore, what they ate, and so on. He thought it was simplistic and condescending, and he was very emphatic about it. "Mau- reen seemed like a tough person," said Kessler, "but Dick could *destroy* somebody if he wanted." She left the party in tears.

It had been a long ten months since Yates had finished his novel, and mercifully the suspense was almost over, if not the hysteria. One way or the other Yates had much to be proud of: Kazin, Styron, Updike* and

---

*John Updike wrote of *Revolutionary Road*: "I was fascinated and, in the end, deeply distressed by Mr. Yates's compassionate, well-wrought, and claustrophobic book." Of Updike, Yates later told *Ploughshares*: "I think [he's] very talented, though none of his novels have been wholly successful for me so far." In private he was more caustic: "Is John Updike *still* only twenty-nine years old?" he'd say on hearing some fresh acclaim for the writer.

many others had blessed his work, and two days before publication a further blurb was wired from Tennessee Williams of all people, who rarely bothered with that sort of thing: "Here is more than fine writing; here is what, added to fine writing, makes a book come immediately, intensely, and brilliantly alive. If more is needed to make a masterpiece in modern American fiction, I am sure I don't know what it is." Sam Lawrence assured Yates that such praise was disinterested ("Don't be concerned about your virility"), and added, "We have never had this kind of response for a first novel since I can remember. . . . This is what makes publishing worthwhile." The two men planned to meet at the Harvard Club on publication day, March 1, to celebrate the fruitful consummation of a long and often dreary ordeal.

Yates was never one to ignore reviews, or for that matter dismiss them with a mandarin chuckle when they were bad. "Oh yes," he responded when an interviewer asked if he paid attention to them, and added with typical candor that he sometimes read them "five or six times over": "When they're helpful is when they're good, and they make me furious when they're bad, which is to say they're probably not helpful at all."

It's interesting to imagine Yates reading certain reviews of *Revolutionary Road*, much less five or six times over, and perhaps it's safe to say that most of them weren't very helpful. With a few exceptions, the good reviews tended to make fairly obvious points, while the bad ones were what Walker Percy called "bad-bad"—that is, bad in every sense: negative, badly written, in bad faith. An early review in *Library Journal* seemed to bode well: "Seldom has the talk of a desperate, ineffectual man been captured with such uncanny precision as in this novel," it noted, and also made the nice point that the book hardly lacked humor in the midst of its general unpleasantness ("such is the nature of life that some of the most pathetic moments are also the most comical"). But at least two of the major reviews on Sunday, March 5, took the line that *Revolutionary Road* must be negligible because it dealt with the tired subject of suburban discontent: "No amount of contrived symbolism can hide what has become a hackneyed theme in the contemporary

American novel," wrote R. D. Spector in the *New York Herald Tribune*, and W. E. Preece of the *Chicago Tribune* went further, claiming the book read like an "intentional parody of all the similarly type-cast novels that went before it." Happily, Martin Levin provided a strong corrective in that Sunday's *New York Times Book Review*. The "excellence" of the book, wrote Levin, lay in the "integrity" of its approach: "Eschewing the pitfalls of obvious caricature or patent moralizing, Mr. Yates chooses the more difficult path of allowing his characters to reveal themselves—which they do with an intensity that excites the reader's compassion as well as his interest."

Leave it to Orville Prescott, the dean of bad-bad reviewers, to rebut in the daily *Times* on behalf of low middlebrows everywhere. The novel, he wrote, was a "brilliantly dismal" tour de force about "two psychopathic characters and their miserable haste to self-destruction." Having thus established that the Wheelers are mentally ill—indeed, Frank is an "absolute psychotic"—Prescott could only wag his head at the folly of such a "superior" writer as Yates wasting his time and talent on characters "so far gone into mental illness that they are incapable of responsible decisions and unaware of the duty and necessity of making them." And lest one forget the main point, he concluded: "No fair-minded reader could finish *Revolutionary Road* without admiration for Mr. Yates's impressive skill; but whether the mentally ill Wheelers deserve the five years of labor Mr. Yates has lavished upon them is another question."

Magazine reviews were mostly positive, though the approval of *The New Yorker* continued to elude Yates: "The Wheelers are young, pathetic, trapped, half educated, and without humor—meaningless characters leading meaningless lives," remarked the anonymous reviewer in the "Briefly Noted" section. "Mr. Yates's attempt to lend drama to their predicament, through an unconvincing introduction of madness and violence in the story, serves only to emphasize the flimsy nature of his work." This weirdly peevish squib was offset by more considered treatment in the *Saturday Review* and the *New Republic*, whose reviewers—David Boroff and Jeremy Larner respectively—made large claims for the novel. Boroff called

Yates "a writer of commanding gifts," whose "prose is urbane yet sensitive, with passion and irony held deftly in balance," while Larner discussed not only technique but also the book's sociological significance: "To read *Revolutionary Road* is to have forced upon us a fresh sense of our critical modern shortcomings: failures of work, education, community, family, marriage . . . and plain nerve." Even *Newsweek* called it "the find of the year," though Yates was perhaps most pleased by Dorothy Parker's panegyric in the June *Esquire*: "A treasure, a jewel, a whole trove is Richard Yates's *Revolutionary Road*. . . . Mr. Yates's eyes and ears are gifts from heaven. I think I know of no recent novel that has so impressed me, for the manners and mores of his people are, it seems to me, perfectly observed."

Finally two insightful and appreciative reviews appeared later that summer: F. J. Warnke in the *Yale Review* made the useful point that the "novel is really about the inadequacy of human beings to their own aspirations, and its target is not America but existence," while Theodore Solotaroff in *Commentary* noted that "Yates has the superior novelist's instinct for the nuances by which people give themselves away." Both reviewers had a few sober misgivings as well: Warnke found the narrative point of view unfocused in such a way that Frank Wheeler and others are alternately sympathetic and the objects of "savage contempt," while Solotaroff objected that the Wheelers' "determinative childhoods" undermined the clarity of the book's social criticism ("the Wheelers probably would have failed under the best of circumstances").

As with his beloved *Gatsby*, Yates's novel got a rather mixed reception despite what many agreed to be its manifest excellence, and like *Gatsby*, too, it would pass in and out of print for many years to the bewilderment of those (especially writers) who continue to think it deserves the status of an American classic. Twenty years ago James Atlas wrote that *Revolutionary Road* "remains one of the few novels I know that could be called flawless," and Richard Ford, in his introduction to the recent Vintage edition, called it "a cultish standard." That it remains a cultish rather than popular standard is perhaps due to two broad factors: (*1*) as the writer Fred Chappell pointed out, the book "strikes too close to home"—that is, the educated general reader is all too likely to identify, depressingly, with a pretentious pseudointellectual such as Frank Wheeler; (2) the book's artistic merit is lost on academic canon-makers who tend to regard it as "merely" another realistic novel about the suburbs. Yates's meaning seems all too plain for the purpose of scholarly explication, and yet this is one of the most misunderstood American novels, both in terms of its meaning and aesthetic approach. As Ford noted, "Realism, naturalism, social satire—the standard critical bracketry—all go begging before this splendid book. *Revolutionary Road* is simply *Revolutionary Road,* and to invoke it enacts a sort of cultural-literary secret handshake among its devotees."

The book's deceptively simple language is like the glassy surface of a deep and murky loch. The first thing one may see is a rippled image of oneself, and then the churning shadows beneath. That Warnke found the Wheelers both sympathetic and repugnant is very much to the point in a novel full of mirrors, windows, and shifting points of view. "I don't suppose one picture window is going to destroy our personalities," Frank remarks when they first examine the house in Revolutionary Estates—and indeed the garish window sometimes rewards Frank with a nocturnal image of himself as "the brave beginnings of·a personage," while other windows and "passing mirrors" sometime surprise him with a very different view: "[His face was] round and full of weakness, and he stared at it with loathing."* And so too with the more admirable April, who from the beginning is shown as two women (at least), filtered through the mingled perspectives of Frank and the rest of the audience at *The Petrified Forest*: She is both "a tall ash blonde with a patrician kind of beauty that no amount of amateur lighting could destroy" as well as the "graceless, suffering creature whose existence [Frank] tried every day of his life to deny." Thus the protean Wheelers embody the thematic (and psychologically valid) discrepancy between romantic and elusively "authentic" selves, a split that applies to every major

---

*The importance of mirrors and windows, as devices of exposure and reflection, is suggested by the novel's French title, *La Fenêtre Panoramique.*

character in the novel with one notable exception—the madly literal John Givings. Such deliberate blurring has led to a certain amount of misinterpretation, as it should. *Revolutionary Road,* no matter how accessible on the surface, rewards a lifetime of rereading and reflection.

Some who view the novel as more or less straight social satire (or social criticism, depending on whether one finds any humor in it) tend to see the Wheelers as an essentially gifted, decent, but flawed young couple who wither amid the sterility of midcentury America as reflected in its suburban ethos. Yates himself dismissed such a reading out of hand. "The Wheelers may have thought the suburbs were to blame for all their problems," he told *Ploughshares,* "but I meant it to be implicit in the text that that was *their* delusion, *their* problem, not mine." It seems fair to assume, then, that the Wheelers "would have failed under the best of circumstances" as Solotaroff points out (deploringly), and hence the need for their "determinative childhoods" by way of explaining the cause, or anyway *one* cause, of this failure. But if the Wheelers are abnormally weak or even mentally ill (as Orville Prescott would have it), where is the universal interest? And if the novel is "really about the inadequacy of human beings to their own aspirations, and its target is not America but existence," as Warnke suggests, why so much harping on suburbia in the first place? Why the suggestive title, *Revolutionary Road*?

Yates, having made the point that the suburbs are hardly "to blame" for the Wheelers' tragedy, goes on to assert that the book's main target is indeed American culture. "I meant it more as an indictment of American life in the nineteen-fifties," said Yates.

Because during the Fifties there was a general lust for conformity over this country, by no means only in the suburbs—a kind of blind, desperate clinging to safety and security at any price, as exemplified politically in the Eisenhower administration and the McCarthy witch-hunts. . . . I meant the title to suggest that the revolutionary road of 1776 had come to something very much like a dead end in the Fifties.

The suburbs (or American culture at large) are not, then, a mass of malign external forces that combine to thwart the Wheelers' dreams; rather the Wheelers—in all their weakness and preposterous self-deceit—are themselves definitive figures of that culture, determinative childhoods and all. Granted, they are somewhat less mediocre than most: They can wax eloquent about the "outrageous state of the nation" as well as the "endlessly absorbing subject of Conformity and The Suburbs," until they begin to convince themselves that they and their friends the Campbells compose "an embattled, dwindling intellectual underground" that is "painfully alive in a drugged and dying culture." But when it comes to the point of leaving the "hopeless emptiness" of it all—or even completing a stone path that would connect their home to Revolutionary Road—Frank, at least, would rather not. As for April, she might never have found herself married to such a man, or living in such a place, were it not for the vulnerabilities created by her "determinative childhood."

In the end, of course, neither Frank nor April can be entirely summed up in social or historical terms, and certainly the novel is "about" human frailty at any time or place. But in 1955 the Wheelers end up in the suburbs for a reason, even while they and any number of bright, skeptical citizens imagined themselves destined for something better. As Chappell noted, such "fuzzy dreams of freedom and 'self-realization'" tend to be peculiar to certain fortuitous moments in history: "[P]lentiful money is required and an easy ignoble means of acquiring it, a good spotty liberal education is needed, and there must be a lack of strong ties to family or even to place. . . . 'If only I didn't have to'—that's probably the commonest excuse we give ourselves." Amid the affluence of postwar America, the temptation was particularly keen to accept the easy rewards of suburban comfort, an undemanding job, and to fill the emptiness that followed with dreams of potential greatness or adventure. But to pursue such dreams in fact—as Yates well knew—required a resilient sense of autonomy that resisted the siren call of, say, a comfortable ranch house in Redding as opposed to a roach-infested basement in the Village. As the mad John Givings says, "You want to play house, you got to a have a job. You want to play very *nice* house, very *sweet* house, then you got to have a job you don't like." And in a society where one's status depends almost entirely on the nice house and "good" job, one must possess a formidable sense of self-worth, and perhaps formidable talent as well, to risk failure by leaving the beaten path. Frank Wheeler, like most, would prefer to believe he's special without putting the matter to a test; meanwhile his sense of inadequacy as the bumbling son of an ineffectual father, coupled with a better-than-average intellect, makes him strident (and almost convincingly so) in his insistence that he's superior to his fate. And April's own deprived childhood helps, in part, to account for her desperate need to believe him.

As characters the Wheelers are meant to be representative and somewhat stylized, but also rounded and plausible individuals in their own right, the better for the reader to identify with them on the one hand, while maintaining a certain judgmental detachment on the other. Yates achieves this kind of double vision—though some would call it inconsistency—with a limited omniscient viewpoint that shifts from character to character, then at apposite moments becomes godlike. For example, the Wheelers' argument during their drive home from the Laurel Players fiasco is given through Frank's point of view, and his frustration toward what seems his wife's unwarranted bitchiness tends to evoke our sympathy; when she jumps out of the car and runs away ("a little too wide in the hips"), we follow with Frank until a car approaches, whereupon we are suddenly looking *at* rather than *through* him: "His arms flapped and fell; then, as the sound and the lights of an approaching car came up behind them, he put one hand in his pocket and assumed a conversational slouch for the sake of appearances." One's heart goes out to the embattled, well-meaning, if rather pathetic man who would have it known he's more than just a "dumb, insensitive suburban husband," while the laughable puppet ("His arms flapped and fell") who worries about "appearances" is contemptible. And yet they are convincingly the same man.

Yates provokes a moral judgment from readers, but not at the expense of their sympathy: "I much prefer the kind of story," he said, "where the reader is left wondering who's to blame until it begins to dawn on him (the reader) that he himself must bear some of the responsibility because he's human and therefore infinitely fallible." This involves, again and again, an uncomfortable sense of *Frank Wheeler—c'est moi* on the part of the reader, though almost any of Yates's better characters will fit this Flaubertian formula. We may not, at first, identify with the silly Helen Givings, a recognizable type of suburban busybody whose insipid patter and hobbies seem a pitiful form of self-hypnotic escapism. It's easy to feel superior to such a person, but less so when suddenly confronted with her despair—as Helen glances at her feet ("like two toads") and begins to cry: "She cried because she was fifty-six years old and her feet were ugly and swollen and horrible; she cried because none of the girls had liked her at school and none of the boys had liked her later; she cried because Howard Givings was the only man who'd ever asked her to marry him, and because she'd done it, and because her only child was insane." This is sad, but later Yates incites us to judgment again: Helen is a woman who can feel pity for herself, but is ready enough to abandon her son to a mental hospital on the convenient pretext that he somehow contributed to April's suicide. Such callousness is at the heart of Helen's shallow everyday pretending—and yet we don't forget her despair either.*

While Yates tried to recover from the psychological fallout of *Revolutionary Road*—the long gestation, revision, relinquishment, and finally the Chinese water torture of its reviews—he was gratified, perhaps, by the epistolary response. For a man who was once a miserable, stammering, skinny kid hiding away in movie theaters or shabby apartments, it must have been gratifying to be told of his greatness by family, friends, and strangers all over the world. His sister Ruth sent a valentine of loving praise; Aunt Elsa (now in her seventies and still looking after her sister somewhat) was especially pleased that her nephew's novel stressed the

---

*The name "Mrs. Givings" was one of Yates's favorite details. According to his friend Robin Metz, Yates had a habit of checking phonebooks in various cities for a listing of "Givings," but never found one. This delighted him: "Doesn't it sound like a real name?" he'd say. "It doesn't exist! Isn't that fucking fantastic?" The reader should consult Ford's introduction to the novel for a nice analysis of Yates's use of "extraliteral" names such as Givings, Wheeler, Prentice, Wilder, Grimes, etc.

importance of a loving childhood; and one can only imagine Dookie's proud maternal bliss.* Yates also heard from his favorite English teacher at Avon, Richard Knowles, who was now in his eighties and more admiring of his pupil than ever, while another English teacher in Houston, Ernest "Bick" Wright, was all but beside himself. For years Wright had scanned the shelves of libraries and bookstores in search of some evidence that his old friend's early dedication had borne fruit, and had almost abandoned hope when *Revolutionary Road* appeared. Wright thought the novel exquisite both as a work of art and a vision of life, and afterward would speak of its author as an almost holy figure who'd devoted everything to the cultivation of his talent.

A few representative bits of mail from the general reader are worth mentioning. A blustery but prescient fellow named Andrew Sinats warned Yates, "You threaten the intellectuals who would accept and receive your work. . . . At the beginning of the book I hated Frank Wheeler, hated you for writing such an awful characterization, and hated that part of myself that was like Frank Wheeler. I even hated you for being right." Donn C. McInturff, a suburban husband and father of two, also identified with Frank, and wondered if the character resembled his creator: "If this was indeed your existence, [how] did you manage to escape from it to get your book written? Was it to Paris?" At the age of thirty-six, McInturff himself wanted to sell his house and "pound out this [novel] that lives in [him]" because (despite an "excellent" credit rating) he was "starving from the inside." And finally Yates received a parcel from one Thalia Gorham Kelly, an elderly lady from San Diego, who wrote in what can only be called a fine old spidery hand, "Not knowing where else to dispense of two such repugnant books as *Revolutionary Road* and *May This House Be Free from Tigers,*† I am sending them to you . . . the author who so industriously presented weak, inferior types." Mrs. Kelly strongly suggested that Yates "enlarge [his] acquaintance" to include "people who face their problems and manage to find other solutions than drunkenness, sex perversion and adultery."

---

*Imagination is particularly required since Yates didn't preserve her letters.

†A satirical work by Alexander King (New York: Simon & Schuster, 1960).

This billet-doux was perhaps a welcome diversion from dwelling on sales figures, which were decidedly meager in the wake of all that "advance enthusiasm and exceptional interest." A week after publication Sam Lawrence reported a total advance sale of 6,100 copies ("very healthy indeed for a novel, first or otherwise"), and a month later he wrote: "We are over 9,000 and the next two to three weeks will tell whether the book will really go into high figures or will resolve its sale in the 10–15,000 category." A last momentum-boosting quote ad was run in the *New York Times,* to no avail: Sales stalled at around nine thousand and stayed there—despite Dorothy Parker's review in the June *Esquire,* despite national newspaper critics naming *Revolutionary Road* one of the "fifty important books published between January 1 and May 30." When the promotional rug was pulled out from under the book in late April, Yates wrote Lawrence a protesting letter: The continuing acclaim, he insisted, justified at least another quote ad. Lawrence disagreed: "I cannot recall when we last launched a first novel in such a powerful and confident way. As a result, more than 10,000 copies* were sold in a few weeks, and this is outstanding for a first novel, but as often happens to new fiction, the demand dropped off sharply." Lawrence reminded Yates that Little, Brown had already spent a relatively lavish $4,500 promoting the book, and "one [more] quote ad will not change anything": "Our goal has been accomplished. You have now established yourself as an important new American writer. . . . I hope you still believe that we have done a good publishing job."

He did and he didn't. Yates never quite got over his anger at the "cheap, vulgar" jacket and "the lousy way the book was marketed," but in moments of sober detachment he "couldn't really blame Sam for that because the true villains were the Little, Brown executives." Such ambivalence resounds in his remarks, ten years later, on the subject of what he would always consider his best novel:

[I]n my more arrogant or petulant moments, I still think *Revolutionary Road* ought to be famous. I was sore as hell when it first went out of print, and

---

*Subsequent accounting by Little, Brown adjusted the total hardcover sales to around 8,900.

when Norman Podhoretz made a very small reference to it in his book several years ago as an "unfairly neglected novel," I wanted every reader in America to stand up and cheer. But of course deep down I know that kind of thing is nonsense.

CHAPTER EIGHT

The World on Fire: 1961-1962

Joseph Heller made the point that "success and failure are both difficult to endure," and by now Yates had enjoyed a fair portion of each. Indeed, he existed in some limbo in between. As Sam Lawrence reminded him, he was now established as "an important new writer": The literary world was keeping an eye on him, and many thought he'd written something very like a classic. On the other hand he was broke again, still living in a basement, and hardly able to write a word without crossing it out. His drinking continued apace. One gloomy night he "reread Fitzgerald's 'Crack Up' for the 400th time" and found that he'd "drawn emphatic pencil lines around these words: 'I only wanted absolute quiet to think out why I had developed a sad attitude toward sadness, a melancholy attitude toward melancholy and a tragic attitude toward tragedy—why I had become identified with the objects of my horror or compassion.'" It occurred to Yates that he'd first highlighted this passage early in the writing of his novel, when he found himself identifying with the feckless Wheelers to an uncomfortable degree. And now he felt worse than ever. "Old Fitz really does have an uncanny way of laying my problems on the line," Yates reflected. "In any case the point is that I just plain can't afford to be as doomed as the people I wrote about."

And yet, like his character Jack Fields in "Saying Goodbye to Sally," Yates took "a certain literary satisfaction" in seeing himself as a "tragic figure." He couldn't help being aware of—and sometimes exploiting—the fact that it was more seemly to be a maudlin drunk if one also happened to be the young(ish) author of a brilliant first novel. It was a role he found hard to resist, and yet its implications troubled him: If he couldn't afford to be as doomed as his own characters, then surely he couldn't afford to be as doomed as F. Scott Fitzgerald either; but then too, he'd arguably earned the privilege of putting a romantic face on his misery, if only for a while. The role was congenial because it was true . . . or was it? He could never quite resolve the question. "The idea of the writer haunted Dick," said his friend David Milch, who described Yates's literary persona as a fifties-style "refinement of F. Scott Fitzgerald": "The ordeal of inauthenticity—what was real versus feigned—was a drama enacted in every gesture of his. Dick had this punitive self-consciousness: Had he integrated the *idea* of being a writer with being a writer?" Or, as another friend generalized it, "Dick was both melancholy and played the role of a melancholic."

But there was more to being Fitzgeraldian than acting melancholy; there was also the impulse to pick drunken fights, to throw one's writerly weight around—the revenge of the weakling who'd spent his youth being picked on by boys bigger and richer than he. "There was a bit of the high school pug in Dick," said John Williams. "He'd become bellicose when he drank, though when sober he was settled and attentive." Seymour Epstein agreed: "Dick always wanted to settle things with his fists," he said, "though I got the impression he always hoped someone would intervene." Epstein performed this function at least once, in a Village restaurant. "Dick was drunk and talking too loud, and a customer seated nearby asked him to keep it down. Dick said, 'How'd you like to go outside?' I got between them and mollified the other guy, who would've torn Dick's head off." More than ever Yates also had a tendency, when drunk, to vent his contempt for people with manqué literary ambitions: "How's the *schoolteaching* going, Hal?" he'd say, whacking the back of a man who considered teaching a degrading and temporary avocation at best. Or, to Bob Riche: "How's the *PR dodge* going, Bob?"—but with nastiness instead of their old conspiratorial glee.

As an acclaimed writer Yates was disinclined to suffer the insolence of waiters, cabbies, and cops who treated him like a common drunk, and this too was a very Fitzgeraldian animus. One day a figure out of the distant past, Doris Bialek, spotted Yates on Fifty-seventh Street; she'd seen neither him nor Sheila in almost ten years, since the couple left for Europe. "He was having an altercation with a policeman," said Bialek. "He was drunk and cursing the man out. He was with some girl—at first I thought it was his daughter, but it wasn't." When Yates heard his name called ("Rich! What are *you* doing here?"), he dropped the quarrel with the cop and became solicitous toward his old friend. Bialek recalled, "By then I'd read *Revolutionary Road* and identified Sheila with April Wheeler. I read how April commits suicide and I thought, 'My God, she must be dead!'" She explained all this to Yates, who hastened to reassure her and even wrote down Sheila's address and phone number for Bialek before saying good-bye.

Yates's friends rarely saw him sober, even during morning strolls in the Village; he'd always greet Warren Owens's wife, Marjorie, with a "big juicy kiss on the lips" that left her dazed with mortification. And then there was the time she ran into Yates in the subway: He'd just been to the dentist, he told her, and found out he had leukoplakia (white precancerous patches in the mouth); the dentist had advised him to stop smoking. "Like hell I will!" said Yates, lighting a cigarette with trembling hands. Many thought he wasn't long for the world, certainly not as a writer, but (oddly enough) they were wrong.

One day Yates got a call from Grace Schulman, a twenty-six-year-old writer for *Glamour* who'd been "enthralled" by *Revolutionary Road* and wanted to include the author in a group of cultural luminaries being featured in the magazine (e.g., Brando, pianist Philippe Entremont, tenor Franco Corelli). Yates had no proper publicity shots to give her—he thought his portrait on the book jacket made him look effeminate—so Schulman arranged a session with the photographer Duane Michals. Afterward Yates and Schulman ducked out of a snowstorm into the Cedar Tavern, and talked for hours. She told him his novel had made the biggest impact on her since Flaubert, and Yates responded with an animated homage to *Madame Bovary*: "When Emma dies, I die," he said. "We realized there was an enormous connection between us," said Schulman, "that we'd be lifelong friends. But there was also this sexual undercurrent." Before things went any further, then, and despite the late hour, she took Yates home to meet her husband Jerry. It was love at first sight all over again.

Yates came to dinner every night that week, and the three became inseparable. "We couldn't get enough of each other," Schulman recalled. "It was that great moment in life when exciting things are *so* exciting. We told each other everything that had ever happened to us, and talked about the books we loved." In certain essential respects the Schulmans were ideal companions for Yates. Grace would later become a distinguished poet, but at the time she was strictly an admiring apprentice, and hence no threat to Yates's ego. Jerry was a medical scientist who was well-read enough to appreciate Yates's work without being inclined to judge it; he was also a kind and decent man, patient with the vagaries of an artistic temperament.

For Yates it was almost like having a family again, or anyway congenial siblings. At night they'd share a pot of boeuf bourguignon, then sit around drinking and talking while Grace strummed the guitar. The Schulmans thought the author of *Revolutionary Road* was a wise and compassionate arbiter of human relations, and Yates worked hard to live up to their expectations. Together and separately the young couple confided their marital problems to Yates, and sometimes he'd suddenly excuse himself to take a walk and think things over; "I've emerged with a fresh insight into your problem," he'd announce on his return. "We never had a friend like that," said Grace, "before or after."

Yates was less temperate on the subject of writing. "Write with *balls,* Grace!" he once exclaimed, and when she protested the impertinent anatomical reference, he said: "Well, write with ovaries, then. It's the same thing." At first she was having trouble writing at all, what with her duties at *Glamour,* and Yates was adamant that she quit: "Any girl in town would give her left breast to have that job," he said, "but you want to write and you should do it." Clearly Yates didn't want his beloved friend to become one of the phony strivers of the world, and he rarely missed a chance to play literary Pygmalion. Indeed, the main points of his *ex cathedra* advice amounted to a nice summary of the Yatesian aesthetic. He suggested she read Jane Austen, who had balls, and avoid Katherine Mansfield, who didn't; Gina Berriault had balls to spare, and one of her stories in *Short Story 1* was "better than any of ours." Cheever was a "dirty old man" who wrote about farts and so forth, and his slick prose didn't compensate for the *sprawl* of his work ("Don't be seduced by prose, Grace; the point is structure"); the same went for John O'Hara. *Billy Budd* was better than *Moby-Dick* because the latter *sprawled*. *Ulysses* ("I stretched my brain for it") was far, far better than *Finnegans Wake*. *A High Wind in Jamaica* and *Invisible Man* were wonderful, classically *structured* books. Characters shouldn't be too "knowy" about themselves; rather they should reveal themselves obliquely, like the narrators in Ford's *A Good Soldier* or Conrad's *Heart of Darkness*. Avoid "privacy" and "preciousness"—neither fiction nor poetry is "a letter home"; one writes with an *audience* in mind.* Nor is "honesty" per se a virtue ("Remember what Anatole France said about the dog masturbating on your leg—'Sure it's honest, but who needs it?' ") And finally, a writer needs to know the difference between sentiment and sentimentality: When Humbert sees the hair on grown-up Lolita's arms and loves her anyway, that's *sentiment,* that's what love *is*—being able to see the hair on somebody's arms.

At the time Schulman wasn't sure whether she wanted to devote herself to poetry or fiction, and Yates insisted on helping her with both. "Bad poems get by me," he said, "but good ones never do." Soon this became "Good poems get by me, but bad ones never do," and Schulman noted the contradiction. Yates waved it away: The same basic rules applied to both fiction and poetry, and to produce first-rate work in either genre required patience, talent, and balls. When Schulman gave up her *Glamour* job to concentrate on creative work, Yates wrote her, "*Don't worry* if it comes slowly at first and fails to give you pleasure, or if your brains feel scrambled, or if you spend whole days staring at the wall. . . . You must expect to produce a certain amount of bad stuff before it starts getting good. *Stay loose*: don't let your high critical standards choke you up and constrict you before you start."

Perhaps needless to say, Yates tended to be more generous when holding forth in the abstract, or rather when sober. "Oh, that *tree* thing—" he

---

*This, said Yates, was the biggest problem with student writing: "It takes many amateur writers . . . a long time to realize that they are addressing strangers with their work. Writing any kind of fiction is a public performance."

sneered tipsily, when one of Schulman's poetic motifs came under discussion. It was Yates who unwittingly canceled her future as a fiction writer—destroying with a vehement black pencil the last story she ever ventured to write. "[I] still feel like a turd," he wrote her afterward, "for . . . having scrawled those inept and booze-soaked half-assed 'comments' all over [your manuscript]." Despite such inevitable remorse, though, the balance between candor and kindness was all but impossible for Yates to maintain in the heat of the moment, much less with a dear friend. "PAY NO ATTENTION to what ANYBODY says about your ideas," he finally insisted, when yet another of his boozy critiques had gone awry. He added that if she'd known him back in 1955—and if she were "as big a bastard as [he]"—she might have said, " 'Ahh, nobody's interested in that Sloan Wilson crap any more' " when he told her about an idea he had for a novel.

The aesthetic perfectionist who spent hours slaving over a sentence, and couldn't resist berating a friend to write better, had a corresponding sense of ethical perfection as well. There was the drunk Yates and the sober Yates, and sometimes one or the other coincided with what Schulman called the "Platonic" Yates—the man who was "always trying to define what was true, what was right," and sometimes even managed to live up to his ideals. "I always thought Dick was incorruptible," Schulman said:

> For example, he believed it detracted from one's own self-esteem to be harshly critical of others, however tempting it was to criticize. Visiting us one evening, he brought us a little bank and insisted we feed it coins (dimes in those days) whenever any of us said unkind words about absent people. The practice took hold, and the bank stayed in our living room. Dick tried to be careful. One day, though, the name of a writer came up—a bad writer, Dick thought—who had won a prize. Dick sprang to his feet, emptied his pockets of change, and only then let loose a stream of invective.

The little bank was called the Physicians and Authors Benefit Fund (PABF), the proceeds of which would send a writer to medical school or a physician to a creative writing program. "I think that remark is fineable," one of them would say when the level of discourse sagged—as it often, wittily, did. Yates aspired to a Platonic self, but he was also a man who tilted at cops and told women to write with balls (and worse, much worse), while at the same time deploring ribaldry-for-its-own-sake and hence taking Cheever to task for being a "dirty old man." And yet amid such contradictions one could divine certain steadfast moral coordinates, indeed almost a puritanical streak. Yates's daughters, for example, were sacrosanct; he'd never violate their innocence by exposing them to a girl-friend, period, and he was appalled when a woman quipped, "Don't you want your daughters to know you have a penis?" Also, he hated pretense even in such harmless, pathetic forms as name-dropping. In college Grace Schulman had been a *Mademoiselle* guest editor, as had Joan Didion and Sylvia Plath, and her mentor at the magazine (and theirs) was one Cyrilly Abels; when Yates met the latter, she lost no time alluding to "Truman" et al., until Yates put his head on the Schulmans' coffee table and went to sleep. "Best regards to Cyrilly," he subsequently wrote his friends, "[and] C.P., Truman, Carson, Alfred, Guvvie, Frank, Ken, and the gang, and do thank them all for being so patient with Jerome (dime enclosed)."

As much as Yates wished to be at his best with the Schulmans, he remained an alcoholic with a severe mood disorder, and this of course made friendship problematic. "The seeds of estrangement were planted from the beginning," said Grace, though the good times outnumbered the bad. Yates was trying to get back to work, and this meant a disciplined avoidance of alcohol during the day (he'd drink tonic water because it tasted alcoholic); usually, then, he could drink steadily at the Schulmans' and still be in control, if a bit charmingly overanimated. But sometimes he'd become difficult, explode over trifles, such that it was hard to tell whether he was drunk or disturbed or both. And when he slept over or they took trips together, Yates tended to be so dour in the morning, and for much of the sober day, that his friends would wonder if they'd done something wrong. Always he required a lot of maintenance. His wild ges-ticulations sent ashes flying all over the apartment, and even though they installed a number of large ashtrays for Yates's benefit, he rarely bothered to use them; worse was his drunken tendency to light and forget his ciga-rettes, leaving them to smolder holes in the furniture.

And then really, their various affinities aside, it's hard to imagine a more curious misalliance than Yates and a sensitive young female poet from a liberal background—which is to say, Yates was not politically correct by most standards let alone Grace Schulman's. Though a self-styled "radical" Democrat, Yates was a social and aesthetic traditionalist who would always believe, not-so-deep down, that a woman was better off as a wife and mother and that most modern poetry was crap. To be a good writer was to write with balls, and when Yates would groan about "that *tree* thing," he often meant the tree in question was affected, fey, and, well, feminine. To Grace Schulman it became clear that Yates was dismissive of certain women because, among other things, they were women. She deplored as "puerile" the way Yates derided a female scholar whose academic specialty was Icelandic literature; she didn't think he'd laugh as hard if the Nordic maven were male. And once she observed Yates arguing with a pregnant novelist over who was more deserving of a Guggenheim: "I have great recommendations," said Yates. "So do I," the woman replied. "Well"—Yates paused—"but you're a girl, and you've got a baby."

Nor did Yates have much use for intellectuals, and Schulman's most revered teacher at Bard College was Theodore Weiss—an intellectual poet, no less. Weiss was head of the literature department, and at Schulman's request he'd agreed to interview Yates for a full-time position the latter badly needed. Weiss had been "moved and more" by *Revolutionary Road,* but must have been puzzled by its author, who seemed to bear him some sort of grudge. To the mortification of both Schulmans, Yates smoked and pointedly flicked his ashes around in brazen defiance of Weiss's request (since he'd been ill) that they all have some candy instead. Their host, wincing but still polite, tried to ask Yates a few interviewish questions ("What about a student who didn't do any work, who just wanted to *think* for four years? Would you flunk him?"), but Yates either ignored the man or gave perfunctory answers at best, until finally—not for the first time—he put his head down and tried to get some sleep. ("I got turned down for that job at Bard," he reported afterward to Barbara Beury.)

Ten years later Yates wrote the Schulmans: "Knowing you both was one of the very few things that kept me sane during all those frantic, dismal years of my second bachelorhood. I know I was an exasperating friend at times, but I can't ever thank you enough, or hope to repay you, for the unflagging moral support you gave me when I needed it most. Please don't ever forget that, either of you." The man who could admit as much was noble at heart, and for a long time the Schulmans loved him no matter what. "We saw the hair on his arms," said Grace.

Yates's favorite possession was a watercolor portrait of him and his daughters, painted by Bob Parker. He hung it over his bed and encouraged visitors to admire it; a girlfriend recalled, "It was the nicest thing in that crummy dump." It was also the closest the woman ever came to Sharon and Monica Yates. Every other weekend girlfriends were banished, not even allowed to call, and Yates would go alone to Grand Central Station and wait for his daughters' train. "I admired Dick's almost painful conscientiousness toward his daughters," said his friend Edward Hoagland. "He really suffered from the loss of their constant company. He'd carry Monica on his shoulders, and Sharon would walk alongside. It made an indelible impression on me. I always made a point of carrying my children on my shoulders after that."

Yates was a poignantly devoted father, but it was an odd arrangement in many ways. The basement was no place for children, however tidy he tried to make it for their visits, and the claustrophobic squalor combined with his vividly ill health made for a somewhat anxious atmosphere. While his daughters tried to sleep in his bed, Yates would set up an old army cot and spend much of the night pacing, smoking, and hacking, all the more insomniac because he was sober. The next morning his daughters would wake him by tickling his feet, and Yates would hold his head in his hands and resume coughing amid whatever playful remarks he could muster. The four-year-old Monica was so disturbed by her father's condition that she developed a habit of putting a hand on her chest and breathing deeply, because he couldn't.

For breakfast the three always went to the Howard Johnson's near the subway stop on West Fourth Street, where they'd try to make plans that reconciled the divergent interests of two girls seven years apart in age. Monica liked going to the Central Park carousel or zoo, perhaps a puppet show, and Sharon was often willing to go along and play the part of a shepherding big sister, though she preferred shopping and street festivals and coffee bars. But both were at pains to defer to the younger Monica, who was often sulky and miserable during these visits: She didn't like the wait and noise and smoke of restaurants, and wanted to be home with her toys, away from the cockroaches swarming in her father's shower stall. Yates worked hard to keep her cheerful, and was enchanted by both his daughters whatever their mood. "He saw us through rose-colored glasses," Monica said. "He thought we were more beautiful, more talented, more everything." When one of the girls would do something memorable—for example, when Monica said "welks" for "you're welcome" as one says "thanks" for "thank you"—Yates would store it away and tell his friends over and over, sometimes for years.

The childless Schulmans were indispensable in making these weekends a success. While Grace and Sharon rented bicycles and went riding around the park, the two men would squire Monica on their shoulders to the zoo, the carousel, the puppet show. "Jerry Schulman was an unbelievably beloved figure from my childhood," said Monica, who tended to "fasten on other guys" as they seemed "so much more together" than her father. Yates would occasionally try to assert his authority with the little girl, but was always more bossed than bossing. He knew that his youngest daughter worried about him, that the gloom of his life cast something of a pall over hers, and he tried to make her laugh whenever possible: He made up songs about her and helped her write plays, called her "Clownfish" or "Bunnyrabbit" or simply "Small." And if she wanted something more stable than a playmate, there was always Jerry Schulman. As for Sharon, she was called "Bigger" and lived up to the name—tall and mature for her age, she demanded that her doting father treat her more like an adult, but Grace treated her that way with far less awkwardness than Yates. Also, as Sharon remarked, "I was very self-conscious about being so tall, and Grace, who was almost six feet, made me feel great about it."

When the Schulmans weren't available, Yates would sometimes take his daughters to Bill Reardon's well-appointed apartment on Bedford Street, near the Blue Mill. Reardon was another divorced father who had children about the same age as Sharon and Monica; he made a good living selling ad space for *Scientific American,* and liked to throw parties for writers and artists who were interested in left-wing causes. The two men would take their children to the Blue Mill, where the waiters would fuss over them, and sometimes the older girls had slumber parties at Reardon's apartment while their fathers sat drinking in the kitchen. When Sharon was fourteen and a Beatles fan, she was very mildly amused when Yates and Reardon showed up at Grand Central wearing moptop wigs.

"The last hour of [his daughters'] visits was always a time of hurrying sadness," Yates wrote in *Uncertain Times.* After the Sunday ritual of window-shopping on Eighth Street, where Yates would buy a little present for each girl, they'd have a last dinner at the Blue Mill or Grand Central. Yates always got emotional toward the end. Unlike his ex-wife Sheila, who was all business when dropping the girls at the station ("Here you are; bye"), Yates would sit with them on the train until the last moment, crooning "Columbus Discovered America" as a sentimental reminder of all the fun they'd had. Little Monica could hardly bear it: "Stop, stop!" she'd sniffle. At last he'd stand on the platform as the train pulled out, waving and blowing kisses until they were well out of sight. "In a lot of ways," said Monica, "he was the same way his mother was: the sad, clingy one you loved helplessly when you were a child, and grew impatient with when you were grown up."

When *Newsweek* calls your first novel "the find of the year," your stock is apt to go up among the opposite sex, and so with Yates. It was a further reminder to the likes of Bob Riche that he and his old friend were no longer on equal terms; Yates would repeatedly leave parties with the best-looking woman there, often the very woman Riche had spent the better part of the evening trying to impress. "After you write *Revolutionary Road* you can screw anybody," Yates remarked with equal parts arrogance and boyish awe, as he'd just managed to bed a gorgeous Ivy Leaguer and was surprised that such "nice girls" could be so easily seduced.

On good days he was no longer the jumpy, drunken swain who scared women off with his needy desperation. He was a witty tippling genius novelist, who also happened to be a gentleman. One night at the Blue Mill the writer Dan Wakefield sat with his friend Sarel Eimerl, who was bemoaning the fact that he didn't seem able to talk to women, and one beauty in particular. "Before the meal was over," Wakefield recalled, "[Sarel] turned pale and said 'Look over there, in that booth, that's her! And *damn*, she's with that fellow Dick Yates, and just look, he's having no trouble talking to her at all! What the hell do you suppose the fellow is saying to her?' " Yates could even afford to be highly selective about the women he chose to charm. A very young and definitively nice girl such as Barbara Beury was near the ideal, worth courting at whatever distance, but a small-time Canadian actress coming out of the past to throw herself at him was not. "You make things most uncomfortable for me by becoming famous just as I am about to take you up on that drink," wrote the star of that mediocre CBC adaptation of "The Best of Everything." She'd seen the *Newsweek* puff and was coming to New York for ten days; could they meet? "You'd be bored to death with me," Yates replied. "I drink too much."

Cocksmanship was one thing, but Yates wanted a proper female companion—he called himself an "incurable keeps-player"—and his "Sweet Briar Sweetie" was proving elusive on the subject of further visits. This became a less pressing concern after a party late that spring at Stephen Benedict's apartment in the Village, where Yates met Natalie Bowen. The encounter was curious but not atypical of the affair that followed. Charles Van Doren, recently implicated in the quiz-show scandals, was sitting off by himself when the drunken Yates bellowed over the crowd, *"How dare that crook show his face in public?"* Van Doren affected not to hear, and a thin pretty woman rushed up to Yates and indignantly shushed him. Yates looked her over: She was wearing a sleeveless blue top with two silver bracelets wrapped around her biceps. "How'd you get those two bracelets up there?" he asked finally. "Elbow grease!" she replied, and Yates laughed. "He wouldn't leave my side the rest of the night," she recalled.

Bowen was a thirty-one-year-old editor at Putnam's with a masters in musicology from Brown—a worldly woman who was charmed but undaunted by a loud, drunken author who seemed "delighted by his own literary fame." She went back to his apartment that first night, and while they undressed Yates paused to examine her bra, plumply padded in the cups: "*That* can take care of itself," he said. Yates was another matter: Like his characters Andrew Crawford, Michael Davenport, and Bill Grove, he proved to be almost totally impotent. "It was ridiculous as far as the sex went," Bowen remembered. "It always was. He was never sober enough to get it up in any particularly gratifying way. But that wasn't the point of our relationship; he needed some female to be close to, to hold him." Yates was a touchingly conventional lover: After a certain amount of old-fashioned foreplay, he'd take a sheepish stab at missionary intercourse, fail, and finally roll over and say "Don't go away" until he fell asleep. The plea was so nakedly insistent that it became embarrassing, and one night Bowen said, gently enough, "Dick, that's *unmanly*." Yates was mortified.*

Bowen was tough, witty, and independent, a refugee from a wealthy dysfunctional family in Fall River, Massachusetts, and for a while Yates seemed to enjoy her feistiness. She called him "a hulking ego in a tweed jacket" and was impatient with his bemused acceptance of certain sordid aspects of his life. "What the hell am I doing here?" he'd say, looking around his apartment as if for the first time. "How did this *happen*?" At one point Bowen took down his Venetian blinds, caked with grime, and made the naked Yates wash them "in that disgusting stand-up shower stall he never cleaned." Grace Schulman pointed out that Bowen was very "elegant and correct," but also "the kind of person who would tell you that your fly is open." When Schulman said as much to Yates, he replied, "Don't you *want* to know if your fly is open?"

Yates's own receptiveness to this sort of remark depended on whether he was drunk or sober. "Dick was courteous and polite," said Bowen. "He always wanted to do the expected thing—always. *If* he was sober." Generally that meant he did the expected thing until noon or so. On weekends the two would sleep late and then go out for Bloody Marys. Yates would insist that the 110-pound Bowen match him drink for drink (it was "one of his gentleman's rules"), and for the most part she was happy to oblige:

---

*From "A Natural Girl": " 'Oh, don't go away. . . . ' That was the cry, or the plea, that had broken from David Clark's mouth as if wholly beyond his control with almost all the women he'd known since his divorce. Several girls had seemed to find it endearing, others had been baffled by it, and one sharp-tongued woman had called it 'an unmanly thing to say.' "

She hated her job at Putnam's, where she edited "control vocabulary books" for children, and was such a heavy drinker that she ended up in AA several years later. Meanwhile the outings with Yates were compelling incentives for going on the wagon. Yates's ambivalence toward Bowen was never far from the surface: On the one hand he seemed pleased that she had "breeding" and an Ivy League degree, but after two or three drinks he'd begin to sense she was putting him down somehow, making light of his own lack of education or déclassé background. Then suddenly he'd be in the throes of another "awful paranoid screaming fit" until finally Bowen would get up and leave. Later he'd show up at her door with a hangdog look, and the whole business would start over. "I was really fond of him," she said, "but I just couldn't handle it."

Yates seemed to cultivate a lack of sophistication, but also (at least in the presence of someone like Bowen) to be rather abashed about it. He always ordered the same thing for breakfast and dinner—scrambled eggs, the "small steak" at the Blue Mill—and it was ill advised to suggest, however lightheartedly, that he try something a bit more exotic for a change. Also he always wore the same daily Brooks Brothers uniform: tweed jacket, blue button-down shirt, gray flannel or khaki trousers, desert boots, a rumpled trenchcoat in cold weather, and for special occasions the tailored suit he'd bought in London. He called all the women in his life "baby," tenderly, but sometimes too in a menacing tone ("Look, baby . . ."). He could knowledgeably discuss a number of writers, but the only ones that really mattered remained the same—Flaubert, Fitzgerald, Keats—and the second was a constant, wistful guidepost for life as well as art. "Fitzgerald inhabited this gilded universe from which Dick felt forever excluded," Bowen observed. "Princeton, football games, Stutz Bearcats—Dick coveted it all intensely. He *hated* not going to college, and his way of dressing was a way of looking Ivy League. He always felt on the outside looking in—*so* ashamed living with his mother on the fringes of that estate [in Scarborough]. I felt sorry for him. I'd say, 'What *difference* does it make, Dick? You have all this talent!' But it didn't matter."

Perhaps Yates thought, at some level, that it was easy for *her* to say: She'd grown up in a beautiful old house as a Fall River Bowen; she had a masters from Brown. And yet, for all that, she was hardly the sort you took home to meet your mother, even if your mother happened to be Dookie. Barbara Beury was a different matter. At twenty she was still a "nice girl" who'd never dream of sleeping with a man she just met, or sleeping with a man who wasn't her husband, period; moreover she was the great-granddaughter of Col. Joseph Beury, a Charleston coal baron, and Bowen or no Bowen, Beury remained the woman Yates wanted to marry. Dookie liked her, too. As Yates wrote Beury in May, "Forgot to tell you that my mother spent approximately forty-nine hours telling me how Lovely and Nice and Intelligent you are—'just the sort of girl you can't help liking right away' etc. etc. etc. and hopes to see you again. I was terribly pleased, like any other gangling slob who hopes his Mom will like his Girl."

Beury had planned—or rather Yates had planned on her behalf—to move to New York after graduation and perhaps work at *Glamour*, where Grace Schulman was trying to arrange a job for her. But Buery was having second thoughts. "I guess I was a bit of a bastard on the phone yesterday," Yates had written her in February, and two months later he was "sorry . . . about all the drunken, shouting, self-pitying phone calls," and by May she was hanging up on him ("poutily," Yates thought). But the *succès d'estime* of *Revolutionary Road* kept her interest kindled, and around this time she invited Yates back to Sweet Briar in order to address her creative-writing class. He was a hit—"charming, witty, impressive"—and Beury was reminded of how glamorous it might be to have a handsome, somewhat famous writer for a boyfriend and maybe even a husband. Afterward they went to her professor's house for a drink, and all went well until the latter ventured to suggest that the one thing that "hadn't quite come off" in *Revolutionary Road* was Yates's use of a "Faulknerian stream-of-consciousness." Yates hated Faulkner. "Dick got furious—cursing, screaming, spilt drink, etcetera," Beury recalled. *"What the hell do you know?"* he shouted. *"You're just some little college writing teacher!"* The man's wife was about to call the police, when Beury at last managed to lead her date away. A few days later Beury's professor took her aside: "Look, it's none of my business," he said, "but if I were you I'd stay away from that man. He's unstable."

Yates wanted to be treated as a proper suitor, and that meant meeting Beury's parents. Since it seemed unlikely that her coal-executive father would make invidious comparisons to Faulkner, Beury was willing to look into it, but the man wasn't interested. Yates was too old, he said, and a writer to boot, the last an anathema that required no inkling of his other vagaries; besides, a nice local boy named George, a friend of the family no less, had given Beury an engagement ring over Thanksgiving. But the girl balked: George was *dull,* and whatever else Yates was, he was rarely that. Clinging to a hope that her life would prove a romantic affair, Beury tried to arrange a meeting between Yates and a great-aunt in Jamestown, New York, hoping that the matriarch might pave the way. At first the woman agreed to see him, but called it off after she'd spoken to Beury's father.

Sometimes fathers really do know best. Early that summer Beury was coaxed back to New York, where Yates acted like such a tiresome drunk that even the Schulmans wanted to get rid of him. He kept maundering about how—if Beury *really* cared for him—she'd take that job at *Glamour* so they could be married; then he'd turn bitter and accuse her of "chickening out." The letter he wrote afterward reflected an awareness that he'd probably blown it for good this time, though he tried to be graceful about it: "Even if you end up marrying George and organizing the bridge club (with washable plastic cards) you'll never be an 'a' to me." An "a" as opposed to a "the," he meant, a hausfrau as opposed to a personage—this a rather shrewd washable card for Yates to play, the better to remind Beury of why she'd liked him in the first place. "My old silver-haired mother keeps asking after you," he added forlornly.

That summer Yates visited Cape Cod with Natalie Bowen and the Schulmans. Bob Riche had taken a cottage in Provincetown, and Yates agreed to deliver an old Volkswagen that a friend was loaning Riche for the summer. It was one of the last times the two friends would meet. When Yates had finished *Revolutionary Road*—thereby reducing Frank Wheeler to his bare essence, a "lifeless man" whose favorite subject is "my analyst this; my analyst that"—his contempt for Riche seemed to crystallize. He inscribed his friend's copy of the novel with a curt "For old times' sake," and told the Schulmans that Riche, like the character he'd partly inspired, was a professional analysand who only pretended to be a writer, but would never be more than a PR hack.

It wasn't a very jolly trip. They started late and got lost, and when the dour Yates snapped a cigarette out the window they were pulled over by the police. That was perhaps the high point: Yates overheard a policeman refer to them as a "band of youths," and took to repeating the phrase whenever he needed a laugh. The phrase was much repeated. Soon it became clear that they wouldn't get to Provincetown by nightfall, and Bowen suggested they stop at her parents' house in Fall River. It was an impressive place—to Yates and the Schulmans it represented the "solidity and stability" the three had never quite known in their own lives—but it soon became clear that in this case a comely edifice was misleading. Bowen's father was a surly alcoholic, her mother "a sweet and ineffectual Billie Burke person" (as Bowen put it), and both parents were openly resentful toward their daughter for neglecting them. Grudgingly the older couple made up rooms for their unexpected guests. "Well, nobody in this family seems to be speaking to each other," Yates said, "but at least we can go to our separate bedrooms and stay there." Each bedroom had its own bathroom.

The visit with Riche lacked even that consolation. "This looks like a slave shack compared to the place we stayed last night," Grace Schulman observed on arrival. Her opinion of Riche was largely informed by Yates's critique, and the two treated their host as though he were the subject of a semiprivate and only mildly amusing joke. Riche tried to be affable but got little encouragement, though Bowen seemed to know what was going on and sympathized. Riche himself was more bewildered than anything: He had a general idea why Yates looked down on him ("I was this asshole writer who wasn't going anywhere"), but never quite understood what seemed to him such a sudden, categorical rejection.*

---

*Five years later Riche was puzzled but touched when Yates called, out of the blue, to congratulate him on the premiere of his play about Malcolm X, *Message from the Grass Roots*. Riche was less than touched eighteen years later, when he read *Young Hearts Crying* and came to the part where Bill Brock discusses his play *Negroes*: " 'Well, sure, it's kind of a stark little title, but that very quality of starkness is what I was after'—and he felt that his gift for dialogue had served him well in exploring the artistic possibilities of American Negro speech. 'For example,' [Brock] said, 'all through the play the characters keep saying "muh-fuh"; "muh-fuh"—and I've spelled it just that way.' "

It was probably a relief for Yates to get back to New York, where he now knew any number of famous writers. As ever, the more he admired a person's work, the more he was apt to find that person congenial as a human being. He'd recently read *The Lonely Passion of Judith Hearne* on the recommendation of Sam Lawrence, the book's American publisher, and eagerly approached its author at a subsequent party: "This confident, good-looking young man came up to me and told me how much he had liked my first novel," Brian Moore remembered. "I was pleased and gratified. I thanked him. He then said: 'Do you ever worry about having written a second novel which mightn't be as good as the first?'" For a moment Moore thought he was being mocked, but Yates's earnest, worried face convinced him otherwise.

The Irish-Canadian Moore had a lot in common with Yates: Both were realistic writers whose characters tended to be lonely, self-deluding failures, and Moore, too, was a witty, voluble man who often became dour and withdrawn. For a while Yates was something of a tipsy fixture at Moore's apartment in the East Seventies, along with the Australian writer Franklin Russell (with whom Moore would eventually exchange wives), who regarded Yates as a "soulmate drinker": "Dick had a steely dedication to destroying himself," said Russell admiringly. "He realized that if you're gonna drink, it's gotta be *serious*." In fact Yates was rather more serious than either man in that respect, and often needed assistance getting home at night. Once Moore asked a young woman to see him off, and Yates became galvanized with indignation: "Outrageous!" he shouted. "A *girl* take me home? I'll take *her* home!" "Are you sure you're competent?" Moore inquired. "Of course I'm 'competent,'" snapped Yates, spinning around and walking full speed into a wall. Another night the men staggered back from a party, and Yates insisted on trudging through the gutter; when he came to cars he'd climb ponderously over the back, jump onto the hood, and proceed as before. "After watching this episode," Moore remarked, "I realize I'm just a country boy."

Yates liked few things better than being admired by writers he admired, but in one case he suspected ulterior motives. He thought it ominous when he got a person-to-person call from "Beverly" ("Beverly *who*?" "Beverly Hills calling, sir") and it turned out to be Tennessee Williams, who wondered if his favorite new writer would like to meet for dinner in New York. Yates felt certain that his "effeminate" jacket photo had something to do with this, but how could he say no to Tennessee Williams? They met at the Forty-seventh Street YMCA, where Williams liked to swim; Yates stood in the lobby when suddenly the playwright appeared, dressed for dinner and still wearing a bathing cap. "How did it go?" Natalie Bowen asked when Yates returned late that night. "We talked books and drank," he reported. "I wasn't his cup of tea." Still, Yates remained convinced that a fair percentage of the reading public regarded him as "queer," and later insisted that Grace Schulman make him look "ballsy" when she photographed him for the jacket of *Eleven Kinds of Loneliness*.

By the summer of 1961, however, such a book had yet to materialize. Sam Lawrence was eager to consolidate Yates's reputation with a story collection, but Yates made him wait while he slowly progressed with his eleventh study of loneliness, "Builders." It was his first sustained fiction in almost a year, and his first short story since the abortive "End of the Great Depression." Work on his war novel had come to a dead end, and at one point he became so desperate that he blamed it on his table: "It's too high," he told Grace Schulman. "I need to get *over* my writing. . . ." So he sawed the legs down, to no avail. He wondered if perhaps it was the material itself that was the problem: He'd never been wholly satisfied with previous attempts at explicit autobiography, which seemed to go against the grain of his favorite Flaubertian principal—"The writer's relation to his work must be like that of God to the Universe: omnipresent and invisible"; and then, too, there was the uneasy sense of exposure inherent in writing (much less publishing) confessional fiction, all the more so while his mother was still alive. "Builders," then, began as an "experimental warm-up" to see if he could make "decent fiction" out of a "direct autobiographical blow-out," and he was tentatively pleased with the result. Indeed, he was sure enough of its basic soundness to be undaunted when Rust Hills rejected an early draft as a "formula story" ("[about] a 'colorful' character encountered by a writer"); Yates went back to work, and told Lawrence that his new book would have to wait a bit longer until he brought "Builders" to its final, perfected form.

Money, as usual, was a problem. Yates halfheartedly cast about for work while hoping that Hollywood's interest in his novel would soon amount to more than occasional teasing. The director John Frankenheimer, who would soon begin work on *The Manchurian Candidate* and was considered the industry's foremost wunderkind, had been trying to get financing for *Revolutionary Road* without success. Yates thought any number of big-name actors would be thrilled to play Frank Wheeler—if they could only be persuaded to read the book—in which case the financing would follow. He particularly wanted Jack Lemmon for the part, and one day he spotted the man in a coffee shop. But the moment passed: Yates didn't have a copy of his novel handy, and was loath to seem just another hustling fan. "But I *knew* he'd buy it!" he told the Schulmans. "I came so close!" By midsummer he was so broke he accepted a book-reviewing assignment from the *Saturday Review*—Jerome Weidman's *My Father Sits in the Dark and Other Selected Stories.* "Jerome Weidman writes three kinds of short stories," Yates wrote: "little sharp ones that are sometimes good, nostalgic ones that are often corny, and long flabby ones that are nearly always very bad. The trouble with *My Father Sits in the Dark* is that the good ones are badly outnumbered."

Yates's poverty was enough to make him long for the fall, when at least he'd have some income from teaching—but such anticipation was rueful at best. Reading students' work was a hateful distraction, and once his double duty at Columbia began he'd have more of it than ever. The previous spring he'd taught a second, nonfiction class at the New School, for which he'd written a course description that read like the jeremiad of a man bracing himself for the worst: "No culture has placed greater stress on the value of 'communication' than ours, and none has produced greater quantities of inept and muddled writing." Yates therefore solicited the "literate non-professional" interested in everything from "the personal essay to the business report," and promised to emphasize "lucid phrasing" and "[how to avoid] dullness." As it happened, mere dullness would have been a blessing. As he'd written Beury in late April:

Had a dreary class tonight after which an enormous fifty-year-old matron who can neither spell, punctuate nor write coherent English cornered me to demand, frankly, whether I thought she Had Talent. Tried to evade the question for twenty minutes and ended up saying sure. Depressing experience. . . . [I've] pretty well decided that teaching *does* sap the old creative energy after all. Why do so many sad clowns want to be writers? It's hard, no fun, scrambles your brains and leaves you unfit for practically all other kinds of human activity. Apart from which there's no dough in it except for Leon Uris and Allen Drury.

And sometimes, in a small way, for Richard Yates. That summer Rust Hills offered him "a considerable amount of dough" to serve as editor of an anthology featuring winners of a fiction contest for unpublished writers sponsored by *Esquire* and Bantam Books. All Yates had to do was read some five thousand stories (with an assistant) and select fifteen or so winners—this in addition to whatever his students at Columbia and the New School saw fit to produce. And meanwhile, too, he was still ghosting the odd speech for an agency in Princeton.

At seventy Dookie seemed tough and talkative as ever, despite a long half century of drinking, smoking, and fiscal emergency. For eight years she'd divided her time between Manhattan and St. James, where she rested each weekend amid her considerable efforts to keep the City Center art gallery afloat. The long commute was brutal in the summer and the hot little garage apartment at High Hedges was hardly an oasis, such that one might have wondered why she bothered to make the trip at all. The fact was, for all her illustrious contacts in the art world, the old woman was socially alone in the city except for an incompatible sister and a beloved son whom she rarely saw. High Hedges couldn't have been much better—her relationship with Ruth was an uneasy truce, Fred hardly spoke to her, and all but one of her grandchildren had grown up and moved out—but her belongings were there, her sculpture, and anyway it was a change.

Yates later told friends that his mother's cerebral hemorrhage (and much of its aftermath) happened exactly the way he described it in *The Easter Parade,* though the only surviving witness—Ruth's daughter and namesake—remembers a few details differently. Unlike the far more dissolute Pookie Grimes, Yates's mother was fully clothed when her fifteen-year-old granddaughter found her comatose in the garage apartment, nor was there any sign of emptied bowels or bottles of whiskey ("Bellows Partners' Choice") strewn about the place. The rest happened pretty much as written: Dookie had failed to emerge after a few sweltering days in mid-July, and Yates's sister had sent little Ruth to investigate.

Yates took it hard. He was with the Schulmans when he got the news that his mother had suffered an "insult to the brain" (Yates was appalled by the term) and that her chance of survival was less than 50 percent. Over the four or five months he'd known the Schulmans he'd always spoken kindly of his mother, and from the depths of his remorse he did so then: She was an elegant, talented woman who'd married beneath her, he said; an artist reduced at one point to sculpting mannequins. He wished he'd taken better care of her, and now she was likely to die or go on living as a vegetable. "I heard she was crazy *before* the stroke," said Natalie Bowen, after Yates caught a train for Long Island.

Dookie had revived somewhat when Yates got to the hospital, but she didn't seem to recognize him or anybody else, and was unable to speak more than a few random words. The doctors said that she could die within days or go on living for years, with or without some significant degree of brain damage. "[They] are talking in terms of 'wait and see' for weeks or months to come—it's amazing how little they really know about things like this," Yates wrote Barbara Beury:

> Meanwhile I've been living with my sister and her family out here in Ass Hole, Long Island, and my time has been wholly given over to the round of hospital visits, conversational banality, drunken slobberings, quarrels and all the other Thomas Wolfean goodies that accompany emergencies like this. My sister is in a constant state of near-hysteria, which doesn't help things much, and she and I have hardly anything in common, which makes it even less jolly. Worst week I've had in years, buddy.

But such was Yates's guilty desire to be a dutiful son that he was prepared to spend most of the summer, if necessary, amid the stormy boredom of

High Hedges (or at least until Dookie's condition was established one way or the other). Lonely and miserable, he called Sheila, one of the few people who could somewhat fathom his conflicted feelings: He wanted to *do* something about his mother, he said, but felt helpless.

A month later Dookie was still holding her own—"physically stronger but mentally off her trolly [*sic*]" as Yates put it—and she was moved to St. Johnland, an Episcopalian "home for the aged" in King's Park, Long Island. Her total monthly expenses came to a relatively exorbitant $260, and the Suffolk County Welfare Department demanded that Yates and Ruth contribute to their mother's care. Both were strapped and the extra burden was unwelcome, to put it mildly; when Ruth reminded her brother that Dookie's doctor at St. Johnland needed a one-time fee of $150 in addition to regular expenses, Yates exploded. Further discussion was impossible, and Ruth wrote him a weary letter instead: "I am not, as you so neatly put it, trying to 'cozy up to this shit-head.' I feel, and Fred agrees, that Dookie needs Dr. Alexander and Dr. Alexander needs $150. It's cut and dried. . . . Don't let's fight anymore." There was one other practical matter: Since welfare benefits still paid the better part of Dookie's care, the State of New York would claim her assets when she died. Therefore Ruth suggested they persuade Dookie to "give" them her sculpture, as it was "just possible that twenty years from now somebody will want to collect 'Ruth Yates.' "*

Dookie tuned in and out of lucidity, but even at her best she lived in a delusional fog. "It was Bob Jones [?] who arranged to have me hit by that car," she belligerently insisted, and wondered what would be done about it. At first she thought she'd "served two years as President of the United States"—it's possible she was confusing the nation with the National Association of Women Artists—and then demoted herself to first mother. She thought Yates was John F. Kennedy, that she lived in an annex of the White House, and that the nurses were pretty insolent under the circumstances. Her place among the "aristocracy" seemed assured at last, but

---

*Neither Yates's children nor Ruth's have any idea what became of Dookie's sculpture. All attempts to trace her work through museums, Pen and Brush, the National Association of Women Artists, etc., were unsuccessful. Except perhaps for some fugitive pieces in private collections, her work seems to have totally disappeared.

soon she became depressed and withdrawn. She stopped speaking of her role in Camelot, and during one of Yates's rare visits she sat ignoring him while she studied her haggard face in a hand mirror; finally, carefully, she painted lipstick on her reflection. The primacy of image over reality was complete.

"The deaths of parents, dreadful and sad as they are, do I think to an extent free writers," said Alice Adams, and this was certainly true of Yates. But it was a long and difficult process, and it exacted a psychic toll. He once told interviewers that the prologue of *A Special Providence*—in which Private Prentice visits his mother and listens to her drunken boasting about her artistic career—was the hardest scene he ever wrote ("I sweated blood over that"), and still more years would pass before he thought he was finally, truly able to "see things in the round" where his childhood was concerned. And the more he saw, the more obsessive and bitter he became, until finally he was as haunted as Stephen Dedalus by the memory of a spurned, beloved, and deeply hated mother.

By mid-August Yates needed a break, and with Dookie bound for St. Johnland he decided to accept John Ciardi's invitation to return to Bread Loaf as a teaching fellow. His friend Ed Kessler was driving to Vermont in rather illustrious company—Julia Child and her husband Paul; Bernard DeVoto's widow Avis—and invited Yates to join them. The five had breakfast together at DeVoto's apartment the morning of their departure, and Yates was on his best behavior. Paul Child had been the art teacher at Avon Old Farms when Yates was a bedraggled fourth former, and both seemed pleased by the subsequent turn of events, though perhaps the happily married Child was a bit more so than his old pupil.

The two weeks passed without major mishap, though the good impression Yates made on the Childs and Avis DeVoto didn't last. DeVoto presided over Treman Cottage, where privileged staff members gathered to eat, drink, joke, argue, and plot sexual assignations, rather in spite of their domineering hostess. DeVoto insisted her guests provide their own liquor and mark the bottles, and if anyone was so much as a minute late moving from veranda or lounge or lawn to the dining room, that person found the door shut. A student who wrote Yates a postconference note, inviting him to visit her, promised, "[W]e don't mark our bottles here . . . and there isn't anyone named Avis within fifty miles, except maybe a car rental agency." Yates seems to have kept his temper in the face of such fussiness, but not without a certain amount of extravagant sulking. "He had the manner of a spoiled child," said Julia Child, who remembered him as a "romantic figure" but a "difficult drunk": "He seemed conspicuously unstable—Byronic, adrift."

Yates was at his best among the unthreatening young, whose work he critiqued with candor and a sense of tact that came naturally in moods of sober detachment. The poet Miller Williams was a student that year, a friend thereafter, and found much to emulate in Yates's approach: "Dick never praised simply to make you feel good, but he never wounded with criticism either." Yates also made his mark in the lecture hall, as a lovingly modest enthusiast vis-à-vis his pet subjects—Flaubert and Fitzgerald, dialogue and the objective correlative.

And finally Yates managed to finish "Builders" and tune up the other stories for his collection, which he sent off to Sam Lawrence as soon as Bread Loaf was over. "I can't tell you how impressed I was with *Eleven Kinds of Loneliness,*" Lawrence replied; he'd read and reread each story with "renewed pleasure" (even the ones he'd rejected over the years) and liked "Builders" the best of all: "It is the most poignant and profoundly moving and it has a kind of prayer at the end which I could not forget."

Back in New York, Yates's life was in flux. His friend Anatole Broyard, at the age of forty-one, had decided to marry—to retire at the top of his form, so to speak. Yates was among the fifty or so guests who attended the Village wedding, where he presented the couple with a crystal decanter. After that he and Broyard saw little of each other: The latter, thus domesticated, avoided Yates as an unpredictable drunk, and in 1963 he and his wife settled in Connecticut; later, when Broyard became a full-time reviewer for the *New York Times,* he'd often be in a position to remind Yates, after a peculiar fashion, of their old friendship.

Yates's romantic life was "lively if somewhat confused," as he put it; two long-term affairs became moribund that fall, while others came and went. Barbara Beury decided to turn down the *Glamour* job and stay in West Virginia, though she continued to write Yates and even spoke of visiting now and then. Yates's response was irascible but gracious on the whole: He was tired of their "endless sophomoric discussions about 'fate' and 'bridge-burning,'" he wrote, just as he supposed *she* was tired of his "instabilities and uncertainties"; but he agreed it might be nice to maintain "an undemanding, friendly-correspondence type thing that would enable us to keep in touch without driving each other crazy." But they didn't keep in touch. A few weeks later Yates decorously confessed to "a new involvement," and though Beury tried to assure him that she wanted to remain friends anyway ("Christ, Dick, you're no cad or whatever, in fact to be honest I've been regarding our relationship as a 'buddy system' since May of last year"), she never heard from him again.

Yates's "new involvement" also superseded his old one with Natalie Bowen. He never did adjust to the combination of her sharp tongue and Fall River pedigree, nor did she grow any more used to the noise. One night the couple met Sam Lawrence for dinner and all got more or less equally drunk, after which they went back to Bowen's apartment for a nightcap. Before long Yates was raving at both of them, muddling his grievances as he addressed one or the other, until Bowen locked herself in the bathroom and Lawrence tried lugubriously to reason with him. For Bowen such scenes had become all too familiar, with or without a third party, ditto Yates's tendency to come banging on her door in the middle of the night to apologize. Toward the end ("as a last resort") he went so far as to tell Bowen he loved her—and then suddenly it was over: He had a new involvement. Unlike Barbara Beury, though, Bowen would continue to hear from him over the years, however sporadically. A few months after their breakup Yates called while she was in the process of moving; he insisted on coming over and helping her unpack boxes. "I remember Dick busily carrying books from one room to another," said Bowen, "one of my friends commenting that she could always tell where Dick had been from the little pile of ashes he left behind." Eventually, more than ten years later, she'd find herself in a position to return this curious favor.

Yates's first involvement after Bowen came to a bad end. The woman's name was Lynn and she was also a writer (not a good sign), a recent divorcée who needed a job. Grace Schulman, obliging as ever, introduced her to the editors of *Glamour,* and the pretty, well-spoken young woman was hired on the spot as a copywriter. She was still working there when she came in one day "looking as though someone had been beating her over the head," Schulman recalled: "moaning, wordless." Yates had just broken up with her, and no wonder: He'd never thought much of her mind—she had "brains of submoronic intellect," he said—plus he'd always been suspicious of the fact that she'd married a wealthy man. At any rate he wasn't alone for long. At a publishing party Bob Riche was glad to introduce his old friend to Sandra Walcott, a "rich, classy girl" who was "too intimidating" for Riche's own taste. Walcott, a reader at Holt, was a great admirer of *Revolutionary Road,* and she seems to have brought out the best in Yates. Indeed she remembers him as "a perfect gentleman," and never experienced the slightest hint of tumult in his presence: "He'd drink wine or beer," she said, "but that was it. He was very sensitive, tender, and courtly. No big ego. He alluded to past problems with drinking, and was thoughtful and honest about it." This of course is a recognizable side of Yates, but when Walcott also recalls his "cute little apartment," the brow begins to furrow a bit: If he managed to tidy the place to such a miraculous extent that someone like Walcott would find it "cute," then that winter must truly have been a halcyon period.

Even Sheila was having second thoughts about her ex-husband. Their relations had gradually thawed since the Bellevue episode, until Yates had taken to spending the night (chastely) when visiting his children in Danbury, where Sheila had moved to be near the teachers' college where she was taking classes for her degree. At one point she proudly brought Yates to the home of her English teacher, a young writer named Lee Jacobus, for whom Sheila was a favorite pupil.* Yates finished off the man's small store of liquor, a little of everything, but remained in control and at one point asked Jacobus to submit a story to the Bantam contest.

For her part Sheila continued to be troubled by Yates's drinking, but her doubts were somewhat offset by his growing stature as a writer, to say

---

*"On the first day of class I asked my students if they'd read various writers—Henry James, for example," Jacobus recalled. "Almost every time, Sheila's hand was the only one that went up. Finally I stopped asking, since I could see she was getting embarrassed."

nothing of his exemplary conduct as a father. Then over Christmas Sheila was so touched by Yates's gift of fine Danish crystal that their rapprochement became heated. A few days later she and the girls drove to Tarrytown to meet Yates for dinner; afterward Sharon woke up in the back of the car and observed her mother canoodling her father's neck: "You know what I want, dear," she was saying. When Sharon inquired about this, Sheila was briskly matter-of-fact: Your father and I *might* get together again, she said, but don't get your hopes up and don't tell your sister.

Otherwise they kept it secret from the children, a situation Sheila disliked as a "hole-in-corner deal." She was sneaking weekend visits to New York, as well as trysting with Yates in and around Danbury, but she wasn't willing to commit to anything more permanent. In some ways the past two years had been the most rewarding (certainly the most peaceful) of Sheila's life: After her abysmal academic performance as a girl, she was gratified to learn that she had it in her to be an excellent student, and she liked keeping an orderly home for her children without interference or mess. But she was lonely. "I have learned what it is to need," she wrote Yates, "to want to go to bed with you and not be able to. . . . I've missed you so awfully much." Not so much, however, that she'd altogether forgotten that she and Yates were "a hell of a lot of trouble to each other." And Yates, too, was a little skeptical—he told Sheila he'd gotten his self-esteem back after the divorce—but the prospect of living with his daughters again, of having a reliable body in bed at night, far outweighed his doubts. Early that spring he parted company with Sandra Walcott: "He was very kind about it," she recalled. "He said he was seeing his ex-wife again, and that he could only see one woman at a time. I never heard from Dick or saw him again."

As the new year dawned, Yates was less inclined to view himself as a tragic figure. The modest abstemious fellow who sipped only wine and beer, who impressed the well-bred Walcott with his "cute" bachelor digs, was at the moment so awash in good news that even he had to concede that the "tragic" label was a trifle inexact. For one thing he'd digested the worst of his "rather exaggerated emptiness and despair that followed *Revolutionary Road*," and in the meantime "Builders" had reassured him not only that he could still write, but also use problematic personal material and avoid what he called "the two terrible traps that lie in the path of autobi-ographical fiction—self-pity and self-aggrandizement." Moreover Holly-wood was coming around at last: Though Frankenheimer had shelved plans to make *Revolutionary Road,* he'd optioned an equally depressing novel by a more famous author who, like the director, happened to be a fan of Richard Yates. Frankenheimer realized he needed a "special type of writer" to adapt *Lie Down in Darkness* for the screen, and while Styron himself wasn't available for such work, he knew somebody who was. "The Movie Deal that seemed so certain for my book all summer and fall came to a dreary end about a month ago," Yates had written in late-November,

> but I'm now almost equally excited and nervous about another deal which is said to be 90 percent of a sure thing—a job to write the screenplay for Styron's *Lie Down in Darkness,* in exchange for such a colossal amount of money that it would buy my freedom for the next two years. If this does happen I will go to Hollywood the first week in January and earn all the dough before summer; if it doesn't I'll stay here in the old mousetrap and continue with other freelance droppings.

Two months later Yates still had "no whiff of a contract yet," but his "endlessly optimistic agent" assured him it was only a matter of time that he'd be bound for Hollywood and the big money.

In general he was too busy to worry about life with his old morbidity. Apart from his teaching duties, some three thousand stories had already been submitted for the Bantam contest, and Yates—never much of a skimmer—was "temporarily out of the writing game" as he made his slow, conscientious way through the vast pile. The work was a bit depress-ing at times, as Yates was made more aware than ever that, where writing fiction is concerned, many are called but *very* few are chosen. One sub-mission came from a New Jersey State Prison inmate, who wrote Yates a long letter admitting, gratuitously, that he wasn't much of a writer, though he did have a number of saleable ideas for a novel, all of which revolved around the same basic premise of a prisoner unjustly accused. No story was enclosed; what the man really wanted was advice: "Mr. Yates, how can I make sure that know one [sic] can use this story concerning me and this whole case? There are a few lawyers thinking about taking this story using it for motion picture."

When the drudgery and waiting got him down, Yates could indulge in the "serene and majestic daydreams" that had sustained him as a hopeful apprentice and now seemed on the verge of realization. In January *Revolutionary Road* was named one of the eleven finalists for the National Book Award, along with such strong contenders as Heller's *Catch-22*, Salinger's *Franny and Zooey*, Wallant's *The Pawnbroker*, and an obscure first novel called *The Moviegoer* by a forty-five-year-old physician named Walker Percy. Sam Lawrence was guardedly hopeful—he knew for a fact that at least one of the three judges that year, Herbert Gold, was a big fan of *Revolutionary Road* ("the book was a shattering experience for him"), and meanwhile there was a growing consensus that such best-sellers as *Catch-22* and *Franny and Zooey* were, after all, ludicrously overrated. Yates emphatically agreed.

After the award ceremony on March 13, Yates and his fellow nominee Ed Wallant went away to commiserate. They were disappointed but philosophical: *The Moviegoer* was a good book and Percy seemed a nice guy, but both had come to believe they had a real chance. Then, two days later, Gay Talese reported in the *New York Times* that writer Jean Stafford had, in effect, waylaid her fellow NBA judges in favor of the underdog Percy.* It was a story that, in bitter moments, struck Yates as all too plausible. Though he later told interviewers that Stafford was "a beautiful writer," for private consumption he called her "a pathetic lush" and would often recount the story of how she'd derailed his career. According to his friend Dan Wakefield, the 1962 National Book Award was "a 'Rosebud' moment for Dick: If he'd won, his whole life would have been different." To be sure, for a writer who often seemed almost self-destructively modest about his own work, Yates could be surprisingly vehement on the subject of the NBA. When a student later asked whether he'd "really wanted"

---

*Both Herbert Gold and the third judge, Lewis Gannett, are on record as having chosen *The Moviegoer* purely as a matter of merit. "I admired Yates's writing," Gold told me, "but I think there's a monotony in the prose—so much *pain* expressed. If writing is no fun, why go on with it?"

it, Yates was incredulous: "Want it? *Want* it? Of *course* I wanted it, I wanted it so fucking bad I could taste it!"

At the time, though, Yates could afford to be stoical. A month before the ceremony he'd been summoned to the Plaza Hotel by John Franken-heimer. "Just to save you anxiety in the elevator," the director told Yates on the house phone, "you have the job." Faced with the staggering prospect of fifteen thousand dollars for a few months' work—to adapt a novel he *admired*, no less—the impoverished freelancer comported him-self with admirable poise in the great director's presence. Amid a suiteful of name-dropping Hollywood types ("Who's going to wet-nurse Warren [Beatty] on the set? *I* did last time," etc.), Yates sat apart with Franken-heimer and explained his thoughts on Styron's work. The director was "very favorably impressed": "Dick was without subterfuge. Very direct and intelligent, no pretense at all. It was clear he loved *Lie Down in Dark-ness* and came well prepared to discuss it."

Yates flew to Los Angeles in mid-March and spent a week or so as Frankenheimer's guest in Malibu. On the plane he felt a bad cold coming on—always ominous for the consumptive Yates—and the milieu chez Frankenheimer was hardly conducive to a quick recovery. As he wrote the Schulmans, "I spent the first week in Frankenheimer's palace by the sea, mostly in a state of continual drunken, shouting story conference with the man himself, while [actress] Evans Evans tiptoed discreetly around in her Mou-Mou [*sic*]." The whole episode is treated at length in "Saying Good-bye to Sally," in which Frankenheimer appears as "Carl Oppenheimer"—"a dramatic, explosive, determinedly tough-talking man of thirty-two." The portrait is not altogether flattering: Oppenheimer is an intellectually pretentious egomaniac who bullies his adoring girlfriend ("Ellie, can you check the kitchen and find out what the fuck's happened to all the bouil-lon?"), and indeed Yates thought Frankenheimer overdid his flamboyant young genius persona. For the most part, though, Yates was struck by how well they got along: "Believe it or not, we made a happy household," he reported to the Schulmans. Frankenheimer was also a divorced father of two daughters, and he obviously respected Yates's accomplishment as a writer. Yates in turn rather envied the man's relationship with Evans Evans—who, though a good sport and attractive enough, was hardly the kind of glamorous starlet Yates would have expected. It occurred to him that he, too, needed such a helpmeet.

Mainly Yates felt intimidated. Apart from the immediate domestic rapport, it was the Hollywood scene writ large: the great pad in Malibu, famous actors calling at all hours for bizarre reasons, power brokers of all sorts coming and going. Yates had never written a screenplay before, and suspected that Frankenheimer—who could have hired anyone in Hollywood—might at any moment realize his mistake. But in fact the two men collaborated well together: The bombastic Frankenheimer found Yates "quite shy" in a pleasant, receptive way, and deferred to his views on literary matters, while Yates was "eager to absorb the whole screenwriting process" from Frankenheimer. Nor did Yates make himself conspicuous as a drinker: "We *all* drank," said Frankenheimer. "We *all* behaved erratically. We weren't prototypes for a brokerage firm. Besides, the Styron piece was really horrid, depressing—we'd *both* be depressed, and one of us would say '*God*, let's have a drink.' We had to boost each other up." Best of all, there was no question of Yates's having to compromise his artistic integrity in exchange for Hollywood lucre; both he and Frankenheimer agreed on a rigorously faithful adaptation of Styron's novel, with due emphasis on its incest theme, and damn the censors. All this came as a great relief to the folks at home, some of whom wondered if success would spoil Dick Yates: Soon after he left for Tinseltown, Sheila reported that she'd been accosted at a party by an almost total stranger, who demanded, "Do you think Hollywood is changing Dick's values?" "Nobody, honest to God," Yates assured the Schulmans, "has tried to corrupt me yet, which in a way is faintly disappointing—there's nobody to hate, and nobody to blame if the picture turns out to be a mess. They all keep insisting that I have Absolute Freedom." If anything the whole business seemed too good to be true, right down to the nature of the work itself, which Yates found "a remarkably easy and interesting kind of writing to do."

Once he and Frankenheimer agreed on the "thrust" of the screenplay, Yates rented the ground floor of a tiny dilapidated beach house in a far more raffish section of Malibu. Like Jack Fields in "Saying Goodbye to Sally," he almost immediately regretted his choice: "He didn't realize until after moving in—and after paying the required three months' rent in advance—that the place was very nearly as dismal and damp as his cellar in New York." As if to convince himself that the glamour of his adventure hadn't faded yet, Yates rented a sporty white convertible and stressed his shack's better features in letters to friends. "Baby, this is Crazyville," he wrote Ed Kessler. "Wobbling around here in a sleek little sunlit beach house while the Pacific thunders beyond my terrace." To the Schulmans he admitted his lodgings were "about as big as 27 Seventh Ave.," but at least the beach was private and it was "picturesque as all get-out, and reasonably cheap, too." But the damp mildewy hovel didn't agree with Yates's lungs, and within a week his cold had developed into pneumonia. The doctor warned him about the possibility of a TB recurrence, and Jerry Schulman mailed a three-month supply of isoniazid ("the drug I've been needling you about for three months"). Yates may or may not have bothered to take the medicine as prescribed, but anyway his health continued to be poor for at least a month or so.

Eleven Kinds of Loneliness was published a few days after Yates arrived in California, and geographical isolation seems to have enhanced his sense of detachment toward a rather disappointing reception. "[The book] is Not Selling at All and being ignored by most New York critics," he wrote Kessler, "but getting excellent reviews in all the places that don't count—Chicago, Detroit, Atlanta, Los Angeles, etc." Yates told the Schulmans he was especially pleased by a Southern critic who'd compared the collection favorably to Hemingway and Fitzgerald: "He's probably some semi-literate cracker with tobacco-juice running down his chin, but it makes delightful reading all the same." Above all he was gratified by the fact that reviewers tended to single out "Builders" as the best story, an advance on the author's earlier work that indicated growth and the brilliant career to come. But very few seemed to think brilliance had already been established, and amply so, on the strength of his first two books.

Perhaps the most representative notice was Peter Buitenhuis's in the March 25 *New York Times Book Review*. Buitenhuis recognized many of Yates's virtues—pitch-perfect dialogue, "exact and memorable" details, the "unexpected rightness [of his endings] that is the peculiar reward of

reading a first-rate story"—but like many critics then and after, he ultimately and rather perversely held Yates's craftsmanship against him. In an
irony that might have struck the author as droll, Buitenhuis (and others)
implied that Bernie Silver's hackneyed "Builders" metaphor constituted
Yates's actual method for writing a well-made story: "Mr. Yates has submitted his considerable talent to the formula," Buitenhuis wrote, "and has
been ground by the mill into mediocrity." Happily he thought that
"Builders" was a hopeful sign Yates was moving away from "formulaic"
O. Henry-like stories toward a more Chekhovian mode, whereby "the
situation grows naturally out of the characters" rather than vice versa.

Other reviews offered a thumbnail sketch of the conventional arguments that tend to be marshaled for and against Yates's work. Richard Sullivan in the *Chicago Tribune* could no more resist the "Builders" metaphor
than Buitenhuis, but at least he used it to express a kind of stolid approval:
"Each story stands on its own. Each is written with its own care and its
own craft. Each is a sturdy structure in revealing prose." Some took Yates
to task for his "limited" range—a charge leveled at everything from the artful economy of his plots to the mediocre character types to a repetitive
bleakness of theme. Hollis Alpert of the *Saturday Review* wondered "why,
over the span of ten years in which [the stories] were written, Mr. Yates
didn't explore farther," and J.C. Pine of *Library Journal* suggested that
Yates needed "a larger canvas" lest "his vaunted 'compassion'" come across
as mere "snobbery."

Perhaps the first indication that *Eleven Kinds of Loneliness* would
stand the test of time came almost two years later, when the critic Jacques
Cabau wrote a long appreciation for the influential French weekly
Express: "A Flaubert formed in the rough school of the magazine," the
review was titled. Cabau called Yates "one of the hopes of his generation,"
and suggested that the perfection of his prose (even in translation) was the
work of a slow, meticulous writer who "searches for hours for the exact
word, and often finds it." Not surprisingly the Frenchman was especially
pleased by Yates's insights into the hollowness of American life: "*Eleven
Kinds of Loneliness*—a courageous theme in America, where loneliness is
a sin, where success is obligatory and happiness is the first duty of every
citizen." Such considered praise, aimed at posterity, was long in coming

on this side of the Atlantic, though an awareness of the book's excellence was—to repeat Richard Ford's phrase on the subject of *Revolutionary Road*—"a sort of cultural-literary secret handshake among its devotees." In 1978 Jonathan Penner noted in the *New Republic* that the collection "stands at the pinnacle of its genre," and three years later Robert Towers made an even more definitive claim in the *New York Times Book Review*: "the mere mention of its title is enough to produce quick, affirmative nods from a whole generation of readers . . . [it is] almost the New York equivalent of *Dubliners*."

The comparison to Joyce's masterpiece is not an idle one, and for that matter the two books have more in common than merit. Each evokes the ethos of a time and place in a peculiarly memorable way, and each reveals aspects of human weakness which are universal and abiding, but flourish better under certain conditions. It's no coincidence that the paralysis of Joyce's Dublin produced characters that might well be called Yatesian. In Joyce's "Counterparts," for example, the frustrated lout Farrington— whose humiliations as a bullied clerk can only be dispelled by violence ("The barometer of his emotional nature was set for a spell of riot")—is the spitting image of Yates's "B.A.R. Man," John Fallon, who returns from the war to find himself in a dismal world of underpaid office labor and a loveless marriage. At a slightly higher social level we find Gabriel Conroy in "The Dead," a kind of Irish Frank Wheeler who affects Continental sophistication in order to distance himself from his petty-bourgeois background—his arty aunts and "country cute" wife—but is finally revealed as "the pitiable fatuous fellow he had caught a glimpse of in the mirror." Postwar America and turn-of-the-century Dublin have niches in store for people like Fallon and Farrington, Conroy and Wheeler, and these tend to be commensurate to their limitations; enticed to act on their longings for something more, be it fame or fulfillment or simple human acceptance, they're exposed like the boy in "Araby"—as creatures "driven and derided by vanity."

The charge that Yates's range is "limited" is particularly unfair in regard to *Eleven Kinds of Loneliness*. Never again would Yates depict such a broad cross-section of society, from the welfare child Vincent Sabella to the expatriate Yalies Carson Wyler and Ken Platt, and all the lonely people in between. That he was constrained by the "formulaic" demands of magazine fiction is true, though one might as well say that a poet is constrained by the sonnet or a composer by the sonata. Yates's talent, like Salinger's, was honed by the necessary discipline of concision, sharply delineated characters, and a clear trajectory of beginning, middle, and end. Both authors would later allow themselves the luxury of "a larger canvas" in their not-so-short fiction—looser dialogue and plots, more ambiguity—and in one case the result was not especially fortunate.

But given only four or five thousand words to tell a story, Yates learned to be ruthless in restricting himself only to the most resonant details. The bleakness of Vincent Sabella's life, for example, is imparted by a single image: "Clearly, he was from the part of New York that you had to pass through on the train to Grand Central—the part where people hung bedding over their windowsills and leaned out on it all day in a trance of boredom, and where you got vistas of straight, deep streets . . . all swarming with gray boys at play in some desperate kind of ball game." As for the characters themselves, Yates sketched them with a few deft strokes; rather like the more contradictory, lingered-over Wheelers, they are both stylized types and nobody but themselves. Thus Leon Sobel, the former sheet-metal worker with writerly pretensions in "A Wrestler with Sharks," is aptly described as "a very small, tense man with black hair that seemed to explode from his skull and a humorless thin-lipped face. . . . His eyebrows were always in motion when he talked, and his eyes, not so much piercing as anxious to pierce, never left the eyes of the listener."

When critics call Yates "limited" what they often mean is *not* that he worries too much about "building" his stories according to some formulaic blueprint, but rather that (*pace* Bernie Silver's instructions) he doesn't put enough *windows* in. Readers want more light, more hope and moral uplift, not such an unremittingly "limited" view of frustration and failure. Few writers can make the reader wince the way Yates can: On the tenth reading it's still uncomfortable to read the passage in "A Really Good Jazz Piano" where Carson humiliates Sid; or when Leon Sobel produces his pitifully pretentious newspaper column (with "a small portrait of himself in his cloth hat" clipped to the top); or when Vincent adds "a triangle of fiercely scribbled pubic hair" to his otherwise loving graffito of Miss Price; or when John Fallon's better-paid wife makes him come back to the table and drink his milk ("you're the one that makes me *buy* milk"), and a page later he avenges himself by scornfully waving a padded bra "in her startled face." Readers who deplore this kind of thing believe Yates is more cruel than compassionate, but this is rather beside the point. As Richard Russo noted in his introduction to the *Collected Stories*, Yates leaves out the "windows" because "he believes this light to be a lie." In real life the light seeps in, if at all, "through whatever chinks and cracks have been left in the builder's faulty craftsmanship"—and certainly Yates, *qua* builder, makes allowance for such occasional rays: hence the grace that allows Ken Platt to recognize a kindred loneliness in his friend's eyes; or Leon Sobel's loving wife who believes in him no matter what; or the memory of being "a damn good B.A.R. man" that will have to suffice for the rest of Fallon's mediocre, loutish life.

"The truth is a funny thing," as Leon Sobel says. "People wanna read it, but they only wanna read it when it comes from somebody they already know their name." Perhaps, but not necessarily in the case of Richard Yates: Readers who already knew his name as author of the depressing *Revolutionary Road*—that is to say, readers who were keen for diversion amid the grim uncertainties of the cold war—might have decided to give *Eleven Kinds of Loneliness* a miss, while those who didn't know Yates at all plumped in favor of Updike's *Pigeon Feathers*. In any case the stories didn't sell despite a number of excellent reviews in the provincial press. When Monica McCall fired off an angry letter to Sam Lawrence demanding a full-page ad—the kind of treatment Updike was getting—the hapless man demurred: The "economics of publishing" wouldn't permit it, he explained, and the Updike situation was "by no means comparable" since the latter had received front-page reviews all over the country; for Yates they'd already spent almost a dollar a copy on advertising, and distributed 543 gift copies to reviewers, critics, authors, and booksellers. But the total sale had petered out at around two thousand, and there it was.

Yates took the news remarkably well, though he did venture to inquire why he couldn't find the book anywhere in greater Los Angeles.

Lawrence replied that at least seven area bookstores had ordered copies, and added a bit of heavy humor to ease the strain: "They're there, and now all you have to do is persuade those starlets and tycoons to buy them. But do they read out there?"

The last week in March, while laid up with pneumonia, Yates set aside work on his screenplay to make a final selection for the Bantam anthology. By then he was thoroughly sick of the whole business—in his introduction he wrote that he'd begun to develop "a kind of literary snow-blindness" amid the "blizzard of manuscripts"—but fairly satisfied with the result: He'd managed to cull fifteen good stories out of the five thousand submitted, and also sent thirty-five runners-up just in case. Rust Hills was "quite impressed" by Yates's selection, though he did decide to rearrange the top two prizewinners so that a quirky, formless story called "Two Semesters at Wagner Inn" got first place instead of George Cuomo's more conventional "A Part of the Bargain." The anthology was titled *Stories for the Sixties* ("Here are some of the writers you'll watch for in the Sixties," trumpets the cover blurb), and Yates's introduction was a precise summary of his own principles whatever the decade:

> There are, I believe, no sentimental stories in this collection. None of them betrays the uncomfortable sound of an author trying to speak in a voice that is not his own, nor is there any in which the voice is not worth listening to. . . . It might be tempting to look for literary trends in these fifteen stories, or to draw conclusions from them about contemporary ways of seeing Man and Society, but that's a risky business better left to scholars and critics. For an editor, it's enough to know that they encompass a healthy variety of style and content, that each writer has accomplished what he set out to do, and that what he set out to do was neither false nor trivial.

Fair enough, though readers who watched for these particular writers in the sixties or any other decade were bound to be somewhat disappointed. Of the fifteen, only one would become at all well-known: Judith Rossner, author of *Looking for Mr. Goodbar*. George Cuomo and Helen Hudson (a former New School student of Yates) would go on to have productive if rather obscure careers, while another, Silvia Tennenbaum, wrote a commercial novel titled *Rachel, the Rabbi's Wife*.

After Yates's first hectic month in California, he was perhaps too exhausted to feel proper elation at the news that he'd won a Guggenheim in the amount of $4,500. He was deflated further by the fact that his friend and fellow NBA-nominee Ed Wallant had just gotten a Guggenheim for $6,000, and had kited off to Rome after submitting his third and fourth novels simultaneously. Yates was gleeful when he got word that both manuscripts had been rejected pending further revision ("Maybe the little bastard will now begin to learn that it's difficult to write good novels"), but shocked into taking a kinder view a few months later, when Wallant died suddenly of a brain aneurysm at thirty-six. "It was almost as if he knew he didn't *have* much time," Yates remarked in a later interview, having noted his friend's hasty working methods.

Yates himself, of course, couldn't help but work with agonizing care, which was hardly the sort of thing his present employers had in mind. "At the rate Yates is going he will complete [the screenplay] about the time we land the first Astronaut on the moon," Malcolm Stuart, his Hollywood agent, reported in May. Meanwhile Yates was "discovering endless problems" in adapting the novel he admired so much: "How can you expect an audience to sit through two hours of unrelieved heartbreak without breaking up into peals of derisive laughter?" he wrote the Schulmans. "The *really* ludicrous part is that I'm going to damn sure have to figure it out before July first or my economic ass will be dragging again—I don't get another paycheck until I've turned in the first draft, and July first is when my dough runs out."

By then Yates was already disenchanted with the whole "diseased" Hollywood milieu, even more so than he'd pessimistically anticipated. It had taken all of two months for his stock as a screenwriter to drop—for his agent to mock his dilatory progress, for his phone to quit ringing while Frankenheimer et al. got on with their high-powered lives—but no matter how bored, lonely, and disgusted he felt, Yates hardly thought he'd find much comfort in whatever "friendships" he managed to make in Hollywood. "Don't think I'm neglecting you, sweetheart," he wrote Bob Parker:

Matter of fact I happened to mention your name to Jerry Wald just the other day—we were grabbing a bite in the Commissary with Frank and Dean and Shirley and some of the group—and I said Jerry, you know why your last four pictures bombed? . . . I said Jerry, you're weak artwise—costumes, set design, the whole schmier. I said Jerry, it so happens I'm personally acquainted with the all-time greatest little art talent of our generation. I said You know the way Judy puts over a song? I said You know the way Marlon puts over a scene? I said Well that's the way this kid puts over a painting. . . . Kid out in Carmel, New York, name of Bobby Andy Parker.

Jerry just looked at me. He said Dick baby you know what I love about you? He said if there's one thing I love about you it's your loyalty to your friends; right, Frank? Frank said That's right, Jerry, that's Dick's whole action: loyalty. Dean said That's right, Frank. Shirley kind of cuddled up and she said You can say that again, Dean. She said That's why we all love you, Dick; that's your whole action: loyalty. Very wonderful; very human; very warm.

Yates went on to write that Wald had rejected his overture in Parker's behalf ("he said Dick baby . . . in this industry you've got to be a businessman"), but begged Parker not to lose heart: He knew of an opening in the "Animation Department (Black & White)" at Disney, where the salary was $67.50 a week, union scale, and in the meantime Yates would find him lodgings at a "very reasonable trailer park out in East L.A." And finally—lest Parker think the target of all this was something other than Hollywood phoniness—Yates added a conciliatory postscript: "This struck me as side-splittingly funny when I wrote it; now it seems much less so, and I'm haunted by visions of Dot saying 'Oh, that's mean.' But I'll mail it anyway because it represents hours of work. If it doesn't make you laugh you have my permission to roll it into a tight cylinder and stick it up the nearest horse's ass." That Yates was willing to spend "hours" composing a clever letter to distant out-of-touch friends speaks volumes about his frame of mind.

Loneliness is perhaps the best way to explain Yates's affair with his agent's thirty-seven-year-old secretary, Catherine Downing, who later turned up as the title character in "Saying Goodbye to Sally."* Sally Baldwin (*née* Munk) was born of working-class parents in an industrial California town, and the same may be assumed of Catherine Downing (*née* Meng) of Lomita, California. Downing was a well-spoken divorcée who did most of Malcolm Stuart's reading for him, and as such had read and admired *Revolutionary Road*. This was the basis of a flirtation that resulted in her "shacking-up" with Yates (as he later put it) for the rest of his stay in California. Yates was surprised to learn that Downing lived in a lavish replica of an old Southern mansion on Coldwater Canyon Drive in Beverly Hills, then a bit repelled as he began to see the whole picture: The owner of the place was a promiscuous single mother who'd enticed Downing to live there not only as a friend but as "protective coloration" for the woman's sordid behavior despite the presence of a young son. For a while Yates was too relieved at having Downing's company to remonstrate much over this arrangement. Like Jack Fields in the story, he romanticized her struggle to rise above the poverty of her early life, and saw their affair as parallel to that of Fitzgerald and gossip columnist Sheilah Graham: "*He* knew she would never be Zelda; that was one of the ways he knew he loved her. Holding himself together every day for her, dying for a drink but staying away from it, putting what little energy he had into those sketchy opening chapters of *The Last Tycoon*, he must have been humbly grateful just to have her there."

Yates may have been humbly grateful, but he was hardly staying away from liquor for Downing's sake; indeed, he was rather hard pressed to keep up with her. Every night was pretty much the same for Downing and her drunken vulgarian friends, and she became ever more willing to linger among them as a way of putting off her return to Yates's mildewy Malibu hovel. After a few drinks Downing's charming facade would fade and she'd become like a parody of the trite Hollywood types Yates had come to despise: She'd use "fudgy little showbusiness" endearments such as "a very dear person" or "a very gutsy lady," and express amusement by laughing "as stridently as an unpopular schoolgirl over things he didn't think were

---

*Catherine Downing died in 1979 at the age of fifty-four, and Yates was in touch with her as late as 1975. When one considers that he undertook to write "Saying Goodbye to Sally" sometime in late '79 or early '80, the title may be understood to have a poignant secondary meaning.

funny at all." Despite such shortcomings, Yates considered Downing a worthwhile if limited person, a pathetic victim of her environment, and the two stayed in occasional contact for years to come. But he had no illusions about her (and perhaps vice versa) after that first stay in California: Three years later, back in Hollywood, Yates alluded to Downing as a cautionary figure while advising another young woman, "You need to get out of here *now*."

After a busy and somewhat chaotic five months, Yates finally submitted a finished screenplay in August. All agreed that it had been worth the wait. "You didn't leave anything for *me* to do," Frankenheimer laughed, noting that Yates had specified almost every conceivable nuance, visual and otherwise, in written form; but then, too, the director had to concede that Yates's choices were inspired. Most gratifying was the reaction of Styron, who thought the adaptation a work of considerable brilliance in itself; for years he advocated its production as a film, and when the screenplay was published by Ploughshares in 1985, Styron helped promote the event with a public reading. Back in 1962, though, such praise was so much gravy for Yates: United Artists had tentatively scheduled production for the following year—starring Henry Fonda and Natalie Wood in the roles of Milton and Peyton Loftis—whereupon Yates would receive "a whole new avalanche of money."

The money was his foremost concern, of course, since Yates had no particular ambition to become a famous screenwriter; and years later, typically, he'd see fit to deprecate his work on *Lie Down in Darkness*: "Good novels—let's say great novels—have almost never been adapted into good movies," he observed, explaining that in the case of Styron's work there were a number of "subtleties that would inevitably have been lost in the translation." That said, he did single out a favorite moment in his screenplay—when Helen Loftis admits to the minister Carey Carr that she doesn't know what God is, and he replies "God is love." "Then, *wham*," said Yates,

instantly there's a cut to the blinding hot sunshine of the Daddy Faith parade . . . and you see these two white-robed blacks carrying a big satin banner that reads GOD IS LOVE. I think that might've been pretty effective. Here's Carey delivering himself of what he thinks is a profound philosophical statement, and then you see these crazy, ignorant Daddy Faith people carrying the same message, and it undercuts it and makes it meaningless for you as well as for Helen.

In fact Yates's adaptation is full of such apposite effects; as George Bluestone noted in his introduction to the published screenplay, Yates skirted such common pitfalls as voice-over narration ("delivering great globs of Styron's prose") in favor of finding, always, some exact visual or aural equivalent.

Perhaps the main challenge that Yates's work poses for any ego-driven *auteur* is how to bring something other than technical facility to the making of a movie that, as Frankenheimer put it, "is all there on the page." Yates took pains to describe facial expressions, sound effects, and camera angles, all of which work to convey in cinematic terms the maximum possible meaning and mood of a given scene. For example, when the jealous Helen scolds her daughter Peyton before Christmas dinner, the stage-directions indicate that Milton's "light, tinny, inexpert" xylophone music (which he plays for the feeble-minded Maudie in order to appear a doting father) be heard throughout the scene. The "music" suggests not only the dissonance between the actual and feigned causes of Helen's rage, but also the gruesome awkwardness of the whole family gathering, the childishness of Milton's not-so-furtive infatuation with Peyton—and so on, level on level. Likewise, Yates managed to find subtle solutions for the novel's alternating points of view, as when the drunken Milton attends the UVA football game in hope of finding Peyton; for the establishing shots, Yates specified "*intentional* newsreel clichés" (a roisterous crowd, players trotting out on the field, and so on), to provide contrast with the same scene as Milton sees it: "narrow concrete steps leading straight down, in dizzying perspective . . . a cheering man's wide-open mouth full of chewed hot dog." Such images suggest a drunkard's viewpoint and more—a sense of foreboding, the grotesquerie of a world bereft of hope or moral center.

Yates was faithful to the novel's episodic, nonlinear structure, which he tightened as much as possible with cuts, dissolves, and motifs linking discrete episodes into a symphonic whole. Perhaps the most structurally crucial sequence in the screenplay is the one leading up to its first climactic plot point, when Milton and the prepubescent Peyton climb the bell tower together. Here as elsewhere Yates evoked character and theme with precise visual economy: After Milton persuades Peyton to apologize for tormenting her sister, the screenplay indicates an immediate cut to father and daughter singing a silly song in the car, like two gleeful children involved in a successful conspiracy; then, as they climb the bell tower, they pause near the top to exchange a look that lingers, ominously, until the clappers fall with a denunciatory clamor to the tune of "Jesus Calls Us"—which we will hear again when Milton passionately kisses Peyton at her wedding, and still again when Peyton climbs the stairs (a *visual* parallel) to commit suicide. Thus Yates suggested the main thematic conflict between illicit love and convention (religious or social) without heavy-handed explication one way or the other, and used the best of Styron's material in doing so. Birds recur in the novel as symbols of flight and freedom, and so too at key points in Yates's version: Pigeons fill the screen when the bell tower clock begins to whir, and later, finally, a flock is disturbed by the fatal impact of Peyton's fall.

Add the sheer perfection of Yates's prose, and the result is a finished work of art that (contrary to his later disclaimer) may well have amounted to a great movie adapted from a great novel. "*God,* it's good," Frankenheimer said forty years later of Yates's screenplay. "I'd *still* like to make that movie."

Sheila and Yates exchanged characteristic letters, at once fond and bickering, throughout his stay in California. "At a distance in time and space of four months and 3000 miles," she wrote, "perhaps we can lay it on the line to each other in a way that will either break the tie . . . or suggest a way to preserve it." For Sheila it was a question of giving up "old, reliable tranquility" for the possibility of a greater happiness, though she realized that disaster and disillusionment were far more probable. She pointed out that he'd be better off with a "literary-type girl," and made it clear that, if they did reunite, things would be different: "I will never—and I mean never—stay home again. Housewifery was my Remington Rand." Also she was "appalled" at the memory of having to clean up after Yates, but knew all too well what to expect: "Judging from your little flat, and your visit out here, [you] are less likely to keep the trash down than you were in the old days." Yates responded with a harsh letter to the effect that Sheila was "less wife than anybody [he could] think of," but later apologized and continued to press for a reconciliation on his return.* By July Sheila seemed almost won over: She asked whether he'd like to settle in Danbury or the city—possibly go back to Europe, even—and as late as mid-August she signed off with, "I love you (and miss you)." Then something happened to remind her, permanently this time, that all such prospects were hopeless.

California had been a draining experience for Yates, and two weeks at Bread Loaf seemed a perfect way to relax and savor his triumph before returning to New York and his novel. Indeed, the first week of the conference went remarkably well, though it was far from relaxing. Yates found himself the most celebrated writer on the faculty, a figure of considerable romantic appeal: tall and handsome, still tan from his stint in Hollywood, the embodiment of literary glamour—looks, talent, money. Copies of *Eleven Kinds of Loneliness* were snapped up by the conferencees (particularly female), many of whom also regarded Yates as the most scintillating lecturer. He discussed, variously, his experience adapting *Lie Down in Darkness*, the matter of tragic design, the influence of Conrad on Fitzgerald (the peripheral narrator, the "dying fall"), and certain postwar American novels he'd take on a "tight boat"—*The Naked and the Dead, From Here to Eternity, Catcher in the Rye*. After his lectures Yates would return trembling to Treman Cottage, the applause ringing in his ears, and try to calm himself with massive amounts of alcohol. "I should, damn it, have known how much you were giving," a rueful John Ciardi wrote him afterward; "you were being so damned great, I guess I forgot everything but my directorial gloat over the way you were rocking the Great Hall."

Yates's breakdown at the 1962 Bread Loaf conference became part of the permanent lore of the place, but details are sketchy at best—a lot of

---

*Yates's remarks are paraphrased in Sheila's letters; his side of the correspondence doesn't survive.

stale, contradictory impressions heard second and third hand from the principal witnesses, most of whom are dead. All agree that Yates was drinking too much, perhaps in an effort to mitigate the rampant pangs of mania—the exhilaration and paranoia, the sense of being stared at and discussed. Yates finally erupted into full-blown, roaring-drunk psychosis at Treman Cottage, where he seems insistently to have helped himself to other people's liquor. When challenged about it (or not), Yates went berserk and began shouting. He apparently called an older woman on the faculty, whom he liked and who liked him, an "ugly fucking battle-ax." Ultimately he thought he was becoming the Messiah (a common delusion of mania), and legend has it he clambered onto the roof of Treman and held out his arms as though crucified. He told Grace Schulman he remembered swinging from tree branches and naming his gawking students after Christ's disciples, though it's hard to imagine someone with Yates's stamina exerting himself to that extent.

Ciardi and Dr. Irving Klompus, a guest at the conference, somehow managed to coax Yates down from the roof (or tree) and conduct him back to his room, where he was forcibly restrained and sedated. Yates was later under the impression that he'd abused Ciardi as a bad poet and dirty old man, but he appears to have made that much sense only to himself. "You can take my word for one thing," Ciardi wrote him: "you did say some fairly hairy things to me in your room, but you weren't sore at me. There was a lot of stuff you somehow had to get out but I'll swear you were throwing it by me, not at me." Typically at the height of his mania, Yates's speech would become a kind of rapid-fire regurgitation of (seemingly) random verbiage—hence Ciardi's impression that it "had to get out" and that it was mostly impersonal, that is, indecipherable; Yates was drunk as well as psychotic after all. In any case he remained "convulsively distraught" (as one witness put it) until the ambulance arrived; a few students stood in the doorway and watched in horror. Sam Lawrence's associate at Atlantic Monthly Press, Peter Davison, was backing out of the parking lot when he was startled by the sight of his firm's most promising author being led away in a straitjacket. It was a brilliantly sunny day.

As always, the worst came later. "After it's over I wince and wither," the poet Robert Lowell wrote apologetically to T. S. Eliot, whom he'd berated on the phone during a "feverish" episode of mania: "The whole business has been very bruising, and it is fierce facing the pain I have caused, and humiliating [to] think that it has all happened before and that control and self-knowledge come so slowly, if at all." And so with Yates. After Bread Loaf he found himself at Mary Fletcher Hospital in Burlington, where he became so despondent with shame that a doctor predicted he'd kill himself within two years.* In *Disturbing the Peace,* Wilder's response to the information that he is *not* the Messiah—rather just a man behaving oddly at Marlowe College in Vermont—may serve to evoke Yates's own devastation at such times: "That was when he started to cry, because what she said did have the ring of reality; and if this was real and all the rest was a dream, then he'd made a colossal fool of himself and everyone at Marlowe College knew it, or would know it soon." A number of prominent writers—including the ancient Robert Frost, no less—knew that Yates had behaved like a lunatic, perhaps *was* a lunatic, to say nothing of all the students who'd admired him. John Ciardi was a generous friend, and Yates had said awful things to him; ditto the woman he'd called "an ugly fucking battle-ax." And still that wasn't the worst of it. When Grace Schulman visited him at the hospital, she made the mistake of sharing a "recognition poem" she'd written based on Seneca's *Hercules Furens,* wherein the protagonist wakes from a spell of madness to learn he's murdered his wife and children. Yates became stricken: As would often be the case, his mania had left him with a terrible lingering delusion that he'd harmed his daughters, or *would* someday, and he felt helpless to do anything about it.

Sheila sympathized with her ex-husband's distress, but at the time she thought his problems were almost entirely alcohol related, and mostly she was exasperated. "Any hope that we can work things out as husband and wife has gone," she wrote a few months after the breakdown, when Yates

---

*Studies show that suicide is remarkably prevalent among bipolar patients: Up to one-half attempt it at least once. Yates's halfhearted wrist slashing went back to 1949, and there were no further attempts as far as anybody knows. His daughter Monica remarked that his whole lifestyle was a "slow suicide," but added that Yates himself "would have poo-poo'd that." His daughter Sharon was even more emphatic: "Suicide was always inconceivable to Dad. Toward the end he said he'd do anything to prolong life, even go on a respirator."

persisted in his visits to Danbury. "I have a sense that I have lost so many, many years, because I was unsure and lonely and confused. . . . If there's anything more you want to know, ask me, but please, by letter. When you put a thing on paper, sometimes you discover you already know the answer. Or maybe that there is no answer, which is the same thing."

CHAPTER NINE

Uncertain Times: 1962-1964

Back in New York, Yates became one of the earliest trial patients of Dr. Nathan S. Kline, a man soon to become world renowned for his work in psychopharmacology. According to his *New York Times* obituary, Kline "revolutionalized the treatment of mental illness" by introducing the use of tranquilizers, antidepressants, and antipsychotic drugs that enabled people to lead productive lives as outpatients—people who would have been considered hopelessly insane just a few years before. Kline was thus instrumental in reducing the stigma of mental illness among a generation that continued to view it as a kind of moral weakness. "The fact that a condition is treated with medication," he said, "somehow guarantees in the public mind that it is a genuine illness."

Yates was delighted to learn that he suffered from something so explicable as a "chemical imbalance," which modern science had the means to redress. No more "Sigmund fucking Freud" for him; all he had to do now was report to Kline's office on West Sixty-ninth every month or so, answer a few simple questions, and be on his way with a fresh supply of "crazy pills" as he called them. And while many creative people who suffer from mental illness (particularly manic-depressives) deplore the effects of psychotropic drugs and try to do without them, this was never the case with Yates. For an absentminded man, and a writer at that, he was remarkably diligent about taking his pills according to schedule, then coping as best he could with the slight mental dullness (and tremor and dry mouth and frequent urination) that followed. By 1974 Yates was taking as many as three different psychotropics a day, in addition to lithium.

But he wouldn't stop drinking. It was the one great caveat that every psychiatrist beginning with Kline tried futilely to enforce: *Do not mix these drugs with alcohol.* At first Yates was wary, but once he learned that no immediate calamity followed, he drank as much as ever—more, perhaps, now that his writing came harder. It was the one reliable pleasure that awaited him after a frustrating day, and most of the time he felt entitled. "He loved the idea that he was mentally ill," said his daughter Monica, "and hated the idea he was an alcoholic"—that is, bipolar disorder *was* a bona fide illness, while alcoholism smacked of a shameful personal failing. As he saw it, he drank because he liked to, and no matter what the doctors said, he refused to concede that alcohol made his illness all but impossible to treat. Again and again he was told that even moderate drinking is ill advised when taking lithium, not to mention the other tranquilizers and anti-psychotics he sampled over the years: Such drugs compound the sedative effect of alcohol, and drinkers tend to urinate the drugs out of their system and hence render them ineffective. Needless to say, too, a drunk is less likely to take his medication as prescribed, particularly if his alcoholism is so advanced that blackouts and seizures become common. "This is what keeps your old daddy in business!" he cheerfully told a friend, dumping a handful of pills into his mouth and washing them down with a slug of bourbon.

For the time being, though, things were looking up. Paul Cubeta, the assistant director of Bread Loaf, visited Yates a month after the conference and was relieved to find him completely recovered and quite confident of staying that way. He had Guggenheim money in the bank and a bit left over from Hollywood, and soon he'd be richer than he ever thought possible: Frankenheimer had assured him that United Artists' reaction to his screenplay was "excellent"; production had yet to be definitely scheduled, and cuts would have to be made, but it seemed only a matter of time now. Meanwhile Yates was covering his bases. He continued to teach at the New School, albeit a bit more lackadaisically than before, and his old friend Verlin Cassill was "ninety-eight per cent sure" he could get Yates a better-paying job at the Iowa Workshop should the need arise.

"It hardly ever happened and it wouldn't last long," the novel *Uncertain Times* begins, "but William Grove felt almost at peace with the world when the new year of 1963 broke over New York."* This was true for Yates, too, and as a final coup before his life went off the rails again, he was chosen one of the "Ten Americans to Watch in 1963" by *Pageant* magazine. Each of these ten, the happy few, had briefly transcended the anonymity of life in the vast republic; each stood to become a dominant force in his or her field of endeavor: e.g., Romaldo Giurgola (architecture), Robert A. Good (medicine), Maxine Smith (race relations), George Grizzard (entertainment), and Richard Yates (literature)—the last of whom mentioned his humble beginnings as a copyboy for the *New York Sun* and remarked that "young writers are not necessarily ruined by Hollywood."

Not ruined, perhaps, but often disappointed. At the beginning of March, right around the time Yates had hoped to be schmoozing with Natalie Wood (since his contract required that he report to the set), he got bad news from a "hesitant and old"–sounding Monica McCall: There would be no movie. As Yates explained it two years later,

Miss Wood's agent decided that it might Tarnish Her Image with the Teenagers if she appeared as a girl who loved her Daddy a little too much— and Blooey. She pulled out, then [Henry] Fonda pulled out, then United Artists pulled out, then John Frankenheimer (the Dedicated Young Director) pulled out—and the whole God damned deal fell through—leaving me with a fraction of the earnings I was supposed to reap. I had been counting on sending both my children through college on the money I'd been promised, so when the axe fell it was something of a blow. . . . That, I guess, is show biz.

He called Styron to commiserate, and a couple weeks later the wealthy, undismayed author wrote a consoling note to Yates: "Frankenheimer's

---

Uncertain Times is the most autobiographical of Yates's novels—which is to say, *very* autobiographical. Since the period in Yates's life covered by the novel is roughly the period covered by this chapter, I *occasionally* quote or paraphrase from the work without explicit/repetitive citation. The reader should be able to detect when I've taken this liberty, and rest assured that I do so only when I have good reason to suspect that the passage in question adheres closely to the facts.

mills, while grinding exceeding slow, seem to be grinding sure. What I mean is that he has just paid me a substantial amount of money in order to extend the option on *Lie Down in Darkness*. This seems to indicate that . . . he *is* eventually going to do it." Alas, no, though the property would be kicked around Hollywood for many years, occasionally shimmering into view like a saving mirage in times of terrible need. As for Frankenheimer—whom Yates had come to consider something of a friend—he soon fell out of touch forever. "I always wondered why better things hadn't happened to Dick," the director mused. "He was such a great writer."

Yates's progress on his novel seemed thwarted by ambivalence toward his material, not to say a lack of clarity. When he first returned to New York that fall, he tried to capitalize on his "Builders" success by writing another short story, but it soon went cold—so cold, in fact, that he came to believe he'd lost his knack for short fiction entirely; some fifteen years would pass before he managed the trick again. So he went back to his war novel, or coming-of-age novel, or whatever it was apart from a journalistic, unformed account of his own experiences as a feckless private who'd played a nonheroic (as opposed to *un*heroic or even *anti*heroic) role in the mop-up action after the Bulge. He asked friends to suggest poems that dealt with "the trials of adolescence"—perhaps he'd find some sort of thematic focus there. Meanwhile he just kept writing: "I'm working hard as hell on a new novel in the hope of finishing it by the end of the year," he wrote Cassill in early February; "don't know if it's any good or not, but the pages keep coming."

Then they stopped coming—just like that—though the rest of his routine remained intact: Each morning he'd put on the same sweatshirt and corduroy pants, take his pills, make coffee, light cigarettes end on end, and stare at the wall. Then lunch and a long walk, the hopeful suspense as he hurried back to his desk, and another afternoon of nothing. Sometimes, in an agony of caffeinated frustration, Yates would force himself into a "spasm of writing"—then reread the pages and throw them away: "All the sentences were weak and lame and even the handwriting looked funny."

Soon Yates was drinking heavily again and wondering whether he'd ever write another page of decent fiction, even as the world continued to honor him. In May, the National Institute of Arts and Letters awarded $2,500 grants to a handful of the most promising young writers in the country, including Yates, William Gaddis, Joseph Heller, William Humphrey, and Peter Matthiessen. An oppressively eminent crowd attended the ceremony at the Academy of Arts and Letters in Upper Manhattan, where an outdoor luncheon was held under a large tent in the courtyard. There was little question of Yates's enduring such an affair soberly, and by the time he and his fellow honorees were herded into the first two rows of the auditorium, he was vividly impaired. Bob Parker watched from the audience as his friend, summoned at last to the dais, "lumbered like Frankenstein" across the stage: "Dick was wearing a tan gabardine suit, the top button buttoned to the bottom hole, his necktie awry—a cartoon of a drunk. He was barely able to say 'thank you.' "

It didn't help that Yates's latest girlfriend was herself an unstable alcoholic, though perhaps a person of more sober habit would have been out of her depth. Craige* was an Irishwoman in her late twenties who worked as a copy editor for a fashion magazine; mordantly witty when coherent, she became (in Grace Schulman's words) "very sick and disturbed" when drunk. She had a way of falling down in public, and in a stupor would sometimes mistake Yates for her father or brother, with all that suggested of an unsavory subtext. And though she was still rather young and pretty, dissipation had already taken a toll: "Even then she had something of the Blanche DuBois agedness about her," Schulman recalled. Indeed, Yates's description of her in *Uncertain Times*—where she appears as "Nora Harrigan"—bears this out in rather pitiless terms: "She seemed to be letting her appearance go in subtle, telling ways: something a little bedraggled about the hair, something flaccid in the lips, a generally unwholesome pallor in the face and neck." Yates even pointed to the character's "toe jam"—the result of being too hung over to wash her feet in the shower.

---

*Her first name.

Such a couple couldn't easily accommodate another lost soul, but when Yates learned the full extent of his sister's predicament he was willing, at least, to take her in. For years he'd been talking about "poor Ruth"—married to such a vulgar oaf, stuck out in "Ass Hole, Long Island" with nothing to do, her looks gone and drinking too much to boot. But he had no idea how bad things had become. By 1963 Ruth was a chronic alcoholic with an enlarged liver, and her husband beat her on a regular basis. "For years we'd hear the beatings," her oldest son recalled. "The shouting and scrambling around downstairs. Finally, when I was seventeen, I walked in on them. They were both surprised. My father had always hit his children, but this time I was determined to stop him. I shoved him in a chair and held him there." Both Ruth and her husband drank—it had always been part of the family culture—but since the late fifties Ruth's drinking had grown steadily out of control. Fred wanted things and people to proceed according to custom ("He was God Almighty," said his son), and it enraged him to come home for the cocktail hour and find his wife already incapacitated. Usually the argument that followed was limited to screaming and weeping, and would end with Ruth tottering upstairs to pass out; but if Fred was in a particularly nasty mood, or a sufficient number of weeks had passed since the last time, he'd beat her. For years Ruth had claimed that she stayed in the marriage "for the children," and then as the children grew up and moved out—and were themselves urging her to leave their brutal father—she'd say it was "[her] problem" and she'd "work it out." Finally it got so bad that she turned to the only person she knew who might be able to help: her brother.

Yates was shocked and furious. He called Sheila—the only person in his life who knew Ruth—and asked her advice: "Dick thought he might go out there and confront Fred," Sheila recalled, "because Ruth was too much of a cipher to stand up for herself. I thought his quixotic ideas were ridiculous, though I was sorry for Ruth. He was considering all options: take her in, confront her husband, whatever." Finally Yates offered his sister a place to stay, but by then the crisis had passed: She couldn't bring herself to leave Fred after all. Her marriage, such as it was, had given her the only "security" she'd ever known, and besides she still loved the man.

And what would she do on her own? Yates may have insisted on bluster-
ing at Fred over the phone, and even threatened to kill him, but that was
pretty much the end of it.

As the summer approached, Yates was all but broke again. He now had a
firm offer to teach at the Iowa Workshop in the fall, but continued to vacillate: There was still a chance the movie would be made, or something
might come up in New York—so he told Cassill, who'd discouraged him
from taking the job unless he could make a full-year commitment. But
now Cassill thought he should come to Iowa anyway and leave whenever
he pleased, no matter what the inconvenience to the Workshop. Cassill
had become disillusioned with the place: Recently a "mentally ill, incompetent" former student had attacked him in the campus newspaper, and
the administration had offered little more than polite sympathy as a show
of support. "Hemingway said writers are wolves and have got to stick
together," Cassill wrote his friend, "and that is exactly how I feel again
now." But Yates remained evasive—the fact was, he didn't want to leave
New York and teach in the sticks any more than he had four years earlier.
He was even willing to take another PR job, though he was having a hard
time convincing interviewers of that: "[H]e was earnestly seeking a kind
of work he didn't want, and that embarrassing contradiction seemed to
leak from his very pores." All this was a long way down from a year
ago—from Frankenheimer's palace in Malibu—and it began to look as
though he'd have to brace himself for an Iowa winter after all. But then his
friend Styron shook another deus ex machina out of his sleeve.

Attorney General Robert Kennedy was losing the sympathy of black
Americans: The long-promised Civil Rights Bill had yet to materialize in
May 1963, when activists in Birmingham were hosed and beaten and
attacked by police dogs. Burke Marshall—the assistant attorney general in
charge of civil rights—went to Alabama and negotiated a truce of sorts,
but many viewed it as a feeble response to a widely televised outrage.
Then, a week after Marshall's return to Washington, Kennedy asked the
writer James Baldwin to convene a group of influential black celebrities
and meet him in New York so they could "talk this thing over." The meeting was a fiasco. Along with Harry Belafonte, Lena Horne, and the

playwright Lorraine Hansberry, Baldwin saw fit to invite a few hard-core activists, such as a young freedom rider who'd been repeatedly beaten and jailed. At one point the latter stuck his finger in Kennedy's stunned face and told him he'd never fight for this country, that he *had* no country. "Was I impressed?" Baldwin's brother David told the media after the meeting. "You see Bobby Kennedys every day, on the street, at cocktail parties. They just don't get it. And he's our Attorney General."

Clearly the administration's message (whatever it happened to be) wasn't getting across, and Kennedy decided he needed a decent speechwriter. He asked an assistant, E. Barrett Prettyman, Jr., to find him a "real writer" who could take his ideas and "turn them into words with a snap and a bite to them." Prettyman called their mutual friend Styron, who said he knew just the man: a superb novelist with extensive experience as a speechwriter, who also happened to need a job. "I don't even know if I *like* the fucking Kennedys," Yates replied when Styron called with the news; Yates pointed out that he'd always been an Adlai Stevenson man, and for that matter couldn't "get much of a hard-on" for politics in general. "What have you got to lose?" Styron said, in effect, and a couple days later Yates boarded the Eastern Airlines shuttle for Washington.

At the Justice Department he was received by Prettyman, who briefly explained the job to him. It was the first of its kind: Before, Kennedy's speeches had been cobbled together by committee, at a certain sacrifice of both style and substance. Worse, Kennedy himself was a rather uncomfortable speaker, who tended to swallow his words and lose the thread, such that an audience hardly knew when to applaud. What was needed, then, were "short, clipped sentences" to match Kennedy's natural speaking style, as well as a lot of "humanity" to put over his civil rights agenda and counterbalance his "ruthless" image.

At the appointed time Yates was introduced to Kennedy, who struck him as remarkably boyish and slight ("part of his shirttail bulged loose on one side"). Kennedy noted with approval that Yates was not only a highly regarded writer, but also had a strong background in public relations. Then he said, "We're living in very uncertain times, Mr. Yates, and those of us in a position of leadership are obliged to be responsive to issues like civil rights, but at the same time I have a great sense of responsibility here. Do you understand that?" As Yates later told an interviewer, he replied, " 'Yes, I do,' without quite knowing what [Kennedy] was talking about." Finally the attorney general asked him what he was currently working on, and Yates mentioned his novel about the last months of World War II. Kennedy observed that that was an "interesting period," and expressed a hope that Yates would find time to work on it if he took the job. They shook hands.

After he left Kennedy's office and rejoined Prettyman and press secretary Edwin Guthman, the latter informed Yates that he was actually in competition with two other writers from *Newsweek* and *Time*; as it happened, Prettyman (who hadn't known this beforehand) wasn't the only one Kennedy had asked to find a speechwriter. Guthman went on to explain that the three candidates would each submit a "trial assignment"—a civil rights speech to be delivered at an "exclusive girls' college in the East." Yates was intimidated by the prospect of competing with veteran journalists, but Prettyman felt confident that he had the edge: He was recommended by *Styron*, after all, and that had impressed the attorney general.

Back in New York, Yates spent an industrious all-nighter writing his trial assignment. Rather to his surprise he found he enjoyed the challenge, the craft, of imagining Kennedy as a kind of fictional character (with a Yatesian outlook, no less)—namely, an attractive young man seductively persuading a group of female admirers to support the cause of civil rights: "School is out, girls. You may sometimes regret your education, for a free mind will always insist on seeking out reality, and reality can be far more painful than the soft and comforting illusions of the intellectually poor." Yates tightened the speech to fit the attention span of its audience, then typed the finished product on his beat-up Underwood and sent it off. A few days later he was summoned back to Washington. He had the job.

A problem remained: The woman he was leaving behind seemed determined to drink herself to death in his absence. One day Yates appeared at the Schulmans' door with the blind-drunk Craige in tow. He had to leave for Washington, he explained. Would they mind looking after his girlfriend? Grace was furious: Just because she no longer worked full-time at *Glamour,* Yates had simply assumed she was free to care for a suicidal alcoholic. "It's up to Grace," said the good-natured Jerry, after which his wife stormed out and stayed in a hotel for the night. Yates's girlfriend, meanwhile, ended up with Grace's elderly mother, and Grace ended up caring for both of them.

"I only took the job because I needed the money," Yates later claimed, "which is an odd thing because everybody else around me was there at some sacrifice of income. I was the only hireling." That Yates always considered himself a "hireling" rather than a "true believer" is indisputable; he was determinedly skeptical where the Kennedys were concerned, and would tell (almost) anyone who asked that he *still* thought Stevenson should be president. But if money had been the only incentive, he might as well have gone to Iowa: As his new employers rather sheepishly put it, the salary was "more of an honorarium kind of thing"—enough for an ascetic writer, but hardly a lure in itself. For Yates, of course, there was more to it than that: "I couldn't resist the opportunity to be that close to the Center of Power in America," he admitted to a friend in 1964, "and it turned out to be a lively and interesting thing for a while. [Kennedy] seemed to like what I wrote, which fortunately was almost all about civil rights, and I think I even managed to put a few words in his mouth that were a little stronger than he otherwise might have used." This is true: While Yates may have wavered in his opinion of the Kennedys, he was eager to enlist his talent in the cause of civil rights, and RFK was a potent mouthpiece. "Dick composed the most memorable phrases the Attorney General ever uttered," said Prettyman, and Kurt Vonnegut went further: "He used RFK as a ventriloquist's dummy."

Happily the work didn't require any particular knowledge of, or interest in, the nuts and bolts of public policy. Yates's job was to convert raw data into eloquence: "BAG [i.e., "Bobby-A.G."] is making speech in [City] on [Date]," Guthman's assignment memo would read; "please look over attached material and let's talk." Yates would do so, perhaps call the sponsors of the event in question, then ask the ultracompetent research assistant to provide further material on, say, B'nai B'rith or Slovak Catholics in Ohio. If the speech was momentous enough, the staff would gather for brainstorming sessions in the attorney general's office, where a shirtsleeved Kennedy would pace around the table and fitfully explain the "main points" he wanted to make. Sometimes Yates would meet with Kennedy alone, or Burke Marshall, and with both men he had a good but impersonal working relationship. "Dick was respectful but not intimidated," said his colleague Jack Rosenthal, "and Kennedy appreciated that."

At first Yates and Rosenthal shared a big sunny room in the Public Information office. Rosenthal, a future Pulitzer Prize–winning editorialist for the New York Times, was then a twenty-six-year-old Harvard graduate whom Guthman had brought in from Oregon to serve as assistant press secretary. Yates was fond of the young man, but found it all but impossible to work in the same room with him. "Sorry I've been so elusive," Rosenthal would say (always) when he returned a reporter's phone call, and finally he'd close with, "You're a nice man." Then he'd return another phone call. And another. For hours Yates would sit rigid at his typewriter, his legal pad, and listen to these exchanges over and over. Often people would wander in to chat. After a few days Yates buttonholed the research assistant and begged her to find him a private workspace, whereupon she led him to what appeared to be a broom closet at the back of the fifth floor: crowded into the narrow space was an old desk, a working typewriter, a few derelict chairs, and dusty storage cartons stacked to the ceiling. Yates called his new office the "Herbert Brownell Room" after the previous attorney general (whose files were stored there); the place was almost like home.

Yates was eager to make his mark, since he didn't expect to be around very long: four months, to be exact. That was usually how long it took, according to Prettyman, for the FBI to conduct a methodical background check. When told as much, Yates confided that he'd had two nervous breakdowns in the past three years, both of which had required hospitalization, and wondered if the FBI was likely to pursue that sort of thing. Prettyman thought it highly probable. Still, some hope remained that they were mostly interested in Communist affiliations—until, a couple weeks into the job, Yates got a letter from Sheila: "The FBI wheels are very much in motion. A bright young man was here on Friday, inquiring closely into everything he could get me to talk about. . . . He did ask specifically about such things as alcoholism and 'stability of character which might affect

Mr. Yates's ability to perform well in the assignment.'" So much for the lone Communist angle. "I questioned *him* a bit," she went on, "and he said the investigation would extend to your 'friends and associates.'" Yates was touched by his ex-wife's loyalty—"I certainly said nothing," she assured him—and others, too, tried to forestall his doom with the same sort of circumspection. Styron managed to skirt the subject of Yates's drinking during the long afternoon he spent in an agent's company, while Grace Schulman was downright uncooperative. Asked if Yates had any "vices," she volunteered that he smoked too much, and when the shrewd G-man inquired whether *Revolutionary Road* was autobiographical, Schulman quoted Yates on the subject: "The emotions of fiction are auto-biographical, but the facts never are." The man looked puzzled, then moved on to another subject.

Nevertheless Yates's days seemed numbered, and since the idea was to save as much money as possible, he was reluctant to take a second apart-ment in Washington. Commuting via the Eastern shuttle was hardly a thrifty alternative, nor was his drunken girlfriend a compelling reason to return to New York on a daily basis. At the beginning of June, then, Yates got in touch with his old army buddy Frank Knorr, whose house in the Washington suburbs included a self-contained basement apartment. Yates moved in, and for the most part proved an amenable guest. His drinking could hardly be less than conspicuous, but he regarded the Knorrs as nice, decent people, and he was at pains not to shock or inconvenience them. "Dick ate dinner with us during the week," Janis Knorr recalled. "At five o'clock sharp he'd come upstairs rubbing his hands: 'Cocktail time!' Then he'd drink bourbon the rest of the night and tell stories. He'd get loud, but he wasn't *too* obnoxious." Yates doted on the Knorrs' three-year-old daughter, Rebecca, who was given the thankless task of waking him each morning when he was "hungover and surly." As with his own children, Yates made a special effort to act playful and pleasant around the girl, though Janis Knorr observed that he seemed "generally unhappy." Around this time his daughter Sharon, during a visit to Washington, first became aware that her father drank too much: "The adults would play cards after dinner," she said, "and Dad would drink steadily but the Knorrs wouldn't." Sharon was thirteen now, and the contrast stuck in her mind.

Whatever his other sorrows, Yates enjoyed his work at the Justice Department. He thought of speechwriting as show business, and assigned a particular persona to RFK depending on his audience—as Bill Grove put it in *Uncertain Times*, "once you've got the character established he kind of takes over, and the rest is mechanical." For a B'nai B'rith dinner in Chicago, Yates imagined RFK as "a fine-looking young man" in his well-tailored tuxedo—the sort of *mensch* who knew he didn't have to mince words with such an educated, receptive audience, but rather address them as fellow liberals who cared about human rights and knew all about persecution: "President George Washington once made a solemn pledge to the Jewish Synagogue in Newport, Rhode Island, when he said 'The American government gives bigotry no sanction.' . . . They must have understood even then, those early Jewish settlers in New England, that bigotry doesn't care whether it has governmental sanction or not." Kennedy, reading over the speech, wondered aloud if Washington had really said that, and Yates replied that it was in *Bartlett's Quotations*; Kennedy, pleased, remarked that it made a good opening statement. Yates's next assignment, the Catholic Sokol Convention in Ohio, called for "a plainer, cornier, dumber Bobby Kennedy," and Yates pictured him "glowing and disheveled in an open shirt with rolled-up sleeves." Such relatively casual speeches tended to end with the same tag—"I think I've said most of what I came here to say now"—just before the folksy, personalized punch line: "Let me salute you with the only two words of Slovakian I understand: '*Zdar Boh!*' "

Yates's first few speeches were so well received that, when President Kennedy prepared to address the nation on civil rights, the attorney general asked Yates to contribute a draft. The speech would be historically momentous—what many Americans had been waiting to hear ever since they'd elected Kennedy more than two years earlier. That same day, June 11, Governor George Wallace planned to fulfill his campaign promise to "stand at the schoolhouse door" and prevent black students from enrolling at the University of Alabama. RFK had dispatched his deputy Nicholas Katzenbach to counter Wallace's "states' rights" rhetoric and enforce the law, and a few hours later JFK would announce to the nation that he was sending an omnibus Civil Rights Bill to Congress.

On Sunday evening, June 9, Yates was assigned to write a version of the President's speech; his deadline was the following Tuesday. He was advised that another draft—possibly several—would be generated by the White House, though it was all but certain that at least part of Yates's contribution would be used: He was RFK's speechwriter after all, and the president deferred to his brother on civil rights. Thus, a little more than two weeks into the job, Yates was already in a position to influence national destiny, and he was eager to make the most of it. For two nights and a day he cloistered himself in the Herbert Brownell Room, consuming coffee and cigarettes and trying to imagine JFK as a character—not "hunched and impassioned" like his brother, but "erect and cool"—a man whose appeal to the heart would seem all the more powerful in contrast with his usual "witty and sardonic" manner.

Early Tuesday morning Yates called his friend John Williams, who was then working on a piece for *Holiday* magazine titled "This Is My Country, Too," about a black man traveling in America. (While in New York he'd planned to stay a few days at Yates's vacant apartment in the Village, but on the second night he heard a scratching noise and discovered— *"Holy shit!"*—a horde of water beetles swarming over his sleeping bag. He packed up and left.) Yates wanted to read his finished draft to Williams, and ask him a few basic questions about civil rights. Williams tried to be helpful, though privately he was taken aback by Yates's frank ignorance over what, exactly, was *meant* by "civil rights." Years later Williams admitted as much in a letter: "Dick, I recall feeling this: 'Yates is okay. I like Yates. He's a good guy. Maybe that's *why* he's got to start this research from scratch.'" But it irritated Williams at the time, who thought it only too typical that a white man would be hired to write about issues he didn't really understand, when there were plenty of black writers (e.g., himself) who did: *"I felt I should have had your job,"* he wrote Yates; "I felt I could have done a better job for my people and for people as a whole." Yates was furious: "If my questioning you about 'civil rights' seemed naive," he fired back, "and maybe even asinine, as I knew even at the time that it must, I thought you were taking it all in good faith and not begrudging me the job. And when I read that damn speech to you over the phone, I thought you liked it."

The fact was, Yates took considerable pride in his work, and he'd been particularly pleased by the way his version of the president's address had turned out. He told the Knorrs that he didn't really expect it to be used, but urged them to watch television with him that night "just in case." When the time came, as Janis Knorr recalled, Yates was taut with anticipation. "He wants to do well for MARR's [i.e., Knorr's] sake," Yates scribbled in the margin of this episode in the *Uncertain Times* manuscript—that is, he'd always admired Frank Knorr as a good soldier who'd accepted him in spite of his incompetence, and he viewed the president's speech as a chance to redeem himself. But it wasn't to be. As Kennedy spoke, the Knorrs glanced furtively between Yates and the screen, and it was clear that each line struck him as a fresh disappointment. At one point he suddenly came alive—"There! I wrote that!"—but it was a false alarm, and when it was over Yates seemed embarrassed. As the scene concludes in the novel: "Grove thought he could see the Marrs exchanging very slight, fond smiles of amusement—smiles suggesting that their houseguest might really not be such an important person after all."*

Other than a slightly more perceptible dislike of JFK, Yates gave little sign of dwelling on the matter. That summer the attorney general had to appear before several congressional committees in support of the Civil Rights Bill, and his speechwriter was kept busy composing his formal testimony. Whatever Yates lacked as a policy specialist was redeemed somewhat by a willing heart and a positive grasp of the moral issues—not to mention a way with words—as witnessed by the remarks he wrote for Kennedy's appearance before the Senate Commerce Committee on July 1:

White people of whatever kind—even prostitutes, narcotics pushers, Communists, or bank robbers—are welcome at establishments which will not admit certain of our federal judges, ambassadors, and countless members of our Armed Forces. . . . For most of the past hundred years we have imposed the duties of citizenship on the Negro without allowing him to enjoy the benefits. We have demanded that he obey the same laws as white men, pay

*President Kennedy's speech on June 11 was written almost entirely by Theodore Sorenson.

the same taxes, fight and die in the same wars. Yet in nearly every part of the country, he remains the victim of humiliation and deprivation no white citizen would tolerate. All thinking Americans have grown increasingly aware that discrimination must stop—not only because it is legally insupportable, economically wasteful, and socially destructive, but above all because it is morally wrong.

Contrary to John Williams's understandable chagrin, Yates may well have been the right person for the job after all, or at least not the wrong one.

One of the secretaries in the Public Information office was a fetching, good-natured young woman named Wendy Sears, the twenty-two-year-old daughter of a prominent Brahmin lawyer in Boston. She and Yates engaged in a hesitant flirtation for much of that summer: Sears felt shy in the writer's presence, but thought he was one of the handsomest men she'd ever seen, while Yates seemed too bewildered those first few weeks to take more than polite notice. One day, during a dull meeting in the attorney general's office, Yates passed her a note—"Bored?"—and Sears scribbled back "Oh, yes!" The practice took hold: While the rest of the (male) staff solemnly discussed civil rights legislation, Yates would mock them either in prose or cartoon form (he was still a good caricaturist), and pass the results under the table to the perky stenographer. At one point Kennedy caught Sears pausing thus in her shorthand and became vexed—"*We've got to get somebody else in here!*"—whereupon Yates sprang to her defense: It was *his* fault, he said, and firmly suggested that Miss Sears be allowed to stay. "That was typical of Dick," she said. "He wouldn't even let *Kennedy* be offensive." Yates was naturally given to chivalry on behalf of attractive young women, though he did find Sears "a little heavy in the leg." She seemed to sense as much, and when she came upon the phrase "unpardonably thick ankles" in *Revolutionary Road,* she approached the author: "Dick, how thick do ankles have to be before they're 'unpardonable'?" Yates recognized his own epithet and laughed. "That got the ball rolling," Sears recalled.

"I have a new girlfriend," Yates announced to the Schulmans upon his return to New York, "and she has really *sturdy* parents." By then he'd come to dread the sight of the slatternly, whiskey-for-breakfast Craige, whose dissolute behavior he blamed in part on an unwholesome family background. But Wendy Sears was the healthy, well-groomed embodiment of good breeding, and what's more she laughed at his jokes. When she was pouty Yates called her "Wendy Serious" (a name that stuck whatever her mood), and he'd go to any length to cheer her up. Their mutual delight was infectious. As Jack Rosenthal put it, "Wendy and Dick were the hub of a circle of laughter—cynical, not necessarily loyal to the powers-that-be, but good-natured."

Another member of the circle was an affable young AP reporter, Joe Mohbat, who shared a cubbyhole at the Justice Department with his UPI counterpart. Yates and Mohbat had a common fondness for certain kinds of sophisticated silliness, and became lifelong friends. Over lunch at the Kansas City Steakhouse or Hammel's, the two would swap "Tom Swifties" while Yates tanked up on vodka martinis (he preferred "something brown" for later) and laughed until he coughed so hard "it hurt to listen," as Mohbat remembered. Often they were joined by Rosenthal and Wendy Sears, and the well-oiled Yates would regale them with table-slapping contempt for some fresh outrage among the "tight-ass political types" back at the office. His favorite expression at such times was *"big fucking deal,"* primarily applied to the brown-nosing toadies who clustered around the Kennedys. He made fun of the way Guthman jumped whenever "BAG" buzzed, or the way a certain young writer for *Look* magazine hung around the office all day dropping the phrase *Bob and I.* "Dick had an objective outsider's eye in a circle otherwise composed of Kennedy admirers," said Rosenthal, who (despite his own youthful earnestness at the time) liked the way Yates sat back in his chair and "laughed at the whole thing."

The group found clever ways to fill downtime in the office. Mohbat filed his wire-service copy as briskly as possible so he could "lurk for tidbits" around the fifth floor, which often meant ducking into the Herbert Brownell Room to cut-up with Yates. The latter liked to boast that he'd worked so hard on *Revolutionary Road* he knew it word for word, so Mohbat and Sears would kill time trying to stump him with his own novel: They'd read the first few words of a random passage, and the author would (flawlessly) supply the rest. Also they played a word game devised by Rosenthal—a former "Quiz Kid" finalist—called "Merkins," taken from LBJ's phrase *"Mah fellow Merkins."* The game entailed contracting syllables according to American dialect—for example (Yates's favorite), "Jeat jet?" for *Did you eat yet?* from Salinger's "Just Before the War with the Eskimos."* All day long they'd leave "Merkins" on each other's desk and keep score, awarding one point per contracted syllable— hence three points for "Shadune?" (*What are you doing?*), two for "Salacornta how you look at it" (*It's all according to how you look at it*), and so on. Such silliness spilled over to dinners at Wendy Sears's Georgetown apartment; because of RFK's crusade against organized crime, Yates would compulsively name his food after mobsters—"Potatoes" Dinado, "Peas" Gambino—and collapse into hacking laughter.

From the beginning, though, Yates's friends at the Justice Department noticed that there was something a little *off* about him. "His rages were tyrannical when he was drunk," said Mohbat. "He'd shout, cough, swear like a sailor. You couldn't believe he wrote so elegantly when he talked like that. And it was all over *nothing*—some neutral talk about politics or whatever." Yates was particularly impatient with Wendy Sears, whose youth and relative passivity made her an easy target for "correction"—as when she'd say something ungrammatical or use a hackneyed expression like *relationship* or *yea high*. Right away Yates insisted on adopting a mentorly role à la Fitzgerald's "College of One" vis-à-vis Sheilah Graham: He gave Sears a list of ten books "she might find nourishing" from the nineteenth and twentieth centuries,† and occasionally treated her to spontaneous disquisitions on, say, the meaning of "craftsmanship." And whenever she'd let some solecism slip, he'd sigh, "Wrongedy wrong wrong wrong" and bemoan how poorly educated even *genteel* girls were these

---

*In 1982, Rosenthal wrote about Merkins (which he spelled "Murcans" for the occasion) when he filled in for William Safire's "On Language" column in the *New York Times Magazine*.
†As follows: *The Great Gatsby, Madame Bovary, Judith Hearne, Lie Down in Darkness, Dubliners, A Farewell to Arms, The Scarlet Letter, The Naked and the Dead, Lord Jim,* and *The Good Soldier*.

days. When Sears happened to mention that she'd attended the same prep school (Beaver Country Day in Brookline) as Yates's former girlfriend Sandra Walcott, his response was to remember how "appalled" he'd been when Walcott misspelled the word "Congratulations." In fact, this aspect of Yates's relationship (*attachment,* rather) with Wendy Sears would survive to the very end: Almost thirty years later, the deathly ill Yates told Sears that he'd enjoyed her latest letter, "except that part where you refer to your daughter as a 'private person.'"

For a while, though, Sears was "enraptured" by Yates. He was quirky and pedantic, yes, but at his best he was the most charming of men. Sears and her roommate Suzie would beg him to sing—especially "I Found a Million-Dollar Baby in a Five-and-Ten-Cent Store," the many verses of which he'd croon with a winsome lilt in his voice. When Sears told him that her father Samuel was a good amateur pianist who'd written lyrics for Hasty Pudding shows at Harvard, the wistful Yates wondered if he'd written, by chance, "Columbus Discovered America" (he hadn't), and then of course Yates would sing that, too. The song reminded him of his daughters (many things did), and he'd happily begin telling stories about them, imitating their voices in turn. For her part Sears was adoring and tactful, a good sport, and as Yates liked to say: "She doesn't tell me long, boring stories about people I don't know."

And finally he liked the fact that she was very young and had a youthful sense of fun. When he mentioned he didn't have a proper typewriter at his apartment, Sears encouraged him to steal one of the many neglected machines at the Justice Department—a caper they pulled off together, under the proverbial cloak of darkness. Around this time, too, Bob Riche came to town and had dinner with the couple at an elegant restaurant, and was "horrified" when Sears casually removed a bottle of wine from one of the tables and stuck it in her purse. As it happened, that was the night Riche informed his friend that he was marrying the woman he'd met at Bread Loaf three years before. Yates remembered her well. "You mean you're gonna marry the *orphan*?" he said.

As the summer ended Yates's speechwriting duties began to pall. The words he'd put in Kennedy's mouth had gone a long way toward improving the man's image and advancing his agenda, but Yates's services were rarely acknowledged except for the odd, casual compliment. Kennedy gave no sign of letting Yates into his inner or even outer circle: He didn't invite him to lunch or dinner or for visits to Hickory Hill. And while Yates certainly hadn't taken the job with the hope of cultivating a camaraderie with the attorney general, he resented what Styron called the "cold transaction" of working for the Kennedys. It became less and less gratifying when the public cheered his speeches, since he never got any of the credit. Of course Yates realized this was his job, but as a matter of principle it rankled that people like himself did all the work while the Kennedys simply accepted it as their due.

Above all he was anxious to get back to his fiction, an attitude that puzzled his colleagues on the fifth floor: As Rosenthal put it, they didn't understand "why anyone would bother with 'mere literature,' when one could be involved in changing the world." Besides, if Yates insisted that speechwriting was "whoring" but he needed the money, why not write fiction in his spare time or vice versa? Why not write *both*? But Yates couldn't compartmentalize that way—"When I'm writing, I'm *writing*"— and it wasn't as if he could alternate fortnights working on one or the other, as he'd done in his Remington Rand days. Meanwhile, as always when he wasn't writing fiction, Yates drank to numb the painful sense of lost time, not to say a bleak suspicion that he was already washed up as a serious writer. Once, after returning to Washington via the Eastern shuttle, he mentioned to Sears that he'd spotted John Kenneth Galbraith on the plane: "God," he said, "if the plane had gone down, all they'd talk about was Galbraith." And when John Williams visited Washington as part of his *Holiday* junket, he was startled by the change in his friend: "Dick was drinking like he needed to get out of himself one way or the other. He said, '*I'm the best fucking writer in America!*' I'd never seen him so full of himself—usually he was laid back and just let the work speak for itself." But there hadn't been any work in a long time (arguably none worth keeping in almost two years), and such boasts were the gasps of a drowning man.

Perhaps there was some consolation, then, in the imminent prospect of a thumbs-down from the FBI. Yates expected as much, and moved out of the Knorrs' house in late August; he rented a basement apartment on Ash-mead Place off Connecticut Avenue, where he could stay close to Wendy Sears and work on his novel in relative privacy once his job ended at the Justice Department. Sure enough, the FBI report landed on Kennedy's desk almost exactly four months after Yates's hiring, and alcoholism and mental instability were its major themes. The interview that followed in Kennedy's office—a stock anecdote in Yates's repertoire—happened pretty much as reported in *Uncertain Times*:

"Would you describe yourself as a heavy drinker?"

"Yes, I would."

Kennedy gave a small nod as if to commend him for honesty.

"But I don't drink when I'm working," he lied. "I've never done that. Be sort of like drinking and driving a car."

"I see. Still, the most disturbing parts of the report for me are these several hospitalizations you've had for mental or emotional illness." Only two, Bob, Grove wanted to say; it's only happened twice, but he kept his mouth shut. A drop of sweat seeped from one armpit and slid down his ribs. "That's a cause of some concern to me," Kennedy said. "Still, your work here has been fine. It's been excellent. . . . Tell me something, though, Bill. When you had these several—breakdowns of yours in the past, has it been possible for you to sort of sense them coming in advance?" . . .

"Yes, I can, Bob," he said, though that had never been true; and to soften it on the side of less flagrant dishonesty he said "At least I'm pretty sure I can."

"I see. Well then, look. . . . Suppose we leave it this way: If that should ever happen while you're working for me—if you ever sense you're in some kind of imminent difficulty of that kind, I mean, will you come and tell me about it?"

"Certainly, Bob."

Yates was allowed to stay. As a speechwriter he wasn't a high-security risk, and the decision was ultimately Kennedy's to make. More mysterious, perhaps, was Yates's willingness to prevaricate in order to keep a job he didn't much want anymore. The easy explanation was that he still needed the money—as of course he did—but a few other factors come to mind: One, he was loath to have it known that he'd been fired because of mental illness; two, at whatever level he actually dreaded the prospect of writing (or rather *not* writing) fiction again, and was somewhat relieved to have an excuse to put it off; and three, at the time he badly needed the esteem he derived from being RFK's speechwriter, and liked to think Kennedy needed him as much as he needed Kennedy. "I think it's sort of important to consider," says Bill Grove after the FBI interview, ". . . that [Kennedy] may not want to lose his voice. . . . I've written every fucking word that's come out of his mouth for the past four months."

Yates's job had been considered "provisional" pending the FBI report, after which the news was finally released to the press: "After searching for months," *Newsweek* belatedly reported in its September 16 issue, "Robert Kennedy has found a new speechwriter. He is 37-year-old novelist Richard Yates . . . who has just finished a screenplay for William Styron's *Lie Down in Darkness*. (Styron suggested him for the job.) The Attorney General started looking after a stormy session with Negro leaders in New York convinced him that his civil-rights speeches were missing the mark."* At last Yates would get some credit in the public mind for RFK's occasional eloquence, though perhaps the most intriguing result of the *Newsweek* announcement was a phone call: Was this Richard Yates the *writer*, a woman wanted to know, and if so how long had he been working in Washington? "Yes," Yates replied to the first question, and "about four months" to the second. The woman sighed, explaining that she'd been seeing a guy in the Village who claimed to be Richard Yates, though various people had suggested he was an imposter. "Can you imagine?" Yates told friends. "People getting *laid* claiming they're me?"

But such glee over reminders (ribald and otherwise) of his literary importance was mingled with rue. It almost hurt to be told that the French edition of *Eleven Kinds of Loneliness* had been selected as Best Foreign Book of the Month, that reviews were ecstatic, when Yates himself had lost faith in his ability to write a short story. As for his stalled

---

*The *Newsweek* item appears almost word for word in *Disturbing the Peace*—that is, to announce the same job for the Yates-like Chester Pratt.

novel, he certainly wouldn't be able to make his January delivery date now that he'd indefinitely committed himself to Kennedy, and really he wondered if he'd ever finish the book at all, or if he should even try. Sam Lawrence tried to goad him back to work with an offer of five hundred dollars a month until the book was finished, but Yates declined: He was already in debt to the publisher and had little incentive to accept further advances at his own risk.

Yates's company became more of a mixed blessing than ever. In the early days of their courtship, Wendy Sears had caught glimpses of his occasional volatility, but never in her life had she witnessed such uncontrollable rage as when she let drop that her mother had questioned whether "Richard Yates" was his real name. Yates was convinced the woman had meant to imply he was some kind of fraud—déclassé, a foreigner perhaps, not worthy of her blueblood daughter and so forth. It didn't help that the woman had also seen fit to belittle the *Back Bay Ledger* ("Never heard of it"), which had provided one of the more glowing blurbs for *Eleven Kinds of Loneliness*. "He went berserk," said Sears, "and he wasn't even drunk. It went on and on—'*What does she know?*'— for almost two hours, shouting, his face red. It was like something snapped in his brain."

Yates seemed to prize the fact that Sears came from "sturdy" Brahmin stock, but it also piqued his deepest insecurities. The worst of his outbursts were almost always related to matters of class, and he often gave Sears the impression of railing against an abstraction rather than her (*"You rich Boston debutantes! Who the hell do you think you are?"*). "It had become important lately to find good reasons for losing his temper at Wendy," Yates wrote in *Uncertain Times**—this in the context of a "fictionalized" account of his meeting one of Sears's cousins: a young man who happened to remark that he wanted to work for the FBI in order to carry a gun. "That cousin of yours," says Grove, "is nothing but a spoiled,

---

* *Sic* "Wendy." In the novel the character based on Sears is called "Holly Parsons," but in the later, rougher stages of the manuscript there are several instances where he'd yet to change real names.

stupid, brutal fucking kid. . . . He's a graduate of Exeter . . . he's a graduate of Brown University; and now all he wants to do in the world is carry a pistol. That's how fascists are made, sweetheart: That's the way the Nazi party was conceived and born." Perhaps, but in real life Sears had readily conceded that such a remark was unworthy of her cousin, that in fact he wasn't a bad sort at all, but anyway why was Yates screaming at *her*? *She* hadn't said anything about wanting to carry a pistol. And why drag Exeter and Brown into it?

The worst lay ahead. In early November Sam Lawrence came to town and took the couple to Billy Martin's Carriage House on Wisconsin Avenue, a "suave, expensive and quiet restaurant" (as Yates described it), where one could have drinks around the piano before adjourning to a gilded dining room. Yates liked that sort of thing and seemed at ease, when suddenly he bellowed that Lawrence was a *son of a bitch* and stood ranting at him for reasons that nobody (Yates included) could later fathom. Sears begged him to sit down and be quiet, Lawrence looked bemused, and finally "four hefty waiters" carried the shouting, writhing author out the door and threw him bodily into the street. The piano played louder throughout the ordeal, like a saloon scene in a Western movie. Sears fled the restaurant and walked home, weeping with humiliation, while Lawrence paid the check and implored the management not to call the cops. "That, I guess, is the kind of awful experience that can sometimes be laughed off," Yates wrote with retrospective serenity in 1972, "as [Lawrence] and I were able to do the very next day, when I crept to his hotel to apologize and retrieve my raincoat." Yates was somewhat less apologetic to Sears, and when he described the scene to Joe Mohbat it was "almost as if [Yates] were talking about a separate person, a person he didn't like, a character in a book: 'Can you *imagine* such an asshole?' "

After the FBI report, Yates made an effort not to drink while at work, but it was a losing battle. Eight or nine hours of sobriety a day, at a job he now actively disliked, meant that he drank with even greater abandon at night and on weekends—so much so, in fact, that temperance at any time became out of the question. Every morning he'd be ashen and shaky with hangover, and the only remedy was to sneak well-paced shots of vodka throughout the day. Neither his heart nor his head was in his work anymore, and people in the office began to notice: His speeches were less original, even a bit lifeless, and Yates himself seemed fed up with more than just the work. When Kennedy and Guthman returned from a trip to the Midwest, the latter remarked that "people out there" were "the *real* Americans"—the folks who paid taxes and fought wars and so forth. Yates held his tongue, but later exploded to Wendy Sears: "That asshole! What does he mean, 'the *real* Americans'? What, the *Negroes* aren't real?" Yates thought it a fatuous, reactionary thing to say, and all too typical of the basic hypocrisy that lurked at the heart of the whole political establishment, however much obscured by the liberal cant of the Kennedys. He wanted out.

Wednesday, November 20, was the attorney general's birthday, and his staff was invited to a White House reception that night for the Supreme Court and other members of the judiciary. For the first and last time Yates shook hands with President Kennedy, the object of his scorn and perhaps wistful envy, and then danced with Wendy Sears in the East Room. At one point he ran out of cigarettes, and was aghast to discover there were none on the premises.

Two days later Joe Mohbat and reporter Jack Vandenburg of the UPI were returning from lunch when they passed the teletype room on the fifth floor, where Yates stood watching the chattering ticker. He waved them inside: "They shot the president!" he hissed. "They shot the fucking president!" The reporters ran to their phones, and Yates left for the airport to spend the weekend with his daughters in New York. He was back in time to watch the funeral cortege pass beneath the fifth-floor balcony of the Justice Department. Unlike many of the others, Yates was somber but dry-eyed. The following Thursday was Thanksgiving, and Yates and Wendy met the Mohbats for a restaurant dinner in Potomac, Maryland. The four hardly spoke. Yates shook his head a few times and said "Holy shit."

Yates had wanted to quit "gracefully," he wrote a friend—"and just about that time the president decided to go to Dallas. And one of the millions of tiny changes brought about by *that* tragic business was that my job was dissolved. So I didn't have to quit after all, and was able to leave Robert with no hard feelings." In the wake of the assassination, at least, Yates had come to think of the attorney general as "Robert"—not the more common "Bob," or even (as in moments of particular ambivalence) one of "the fucking Kennedys." Whatever else Yates thought of the man, he didn't doubt his basic decency anymore: Not only had Kennedy treated him with kindness and tact over the FBI matter, but it was hard not to have tender feelings for a man as ravaged with grief as the president's brother.

Yates continued to take a dim view of JFK. In the words of John Wilder in *Disturbing the Peace,* he considered the president "a rich boy, a glamour boy, a senator who'd never once spoken out against McCarthy even after it was safe for anyone to do so, a candidate who'd bought the primaries and rigged the convention." In fact Yates made that exact remark, more or less, while explaining to Arthur Schlesinger Jr. why he (Yates) remained "an unregenerate Stevenson man"; and Schlesinger's reply was essentially that of Paul Borg in the novel: "I think we have to agree that Stevenson was a Greek. Kennedy's a Roman. We need Romans in the country now."* But Yates didn't buy that. To him Kennedy was a shallow opportunist, the ultimate triumph of surface over substance, and such a president should be deplored no matter what he manages to accomplish (via the efforts of others, as Yates would have it). Perhaps to mock his own unworldliness, though, Yates considered the following quote from Schlesinger as a possible epigraph to *Uncertain Times*: "Never look for political ideas in a literary mind."

Yates's sister Ruth had deteriorated rapidly since her decision, a few months before, to remain with her husband. That summer she'd been too drunk to attend her daughter Dodo's high school graduation, and Fred

---

*Wendy Sears witnessed this exchange at a party Schlesinger gave in August 1963. In his biography of Robert Kennedy, Schlesinger baldly declared: "Richard Yates, the novelist . . . did not like [Robert] Kennedy." Perhaps he assumed (not without cause) that Yates's contempt for JFK embraced both brothers, but it doesn't seem that Yates explicitly disparaged RFK in Schlesinger's presence.

was far from sober when he arrived (late) for the ceremony. "Everybody in town knew about the situation," their daughter recalled. "It was a horrible experience growing up in that house, especially after Fred [Jr.] went into the service and Peter went off to school." Dodo had never really known her mother as a sane, functioning person: By the time the girl reached puberty, Ruth had given up most of her avocations at Fred's behest; she drank in the morning and tried to sleep it off during the day, in hope of being "fresh" when her husband returned from work. Their daughter would find bottles stashed all over the house, even around the mailbox where she waited for the school bus; one morning Ruth caught the girl trying to remove the hidden bottles and came after her with a kitchen knife. Another time Dodo found her mother in the closet trying to hang herself with knotted neckties: Fred had been out of town, and Ruth was terrified of his coming home that evening and finding her drunk again.

"She felt like everything was drifting away from her," said her sister-in-law Louise. Not only were the children gone most of the time, but her husband had gotten into the habit of "working overtime" and leaving town as often as possible "on business." A few months after Ruth had called her brother for help, she turned up at Louise Rodgers's Manhattan apartment in the middle of the night. "Your brother doesn't love me anymore," she was sobbing. "I have nothing to live for." That Fred had girlfriends was hardly a mystery ("He was spoiled, from a good family, so he figured he could do what he wanted," said his daughter); more puzzling to his children was why he wouldn't arrange (or let anyone else arrange) some kind of long-term care for his alcoholic and now suicidal wife. When confronted, he'd say he was "handling it."

That winter, Ruth called her brother again and asked if she could come stay with him in Washington. This time Yates gently talked her out of it: He was working hard on his novel and needed privacy; besides, his apartment was too small, and most of the time he shared it with Wendy Sears. The truth was that he'd come to believe his sister was a hopeless case, and felt contempt for the way she'd "fucked up her life"—become the victim of a man like Fred Rodgers, whom (Yates was sure of it now) she'd never really leave. And even though Ruth's call depressed him, he told Sears he was "glad it happened." It brought him back to the "hard facts of life," he said, so he could get on with putting those facts on paper and not worry about being so goddamn "literary."

A few weeks later Ruth was in Central Islip, the state mental hospital on Long Island. She'd crashed into a parked car, and a boat anchor in the back of her station wagon had shot forward and hit her in the back of the head. When Yates visited her at the hospital, her shaved scalp was swathed in a large turbanlike bandage; but the injury was incidental to the main diagnosis of acute alcoholism that had brought her to Central Islip. Somewhere, too, among the 122 buildings of the vast asylum was Dookie, who'd been moved there after St. Johnland became too expensive.

Ruth would be in and out of Central Islip for what remained of her life, but she no longer discussed such matters with her brother. A few weeks after her first hospitalization she typed a letter to Yates full of chatty domestic news: Her son Peter had presented her with a secondhand Underwood portable for her birthday; Fred Jr.'s wife had just given birth to a baby girl who looked exactly like Fred Sr. ("this makes [my husband] very angry, because it makes him tend to feel like a grandfather, and he doesn't care for the idea"); she'd been harvesting blackberries all week even though she hated blackberries ("I do this, remembering what the man said when asked why he wanted to climb Mt. Everest—'Because it's there' "); and finally she hadn't visited Dookie lately because her driving was "limited to strictly local stuff, at least until I gain a little more self-confidence and grow a little more hair." The entire letter was transcribed almost word for word in *The Easter Parade*, where it serves as evidence that Sarah Grimes has surrendered herself to the illusion that she is "the happiest, most contented little housewife in the world." For the purpose of his novel, though, Yates saw fit to cut the last line of Ruth's actual letter: "It's quite lonely around here."

The night before he left Washington for a Christmas visit with his daughters, Yates stayed up until three A.M. wrapping presents; Wendy Sears offered to come over and help, but he wanted to do it himself. He'd arranged to spend the holiday with Sharon and Monica at the Plaza Hotel.

By then the girls had moved back to Mahopac, and their father was eager to compensate for what he called "that proletarian town" by giving them a taste of high life during their visits—nice restaurants, the theater, the Plaza. It was an almost wholly successful Christmas: The girls ordered butterscotch sundaes from room service and read *Eloise* with Yates; they romped in the hallway and wished they could live there forever. Monica recalls that the only dark moments came when she—then six—sensed her father's almost oppressive need to please them; she wondered if he could really afford such gestures, since he usually lived in a basement.

Yates was briefly in better spirits now that his work for the Kennedys was over. He took Wendy Sears to New York for the first time and introduced her to friends. They had dinner at the Blue Mill with Broyard, who seemed to like Sears in an unsalacious way, and spent a jolly evening with the Schulmans, who were naturally relieved to have the sodden Craige off their hands. In fact the visit went remarkably without a hitch, though Sears vowed never to pass another night in Yates's "dark, awful, dirty" apartment at 27 Seventh Avenue South.

Yates continued to live in Washington until early April; he claimed to like the town well enough, but it was mostly a matter of having a warm body in his bed at night. Wendy Sears, however, was almost frantically longing for freedom. She was still fond of Yates and awed by his stature as a writer, but as a constant companion he was a disaster. Even times of relative calm were nerve-racking. The air was forever charged with some dire emotion—as when Sears gave him, for his thirty-eighth birthday, a black leather album with the gold-embossed title, *The Speeches of Robert F. Kennedy, by Richard Yates*. "I thought he was going to cry," she said. "He was always so *astonished* when you gave him a gift, or did anything nice for him." Then in March they took a larky drive through the Virginia countryside to visit Yates's old friend Ed Kessler, who'd taken a job at William and Mary. As with the New York trip, the weekend was almost ominously tranquil: Kessler led them on a droll historical tour of Williamsburg, and later they attended an elegant cocktail party where they mingled with the likes of Winthrop Rockefeller.

But Sears knew it was only a matter of time, and when the storm broke it was worse than ever. Looking back, she can't remember why they stopped at that motel outside Washington, or why Yates started screaming and throwing things, only that it went on for a long time and was definitely the last straw. It wasn't a question of his being menacing, or actually throwing things *at* her, or even taking her into account one way or the other. But the episode was terrifying all the same, not to say exhausting, and when Yates left Washington a few weeks later they agreed to part as friends. He *lerved* her, he said, which was a little less than love but more than like. Sears was just glad he was at a safe distance now, so she could enjoy his finer qualities via letters and phone calls.

Granted, he was under a strain. At the end of December he'd finally decided to accept Lawrence's arrangement of five hundred dollars a month up to three thousand—this for a novel he was by no means confident of finishing, at any rate not within six months, and meanwhile the money was just enough to cover child support and alimony with a pittance left over. Monica McCall continued to make encouraging noises about the lucrative prospects of *Lie Down in Darkness,* but that bubble burst (again) in January when Frankenheimer decided to let his option lapse. The following month Yates learned he was the recipient of a Brandeis University Creative Arts Award ("for recognition of promise") in the amount of a thousand dollars, to be awarded at the Waldorf in May; Nabokov was slated for special recognition that night, and certainly Yates hoped to meet the great man,* though his own award hardly altered the fact that by the end of the summer he'd be broke. McCall tried to interest him in writing a sixty thousand–word social history of Saratoga Springs, New York, for Prentice-Hall ("There are of course a number of elements involved: money, society, health, gambling and horses, and I think that such a book could be fun to do"), but Yates was not interested. Finally by mid-February his outlook was bleak enough for him to accept, at long last, a teaching position at the Iowa Workshop beginning that fall. Cassill was pleased to gain another ally, and replied with the cheerful news that Yates would be getting eight—rather than the aforesaid seven—thousand dollars a year; he was advised to buy a car, however.

---

*Nabokov remained in Switzerland rather than accept the award in person.

Money was one thing, but Yates's erratic behavior was mostly fueled by despair over his work. More than three years earlier he'd conceived his novel, all too ambitiously, as a bildungsroman to rival Joyce's *A Portrait of the Artist as a Young Man*; but on bad days he saw the thing as little more than so much pointless confession, and wondered whether he should simply cut his losses and write something else. On what appeared to be a relatively good day in mid-March he wrote his friend Miller Williams,

> I'm working like a bastard on this second novel, which is at the stage now when I sometimes think the only respectable thing to do is burn it, but on betters days I continue to hold pretty grandiose hopes for the damn thing. It's a tough one, about five times more "autobiographical" than *Revolutionary Road,* with all the possibilities for Naked Embarrassment implied in that statement. But if I *can* bring it off it might be good.

Such occasional confidence was mostly due to the novel's excellent self-contained prologue, in which Prentice visits his deluded mother in New York while on leave from the army. *That* part of the book was finished, was "formed" as Yates put it, but the problem he couldn't solve was how to relate it to the rest of the novel—that is, how to find some plausible connection between Prentice's war experiences and his disenchantment with (and subsequent liberation from) his mother. Was any such connection really valid? And wasn't the whole point of the prologue to suggest that Prentice is *already* disenchanted with his mother, even before he goes overseas?

So Yates brooded. And while there were days when he worked "like a bastard," there were others he spent writing letters to Wendy Sears, or making lists, or "doing research" and drinking. He asked Sears to find books about the Seventy-fifth Infantry Division, the Ninth Army, and wondered what she thought of such prospective titles as *Rite of Passage, Prentice,* and *The Straggler* (one of the many rejected titles for *Revolutionary Road*). Sears was nothing if not obliging: She visited the Library of Congress on his behalf, and tended to prefer whatever title was presently on his mind.

A representative artifact of this period is a curious group of poems Yates wrote amid the inertia of evading his novel. The title pretty much says it all: "QWERTYUIOP½: Six Efforts To Achieve Coherence While Using Only the Second Row of Keys on the Standard Typewriter." The novelty of such an exercise suggests a writer with far too much time on his hands. Fittingly the theme of all six "efforts" is literary failure. A few samples:

A CONFESSION OF FULBRIGHTS

We were poor, we were witty,
Our poetry tip-top, our Europe pretty.
We quit our torpor, quit our rue—
Yet O!—we quit our typewriter, too.

A RELIGIOUS-CONVERT WRITER'S LAMENT

O Piety, Piety, prior to you
I wrote poor yet I wrote true.
I wrote out worry, wrote up riot.
O Piety, Piety, Piety—Quiet!

A LOVE SONG

Pet, I owe you poetry.
I write to you; yet, eye-to-eye,
You pout, you weep, require rye.
O Pet, I owe you poetry.

Yates recited his verse during a boozy night with Styron in Martha's Vineyard, and the latter was so impressed that he wanted to see about getting it published in the *New York Review of Books*. Alas, Styron misplaced the one rumpled page Yates mailed him that summer, which naturally turned out to be the only copy of the manuscript. Eventually Yates got around to rewriting the poems from memory, and they appeared in *Esquire* two and a half years later. Twice as many years would pass before Yates's second novel was published.

• • •

At Sam Lawrence's suggestion, Yates arranged to spend the summer at the MacDowell Colony in Peterborough, New Hampshire, where in theory he would finish his novel in a placid yet stimulating environment—as Lawrence described it, "you work all day and carouse from 5 to 6 p.m. on: writers, painters, sculptors, composers." Monica McCall had another client who lived in the area, the writer Richard Frede, and Yates stopped at the man's house for a dinner party en route. "Yates was pleasant enough," Frede remembered, "but still it was a rather fearful experience: He seemed to be drinking compulsively, *hurting* himself with drink. One after another."

At the colony Yates was given a secluded cabin with a desk, bed, and fireplace, where at first he was able to settle down to work; the only interruption before cocktail hour was a pickup truck that delivered box lunches between 11:30 and noon, with one's letters tucked next to the sandwiches. Wendy Sears wrote almost every other day, and Yates also got some rather nostalgic gossip from Sheila and the Schulmans: The first reported that her brother Charlie was now working at *Reader's Digest* (something to do with computers) as part of a program prescribed by his doctors to help him "get along with people," while Grace mentioned that Barbara Beury had been in touch asking if she still had a chance at that *Glamour* job ("I'll put in a dime if you like," Grace added wryly. "Clinkety, clinkety clink. The last one was Jerry"). Such news of his previous lives in Washington, New York, and beyond was calmly received at a distance, and during the first week Yates managed to write fiction at the astounding rate of three to five pages a day.

It didn't last. As he became better acquainted with his fellow colonists, the nights grew longer and more bibulous, and soon he was entangled in a distracting affair with a "rich, waspy" painter manquée named Victoria. He continued to write a fair amount, but there were days of crapulent depression when he wondered why he bothered. At the beginning of August he called Wendy Sears and told her he'd finished the last chapter, though he didn't seem pleased about it, and a few days later he vented his frustration in a letter to the Schulmans:

The damn place [MacDowell] is a little too Bread-Loafy for comfort—by which I mean that too many evenings get wasted having Brilliant Conversations with the Nicest and Best People you've Ever Met, and then waking up with a terrible hangover and going to the damn typewriter as if it were an instrument of torture. Sometimes I get good working days in and hardly drink at all; other times everything goes to hell. Worst feature now is that I'm horribly aware of the time slipping away, and feel a compulsion to finish the effing book by September First whether it's any good or not—and this, of course, is not exactly a healthy attitude.

One good thing: there's a guy here with a collection of old-timey phonograph records, and I've mastered both lyrics and tune of an absolutely great Al Jolson item called "Where Did Robinson Crusoe Go with Friday on Saturday Night?"—I promise to sing it for you loud and clear the minute I'm back in town.

By then his friend Victoria had left MacDowell to go abroad, and Yates was all the more free to write or drink or sing or sit in his cabin and brood. When Edmund Wilson visited the colony for a weekend in mid-August, the languishing Yates declined an invitation to deliver the salutatory remarks; Wendy Sears called to ask him about it, but Yates was too drunk to give a coherent account—"Oh well," he managed to sigh. The next day Sears wrote him a scolding letter: "Brendan Behan drank because when he did, he knew he couldn't write and this was his excuse."

After he left MacDowell at the end of the month, Yates stopped in New York for ten days to wrap up his affairs before moving to Iowa City. After exactly five years of Dostoyevskian habitation, one imagines a faint pang on Yates's part as he carried his few possessions out of the basement at 27 Seventh Avenue South (never to reclaim them: When he returned to his storage locker a year later, he found it full of a stranger's things; nobody could tell him what had become of his old sling chairs and bookcase and Bob Parker portrait). He lunched with Sam Lawrence and broke the news that he hadn't finished the novel after all, but hoped to do so by Christmas "at the latest." And finally, per the advice of Verlin Cassill, he bought a "snot-green" used car for the long rural backroads of Iowa. "Richard Yates?"

said the man taking his order at the car-painting shop. "There's a good writer who goes by that name." As it happened, the car painter was himself an aspiring writer who took classes at the New School; the paint shop, he explained, was only a day job. Yates asked him to paint the car gray.

CHAPTER TEN

A New Yorker Discovers the Middle West: 1964-1966

Before the poet Paul Engle and others began to teach creative writing there in the mid-thirties, the University of Iowa was a minor member of the Big Ten with nothing much to recommend it other than a picturesque locale (Victorian architecture, the Iowa River winding through campus). Thirty years later, the "Workshop" was by far the most famous writing program in the country, rivaled only by its counterpart at Stanford established by Wallace Stegner, an Iowa graduate. The Workshop was composed of a hundred or so carefully selected graduate students who prided themselves on being part of a bohemian community of writers coexisting with, but remaining aloof from, the conservative bumpkins of both town and campus. "Greenwich Village West" they called it, and tried to live up to the name by smoking pot, getting drunk, and enjoying a certain amount of "free love" long before such a lifestyle was assimilated into the national counterculture. Just beneath the surface of this self-styled Arcadia, however, was a snakepit of internecine strife between poets and fiction writers, traditionalists and experimentalists, the talented and not-so-talented, the drunk and not-so-drunk, the faculty and administrators.

Yates would have preferred to stand apart from all that, or most of it anyway. He'd come to Iowa for one reason—as he liked to say (echoing Vonnegut), "The business of teaching creative writing offers solace to writers who are down on their luck." *He* was down on his luck, and grateful for the chance to make a living, but continued to think the whole idea of "teaching" writing was ridiculous. He felt no particular solidarity with the whole noble experiment—a Community of Writers—much less its affected bohemian nonsense, though he was glad enough to know that liquor by the drink was now legal in Iowa City. And certainly he could use whatever comforts were afforded by an emancipated sexual ethos, whether he quite subscribed to it or not. As he'd written Cassill, "I must admit I'm a little leery about the idea of living in Iowa as a bachelor—what if anything does a fella do for laughs on those long winter nights out there?" Cassill replied that the night life of the town was fairly dull—"few places interesting to eat out in, even fewer to drink in"—but assured him that he'd be invited to a lot of parties, and that "a great deal of flexibility" was possible in one's private life: "That is, everyone will know what you are up to, but no one will interfere."

Yates's arrival in Iowa was far from auspicious. His car overheated and caught fire on the way, and what few worldly possessions weren't in storage (and hence lost forever) were scorched in the mishap. Somehow he managed to be only a few minutes late to his inaugural guest lectureship, but was ill prepared and utterly cowed: "I found myself talking about Bellow," he said later, "about whom I knew nothing. And they were writing it down!" When that ordeal was over he was conducted to his lodgings, which Cassill had found within the specified price range of eighty dollars a month or less: a drafty ramshackle Victorian mansion divided into four apartments at 317 South Capitol Street ("Turn at the sign that says 'Save Two Cents,'" Yates would instruct visitors in a despondent drawl), where he would dwell for the next nine months with a table, bed, typewriter, and little else. One of the first things he did was write a letter to his daughter Monica, at the bottom of which he drew his signature cartoon of a sad daddy with a thought balloon above his head filled with the face of a pretty girl: "Thinking of you."

Yates was a celebrity at the Workshop as soon as he arrived—many regarded *Revolutionary Road* as the most important novel written by a faculty member—and before long he became something of a legend. "I think we all wanted to be Richard Yates," his student Robert Lacy remembered. "I know for a fact that I did. He was tall, lanky, and moviestar handsome back then, and he moved in an aura of sad, doom-haunted, F. Scott Fitzgeraldian grace. He was Gatsby and Nick Carraway and Dick

Diver all rolled into one." Gaunt and dapper and courtly, coughing mortally as he lit one cigarette after another with palsied hands, he was "everybody's idea of a writer" as David Milch put it. And for many Iowa students, learning how to *look* like a writer was at least as important as learning how to write—of course, one had to cultivate a fair amount of misery to look as "doom-haunted" as Yates, though perhaps that was a price worth paying.

Yates wasn't much comforted by the admiring eyes that followed him around. Not only was he losing faith in himself as a writer—a little worse than dying—but he'd *never* had any faith in himself as a teacher, and now he was being scrutinized by people, *intellectuals,* who took the whole business very seriously indeed. It was one thing to "teach" nice-biddy hobbyists and car-painting dreamers at the New School, another to be exposed as a fraud in the eyes of some of the brightest, most talented young writers in the country, many of whom hailed from the dreaded Ivy League. And the earliest signs seemed to indicate that Yates and the Workshop wouldn't mix. At one of his first parties he was approached by an admiring new student named Robin Metz; Yates was tipsily cordial until the young man happened to mention that he'd gone to Princeton. Yates squinted at his necktie. "What's this," he said, flipping it into Metz's startled face, "—a fucking *club tie*?" Then, to make matters worse, the two found themselves having brunch together the next day, in a group that included Richard Baron and E. L. Doctorow (both with the Dial Press at the time), who were in town for a publishers' conference. At one point it came to light that Metz had been a student of Philip Roth at Princeton, and Yates's face darkened as Baron went on about what a *prodigy* Roth was as a teacher and a writer—the National Book Award at age twenty-six! Verlin Cassill and Vance Bourjaily heartily concurred. Then Metz ("still irked") mentioned the tie-flipping incident of the night before, and the mortified Yates explained to the table that he didn't remember that *at all.* By the end of the brunch both men were miserable: Metz, because he'd alienated the writer he most admired on the faculty; Yates, because some Princeton snotnose had just made him look like a fool in front of his new colleagues—and for that matter he was stuck in a place where people made a *big fucking deal* out of Philip Roth, whose lack of basic human sympathy was evident on every page of his books (and who'd won the NBA at age twenty-six).*

A week later Metz got a message to meet Yates at Donnelly's Bar. Warily, the young man arrived at the appointed time and found Yates sitting in a booth with a coterie of three or four older students he'd already picked out as drinking buddies. "There he is now," one of them hissed. Yates sprung to his feet and shook Metz's hand: "I read your story 'Doughboy,'" he said. "That's one fucking good story! I've wanted to meet you ever since." Metz, a little puzzled, pointed out that they'd already met—the necktie and Philip Roth and so forth. Yates waved his hand: "Oh, well, I don't care about *that*. . . ."

And (beyond the heat of the moment) he *didn't,* and that was one of the things that proved a bit of a revelation to Yates's more smitten students: He cared about the *writing*—whether Hemingway's or Metz's or whosoever's—more passionately than any jargon-spouting literature professor, such that life itself was somewhat less than secondary. In the World War II–era Quonset huts where Workshop classes were held, Yates would sit on the edge of a desk with his long legs dangling, as he lovingly flipped through and finger-thumped the ragged paperbacks he taught from. His student Luke Wallin called him a "sublime, rugged presence," and particularly looked forward to his seminar on contemporary fiction:

> His lectures were like his narrative voice: gentle and careful, honest and clean and surprising. He was something to watch, with his aging good looks, his shyness (he was extremely polite to his students, almost afraid of them), and best of all his personal, thought-out views of each novel we read. He, too, had an incredible voice, expressing such pain and such love for American writing. . . . His views were presented in quiet, open

---

*In those days Yates thought Roth "condescended" to his characters—that is, made them into so many foolish stereotypes. "I thought Philip Roth was vastly overrated for years until I read *Portnoy's Complaint*," he told *Ploughshares*; "then I forgave him everything including his millions of dollars."

challenge to the class, and it always amazed me how little his otherwise boisterous students would take exception and argue. His criticism reminds me most of Kazin's, about as nonacademic as one could find, and full of power. His lasting example was of a writer who had taken his tradition deeply to heart.

As his listeners at Bread Loaf had also learned, Yates had a gift for imparting his very subjective enthusiasms; he rarely if ever approached a text in any kind of systematic way, but rather pointed to a line, a detail, a bit of dialogue, and said in effect, *See?* His fixed ideas remained the same—revealing dialogue, objectification, structural integrity, *precision*—but he digressed more than ever in discussing them. The "controlled sentiment" of *Lolita* might remind him of "Guests of the Nation" or "The Girls in Their Summer Dresses," and (legs softly kicking, head wagging in awe) he'd enumerate certain pertinent aspects of those stories, and perhaps others, until it was time to go. And then the following week he'd discuss an entirely different novel, as dictated by the syllabus, and *Lolita* would be forgotten unless it happened to cross his mind again for whatever reason. Such an approach would explain the rather inchoate notes that student Loree Wilson took as she tried to follow the thread of Yates's "lectures":

> *The Sun Also Rises*: Pathos of the book—it's almost as if . . . Story of a nymphomaniac, a romantic, and an emasculated. . . . Book is pernicious if read the wrong way. Hemingway is not speaking—Jake Barnes is speaking.
>
> *All the King's Men*: Road company Faulkner. Melodrama is pejorative term.
>
> *Babbitt*: Can't look for grace and tightness in Sinclair Lewis. Babbitt is an accidental work of art. Worked in the 19th c. tradition. Ear for American speech. Scene—education between father and son p. 66, hilarious. Babbitt man going to pieces before our very eyes—contradictions.
>
> *Lolita*: Beautiful book—funny and tragic. N. takes such pains setting up this complicated voice of Humbert. Very first pages brilliant. A story about love—but not how Humbert loved Lolita—but the generative writer's love of Nabokov for Humbert Humbert. . . .

"Uncle Wiggily in Connecticut": Eloise a type—a neurotic—standardized suburban wife (surroundings and furniture of mind). . . . Big action doesn't amount to much, but the little bits of dialogue—delicacy—finally make the shape of things. "Down at the Dinghy" a flimsy story . . . because we're told to love Boo Boo. Mistake of kite and kike is sweet and icky and sentimental. . . . "Teddy": annoying damn story. Dick suspects Salinger's zen kick.

The few lines quoted above represent the whole gist, more or less, of what Yates had to say about each book; ellipses indicate either where he left a thought unfinished, or the omission of a line or two (but no more) from Wilson's original notes. What she didn't write down, of course, were all the points where he quoted from the text, as well as his various conversational glosses and digressions ("By the way, for a good example of that kind of rhetorical style you might want to read Katherine Anne Porter's 'Flowering Judas'. . . ."), in the course of which he'd come up with the best of those "clean and surprising" aperçus of which Luke Wallin and others were so enamored. Finally, while students waited for him to return to the subject at hand—be it *Lolita* or *Babbitt* or whatever—Yates would abruptly stand up and announce: "I'm going to the Airliner [bar] for a martini. Would anyone care to join me?" There were no exams.

Yates's approach didn't appeal to everyone. It was true that "otherwise boisterous students" tended to defer to him, but not always because they agreed with his opinions; rather the man's extreme politeness—so anxious and unsettling at times—could turn into something else when he was put on the defensive. "Now that is fucking good writing!" Yates would exclaim after reading dialogue from *Gatsby,* say, then thrum a few pages to the next example—perhaps the part where Daisy sobs over Jay's "beautiful shirts": "Now, if that's Daisy talking, and not Fitzgerald, we've got a great novel!" *Thrum* . . . If a hand went up, and a puzzled (or cocky) student asked *why* it was so great, Yates would often get irritated, and suddenly the soft-voiced monk of literature would vanish, replaced by a hungover curmudgeon who hated show-offs. "There's Murray, squirming in his chair to tell us the news again," Yates said of one student who (until that moment) had a tendency to talk too much, and who happened to be an Ivy Leaguer. And while Yates was compellingly reverential toward the books he loved, he became downright antic on the subject of books he loathed, and dissent was hardly encouraged. Southern students—or those such as David Milch who'd been protégés of Robert Penn Warren at Yale—would blanch at Yates's (literal) trashing of *All the King's Men* as fake, derivative, melodramatic *shit*.

"We all adored him," said Cassill, and by "we" he meant all the people at Iowa who "got" Yates. "We found him stubborn and foolish sometimes, but he was constantly turning up with his heart in the right place." While Yates would sometimes overexcitedly praise or damn a book, or put certain students in their place, usually he was the essence of modesty and tact. Though he didn't much like to have his convictions challenged (especially since such a response tended to have faintly mocking overtones), he often wanted to know what students thought, and would listen with an almost disconcerting intensity to any well-meant comment or question. And when a student would say something that seemed (inoffensively) "callow and absurd," as Geoffrey Clark recalled, Yates was at his best: "[H]e'd take special pains to be gentle with you; it hurt him to inadvertently discomfit a student. . . . About the only things that really aroused his contempt or derision were pretension or condescension of any kind."

Accordingly Yates preferred underdogs: students who were socially inept, who were talented but hadn't found their voices yet, and who tended to be the target of mean-spirited sallies from the smart-ass contingent. "Oh c'mon, you don't really mean that!" Yates would admonish the latter, if they unfairly attacked a person's work or observation. When one of his more awkward students went on to become a well-known critic and novelist, Yates fondly reminisced how "smelly and shy" the man had been at Iowa, how others had mocked him as a crackpot. Yates lavished attention on such students, and protected them both in and out of the classroom. John Casey remembers how "furious" Yates became with him and David Plimpton for bullying their roommate (and Yates's student) Robert Lehrman: The three young men had rented a farmhouse together, but the suburban Lehrman was ill-suited to country life; he'd tag along in his loafers while the older, bigger men shot birds and turtles, ridiculing Lehrman the while. Both Casey and Plimpton were from genteel backgrounds—Casey had prepped in Switzerland and attended Harvard Law, Plimpton (like his cousin George) was the product of an illustrious New England family—and Yates considered their treatment of Lehrman a typical instance of the rich picking on the (relatively) poor. Yates let Casey know that he wouldn't stand for it.

But, as Lehrman himself remembers, it was always a student's work that mattered most: "Yates had no doubt that writing was important. Unlike some of the other writers on the faculty—Nelson Algren, for example, who was shocked that he had to actually read student work— Dick threw himself into helping us." Yates put himself at the disposal of those who wanted to discuss writing—whether their own or others', at the Airliner or in his office—and he'd not only read their work, but cover it with scribbled commentary in his own recognizable voice. Once Lehrman wrote a demurring essay on Yates's pet concept of literary "condescension," as it applied (or rather *didn't* apply in Lehrman's view) to Roth's *Goodbye, Columbus*; Yates's marginal notes (given below in italics) were typically prickly but amused. " 'Condescension' is not a part of the official language of criticism," Lehrman began, "—certainly Northrop Frye would disapprove of it [*big deal*]—for good reason. . . . The word doesn't apply to literature [*Why not?*]. . . . Sinclair Lewis, for example, feels superior to Babbitt [*says who?*], Flaubert had great difficulty convincing himself [*But he did, which is the point*] that Emma Bovary wasn't too petty to write about, and so on." Lehrman went on to claim that writers of farce (e.g., Roth) necessarily "condescend" to their characters, and noted: "It is not that Roth satirizes the Patimkins but that at the same time he takes Neil Klugman seriously [*Right! And there goes your argument about 'Farce'*]." And so on. Yates's good-natured sniping continued to the last page, at the bottom of which he wrote: *Okay. You finally convinced me—but it was touch and go for a while there, buddy. R. Y.* He gave the paper an A.

Actual "workshop" sessions—in which student fiction was read aloud and discussed, often viciously—were held once a week in the afternoon. Each writer on the faculty had a section of fifteen workshop students, assigned somewhat on the basis of mutual affinity: That is, if a student wrote in a purely realistic mode then he or she might be apt to sign up for Yates, and if Yates liked his or her work then he might be apt to accept the student into his section. Sometimes he'd give the person a call first. DeWitt Henry had been so "galvanized" by *Revolutionary Road* that when he left his Harvard Ph.D. program to transfer to Iowa for a continued draft deferment and time to write, he was thrilled to discover Yates among the staff and left a writing sample for him. At a dingy table in one of the Workshop Quonset huts, Yates praised "The Lord of Autumn"— then told Henry to scrap it: Too influenced by Faulkner, he said, but a talented piece of work nonetheless. Henry handed him the tentative pages of a new story, and a few days later was even more thrilled by an excited call from Yates, announcing that these pages were "the real thing" and had to be a novel. "The sword fell on my shoulder," said Henry.

Where his students' fiction was concerned, Yates was polite if he could help it, but also emotional, blunt, and uncompromising: Either a story (a scene, a line, a word) came alive or it didn't, and he was eager to explain *why* it didn't and how (if possible) to fix it. Intellectual exercises, ideas, abstractions, didacticism, pretension, or implausibility of any kind were fatal errors. Mark Dintenfass was startled when Yates called to discuss his first three stories, and dismissed two of them as "crap": Dintenfass was trying to write like Nabokov, Yates explained, and only Nabokov could do that; Dintenfass's *other* story, however, was about *real life*, the life he knew, and *that's* what he should be writing about. "It's the most important thing anyone ever told me as a writer," said Dintenfass, who turned away from "fruitless experimentation" and started a novel about Jewish life in Brooklyn. Yates encouraged him to send opening chapters to Monica McCall, who eventually sold the book.

Yates could get away with calling a piece of fiction "crap" (though he'd rarely say as much unless he had some kind of compliment in store) because his goodwill was never in doubt. Flattery was bullshit; what was good for the work? "Would it *really* happen that way?" he'd expostulate. "I don't think so." He wanted students to see the "Platonic form" of the work—its latent state of finished perfection—and this involved examining every nuance in terms of precision and truth. "Dick demonstrated the keenest eye I've ever seen for the flaw, great or small, in fiction," said Geoffrey Clark; "and for the small telling detail that transfigures or transfixes; and for cant, cheap tricks, and especially *unfelt* fiction." A student's ego never stood in the way of Yates's insistence that something could be improved, even if the story or novel in question had already been accepted for publication (or published). "They're rushing you," Yates told James Alan McPherson, whose first collection *Hue and Cry* was in press at the time. "Slow down." And he proceeded to tease through McPherson's paragraphs, pointing out all the little things that needed to be "fixed" prior to publication. "I hope this won't make you sore," he wrote DeWitt Henry, "but I'm not too crazy about your story"—a typical preamble to an epistolary critique, both in terms of candor and modest reluctance.

If a story was a total loss, was "crap" in short, Yates would summarize the reason(s) as briefly as possible and elaborate only if challenged. And he much preferred to say he *liked* a given story, then list his various quibbles at length—e.g., "I simply can't imagine a man polishing off a whole fifth of whisky in a single drive between Philadelphia and New York. Better make it a pint"; "You have her kick off her shoes, flop on the couch, throw back her head, eyes closed, and rub her throat (hardly the gestures of a frightened girl, or even a wary one)."

Yates was more diffident during the formal workshop sessions. At the New School he'd never felt comfortable criticizing students' work in front of their peers, and amid the ruthless crucifixions of Iowa the best he could do, at times, was serve as a gentle referee. "Hm, did you really have to say that?" he'd intercede, and try to silence the more rabid critics by pointing out the better qualities of a given story, while (in accordance with workshop protocol) its reeling author would have to weather the onslaught in red-faced silence. Occasionally Yates was so startled by the carnage he'd simply withdraw into chain-smoking bemusement. His student Bill Kittredge described a session in Yates's workshop as "the most savage thing [he'd] ever witnessed": "This guy from Spokane just got *shelled*. People were reading lines aloud from his story and everybody would laugh. Dick let it get out of hand. There were a lot of strong personalities in the class— Ivy Leaguers, New Yorkers. The guy from Spokane left town after that, and nobody ever saw him again."

More often than not, Yates was less tolerant of such excesses. Sometimes he'd check a student with a look of baleful disapproval, slowly shaking his head ("Bill, Bill, Bill"), or else he'd let others express views that decorum forbade to himself. *"You motherfuckers wouldn't know literature if it ran you down in a car!"* shouted his student Jane Delynn in defense of a story under attack. There was a silence. "As the lady in the rear suggested—" Yates sighed approvingly. Above all he became fed-up with the condescending sarcasm of certain students, perhaps most notably David Milch. As one student recalled, "Milch was a slasher in workshops. He was part of a new wave of Ivy League students at Iowa, and some of these students were contemptuous about Iowa's casual nonacademic milieu. Milch thought Yates was a joke—too nonprofessorial, stumbling, and shy. Too conversational." Robert Penn Warren had helped Milch get a teaching fellowship at Iowa, where he was touted as a writer of tremendous promise. At twenty-one he was brilliant, learned, and witty, and apt to make light of other students' writing. "Oh, for Christ's sake, Milch!" Yates would erupt. "Who's interested in your jokes? What do you think it feels like to be at the other end of a barb like that?" Not only did Yates object to Milch's wisecracks, but he wasn't much inclined to praise the young man's work either: Sometimes he'd begrudge Milch's (vaunted) facility for writing dialogue, but was often exhaustive in taking him to task for other lapses.

The enmity between the two doesn't call for a lot of subtle analysis. Milch was a catalogue of Yates's foremost bogeys: an unapologetically intellectual graduate of Yale who'd arrived at Iowa under the aegis of the world-famous author of *All the King's Men*, no less; a condescending young man who sneered at both students and Yates alike. Milch, for his part, deplores the arrogance of the young man he was, but points out that *all* the Workshop people, teachers as well as students, were "unfinished spirits" in one way or another: "Self-taught writers like Yates and Vonnegut who'd developed their talents outside the citadels of culture—the 'apostolic succession' of Harvard, say: William James teaching Gertrude Stein and so on—had this *rage* against the Tradition even as it attracted them. They had an adolescent relationship with the authority of culture." Certainly *Food Field Reporter* and Remington Rand were about as removed from the citadels as one could get; in any case Yates let himself go one night at Kenny's Bar. "*Who wouldn't want to be David Milch?*" he announced to an audience of Workshop people, on whose periphery was Milch. "He went to Yale! He graduated first in his class! Warren said he has an ear for dialogue that rivals Hemingway! And here he is *twenty-one years old.* . . ." It went on and on. The whole spiel, said Milch, "was a devastating encapsulization of everything pretentious and self-important." Many years later, though, Milch would be in a nice position to get his own back.

For the most part, Yates chose not to socialize with his fellow faculty members, except for Cassill. "*That* many writers were never meant to be together in the same place," he said of Bread Loaf, and so with Iowa. He never felt particularly at ease with rival authors unless they were the sort who wore their eminence lightly—"good guys" as Yates would have it. His colleague Vance Bourjaily was a good guy, modest and affable, though perhaps a bit too much of an outdoorsman for Yates's taste. The two were cordial but not close. Yates would make a point of attending the frequent parties at Bourjaily's farm (or any party to which he was asked), but if the guests were mostly faculty Yates would recede into a quiet corner where he could soak in peace.

He preferred the company of graduate students, the more down-to-earth the better. The first to accept his invitation to the Airliner was a burly Texan named Jim Crumley, and soon they were joined by others who, like Crumley, tended to be married ex-servicemen in their late twenties: Bob Lacy, Jim Whitehead, and Andre Dubus; Ted Weesner and Robin Metz also became part of the circle. After a few hours of noisy, drunken argument, one of the young men would call his wife to say they were coming over (while the others would call theirs to say they weren't), and the evening would continue until three or four in the morning.

Dubus belonged in another category—perhaps the closest thing to a soulmate Yates ever had (though both men would have cringed at the term). Dubus was a shy, plain-spoken ex-marine who became raucous and swaggering when he drank. As his third wife Peggy Rambach observed, "Andre wanted to be a tough guy. He was picked on a lot as a kid, and both he and Dick grew up in a time when men couldn't be sensitive." The two friends would sit drinking on Dubus's porch for hours—sometimes bellowing at each other amid skirls of laughter, sometimes hushed—and Dubus got to where he could mimic Yates so perfectly that others couldn't tell them apart. Along with their temperamental affinities, both had unqualified admiration for the other's work. Within three weeks of his arrival Yates decided that Dubus was by far the most talented student at Iowa: "Most of the clowns here will never be writers," he wrote Miller Williams, "and it's depressing to think of their getting degrees called 'Master of Fine Arts'—Good God!—but [Dubus] is one of the very few exceptions to the rule. I haven't read much of his work—he's Verlin Cassill's student here, not mine—but I read a story he published in the *Sewanee Review* a while back that really knocked me out. He's also a fine guy, which supports my rather shaky theory that good writers tend to be good men." Almost seven years later, when Yates left Iowa for good, he still considered Dubus the most talented student he'd ever encountered there, while in turn Dubus revered Yates as a master comparable to Chekhov.* As he wrote in a 1989 tribute, "Richard Yates is one of our great writers with too few readers, and no matter how many readers he finally ends up with, they will still be too few, unless there are hundreds of thousands in most nations of the world."

Dubus and the other married students were almost ideal companions for Yates: Most were hard-drinking men's men who loved to stay up late and talk about books, and they admired Yates both as a writer and a personality. When he wasn't shouting them down on some literary point or lost in the throes of another hilarious coughing fit, he'd teach them his vast repertoire of show tunes, ribald ditties, and patriotic anthems. He loved the clever rhymes of Cole Porter and Lorenz Hart (particularly the latter's "Mountain Greenery": "While you love your lover, let/Blue skies be your *coverlet* . . ."), which he'd linger over with leering relish as he sang verse after verse in their Quonset-hut duplexes. Along with his occasional cartoons, the nearest thing Yates ever had to a hobby was learning

---

*Dubus wrote in a 1970 letter to Yates: "Getting a letter from Richard Yates mentioning Anton Pavlovich Chekhov is somewhat like getting a letter from Jesus Christ mentioning the Holy Spirit."

old songs and working out routines for performing them, and his memory for lyrics was flawless. Sometimes he'd prefer obscurity for its own sake, whether a parody version (e.g., "Honey Suck My Nose" for "Honey-suckle Rose") or an old Wobbly* variation ("You'll Get Pie in the Sky When You Die [That's a Lie]")—but the climax of almost any night's recital was an old WWII hillbilly anthem called "There's a Star-Spangled Banner Flying Somewhere." The sentimental vet Yates would become when singing this song was an affecting sight, and fellow servicemen such as Bob Lacy couldn't resist joining him in joyous harmony. One verse in particular elevated them into a kind of ecstasy:

> *Though I realize I'm crippled that is true, sir,*
> *Please don't judge my courage by my twisted leg,*
> *Let me show my Uncle Sam what I can do, sir,*
> *Let me take the Axis down a peg.*

"God, how we loved that song!" Lacy remembered. "And, God, how Yates used to love to lead us in it! No doubt there were happier moments in his life. But those were the happiest I ever saw. We'd be gathered in someone's kitchen, our heads, including Yates's, all leaned in close together in a drunken bouquet, and the look on his face as he put us through our musical paces would be positively beatific. Occasionally a spouse or girlfriend might stick a head in the door to see what was going on, see what all the racket was. But after one look they'd shake their heads and go away."

Yates's high spirits were a necessary outlet, because he was miserable in almost every other department of his life. "Dick walked around with the weight of the world on his shoulders," said Kittredge. "On the one hand you had the poet Marvin Bell, who'd just written a poem that day and would write another tomorrow, whistling on the way to his eleven o'clock class. Then three o'clock would roll around and here comes Yates

---

*"Wobbly" stands for "Industrial Workers of the World," a labor movement founded on revolu-tionary principles in 1906.

shambling down the hallway, depressed as hell because he's got a six-hundred-page novel and doesn't know if it's any good." Somehow he needed to make his unwieldy manuscript cohere by Christmas, but teaching proved too much of a drain on his time and energy. "If that goddamned movie thing had panned out I wouldn't be fucking around here!" he'd grumble, faced with at least two hundred pages of student writing a week—with lectures and conferences and chaotic workshop sessions—all in exchange for a gross income of $666 a month, almost $400 of which went to alimony and child support.

Then in October, to make matters worse, he was hospitalized with pneumonia. The Iowa weather was ill suited for a consumptive chain-smoking alcoholic: Scores of pigs were slaughtered each year by hailstones, and it was all but suicidal to run out of gas on a country road in winter. But whatever the season, the creaky old wind-moaning mansion on South Capitol Street was meager shelter at best, and Yates was felled by the first bitter drafts. For two weeks he lay abed in the hospital, deathly ill, alone in a cold alien land, thinking he could scarcely afford to be there. He said as much to Wendy Sears, and sounded so weak and depressed she wanted to "hug [him] to pieces," while the stolid Sheila was moved to write a kindly note advising him to get well and stop worrying about money (for now). He was somewhat cheered by the concern of his students—one of whom, Jonathan Penner, recalled their hospital visit as an unexpected lesson in Yatesian style: "Steve Salinger sneaked in whiskey. Immediately, Dick poured a shot for his roommate, an elderly farmer. We studied that. That was style." But such admiration went only so far to alleviate loneliness, to say nothing of paying the bills. "I don't think I'm at all cut out for this teaching scene," the convalescent Yates wrote Monica McCall. "It becomes increasingly clear that screenwriting is the only way I can ever hope to achieve minimal solvency and still have the freedom to write fiction." McCall replied with maternal reassurance: She'd look into getting him that Hollywood job, and meanwhile a further advance on his novel was forthcoming.

Even before his health took a turn for the worse, Yates was an object of tender regard among female students and wives. "He really listened to women when they talked," said Pat Dubus, "and that was a new experience for us." Lyn Lacy agreed: "Dick saw more in me than I did myself at the time, and I adored him for it. He was sort of an uncle or brother figure—so friendly, open and *interested*." Such intense solicitude on Yates's part was touched with desperation: More than anything he missed the intimate company of women—a wife, a girlfriend, his daughters. And while the young women at Iowa, married or not, were used to predatory advances (particularly from distinguished authors), there was little of that from Yates: Soft-spoken and handsome, the picture of a gentleman in his coat and tie, he'd prolong the sweetness of their company with fervent curiosity, the only selfish aspect of which was a naked fear of being left alone. "Dick attracted women as a victim," said Robin Metz, "a kind of Keatsian figure who needed to be cared for." At least in that respect he'd come to the right place.

In the Workshop there was no particular stigma attached to the rather common phenomenon of love affairs between teachers and students; in principle they were all writers together, and "human moments" were to be expected. Cassill—who looked after Yates in a fraternal way, and was distressed by how sickly and morose he was becoming—urged their friend and mutual student Loree Wilson to help care for him. A single mother who got by on a graduate assistantship, Wilson was strong, voluptuous, and warm hearted, and she adored Yates. "Dick appealed to one's deepest sympathies," she said. "He was so clearly unwell, and seemed to be reaching out with those big, soulful eyes, but he could be insatiably needy. He was the loneliest man I ever knew." As Wilson soon discovered, Yates required at least as much care as that soulful aspect of his seemed to suggest. Mornings she'd find him sitting alone in a booth at the Airliner, forlornly eating a hard-boiled egg with his beer as he listened to Barbra Streisand on the jukebox. Other times he'd call from his apartment—"I'm sick, I'm cold, I'm sitting here in a sweater"—and, if possible, Wilson would drop everything and go make him warm. One day Cassill called and told her something was wrong with Yates, that he'd "lost it" and needed to be calmed down. She rushed over, but by the time she arrived Yates had already taken his "emergency kit" of pills prescribed by Kline. "You're a good kid," he murmured as he fell asleep.

Perhaps the best part of the arrangement were Wilson's children, a boy and girl aged seven and eight. It was widely known how much Yates suffered from the absence of his daughters: He blamed himself for being a bad father, and fretted incessantly over whether he'd be able to provide for them. A necessary solace for Yates was lavishing affection on whatever children were available, whether Wilson's or the Dubuses' or the Lacys'. He'd give them his undivided attention and refuse to discuss adult matters in their presence. He was particularly attached to Wilson's daughter, who sometimes joined her mother in bringing soup and other comforts to Yates's dismal apartment. Both children were disturbed by his gaunt appearance, his wheezing, and for Christmas they gave him a muffler to keep him warm. Yates had nothing to give them in return, and later became so enraged at himself that he began weeping and beating his fist on the car.

Sam Lawrence's career had taken some curious turns of late. The previous April, as Yates prepared to leave Washington, Lawrence had come to town and gloomily announced that he'd parted company with Atlantic Monthly Press. As Yates remembered the episode a few years later, "He talked of prospects for·a big job at Knopf and asked me, shyly, if I'd stick with him. . . . Not only did I promise, but we firmly and maybe even mawkishly shook hands on it." As good as his word, Yates severed his connection with Atlantic as soon as Lawrence was established at Knopf—a somewhat sturdier firm, after all. But Lawrence had gotten used to being in charge of things ("I'm a publisher, not an editor"), and a few months later he took a leap of faith and hoped Yates would follow again: "I resigned from Knopf early this week to embark on my own and establish an independent imprint here in Boston. I want you to be on the First List which will appear in the Autumn of 65. There will be 5 or 6 books and you will be in good company: Brian [Moore], Anatole, Katherine Anne Porter, Alastair Reid."

This, Yates thought, was getting a bit thick. Certainly it was the wrong time for him to be taking any kind of financial gamble: He was already in debt for a novel he couldn't finish, his teaching income was a joke, and there were no other prospects in sight. He and Sheila had also decided to take Sharon out of that "dumb, blue-collar" high school in Mahopac and send her to a proper boarding school ("I don't want Bigger to be finger-fucked by the motorcycle crowd," he told the Schulmans); just the week before, in fact, both mother and daughter had visited—and set their hearts on—a Quaker school called Oakwood, where the annual tuition was a whopping $2,435. Sheila thought she could arrange a partial scholarship ($800), but either way the expense was grim for a man who could barely pay his bar tab. And though they'd made a gentleman's agreement, Lawrence's recent employment record hardly inspired confidence. Monica McCall was adamant: "Sam's attitude is rather deplorable, certainly arrogant. Not for one moment could I advise you to commit yourself to any editor, I don't care who it might be, only just starting out on their own. . . . I told [Lawrence] that your illness had set you back desperately in regard to your work . . . and that probably he wouldn't get any answer to his letter. So that lets you off *that* hook!"

Yates's poor health, poverty, and general malaise made for a strained Christmas. In New York he stayed with the Schulmans, who were shocked by his deterioration over the past three months. That first evening, as he dined with Grace at the Blue Mill (Jerry was out of town), he told her he was badly in need of medication and had an emergency appointment with Kline in the morning. But any further mention of his mental state became redundant when they returned to the Schulmans' apartment, where Yates began shouting and kicking furniture. For the first time Grace felt a little afraid of him; they were alone together, and he seemed capable of anything. More than fear, though, she felt a kind of weary exasperation: "Insanity is no excuse for bad behavior," she told him, then turned around and went to bed. Yates was demonstratively calm the next day, though further outbursts followed and it was a long visit all around.

"I know apologies are a bore," he wrote afterward, "but I *am* sorry as hell about those several loud-mouth evenings, and am filled with admiration for your patience in putting up with me." The Schulmans replied graciously as ever ("people don't stop caring for one another because of some silly thing like that"), though they were slowly but surely coming to the end of their tether. After a ruckus Yates was sometimes sorry, but seemed incapable of conceding actual insanity and often blamed others for his behavior. If the Schulmans asked him to leave when he lost control, or offered to take him to the hospital, he'd only wax more belligerent—and later, in moments of seeming lucidity, he'd *still* look back on the incident with a sense of injustice ("Why'd you ask me to leave? Obviously there was nothing wrong with me!"). Though he often complained about his awful childhood—indeed more so all the time*—any suggestion that he augment drug treatment with some form of psychotherapy was met with table-pounding scorn: "Why go to a two-man to tell me what a ten-man has discovered?" By "two-man" he meant an ordinary shrink, and by "ten-man" he meant Freud—or rather (since he didn't like Freud) some personage of ideal wisdom and tact, which pretty much ended the discussion.

Back in Iowa Yates was "lonesome as hell." If nothing else, New York had been a blessed respite from his novel, during which he'd almost managed to convince himself it wasn't as bad as he thought; on his return he resolved to undertake "a crash program to get the bleeding book finished by March One." But within days he was gloomier than ever—the novel simply wasn't working, and he didn't know what to do about it. Also Iowa was cold, he felt sick all the time, and other people weren't much of a comfort; as for his job, it was a daily torment. "[T]he 'teaching' routine grows increasingly dreary," he wrote the Schulmans. "It's easy work, but so basically lacking in substance—and even fraudulent—that I'm damned if I can understand how full-grown men can find it rewarding in its own right, year after year. I've now firmly decided not to come back here next fall, even if they ask me real pretty. . . . I'd rather rot in Hollywood than go on performing the ponderous bullshit-artist role I'm expected to play in this place."

But the privilege of rotting in Hollywood remained purely speculative, and his only immediate chance for escaping the Middle West lay in finishing his novel. So far the only part he'd dared show around was that unimpeachable prologue; meanwhile he'd "tinkered and brooded and fussed" so much with the rest he could scarcely see it anymore—though he sensed

---

* "Maybe this is silly," Wendy Sears had written him the previous summer, "but I think it's about time you stopped dwelling on your past—unfortunate though it may be."

something was terribly, organically wrong—and in February he finally accepted the fact that he'd have to get an outside opinion before he went any further. His friend Cassill was the inevitable choice: The author of *Writing Fiction* and one of the leading practitioner-teachers of same, Cassill was an astute if somewhat captious critic, who for months had bullied Yates to quit "digging himself into a trap" and move on. Yates could count on the man's probity, but that was rather the problem—if Cassill said the book was bad, the book was bad. And Yates had once told him it might turn out to be better than *Revolutionary Road*!

"Verlin Cassill's verdict on my book could not have been more negative," he informed the Schulmans. "He talked for a long time, some of it incomprehensible but most of it all too painfully clear—he said at one particularly unkind point that it 'reads like a book written by a man on tranquilizers' (Jesus!)—and I was pretty shattered for a few desperate and boozy days." Cassill himself doesn't remember it that way, and particularly disowns the "tranquilizer" remark. What he recalls telling Yates, in effect, was that the book probably *wasn't* as good as *Revolutionary Road,* but it did have a "Hardyesque compassion" to it and a number of fine incidental things. But at that stage of composition the story of Prentice's mother wasn't developed much beyond the prologue, which after all was the strongest section of the book. Hence Cassill suggested that he either balance the war sections with more stuff about Alice Prentice, or just finish the damn book as it was and write an entirely *different* one about his "crazy sainted mother." Yates would eventually take most of this advice to heart, but for a while his almost total despair was akin to "a kind of peace": "I can remember the same kind of thing happening fifteen years ago, when the first X-ray showed that I really did have TB, and could therefore stop worrying."

After an all-night celebration of his thirty-ninth birthday, Yates became increasingly withdrawn from the communal world of the Workshop. Partly this was a matter of depression and ill health, but a number of other factors conspired to make the whole atmosphere distasteful to Yates. For one thing Cassill was engaged in an ugly feud with the head of the English department, John Gerber, who wanted to absorb the Workshop into the regular academic program. Cassill thought that writers (à la Hemingway's "wolves" who ought to stick together) should be immune from the bureaucratic, bourgeois rigmarole of conventional academia, and that the MFA should be regarded as a legitimate terminal degree.* Yates agreed with his friend, more or less, but lacked the man's crusading fervor. "I think my loyalty has been called into question at least once," he wrote in a later tribute to Cassill, "but then, calling people's loyalty into question is as much a part of Verlin as his endless conspiracy theories, or his wrong-headed rages, . . . or his ominous way of saying 'Ah.'" Reluctantly Yates attended a dramatic meeting at Cassill's house, where the charismatic host conducted himself like the leader of some revolutionary fringe group. "What will *you* do?" he hectored each person in turn. "And *you*?" He thought they should all resign from the Workshop if their demands weren't met, and insisted on an overt pledge of loyalty from everyone in the room. Yates looked miserable: "Oh Christ, Verlin, do we have to go through all this? Can't we just talk it out?" Cassill shushed him as if he were a callow little brother: "Dick, you just don't understand." At one point Yates looked ill and left the room ("It just seems so *concocted*—"), and when he finally returned Cassill was pacing and shouting as before. "Is this shit *still* going on?" Yates sighed. "C'mon, let's all go have a drink."

But a tiresome, divisive political situation wasn't the main reason for his low profile. That spring, as his health and spirits continued to flag, his friend Andre Dubus offered Yates the greatest conceivable form of succor— his wife Pat. At the time he thought it the least he could do where both parties were concerned: Dubus ("a cherry when I got married," as he put it) had spent the first years of his manhood raising a family, and now amid the swinging milieu of the Workshop he openly made up for lost time with various students and wives; it seemed only fair, then, that Pat be allowed to follow her heart and comfort a talented man who needed all the comfort he could get, and who happened to be one of her husband's dearest friends.

A nice gesture, perhaps, but hardly one that enhanced the friendship. As Dubus later wrote Yates, "I wasn't so Goddam happy because, as you

---

*After Cassill resigned from Iowa the following year, he founded the Associated Writing Programs as a rival to the more academically oriented Modern Language Association.

know, Pat loved you then and still does, and I reckon I got jealous, not about the boudoir, but the heart." The tension between them became so sticky that Yates almost gave up going to parties altogether, particularly since a lot of them took place at Dubus's house down the street from a certain sign on South Capitol that said "Save Two Cents." Yates felt terrible about the whole thing—he was "a moralist at heart" as Milch pointed out—but not so terrible that he was willing to go without female company. It was certainly a trade-off, though; Yates sometimes had to be seen in public, after all, and Iowa City suddenly seemed a very small place. One day, after Pat had spent the night with Yates, the two men bumped into each other on the street. Dubus's first novel had just been rejected by Viking, and Yates tried to console his friend over Bloody Marys at the Airliner. "[But] all the time you were feeling bad," Dubus wrote, "and I knew you were, so I was uncomfortable, and I kept thinking what an ass I was, how I was ruining all those fine moments in all of our lives." They would not reconcile while at Iowa. Dubus knew that Yates had no intention of returning in the fall, and decided to bide his time until the affair necessarily ended in May. But the last months were sad for both men: They adored each other, and the constrained civility between them was perhaps more painful than outright hostility. For Yates, the year was shaping up as an all but total loss.

Meanwhile another, far older friendship was in danger. In late March Sam Lawrence had finally made a deal with Dell-Delacorte to finance and distribute books under his own imprint; he assured Yates that he was prepared to offer a larger advance and better terms than he was presently getting at Knopf. The month before, however, Yates's project had been passed on to a brilliant young editor, Robert Gottlieb, who lost no time getting off to a good start with his new author: "I've wanted to publish you ever since reading *Revolutionary Road,*" Gottlieb wrote, "which I loved." As for Monica McCall's advice, it was predictably anti-Lawrence: "Was Sam ever useful to you as editor?" she knowingly inquired.. "I have had no particular experience with him in that respect, though I have had with Bob Gottlieb and do know that he is magnificent." Having insinuated the point that Gottlieb was precisely the kind of hands-on man that Yates might require this time around, McCall addressed the main issue:

"Sam's present position could result in one of two things: either further monies from [Knopf] or more money from Sam now that he has Dell-Delacorte behind him." For the moment, though, McCall urged Yates to stay put.

But at this point the real question was whether he had any book to sell. After Cassill's withering (or perhaps only ambivalent) critique, Yates had despairingly informed his agent that the novel wouldn't be ready that spring after all—despite the fact that he'd already promised as much to Gottlieb, despite the fact that Rust Hills had already bought the prologue as an "advance excerpt" for the *Saturday Evening Post*. McCall replied that he "mustn't worry": They'd simply show the manuscript "unofficially" to Gottlieb as a first draft, and the prologue would run in the magazine without any reference to the novel. Official or not, though, Yates dreaded the prospect of presenting inferior work to an admiring new editor, and spent feverish weeks "making notes and drawing spooky diagrams and trying to figure out some way to break [the book] open and take it apart and put it back together a different way." He even consulted a somewhat more accomplished work, which now seemed to have been written a long, long time ago: "[M]aybe it's a kind of literary masturbation," he wrote, "but I'm rereading *Revolutionary Road*, studying the way *it's* put together as if it were written by somebody else, in the hope that it will give me some clues."

But the mystery remained unsolved, and Yates's latest *annus horribilis*—the academic year 1964–65—came to a kind of logical end in early April, when he went to New York and was told by both Gottlieb and McCall that his novel was unpublishable. "I'm afraid we really are in trouble this time, dear," says Grove's agent "Erica Briggs" in *Uncertain Times*. "It doesn't work as a book. It's not a war novel because there's not enough war in it, and it isn't a coming-of-age novel because the boy doesn't really come of age." All was not lost, however: Briggs-McCall suggested (not unfamiliarly) that Grove-Yates expand the narrative to tell more of the mother's story:

"She's one of the world's lost people, isn't she? And you always do that kind of thing so well."

"Jesus, I don't know [Grove replied]. That would be opening a whole new can of worms."

"I suppose it would, yes. But I know you can work it out. . . . The point is I can't handle the manuscript as it stands. I don't want to represent you with this."

"So there went the ball game," Yates wrote friends. If Cassill's verdict had been the moral equivalent of TB, this was advanced cancer. It was awful on so many levels that it might have inspired a kind of vertigo. The very idea of "expanding" the novel to write in detail about his mother (and hence the ghastly childhood of a character "clearly and nakedly" himself) was "a whole new can of worms," to put it mildly, and never mind that Dookie wasn't even dead yet—indeed, still enjoyed the odd moment of fleeting lucidity. Moreover he was sick to death of "that crummy novel" one way or the other, his credibility as a promising writer was waning fast, and he didn't know what to do next or even if there were any more books in him. And finally he was broke and had no definite source of income that summer, and if it came down to living in Iowa another year he'd pretty much rather die.

"If calling me when you get into your worse moments of panic helps you at all," McCall wrote him in early May, "then I want you to know that I don't really mind, except that you create a sense of frustration and failure and pressure, pressure which you know realistically is not necessary! . . . I know these are *hideous* days for you, but urge you to try not to panic." She was pursuing every possible lead in Hollywood: The producer Albert Ruddy presently held the option on *Revolutionary Road,* and might be persuaded to hire its author to write a screenplay; Ross Hunter or Elliott Kastner might have work, or a man named Richard Lewis who produced TV dramas, or even Johnny Johnson at Walt Disney (though McCall had to admit she could hardly picture Yates as a Disney writer— "however if you can write speeches and articles for Remington Rand . . ."); and finally Yates's old Hollywood agent Malcolm Stuart handled a young B-movie director named Roger Corman, who'd just signed a big contract with Columbia and was shopping around for a screenwriter. McCall doubted, however, that anyone would hire Yates sight unseen;

he'd simply have to go west and hope for the best. "Train yourself to go into appointments where for the moment it is talk and not necessarily a firm offer of a job," she advised, "[and] get in the mood where you don't care if there is a job or not." Sensing, perhaps, that this was a tall order for such a desperate man, she added two lines from "Chaucer's translation of the Boethius Cancellations [*sic*] of Philosophy. . . . 'Ne hope for nothing/ Ne drede not.'" Yates was well on his way to mastering the first part of that formula.

At the end of May he stopped in New York to see his daughters, but the eight-year-old Monica was upset over the brevity of his visit, and acted moody and unresponsive. More depressed than ever, Yates confided his fears about Hollywood to Nathan S. Kline, who made a referral Yates scribbled on his bill: "Dr. Robert T. Rubin, Neuropsych Inst UCLA."

Yates's luck took a temporary turn for the better. Roger Corman hired him in mid-June for "ridiculous amounts of money," and Yates splurged on a "sleek" Hollywood apartment at 1215 North Harper in hope of attracting visits from his daughters. Frugal as ever, though (where his own needs were concerned), he made up for this extravagance in other ways: His tendency never to change the oil had reduced his previous car to a smoldering husk, and now he replaced it with the cheapest thing he could find—a yellow Volkswagen (used), which he regarded as "Hitler's car" and cursed himself for buying.

It was a relief to be solvent again, though money went only so far to ease the pain of being back in Hollywood. Phoniness and impermanence were writ large in the very landscape of the place—the ornate plaster façades of drugstores and gas stations and office buildings, the "grubby white edifice of the Hollywood Palladium," the ubiquitous Orange Julius stands—all around the corner from Yates's apartment. As for the movies themselves, as for The Industry: "Don't get me started," he'd say, but by then he was already started. "The goddamn movies" had a malignant effect on society; they were made by greedy, dishonest, untalented, manipulative bastards, and created a wholly false version of reality that made people think love or success or whatever was right around the corner, when in truth (as they were soon reminded) it wasn't. "I used to *like* the movies," he'd sigh, shaking his head. It was a lousy way to make a living.

But he never lost sight of why he did it. "Guess what, hey," he wrote Wendy Sears two weeks after his arrival. "Remember how down-in-the-mouth I was because Monica Jane and I didn't hit it off very well that weekend? Well, by God, today I received my Father's Day package . . . and among other goodies there was the following: an illustrated poem by Monica Jane which damn near made me burst into tears, and which I can't refrain from quoting in full to you." His daughter's poem was titled "Father's Day" and included the lines, "I love you when your near./Little as your here,/I'll still love you always." "How's *that* for a heart-breaker?" Yates continued. "It's the 'Little as your here' line that really tore me up. . . . It's also a little disturbing, because anybody who can write that well at the age of eight is almost certain to have a complicated and diffi-cult life." Perhaps he also sensed that any daughter of his was bound to have a difficult life no matter what, though it cheered him to be a good provider again—indeed, that fact alone made the situation bearable: "[W]hatever kind of place Hollywood may be," he wrote the Schulmans, "it certainly beats the hell out of Iowa City."

He was also fortunate in his employer, whom Yates forever exempted from his general indictment of the industry: "[Corman] turns out to be a very nice and smart and gentlemanly fellow," he wrote, "nothing at all like Frankenheimer, and he seems to like what I've done so far." Still in his thir-ties at the time, Corman had already made some seventy movies and man-aged to turn a profit on almost every one; unlike Frankenheimer, he didn't consider himself an Artist in his own right, though he took a pardonable pride in his proficiency for cutting corners, and the quality of his product set an almost legendary standard for watchable schlock. His approach to collaboration was also highly agreeable to Yates: After the basic idea was worked out, he'd modestly insist on a few fundamentals (story structure, the visual nature of the medium), and leave nuances of character and dia-logue to the writer—in this case a writer whose work he deeply respected.

In fact Corman hadn't hired the author of *Revolutionary Road* for just another B-movie. Rather, the director's first vehicle for Columbia was meant to be something of a breakthrough in his career—a big-budget feature about the Battle of Iwo Jima called *The Inevitable Island*, to which Corman wanted to take an innovative approach if at all possible. "I poke around trying to find some wrinkle in the Iwo Jima story that hasn't already been crushed flat by John Wayne," Yates wrote the Parkers, and after a couple of weeks he came up with a treatment that satisfied Corman as well as himself—that is, the battle as seen from *both* sides, Japanese and American, with all that implied of sympathetic ambiguity, a very Yatesian refusal to reduce any character to a demonized stereotype.

Except, perhaps, certain Hollywood characters. As long as Yates was out on the Coast, he thought it wise to take a meeting with Al Ruddy (the future producer of *The Godfather*), who professed a grim determination to make a faithful adaptation of *Revolutionary Road* despite the obvious obstacles of the industry. As Yates told this "funny Hollywood story" to the Schulmans,

[Ruddy] turned out, predictably enough, to be a very agreeable, friendly bull-shit artist, the kind of young man who has read somewhere that 'vitality' and 'magnetism' and 'integrity' are considered attractive traits. For the first five minutes he's elaborately, embarrassingly respectful, creating this atmosphere of Hushed Reverence, see, because he Admires my Work so much (so very, very much) and because he's always, always wanted to meet me. Get the picture? Okay. Then pretty soon he turns into this brusque, ballsy, rough-diamond kind of guy: hell, maybe he's crude and maybe he's coarse, in his own lovable way, but no son of a bitch in This Town, in This Industry, can ever say he's copped-out on a property yet. For instance, let's take a property like Revolutionary Road. Let's take the ending. Is that a problem? Why hell, let's face it, of course it's a problem. Nine guys out of ten in This Town would cop-out on a problem like that—but wait. Listen. Do I know what *he's* gonna do?

Then he moves into his third phase: he becomes Creative. Suddenly he's pacing the floor with wild eyes, waving his hands around to show me different camera angles—he's gonna cut into this flashback here, lay-in this dialogue there, match-dissolve to this track-shot, then dolly-back and pan and zoom into this close-up. . . . His plan is to make the ending of the picture so artsy-craftsy, so impossibly full of tricky camera work, that the audience is left hanging in doubt as to whether April Wheeler is dead or alive. And the punch line of the whole story is what he said when I asked him if he didn't think that might be a little confusing, or a little ambiguous. He said, and this is an exact quote:

"Well, but don'tcha see? I'm trying to eat my cake and have it *too*!"

In the end, of course, it came to light that he has absolutely no plans for producing the picture in the near or even foreseeable future . . . and that the whole afternoon was really just an opportunity for him to try out his personality on me.

. . .

Though he halfheartedly resumed his affair with the aging Catherine Downing, Yates was almost entirely alone those first months in Los Angeles. Roger Corman saw little of him, and what little he saw was reassuring; rather like Frankenheimer he dimly remembers Yates as a "friendly but reserved" man who drank a little more than normal, maybe, but otherwise gave no sign of being troubled. After Corman okayed the initial Iwo Jima treatment at the beginning of July, there wasn't much need to speak until the screenplay (which would take a certain amount of research) was finished three months later. Unknown to Corman, Yates spent roughly half that time hospitalized at the UCLA Neuropsychiatric Institute.

Apart from Dr. Robert T. Rubin,* the only known witnesses to Yates's breakdown, Catherine Downing and Bill Reardon, are both dead. Yates's address during much of his hospitalization was "c/o Catherine Downing, General Artists Corp.," and ten years later she wrote a brief note to Yates after reading *Disturbing the Peace*: "There's really not much that I am able to say. . . . It's just that I have always known you would eventually write the book and that reading it. . . . would be a painful experience for

---

*Rubin declined to be interviewed, though he did admit that he remembered Yates *qua* patient very well indeed. The psychiatrist, a young man in 1965, is almost assuredly the model for Dr. Burton L. Rose in *Disturbing the Peace*—"a small, slight, pale man who couldn't have been over thirty, . . . His office, deep in the labyrinthine complex of the [UCLA] Medical Center, was barely big enough to contain a desk, two chairs, and a psychiatric couch. . . . How could anyone 'talk' to this solemn, staring boy in this claustrophobic room?"

me. I want to give you the well-deserved words of congratulations and praise, but I can't just now. Today is a fragile day for me." Monica Yates attests that John Wilder's third, most devastating breakdown in the novel was "as true as [her father] could write about how [his breakdown in Los Angeles] went," and what slender evidence exists would seem to confirm as much. Such a meltdown may explain Downing's lingering trauma ten years later, as well as the fact that she and Yates mostly avoided contact after the summer of 1965.

Yates's relief over the "ridiculous amounts of money" he was making didn't last long, and the main theme of his letters throughout July was loneliness. When he wasn't working on the Iwo Jima script—which hardly engaged him the way *Lie Down in Darkness* had—there were long nights of despondent brooding over his distant daughters, the writer he used to be, everything. He made a number of drunken phone calls to his Iowa friend Jim Crumley, who was going through a divorce at the time. Mostly they talked about broken homes, but once Yates mentioned that he'd just spent a night in jail for drunk driving; he'd gotten lost in one of the hilly sections of Los Angeles, he said, and the contemptuous attitude of the arresting officers had enraged him.

As with other breakdowns, Yates's drinking became more compulsive as he tried to medicate his rising mania, and like John Wilder he probably stopped sleeping (hence the late-night drives). In the novel Wilder complains to Dr. Rose at UCLA that he needs his prescriptions refilled, but the young man won't oblige him without a records-release form from "Myron T. Brink" (the Nathan S. Kline character) in New York; meanwhile the best he can do is advise Wilder to stop drinking immediately. What happens next was perhaps the sort of thing Rose's real-life counterpart, Robert Rubin, remembers so vividly about Richard Yates:

> For the fourth night in a row—or was it the fifth?—[Wilder] hardly slept at all. No amount of whiskey could make him drowsy as he sat or sprawled on the sofa and tried to think things out, and he watched the morning break through the closed blinds. . . .
>
> "Mr. Wilder [said Dr. Rose], these phone calls are becoming a little bizarre."

"Whaddya mean? This is the first time I've—"

"You called me four times yesterday, three times at the office, and once at home, and you called twice the day before. I've heard a great deal about 'emergency kits' and 'shots' and all sorts of disconnected talk, and I've given you the same advice each time: 'stop the alcohol.' "

Yates was perhaps desperate enough to take such advice to heart, but by then it was too late. In an earlier fragment of *Disturbing the Peace,* the protagonist (a tall man named "William Jeffries" in this version) tells a doctor that he realized he'd been drinking too much prior to his break-down and poured a whole bottle of Jim Beam down the sink; as for Wilder, he smashes his bottles against the wall of his apartment. But like both characters Yates nonetheless ended up wandering Sunset Boulevard (so he told his second wife) dropping large bills out of his wallet while a mob gathered in his wake—an interesting gesture, given Yates's loathing for the way he'd made such "ridiculous amounts of money." In any event, he seems to have acted on *some* sort of expiatory impulse: When he was arrested for disturbing the peace, Yates apparently told police that he was Lee Harvey Oswald; he also thought (once again) that he was Jesus Christ.

What happened next was a blur to Yates and hence to posterity. On the aforesaid novel fragment he scribbled a note to himself: "West Hollywood Sheriff's Office. Los County Gen Hospital Psych Unit. Zonal Ave." Thus a doctor tries to reconstruct for "William Jeffries" (while the latter enjoys a brief spell of Thorazine-induced lucidity) what happened over the past week—namely, that Jeffries was taken from the police station to the County Psychiatric Unit for three days, then removed to Hollywood Pres-byterian Hospital (where John Wilder also finds himself at a similar junc-ture). It's likely that Yates checked himself out of the hospital prematurely—as he was wont to do, especially in later years—and went on a rampage of sorts. At some point he made the usual raving phone calls to Sheila, convinced that he'd hurt or possibly killed their children; again and again she assured him they were *fine,* they were right here, but it was no use; sometimes, too, he sang nursery rhymes. Either Sheila or Yates or Catherine Downing got in touch with Bill Reardon, who caught a flight to

Los Angeles and helped his friend commit himself to UCLA. As Reardon pushed the necessary documents under his nose, Yates thought he was certifying his identity as the new Messiah, or else signing confessions of one sort or another. ("In the bughouse I thought I was Jesus," he told a girlfriend. "How does that grab ya?")

All this was during the first week in August. By August 10 his daughter Monica had written a get-well card, though she was misinformed about his illness. After the latest disturbing phone calls, Sheila bluntly announced to Sharon that her father had suffered a nervous breakdown, and added that Monica should know *nothing* except that he was in the hospital. From now on, Sheila insisted, either she or Sharon would answer the phone—never Monica, unless it was one of their father's regular Sunday-morning calls. She then wrote Yates a comforting note: "We have had a wonderful, relaxed summer, and the only cloud on our horizon has been your illness. . . . All your worries are just terrible dreams you are having. . . . If there were anything more serious than a cold wrong with either of the children, I would let you know immediately."

In the meantime word of Yates's predicament had spread, at least on the other coast. "I am awful sorry to learn of your dark passage," McCall wrote on August 23, "but *very* happy to learn you are at the psychiatric department of UCLA." As soon as he was sufficiently sane to do so, Yates had written or phoned such people as McCall, his children, Wendy Sears (who'd written on August 18, "Are you still alive? Where are you? Why aren't you writing or calling?"), and the Schulmans; his friend Reardon had notified everyone else. "I had a full report from Bill Reardon," wrote his old girlfriend Natalie Bowen, who congratulated Yates for doing "the right thing" by committing himself. "The only thing that worries me is that you're so leery of psychiatrists. I hope you'll let one of them get at you this time, no matter how painful it is at first. It'll be much better for you than all the pills in the world." Yates may or may not have appreciated such well-meaning advice, but he was clearly alarmed by the extent of the gossip. He obliquely queried people in the publishing world, and the response was less than reassuring. Marc Jaffe at Bantam wrote that he hadn't heard "much" gossip, and promised not to "spread any unfortunate word around Madison Avenue and/or East

Hampton"; but Rust Hills had heard plenty, and hectored Yates to write more and drink less: "The fact of talent is really given to very few; Faulkner, Fitzgerald, and Wolfe—they all drank like fish and seemed to us to have acted in self-destructive ways. It's very romantic—but they all did their work. . . . [Your friends] don't gossip about you, but they sure worry about you."

As the whole thing began to sink in, Yates seems to have accepted such lectures as his due. Time would tell how much this latest fiasco had cost him, financially and otherwise, but for now he was determined to limit the damage as much as possible. In the hospital he worked steadily on his screenplay, impressing staff and patients alike with his industry. Also he met regularly with Dr. Rubin, whom he described to the Schulmans as "voyeuristic"; to what extent he let the young man "get at" him is a mystery, though there's no question Yates was at least somewhat persuaded that alcohol was a big part of the problem. By the time he was released on October 2, he was taking Antabuse and attending AA meetings; also his screenplay was finished and by his own account he looked five years younger. Unfortunately a few specters lingered from "the great travail": A shady character named Dr. Salem insisted that Yates was still under his care, and was calling around to inquire into his patient's whereabouts ("he is *not* my doctor," Yates warned McCall, "and not to be trusted"); also Yates discovered that he was persona decidedly non grata at his former apartment, and in a rush he was forced to take rather seedy lodgings on Clark Street—"the kind of place you commit suicide in," as he put it.

While in the hospital Yates was somewhat heartened by the reception of his novel's prologue, published as "A Good and Gallant Woman" in the September 11 issue of the *Saturday Evening Post*. "People found it very warm and moving," Rust Hills wrote, "and so well made that they are astounded when I tell them it is a novel sequence." A second excerpt titled "To Be a Hero" ran two weeks later, and was also successful despite Yates's being too deranged to approve galleys in time for a rushed production schedule. "I made it as good as I possibly could," Hills reported a bit defensively. "It was certainly your job to do, not mine." Some of Yates's friends remarked on the abrupt ending of the second excerpt, but both stories were listed in the 1966 "Best" volume, and "A Good and Gallant Woman" won an O. Henry Award.

Meanwhile Corman was delighted with the screenplay: The only immediate change he made was to scotch the fancy title and go with the more saleable *Iwo Jima*. Yates was emboldened to send a few copies of the script to friends, though he tried to downplay it as so much craftsmanly hackwork: "There are several good things in it," he wrote Cassill, "but basically it'll be just another combat flick, the kind you forget five minutes after finishing your popcorn." One of the copies floating around Iowa fell into the hands of Andre Dubus, which prompted an icebreaking postcard: It was a "fine well-focused script," Dubus wrote, though he couldn't help but point out that "Marines call 'em NCO's, not non-coms."

The movie was never produced. "Dick wrote a very good script," Corman recalled, "but it was turned down by Columbia—some misunderstanding, or double-dealing, or misinformation. Turned out they wanted me to go on doing medium-budget films." Not only did studio executives want a less elaborate, more commercial picture, but they were also unimpressed by the whole Japanese-are-people-too angle, and thought the two lead characters on either side of the battle should meet at the end (a convention that Yates and Corman had expressly nixed). Hence the project was killed; Corman was assigned to shoot the kind of slapdash Western he did so well, and a few weeks later the studio fired him after he gave a disgruntled interview to the *Los Angeles Times*. Yates had since moved on: Days after his release from UCLA, he was hired by producer David Wolper to do a rewrite of another World War II movie, *The Bridge at Remagen*.

Yates was busy enough but lonelier than ever. He no longer had a female companion, his apartment depressed him, and he was sober. That summer he'd sustained himself (or not) by looking forward to his daughters' visits—they'd definitely planned to come for Christmas, and he hoped to coax Sheila into letting them have at least one other visit in between. But recent developments had changed all that: "This is your third breakdown," Sheila wrote, "and you are, as you yourself are now recognizing, an alcoholic. . . . I can understand your wanting to mend your fences as fast as you can, but it would be better for [the girls] if you let the past lie and concentrate on getting well. You have been a good father, and they love you."

Worried that Yates's sobriety was unlikely to last under the circumstances, both Wendy Sears and Sam Lawrence made a point of informing him that his old friend Brian Moore was also now in Hollywood, writing a screenplay for Alfred Hitchcock (*Torn Curtain*). Yates, however, seemed in no hurry to get back in touch—his respect for Moore as a writer was unwavering, but he'd come to regard the man as "kind of fat and grumpy and sour": "He's a very, very touchy guy," Yates wrote a friend. "He absolutely hates to have anyone praise *Judith Hearne,* however elaborately, with even the faintest implication that it's his best book (which of course it is)." Meanwhile the vast sums Moore was making as Hitchcock's screenwriter might have served as a further disincentive for resuming the friendship. But finally Yates got lonely enough to leave a message at Universal, and Moore replied with a note inviting him to his house in Malibu.

Yates reported afterward that he'd "never seen such a change in a man": Moore—married to a "stunning new wife" (that is, his old friend Frank Russell's ex)—was "trim, expansive and happy as hell." On the other hand, now that Moore was something of a Hollywood bigshot, Yates also found him rather "abrupt and impatient" at times, and noticed that he seemed to prefer the company of other bigshots. The most agreeable exceptions were their mutual friends Joan Didion and her husband John Gregory Dunne—or rather, as the latter liked to say (or as Yates liked to tell it): "I'm John Gregory Dunne, the writer"—pause—"and this is my wife, Joan." "What a colossal ego!" Yates would hoot. "Joan is the *real* writer in that family." A year later Didion used Yates as a reference for the Guggenheim she needed to complete her second novel, *Play It As It Lays,* which Yates considered something of a masterpiece ("you are one of the very few people I hoped would [like it]," Didion wrote).

In mid-December Yates flew back to New York for five days—time enough to deliver presents to his daughters and see a few friends—but on Christmas Eve he was alone again in Hollywood: a ticklish business for a recovering alcoholic outpatient living in a stark apartment off the Sunset Strip. At 6:45 that evening he called the switchboard at the Hollywood

Studio Club (a sort of YWCA for would-be starlets) and asked for Frances Doel, who was out; Yates left a message but no number. A little before midnight he called again: "Where've you been?" he asked. The young woman, flustered but not displeased, replied that she'd been out with friends. "Of course," Yates sighed. "That was dumb of me." Then he asked if she was doing anything for Christmas Day, and if not, would she like to have dinner with him? She was not, and she would.

Doel was Roger Corman's twenty-two-year-old assistant, who'd just arrived in the States that summer after taking a degree at St. Hilda's College, Oxford. One of her teachers had recommended *Eleven Kinds of Loneliness* as "an example of good American writing," and a year or so later who should appear in her boss's office but the good American writer himself. "He was my romantic ideal," said Doel—meaning, more or less, that he was a handsome, talented man who appeared to be down on his luck ("I'd grown up in a culture where failure was glamorous," she added). Doubtless Yates sensed her interest but kept her in reserve for some emergency: During the *Iwo Jima* project he'd been polite and bantering at times, but not very attentive. They'd exchanged a few greetings at the Copper Skillet, near the studio, and once during a script conference he'd suddenly asked Doel if *she* had any ideas: "No," she said, and Yates shouted, *"Think! That's what you're paid for!"*—then burst out laughing. But that was pretty much the extent of it until Christmas.

They went to a meat-and-potatoes place called Tail of the Cock and had a low-key conversation about books, Hollywood, and their awful childhoods. Yates brightened when Doel mentioned that her father, killed in the war, had worked for General Electric, but his glee waned quickly as he recounted his own father's career in the Mazda Lamp Division, as well as the man's almost total absence during his childhood. Doel was in a position to suggest, however, that it might have been worse: She told Yates that her stepfather was a miserly, ineffectual man who'd treated her with such cruelty that her mother had tried to kill him. This seemed to chasten Yates, who was gentle and protective toward Doel from that point on. Later they went back to his melancholy apartment, for which he apologized. "Dick generally expressed bewilderment at finding himself in a particular place and time," Doel remembered.

. . .

While in New York, Yates had seemed stable enough to warrant a Holly-wood visit from his daughters in late January, and in preparation he moved to a nicer apartment on Sweetzer Avenue—a small two-bedroom that opened on a catwalk balcony. As he counted the days and struggled to make progress on the stalled *Remagen* script, he was hourly tormented by the glibly clicking typewriter of Charles (*True Grit*) Portis, who lived on the same block. As ever, Yates wasn't able to write fiction while he worked on something else, though he did brood and make notes about it every so often. "Haven't done any more wrestling with the abortive manuscript you read last year," he wrote Cassill, "and doubt if I will for some time, if ever. A whole new novel is more likely and I've got the barest beginnings of one started." But that soon petered out, and again Yates wondered if he was all washed up; he wrote Dubus that he was sober and functioning, but couldn't seem to write a single decent line ("Is just 'functioning' being alive at all?"), and one awful night he told Loree Wilson that maybe it didn't matter if he ever finished another book.

But later that spring he wrote Cassill, "I'm feeling pretty jaunty for a change. I'm loaded with ideas for maybe salvaging that crummy novel—mostly, oddly enough, along the lines you suggested last year: more stuff about the mother, less about the kid." Meanwhile Bantam had reissued paperback editions of Yates's first two books, and while sales were thin ("Not an unhappy experience for [Bantam]," Marc Jaffe reported, "but not up to expectations either"), the mass-market printing would at least bring *some* new readers and remind others that Yates was still alive. And finally the altruistic Cassill was doing his best to liberate Yates from Hol-lywood, if only for a while; he'd learned that the National Council on the Arts was awarding ten thousand dollar grants to eight novelists that fall: "[Yates] has been in Hollywood for the past year," Cassill noted in his recommendation letter, "doing the kind of bitter work one does there when he is neither quite in or out of the screen writers guild. The year before that he taught in the Workshop at Iowa—and with all the sordid, backbiting politicking that went on that year, I can't think we gave him much of any chance to write." He concluded that Yates was the "most deserving" of any writer he knew, and urged a quick decision in his friend's favor (though as it happened recipients wouldn't be notified until August).

Amid such ups and downs, his daughters' visit helped "take the curse off this loathsome town," as Yates put it. This time there was no sitting around Howard Johnson's debating the day's activities; Yates had planned almost every hour in advance. The girls flew first-class and ate lobster on the plane, and were duly impressed by the fact that, for once, they had a bedroom all to themselves. They went to Universal Studios, visited Brian Moore's swanky home in Malibu, and met a number of pleasant grown-ups who paid attention to them. They also took a day trip to Tijuana, though this outing proved a bit much for the cranky Monica; at one point she stood, arms folded under a giant souvenir sombrero, and imperiously commanded her father, "Take me to the car!" (For years afterward, Yates delighted in saying "Take me to the car!" whenever she started pouting.) Monica invented a game during the long drive back that was much to her taste: It involved making her father say "What?" so she could retort, "Shut up!" Lest his older daughter feel slighted, Yates arranged for some "irresponsible college kids" (as Monica remembers) to baby-sit while he and Sharon went to a fancy restaurant and saw *The Sound of Music* at Grauman's Chinese Theater.

After the girls had left, Yates became increasingly morose. One night he and Frances Doel drove to Van Nuys to have dinner at the home of Peter and Polly Bogdanovich, but the evening was not a happy one for Yates. At the time Bogdanovich was a bright young man trying to get started as a writer and director; he'd met Yates through Corman, and deferred to him as the author of a distinguished novel. Bogdanovich, however, depressed Yates on almost every level: The young man was determined to be a serious artist in Hollywood, while Yates hated the place and was stuck plugging away at his "loathsome" *Remagen* script; worse, Bogdanovich's then-happy marriage was a painful reminder of Yates's own broken home (much on his mind at the moment). As Doel summed it up, "Peter represented lost opportunities for Dick." On the whole Yates was far more relaxed having casual chats with his neighbor Portis, who understood what it was like to spend most of one's life alone, writing fiction of whatever sort.

Yates began drinking again in March. He considered AA meetings a maudlin bore, and as for the twelve steps—well, he'd tried to seek out a few people he'd harmed and ask their forgiveness, but he hated that part almost as much as being sober. Perhaps the last straw was in late February, when he got in touch with his old girlfriend Craige because he blamed himself for pushing her into hard-core alcoholism. Sure enough, the woman was still plastered. "Is this some kind of AA thing?" she asked. When Yates admitted it was, she berated him with a slurred tongue and hung up on him again and again. "The purpose of this letter is really to apologise for my extraordinary conduct on the telephone," she wrote afterward. "It must have cost you pots of money and been terribly depressing. I really don't remember much after you called back the last time except that it must have been pretty bad on my part." On Yates's part, too.

Another reason sobriety was out of the question was *The Bridge at Remagen*—an experience that made Yates long for the halcyon days of *Iwo Jima*. As he wrote Cassill,

[The story] is all tricked out with sinister Nazis, plucky GI's and more cliches than Louis B. Mayer ever dreamed of. On Iwo I was left pretty much alone; this time I'm stuck with a pea-brained "Story Editor" who wants to control the whole project and has his own dreary and emphatic ideas for each scene. But the money is far better than I got for Iwo, so I'm keeping a tight asshole and ought to be done with it by April, when I hope to buy a little free time.

Yates was looking forward to an additional ten thousand dollars when he submitted the finished script (in its "final-final stages" as of late-March), but Wolper apparently wanted another rewrite and fired Yates without further payment.*

For whatever byzantine Guild reason, though, Yates was given lead screenwriting credit and hence received the odd residual pittance once the

*It's likely that Yates balked at Wolper's demand for another rewrite, and perhaps that's why he was fired, but all that's definitely known is that (a) further rewrites were done, and (b) Yates *was* fired (sans ten thousand dollars). See endnotes.

movie was finally released in 1969—though Yates had disowned it so completely that he even refused to list *Remagen* on his otherwise all-encompassing résumé of 1973. He told friends he was appalled to have his name associated with such a "dog," and claims the final version was an almost total rewrite. But the basic idea Yates brought to that original, cliché-ridden script does seem to have remained intact—to wit, the whole Germans-are-people-too angle: *The Bridge at Remagen* cuts between "plucky GI's" (George Segal et al.) and not-so-sinister Nazis (Robert Vaughn et al.), the better to suggest that war is hell no matter what your nationality. And that's not the only abiding Yatesian touch, as the author himself pointed out during Thanksgiving 1969 with Robin Metz's family, when they all piled in a car to see the movie at a local drive-in. Yates took a sheepish bow as Metz blared his horn—*"This is the guy who wrote it! Right here!"*—but as they settled down to watch, Yates began shaking his head ("Nope, didn't write *any* of that . . ."), then suddenly bolted upright and thrust a finger at the screen: *"There! I actually wrote that part!"* The "part" was a gold cigarette case that's fumbled on the bridge by Nazi Vaughn and recovered by GI Segal, for whom it becomes a prize possession while its previous owner is reduced to cadging a last, sad fag before he's shot for desertion; thus the gold case serves as a neat little objective correlative suggesting the spoils of war, the common bonds of humanity, and so forth. Suffice to say it's the best thing in the movie.

After the *Remagen* debacle Yates was finished with movies, or so he thought. "I wouldn't want to try it again," he said as late as 1981. "It's a brain-scrambling business." That left teaching, though if possible he was even less enthused by the prospect of Iowa than a year before: Cassill had bitterly resigned, while most of Yates's old grad-student pals, including Dubus, had taken degrees and moved on. Even after the Workshop officially invited him back with a three-thousand-dollar raise, Yates continued to test the waters elsewhere—the University of Arkansas, San Francisco State, University of North Carolina at Greensboro—but there were no takers, and in June, Yates accepted his fate. "We are delighted," Bourjaily replied, offering his family's old apartment ($155 per month) to Yates when he returned in the fall.

He was in no hurry to move. "Still hate [Hollywood]," he assured Cassill, "but I think I'll hole up here anyway to work on the book, rather than spend the dough and time necessary to go back to New York or somewhere else. In a way it's a good place to work because it *is* so lousy—no very tempting distractions." By then, however, it didn't take much to distract Yates. That summer another refugee from the Workshop, Murray Moulding, came to Los Angeles to join his clinically depressed wife who was in the midst of intensive psychotherapy. Moulding was the kind of rich Ivy Leaguer whom his former teacher had scorned ("There's Murray, squirming in his chair to tell us the news again"), but now Yates was just relieved to have a reliable drinking buddy. He didn't even begrudge Moulding the large inheritance that enabled him to buy a fancy home in Brentwood: "Hey, Styron was a rich guy, and *he* did okay," declared a newly pragmatic Yates.

Fair to say the two were not a good influence on each other, despite Yates's occasional stabs at being a wise big-brother type. "One of these days I've got to *do* something about this," he said frowning at his glass; Moulding tipsily suggested he go back to AA, but Yates shook his head. "Nah. Once you've done it, it doesn't work again." Add to the picture a melancholy, neglected wife, and the household might have resembled a Eugene O'Neill play. Attempts to seek more wholesome diversions were less than successful. One night they bought tickets to *The Fantasticks,* but the Mouldings got in a fight and were an hour late picking up Yates, who sat placidly drinking on a wall outside his apartment. A few minutes into the play he was fast asleep, and incoherent when they roused him for intermission.

Frances Doel remained a port in the storm, but the young woman's extreme adoration seemed to make Yates uncomfortable, especially as he began to fall apart in earnest. He'd try to act jaunty as he drank his morning martinis, but Doel would insist on gazing into his eyes, which (she recalled) "betrayed feelings that went against the grain of his conversation." Impotence was again a problem. Earlier, when he was sober, Yates had responded to the odd lapse with a kind of fatherly aplomb: "Well, I guess this has never happened to you before—you're too young," etc. But now that he was drinking again, impotence became a suggestive aspect of his overall desperation. "Don't leave me!" he'd plead as he was falling asleep, though the smitten Doel hadn't the faintest notion of doing so; indeed she was flattered by his need (though she could scarcely help but detect something a little impersonal about it). Even if she hadn't been in love, it would have been hard for Doel to abandon such a tormented man. When Yates disappeared for several days in mid-July, Doel was convinced he'd had another breakdown: "Forgive me," she wrote him, "but I called the UCLA place in case you were there. I wanted to come and see you . . . but I didn't because I thought you probably wouldn't want that. Then again, it might be that your family would be here with you, so whatever the circumstances it seemed I shouldn't worry you."

He wasn't quite crazy, nor was he with family. Rather, he'd received a long, semiarticulate fan letter (and perhaps a photo) from a woman in Texas named Carole,* whom he tracked down by telephone and offered to fly expenses paid to Los Angeles. Her two-year-old daughter from a previous marriage was also welcome. Murray Moulding described the woman as a "free-floating opportunist" and "groupie," while Robin Metz called the episode "a Maureen Grube–type affair: life imitating art." Like Maureen Grube (in *Revolutionary Road*), the woman had a bad complexion beneath heavy layers of makeup, but also a voluptuous body and a kind of coquettish vulnerability that made her attractive, at least to Yates. Also she was willing to match him drink for drink.

Yates later told his second wife that he knew he'd made a mistake the minute this woman walked off the plane, but the truth is somewhat more complicated. She was, after all, bright enough to appreciate his work (whole paragraphs of which she could quote verbatim), and a letter she wrote Yates in 1970 reflects a kind of grandiosity that might have seemed intriguing at first: She describes herself as "brilliant," an "emotional genius," and so on; she also calls herself Yates's "soul-sister" and cryptically alludes to the "things that went on between [them]" that he "may have completely forgotten." Her intellectual pretensions almost surely annoyed him, as she claims to have made him feel "edgy and challenged all the time": "I made you nervous, even when I tried to play the role of a

---

*Last name deliberately omitted.

background stage-setting. What all this amounts to is HELP! 'Where did I go wrong?' "

At the time Yates seemed rather sheepishly pleased with himself. He wrote friends that he'd "found a girl"—his "fair Texan"—and broke the news to Frances Doel as though he expected her to be happy for him. After his mysterious disappearance, he asked Doel to meet him at an old haunt, the Raincheck Room on Santa Monica Boulevard, where he greeted her with a "guiltily triumphant" smile: "You thought there was something wrong with me, didn't you? Well, there isn't." He then explained about the "healthy woman" who'd helped him over that "problem" he was having. He spoke to Doel as if she were a fond old confidante who happened to be familiar with the problem in question. The young woman was stricken but tried to seem pleased.

This meeting was meant to be good-bye, though Doel didn't know it at the time. When the days passed and she didn't hear from Yates again, she paid him a visit on the pretext of returning some books; he was sitting alone amid some boxes, about to leave Los Angeles. Doel burst into tears: "I tried to be stoical—not to let my emotions go to the point where they became false, as Dick would have it—but I couldn't help it." Yates tried to comfort her, then rummaged through some boxes and came up with copies of his two books. Doel had once mentioned how much she used to love Christmas pantomimes in England, and that she'd always preferred playing the principal boy in Shakespearean productions at school (she found it oddly fascinating that the audience knew she was really a girl). Hence Yates inscribed *Revolutionary Road,* "For Frances—Who may once have wished to be a Principal Boy but who, in a far larger and more desperate pantomime, has been unforgettable as my principal girl. Love, Dick." Then he took her hand and walked her back to the apartment she'd recently found on the same block.

"The world was out of sync for days after," Doel recalled. To cheer her up, the Bogdanoviches took her to see *The Man Who Shot Liberty Valance,* which turned out to be a "terrifying" experience: "I couldn't make sense of it. I couldn't match the words with the images." Yates wrote her a last kindly letter, but she never saw him again and remained haunted by his memory. "I obsessively studied the jacket photos: He looked ill, rapidly aging, and I guessed things weren't going well. Then there were no more books, and then I saw his obituary. I'd always had a sense that I could call him, that he was at least around, and suddenly it was no longer possible."

CHAPTER ELEVEN

A Natural Girl: 1966-1968

Yates drove straight to Iowa City from Hollywood, but when he arrived he couldn't find his new apartment at 800 North Van Buren. His old friend Loree Wilson—who'd recently finished her thesis and was about to leave town—was with a new arrival, Mark Costello, when the phone rang. Yates was at the Airliner and needed her help, but there was no hurry. ("Dick's helplessness over logistical details was learned," said Costello; "he didn't want to fuck with it and wanted other people to take care of him.") When they arrived at the bar Yates was "drunk out of his gourd"; happily he only had a few more blocks to drive.

A year ago he'd been depressed about being in Hollywood, but grateful at least that it wasn't Iowa; now it was the other way around. He'd returned almost a month earlier than necessary, simply because he couldn't wait any longer and hoped to "get [his] brains into some kind of focus" before classes began and his "fair Texan" arrived with her daughter. (He and Carole had decided to live together.) He'd been in Iowa less than a week when he got some very good news: Along with such writers as Grace Paley and Tillie Olsen, he'd been awarded that ten-thousand-dollar grant from the National Arts Council. "So I'm no longer in much financial stress and can pay off some of my debts," Yates wrote, "and I guess it tends to prove that I'm a good deal luckier than I care to believe."

So it seemed. The old Bourjaily place where he now found himself was on the ground floor of a stately Victorian mansion, and his typewriter was parked beneath a crystal chandelier; the dusty baubles gave him something to look at, but still the place struck him as big and empty and strange. Really, he didn't feel lucky at all. The change of scenery hadn't affected his writer's block a whit, and what the hell was he doing back in Iowa anyway? Why had he invited some feckless woman (and her two-year-old daughter) to live with him? After a couple of weeks beneath the chandelier he was miserable enough to write a rare letter to his sister, the contents of which are suggested by her reply: "If we stick together," Ruth wrote, "we'll both live through it." (By "it" she meant life in general.) "Don't 'adapt,' dear; persevere."

It wasn't half-bad advice. By the second week of September, the gloom had lifted somewhat: Workshop people were back in town, and the first big social event was a welcome-back-from-Hollywood party for Yates. There was a swimming pool and Sinatra tunes, old faces as well as new, and the guest of honor was in good form—just drunk enough to wax droll on the subject of Hollywood without becoming bitter and obsessive about it. Once again he was the most glamorous writer in Iowa, certainly the best dressed, and what's more he seemed to sense as much. Suavely he approached one of the youngest women at the party (about a week shy of her twenty-first birthday) and asked her out on a date. She accepted readily enough, though she seemed reserved almost to the point of indifference; in fact she was "bowled over" by the handsome celebrity.

Martha Speer was the fourth of nine children born to a well-to-do doctor in Kansas City, and she'd always wanted to be an artist of some sort. At Carleton College she'd auditioned for plays but ended up designing sets, and this soon became part of a larger disenchantment: The school was too staid and "goal-oriented" for her tastes, there was no art department per se, and anyhow such an environment was hardly the "real world." So she dropped out and returned to her appalled parents in Kansas City, where she worked as a waitress for a few months. After that she went to Mexico for the summer, then followed a boyfriend to the University of Iowa and enrolled as an art student because she "couldn't think of anything else to do." Around this time she found herself talking to Yates at the party in his honor; she'd attended as the date of a fellow art student who was not the young man for whose sake she'd come to Iowa.

Within days she'd moved most of her things into Yates's apartment. "He swept me off my feet with his personality," she explained. He was a well-known writer, and though she was "a nobody" he listened to her with what appeared to be real interest, with humility and humor, and of course he sang the old standards for her. She couldn't quite understand why this charming, distinguished man of letters was paying so much attention to her—was, for that matter, practically goading her into merging her life with his. When she returned to Kansas City for a few days before the semester got under way, Yates suggested she persuade her parents to let her move out of the dorm and into Black's Apartments (where a lot of Workshop students lived), which would make it easier to deceive them about the fact that she was living neither at the dorm nor Black's, but rather with a man twice her age. Speer was happy to go along with that or whatever else he advised: "I was ready to strike out on my own," she remembered. "I detested the role of the little Midwestern kid from an upper-middle-class family."

There was, however, one immediate hitch. "I'm sorry your friend is having trouble disinvolving herself, sorry you have to argue with her," Speer wrote Yates from Kansas City. An awkward business, to be sure, when the woman named Carole arrived from Texas with the rest of her things and a two-year-old daughter in tow, only to find she'd been superannuated in the meantime. One doubts she took it lying down either, as three years later she was still inclined to castigate Yates for the "traumatic and cowardly way" he'd ended the affair; but then, too, she allowed that he was "at least honest." What he seems to have been most emphatically honest about was his obsession with Martha Speer ("I want the *hell* out of her," he said), and nothing in the immediate future was liable to change that. He also reminded the older woman that it was essentially *her* idea to come to Iowa—he'd promised nothing.

The sequel was sordid, and one can only speculate to what extent it interfered with Yates's newfound happiness. Evidently Carole had little reason to return to Texas, since she went on living aimlessly in Iowa for at least another year. At first she had a few brief affairs with Workshop students, then took a campus job in the chemistry lab and pretty much disappeared from Yates's purview. The following summer, still in Iowa, she took an overdose of sleeping pills; after two days she was found comatose in her car, and almost pronounced DOA at the emergency room ("until some smart-ass intern found a flutter of a pulse," as she put it). Finally, after three more months in an Iowa City mental hospital, she returned to Texas. "If you ever blamed yourself for my suicide deal," she wrote Yates, "let me assure you . . . that you were only indirectly or passively concerned with it. The guy I was living with was the main reason. I was very depressed when I met him and he . . . terrorized me into a paralysis which nothing could alleviate except death." However, she wasn't willing to let Yates entirely off the hook for at least his "passive" culpability—she pointed out that he'd started a "flow of love" in her that had proved "drowning": "My suicide was an act of love, Dick, not an act of hostility or hurt." Whether Yates had wondered much one way or the other is a mystery.

He'd solved his problem in time for Martha Speer's return, and two days later (September 19) he gave her a dozen yellow roses for her twenty-first birthday. Yates's students and colleagues could scarcely believe the change that was coming over him: Suddenly he seemed content, steady, even somewhat soberly so. He'd dispensed with the morning martinis and drank according to a disciplined regime: a quarter of a fifth of bourbon per night, neither more nor less (except for the occasional party), and never before five P.M. As for Speer, who'd also been going through a bad patch, she felt exalted by all the attention—not just from Yates, but from those who admired him and valued her as his beloved. She liked being the only woman included in those raucous chats at the Airliner, and for a time she even liked the fact that almost all the talk was literary (as when Yates would spend half an hour discussing, say, how certain ceiling tiles might be described in fiction), which only served as another reminder that a brilliant man was in love with her.

That she didn't really love him back was a problem, though perhaps not an insurmountable one. For a long time she'd craved purpose in her life, and what better than caring for a man who stood a good chance of becoming a bona fide famous writer? And it wasn't just a matter of self-interest—she *was* fond of him: He made her laugh and "elicited a sense of protectiveness," as she put it, "coupled with respect." On the other hand, she sometimes felt as if she'd been "swept along into his life," and worried over the heedlessness of it all. Before she could quite parse out her feelings, she was insolubly linked with Yates in the eyes of Iowa, and the man himself was cleaving to her for dear life. And then, too, it became increasingly clear that her role was to listen and sympathize and support, with very little coming the other way, to the extent that one's ego was liable to vanish in the process. As Monica Yates pointed out, "Dad didn't notice other people. He picked up on asshole people, he could figure people out in general, but in another way he saw himself projected out, and that's another thing that made Martha angry: She thought he was going to be so perceptive, but really he was very self-regarding."

But what else was she going to do with her life? That (at the time) was very much the question. "I was afraid to face people, afraid of my inadequacy, convinced I was boring and untalented," she wrote Yates several years later. "You told me I was pretty, talented, and smart, while at the same time making it seem unnecessary for me to ever use any of these things." Still, it was nice to know she was worthwhile in the abstract, or at least as Yates's caregiver, and of course there was always the chance things would get better.

After that first bumpy month the year was off to a good start for Yates in almost every respect. His novelty verse "QWERTYUIOP$\frac{1}{2}$" appeared in the October *Esquire,* and prompted a fan letter from Roger Angell of *The New Yorker*: "As an occasional palindromist and part-time anagrammist," he wrote, "I have had occasion to study this curious back-corner of letters, and I think you may have invented a new form. Invented it and exhausted it, all at the same time." For Yates's private reading pleasure, Angell enclosed a kindred performance of his own—a long ribald poem wherein every line is an anagram of the title, "On a Festival Aire": "O, a vile siena fart!" it begins. This would prove one of the most gracious letters Yates ever received from *The New Yorker,* and particularly Roger Angell, who wrote in a very different vein some fifteen years later.

Even with his friend Cassill gone, the Workshop—or the "Program in Creative Writing" as it was now known (since Cassill's battle had been lost)—seemed rather congenial, at least for a while, and certainly more peaceful. Paul Engle, though still a force, had resigned as director to devote himself to the International Writers' Workshop, and his successor, the poet George Starbuck, soon became a friend and sometime protector of Yates. Workshop classes had moved out of the barracks and into the better-ventilated English Philosophy Building, and as a teacher Yates was more in demand than ever. His legend had spread in his absence, such that he was at the top of many preference lists and could pick and choose among the more talented students—the realists, anyway.

A vague source of disquiet was the new, experimental element on the fiction staff, including the surrealistic Chilean novelist José Donoso and a man named Kurt Vonnegut, who was known as everything from a black humorist to an intellectual science-fiction writer. Yates steered clear of Donoso but struck up a respectful friendship with Vonnegut. The latter was still three years away from the wealth and fame that *Slaughterhouse Five* would bring, though he'd made a minor splash with such novels as *Cat's Cradle* and *Mother Night*. At the time, though, it's likely that Yates was still the better known of the two. What mattered was that both men deeply admired the other's work. In his *Ploughshares* interview, Yates made a point of exonerating Vonnegut from the charge that he was one of the detested "post-realists": "The difference is that there's real fictional meat in his best work, despite the surface flippancy of his style—real suffering, real passion, real humor. . . . When I hear kids today mention him in the same breath with some silly clown like Richard Brautigan it drives me up the wall." Vonnegut, in turn, thought *Revolutionary Road* was "one of the best books by a member of [his] generation," and over the years nobody was more instrumental in promoting Yates's reputation.

The two men never saw much of each other, but from the beginning they had a kind of brotherly rapport. Both had served as enlisted men in the war, and both had supported families with egregious jobs (Vonnegut at General Electric for a time), followed by many bleak years of the freelance grind. They were amused by Workshop students who worried that such jobs would "damage their machinery," and each year the two gave "a very unpopular lecture" on the subject "The Writer and the Free Enterprise System": "We would talk about all the hack jobs writers could take in case they found themselves starving to death," Vonnegut said. "Dick and I found out you can almost always get work if you can write complete sentences." But what bonded the two most, perhaps, was the fact that they were essentially melancholy men who sometimes took refuge in antic behavior—Vonnegut also liked to sing and dance ("I'd rather be Astaire than anybody other than Chekhov")—to say nothing of cigarettes and alcohol. Vonnegut referred to Yates as "Eeyore" and insisted that his depression was mostly "existential": "Dick was a man of big dreams," he said, "but modest expectations."

What Yates expected in the way of decent writing was another matter, and he felt annoyed and somewhat threatened by a now-rampant tendency—even among his own students—to indulge in what he considered gimmicky fiction: incredible characters and situations, fancy word stringing, fey whimsy, political diatribes, and so forth. For Yates such effects were "violations, bullshit" (as Bill Kittredge put it), whose proliferation sorely tested his vaunted sense of tact. When one of his more promising students submitted such a story for workshop critique, and others proceeded to praise it lavishly, Yates stood frozen at the lectern as if stricken with stunned distaste; after some forty-five minutes he suddenly broke out with, "*I think you're all just fucking around*—let's go on to the next story." "It was like a bomb went off in the room," said Kittredge, who to this day can hardly write a tricky line without picturing Yates's "sad old eyes" and hearing his anguished "For Christ's *sake*, Kittredge . . ."

But experimental fiction was the coming thing in the mid-sixties, and traditional writers such as Yates were widely considered passé and sentimental; the oppressive reality of current events seemed to call for a more subversive approach. "Oh, the hell with that," said Yates in *Ploughshares*. "I find that reprehensible." In fact he was pleased by his own pithy restraint here, since he'd been tempted to say so much more; as he subsequently wrote interviewer DeWitt Henry:

I wanted very much to mount an all-out attack on the whole fucking "Post-realistic School," and I think I brought that off rather nicely in a short space. I didn't mention one of the most loathsome of that breed—Robert Coover— by name, because I know the little sonovabitch personally, and a good many people know I know him, and it might have read like a vindictive personal vendetta.

Coover's arrival at Iowa the following year was like the advent of a literary Antichrist to Yates—the incarnation of everything he deplored, and a constant reminder that he himself was perceived as old hat. Amid an increasingly radical ethos, Coover became the star of the Workshop, gathering around him a claque of students who wrote the same kind of "lazy" and "soulless" fiction as Yates would have it. And what really hurt was that some of these students were talented defectors from his own class—Kittredge, for instance, who remarked that he'd found such divergent influences a "good combination": "From Coover I learned to see what I was doing in terms of traditions and possibilities more universal than realism. From Yates I learned something I can only sum up as responsibility, to my characters and story, to readers, and to myself."

Yates would have shaken his head and sighed, *For Christ's sake, Kittredge*; for him there were no "possibilities" beyond the necessary craftsmanship of depicting "apparent reality" in all its intricacy, and people who ignored the rules were phonies—"chessmasters," maybe, but not writers. Toward Coover and his coterie Yates maintained a more or less civil distance; whenever he was tempted to register some kind of aesthetic demurral, he tended to preface it with a phrase like "Well, I'm just a dumb guy, but I think . . ." In *The Easter Parade*, though, he channeled his frustration through the Yates-like Jack Flanders, a "traditional" poet who accuses his experimental colleague "Krueger" of having "thrown everything overboard": "His favorite critical adjective is 'audacious.' Some kid'll get stoned on pot and scribble out the first thing that comes into his head, and Krueger'll say 'Mm, that's a very audacious line.'"

The political concomitant of all this "subversive" writing was no less distasteful to Yates. The Workshop to which he returned in 1966 was, as Robert Lehrman described it, "a seething mix of creative ferment and rage about the Vietnam War." A number of students had sought refuge from the draft by enrolling in the program, and teachers such as Vonnegut expressed solidarity by refusing to flunk anyone even if they never wrote a word. Director George Starbuck insisted on being arrested with a number of Workshop students who'd protested CIA recruitment by blocking the entrance to the student union. Yates's rather paradoxical liberalism produced a complex but characteristic response: He opposed the war, but even more adamantly opposed the counterculture. He loathed the shaggy incivility of the protesters (whom he privately called "faggots" and worse) and was outraged by their tendency to blame the war on the soldiers. In *Young Hearts Crying*, Davenport's response to a popular mock–recruitment poster (JOIN THE ARMY/VISIT EXOTIC PLACES/ AND KILL PEOPLE) was also Yates's: "And I mean what kind of horseshit is that? . . . Soldiers are the *victims* of wars; everybody knows that." But any number of people at Iowa disagreed: Soldiers *are* to blame, they argued, since they might have chosen to be conscientious objectors rather than murderers—to which Yates would respond, in effect, that one couldn't expect a bunch of naive, patriotic kids to be so *enlightened*. (Martha Speer sympathized with such a view: "I myself had enlisted in a hopeless cause: Richard Yates.") Yates thought the general disorder of the counterculture—ideological and otherwise—threatened the integrity of the Workshop, such as it was, and by the end of that first semester he was already casting about for openings at other, less radicalized universities.

But these were incidental matters, for the most part. Yates could coexist with a postrealistic counterculture as long as his own work and domestic life were in some kind of order, and in that regard he was having the best year "in the past four or five" as he reported to Cassill: "This is partly because I'm making slow but steady progress on my book (yeah, yeah, the same damn book, but different now), . . . but mostly because of Martha Speer." For Martha's sake he'd curtailed his drinking, curbed his temper (somewhat), and "learned a few tricks about how to keep students from bugging me and how to keep a safe and cordial distance from what I believe is called 'Social Life.' " The young woman had probationally agreed to marry Yates in the not-distant future, and he was careful to stay on his best behavior. He also tried to help her find a few companions among his students' wives and girlfriends—without much success, as Martha tended to be even more reticent than usual among women her own age. In fact she was rather opaque in general, though Yates could hardly fail to detect that she was a little conflicted about things, and he wondered whether age might be a problem after all; as he told friends, he didn't want to seem "like fucking Sinatra" going after Mia Farrow. Andre

Dubus, who sympathized with Yates's tastes in women, sought to reassure him: "Good work to you down there, and I don't really see why a twenty year age-gap should prevent marriage . . . but I'm impulsive and I'd probably tell the chick, like unto Sinatra, Come fly with me, come fly come fly away. . . ."

Meanwhile neither of their families knew anything. Martha's parents continued to believe that she resided chastely at Black's, and it was convenient that she return to Kansas City for Christmas that year, since Yates's daughters were visiting Iowa and there was no question of their meeting Martha unless marital plans were definite. Indeed, the couple's holiday separation may have decided things, at least in Yates's mind. Though he enjoyed showing his children the rural splendors of Iowa, Martha's long absence was an intolerable wrench. At least one night, though, he was diverted by welcome voices from the past: Wendy Sears was working for Mayor Lindsay in New York, and Joe Mohbat had visited her from Harvard where he was a Neiman fellow; they'd just finished dinner when they decided to have a phone reunion with their forlorn friend in the hinterland. "Dick, guess what we're doing?" said Sears. "Joe and I are sitting here smoking *pot*." Yates affected to be aghast—"*You fucking hippies!*" etc.—though he was touchingly happy to hear from them.

Financially it was the best and worst of times. In March, Al Ruddy bought out the motion picture rights to *Revolutionary Road* for $15,500, about $12,000 of which went to Yates after 10 percent was subtracted for Monica McCall and Little, Brown respectively. But really he saw very little of this windfall, as he passed most of it on to the parsimonious Sheila to divide between a college fund and down payment on a new house. As for the $10,000 federal grant, much of that had already evaporated toward debts incurred when *The Bridge at Remagen* fell through.

Meanwhile Sam Lawrence was pressing him to make good on their gentlemen's agreement of three years before. "We would be prepared to make a substantial offer on your next book or books," he reminded Yates. "I would very much like to be your publisher again." As if to demonstrate his largess, Lawrence struck a deal with Yates's friend Vonnegut for a

$25,000 advance on his next book. Again Yates appealed to his agent for guidance, and again she guided him away from Lawrence: While she conceded that his Knopf advance was only $20,000 ($7,000 of which had gone to reimburse Little, Brown), she also pointed out that Lawrence would actually be paying for both hardcover and softcover rights, and hence Yates stood to lose "anywhere between $50,000 and $400,000" on a big softcover sale. "I do know that the pressures on you are appalling," she wrote, "and I'm sure that your main nightmare must be a buying of time in order to finish the book. But I would hope never to have to see you pay too high a price for the time." McCall couldn't have known that a big paperback sale was hardly in the cards for Yates's next book, but it was bad advice nonetheless. Lawrence subsequently assured Yates that he was willing to "repay the outstanding advance on your current novel and at the same time provide for additional income"; also the author would receive both hard *and* softcover royalties, *pace* McCall. But as Yates reminisced a few dreary years later,

> In the end I told Sam I just couldn't afford to keep my promise—told him (and this is the kind of memory that *really* rankles) not in a letter or in person over a drink, but in an abrupt, testy little conversation over the God damn telephone. That was splitsville between us.
>
> And the rest is history. Within two years his "venture" had burgeoned into the multi-million-dollar Delacorte empire—one best-seller after another.

As such matters came to a head, and progress on his novel stalled again in late spring, Yates's precarious well-being began to slip. When a young editor named Gordon Lish came to Iowa to interview Yates for a collection of taped readings, he found the author obliging but "lugubrious." The two got "roaring drunk" (their tinkling glasses are audible on the tape), and afterward Yates insisted on driving his guest to the airport. They arrived early and sat in the cocktail lounge, where Yates bitterly maundered about having to "teach" for a living. At one point they discussed a mutual friend, Anatole Broyard, the mention of whom only reminded Yates of his main theme: He remarked on Broyard's new career as a critic—the fact that Broyard, at least, didn't have to demean himself by teaching anymore, much less in the sticks.

Yates's colleagues began to notice something amiss. When Peter Davison of the Atlantic Monthly Press came to Iowa in May, Yates gave a crowded party at which his behavior seemed oddly "elevated." Davison—who'd witnessed the spectacle of Yates's being taken away in a straitjacket five years before at Bread Loaf—suddenly had a "clear impression" that the man was bipolar. Such conduct was all the more conspicuous to faculty and staff, toward whom Yates had tended, in the past, to be nothing if not reserved. But one night he startled his colleague Bill Murray by staying late after a party to discuss his daughter Sharon, who (Yates said) was romantically involved with a Negro.* Murray, though on good terms with Yates, was taken aback by such abrupt and bizarre intimacy. "The Workshop was very incestuous," said Murray, "but I thought a wall of privacy should prevail."

Martha Speer didn't know what to make of the rather gradual change. For no particular reason Yates began to drink more and grow irritable; he paced around the house at night, sleeping less and less. He'd already told her about his psychotic episodes in the past (hence the pills), but hadn't characterized himself as suffering from chronic mental illness. Martha wondered if others noticed the change, but nobody told her anything (until later) and she didn't know whom to confide in. "I was left to my own devices," she said. "It was horrible. I wanted to escape quite often, but I felt it was a commitment and I was stuck with it." As Yates's paranoia began to escalate, she thought she could somehow arrest the process by being steadfastly rational—by explaining, again and again, that she and others *weren't* looking at him in any particular way, that a certain person *wasn't* plotting against him, but of course it was no use. Repeatedly Yates

---

*"Dick wasn't racist about it," Murray recalled, "simply concerned [about Sharon] in general." Sharon Yates points out that she was not involved with a black man, then or later. Around that time, however, she *was* entering a phase of adolescent rebellion in which she'd test her parents' liberalism with provocative hypothetical questions, such as "What if I dated a Negro?" She assumes that's where her father got the idea, but it was a delusion—"part of his nuttiness."

went berserk—raging over grievances old and new, hurling furniture at phantoms out of his past. The nurses who lived upstairs complained about the racket to the landlady, an eccentric woman who adored Yates and did nothing. One night he arrived drunk at a dinner party for a man who'd been hired as "executive secretary" of the Workshop. *"Where's the pencil pusher?"* Yates roared—and when he found the guest of honor in the kitchen: "Are *you* the pencil pusher?" The latter stammered some kind of protest, and Yates dumped a bowl of spaghetti over the man's head. Finally, as a state of total psychosis set in, Yates began to hallucinate so badly he mistook old acquaintances for other people; once, elated, he told Martha he had a plan to save the world.

Yates's students had known for some time that he was unwell: He was often drunk in class and at least once had lapsed into a crying jag. Such was their devotion, though, that they hesitated to say anything lest they get him in trouble. In the end it was Yates himself who spoke up. One morning he approached Vance Bourjaily and explained, shakily, that he had to commit himself for treatment; he thought he'd killed JFK, and though in a way he knew it wasn't true, at the same time he was convinced of it. Unfortunately, he was determined to teach a two-hour class before he went to the hospital. Fortified with alcohol, Yates slumped over the lectern and stood blinking into the bright fluorescent light: "[He was] clearly upset," Robert Lehrman recalled, "his voice even raspier than usual, and [he] stunned us with a long, rambling, only partly coherent monologue about a writer who turned out to have the luck of being a great writer— and married a woman of great wealth—the punch line of which was that it was William Styron." Yates was at pains to make it clear he didn't resent Styron—hell no, he *admired* the man—but it was just that he'd had such an easier *life*.

Yates was admitted to the hospital for a month. His friend Robin Metz paid him a visit, but felt "hopelessly inadequate" to the situation. Yates was in a locked ward for acutely disturbed patients, and Metz tried to think of cheerful things to say while others wailed and moaned and gibbered around them. Insofar as he was aware of Metz at all, Yates was abject at being seen in such a place; he sat on a couch with his knees pulled up to his forehead, "shrunk into himself," and hardly acknowledged his visitor at all. "I realized that being a friend wasn't always enough," said Metz. "For the first time I realized how bad a situation Dick was in—how wretched and miserable he was."

Martha Speer felt almost as miserable. Apart from Yates and a family whose way of life she'd rejected, she was pretty much alone in the world, and too depressed at the moment to judge things clearly. Yates's psychiatrist at the hospital, a Dr. Brown, took pity on the bewildered young woman: "You may want to get out of this," he urged her. "This man is going to have serious mental health problems." Speer would always remember Dr. Brown with gratitude, as he was the only person at the time who tried to deal honestly with her. But she had a "savior complex" and chose to ignore his advice. As she later explained to Yates, "I thought 'this is life,' that my childhood had protected me from reality, that I could find both escape and meaning for myself in an almost religious kind of identification to another."

Thus committed, the first thing she did was rent a smaller, cheaper apartment two blocks down the hill on Van Buren. Money, after all, was one of the things that preyed on Yates's mind, and at least in that respect she could be of some definite use to him. But when he got out of the hospital he was displeased. "Don't be ridiculous!" he told her, shaking his head at their "boring" new digs. "Money is to spend!"

That summer Yates rented a cottage in Montauk Point, Long Island, where he could "hole-up" and get some writing done: "No chance of finishing the book in that time," he wrote Cassill, "but there's a considerable chance that I might get it sufficiently in shape to finish next year." As it turned out, he was in far too deep a funk for creative labor. Kline had given him powerful new tranquilizers on the strict condition that he stop drinking, and the drugs combined with alcoholic withdrawal left him dopey and depressed. For days at a time he hardly spoke, except to complain about his writing: He wished Martha had known him when he was "younger and smarter," when he "knew what the hell [he] was doing." It got very monotonous, and Martha's depression deepened as well.

Yates put off seeing his sister almost to the end. More than three years had passed since their last meeting at Central Islip, and he dreaded what he and his fiancée would find at High Hedges. If anything it was worse than he imagined. The forty-six-year-old Ruth was now a toothless invalid who could hardly speak or walk without assistance. Yates sat beside her on the sofa and made kind, encouraging noises as she fumbled with his hands and talked about their childhood in a slurred, meandering way. Her husband Fred chatted with Martha and made sure Ruth's glass was filled, while their well-mannered son Peter answered questions about his seminary and patiently weathered his mother's inept sallies of affection. He alone seemed at ease with the situation. "The family was used to dealing with [Ruth]," Martha recalled, "they kept her propped up, but Peter had the best idea of her condition. The others sort of pretended it wasn't there." Yates endured things as long as he could, then abruptly stood up and said good-bye to his dazed older sister for the last time.

He also had a last (but one) meeting with Sheila that summer. Over lunch at Grand Central, he broke the news of his engagement to Martha, and Sheila wasn't entirely successful in masking her skepticism. "Does she know about your problems?" she asked, and Yates replied, "Oh yes, she knows everything" in a rushed, rather touchy voice. Sheila tried to be properly congratulatory, but was further bemused by the whole age business and couldn't help but wonder whether Yates was trying to recapture something irretrievable. Both were feeling a little awkward toward the end, and sad, and later that day Sheila wrote her ex-husband a note expressing what she'd failed to find words for in his presence:

I hope you're not sorry for our talk today and I want you to know I don't think you're foolish in what you're thinking of doing. What I really wanted to say is to do with those memories I mentioned of our romance of long ago when you and I were very young. They mean a great deal to both of us and I've known for a long time that nothing can come of trying to find that again with anyone else—something completely different, yes . . . but that particular agony and delight, never. That's the Garden of Eden and we've gone out. There are other Edens, though, and if this is truly another one altogether and you're not battering at the gates of the old one, then it's not foolish. . . . Love, and good luck, Sheila

In later years she'd rarely speak of Yates—much less in Edenic terms—but then she never remarried either.

Yates's dosages were adjusted before he left New York in mid-September, and by the time he was back in Iowa he felt like a new man. He returned to his sensible drinking regime and vowed not to let teaching duties monopolize his time; he informed his workshop that he refused to read any more stories "about the sex lives of graduate students in English." He was determined to devote at least four hours a day to his novel until the damn thing was finished, and in fact Martha Speer can hardly remember his ever missing those four hours again, no matter how blocked or addled he sometimes became. He'd work with his door open, smoking or pacing with a pencil in his teeth, occasionally reading something aloud to her. She became adept at responding in a way that seemed both candid and appreciative.

The shared trauma of Yates's breakdown had "glued" the couple together, as Martha put it, but no definite wedding plans were made until early that fall, when Mrs. Speer tracked her daughter down by telephone to Yates's apartment. Things happened fast after that: Martha admitted they were living together but were engaged to be married, whereupon an immediate visit to Kansas City was arranged so Yates could meet the parents. Anxious at the prospect, he made a rather good impression: He and Dr. Speer were about the same age and found a number of tastes in common (music for one), and both parents deemed him a gentleman; for Yates's part he was in awe of the family's bland, putative stability, while they were duly impressed by the information that he was a celebrated author. The father was quietly dubious over Yates's ability to generate a steady income (to say nothing of his age and apparent health), but as the man quipped, "I have so many daughters, letting one of them go won't bother me too much."

Yates was gleeful in announcing the wedding to friends. "I'm getting married," he wrote Cassill. "She's twenty years younger than me but I keep thinking about Picasso, Charlie Chaplin, Frank Sinatra and Justice Douglas, which makes it okay. Anyway I'm drinking less and showing many other signs of health including a protuberant gut and a winning smile." He'd asked Sheila not to tell their daughters until it was definite, and a couple of weeks before the ceremony he called to break the news: "I'm getting married! Isn't that exciting?" They'd had no idea of Martha's existence, much less of the fact that she was just four and a half years older than Sharon—but if he was happy, so were they.

The Workshop turned out in force for the event: Everyone seemed deeply moved that the lovable, troubled Yates had found someone to take care of him; as Lehrman noted, "We wanted him to have a happier life." Jerry Schulman was best man, and both he and Grace were struck by the way students and colleagues doted on Yates, how eager they were to accommodate the Schulmans simply because they were his friends. One rather ominous specter at the feast, however, was the poet John Berryman, about whom Grace had published an essay in the journal *Shenandoah*; as a pleasant diversion during the wedding rehearsal, Yates had arranged for her to attend a tea in Berryman's honor. The plan began to backfire the night before, when the boozy, disturbed poet accosted Yates after a concert and began ranting about marriage—whether for or against was hard to tell—while Yates listened with perhaps a grim sense of recognition. The next day at the tea Berryman was owlishly tipsy, and began dictating poetry at the table ("He said it was a Chinese stanza," said Grace; "it wasn't"). When he learned of Schulman's paper on the subject of his auto-biographical *Sonnets,* he asked her whether they'd been too private to publish. He seemed genuinely upset about it.

The day of the wedding—January 20, 1968—Yates was badly hung-over. The night before, he'd been the happy, silly, singing life of a party given by Bourjaily in the couple's honor. Martha's eight siblings were in town, and while they didn't know much about writing, each of them thought Yates was a delightful fellow. He made a resplendent groom, too, in his Gieves and Hawkes suit—"tall, fair-haired, gorgeous," as Grace Schulman remembered him that day—and after a few nips from a student's flask, his crapulence faded and he entered the First Presbyterian Church with a merry grin. When the four-year-old ring-bearer, Lisa Metz, paused warily in the aisle, Yates dropped to his haunches and gave her a look of ecstatic reassurance. "Dick was so handsome when he smiled," said the ring-bearer's father; "he was so full of joy at having this sweet little kid involved. His eyebrows would go up, up, *up* as he coaxed her on." The bride was a little dismayed to smell liquor on his breath—in a church, no less, on this of all days—but once they were man and wife and a mass of people were happily pelting them with rice, she managed a flustered smile. For better or worse, the thing was done. "I just placed my bets in that direction," she later mused. "It might have turned out great. Who knows, he might have written another *Revolutionary Road* and become really famous."

In fact a number of excellent books would follow, though by the time they were written Martha had lost all interest in Yates's career. And whatever the case, fame or no, he would have still been the man she married. As Bill Murray remembered, "Here was this very ordinary, sweet girl, dressed like a June bride, walking into a maelstrom. I thought, *Oh my God, what's going on here?*"

CHAPTER TWELVE

A Special Providence: 1968–1969

A month or so after the wedding, Yates overcame his aversion to the outdoors and rented a picturesque stone cottage about four miles north of Iowa City near the Coralville Reservoir. Their landlady was the same woman who owned the Victorian house where Yates had had his breakdown, and perhaps she understood his needs better than most. Save for a single neighbor in the vicinity—a "chummy, bubbly, tolerant" woman in her mid-thirties named Jill Van Cleve, who became a good companion to the couple—they were pretty much on their own, and both seemed to like it that way. The cottage was a former soap factory that had been moved stone by stone from the Mennonite colony in nearby Amana: Apart from a small bedroom it was all one space, the most arresting feature being a large fireplace with wrought-iron arms that pulled out. The house had a furnace, too, though it pleased the wistfully masculine Yates to chop wood on cold days and build roaring fires. Soon they inherited a dog named Cindy, who accompanied them on long walks and seemed to complete the household.

Except for his work, these were happy days for Yates. Around this time he grew a permanent beard whose relative tidiness (particularly later) was a telling indicator of his well-being; it lent a certain somber dignity to his features and solved the problem (as he saw it) of a weak chin and effeminate mouth. Life was starting over, and he was eager to leave behind the bewildered-looking bachelor who for years had lived in one anonymous den after another, eating restaurant meals and drinking too much. Now he had a pretty wife who was content to cook and clean and trim his whiskers for him, and he was anxious never to go back.

His daughter Monica was especially pleased with the change: In the old days her father's odd, transient life had made her too nervous to enjoy her visits, but Martha created a cheerful environment even when Yates was grumpishly stalking about with a pencil in his mouth. Also, the girl relished the company of handsome, robust graduate students such as Bob Lehrman and Jody Lowens, who were frequent guests at the cottage and assumed the role of attentive big brothers. One night Lowens put Monica on his shoulders so she could pry open a mysterious door above the fireplace, where she found an alcove filled with squirrel droppings. She promptly appropriated the space as her own, and Yates (who enjoyed such projects) provided a rope ladder and helped her clean it out. More than ever, father and daughter were a curious pair. "Monica always wanted him to shape up," said Martha. "It made her mad when he didn't live up to his own ideals. She'd get disgusted with him, but she loved him dearly." Almost from infancy the girl had gotten used to being hard on her father, often brazenly so, and as she got older her barbs became more incisive and somewhat less adorable. "Oh, babe, give me a break here!" Yates would bristle, or "Yeah yeah, I *know*"—this when she'd nag him about smoking, say, which only unnerved him into smoking more.

Meanwhile the world continued to wait patiently for another novel by the author of *Revolutionary Road*. With the help of his friend Styron, Yates was awarded a Rockefeller grant that winter for eleven thousand dollars, even while he agonized over the merit of the project that continued to attract such lavish subsidy. Styron himself had taken seven years to write his latest novel, *The Confessions of Nat Turner,* which won the 1968 Pulitzer and left Yates "almost wiped out with admiration and envy"; he wondered whether he'd keep such a man's respect, much less the world's, once his own tardy opus was revealed for what it was. The problem—and his editor Gottlieb agreed—remained one of *structure*: that is, whether to stitch the new material (i.e., Prentice's childhood with his mother) into the main narrative as so many intermittent flashbacks, or lump it all into a long discrete bridge in the middle; either way was far from seamless, and Yates couldn't help but suspect that he'd essentially written *two* novels which didn't go together and yet couldn't stand apart.

He was more vulnerable to criticism than ever. That spring he was invited to give a reading at Knox College in Galesburg, Illinois, where his friend Robin Metz had taken a teaching position. The visit got off to an awkward start when another Workshopper-turned-Galesburgian, Murray Moulding, had Yates over for dinner. Yates seemed somber and out-of-sorts, and when the seat of his lawn chair broke and he hit the ground, he didn't crack a smile amid the nervous laughter that followed. The next day he was scheduled to give a public reading for students, then meet with faculty from various disciplines to discuss his story "Builders," which they'd been given to read in advance. The first part of the agenda went fine; the faculty session, however, proved a kind of moral equivalent of that pratfall Yates had taken the night before. Such meetings were meant to be relaxed but scholarly, and usually the work under discussion was somewhat more abstruse than Yates's story. "I felt like I'd led Dick to slaughter," said Metz. Yates sat glowering as one academic after another implied—or seemed to imply—that the story was a bit *sentimental* and overly *autobiographical* (and really was it *fiction* at all? and really what does one *mean* by "fiction"?). Finally a math professor from the Orkney Islands, trying to be kind perhaps, wondered aloud how one *does* go about distancing oneself from one's work and hence *avoiding* sentimentality? Yates slumped so low that Metz thought he might put his head down on the table; on top of everything else, the math professor had a funny accent and that seemed the last straw for Yates. *"I don't have to answer the goddamn question!"* he suddenly erupted. There was a silence, and then the meeting was adjourned. Yates remained in his seat until he and Metz were alone. "Fucking sons of bitches!" he resumed. "Why do I come to these goddamn academic conferences?"

Once the ordeal was over, though, Yates made a remarkable recovery. That night Metz gave a raucous party, during which they broke out a twelve-foot collapsible tunnel for children; the idea was to crawl through without spilling your drink, as well as to peek at and poke the behind of the person in front of you. Yates was delighted by the high jinks, and finally transported into laughing, cheering, floor-pounding ecstasy when three pretty coeds did a dance-and-kick rendition of "Shuffle Off to Buffalo."

Yates's sister died in May, three months short of her forty-seventh birthday. Oddly enough, she'd briefly managed to quit drinking a few months prior to that final visit from her brother the summer before; her son Peter had researched a rehabilitation facility in Vermont, and while Fred vetoed the idea, his son's concern seemed to shame him into making a last effort to "handle" the matter on his own. For a while, then, the goaded Ruth gorged herself with sweets and stayed mostly sober—but Fred kept drinking, and soon she gave up the struggle for good. "With a different husband she might have pulled through," said her sister-in-law Louise. "But Fred and Ruth had a symbiotic effect on each other—it was a 'Days of Wine and Roses' situation." One night their oldest son, Fred junior, got a call from his father, who was in a drunken stupor and needed the young man to drive Ruth to the hospital: She was sick, he said; she'd taken a fall. Fred junior found his mother more or less sober, though she had a large bruise on one side of her face—hardly uncommon, since she often fell and bruised easily because of liver damage. Three days later she died in the hospital of cirrhosis.

Yates was not surprised by the news (nor was Martha, whose immediate thought on meeting Ruth was "She's done for"); he professed to be relieved that her "miserable life" was over, and arranged to leave immediately for an early-summer trip to New York. The graveside service in St. James was remarkably similar to Sarah Grimes's interment in *The Easter Parade*: Fred Rodgers arrived at the cemetery tipsy and befuddled, supported by a huddle of friends from Grumman, and like his alter ego Tony Wilson he repeatedly "knif[ed] the flat of his hand straight ahead from the temple" and mumbled something like, "Straight ahead: don't look right, don't look left, don't look back." Later there was a beery gathering at High Hedges, where Fred's buddies jollied him along with old stories, and his son Peter alertly attended to the other guests. Martha approvingly described the mood as "joyful" ("Ruth had been out of reach for a long time—whatever they'd known of her was gone"). But Fred junior left early that night—"sick, in shock"—and later, after most of the guests had gone, Fred senior sat in the dining room with his sister and broke down crying. "He wasn't good at communicating deep feelings," she said, "but in an odd way there was a great love between him and Ruth." Fred remarried less than a year later but often spoke vaguely of "mistakes" he'd made in his first marriage. He outlived Ruth by twenty-seven years.

"Your brother killed my sister," Yates said to Louise Rodgers on the train back to Manhattan.* She replied to the effect that the matter was more complicated than that; she'd always regarded Yates as something of a malcontent, particularly where family was concerned. As for Martha, she found it fascinating that Louise, a charming, intelligent woman, had nothing but admiration for *Dookie* of all people and would only laugh when Yates tried to remonstrate with her. He'd always led Martha to believe that his mother was ridiculous at best, and at worst a monster of feckless egoism.

Yates was still in New York when Robert Kennedy was assassinated. A month before, he'd written his old Justice Department colleague Barrett Prettyman that the world seemed "more hopeful now than at any time since God knows when—Johnson out, the Paris talks on, and an election shaping up in which Our Side looks likely to win." By "Our Side" Yates meant liberals in general who opposed the war, *not* die-hard Kennedy partisans such as Prettyman: "I don't mean to be disloyal," he added, "but I'm wearing a McCarthy sticker on the back bumper of my car. It was purchased before RFK declared his candidacy, but I haven't taken it off yet because RFK hasn't yet said anything big enough to convince me that he'd be a better President." Such sentiments notwithstanding, Wendy

*According to the oldest son Fred—who takes a very dim view of his father—Ruth's autopsy showed cirrhosis as the sole cause of death, and indeed most (if not all) of her occasional bruises seem to have been caused by the falls to which she was prone in later years. Yates's reasoned view of his sister's death was not so much that her husband caused it with a single beating or shove, but rather "with twenty-five years of brutality and stupidity and neglect," as Emily Grimes puts it.

Sears spotted Yates at the requiem for RFK at St. Patrick's Cathedral; he made himself conspicuous by proceeding uncertainly up the aisle to take a Communion wafer. Afterward she caught up with him outside the church: Had he converted to Catholicism, or was his interest in the Eucharist just a tribute to his old employer? "Jesus," said the flustered Yates, "I was just following the crowd!"

He wouldn't follow it for long, though not even Yates was wholly immune to RFK's peculiar charm. Later that summer he wrote another, condoling letter to Prettyman, referring to Kennedy's death as a "hideous loss" and expressing chagrin over the unseemly pro-McCarthy message of his previous letter: "I didn't realize how ready and eager I was to have my mind changed until it was too late. For whatever it's worth, let me tell you that McCarthy now seems very pale indeed, as does every other national political figure." This was somewhat for Prettyman's benefit, but at the time Kennedy's death genuinely affected Yates as a sorrow both personal and political. As the years passed, however, he became more and more impatient with any hint of Kennedy hagiography, until he eventually lumped RFK into his general indictment of the brothers as overrated, phony, out for number one, and ruthless.

Yates spent much of the fall in pencil-chewing seclusion with his manuscript; he'd recently stumbled on the information that more than 50 percent of first novelists never publish a second novel ("that scares the shit out of me"), and more than ever he just wanted to be shut of the thing. In November he mailed what he "hoped was a finished novel" to Gottlieb, who "didn't like it but came up with three or four very good ideas about how it could be revised and improved": Apparently Gottlieb suggested that he cut a gratuitous final chapter, as well as tweak the Alice Prentice material in ways that might bring about a slight further refinement of the structure.* For another two months, then, Yates was "up to [his] ass" in

---

*Unlike the rest of his published work, Yates did not preserve any drafts of *A Special Providence*, his least favorite novel. Beyond a point, then, one can only speculate on the revision process, based on oblique references in letters as well as the uncertain testimony of a few interview subjects. As for Robert Gottlieb, he vaguely remembers Yates ("a tall, good-looking fellow"), but has entirely

further repairs, but finally relinquished the thing for good in February. He'd even come up with a title—*A Special Providence*—after discarding such recent ideas as *A Letter Home* and *The Wine of Astonishment*. Indeed the title may have been the one thing about the book he definitely liked, though he had to concede a heady sense of liberation now that his joyless, eight-year ordeal was over. As he wrote Prettyman, "[The novel] may not be very good—I suspect it is nowhere near as good as my first one—but the beautiful thing about it now is that it's done and off my back, leaving me free to write other and maybe better novels." And then there was always the chance his pessimism was misplaced: Not only did Gottlieb profess to like the book, he even went so far as to list by name all the *other* people at Knopf who liked it—sales and publicity people at that.

What with his regular income and leftover Rockefeller money, Yates found himself rather flush when he received the nine thousand dollars due on delivery of his manuscript. Never mind that he now had a daughter at Bennington, one of the most expensive colleges in the country; it was time to celebrate—the curse of his second novel was lifted (so it seemed), he'd never given Martha a proper honeymoon, and after all, *Money is to spend*. Thus he decided to take his wife on a grand tour that summer.

They departed at the beginning of June, stopping in New York on the way. A night was spent with the Styrons in Connecticut, and Yates was in high spirits for most of the visit: His hosts went out of their way to put his shy wife at ease, and it may have gratified Yates for Martha to witness his friendship with such an eminent man. Later, however, they had dinner at the home of playwright Arthur Miller, whom Martha described as a "full-time celebrity": "He was very imposing and gruff," she recalled. "Everything was *Marilyn* this and *Marilyn* that, or else he'd name-drop some other famous person." Intimidated, neither Yates nor Martha said a single word during the entire meal.

---

forgotten the fact that he worked on Yates's second novel. It seems improbable, anyway, that Gottlieb "didn't like" that penultimate draft; his correspondence is nothing but encouraging.

They'd originally planned to rent a flat in London, though Yates may have figured the nostalgia would soon turn sour. Whatever the case, they passed only a few "idle, boozy" days there: Yates visited his old neighborhood in South Kensington, and possibly became as moody as his character Jack Flanders when he encountered his old flat at Two Neville Terrace, or when the bartender at the Anglesea failed to recognize him. Maybe not, though: Martha doesn't recall any such tiresomeness at that stage of the trip, and in fact Yates received some very heartening news there: His agent in London, Monica McCall reported, was "*very* high on [his] book."

He was in excellent fettle by the time they got to Ireland, where they rented a car and drove around the countryside for two weeks. Yates loved everything about the place—especially the people, who shared his fondness for drinking, singing, and talking (unpretentiously) about literature. Yates made friends at every pub; they valued him as a writer, and laughed when he'd mention, for instance, that *his* favorite lines of poetry were "*Fly*/ing too *high*/with some *guy*/in the *sky* . . ." The only drawback was Yates's driving—as ever, he refused to let a woman take the wheel, while he himself drove "like he'd never quite caught on"—which made their progress "maddeningly slow" as the white-knuckled Yates negotiated narrow winding lanes. Still, Martha considered Ireland the happiest time of the marriage.

They should have stayed in Ireland. The reasons Yates hadn't liked Paris almost twenty years earlier still applied: His French was a joke and the Parisians treated it as such, and all he wanted in the way of haute cuisine was a good steak. Also, though Martha herself spoke a little French—ergo a little more than her husband—Yates wouldn't let her order in restaurants, while he invariably became flustered when a "snooty" waiter seemed amused by his accent, to say nothing of his philistine tastes. Soon—quite like his own Jack Flanders—Yates was "trudg[ing] along with a look of petulant bewilderment in his eyes . . . the picture of a bumbling American tourist."

But amid such dreariness he'd at least looked forward to dinner with his French publisher, Jean Rosenthal, a charming man who'd personally translated Yates's first two books to impressive acclaim. The evening promised to redeem the whole Paris debacle: Rosenthal and his wife took their guests to an excellent restaurant, and far from snickering at Yates's preference for *bifteck saignant* (while Martha tried snails for the first time), Rosenthal lauded the author as one of the great hopes of American literature and so forth. Alas, all this was by way of sweetening the pill, and once the plates were cleared the Frenchman got down to business: He regretted to report that Éditions Robert Laffont had decided *not* to publish Yates's second novel. Rosenthal had found the book very "moving and sensitive," and if it had been written by a French author they wouldn't have *hesitated* to publish; *however.* . . . "Dick was like a deflating balloon," Martha recalled. When Rosenthal noticed the effect his words were having, he hastily dropped the matter and cast about for happier themes. But the damage was done, and Yates proceeded to get drunker than his wife had ever seen him. Later Rosenthal wrote a letter expanding tactfully on the points he'd deferred over dinner. He discussed the commercial risk of foreign novels—translation costs, sparse reviews, the high retail price of a longish book such as Yates's—none of which would have mattered, of course, were it not for the following: "I do like the book and I think that the portrait of Alice is excellent and of a vivid accuracy. But as I had begun to tell you in Paris, the war part—interesting as it may be—has not the same stamp of deep originality. To put it bluntly, it is in the same vein as many war novels and it is a long section of the book."

That was pretty blunt, all right, and for the rest of the vacation Yates was decidedly poor company. Rosenthal, a man whose judgment he trusted, had told him almost exactly what he'd feared all along: He'd be a laughingstock once the novel was published, and everyone would say *Revolutionary Road* had been a fluke.

Martha tried to cheer him up, but it was no good. "He was a mess. *Very* depressed: not just flat, but very very *sad*. Everything was pointless, ridiculous." While in Cannes—where Yates had written his first publishable fiction as a sickly yet still hopeful young man—the enraptured Martha ventured to remark on the beauty of the prospect: the moonless Mediterranean, the glittering lights of town, the marvelous blackness of the sky. *"Don't give me that poetic bullshit about a black sky!"* Yates exploded.

They also went to Rome, Lisbon, and finally Madrid, where all the gifts Martha had bought for her family were stolen out of the rental car. Yates told her to buy more, and kept drinking. The only time he laughed, and then bitterly, was when she worried about how much money they were spending.

Shortly after their return to Iowa in August, Yates received the rather anti-climactic news that his mother had died. Martha and Monica were on hand when he got the phone call from Central Islip, and both remember his matter-of-fact tone as he agreed to the various funeral arrangements.* But afterward he seemed pensive and remote—"perhaps fretful over the fact that he didn't feel worse about it," said Monica. He also might have been somewhat bemused by the way his mother's death had coincided with the publication (two months later) of a book that would have destroyed her if she had been alive and lucid. His "fair Texan" Carole had once observed that he couldn't finish the novel "because it is much harder to kill a mother than it is to kill a wife," and she remarked on how "scared" Yates had looked when she said as much (though it's possible she misconstrued an exasperated silence on Yates's part).

A far greater concern at the time was his daughter Sharon, who'd flunked out of Bennington after the spring term. In recent years her adolescent rebellion had taken increasingly disturbing forms: In Mahopac she fought constantly with her mother, and broke curfew to attend forbidden

---

*Martha said that Yates settled the matter over the phone and didn't go back to New York for the funeral. All three of Ruth's children, however, recall seeing him there—indeed say it was their last meeting with "Uncle Dick." Also (for what it's worth), Emily Grimes attends Pookie's funeral in *The Easter Parade*—a scene depicted with the same vivid particularity as the graveside service for Sarah Grimes, which of course *was* based on firsthand observation. Still, I can find no compelling evidence that Yates made a special trip to New York for his mother's funeral, nor do I find it plausible for any number of reasons. As for the hesitant testimony of his niece and nephews, I daresay they've conflated the memory of Yates's presence at their mother's funeral, which, after all, was just over a year before Dookie's.

parties at the old Babaril estate; she drank, smoked pot, and was rightly suspected of worse. Sheila accused her of becoming unstable "just like [her] father," which tended to provoke Sharon into a shrill defense of the man as one of the most *feeling* people she knew. But when Yates himself expressed pique over her "irresponsible, aimless" life, she'd accuse him of trying to "control" her and make her a "carbon copy" of him. Finally, having finished high school a semester early, she ran away from home and joined some "cool creeps" (as Yates called them) in Andes, New York, where they proposed to start a ski lodge but mostly sat around getting stoned and sleeping.

Yates was somewhat mollified when Sharon started college in spring 1968, though he'd hoped for the corrective gentility of a proper "Eastern women's college" rather than an "arty-farty," dubiously coed place like Bennington. When Yates heard she had a boyfriend of sorts, he was disgusted: "What kind of *guy* goes to Bennington?" he remarked to a friend. "And then hangs around! And he's with my daughter!" Before long an effete boyfriend would be the least of his worries. For her winter work-study interval, Sharon packed off to yet another hippie "ski resort" in Manchester: "With time on my hands," she wrote her father, "in the hills of Vermont, I'll be able to work on learning to sit and concentrate on one thing"—a habit she'd admittedly failed to cultivate at Bennington. "My whole generation is running," she noted in closing, "just as hard as I was, and we all help each other." At the very least Yates must have rolled his eyes at that particular envoi, and meanwhile his disdain for hippies would have certainly been aroused by the scene in Manchester, which was rather like the scene in Andes the year before.

The bewildered girl bottomed out that summer in Boston, where she'd washed up with one of her classmates. The latter's boyfriend was a chemistry major from Brandeis who supported himself by making and selling LSD, and Sharon spent much of the summer in a psychedelic haze. It was tolerable as long as she had companions, but in the fall her roommate went back to Bennington and suddenly she found herself stoned among relative strangers, and living in a "horrible flop." Around this time she was "rescued" by her father—an incident he reluctantly saw fit to fictionalize in *Young Hearts Crying*, though Sharon claims she

wasn't as luridly strung out as Laura Davenport. "Dad called one morning after a party, and I was a little fuzzy," she remembered. "He got all
worked up: 'My God, what are you taking? I'm gonna come out and get
you!' I decided maybe it wasn't such a bad idea." As good as his word,
Yates caught the first plane to Boston and brought his daughter back to
Iowa with him.

For the rest of that year she lived in the stone cottage with Yates and
Martha. At first she remained a bit slow on the uptake, and her father
arranged for her to see a psychiatrist; the man diagnosed her as having
suffered a drug-induced psychotic episode and prescribed Thorazine,
which she soon stopped taking. "I was depressed and found it hard to
concentrate," she said, "but not really psychotic—I felt *overwhelmed* by
reality, not out of touch with it." Meanwhile her father's attitude seemed
rather inscrutable at times: On the one hand he was glad to have her
home and eager to do what he could to help, but often he seemed very
irritable about things. Her depressive moping grated on his nerves, and
when she confided details of her life in Bennington and Boston, he'd
sometimes respond with neutral interest and sometimes with rage. "How
could you *do* something so stupid!" he erupted—understandably—when
she mentioned how she'd once spent her entire semester's allowance on
wholesale hash, most of which she'd smoked herself rather than selling at
a profit as intended. What seemed odd, though, was that Yates's
responses one way or the other were hard to predict, no matter *what* was
being discussed. "He was never really well even when he was well," said
Sharon, who around this time gained particular insight into her father's
condition. "Just in general he'd often say irrational, irrelevant things."
She once mentioned a roommate who had a black boyfriend,
and Yates said the girl was just trying to spite her parents; when Sharon
calmly tried to explain ("No, they went to high school together and he's
really a nice guy" etc.), her father snapped "Why *else* would she do that?
Girls like Negroes because they have big penises!" At his best, Yates was
incapable of such a benighted remark—but there it was. "I'd blink at
him and get quiet," said Sharon, "and he'd go off and have a drink. He
didn't seem aware of his own strange behavior, though if I got tearful
he'd apologize."

Martha made the situation not only bearable but "pretty jolly." The better to leave Yates alone during his grouchy working hours, the women enrolled in a typing course and kept each other company. Each acted as a kind of calming buffer between the other and Yates, and there was no friction whatsoever between themselves. ("Will you guys stop *fighting* already?" Yates wryly remarked, when the two had a laughing disagreement over how to cook mushrooms.) Still, Yates was eager for his daughter to go back to college, and she was only too happy to oblige, as she missed the company of people her own age. Martha advised her to look at small liberal arts colleges—less conservative than Carleton, if a bit more so than Bennington—but Sharon disliked the hassle of ordering catalogs and writing application essays. One day she stopped at the Iowa admissions office and filled out an application (no essays), and was promptly accepted for the following semester. In January she moved to a dormitory.

Publication was always an unnerving experience for Yates, particularly so in the case of *A Special Providence*: He remained convinced that the book was an inferior performance, that after the eight-year wait reviewers were bound to be disappointed. What made matters worse (throughout his career) was the baldly autobiographical nature of the work: Though in time Yates would grow convinced that such material—*if* properly crafted—was not only valid but rather crucial, he never got used to the humiliation of exposing himself in public, of "dropping [his] pants in Macy's window" as he put it.

His terrible fragility was well known to friends, who did their best to reassure him. "I imagine you are now going through the traditional big sweat in anticipation of the publication of a new book," wrote Vonnegut, "and I'll guess that it is tougher for you than it is for most people. . . . Because you're you. For you, things are tougher." Vonnegut urged his friend to keep it all in perspective: "Every good writer I know acknowledges you as a master. . . . So—carry on. But you've already won." When the book was published in October, though, such personal admiration did little to lessen Yates's gloom over poor sales and scant reviews. "It is a beautiful book," wrote Joan Didion, and Styron sent a congratulatory telegram: HOPE YOU SAW EXCELLENT REVIEW CURRENT HARPERS FINE STUFF I FIND CRITIC AND ALL TRUE. Yates may have been relieved to know he still enjoyed Styron's good opinion, and the *Harper's* review was indeed fine ("Yates presents with no sentimentality a story that is all but heartbreaking"), but he couldn't help dwelling on the fact that, say, the daily *New York Times* had ignored the book entirely. And still his friends assured him that, far from disgracing himself, he'd written a very good novel—certainly better than what he'd led them to expect. "I remember how many times you called your book . . . a piece of shit," wrote Dubus. "So I expected [it] to be a piece of shit, barely and finally released from the anguished bowels of a weeping man. . . . Not so. I find it a wonderful fucking novel." But in the meantime Bantam had passed on the paperback rights, and such slights meant to Yates that the novel was *no damn good,* period. By the end of November he was so despondent that Martha called Robin Metz (and presumably others), begging him to hurry up and finish the book so he could praise it, persuasively, to Yates. This Metz did, addressing what he knew to be the particular concerns of the author: "What do Alice Prentice's dreams and delusions *mean* unless we see them juxtaposed against the mud and slop, the weariness of marching?" In short the book held together after all, and wasn't the mishmash Yates suspected it was.

Because the novel wasn't widely reviewed, Yates assumed that "a lot of people didn't think much of it," which may or may not have been so; nevertheless, the actual reception was by no means the disaster he'd anticipated. There were no outright pans among the major reviews, all of which acknowledged Yates's skill. Joyce Carol Oates in *The Nation* noted the novel's similarity to the "disturbing and prophetic" *Revolutionary Road,* insofar as both explore "various contemporary delusions" such as the common tendency among Americans not to accept "[their] own mediocrity": "A sad, gray, deathly world," Oates concluded, "—dreams without substance—aging without maturity: This is Yates's world, and it is a disturbing one." John Thompson's review in *Harper's* (the one that caught Styron's eye) was an almost unequivocal rave: He called the novel "straightforward, intelligent, and clearly written," and referred to the "bad luck" of Alice Prentice as being "so quotidian, so possible, so plausible, that it is more terrifying to read of it than to read of the disasters and massacres of kings."

Yates's pessimism was somewhat vindicated by Elizabeth Dalton's belated notice in the December 14 *New York Times Book Review*: "[*A Special Providence*] is in some essential ways an honest and intelligent novel," she began, "and yet it fails, finally, to be a moving or exciting one." Dalton thought the war sections the strongest of the book, though "the effect of [Prentice's] mediocrity is to deprive his conflict of urgency and significance." As for Alice, she is "simply too thin and pathetic a character to support much attention." Even Yates's "clarity and precision of detail" was viewed as a lapse of sorts, since "so heavy an air of patient skill hangs over much of the writing that the book seems almost embalmed in good craftsmanship." And finally one can almost picture Yates nodding his head in masochistic agreement with Dalton's coup de grace—to wit, that the childhood section "seems remote" to the rest of the narrative, "and its placement in the middle, between the two halves of Robert's war adventures, gives the novel a queer, broken-backed structure."

Revealingly—though hardly for the first time—Yates's craftsmanship was held against him, damned as both excessive *and* lacking, at a time when a fastidious concern for "structure" and "style" was viewed with suspicion or outright indifference. Somewhere in the subtext of Dalton's review was perhaps a thought shared by other critics who were too bored by Yates's latest to bother reviewing it: Namely, if the man insisted on writing a traditional realistic novel—a *war* novel for that matter, a *coming-of-age* novel—then it had better have a sound narrative structure, but really, why write such a book in the first place? Hadn't anyone told Yates that "the true enemies of the novel [are] plot, character, setting, and theme" (as postmodernist John Hawkes had summed it up)? That the so-called New Journalists had usurped the conventions of fiction in order to dramatize a reality that seemed to baffle the imagination, while novelists were left to challenge the very nature of "reality" itself (and hence the authorities behind it) with wacky surrealistic satire and/or formal experiment?

Yates knew all about it, of course, though perhaps even he was startled by how far things had gone. Fred Chappell, in his 1971 essay on

Revolutionary Road, noted the "inglorious" literary fads that had helped consign Yates's reputation to near-oblivion in the space of ten years, and quoted the poet Randall Jarrell to good effect: "It is hard to write even a competent naturalistic story, and when you have written it what happens?—someone calls it a competent naturalistic story." With *A Special Providence* Yates had again written such a story, and to detractors he'd chosen an even more hackneyed subject than the suburbs—that is, World War II, about which any number of sensitive young men had been writing for almost a quarter century. Such a novel should at least possess the stylistic verve or the *relevance* of a *Slaughterhouse Five* or a *Catch-22,* whose "black humor" pointed up the absurdity of war at any time or place, and whose "real" subject was of course the contemporary war in Vietnam.

But finally what galled Yates most was that *A Special Providence* simply wasn't good enough to overcome current trends; also, that he'd wasted so much time on it. Eight years ago he'd had the idea of writing a "direct autobiographical blowout" about the war—to be exact, about a young man who is disabused of his romanticism by the ordeal of war. But such a story was familiar, to say the least, and whatever had struck Yates as momentous about his own experience seemed less so in retrospect; hence the long struggle to *form* the material in such a way that made it fresh and avoided what Yates called "the two terrible traps that lie in the path of autobiographical fiction—self-pity and self-aggrandizement."

The result was a noble failure, at least by Yates's standards. Jean Rosenthal had it right when he called the war sections "interesting" but not particularly original. Yates remembered his own infantry experience as alternately tedious and terrifying, and he rendered it with a number of vivid details: the "smell of mildew and rubber and his own breath," as Prentice tries not to vomit in his gas mask; the corpses' eyes "like dusty marbles"; the soldier Krupka who "sat on the chest of the bespectacled corpse and spooned up his can of dehydrated eggs, which were almost exactly the color of the dead man's flesh." But the images of corpses and basic training and war in general had long been exhausted by books and the movies, and their reanimation required a more novel viewpoint than that of a romantic and rather typically self-conscious young man. Yates knew this, and "after much labor and much to [his] chagrin" realized that no amount of polishing and fine writing and craft could quite overcome the fallacy of his approach, to say nothing of the fundamental insincerity at the bottom of it—that is, the fact that Yates himself was *not* particularly disillusioned by the war, and really had no strongly defined point of view at all, much less a novel one.

But faced with the artistic challenge of posing *disillusionment* as the defining factor in Prentice's development—and thus linking the latter's war experience to his childhood—Yates resorted to the mechanical formula of a movie motif, whereby the reader is reminded every so often that Prentice has yet to cast off his mother's romanticism: Thus he imagines himself carrying a wounded buddy in the manner of Lew Ayres in *All Quiet on the Western Front,* or labors at seducing a woman by lighting two cigarettes at a time like Paul Henreid in *Now, Voyager,* and so on. All of which culminates in a labored epiphany devised to meet the needs of Yates's synthetic theme, however lacking in spontaneity or psychological plausibility. "No account ever really needed to be settled," Prentice reflects after bravely taking a beating from a bigger soldier;

> nothing ever really needed to be proved. Everything would always come right in the end as long as a couple of good guys went up behind the barn and had it out, as long as a mother fell on her knees and offered all her thanks to God and they played the Star-Spangled Banner on the radio. That was what these voices had to say; that was their lying sentimental message, and it all went down as smoothly as the pancakes and jelly.

Whereupon Prentice vomits up the pancakes and jelly, and hence rejects the sentimental values of America, the movies, and his mother—rather patly, not to say sentimentally, as doubtless Yates himself suspected. And so as a kind of corrective he finally asserts that "all [Prentice] knew with any clarity was that he was nineteen years old, that the war was over, and that he was alive." That was all the nineteen-year-old Yates had known as well.

But he never had to strain after meaning or originality where his childhood was concerned, and the book comes alive whenever it returns to Alice Prentice. The theme associated with the character, that of a "special providence," is not superimposed for the sake of craft, but rather reflects the essential delusion of people such as Alice-Dookie—that is, that they are gifted, among the world's golden people, and that God (or somebody) will always provide. Alice's refusal to face reality leads her and Bobby into disaster time and again, and yet if she were level-headed like her "dreary" ex-husband ("I've got a good amateur voice, that's all"), life would be intolerable. Having committed herself to the fiction that she is "remarkable and gifted and brave"—a noble fugitive from a dull provincial family and husband, from all the dull conventions of average people—Alice would rather endure hardship than resign herself to being merely "reasonable." And in fact the bland, uncertain rewards of reality aren't enough for *anybody,* much less modestly talented people such as Alice, though most of us learn to live with our compromises. Those who don't are ultimately left with only God to believe in them, and perhaps with the comfort of a cocktail that's still nearly two-thirds full.

Alice's self-deception borders on the pathological, so that her striving has both a universal and larger-than-life aspect. Her son Robert, though, is not so compelling: His desire to be a hero, or at least a competent soldier, is surely typical of most young men at war, and hardly requires a fantastically deluded mother as an explanatory factor. Moreover, Robert's role in the flashback section is rather incidental, while Alice is all but absent (even by implication) from the war section; if the flashback had been given from Robert's (rather than Alice's) point of view, it might have related more clearly to the rest of the book, but then those particular scenes would have been weakened in the process. Which is to say, alas, that the two stories really *don't* belong in the same novel—not ideally anyway, not in a novel written by a man who believed *structure* was among the highest virtues of narrative art ("Don't be seduced by prose, Grace; the point is *structure*").

But Alice alone is worth the price of admission, so to speak, and there's much to commend in every part of the book, whether or not it all works as a whole. In a better world, then, *A Special Providence* would have been treated as a noteworthy transitional effort by a writer of the first rank, who'd already produced two arguable classics; instead it was all but ignored by reviewers and public alike, dismissed as Just Another War

Novel. And meanwhile nobody loathed the book more than its author, who considered omitting it from future pages listing "Other Books by Richard Yates." At the time he comforted himself with the prospect of writing "better and easier" books, but first he'd have to get his confidence back, and that would prove a long, ravaging process. "Let's see," he later said to a friend. "I guess I first got to know you right around the end of the sixties, right? Just about the time I started falling apart. . . ."

Richard Yates and his sister, Ruth, shortly before their parents' divorce in 1929. Ruth would always say that her childhood in Hastings-on-Hudson was the happiest time of her life. *(Courtesy of Peter Rodgers)*

LEFT: Ruth Maurer ("Dookie") Yates, sculpting one of her garden figures: "Her idea was that any number of rich people, all of them gracious and aristocratic, would soon discover her . . . and they would want to make her their friend for life." *(Courtesy of Sharon Yates Levine)*

RIGHT: Vincent Matthew Yates, "an operatic tenor lost among the salesmen." *(Courtesy of Sharon Yates Levine)*

Mrs. Ruth Yates' latest carving for the "Sports Hall of Fame" is a head of Joe Louis, heavyweight champion boxer. Mrs. Yates, a celebrated New York sculptress, is shown here with her work. The admirers are her children.

Dookie's children watch admiringly as she sculpts a head of heavyweight champion Joe Louis. *(Courtesy of Ruth Rodgers Ward)*

Yates as an unhappy fourth-former at Avon Old Farms: "The kid was a mess. His tweed suit hung greasy with lack of cleaning, his necktie was a twisted rag, his long fingernails were blue, and he needed a haircut."

A behatted and somewhat happier Yates during his second year at Avon. *(Courtesy of Lothar Candels)*

Top Row (*left to right*) Richardson, Allen R., Zabriskie, Covey, Laird, MacMath, Sproule, Peck
Bottom Row (*left to right*) Jennings, Ordway, Wright, Yates, McMichael, McCorkle, Olney, Pratt

Yates was a conscientious editor-in-chief of the school newspaper, *The Avonian*. His friends Ernest "Bicky" Wright and Hugh Pratt were also on the staff. "Dick ran everything of a literary nature," one classmate recalled. "He might have been the only one of us who knew exactly what he wanted to do with his life—become a writer of fiction." *(Courtesy of Avon Old Farms School)*

Yates's persona as a maverick littérateur—and devoted smoker—was complete by his senior year: "Cigarettes were a great help because any big-eyed, full-lipped boy could be made to look all right if he smoked all the time." *(Courtesy of Avon Old Farms School)*

RICHARD WALDEN YATES
NEW YORK, NEW YORK

FELLOW members of the Midnight Oil League, stumbling into a
blue hazed room have often found Dick bent over his half-written
novel. Of course the ever present pot of coffee and pack of cigarettes are
found beside his manuscript, temporarily neglected in favor of a nocturnal
bull session. In Dick's opinion cigarettes, coffee, and night hours are essential
to the art of fiction.

Dick has his less abstract side too. After Bicky's departure he took over
the dormitory inspectorship in the top of one
building. The school paper is another of his
fields. As Editor during his last two years,
Dick's familiar figure has been seen many a
Tuesday afternoon, draped in a pair of gray
trousers and a wilted blue shirt, as he strides
about with a harassed look. At five fifteen he
totters into the Avon Club, lights the usual
cigarette, and falls on the most comfortable
sofa. The crisis has passed and our next
Avonian will come out after all. When not
engaged in any of these activities Dick could
be found cartooning, either for amusement or
for the *Winged Beaver* where he served two
years as Art Editor. This year the *Winged
Beaver* also received his services as Associate
Editor. He does plan a college education and
a career as professional writer, but that must
wait until peace.

One of Yates's cartoons for the
Winged Beaver. Almost the entire
class of 1944 was inducted into the
army upon graduation. *(Courtesy
of Avon Old Farms School)*

Sheila Bryant in the late-forties, when she first met Yates: "She was tall and slender with rich dark red hair and a pretty, bony face that could sometimes look warily stern, as if the world were trying to put something over on her." *(Courtesy of Sharon Yates Levine)*

Yates's sister, Ruth, and her husband, Fred ("He looks just like Laurence Olivier!"), with their children, Fred Junior and Peter, in 1945. *(Courtesy of Fred Rodgers, Jr.)*

Yates and Sheila in the early fifties. *(Courtesy of Sharon Yates Levine)*

Yates, Sheila, and their daughter Sharon in the South of France, 1952. Yates, recently released from a tuberculosis sanitarium, spent his days writing and smoking. *(Courtesy of Sharon Yates Levine)*

Yates and Robert Riche after the 1956 Harvard-Yale game. Riche was a partial model for Frank Wheeler in *Revolutionary Road* and sole model (to his great dismay) for Bill Brock in *Young Hearts Crying. (Courtesy of Robert Riche)*

Yates's publisher and sometime friend, Seymour Lawrence, in 1955. *(Courtesy of Merloyd Lawrence)*

Yates with his daughters Monica (the toddler) and Sharon in 1958, at home in their rented cottage on the "Babaril" estate in Mahopac, New York. *(Courtesy of Sharon Yates Levine)*

Yates's sister, Ruth, in the late-fifties. *(Courtesy of Fred Rodgers, Jr.)*

Barbara Beury, Yates's "Sweet Briar Sweetie." *(Courtesy of Barbara Beury McCallum)*

Jerry and Grace Schulman in the early sixties. "Knowing you both was one of the very few things that kept me sane during all those frantic, dismal years of my second bachelorhood," Yates wrote the couple. *(Courtesy of Grace Schulman)*

Natalie Bowen, partial model for Emily Grimes in *The Easter Parade. (Courtesy of Natalie Bowen)*

Yates and Wendy Sears outside her Georgetown apartment in 1963. "I have a new girlfriend," Yates informed his friends, "and she has really *sturdy* parents." *(Courtesy of Wendy Sears Grassi)*

Yates trying to look "ballsy" for the jacket of *Eleven Kinds of Loneliness*. *(Courtesy of Grace Schulman)*

Yates in a vulnerable, unposed moment. His "girlishly round" eyes and "Aubrey Beardsley mouth" were features he despised, and usually he squinted and grimaced a little for photographs. *(Courtesy of Wendy Sears Grassi)*

A rather sickly, depressed Yates during his first year at the Iowa Workshop, 1964. "I think we all wanted to be Richard Yates," said his student Robert Lacy. "He was tall, lanky, and movie-star handsome back then, and he moved in an aura of sad, doom-haunted, F. Scott Fitzgeraldian grace." *(Courtesy of Lyn Lacy)*

Yates and Martha's wedding at the First Presbyterian Church in Iowa City, January 20, 1968. Said Yates's colleague Bill Murray, "Here was this very ordinary, sweet girl, dressed like a June bride, walking into a maelstrom." *(Courtesy of Martha Speer)*

Yates in his classroom at the Iowa Workshop, 1969. Standing beside him is the novelist Tom McHale, a student. *(Courtesy of John P. Lowens)*

Yates and Martha entertain friends at the stone cottage in Iowa City, 1969. From right: Yates, Martha, Jill Van Cleve, Phyllis and Bob Lehrman. *(Courtesy of John P. Lowens)*

Martha and Yates in Ireland during their belated honeymoon, 1969. Martha remembered the first two weeks of this trip as the happiest time in their marriage. (*Courtesy of Martha Speer*)

Yates and Martha were interviewed by the local newspaper shortly after their arrival in Wichita, 1971. Yates frequently referred to Kansas as "up the river." (*Courtesy of Martha Speer*)

Martha, Yates, and Monica in
Wichita, 1971. *(Courtesy of
Julia Munson)*

The Crossroads Irish Pub on the corner of Beacon Street and Massachusetts Avenue. Yates ate almost every meal
there during his eleven years in Boston. *(Courtesy of Emma Brinkmeyer)*

A cartoon Yates drew of himself
and his youngest daughter, Gina.
(Courtesy of Martha Speer)

GINA AND DAD

Yates and Gina in Durango, Colorado, 1979.
(Courtesy of Gina Yates)

Yates and his friend Seymour Krim in New York, 1982. The two writers were both in the midst of a long and lonely bachelorhood. *(Courtesy of Sharon Yates Levine)*

Yates and Andre Dubus after a reading in the early eighties. The two men loved and admired each other to the end. "Richard Yates is one of our great writers with too few readers," Dubus wrote, "and no matter how many readers he finally ends up with, they will still be too few, unless there are hundreds of thousands in most nations of the world." *(Courtesy of Suzanne Dubus)*

Yates chats with his daughters Sharon and Monica at a publication party for *Young Hearts Crying* at the Plaza Hotel in Manhattan, 1984. *(Courtesy of Sharon Yates Levine)*

Yates at the Crossroads, 1986. "This is the only time I can ever remember Dick sitting at the bar," remarked the owner (and Yates's landlord) Michael Brodigan. Usually Yates preferred a booth facing the door. *(Courtesy of Michael Brodigan)*

Yates at Brodigan's house, 1986. *(Courtesy of Michael Brodigan)*

Yates sitting on the hood of his ancient Mazda, 1991. He alternately smoked and sucked air from an oxygen tank while driving, such that his students in Tuscaloosa called the car "a bomb on wheels." *(Courtesy of Gina Yates)*

Yates and Gina in front of his duplex apartment on Alaca Place, 1991. *(Courtesy of Gina Yates)*

"In the bright winter of life": Yates sitting at his L-shaped desk, about three months before his death. *(Courtesy of Gina Yates)*

CHAPTER THIRTEEN

Fun with a Stranger: 1970-1974

A *Special Providence* sold fewer than seven thousand copies and left Yates in debt to Knopf for almost thirteen thousand dollars; Dell paid only twenty-five hundred for the paperback rights and made it clear they weren't hopeful for a large sale. "But you must not brood over this," wrote Monica McCall; "it will simply be up to me to get you a sufficient advance from Bob on the new book." Meanwhile Dell was considering a new edition of *Revolutionary Road* (out of print by then) for their Contemporary Classics line, so that was a comfort.* Nor was it the only sign that Yates wasn't entirely forgotten as a force in American literature: That spring he was approached by Boston University, whose representatives were "most desirous of establishing the Richard Yates Collection," as they were certain future scholars would be studying his life and work. Yates was happy to oblige with whatever papers he had, though he regretted to inform them that he'd already "lost" all working drafts of his latest novel, *A Special Providence*.

It had taken Yates almost fourteen years to produce his first two novels, and now that he faced "the added disadvantage of being middle-aged and tired," he doubted that his output would increase. As fame and fortune had ceased to be imminent prospects, Yates was ready at last to commit himself to teaching as a career. "I've sort of decided I like [Iowa] after all," he wrote a friend, "which I never thought would happen. I guess what it amounts to is that I've proved I can't make a living in

---

*Sam Lawrence, whose imprint was then at Dell, had nothing to do with these transactions.

Hollywood or New York without scrambling my brains, which leaves the Groves of Academe as the only reasonable alternative—and these particular groves are the only ones I know." As jaded as Yates remained on the subject of "teaching" writing, the truth was he rather enjoyed it: His students brought out the best in him—modesty, candor, generosity—and more than ever he needed their admiration. Unfortunately it was "almost impossible" for Yates to write and teach at the same time (since both "require the same kind of energy"), but such was also the case with every other kind of wage slavery he'd tried, and meanwhile a man and his family had to eat.

Now that he was married and settled, Yates wanted the security of tenure as well; he was now in his fifth year at Iowa and still only a lecturer with an annual salary of twelve thousand dollars, which he bitterly attributed to his lack of an academic degree. In fact tenure was rarely awarded to Workshop faculty, since a brisk turnover was regarded as desirable for any number of reasons—not the least being that many writers were prone to burnout and proved to be mediocre teachers besides. But whatever else one could say of Yates, he wasn't mediocre, and his friend George Starbuck had recommended him for tenure before resigning as director at the end of the 1968–69 academic year.

In the fall Yates's promotion was passed by the Executive Committee of the English Department as well as the dean of the College of Liberal Arts, but his final appointment had yet to be approved. Meanwhile, a writer and Houghton-Mifflin editor, Jack Leggett, was brought in from Boston to serve as temporary director of the Workshop, and he promptly invited Yates to dinner and vice versa. Leggett was an affable man who knew of Yates through their mutual friend Sam Lawrence, and Yates assumed he'd be an ally. Frankly and rather tipsily, Yates confided his frustration over the tenure question: He'd been given to understand that approval was little more than a formality at this point, but as time dragged on he'd begun to suspect that Paul Engle "had it in for him." Engle had retired as director a few years ago when the Workshop was absorbed by the English Department, but he still exerted considerable influence behind the scenes, and Yates thought he looked like a man "slinking around with a secret."

In any case Yates hoped that Leggett would fix the matter as soon as possible. Leggett remained affably noncommittal.

Yates's suspicions were not idle paranoia. Though Paul Engle was regarded as a kind of benignant Carl Sandburg figure, he could be ruthless in protecting the interests of the Workshop—his own brainchild, after all—and that meant weeding out undesirables. Engle had attended Yates's wedding to Martha, and the men were cordial if not close; privately, though, Engle had always had qualms. During Yates's first sodden year at Iowa, he'd been protected by the formidable Cassill, who thought the vagaries of writers and Yates in particular should be pardoned as part of the psychic territory. To some extent Engle agreed, but at the same time he recognized the need for diplomatic restraint on the part of teachers and students alike, lest the Workshop's dubious reputation in the community suffer further.

Probably Yates's 1967 breakdown, what with all the odd behavior that attended it, had sealed his fate as far as Engle was concerned. After Cassill's departure Yates still had influential friends such as Bourjaily and Starbuck, but the latter was gone now, too, and other poets on the faculty were not so well disposed. While Yates was careful not to insult colleagues to their faces, he was rather infamous for regarding poets with disdain. As Robin Metz explained, "Poets were open to a kind of effete sensibility—still affected by the modernist idea that they were an academic priesthood, and they engaged in the sort of esoteric literary talk that always intimidated and angered Dick. He thought they put on pretentious airs, while prose writers were foot soldiers doing an honest and difficult job."

Ultimately, though, the poet whose opinion mattered most was Engle, and whether or not he was aware of Yates's aesthetic prejudices was probably beside the point; when he learned that someone so "unbalanced" was about to get tenure, he took immediate action. "Engle let it be known in a whispered way that I had to get rid of Yates," Leggett recalled. " 'This guy must *not* have tenure,' he said, 'otherwise we'll *never* get rid of him,' etcetera. I was the cop-sergeant getting orders from above. And [English chairman] Gerber must have concurred with Engle, since I wouldn't have done anything without his order." Leggett also remembered being approached that year by some of Yates's students, who "loved Dick but thought he was too sick to be teaching": Apparently Yates had missed a few classes and begun behaving erratically again. Martha, however, claims that his mental health and drinking were more or less under control at the time, and (as far as she knew) he never missed another class after his breakdown three years before.

The fact remained that Yates had been *promised* tenure, that he desperately needed the security to go on with his writing, and nobody wanted to break the news to him. Leggett noticed how Yates seemed to grow hostile as he began to suspect the deception, but the year passed and nobody said another straightforward word on the subject to Yates.

They waited until he'd left town in June to attend the Hollins Writing Conference in Virginia, an occasion Yates might have enjoyed under other circumstances. Organized by writer-in-residence George Garrett, the two-week conference turned into an almost legendary debauch, featuring some of the leading lights of American literature (for whose services Garrett had paid upward of five thousand dollars a head): Ralph Ellison, Styron, Peter Taylor, James Dickey, and some fifty others. "They turned the dorms into Dodge City," said Garrett, "swimming in the nude, drinking all night. Dickey came to town with a blond hooker from Miami, and the couple appeared in the Hollins alumni magazine as 'Mr. and Mrs. Dickey.'" Amid the fun Yates somberly attended to his duties and got quietly "stewed" at night. "Martha seemed a nurse," the writer Bill Harrison observed. "She propped Dick up and sat stroking his arm. My wife would just look at her and shake her head."

Yates needed the nursing. He'd received a letter on arrival ("c/o The Hollins Writing Conference") signed by his Iowa colleague Bill Murray, who sheepishly identified himself as "Acting Director" in the summertime absence of those from whom he was taking orders:

A problem has come up regarding your appointment to Associate Professor. The Administration questioned it on two grounds—the usual "ladder of promotion" is from Lecturer to Assistant Professor: Vance was promoted in this way. They also questioned the validity of making a tenured appointment when the Workshop has no Director. You know, of course, that the initial proposal for your promotion passed the Executive Committee of the Department, and through the Dean of the College of Liberal Arts as well. The question came from the Provost of the University.

John Gerber called a special meeting of the Executive Committee, and it was decided to recommend your promotion to Assistant rather than Associate Professor. The Assistant Professorship is a three-year appointment, renewable. . . . Though the promotion now is to Assistant Professor, your salary will be that promised you as Associate Professor.

Yates was devastated—as much by the cowardice and petty chicanery of it all ("The question came from the Provost of the University") as by the professional consequences to himself. Back in Iowa, he made a beeline for Leggett's office and stood glowering in the doorway while the man let him know, affably as ever, that he hadn't written a recommendation for Yates's tenure and now—well, he didn't see how he could. "That told Dick all he needed to know," said Leggett. "It was time for him to fish or cut bait."

Yates had no desire to accept the guilty sop of an assistant professorship, but as it turned out he'd be stuck at Iowa for another disgruntled year while he hunted for a job, *any* job, with a somewhat comparable salary. He even wrote to his old friend Hayes Jacobs at the New School, who jovially replied that he could get Yates as much as eight hundred dollars for a fifteen-week term, which was more than "80% of the writing faculty" were paid. Yates kept looking.

He didn't want to spend a day more in Iowa City than strictly necessary, and much of that summer was spent traveling. For a long time he'd been eager to get started on a novel about a man who goes "progressively, irredeemably crazy," and for the sake of mnemonic atmosphere he returned to the sites of his own breakdowns. For a month or so, he and Martha lived in the same raffish part of Hollywood where Yates had been arrested while emptying his wallet on Sunset Boulevard. Such research had a less than salutary effect on his morale, though he was careful not to drink too much and invite a sequel to the summer of 1965. Meanwhile Brian Moore rallied round with a party or two in the Yateses' honor. Martha observed that her husband's Hollywood friends seemed "relieved that someone was taking care of him," though Joan Didion was "chilly" toward her, and apparently Didion wasn't the only one. Years later, long after his second marriage was over, Yates was still grumbling about how certain "Hollywood writers" had been rude to his wife, though Martha wasn't particularly bothered one way or the other ("that's just the way it was"). For Yates, though, it was further proof of the corrupting influence of the place.

After a teaching visit to Central Oregon Community College, the Yateses spent a week at Bill Kittredge's home in Missoula, Montana. Yates's old roughneck buddies Bob Lacy and Jim Crumley were on hand, and the reunion was a festive respite in the midst of a trying summer. Despite the rowdiness of the younger set, Yates was adamant about sticking to his sensible drinking regime for Martha's sake. "Dick waited until the cocktail hour," said Kittredge, "but around 4:30 he'd start pacing through the house straightening pictures and checking the thermostat." As it happened, the visit was the last Kittredge ever saw of his old teacher (except for the "sad eyes" that sometimes appeared whenever he lapsed into tricky prose).

Yates continued his research in New York, lurking around Bellevue and St. Vincent's and various old haunts in the Village. Memories of his tormented "second bachelorhood," mingled with a sense of unfulfilled literary promise, left him depressed and on edge. Bob Riche was struck by the change in Yates when the two met at Warren and Marjorie Owens's house in Bethel, Connecticut. As Riche remembered, "Dick used to be so funny, but no more. Just to be provocative, I mentioned a few postrealist authors like Barth, and Martha took me aside and said 'Please don't get him upset.'" Warren Owens also noticed Martha's tendency to "cringe" at her husband's outbursts, and later she unhappily confided that she'd been having problems calming him down. Most of the night's discussion was political: One of the guests, Penny Miller, was the wife of a CBS correspondent who'd recently been killed in Vietnam, and Yates was alternately consoling and volatile in his ranting against the war— incited somewhat, perhaps, by Riche's competitive tendency to remind the room that he himself was not merely "radical" but "revolutionary." "I recall trying to say a good many loud and raucous things on *all* sides,"

Yates wrote afterward, "and finally spoiling the whole party by puking my guts out into what I believe was a very nice toilet bowl (yeah, yeah, drunk again)."

But the night had piqued Yates into thinking about the past, his own generation's political convictions, and on the plane back to Iowa he began to consider a rather peculiar nonfiction project—all the more alluring, perhaps, because his new novel had left him blocked and haunted and he was eager to put it aside, and perhaps too because he was tempted to prove he could be as "relevant" as the next writer. That fall, anyway, Yates appeared at a public reading in Iowa with two manila envelopes under his arm, one marked DISTURBING THE PEACE and the other VETERANS; he told the audience he wasn't willing to read from either, but would answer questions, most of which were in regard to the latter. As Yates subsequently described *Veterans* to the man whom it most concerned, "the 'book' might be in the form of one long letter, or possibly a series of letters, to an old friend . . . John A. Williams." He went on:

> But there *has* been a lot of "veteranship" between you and me—combat service in WWII, early marriages that didn't work, touch football, boozing, and meeting Famous Writers at Bread Loaf, the many times you tried to explain different kinds of jazz to me . . . those phone calls between us when Ed Wallant was dying; the time I woke you up . . . and made you listen to the Kennedy Civil Rights Address that never got delivered; the time you stayed in my Washington D.C. apartment during your Holiday Magazine trip, and much, much more.

Who knows where this bizarre career move would have taken Yates— this impulse to rebut the radical youth of Iowa who, he noted sardonically, were "On the March (. . . one of the more bewildered undergraduates is my older daughter, Sharon)"—had it not been for John Williams's intrigued but rather barbed reply. Among other things Williams remembered that their first conversation at Bread Loaf in 1960 had concerned what Yates allegedly called "the mediocre record of black soldiers in World War II"; Williams then proceeded to confess his irritation over being used as a sounding board for Yates's civil rights speeches in 1963. It took Yates many months to regain his composure, and finally he wrote a measured but seething response: Their "first conversation," he amended, was not at *all* as Williams described it, but rather "about the hideous whim of the federal government that consigned virtually all Army blacks to rear-echelon service and support duty." What angered Yates most, though, was his old friend's belated frankness about the speechwriting episode. "I guess all this just goes to show how many secrets lie under the surface of any friendship," Yates concluded. "But it tends to make my 'Veterans' book a much harder piece of work than I thought it was going to be and so I have temporarily shelved it." "Temporarily" soon became forever, and apparently neither *Veterans* nor any other nonfiction book, relevant or otherwise, was undertaken again.

Perhaps it was for the best. Such diversions seemed the baffled groping of a lost man, but that fall he was summoned back to the true path. He'd been "sore as hell" when *Revolutionary Road* first went out of print ("Do you know what being out of print is like? It's like being dead"), but now Dell was preparing a new paperback edition for the lucrative college market. Moreover, his famous friend Vonnegut had provided a blurb in which he called the novel "*The Great Gatsby* of [its] time": "All the time I praise books I don't give a shit about," he wrote Yates. "This is a sickness of mine. I thank you for the opportunity to do something healthy for a change—to boom one of the best books of our generation." And finally Fred Chappell's rueful vindication of the novel was published that April (a month after the Dell edition) in a volume titled *Rediscoveries*. Martha seized the moment to rally her husband with a "Rebirth Announcement" mailed to friends: "*Revolutionary Road* is back in print now. Richard Yates Club International. Martha Yates, President." And by the end of that last, otherwise uneventful year at the Workshop, Yates was able to write that he was "deep" into his new novel "and working with qualified optimism." It was a start.

Yates was sufficiently eager to leave Iowa that he decided to accept a job as "Distinguished Writer in Residence" at Wichita State University, though he had to do a certain amount of soul-searching first. Jack Leggett had assured him that his three-year term as assistant professor would remain intact no matter what, so really there was no hurry to settle for a venue like Kansas, which seemed the quintessence of what Vonnegut called "up the river." On the other hand the salary was decent (sixteen thousand dollars a year), and Martha was in favor of living closer to her family. Nor was he likely to get a better offer. The fact was, even in the darker plains states Yates's drinking and odd behavior had become all but proverbial—indeed, had been much discussed in advance at Wichita State, where the head of the writing program, Bruce Cutler, was a former Workshop student of Yates. "There's a great deal of interest among the students here in your arrival," Cutler wrote his old teacher, on whom he'd promised to keep an eye. At any rate it was only a temporary appointment, renewable or not at the end of the year, whereupon Yates could always return (temporarily) to Iowa.

Moving out of the stone cottage was a melancholy business: Yates was fond of the drafty old conversation piece, where he'd hoped to settle for however long it took to write the novel that would end his teaching days forever. But then he was hardly one to become overly attached to (or even much conscious of) wherever he happened to dwell, and after a big garage sale they moved in August to a suburban tract house in Wichita. The place was soulless, though Yates was impressed by its efficient, no-nonsense modernity, and he went right to work in climate-controlled comfort without any more picturesque distractions.

Things got off to a good start. Yates was promptly interviewed by the local newspaper, and a flattering article with a photo of both Yateses followed; also he was pleased to find that he had two or three students who gave hints of talent and were good occasional companions as well. He felt as if he'd landed on his feet, more or less, and was careful to keep his balance: He stuck to his sensible drinking regime, avoided faculty parties, met his classes on time, and got his work done. One drawback was that Martha's life was duller than usual, and (with whatever misgivings) she decided it was time to have a baby. Yates saw her point, and within a month of their arrival she was pregnant.

With another child on the way, the long-term prospect of ill-paying academia—whether in Wichita or Iowa City or whatever godforsaken place he landed—looked grimmer than ever, such that he was even willing to consider Hollywood again. In October he asked McCall to find out whether Al Ruddy would hire him to write a screenplay adaptation for *Revolutionary Road*. McCall urged him to "dream up an original" screenplay if possible, since "material in this form is more easily saleable than in the novel or play form." Meanwhile Ruddy claimed he was still interested in making a movie out of Yates's novel, but already had two projects lined up after *The Godfather*. He did tell McCall that it would "break [his] heart" for another person to produce *Revolutionary Road,* though if someone made him an "irresistible offer" he wouldn't stand in the way. But nobody did, and Ruddy kept busy with other things, and Yates decided to forgo "original" screenwriting and get back to work on *Disturbing the Peace* ("in something of a muddle" by the end of November).

That spring Yates scheduled back-to-back readings at the University of Arkansas and Roger Williams College in Rhode Island; clearly, geographical convenience was not the guiding principle. During three years of marriage he and Martha had rarely been apart, and except for the odd lapse Yates had been on his best behavior. But with a baby due in June, and his financial future uncertain as ever, the Easter break would be his last chance to go on a quick cathartic bender in congenial company—namely, with old friends and/or students such as Miller Williams, Jim Whitehead, and Bill Harrison in Arkansas, and Geoffrey Clark, DeWitt Henry, and the Cassills in Rhode Island. Martha spent the time with her family in Kansas City.

The Arkansas part of the junket remains something of a blur to all concerned. Yates put in a few workshop appearances and gave a reading, after which he got "over the top" drunk at Bill Harrison's house and passed out on the floor ("students stepped over his body on the way out," Harrison recalled). Rhode Island was somewhat more memorable, though hardly more sober. Yates's host, Geoffrey Clark, was a devoted protégé who introduced Yates to his students as "the best teacher I ever had."* "Say,

---

*Clark was kind enough to send me a tape of Yates's reading ("Doctor Jack-o'-Lantern") from this visit—the only time I've ever heard Yates's voice: Sonorous, doleful, with a barely perceptible lisp,

Geoff, tell me the truth," Yates later asked him. "Did you *really* mean that about being the best teacher you ever had? Are you kidding me?" Clark assured him that he was not, and Yates's face broke into "a shy, pleased smile" as Clark described it, "a Gatsby smile." Yates was less pleased when he skimmed through his ex-student's teaching copy of *Revolutionary Road* and encountered the marginal gloss "use of cliché": "[Yates] seemed to recoil from it as from a hot poker," Clark recalled, "then go glum, until my explanation: The note was a reminder to me to point out to my class how he'd use spoken clichés to capture the character of the speaker."

The main item on the agenda was an interview for the journal *Ploughshares,* which DeWitt Henry had founded in Boston the year before as a corrective to the tide of experimental postmodernism sweeping the country. The interview was a chance for Yates to discuss the principles of traditional fiction in terms of his own work, as well as to recommend a number of other writers who were in danger of being overlooked amid present trends. The published interview is perhaps the most useful source of Yates's opinions on his craft and career, as well as the most vivid record of his distinctively candid yet diffident voice—all of which is a bit remarkable given that the actual interview was something of a fiasco and had to be rewritten almost from scratch.

Henry had driven down from Boston with two *Ploughshares* associates, David Omar White and Peter O'Malley, as well as the latter's fiancée, the poet Richard Wilbur's daughter Ellen. The interview was taped over the course of several boozy hours at Clark's house, and the interviewee was besotted in more ways than one—flirting blatantly with "that luscious Wilbur girl," as he called her. "I felt like a teenybopper because I admired *Revolutionary Road* so much," Wilbur remembered. "But I was also alarmed: I told [Yates] he had the most brutal eye for human flaws of any writer, and it frightened me to think he was casting the same eye, right now, on me." Yates was flattered, and when Wilbur

---

he sounds to me like a rather less jaunty version of the actor Donald Sutherland. By all accounts— when in good form—Yates relished the opportunity to read for a receptive audience; on the tape, his imitation of Vincent Sabella's New York accent earns him a well-deserved burst of laughter, and the final applause is properly enthusiastic.

further confessed a kindred fondness for Cole Porter and Gershwin, he became enthralled. When she wondered if he could supply a forgotten line from a favorite song, his face "lit up at the challenge": " 'You're the cream in my coffee,' " she prompted, " 'you're the—' . . . ?" " 'Lamb in my stew'!" he crowed, and the two proceeded to sing the rest. Wilbur's fiancé grew increasingly glum as Yates implied that such an elegant woman deserved better ("I seem to recall being not very nice to that Irish clown," Yates wrote afterward). And finally they all adjourned to Howard Johnson's, where Cassill (then at Brown University) met them in order to take his worse-for-wear guest home for the night. Alas, amid "all the boozing and bullshit," as Yates put it, he'd "totally [failed] to apologize to DeWitt for having flubbed his interview." Indeed, Henry found his transcription "fragmentary, diffuse and frustrating," but hoped the subject would agree to expand and clarify in written form, and this Yates was happy to do.

There was another, less festive bit of business in the East. David Milch had returned to Yale to teach alongside his old mentors Robert Penn Warren and Cleanth Brooks, and had recently intimated that he might be able to arrange a writer-in-residence job for Yates. The latter's distaste at assuming the role of supplicant vis-à-vis an old bête noire like Milch can scarcely be conceived—or rather it can, since it wouldn't be the last time it happened. But at the time he was simply too desperate not to pursue the lead, however specious: More than ever Yates wanted to end his exile in the sticks and live in or around New York again; also he'd prefer to say he taught at Yale rather than Wichita State. Yates visited Milch's seminar a few times that spring and summer as a guest lecturer, and though he was visibly cowed by the dreadful ambience of the Ivy League, he acquitted himself well enough for Milch to report somewhat plausibly that "chances [were] very good" he'd be hired: Milch had broached the matter with the author of All the King's Men, whose "reaction was very favorable, as was that of Cleanth Brooks." He added, however, that Brooks was "angling for Walker Percy," though Percy's health was such that he seemed "reluctant to come north."

Nothing came of it. "Maybe I didn't follow through," said Milch, "or maybe Dick gave the impression he was having a lot of problems."

Whatever the case, Milch concedes his "ambivalence" toward Yates in those days: "Probably I didn't go out of my way to put Dick at ease—inviting him in, but not letting him *know* he was in. That was the kind of asshole I was at the time."

Gina Catherine was born on June 15, 1972, more than fifteen years after Yates's previous child; her belated advent seemed a promise that Yates (if he played his cards right) would have the comfort of a doting girl for the rest of his life, and thus was cause for great rejoicing. "She's lovely!" he wrote friends. "Looks just like her mother." Her namesake Gina Berriault (who'd finally met Yates in the flesh while teaching at Iowa two years before) wrote that the baby "must be beautiful and delightful, she can't be less, given her parents who answer to that description themselves." And so she was, and for a little while Yates was the happiest he'd been since he first met the baby's mother: Love-struck, he fussed over Gina constantly and even seemed to enjoy changing diapers and so forth. Such was his contentment that he was able to work better, though he had less time for it, while Martha installed a darkroom and got on with both motherhood and photography. The baby's presence was a decided improvement.

That summer DeWitt Henry sent a somewhat worked-over transcript of their "interview," and Yates was so appalled by what he'd apparently let slip while in his cups that he rewrote almost every word, including a number of the questions. "Believe it or not," he informed Henry, "I *have* put an awful lot of work into this thing—a solid week, working damn near around the clock, neglecting everything else I was supposed to be doing—and I do feel satisfied with it now, though you may not." The project posed an interesting challenge to Yates. As he began to consider seriously what he'd so "dumbly" put on tape, he found himself working out certain convictions that hadn't been quite so clear in his mind before. For example, his frustration over the failure of *A Special Providence* had provoked "a half-assed outburst against autobiographical fiction," which on sober reflection struck him as "pure nonsense." In the published interview, then, Yates nicely amended the matter with a detailed apologia for his own evolution from a mostly "objective" writer to one who'd learned the hard way that he hadn't "earned the right" (*yet*) to translate personal experience directly into fiction—which was *not* to say it couldn't be done, given the proper "distance" and "detachment."

Perhaps the most ticklish issue was that of *neglect,* both with respect to his own reputation and certain others'. The last thing Yates wanted was to come off as a crybaby who felt he'd been treated unfairly by the literary establishment, or had the bad luck of going against the grain of egregious fashion. His original response (or rather Henry's touched-up version of it) is arguably a bit closer to Yates's true feelings on the subject than what he allowed into print, and deserves to be quoted at length:

> A popular writer, a writer who gains a broad and sustained contemporary audience, I guess, like any other writer wants to know he's good, and the bestseller lists and talk shows and his annual income all repay whatever faith it was that sat him down in front of his typewriter in the first place. But if he's a serious writer that's got to come second. . . . Much more common, and I think the case is mine, [is when] the good work is its own reward and you share it with as many readers as you can and it stays alive, and has some hard-won clarity and richness, some distillation of human investment, that continues to claim some kind of permanent interest no matter what angles fashion may dispose new readers towards. . . . My first book made a big, popular splash and that kind of success was intoxicating, and I was in the racket, in the race, but the down that followed it was miserable, and the real success has been a quieter, more solid kind of thing. I know the book's good. It's there. It wins new readers. That level is there to be reached, and I don't need a cheering crowd to tell me that it's worth it. It would be nice to be the fashion, to be recognized for what I'm trying to do—in the sense that Mailer is, for instance—life would be easier in a lot of ways—but the price of doing something difficult and honest, something true, as April Wheeler learned, is doing it alone.

Yates cut the entire speech, which perhaps struck him as pontifical or protesting too much, though surely he believed every word of it: To Yates writing *was* a lonely business (it would become more so over time), and *had* to be its own reward.* A little more fame, however, would have been "nice."

As for the question of other neglected contemporaries in the realistic tradition, Henry had originally suggested three: Edward Wallant, Brian Moore, and Evan Connell. Yates agreed they were neglected after a fashion, but for very different reasons (e.g., Wallant because of his early death), and hence in revision he made a separate, qualified case for each—"and then," as he wrote Henry, "once I got started, I couldn't stop. There are simply too God damn *many* neglected contemporary writers, and I felt I had to mention at least a few of them." The few? Anatole Broyard, Gina Berriault, R. V. Cassill, George Garrett, Seymour Epstein, Fred Chappell, Helen Hudson, Edward Hoagland, George Cuomo, Arthur Roth, Andre Dubus, James Crumley, Mark Dintenfass, Theodore Weesner, and on and on—mostly friends or students, but still writers whose work Yates admired, and whose careers he was loath not to boost when given the chance.

"Anyway," Yates's letter to Henry continued, "that got me started on the making of still another damn list—

> a list of traditional, realistic writers who *haven't* been neglected, who *have* made major critical and popular reputations—and in a way that was the most maddening part of the whole damn thing. In one of my early drafts, for example, I launched into a furious, splenetic diatribe against Saul Bellow, and another equally nasty assessment of J. P. Donleavy. But I tore all that stuff up in the end; I finally decided the best way to do it was simply to leave out the

---

*In the published version of his response *re* "neglect," Yates avoided any kind of general statement, restricting himself to the facts of his own career with characteristic modesty: He admitted occasional irritation that *Revolutionary Road* wasn't better known, but pointed out that "it did quite well for a first novel"; then he blamed himself for having "tinkered and brooded and fussed" so long over *A Special Providence*, and concluded, "I can't honestly claim my stuff has been neglected; it's probably received just about the degree of attention it deserves. I simply haven't published enough to expect more—not yet, anyway."

writers whose work I don't respect . . . and mention only those whose work I do. It's really a short list, as you'll see.*

Another diatribe that required a great deal of temperate revision was the one against "the whole fucking Post-realistic School' "—from which he felt obliged explicitly to exempt Vonnegut despite the "tricky business" of the nice blurb the man had provided for *Revolutionary Road*: "[S]o I guess some of your more small-minded readers are going to think I'm kissing his ass in return for that favor," Yates advised Henry. "And the point *I'd* like to make, to you, is that I don't give a shit if they do." Finally he asked Henry to "read this damn thing carefully, and bear in mind that my whole effort has been to make it clear, sane, rational and fair."

It was all those things, and Yates's pains in making it so were not in vain. A few months later Henry walked down the street to Sam Lawrence's office in order to submit his own work-in-progress, as well as to show a sample issue of *Ploughshares* and the Yates interview in proof. Lawrence was impressed by how "cogent and back-to-work" his old friend seemed. The two men had been out of touch for almost five years; Yates was hurt but unsurprised that Lawrence had sent no word when *A Special Providence* was published ("in all its carefully-edited sloppiness," as Yates put it). He assumed Lawrence had given him up for dead— another washed-up author, and a treacherous friend at that—and thus was "very touched" to hear again from Lawrence that November: "I've just finished reading proofs of a very fine interview you gave to DeWitt Henry and I could hear your voice clearly," Lawrence wrote. "If for any reason you decide to change publishers, please let me know." "So who knows?" said Yates. "I might still bring out a Delacorte 'Seymour Lawrence Book' and have money coming in by the bushel-basketful."

---

*To wit: Styron, James Jones, Mailer, and Salinger (except for "those convoluted Glass-family chronicles"); also—with dire reservations in some cases—Updike, Philip Roth, Nabokov, Isaac Bashevis Singer, Jean Stafford, Peter Taylor, Flannery O'Connor, Cheever, Malamud, Bruce Jay Friedman, Thomas Berger, and Joan Didion.

. . .

Meanwhile he was still in Wichita. His writer-in-residence appointment had been renewed for another year, and might indeed become permanent if he wasn't careful. By then the idea of getting out of Kansas and going home to New York had become an obsession, and Yates was far from particular about the means. He asked Hayes Jacobs—an old freelancer like himself—to find him an employment agent who could scout the New York job market for anything from PR to publishing to teaching to whatever, preferably on a part-time basis. Jacobs was less than sanguine ("devilishly hard to place you at the price you're seeking"), but put him in touch with Elise Ford at the Prudential Placement Agency.

For Ms. Ford's benefit, Yates spent much of his Thanksgiving vacation updating his résumé—a two-and-a-half page, single-spaced summary of a singularly varied career: Its subject (a "Free-lance Writer") was an NBA-nominated author of three books who'd received several major grants, served as "sole speechwriter" for Robert F. Kennedy, written screenplays for John Frankenheimer and Roger Corman, and published short stories in numerous anthologies and major magazines (though not, alas, *The New Yorker*); along the way he'd also written for *Food Field Reporter, Trade Union Courier,* UPI, Johnson & Johnson, and of course Remington Rand (about which he spilled the most résumé ink of all, detailing his various duties on behalf of the UNIVAC); and last but hardly least, he'd taught at four universities and his list of references included Styron, Vonnegut, Cassill, Kazin, Bourjaily, and Dr. Frank Kastor at Wichita State University ("This is my present position").

Such a résumé would seem to suggest an eminently can-do kind of guy, but amid what Jacobs called the "big Nothing" of the New York job market, the only initial nibble it elicited was from N. W. Ayer and Son, Inc., who thought they might be able to get Yates an occasional PR assignment concerning the "U.S. Army's second centennial." The academic world was even more categorical in its rejection. Hostos Community College was willing to interview Yates (but wouldn't pay travel expenses), while Sarah Lawrence, Rutgers, Queensborough Community College, Rider College, Princeton, Wellesley, Skidmore, and SUNY at Stony Brook—just to mention the few that favored Yates with a reply—had no openings at the time.

As a kind of dismal postscript, Yates's old New York friend Arthur Roth wrote in January that his last two novels had been rejected ("a lot of commitment down the drain") and for the past nine months he'd been working as a carpenter's helper. "I often wonder how you are doing and how life is treating you," Roth remarked.

At the moment Yates was of the opinion that life was treating him poorly. Perhaps as a favor to Sam Lawrence (with whom McCall was tentatively negotiating a contract for *Disturbing the Peace*), Yates agreed to review a Delacorte novel for the *New York Times Book Review*—something called *The Morning After,* by Jack B. Weiner. All Yates knew at the outset was that the book was about a drunk, and by the time he finished it Yates was a drunk again, too. Martha never quite understood the coincidence: "The fact that he'd review such a book gave me the creeps," she said, "and afterward he seemed to make a decision to give up'. The book seemed to remind him that drinking was something he could do."

The book also made him aware of the fact that a Delacorte author had just published a novel almost exactly like the one Yates himself had been writing for three years. Ninety percent of Yates's *Times* review is a dogged plot summary, as if he were bemusedly enumerating all the ways in which Weiner's book resembled his own: The alcoholic protagonist Charlie Lester is a PR man who's "cynical about his work"; he decides to consult a "vain, supercilious" psychiatrist who "appears to doze through Charlie's hapless monologues"; after a few sessions Charlie "quits the man cold" and goes on a vacation to dry out, but ends up "screaming drunken obscenities to [his wife] on the phone"; he makes his ten-year-old son feel "so unhappy and embarrassed" that all the boy can muster is a mumbled "Fine" or "OK" or "No" (the constant refrain of John Wilder's son is "I don't know. I don't care"). And so on. Toward the end of his review, Yates pointed out a few flaws such as Weiner's "dreadful images" (for example, the surf rolls in "as if to the slow rhythmic beat of a giant, salt-encrusted metronome"), but then manfully calls it a "compelling piece of work": "Charlie Lester's real 'problem' is the agony of his total isolation, and it comes to serve as an eloquent, unforgettable metaphor for the secret loneliness in us all." A very Yatesian theme, that, and an apt description of Wilder's (and Yates's) "real 'problem' " as well.

So began what might arguably be called the worst year (or two) of Yates's life, which of course is no mean assertion. "He started drinking during the day," Martha remembered. "One of his students was a big drinker, and the two of them would get drunk a lot until three A.M. or so. I hated it." In despair over his novel (to say nothing of life in general, the steady drumbeat of rejection coming his way from New York), Yates tried writing a short story for the first time in ten years. Titled "Forms of Entertainment," it was promptly rejected by *The New Yorker* and then sent to Gordon Lish at *Esquire,* who'd solicited work from Yates as soon as he arrived at the magazine a few years before. Monica McCall reported that Lish was "putting the story through"—that is, "sending it upstairs to [Editor in Chief] Harold Hayes for confirmation of purchase, which does not necessarily mean a firm acceptance because apparently Hayes could . . . turn it down." Yates was frantic enough to call Lish on the phone, which resulted in the following note: "Dick—I'm doing all that can be done; trust me. But for God's sake, man, keep this thing in perspective."

A few days later the story was officially rejected. As Lish recalled the episode, "I wanted to get Dick into *Esquire,* because I felt bad for him and wanted to do something for him: He was so miserable, that I extended myself." But the truth was that "Forms of Entertainment" had never made it past the magazine's associate editors, and Lish ("in defiance of [his] better judgment") had tried but failed to change their minds about it. Yates responded to this latest rejection by calling Lish on the phone and abusively accusing him of favoring only "name" writers; finally he threatened to "get on a plane and shoot [Lish]." "Dick was unappeasable, shouting," Lish remembered. "His wife was screaming in the background: 'Don't pay attention! He's drunk! He's drunk!' Afterward she called me to apologize." The next day Lish wrote Yates a letter:

> Your performance was an appalling piece of self-destruction. How absurd to make an enemy of me and of *Esquire.* . . . Your calls, your letters, the whole matter of your offering of "Forms" and your response to the rejection is ugly and sad. Your rage should be directed elsewhere; if you had the maturity of your years, you'd see this. And as for your threats of

violence, come ahead, old buddy: you'll find me as passionate in this as in friendship.

It would take almost three years for a somewhat recovered Yates to apologize; meanwhile he decided not to submit "Forms of Entertainment" elsewhere, and the manuscript doesn't survive.

"It was a Jekyll and Hyde thing," Martha said of her husband's abrupt decline. "It was like something clicked in his brain: Suddenly he wasn't there anymore. He was irrational, drunk all the time, and it was willful, in-your-face drinking." Consumed with self-loathing over his work and desperately anxious about the future, Yates began to suspect that the world was conspiring against him. Shortly after the *Esquire* contretemps, he called Styron and held the man captive for some two hours while he railed against all the people who'd let him down: friends, family, Hollywood people, Iowa people, on and on. Soon Martha became the enemy—particularly when Yates discovered a paperback on alcoholism she'd recently purchased and stashed in a drawer. "He hit the ceiling," she recalled. "*Furious*. I couldn't deny it was to read about him; it was the first time, by default, I'd confronted him that I thought he was an alcoholic." Many "endless conversations" followed—the long lesson in futility that Sheila had learned so thoroughly more than a decade before. As ever, Yates proved an adept, indefatigable arguer, and would *never* concede that he was an "alcoholic." The word enraged him: Whoever used it didn't understand where the "real 'problem'" lay.

Into this nightmare came his daughter Monica, who for fifteen years had somehow been spared the knowledge of her father's mental problems. This time he was too far gone to pull himself together for her visit, though during the daytime, at least, he was sober if morose. But night after night she'd hear him pacing the hours away and hissing abuse at his wife, the word *bitch* recurring every so often amid the general mutter. One morning she found Martha sitting in the kitchen weeping. "Why is he being so *mean?*" Monica asked, and the hollow-eyed woman said he had a "drinking problem." By then Martha herself was so depressed that she'd stopped doing housework, and Monica tried to cheer things up by mopping floors and taking care of the baby. But mostly she stayed away on her bicycle, and when she returned to Mahopac she asked her mother about Yates's "problem." Sheila had made it a point never to malign her ex-husband to the children (though "she *always* spoke badly of him later," Monica points out), but this time she calmly explained that, yes, he was an alcoholic. "I am your daughter and I love you," Monica wrote her father, "and I hereby order you to be no longer depressed or sad or feeling blue. . . . When you finish reading this I want you to go look at your neato wife and your little cute daughter and think of your two big daughters and be overjoyed."

But Yates was almost beyond noticing his wife and daughter, much less deriving comfort from them. As Martha put it, "He was so self-absorbed by then he couldn't part the curtains of his own problems and relate to the world." Determined to confront him with indisputable proof of his sickness (and also, perhaps, to have something to show a doctor when the time came), Martha prepared a list of symptoms that gives a vivid idea of what it was like to live with Yates at his worst, and why it was sometimes difficult to make a proper distinction between alcoholism and mental illness. According to the memo, Yates had taken to "spook[ing]" around the house in his underwear ("usually fanatic about body exposed," Martha noted, "—skinny legs, etc."), and sometimes standing still for long intervals, obliviously, as if in deep concentration. He was now smoking "*constantly*" and "inhal[ing] deeply," though all the while he was obsessed with a fear of death from lung cancer or heart disease. Like his idol Fitzgerald, he made constant lists in "very emphatic script" while "talking to self and constant whispering (extreme)." Sometimes his grandiosity was such that he became convinced he had an urgent "message to the world" and was on the "verge of something big." But perhaps the most definitive symptom was an agitated inability to communicate, to understand and make himself understood amid the depths of his own bewildered dread. As Martha wrote:

Mostly quiet and brooding but when gets to talking easily worked up into panicky declarations: "I *hate* psychiatrists." "What do *you* know" "They *do* watch what you're wearing." . . . Increasingly jumpy to being asked simple question while working or charged with simple tasks or put something on calendar. [E.g.,] "Breakfast is ready." "God *damn* it." Time—calendar and clock great source of consternation, confusion and panic. . . . Simple phrases and cliches are not understood for their common meaning. [E.g.,] "Which Saturday is this Saturday?" (It could be any in the year) . . . Recurring conversation. D: Martha? M: What, honey? D: Oh nothing. Recurring: "I'll be okay just as soon as . . . Don't go away.[. . .] How am I doing? [. . .] I'm all right. [. . .] Who says I'm crazy? (then a hug) [. . .] How could you love a crazy man? [. . .] What's going to become of me? ["] . . . As time passes more and more fearful of hospitalization or being doped up and brought down too far (a legitimate fear) and more suspect of my motives—"You think I'm crazy" "*You* don't understand."

The more Martha begged him to get help, the more sarcastic and spitefully drunken he became. And though he was wholly dependent on her (*Don't go away*), he seemed unmoved by the distress he caused with such obnoxious behavior. When she finally lost her temper and flew at him with her fists, the inebriated Yates seemed to enjoy the spectacle, holding her off and laughing.

After a while she gave up. "I remember sitting on the couch," she said, "holding Gina, my tears falling on her, and Dick yelling at me. It was so senseless it sticks in my head: *What's wrong with this picture?*" Since she didn't argue anymore, Yates seemed to assume he'd finally brought her around to his point of view—namely, that he *didn't* need help, that all would be well as soon as certain enigmatic factors fell into place. In fact she'd made "a cool-headed, deliberate decision": She'd do whatever was necessary to help him get back to New York ("I felt responsible for Wichita"), then wait a year or so "for him to be lucid enough to fend for himself." Then she'd take the baby and leave.

By the time Yates's luck changed he was in no condition to enjoy it. His red letter day was March 21, 1973, when he was offered a part-time position at Columbia beginning with the spring 1974 semester; far more importantly, a lucrative deal (by Yates's standards) was finalized that same day with Sam Lawrence, who offered a fifty-thousand-dollar advance for *Disturbing the Peace*. At the time Yates was too relieved to be bothered much by the somewhat eccentric method of payment, which would persist for the rest of their association: He was to receive twelve thousand dollars on signing, and then equal monthly payments of fifteen hundred dollars until he delivered the manuscript on July 1, 1974, whereupon he'd receive the balance of twenty thousand dollars—or rather, he'd receive ten thousand dollars for delivery and another ten thousand dollars when the book was published. The idea was to provide a steady long-term income for an unpredictable man. "Those monthly payments were a kind of salary," Lawrence proudly observed, "and they sustained him."

They also signaled the beginning of an even more ambivalent phase of the friendship. When sane and solvent, Yates was mostly grateful for Lawrence's belief in him as a writer, for his financial as well as moral support. ("How much do you need, Dick?" Lawrence had said when Yates complained of his Wichita predicament.) It was true that he thought Lawrence a bit pompous, but, as he wrote a friend, "at his best he's a solid man with good instincts"—moreover, "he'll never try to fuck around with your manuscripts, as many editors do; he's never asked me to change a word." After the "carefully-edited sloppiness" of Knopf, Yates had decided that Lawrence's laissez-faire approach was a virtue after all; as for the man's "good instincts," he found favor with Yates by turning down such novels as *The World According to Garp* ("On the other hand," Yates noted, "he's an enthusiastic supporter of Richard Brautigan, so what the hell are we going to do?"). Lawrence's view of Yates, meanwhile, was characterized by a kind of complicated magnanimity— "a mixture of admiration and concern," as their mutual friend Dan Wakefield put it.

It was the "concern" part that rankled. Concern meant that he was mawkishly aware of Yates's failings—his drinking and instability and general incapacity to care for himself. Lawrence, too, was a heavy drinker and rather strange man in his own right, but he was also prosperous, and proprietary toward his authors; what he demanded (implicitly) in return for his largess was that they do their work and show a seemly gratitude, a sentiment Yates sometimes felt and sometimes didn't. Lawrence's later eulogy of his old friend, while touching in parts, reads almost like a litany of unacknowledged favors, as it's largely comprised of data relating to their various contracts. "Dad would've *hated* that eulogy," said Monica Yates. "[Lawrence] went on and on about the money. . . . That was a love-hate relationship big-time." Another aspect of Lawrence's *concern* that bothered Yates was the fact that it was mostly transmitted at arm's length (usually in the form of a check)—all the more so later, when Lawrence seemed unwilling to "soil himself" with Yates's difficult life. Yates would mimic him bitterly—"D-d-d-don't m-m-mix b-b-business with puh-pleasure!"—or so Lawrence liked to tell Yates, though the former's social life was actually consumed by "business" with and on behalf of his authors. "Yates was always angry at Lawrence," said psychiatrist Winthrop Burr, "but at the same time he wanted to be more accepted by him."

For a while, though, it sufficed that Lawrence had rescued him from Wichita, and Yates lost no time traveling to New York, alone, to find an apartment. Needless to say, he was in no shape for such a trip, which would serve as a bleak foreshadowing of the move to come. Perhaps the first blow was his discovery that he couldn't afford to live in Manhattan after all; he'd have to settle for one of the outer boroughs, which to Yates was only a slight step up from Kansas. For that and any number of other reasons, he began drinking even harder than before, which provoked a fresh and frightening symptom of advanced alcoholism: epileptic seizures. His first attack took place at Bill Reardon's apartment in the Village, and later that day he had another in Jerry Schulman's car, while the latter drove him to Staten Island to view an apartment. Yates—already drunk and semideranged when Schulman arrived to pick him up—began thrashing and frothing at the mouth while they passed through the Brooklyn Battery Tunnel, then tried to jump out of the car. Schulman had to hold the writhing man in place until they could turn around.

After a phone call to Nathan S. Kline, Yates thought he was calm enough to make the trip back to Staten Island, but once they arrived he had another seizure, this time in the presence of his prospective landlord.

As his convulsions subsided he tried to stand up and tripped on a toy car, which (according to Schulman) prompted "a stream of hideous invective." The landlord proved remarkably sympathetic; no doubt mollified by the relative sanity of Yates's companion, he agreed to rent the apartment to this disturbed man, perhaps on the theory that he was having a bad day. It continued badly. Schulman drove his friend to the airport, where Yates began to have second thoughts about catching his flight: It was late, he felt lousy, and besides he usually called Monica at this time of day. When Schulman offered to take Yates to a hospital, Yates became indignant: "Don't tell me what to do!" he shouted, and staggered off to find a phone. Schulman, meanwhile, called Martha in Kansas and asked her advice: With a baby screaming in the background, she mentioned a number of pills her husband should take and urged Schulman to get him on the plane no matter what. When the exhausted man tried to do as he was told, Yates exploded as if mortally offended by his friend's presumption. "It was humiliating to be with him," said Schulman. "After that I realized you couldn't do the right thing for Dick, because he'd always insist on taking care of himself."

The episode officially killed whatever was left of Yates's friendship with the Schulmans. Grace had been drifting away for some time—apart from a general exasperation with Yates, her life had simply settled in such a way that commotion makers were no longer welcome: She was a professor at Baruch College as well as poetry editor of The Nation and director of the 92nd Street Y Poetry Center; also, she was sick of "literary people" who exploited her husband's good nature. "Often I had to be the heavy in protecting [Jerry] from what I felt to be insulting responses to him for his kindness," she said. "And when I heard about his patience with Dick that day, I thought—enough. Enough of Dick's bad behavior." As for Jerry, he accepted a last goodwill invitation to dine with the Yateses in Staten Island, but the evening was awkward and neither man made an effort to contact the other again.

By the time they moved to New York in June, Yates was a "total wreck," as Martha put it; even he himself admitted, a month after their arrival, that he'd "become such a wallowing whiskey-head" (not to be confused with alcoholic) that he could "barely hold a pencil straight." As ever, his drinking both worsened and commingled with the vagaries of mental illness, such that it was impossible to predict what he would do or say next. Shortly before leaving Kansas, he'd invited his daughter Sharon to come take his car off his hands, as long as she agreed to arrange such matters as insurance and title transfer; after she'd done so, she called from Iowa to apprise him of her progress ("Okay, I got the insurance; now we have to—") and Yates blew up: *"What d'you think I am? Some sort of Jewish father?!"* Sharon didn't know what to make of this (certainly the ethnic slur was uncharacteristic): Was he angry because she'd called about practical affairs and hadn't attended to the proper daughterly preliminaries?

The apartment in Staten Island was still being painted when they arrived, so they spent a few days at the Americana Hotel near Times Square. Yates checked in with Dr. Kline, who prescribed the anticonvulsant drug Dilantin and strongly urged Yates to stop drinking. Probably during this visit, too, Kline prescribed (or represcribed) Antabuse, which Yates took sporadically if at all; his private compromise was to give up whiskey and drink only beer, and his relative initial sobriety had the usual depressive effect. When his Iowa friend Jody Lowens visited him at the hotel, Yates wanted to talk about the death of his former teaching colleague Richard Gehman. Gehman, called "King of the Freelancers" because of his mammoth output, had rated a very brief photoless obituary in the *Times*. "Three thousand articles and over a dozen books," Yates sighed, "and they give him five inches for his obituary. I'll be lucky to get two."* Lowens recalled that the whole matter "seemed to trouble him tremendously," and Martha agreed—Yates's indifference toward fame, she always felt, was deceptive: "Dick had to be recognized for his talent, to be one of the literary elite—anything else amounted to failure. A good marriage and child should have been enough, but it wasn't."

Granted that he could scarcely get worse, Yates showed a few signs of improvement in New York. Staten Island wasn't so bad after all. Their apartment was a cramped two-bedroom on the seventh floor of a drab

---

*Yates received almost ten inches and a photo.

modern building, but it had a view of sorts and was nice enough by Yates's standards ("all the places where he lived with Martha were nicer than other apartments in his life," Monica pointed out). He'd always enjoyed crossing on the ferry, and now that he didn't have to bother with a day job for a while, he spent leisurely afternoons walking around Manhattan and seeing a few leftover friends. He visited Bill Reardon and John Williams, and was gratified to find that Vonnegut was "taking his enormous success very gracefully" and had even promised to "come slumming" in Staten Island with his new girlfriend, Jill Krementz, an "ultra-fashionable young photographer." But mostly Yates kept to himself; he was bemused by what he found in the city after his "nine-year exile," and noted "a certain Rip van Winkle quality to [his] prowlings in Manhattan." As he wrote his friend Geoffrey Clark:

> Christ, how things have changed! The Empire State Building is no longer the tallest in the world, the whole West Side is swarming with guys who look as if they've got switchblades in one pocket and hypodermic syringes in the other; the whole Village is a morass of cruising fags and teenyboppers; all the good restaurants and bars have become tourist traps, and all the taxicabs have plastic or wire-mesh partitions to keep the passengers from garrotting the drivers. But it's home, and I guess I'll get used to it.

But he never quite did. Like his character Emily Grimes, Yates had begun to "[live] in memories all the time," and New York was haunted by too many ghosts.

Friends didn't notice anything particularly amiss between the Yateses: Martha tended to be a courteous hostess, if a bit stiff and withdrawn. ("By then I was so radically disenchanted by the world of writers that I'd rather do anything than listen to them talk.") Yates liked to mention that this was actually his *second* time in Staten Island, reminiscing about his eight months in the TB ward at Halloran. Generally, too, he'd pay his wife the gentlemanly tribute of showing off her artwork on the walls ("trees and dogs, things like that," DeWitt Henry recalled) with many a lavish compliment. Toward Gina he seemed "clumsy and devoted," said Mark

428 । A TRAGIC HONESTY

Dintenfass. "He was almost afraid to hold her because he thought he might drop her." One night the family bumped into Bob Riche and his wife at a Broadway show—the last time Yates and his old friend ever laid eyes on each other—and the Riches cooed appropriately over the somber toddler in their midst. "She's cute when she doesn't have that *thing* stuck in her face," said Yates, and abruptly plucked the pacifier out of his daughter's mouth.

Those were the good times. "Dick acted normal around friends," said Martha. "He could sort of turn it on and off, but his tirades would continue as soon as they left." Yates spent most of his days anxiously taking pills, trying to write, and stalking around the apartment shouting. It didn't matter if Martha was present; he wasn't addressing her, after all. *"Lish, you son of a bitch!"* he'd suddenly erupt, or else some ghost from a more distant past would provoke his wrath. Martha worried a little what the neighbors thought—surely they heard—but otherwise she was used to it. "Dick's tantrums were so much background noise by then," she said. "If he didn't come out of it, well, I'd already decided to leave. Still, I'm amazed now that I stuck it so long; I'd come to accept things no human being should ever have to accept."

Yates conserved the better part of his sanity for work. Though Martha had "no idea how he managed at Columbia," he nonetheless ventured into Manhattan once a week to meet his two-hour class and hold conferences before and after. His novel was a little behind schedule, but not much, and Sam Lawrence was so "overwhelmed" by the first 122 pages that he urged him not to rush: "What's most important is to have the book right." One night the publisher came out to Staten Island for dinner, and Martha bought a special antique chair for the occasion and cooked a sole with cream sauce and mashed potatoes; otherwise she might have been invisible. Lawrence commended her for putting rolls on the table ("Good, rolls. Can't possibly eat until I've had rolls. Ulcer."), then the two men commenced drinking and talking books. Yates was already thinking about his next novel, the subject of which he proposed to be a "lovable Irish alcoholic" who performed "spontaneous tap dances." Lawrence winced: "No more desperate characters, Dick. *Please.*"

Soon Yates got a better idea. Ever since *A Special Providence* he'd wanted to take another shot at writing an explicitly autobiographical novel, but properly formed this time; one night it occurred to him that a nice way to objectify "the Me character"—as Yates called it—would be to make him a woman. In order to bring it off, though, he'd need more material than his own life could provide. "Dick called me out of the blue," remembered his old girlfriend Natalie Bowen. "He was drunk, of course, and woke me up, but I was glad to hear from him. He said he was starting a new novel and wondered if I'd be willing to talk about my own life." Bowen was happy to tell him whatever he needed to know. As Yates was already somewhat aware, she'd led just the kind of independent and rather lonely life he had in mind for his character: She'd been married briefly to a man who told her he "hated [her] body" (referring mainly to her flat chest); she'd had two abortions in the fifties; she'd lived in a "high, spacious apartment near Gramercy Park" where somebody had penciled a "long, thick penis" on one of the wallpaper horses in the hallway, and as her drinking got worse she would occasionally wake up with strange men in her bed; for a while she'd collected unemployment and stayed drunk all day, until finally she went to the Payne-Whitney walk-in mental health clinic and started seeing a psychiatrist.

Yates was delighted, and invited Bowen to come out for dinner and meet his wife. He may or may not have had ulterior motives for exposing Martha to this partial model for the embryonic Emily Grimes—"the original liberated woman" as her nephew Peter remarks with unwitting irony in the novel. That such liberation leads (if only for a while in Bowen's case) to promiscuity, poverty, and despair was a point Yates would have been eager to impress on Martha, who'd begun to intimate her plans for leaving him.

Largely to spare his feelings, she'd spoken in rather vague terms about wanting to "find herself," and Yates concluded that she'd become a "womens'-libbing bitch" as he sometimes put it. He couldn't speak calmly on the subject; partly, perhaps, because his mother's "independence" had caused him so much grief, Yates's hatred for all "feminist horseshit" bordered on the pathological. As usual in such matters, he found a sympathetic ally in Andre Dubus, whose own marriage was breaking up around the same time: "Trouble with me and my friends," he wrote Yates, "is we're married to women who're making the transition between the old type woman and the new type and we're getting the best of neither and the worst of both." In fact Martha was not at all active in the movement, though its ubiquity could hardly fail to affect her state of mind—as might be surmised by a letter she wrote Yates almost three years later: "Women have been oblique, mysterious, evasive out of fear of telling the truth, . . . fear of hurting the vulnerable emotions of a man, fear of being scorned or laughed at, and out of shame. I made for myself a perfect trap out of my inability to speak. And the longer I went—taking my self-definition from you . . . the less you knew me." At the time, though, she tried to avoid discussing such notions with him—"I didn't want to throw kerosene on the fire"—but it was typical of Yates to blame his wife's disaffection on a pernicious ideology (as he saw it) rather than his own behavior.

She left him that spring. Yates would later tell friends that "A Natural Girl" was a "wholly autobiographical" account of their breakup, and while Martha dismisses the story as a "crock," much of what her fictional alter ego tells the devastated David Clark rings true:

"We haven't been all right for a long time and we aren't all right now and it isn't going to get any better. I'm sorry if this comes as a surprise but it really shouldn't, and it wouldn't if you'd ever known me as well as you think you do. It's over, that's all. I'm leaving. . . ."

"You don't—love me anymore."

"That's right," she said. "Exactly. I don't love you anymore."

By then Martha was apt to say all those things, and indeed Yates *was* shocked when the time came, though as the wife in the story points out, he shouldn't have been. Martha's decision was hardly the bombshell hurled by the morbidly callous Susan Andrews. She'd spent almost a year preparing him for her departure ("he was too out-of-it to remember from one day to the next"), and when she finally told him the time had arrived, Yates drew the same conclusion as fifteen years before: Martha's "inability to love," like Sheila's, was a manifestation of insanity.

He made an appointment with Nathan S. Kline for all three of them—baby too—and at length the exasperated Martha agreed to go. For most of the session she was left waiting outside Kline's office with Gina on her hip, while the two men discussed the matter between them. Finally Kline asked to see Martha alone. "So," he said. "You're pretty determined to leave." "Yes." "Tell me one thing," he continued. "I want you to think about this really carefully. Has your primary feeling for Dick always been pity?" "*Yes.*" "That's all I need to hear," said Kline, and rather contemptuously dismissed her. She was then handed over to a psychologist next door ("Kline was just a pill pusher," she remarked, "not a talk psychiatrist"), who gave her a book with some such title as *On Becoming a Human Being.* "I almost threw it at him," said Martha. "Probably the guy was just trying to be helpful, but the book had an unfortunate title." Both Kline and the second man seemed to "read the anger on [Martha's] face" and realize that there was "no point in going on." They were quite right: "I resented being left out of the whole process of Dick's treatment until then. Nobody had ever asked me *anything,* and I was the person who had to live with him!"

The actual leaving proved a protracted, problematic business. Martha had tried to go at least once, while Yates was ranting at her, but realized she didn't have the means: no money, no friends to speak of (outside the marriage), and her family knew nothing of the whole business. Finally, on a day when Yates had gone into the city to teach, she worked up the nerve to call her parents and tell them everything. It came out between sobs, and they arranged to send a plane ticket and money. When Yates returned that afternoon, Martha told him she was going home for a month to "think things out."

"Dick called me a lot in Kansas," she remembered, "and he was *still* verbally abusive, even though he wanted me to stay. He didn't have the sense to realize he was making matters worse." When bullying failed to have the desired effect, he began to plead: He'd stop drinking and try to be nicer and so on. But it was no use. Martha wanted an immediate separation, and had already made plans to move to Washington, D.C., for Montessori teacher training.

Back in Staten Island the couple divided their belongings into two separate moving vans; Yates could now afford to live in Manhattan. He was so vividly crestfallen that several of their neighbors asked him what the problem was. "The problem," he might have reflected à la Michael Davenport, "is that my wife is leaving me, and I think it's going to drive me crazy."

CHAPTER FOURTEEN

Disturbing the Peace: 1974-1976

Yates never entirely recovered from losing Martha, and once she was gone, whatever last threads of sanity had bound him to the world began to fray. Sharon visited her father while Martha was "think[ing] things out" in Kansas City, and found him "very shaky": He said nothing about marital problems, but drank heavily and bickered as if to distract himself. Around this time, too, he attended a CUNY writers' conference, where John Williams noticed his friend was "ill, or getting that way": At a festive lunch attended by such rivals as Joseph Heller and E. L. Doctorow, Yates looked as if he were stupefied with depression.

He tried reaching out to a few old friends, though he was embarrassed by his own wretchedness and could barely bring himself to speak. "Martha got mixed up with those libbers," he told Cassill. "They put ideas in her head. I'm not the easiest person to live with, Verlin, but I tried to be decent with her. She's taken off and gone away." He also commiserated with Dubus, who was then going through "that loneliness shit" too; but Yates was far more desolate, and his worried friend encouraged him to call one of his (Dubus's) former students in the city—a woman, he noted, who was "attractive, tall, intelligent . . . divorced, childless." But Yates only wanted Martha, and was so ashamed of losing her that he couldn't bear telling most of his friends, especially those who'd been at the wedding. "Dick was out of touch for over a year after the breakup," said Robin Metz. "He felt he'd disappointed people." "Damn," Loree Wilson Rackstraw wrote when she finally got the news. "It always made me pleased to envision you with Martha, and to know you were happy."

These were people who knew better than most what Yates had been like without a full-time caretaker.

One day the bewildered man showed up at Vonnegut's apartment on East Forty-eighth Street: He couldn't remember where he'd left his dry cleaning, he explained, and his wife had left him. "I'm leading a very unnatural existence," he said. The kindly Vonnegut invited him to rest there as long as he liked, and Yates shambled in and stayed for almost two weeks. He seemed aware that whatever he said or tried to say seemed a little odd, so he hardly spoke at all; Vonnegut described him as a "black hole in the room": "He had nothing to be proud of or look forward to at that point. Quite neutered. This was a sick man, carrying himself around in his arms."

According to the "PERSONAL RECORD OF ILLNESS" Yates wrote for himself on August 9, 1974—an attempt to reconstruct his lost summer as best he could, while mysterious hospital bills continued to pile up—the most sustained mental collapse of Yates's life began with an alcoholic seizure on the street ("Epileptic fit" Yates wrote in quotes) on May 21. He knocked two teeth out and was taken to a hospital where he was visited by Monica McCall, after which Yates noted "SEVEN MISSING DAYS." In the meantime McCall's companion, Muriel Rukeyser, tried to arrange a room at Yaddo for Yates, who'd apparently told McCall how desperately he needed to get out of the city; but there were no available rooms that summer. On May 31 Yates was found wandering around Staten Island in a daze, and was taken by ambulance to South Bay Hospital: "Records show [I] gave my address as 20 Cliff Street" (Yates's old Staten Island address, though he'd since moved to a tiny apartment on the Upper West Side), "my 'spouse' as Martha and my age as 29." The next day he was removed to St. Vincent's Medical Center in Richmond, Staten Island, where he stayed for a week and was billed $1,222.

Perceived as indigent, perhaps, Yates was then taken to the State Hospital at South Beach for three days, where he was visited by Bill Reardon— *"Don't yet know how he found out I was there,"* Yates wrote (and double-underlined) two months later, which suggests Reardon was sworn to secrecy on the subject. (It can hardly be overemphasized that one of the worst aspects of these ordeals, for Yates, was always the awful shame he later felt once he learned how widely the word had spread.) On June 11 he was transferred to Kirby–Manhattan State Psychiatric Hospital on Ward's Island, where he stayed until July 18: "I remember all 47 [37] days at Ward's Island," Yates wrote. "Suffered two more 'epileptic seizures' while there.* No memory of homecoming." Yates was under the dubious impression he was released from the hospital without a wallet, wristwatch, or "any clothes of [his] own," though such alleged losses could have occurred at any point that summer; without some kind of supporting documentation, Yates was simply too disoriented to know when, what, or how. "Have dim memory of being mugged by a black gang in a subway station," he wrote. "Other dreamlike memories: Arriving at Jerry Schulman's apartment dressed in nothing but a hospital gown, begging for shelter. He refused, gave me shirt, pants and underpants of his own and told me 'Go to a hospital.'" Schulman flatly denies that this ever happened.

Sometime during the summer Monica Yates finally discovered the extent of her father's mental illness. The seventeen-year-old answered the phone and listened in horror as Yates told her in a panicky, begging, barely coherent voice that he'd been rolled in the subway and the police had taken his clothes and he was at the station and somebody had to get him *out* of there. "I was frantically scared," Monica recalled; "my mother was away. I called Bill Reardon, who gently explained, 'He's in the hospital. I'm sorry. You have to talk to your mother about this.'" By the time Sheila got home, her daughter was hysterical. "I tried to explain the gist of [her father's illness] between her sobs," said Sheila.

Yates was at liberty for one week after his release from Ward's Island. On July 25 he went to see a new psychiatrist,[†] Dr. Carol Keban, whose office was on East Eighty-seventh Street. His taxi got stuck in traffic, and Yates asked to be let out a few blocks away. "Didn't have proper address

---

*Another potential cause of Yates's increasingly common seizures was the volatile mixture of drugs he was then taking—none of which, needless to say, should have ever been mixed with alcohol. At Ward's Island he listed the following as "regular" medications: lithium, Dilantin, Antabuse, Sinequan (for depression and/or anxiety associated with alcohol abuse), and Trilafon (an antipsychotic). "Epileptiform seizures" are a common side effect of lithium in large doses, as well as almost any antipsychotic mixed with alcohol; withdrawal from Dilantin also lowers the seizure threshold.

†By that time Yates was disenchanted with Nathan S. Kline, for any number of conceivable reasons.

on me," he wrote; "wandered for hours asking innumerable doormen for 'help' until all the old delusions came back. Must have come home well past midnight, after one doorman called me a 'bum.'" When he returned to his apartment he phoned Martha and tried to explain what had happened; she told him to take a tranquilizer and go to bed—when he woke up, she said, he'd be "in good hands." The next morning she tried to get in touch with Monica McCall, who was on vacation; her associate Jo Stewart was familiar with the problem, though, and promised to do what she could.

An out-of-work actor named Mitch Douglas was in the office as a temporary employee; it was, in fact, his first day on a job that would soon become a permanent career—the beginning of a long association with McCall and her clients. The first client he ever served was Richard Yates. Jo Stewart gave him the author's address, and told him to go there with a mailroom assistant and take Yates to Bellevue: "Whatever you do," she advised, "don't let him know you're taking him to the psych ward." When Douglas arrived at the dingy, devastated little apartment on West Seventy-third, he found Yates hunched in the corner "like a trapped animal," but otherwise subdued. "Would you like to go to the hospital?" Douglas asked. "Oh yes," said Yates in a small voice, "I'd like that." Douglas had told the taxi driver not to divulge their exact destination, but as they approached Bellevue the man loudly inquired, "Which entrance to the psych ward you want?" Fortunately Yates was disinclined to protest at that point. "The lobby was crowded with homeless people trying to get in," Douglas recalled; "they were talking and fighting with imaginary people—total chaos. Dick was interviewed as soon as we got there: 'Are you married?' 'Yes.' 'Where's your wife?' 'Somewhere farrr a-way.' They admitted him on the spot, ahead of all the others doing their tricks." Yates went peacefully.

"In Bellevue," Yates wrote in his memorandum, "[I was] treated by Dr. Rosenberg who became very exasperated with me." Meanwhile a devoted former student of Yates, Jim Goldwasser, asked a young psychiatrist friend named George Hecht to visit Yates and give him a sense that someone on the outside was looking after him. "Yates was absolutely nonfunctional," said Hecht. "I had just finished my residency, and it was hard for me to believe a human being could degenerate to that extent." "Visited by

Dr. Hecht," Yates noted, "but our communication fragmentary and I remember nothing of his talk. Discharged [on August 1] with supply of pills and stern lecture by Rosenberg, who called me 'infantile.' REMEMBERED." One may assume that Rosenberg became frustrated with Yates's refusal to acknowledge his alcoholism, or the extent of his problems in general. In any case his latest confinement at Bellevue had left him demoralized and furious—all the more so when he got the bill: $1,150. Among his first acts as a free man was to call Mitch Douglas. As the latter remembered: "Dick shouted at me, *You little motherfucker, you checked me into the psych ward!* And I said 'No, Dick. You checked yourself in.'" Douglas paused. "And that was the beginning of our adventures together."

After the dismal events of the past two years, Yates tried to reconcile himself to loneliness and get on with his work. Indeed, from this point on, Yates's life would gradually shrink around his writing, a necessity imposed both by himself and the world. A great admirer of Fitzgerald's letters to his daughter Scottie, Yates doubtless took one quote in particular to heart: "What little I've accomplished has been by the most laborious and uphill work, and I wish now I'd *never* relaxed or looked back—but said at the end of *The Great Gatsby*: 'I've found my line—from now on this comes first. This is my immediate duty—without this I am nothing.'" In later years the only regret Yates would allow himself to express publicly was over "the desolate wastes of time" that had diminished his productivity. But for the rest of his life, amid a number of terrible infirmities, Yates remained fully focused on his "immediate duty."

That fall he began the deliberate task of putting his affairs back in order. As before in 1960, he'd promised Bellevue authorities to seek "voluntary psychiatric assistance" on release, and so presented himself to the man who'd visited him *in extremis*, George Hecht. Again Yates managed to startle the young psychiatrist: "He came to my office a few days after Bellevue," Hecht said. "He seemed fine. It was amazing he could resurrect himself like that." Unfortunately Hecht declined to accept Yates as a patient on ethical grounds (because he was the friend of a friend). Hecht recommended a number of other doctors, but for the next few years the irascible, psychiatrist-hating Yates only availed himself of such services (voluntarily) when he needed more or different medication.

By September he was at Yaddo, working steadily. As a testament to his resilience, he was all but caught up with his contract deadline despite recent cataclysms.* Sam Lawrence was planning to feature *Disturbing the Peace* as the lead fiction title on his summer 1975 list, and meanwhile he'd picked up the latest *Ploughshares* and read "Evening on the Côte d'Azur—1952" (the strongest of Yates's hitherto unpublished stories): "It may be an old one," Lawrence wrote the author, "but is it good." That same month *Variety* reported that the actor Patrick O'Neal had made a deal with Al Ruddy to produce and direct *Revolutionary Road*, which O'Neal was then in the process of trying to finance. This last development seemed to complete (however deceptively) the overall positive trend, at least where Yates's career was concerned.

He'd done whatever he could to help Martha get settled in Washington. He called Joe Mohbat, who arranged for her and Gina to stay at his fiancée's place across from the National Zoo; also she stayed briefly with Jim Goldwasser's twin brother Tom and his wife Joan, who helped Martha find a suitable one-bedroom apartment in a tough market for single mothers. Whatever her difficulties, Martha was nothing but relieved to be on her own: The chaos of Gina's first two years had turned her into a quiet, frightened child who had trouble sleeping, though amid the relative calm of Washington she'd begun to show signs of cheering up. Meanwhile Martha felt more pity than censure for the child's father, particularly at a distance, and their lonely lives remained somewhat linked. There was the kindness of Yates's friends—they could imagine what Martha had gone through—as well as the companionship of his daughter Sharon, who was also living in Washington and also lonely. Sharon had moved there for the sake of a college boyfriend who'd since gone off to graduate school; she was planning to move back to New York in the near future, but for the

---

*It's worth bearing in mind that, while *Disturbing the Peace* followed his previous novel by almost six years, Yates hadn't actually begun writing the final John Wilder version until sometime in mid-1972—that is, not far from the time he entered one of the most alcoholic, disturbed phases of his life.

time being she kept her stepmother company and played with Gina. All of which made Martha rather wistfully well disposed toward Yates: "I think about you often, Dick," she wrote in September, "especially of those times when we were the best company for each other. I hope you are not completely miserable and depressed."

Yates finished his novel that fall and made a number of trips to Washington—to visit Gina, but also to make a good impression on Martha if possible, since he desperately hoped (and would go on hoping) for a reconciliation. He was subdued and dignified, doting toward Gina, but of course Martha had no intention of taking him back. She endured their "awkward" outings for the toddler's sake: "I always wanted to make sure Gina had contact with Dick, because I wanted her to know the good as well as the bad. I didn't want her to get some romantic notion of him based on what people said who knew him when he was young." Lest Yates think Martha was warming to his charms, she wrote a letter that November gently prompting him to get on with the divorce: "[M]y mind just wants things to be definitely resolved," she explained.

By then Yates had moved to somewhat less cramped quarters on Twenty-sixth off Fifth Avenue, though he could barely manage the seven flights of stairs: "Jesus Christ," he'd gasp, coughing, "I just hope I don't have a heart attack and be found dead in this grungy place." His apartment was a long studio with a few random sticks of furniture—an orange sofa bed where he slept, a wobbly table in the narrow sit-down kitchen, two or three chairs and a desk by the plaid-curtained window; also he installed a bookshelf where he mostly kept the work of friends and students, as well as a handful of novels he couldn't do without. A Manhattan bachelor again, Yates's mode of habitation immediately reverted to that of his basement days at 27 Seventh Avenue South, complete with staple cockroaches. Nor did he bother to get out much—so many stairs—except to take meals and teach his weekly class at Columbia, where he found more experimental writing per capita than ever before. Happily his new novel was progressing at an unprecedented pace, and Lawrence had high hopes for *Disturbing the Peace*; he passed along a memo to Yates from the Delacorte sales manager, who'd remarked, "We should approach this for what it is—a major book with potentially very large sales."

Yates was a bit less lonely when Sharon moved back to New York in December, though he didn't see as much of her as he might have liked. Along with her sister Monica, she'd also received a deranged phone call or two the previous summer, and wasn't sure whether she was equal to coping with more of the same. Besides, she had her own problems—she was unemployed and had little idea what to do with her life. Certainly she didn't need any more tumult and worry, and in recent years her father had been difficult even at the best of times. For a while she stayed away in Mahopac, then found a job as a file clerk with a Wall Street firm and moved to a small apartment in Brooklyn Heights, whereupon she began seeing her father on a consistent, if not frequent, basis. He seemed somewhat better, though still crotchety: Sharon had begun dating an older man whom Yates thought an awful bore (she agreed for the most part), and he scolded her for wasting time with a man she didn't love; there should be romance and the possibility of marriage, he insisted, otherwise why bother?

Among the many people in the city he used to know, the only one he saw regularly was Bill Reardon, whom he met every week or so for boozy dinners. Yates was comfortable with Reardon, all the more so since the latter had fallen on hard times—the result of a long run of alcohol-related bad luck. A second marriage in the late-sixties had soon ended, after which Reardon lost his job at *Scientific American,* set his apartment on fire, and declared bankruptcy. By the mid-seventies he'd moved to a squalid loft space in TriBeCa, where he supported himself as a chauffeur of sorts. He was, in short, one of the few people who could make Yates feel almost fortunate by comparison, and it was a blow when Reardon died later that year of liver failure. At a memorial gathering on the Upper West Side, Yates mingled somberly with half-forgotten friends from the past, most of whom he was seeing for the last time. "You and I were the only ones who'd sit up and talk all night to Bill," he told Marjorie Owens in a husky whisper.

An improbable figure came along to fill the void. In the fifties and sixties, Seymour Krim had been a devoted hipster who wrote antiestablishment articles for the *Village Voice* and edited a magazine called *Nugget,* whose audience he envisioned as "call girls, dope addicts, jazz musicians and prisoners." He was among those who espoused the idea that the weirdness of actual events had made realistic fiction obsolete, and while teaching at the Iowa Workshop he'd been a great enthusiast of experimentation, praising students for such audacious effects as scribbling in the margins of their stories. Yates and Krim had overlapped at Iowa for just one year, 1970–71, and remarkably Yates had seemed more amused than offended by the aging hipster. They put their workshop sections together on the first day of class, and the neophyte Krim asked his colleague what he did about grades. "Oh, I just give everybody an A," Yates replied.* The following year Krim's provocateur tendencies (to say nothing of his drinking and pot smoking) led to a fiasco at least as damning as Yates's breakdown five years before: A drunken Krim insulted the writer Angus Wilson at a public symposium, then turned on the audience. "Oh, bullshit!" he sneered at an elderly woman who'd wondered why nobody wrote novels for ladies anymore, and when a female student got up to leave, Krim hooted: "She's bored with this goddamn symposium! Who wouldn't be? She's going to find her boyfriend and get laid."

Despite such antics Krim was the kindest of men—"a great generous soul," Dan Wakefield called him—especially where other writers were concerned. For decades he made a practice of sending encouraging postcards ("loved the piece") whenever a friend's work appeared in print. And while he and Yates might have differed aesthetically, by 1975 they had just about everything else in common: Krim, too, was a lonely middle-aged bachelor in bad health who drank and smoked too much, and if anything his apartment was even grimmer than Yates's—a tiny studio in the East Village where he washed his dishes in the bathroom sink. The two men were a comfort to each other. Krim was able to make the gloomy Yates laugh, and the latter became so dependent on Krim's postcards that he threw tantrums when they didn't arrive: *"Where's my mail?!"* he yelled in front of one companion; by then Krim's notes had become so regular that Yates almost suspected the postman of theft.

---

*This appears to have been the case—still another reason for Yates's general popularity among students.

The friends would meet at the Lion's Head and discuss books, mostly, but also more general issues relating to their common predicament. One night Yates broached the subject of suicide, perhaps aware of the fact that he himself was widely viewed as a prime candidate. Both Monica McCall and Sam Lawrence had openly worried about the possibility for years, now more than ever, but Yates was adamant in denouncing the act as "self-indulgent"—which is not to say it didn't exert a pull. The year before, Loree Wilson Rackstraw's second husband had killed himself, and when Yates called to offer condolence he seemed "envious but scornful": "[Dick said] something like, 'How did he do it,'" Rackstraw recalled, "with a tone of voice that said, 'How did he have the right to do it?' I believe he had a kind of hero's pride that *he* didn't kill himself. And also pride that he could drink and smoke so much and still stay alive. He wasn't going to be a wimp and stop drinking or off himself!" But something about Krim's response made Yates drop the subject—an awkward moment that Krim sought to clarify in a subsequent letter: "My mother did the Dutch Act when I was 10 and it's always hung over my life as a possible way out if and when things got too tough. . . . But I enjoy discussing such things with you and please feel no sensitivity at all for categorizing all such acts as self-indulgence."

By that summer, in fact, Yates was able to dismiss the idea with more than just abstract distaste. He was never more content than when his work was going well, and by August he had half-finished a novel that promised to be on a par with *Revolutionary Road*. As for the novel about to be published, he viewed it as a respectable "plateau performance"—if nothing else, an improvement on *A Special Providence*. The usual dread that attended publication was all but entirely absent this time, perhaps because he had neither high hopes to be dashed nor expectations of disaster; also he felt he'd mostly disguised the autobiographical nature of the work behind the deceptive persona of John Wilder, so there was less question of any humiliating public exposure. Meanwhile Vonnegut had come through with another supportive blurb ("Richard Yates has regained the wonderful power he demonstrated in *Revolutionary Road*. It is a cause for celebration"). George Garrett called the book "the best novel [he'd] read in ages," and Sam Lawrence was nothing but optimistic.* What mattered most to Yates, though, was that he himself believed in his talent again: "I think it's okay," he wrote of his third novel, "though not as big or as rich as I'd hoped. Am trying to make up for that in my next one."

Around publication in early September he went to Washington for a festive weekend with Joe Mohbat and his new wife Nancy. Yates was in such high spirits that he inadvertently spat in the young woman's eye while in the middle of an excited bit of storytelling. "Things I regret," he wrote the couple afterward: "1.-Smoking and coughing all the time. 2.-Bending your ears so much. 3.-Pulling that half-assed poetry recital on you in the restaurant.† 4.-Spitting on Nancy. If you can find it in your heart to forgive me for these four . . . then there would seem to be every chance that we might somehow get together again soon. Hope so." At his best Yates was still a lively companion, if a bit hard to take in large doses (as he was coming to realize himself). His friendships with the Mohbats and various others remained viable for the very reason that they were conducted at a certain distance of space and time.

Disturbing the Peace earned the kind of reception that Yates had expected. Gene Lyons in the *New York Times Book Review* came closest to summing up the consensus, commending the book's "exact precision of style and flawless construction," but finding Wilder a simplistic pawn whose fate is too predictable to engage the reader much: "*Disturbing the Peace* is an eloquent minor novel," Lyons wrote, "by an author whom one begins to suspect of systematically denying himself major possibilities." Yates's old friend Anatole Broyard, who reviewed the book in the daily *Times*, was markedly grudging in his praise. He allowed that the novel succeeded "to a degree," and particularly commended the Bellevue scenes,

---

*If Lawrence noticed any similarity between *Disturbing the Peace* and Jack B. Weiner's *The Morning After*—the book that had plunged Yates into such alcoholic misery two and a half years before—he seemed never to mention it. Probably the likeness (such as it was) didn't occur to anybody but Yates.

†"I don't remember what poetry," said Mohbat. "The restaurant was in Georgetown."

but dismissed Wilder's repetitive drunkenness as "about as interesting as having someone throw up on you" and suggested the story's deeper meaning was muddled if not entirely absent. William Pritchard paid the author a compliment in the *Hudson Review* which may have caused unwitting offense*: "One hopes we will begin to be more grateful for American writers like [Yates]: if you can't be Pynchon why try to be second best? Richard Yates works superbly within the limits of his strength." The one notable outright pan was Peter Prescott's notice in *Newsweek,* which granted the novel's "readability" but declared it an ignoble performance on the whole: "Wilder is an . . . unsympathetic wretch, and his wife a dismal cow. . . . Of such stuff is melodrama, not tragedy, made."

Perhaps. As a character Wilder is unremarkable when he isn't utterly loathsome, and while this is in line with Yates's intention, it does diminish the emotional impact: By the end of the novel, when the lifeless Wilder is left permanently institutionalized (implausibly enough), it's all but impossible for the reader to care. As for the rest of the characters—from the pompous Paul Borg to the bovinely patient Janice Wilder to the fickle Pamela Hendricks—they're little more than embodied traits, figures in a morality play, and while such flatness lends itself to the macabre comedy of the novel, the basic effect is a cold one.

Such apparent flaws aside, *Disturbing the Peace* is a remarkable work of art, an advance on Yates's previous work in almost every technical sense. Even its flaws can be justified in terms of craft: That Wilder is one of life's losers, and obnoxiously bitter about it, is an essential requirement of the story Yates meant to tell. And this ceases to be a liability if one considers the novel as the black comedy it is, and so views its hero as a laughable victim rather than a tragic figure meant to evoke pathos. When a friend informed Yates that she'd *cried* at Wilder's fate, he responded with mild exasperation: "I had hoped people might wince a little . . . or shudder, but really didn't expect anyone to cry. Maybe someday I'll write a book that makes people laugh, which is a good deal harder to do."

---

*This would help to explain Yates's conduct (described below) when the two men met shortly thereafter.

Harder still when the material is so repugnant, but not impossible given a receptive reader. Again, those who insist on sympathetic, well-rounded characters in serious "realistic" fiction are bound to be disappointed here—particularly by the supporting cast, since the world of sane society in *Disturbing the Peace* is largely perceived through the eyes of the misfit Wilder, for whom it is monstrously bland and smug: a mass caricature, in short. His wife is "fond of the word 'civilized' . . . and of 'reasonable' and 'adjustment' and 'relationship,' " while she is terrified by "things she [doesn't] understand." Even scenes that ostensibly aren't from Wilder's point of view, but reinforce his basic perspective, might be understood as enacted in his mind—for example, when his friend Paul Borg pauses in traffic to "admire the sober maturity of his face," or when Wilder's triumphant rival Chester Pratt is commended by Pamela Hendricks because he's "so nice and tall." The world from which the diminutive Wilder finds himself excluded is a place where nuance is equated with aberration; aptly its ruler is the "glamour boy" Kennedy rather than the problematic egghead Stevenson (Wilder's choice). And the response to being lumped among the "losers of the world" is rage, as Wilder's fellow Bellevue inmate Henry Spivack—another aberrant and hence more nuanced character—makes explicit when he rails against the complacent normality of his family: "Dear Sis; dear Miss Priss," he writes. "This is important. This is *reality* [italics added]. 1.-Call Dad. 2.-Call Eric and Mark. 3.-Tell your husband he is a simpering, pretentious little fool. 4.-GET ME OUT OF HERE."

But finally, of course, "reality" is perceived imperfectly by both the outcasts of Bellevue and better-adjusted citizens such as Borg and Janice, who are frightened and repelled by the abnormal. For that matter, a novel whose main character is a drunken lunatic might be pardoned for straying from the conventions of reality *and* realism, and in fact *Disturbing the Peace* is no more "realistic" than, say, the early novels of Evelyn Waugh (which it resembles). As a writer Yates was constrained by his own standards of craft, never by the requirements of so-called realism per se, and with this novel he adopted an approach to fit the matter at hand—to wit, a satire on the relative nature of sanity in modern society. That such a work entails certain surrealistic, metafictional effects is underappreciated by those who think Yates was forever at pains to avoid comparisons to Coover, Pynchon, et al. For example: One of the main themes of the novel is the disparity between art and life, "reality" and madness, and hence it's a valid (and funny) narrative tactic for the "gentleman producer" Carl Munchin to propose a rewrite of Wilder's Bellevue script that mimics (metafictionally) the very plot of the novel we're reading: "How does Bellevue change his life?" says Munchin. "I want a revised version of this script of yours to serve as part one, you see. Then I want to see a part two and a part three. . . . I'd say build him up for another breakdown . . . in part two, and then in part three let him have it. . . . Wipe him out." Similarly the weary hack who does the initial rewrite, Jack Haines, fleshes out the script's protagonist in a way that accidentally divines the actual nature of Wilder's life simply by sticking to the usual clichés: "He's unhappily married and he's got kids he can't relate to and he feels trapped. He's solidly middle-class. I don't know what he does for a living, but let's say it's something well-paid and essentially meaningless, like advertising."

Ironically the most "unrealistic" scenes are perhaps the most mimetically exact—namely Wilder's psychotic delusions, which evoke the actual process of going mad with compelling accuracy. And while the overall effect is harrowing and never less than convincing, the comic tone of the novel is held precisely in balance. Thus Wilder smells dogshit on his thumb to remind himself that "he was earthbound and mortal," and imagines a series of impatient tabloid headlines as his Messiah delusion takes over: SAVIOR OR FRAUD? . . . A GLIMPSE! . . . IS HE OR ISN'T HE? . . . THIS IS GETTING SILLY. . . . THE MILLENNIUM! Such a tour de force is the very "order in chaos" to which the hapless Wilder aspires, but which only the rare artist can ever impose—a point reinforced by the presence of the Nabokovian doppelganger (and Yatesian "Me character") Chester Pratt, yet another apposite touch in this singular novel.

One last felicity needs to be mentioned, if only because it was important to Yates: "Generally," he remarked, explaining his own growth as a writer, "I've acquired a better sense of pace." Whereas A Special Providence often languishes amid a welter of detail, Disturbing the Peace is impressionistic in the best sense. Thus Dr. Brink calls Wilder's attention to an article about himself (Brink) in the August 1961 issue of *American Scientists,* after which more than six months pass in the course of a few sentences:

> There wasn't time to read it in the office, but [Wilder] took it home and promised himself to read it soon. In the end the magazine somehow found its way to Pamela's apartment, and when he asked her about it at Christmastime, long after it had ceased to matter very much, she said she guessed she'd thrown it away.
>
> All at once it was spring again. . . .

Such compression would prove an even more crucial aspect of the novel that followed.

Those who consider Yates a "writer's writer" are particularly advised to take another look at the underrated *Disturbing the Peace.* Readers who need to *care* about fictional characters will be left cold, as will readers who require a certain clarity of message. (The novel proposes no solution to the problems it raises: Modern reality is insipid, Yates suggests, and those who can't take refuge in art or illusions or "success"—of whatever sort— are probably condemned to addiction or madness, and there you have it.) But the novel is as strange and perfect in its way as a Fabergé egg, and almost as beautifully useless.

Though an alternate selection of the Book-of-the-Month Club and Psychology Today Book Club, *Disturbing the Peace* sold no better than Yates's previous novels. He was somewhat consoled, though, when it was chosen to receive the Rosenthal Foundation Award of two thousand dollars from the National Institute of Arts and Letters for "that literary work . . . which though it may not be a commercial success, is a considerable literary achievement." The citation referred to *Revolutionary Road* as a "modern American classic," and at first Yates seemed almost giddily pleased; then his face fell and he grumbled, "Oh, what the hell, it's only worth $2,000." Perhaps he noticed in the enclosed brochure that Robert Coover was slated to receive an award for three thousand dollars at the same ceremony.

Work was its own reward as ever, not least because it was the best way to avoid dwelling on life. By the end of the year *The Easter Parade* was "in the home stretch, for better or worse," and a fruitful month at Yaddo yielded not only a finished typescript but also the first chapter and outline of his next novel—"about that second-rate school my mother got me a scholarship to," Yates chuckled. He thought he could make such a book "pretty funny," and besides the idea provided ready means of getting "more dollars from Delacorte." But the main thing was just to keep busy. When his old Iowa disciples Bob Lehrman and Jody Lowens came to Manhattan for New Year's Eve 1975, the only heartening item they found in Yates's bare, chilly apartment was the neatly squared manuscript on his desk. Otherwise the place gave them "an overwhelming impression of loneliness": "The tenants were on rent strike and there was no heat in the building," Lowens recalled. "Dick had the stove burners turned up, the oven too, and he apologized about the cold." Sensing his guests' discomfort, physical and otherwise, Yates invited to buy them a drink at a nearby hotel on Fifth Avenue. It had grown dark by the time they returned to Twenty-sixth Street, and the young men invited Yates to come out and celebrate New Year's Eve with them. "Nah," he said, "I'd better get back to work." "I lost contact with Dick after that," said Lowens. "His life was just too depressing."

For a while, though, he did have "a girl"—as Yates would forever say, though in this case the girl was in her late-thirties. A decade before, Carolyn Gaiser had been a promising young woman who worked at *Harper's Bazaar* and *Glamour* (where she was friends with Grace Schulman), wrote poetry and fiction (including a story published in the *Paris Review*), and went to Italy on a Fulbright. Then she suffered a breakdown of sorts and spent a number of years in and out of hospitals. Once the worst had passed, Gaiser was like "an aging Sally Bowles" in the words of a friend: "She had a kind of bleak, bittersweet humor." She was still in a rather convalescent mode when she met Yates—"two lost people bumping into each other in the dark," as Gaiser put it.

Seymour Krim introduced the two at the Lion's Head. "I understand we have some ex–mutual friends in common," Yates said, meaning the Schulmans. Perhaps because he was aware of Gaiser's own troubled history,

Yates didn't hesitate to admit that he found himself virtually alone in the world. "I have two close friends left," he said. "Sam Lawrence and Sy [Krim]." They compared notes about the Schulmans: Gaiser also felt she'd been banished for becoming difficult, and while Yates conceded that in his case he was mostly to blame, he remained deeply bitter toward Grace. Jerry he forgave as a sweet man who'd been provoked beyond endurance, and by way of example Yates recounted what he still thought was their last meeting—when Schulman "threw him out in the street": "I must have gotten out of line," Yates shook his head. "I can't remember much about it." The Schulmans had been separated since 1971, and Yates described how Jerry lived alone in a "tiny dismal apartment" hoping Grace would take him back—"but she never will," he said knowingly.* Gaiser agreed that it was "tragic," and Yates nodded: "Yeah, but it's true." Then his face lit up. "Hey, that's a great new game! We can start a list of 'tragic but true' people!"

As they prepared to leave the bar and get dinner somewhere, Krim took Gaiser aside: "Don't let him drink too much," he warned. "He's on antipsychotic medication." Gaiser was reminded of her time at Bread Loaf in 1963, the most memorable aspect of which was her involvement with Nelson Algren; a close second, though, was the pervasive gossip about "the man who'd threatened to kill Ciardi" the year before: Richard Yates. Now that man was sitting across from her at Jimmy Day's, drinking too much beer and railing against his "child bride ex-wife" who was then dating a carpenter: "Can you imagine?" he said. "A carpenter! I don't want my little girl Gina exposed to that kind of proletarian stupidity!" He persisted with the subject for some time, then asked for Gaiser's phone number. She gave it to him.

Soon they were spending weekends together. On their first official date Yates appeared in a trench coat, and Gaiser remarked that he looked like Holden Caulfield grown up ("Dick treasured this as a compliment"). That was perhaps the high point of their three months together. Gaiser was a Swarthmore alumna who spoke with what Yates called an affectedly "lockjaw" accent. She also tended to compensate for

---

*The Schulmans did in fact reconcile.

a hobbled self-esteem by insinuating past successes, all of which had a provoking effect on Yates, to say the least. When she mentioned her *Paris Review* credit and regretted that she'd yet to finish a novel—a lingering ambition of hers—Yates hooted, "If you haven't written a novel by the time you're forty [she wasn't forty, but close] you never will!" Gaiser defensively presented Yates with specimens of her published work from the sixties, but he wasn't impressed. Nor was she when Yates, after a certain number of drinks, would start crooning the old standards that used to wow Wendy Sears and the like: "I'd try to look breathless and thrilled," Gaiser recalled, "but it got really tiresome." Later they'd go out for dinner, and Yates would lapse into ungovernable coughing (while talking obsessively about Martha and the carpenter), which attracted kind strangers to their table offering water and smacking the mortified man on the back.

One day in March he was vividly downcast. He'd just gotten proofs for *The Easter Parade* with the following copy editor's memo still attached:

This is *not* a rush book! However it is a difficult author who may call you in his natural state which is a drunken stupor, to check out a comma or something. The editor's note says light copyediting, which is exactly what is needed. Please do not use whoever did his previous book as the author is disenchanted with him/her.

"Dick *agonized* over whether they'd left it there on purpose or accident," said Gaiser. Given that almost exactly the same note would later be attached to *Liars in Love*, it's fair to assume that the Delacorte copy editors were trying to send Yates a message. By then his perfectionist quibbling, excited by alcohol, had become something of a legend among editors and friends alike. "Nobody was up to Dick's long-winded colloquies," said DeWitt Henry, with whom Yates once spoke for several "deadly serious" hours on the subject of whether "toe-jam" was the *mot juste*. Yates was nothing if not dogmatic on matters of punctuation and grammar, and relentless whenever he required information of any sort. While writing about the Dorset printshop in *A Good School*, he pestered Henry to provide pertinent technical data ("quoins" and the like), ditto when he needed fodder for his Washington novel, *Uncertain Times*: "He leaned into conversations and always wanted more detail, detail," said Joe Mohbat, "[then] he'd call months later and say, 'Remember you were talking about . . . ? Where *was* that? Tell me more about that.'"

But what ultimately made Yates the scourge of copy editors was his simple aversion to criticism; any emendation in his manuscript, be it a single semicolon, would cause dark alcoholic brooding, which would finally erupt in long, hectoring, semicoherent phone calls. Meanwhile the foregone end of his affair with Gaiser was hastened somewhat when he canvassed her opinion of *The Easter Parade*, which he'd given her to read in galleys. "Do you think it compares to *Revolutionary Road*?" he pressed, after she'd repeated that it was "very good." "Well," she said, "I think it's very good, but I don't think it's brilliant compared to *Revolutionary Road*." "Damn! Well, I knew that!" said Yates with a kind of bluff stoicism, though from that point on the phrase *good—but not brilliant*! would resurface nastily when he was drunk.

During their last few weeks together, Yates made the woman "pay and pay and pay" as Fitzgerald would have it. "You must have gone to a posh girls' school to get that accent," he'd insist at every opportunity, though she assured him this wasn't the case. Once while they were having dinner in the Village, Yates spotted a former Iowa student and delightedly invited him to join them. "Did you know Algren?" Gaiser asked, after a long silence on her part. "Jesus Christ!" Yates turned on her. "Can't I take you *anywhere* without you dragging up Nelson Algren again?" He made it generally clear that almost any company was preferable to Gaiser's, and urged her to bring friends whenever possible to their meetings. She was amazed by how Yates would metamorphose in the presence of anyone he wished to charm. "How can you help but be in love with this man?" asked a girlfriend whom he'd regaled with witty RFK anecdotes, accent and all. In this case, though, it turned out he was just keeping his hand in: "Well, your friend is delightful," he told Gaiser later that evening, "but I can't stand fat girls. Just can't tolerate it." Soon Gaiser herself became the victim of Yates's "ruthless aesthetics" where women were concerned. One morning she found him staring at her "as if there were a tarantula on [her] shoulder": "Good God, what *is* that?" he said, shakily pointing. "Sort of a *ridge* under your eyes—" "Cheekbones?" asked Gaiser, but Yates shook his head. "No, I mean that padding of *flesh* over them . . . well anyway, it's very unfortunate."

The end came sometime in April. One night at a restaurant, Yates was holding forth on a favorite theme—wishing he'd gone to college—when Gaiser mentioned an old friend from Swarthmore who'd joined the faculty of an Ivy League school, which later paid for the man's occasional stints in pricey rehab facilities. Not only did Yates detect an injustice here, he seemed to think Gaiser tactless for even bringing it up. "Why should that fucking guy have Ivy League colleges picking up tabs for his breakdowns when I have to stay at these ratty hospitals?" he ranted, until a waiter asked them to leave. By the next weekend Yates's mood had only darkened further. Having evidently spent the interval brooding over pretentious Swarthmore girls who presumed to criticize his work, he burst out in a Village restaurant: "*Who the fuck do you think you are? What do you have to show for yourself but some yellowed newspaper clippings and that snotty accent you picked up at some posh girls' school?!*" Gaiser thought this gratuitously cruel, but gamely rejoined that she *hadn't* gone to a posh—"Ahh, who the fuck cares?" said Yates. "As I fled down the street," Gaiser recalled, "Dick ran after me. Between coughs, he said, 'Okay, break up with me. But will you still be my date at the Academy of Arts and Letters?' If I hadn't been so angry with him at the time, I might have recognized the pathos of that remark."

By 1976 Monica Yates had begun to distance herself from her father. Her sudden exposure to the worst of his mental illness two years before had been bad enough, but even when he was relatively stable it was distressing to speak to him; Monica was less passive than her older sister, and after a lifetime of hearing Yates complain about one thing or another—"pulling for pity" she called it—impatience had taken over, and she often hung up on him. Also, of course, he was rarely sober: "There was a window," she said. "He'd wake up tremendously hungover, and put himself together for about two hours. Then he wrote, and then he went out and got drunk for the rest of the day." Meanwhile her mother was "the opposite extreme"— briskly pleasant and self-possessed to the point of aloofness—and Monica was sick of them both. She graduated high school early and considered escaping via the Peace Corps; instead she spent a year at nursing school and then enrolled at the University of Massachusetts (Amherst) as a chemistry major—mainly because pure science was the last thing her father would have picked himself, and Monica wanted to avoid the "self-indulgence" of anything connected with the literary life.

In late March Yates was asked to interview at Amherst College for an opening as writer-in-residence. Though he hated the idea of teaching full-time again, he needed the money and was anxious for almost any change in his present situation; above all, it would mean living near his daughter, who still had little idea of his importance as a writer. And the job seemed his for the taking: The chairman of the English department, William Pritchard, was a great admirer (as Yates might have surmised from the man's review of *Disturbing the Peace* a few months before), and was thrilled to learn from DeWitt Henry that Yates was available. Whether the fix was in or not, though, Yates was so terrified of making a poor showing in his daughter's eyes that, as the date approached, he was almost on the verge of a breakdown. He had to give a reading in addition to the interview, and felt certain that his stories would seem dated to Amherst students, while he himself would come across as a "whiskery old bullshit artist."

The trip got off to a good start. He went to Rhode Island first and gave a reading at Roger Williams as the guest of his protégé Geoffrey Clark, whose unconditional esteem always brought out the best in him; also, he made the acquaintance of another admiring writer and "good guy," Robert Stone. He then moved on to Amherst. Monica lived in a walk-up apartment, where her father's arrival was heralded by a hideous burst of coughing that brought her "health-freak friends" out of their rooms to gaze, appalled, at the bewhiskered apparition pausing every few steps to gasp for air and/or light another cigarette.

Prior to his interview with Amherst president Bill Ward, Yates and Monica had lunch with Pritchard and a colleague, neither of whom knew what to make of the coughing, laconic, oddly hostile Yates. "When do I see the head honcho?" the latter kept asking between paroxysms, or whenever the two men's genial patter subsided. Pritchard wondered if

Yates had any idea who he (Pritchard) was; perhaps Yates hadn't read that admiring review of *Disturbing the Peace*? Pritchard's colleague, meanwhile, spoke with a kind of British accent that seemed to set their guest's teeth on edge.

After his interview with Yates, President Ward took Pritchard aside. "My God, Bill, you think this is going to work out?" Pritchard just shook his head. (Ward was an affable Irishman and heavy smoker himself; it was a bad sign that Yates hadn't warmed in his presence.) By then Yates had given his reading to a group of students in Pritchard's living room, followed by one of the most gruesome Q&A sessions anybody had ever witnessed. Yates, who coughed more than he spoke, may or may not have known that the students had input into the selection process; perhaps he thought the whole thing was just a formality, and a tiresome one at that. "He was the opposite of ingratiating," Pritchard recalled. "Some of the students' questions might have been pretty inept—like, 'Where do you get your ideas?'—but Yates didn't give an inch. His responses were sour, superior, humorless. Sort of like, 'Take it or leave it.' "

"Went through the sweaty business of reading and asskissing at Amherst," Yates wrote Geoffrey Clark, "then waited more than a week only to have them give me—you guessed it—the cough drop." *The cough drop* was one of Yates's favorite terms for rejection, derived from John O'Hara (who used it to characterize his treatment at the hands of the literary establishment): The idea was that when a teacher hands out all the candy, she gives the last hapless kid a cough drop. Yates was not only hurt and embarrassed by the whole fiasco, but puzzled to boot: "Still can't figure out why," he wrote, "since I thought I'd played my cards pretty well up there. The department chairman's letter was some lame nonsense to the effect that there is agitation to hire a woman or a black." Pritchard remembers all too well the "equivocating" letter he'd had to write, as well as Yates's poignant response: "I'd said, 'Send me your expenses.' Yates had come up on the bus, and he mailed me this scrap of ugly brown paper in an envelope with something like '$36.03' scrawled on it."

Denied a prestigious job and lowered still further (he thought) in his daughter's regard, Yates holed up in his apartment and tried to comfort himself with some marijuana Clark had given him in Rhode Island—but the highs, he found, were too much like going crazy. "Or maybe," he wrote, "it's just that I shouldn't do it alone." By then he didn't have much choice in the matter.

Not uncommonly, though, Yates's work was flourishing in inverse proportion to his personal fortunes. He was making excellent progress with his new novel, and *The Easter Parade* was scheduled to be a Book-of-the-Month Club dual main selection (with Judith Guest's *Ordinary People*) for September. The deal would help pay off his debt to Delacorte, but far more important to Yates were all the new readers he'd gain—more than one hundred thousand if only one in ten subscribers took the book. Yates cheerily noted that Delacorte's first response to his novel had been "tepid," but now they were "climbing all over" him. As Sharon Yates remembered, "There was a general sense of *this is it*"—the rediscovery would soon be in full swing.

Then in late June Yates set his apartment on fire. "Three guesses how," he later told Dubus, "and the first two don't count." As ever, he'd started the day with a cigarette in bed, then gone to the bathroom to throw up and shower. Apparently Yates put the butt in an ashtray on the arm of the sofa bed, and the sheets began to smolder when he threw them off to get up—then he opened the bathroom door and created a cross-draft that caused the bed to burst into flames. According to the "funny story" Yates later made of the incident, when he discovered the fire he ran all the way to the ground floor and woke everybody in the building, knocking on all the doors as he made his way back up.* By the time he attempted to reach his desk and recover the one-hundred-page manuscript of *A Good School,* he was prevented by a wall of flames that badly burned his face and hands. He also inhaled a lot of smoke, and was perhaps only semiconscious when the firemen arrived through the window, from which they thoroughly doused the apartment and destroyed whatever of Yates's effects the fire

---

*This part may be so much raconteurish filigree, given that the "funny" version he told Dubus et al. came later. As we shall soon see, the morbidly modest Yates was naked when the firemen arrived, and to put it mildly it seems implausible that he'd run about the hallways thus. The main thing Yates wanted to impress on people (particularly Sam Lawrence) was that the fire had nothing to do with his being *drunk,* which was probably true.

had missed (with at least two exceptions, noted below). Yates was rushed to the Bellevue ICU and was all but inconsolable when, coming to, he learned that firemen had seen him naked. Meanwhile the hair was scorched off his face, his hands were bandaged mitts, and his lungs were in even worse shape than before.

Word traveled fast. Sam Lawrence, who knew Yates could never be bothered to make copies of his manuscripts, called their old friend Frank Russell in East Hampton and begged him to go to Yates's apartment immediately and find out if *A Good School* could be salvaged. Russell obliged, and when he squinted into the drenched, smoky room he spotted a crisp black square on Yates's desk. A former intelligence operative in Southeast Asia, Russell soaked the manuscript in glycerine for a few hours, then peeled the pages apart and Xeroxed them between sheets of acetate. Also intact was a large steamer trunk in which Yates kept letters and original manuscripts; Lawrence subsequently urged him to relinquish the latter into the care of Boston University without further delay.

Among Yates's visitors at Bellevue was Kurt Vonnegut, who found his friend in a fetal position amid hissing oxygen equipment. "Aren't you celebrating the Bicentennial a little early?" Vonnegut quipped. Yates gave him a sheepish, so-what-else-is-new look and asked for a cigarette. Now he'd have to buy an entirely new wardrobe, he mused. Worse (though he kept this part to himself), he had no health insurance, and Bellevue was costing him hundreds of dollars a day for however long it took for smoke-damaged lungs and third-degree burns to heal. From this potentially disastrous situation arose what would prove to be one of the great blessings of Yates's later life: Sharon, sifting through the rubble of her father's apartment, found his honorable discharge in the steamer trunk and got the idea to transfer Yates to the VA hospital across the street from Bellevue. His medical records followed, and thereafter were readily available whenever Yates found himself back in the care of the Veterans Administration. Rarely would he be hounded anymore by exorbitant bills from private doctors.

Around this time he was visited by an attractive stranger from Boston— a woman in her early thirties named Joan Norris, whom Lawrence had hired to handle PR for *The Easter Parade*. The novel had so overwhelmed her that when Dan Wakefield mentioned Yates's predicament, she impulsively caught a plane to New York. Early rumors suggested that Yates had been blinded in the fire, so Norris was relieved to find the man browless and blistered but decidedly able to see. "You look fabulous in green," she said, and Yates chuckled and croaked for a cigarette. She held it to his lips and told him of all the people in Boston, her friend Wakefield for one, who *adored* his work and wished him a full and speedy recovery. The information stayed in his mind.

A week after the fire Sharon Yates found her father muttering and rocking in bed, and when she tried to speak to him—"Here's the bathrobe you wanted"—he answered with non sequiturs: "Bathrobe on the rooftop? Clothes on the barn?" Disoriented by his injuries, Yates had forgotten to mention the matter of psychotropic medication to his doctors; also, as he got older, physical problems tended to lead to a concomitant mental collapse. Anyway Yates was moved to the psychiatric ward, where he soon became merely eccentric again. "I figured out what happened," he told Sharon in a calm but intense voice. "See, the reason I'm like this is I lost my glasses. And I can't see! And if I can't see, my brains get scrambled."*
A couple weeks later he called Sam Lawrence and expressed agitated concern that Delacorte planned to promote *The Easter Parade* as "a woman's book"; mostly, though, he vented frustration over the fact that he was still cooped up in a hospital. A few days later he checked himself out.

At first Yates was homeless but otherwise in fine fettle. He cashed his latest monthly check from Delacorte and took a room at the same raffish hotel where he'd gone to eat breakfast for the last year or so; presumably, too, he bought a few items of clothing. Then he called Frank Russell and offered to take him to dinner as a show of gratitude for saving his manuscript. Russell and his friend Galen Williams (founder of the organization Poets and Writers) met Yates at the specified location—a dingy bar in the twenties called Three Ravens, where the awful food was somewhat

---

*Yates wore glasses for reading and driving only. His idea that the loss thereof led to scrambled brains was recurrent; he'd said something similar to Monica McCall two years before, and she'd humored him by typing her correspondence in capital letters so he could read it better.

redeemed by the liveliness of their host, who waxed in charm and animation as the evening wore on. Yates wanted to go barhopping, and began drinking brandies one after the other without visible effect. Williams had never smoked before, and Yates persuaded her to match him cigarette for cigarette. The night ended around three in the morning. "I'm looking for a girl," Yates told his friends, and they invited him to dine at Williams's apartment the following night, a Friday; they promised to find him a date in the meantime.

Williams awoke feeling so ill from cigarettes that she almost went to the hospital. Despite her frailty, she managed to get Yates a date—an attractive colleague from Poets and Writers—but the whole business exhausted her, and she could hardly move for the rest of the evening. Happily Yates proved a low-maintenance guest. Quite content with the Chinese takeout Russell ordered for the four of them, Yates coaxed his date away at a seemly hour to join him for a nightcap elsewhere. Before he left, he accepted his friends' invitation to stay at their house in East Hampton for as long as he liked, the better to rest up from his recent ordeal. Russell and Williams agreed to call at his hotel in the morning.

The next day Russell was stopped in the hotel lobby by police, who informed him that a man upstairs had a gun. Russell (familiar with Yates's condition, all the more so because he was bipolar himself) explained that he was a friend of the suspect, who was having mental problems as the result of injuries suffered in a fire. He assured police that Yates was harmless, quite a well-known writer in fact, but in any event Russell would take full responsibility. They let him pass. "Oh hi, Frank," Yates greeted him. He was crouched behind a sofa with a large stick in his hands. "Listen: The place is surrounded by Germans at the back. Some of my guys are in front with automatic weapons, but we've really got to be careful." (Words to that effect.) Russell said the cops downstairs were on their side, so that Yates could slip out a side door while Russell covered him with a B.A.R. Yates thought it just might work, and once he was outside Russell waved him into the car and they took off for Long Island.

"Dick got crazier and crazier," Russell recalled. Like a mantra he kept insisting he needed to get to a telephone, then he rolled down the window and began shouting at passing cars: *Look out! Look out! Tanks on the horizon! Watch out! Get covered!"* They decided to pull into a gas station and assess the situation while Yates made his call. After they let him out of the car (*"Clear the area! Goddamn Germans are coming!"*), Williams told Russell that she'd really rather *not* have Yates in their house; what about Arthur and Ruth Roth? Russell agreed it was worth a try. Meanwhile Yates was unable to get the phone to work. Russell persuaded him to take five and made a number of calls himself: to the Roths (they were happy to put Yates up) and to Sam Lawrence, who called back a few minutes later with the name and number of Yates's doctor at the VA; Russell got hold of the man and arranged for Yates's various prescriptions to be phoned in to a nearby pharmacy. They picked up the pills on the way to the Roths' house.

By the time they arrived Yates was already sedated. Williams took Ruth Roth aside and explained that he was having problems; the tranquilizers helped, but the other pills might take a few days to kick in. Ruth, who was fond of Yates and used to his quirks, assured Williams that she and Arthur could handle him and were happy to do so. Sure enough, when Russell and Williams returned a few hours later for a backyard barbecue, they found Yates agreeably listless with liquor and pills. He hadn't slept for the past few nights, and was finally succumbing to a salubrious exhaustion. The worst had apparently passed.

The next day Russell got a call from Arthur Roth. "For Christ's sake," said Roth, "get over here! Dick's gone totally off his wicket!" Yates had slept poorly the night before, and in the morning the Roths found him jittery but composed, or so they'd hoped. Suddenly he asked Ruth to pick up a broom and start sweeping—he wanted to describe the action in his writing—and when she balked he got angry. The situation deteriorated until Yates locked himself in a bathroom and refused to come out. Afraid that his friend was perhaps taking an overdose of pills, Roth called the police and then Russell.

By the time Russell arrived, a tractor-trailer had come to a ragged stop near the Roths' house and its driver was animatedly discussing the matter with police. "This fucking naked guy comes running into the middle of the road!" he was saying. "What the hell am I supposed to do?" The naked Yates, meanwhile, was racing around Roth's house urinating on the walls. The police watched with folded arms. Russell approached and asked if they intended to remove Yates from the premises, and an officer shook his head: In mental cases they couldn't act, he said, though an ambulance was on its way. Russell began spraying Yates with a garden hose in an effort to calm him down.

The two ambulance attendants were actually volunteer firemen from the neighborhood, and Roth later commended their "ennobling brotherhood" for helping to wrestle Yates to the ground and put him in the ambulance. While the firemen rode shotgun, Roth agreed to sit in the back with Yates. "Driving behind that ambulance," Russell remembered, "was like watching a washer-dryer with limbs and body parts spinning into view." The ambulance disgorged two bloody men on arrival at the hospital in Southampton, where emergency room workers were willing to tranquilize Yates but otherwise flatly refused to admit him as a patient. When it came to light that Yates was a veteran, though, they suggested that Russell and Roth drive their friend to the Northport VA.

"My father spent years in Northport as a mental patient," Roth later wrote Yates. "In fact he died there. The experience of helping commit you unloosed all sorts of guilt feelings in me." While Roth lapsed into a speechless funk in the hospital lobby (an "Abreactive Experience" he called it), Russell was all action: He strapped the heavily sedated Yates into a wheelchair and demanded that he be committed on the spot. A clerk asked a number of questions about Yates's service information, which Russell answered off the top of his head ("Rank?" "Captain." "Serial number?" "55-666-777," etc); finally the clerk became suspicious and summoned the head psychiatrist—an Armenian whose command of English was spotty. "I am the big person here!" he announced. "This whole hospital is mine!" Noticing the distraught Roth, he began to lead him away by the elbow for questioning, but Russell indicated Yates. "*What is your name?*" the doctor asked the seated, bleary-eyed man, who managed to mumble "Dick." The doctor insisted on calling him "George," despite repeated correction. ("At one point he asked me what I thought was wrong with you," Roth wrote Yates, "and it was only with the utmost self-control that I prevented myself from saying, 'He keeps thinking people are calling him George.' ") But it seemed the doctor was just passing time, as he ended the interview by declaring that no beds were available.

By now Russell was desperate, as much for his own sake as Yates's. Roth had wandered off somewhere, and as Russell began to wheel their friend toward the exit he got an idea. He continued down the long corridor until he came to a janitor's closet at the back of the hospital. He trundled Yates inside and shut the door. An orderly seemed to eye Russell suspiciously as the latter returned, alone, to the lobby and hurried out to the car, where he found Roth sitting in the passenger seat with a stunned look on his face. "My father died there," Roth explained, dully, as they drove away. "They haven't even changed the paint."

Years later Russell wrote in a personal memoir: "The abandonment of Yates . . . in the janitor's closet of a madhouse, was an act of kindness by a friend, not so much to help him get sane again, but to protect him from the lunacy that he had revealed [i.e., in his fiction] pullulating outside the madhouse walls." As for Arthur Roth, he recorded what he considered "the most intensely dramatic six hours of [his] life" in the regular column he wrote for the *East Hampton Star,* praising the communal spirit and physical strength of neighbors and police who'd helped "cart [Yates] off." He didn't mention Yates by name, though already the story was more or less common knowledge in the parochial world of literary New York. "I was surprised and disappointed in that article," Grace Schulman wrote Roth.

I feel that it was tawdry to betray your long friendship with Dick Yates . . . [and that] you have made . . . a shabby thing of what friendship is all about: privacy, trust, discretion. . . . Usually [Dick] is a good person, capable of free choice under most instances but given to a severe illness that might befall any of us at any time. . . . Close feelings continue long after friendships cease to be active, and somehow I feel that the friendship we all shared years ago is still too important to be treated in that way.

It's doubtful Yates was aware of Schulman's protest (which would have touched him, albeit a bit ruefully perhaps), as he'd been discovered in the janitor's closet by then and duly admitted as a mental patient to the Northport VA, where he languished into the month of August. Still, things could have been a lot worse. Along with his salvaged manuscript and other effects, Sam Lawrence was holding eleven hundred dollars in cash they'd found in Yates's pants; in fact the publisher had taken care of everything, and meanwhile had every reason to hope Yates would be free in time for publication of *The Easter Parade* at the end of the month. Yates was irritated at Lawrence for "hyping himself as a hero," but otherwise seemed cheerful enough. When Bob Lehrman visited him at Northport, Yates pointed out the more interesting lunatics and reflected on some of the lesser-known effects of losing one's reading glasses. All he asked was that Lehrman bring him a few cartons of cigarettes.

CHAPTER FIFTEEN

Out with the Old: 1976-1978

W hat Yates called the "ugly and humiliating" events of that summer had taken a lasting toll. Though he hadn't been badly disfigured by the fire, his good looks had assumed a rather battered quality: His nose was "red and potato-y," as his daughter Sharon put it, and his beard's foremost cosmetic purpose was now to conceal the slight burn scars on his cheeks. Smoke inhalation had further damaged his lungs, and his hacking cough became an even more constant nuisance. Mainly the ordeal seemed to age him: Friends who hadn't seen him in a while were shocked by the difference. He'd become a peculiarly feeble fifty-year-old man.

The destitute Manhattan of the mid-seventies had always seemed alien to Yates, and the fire served to underline the fact that nothing much was left for him there. The last three years had been one disaster after another, the latest of which had left him even more *non grata* among old acquaintances, not to mention a disturbing burden on his daughter. Still, as long as he had a roof over his head he could always bear up, more or less, and after the fire he called his friend Edward Hoagland about a possible sublet in WestBeth—a HUD housing project of four hundred apartments in the old Bell Lab Building on Hudson Street, where artists with low incomes could live cheaply. But there was a long waiting list, and as Hoagland tried tactfully to explain to Yates, WestBeth wasn't really his style. "Dick was an O'Hara-Cheever type," he said, "and there were too many arty beatniks at WestBeth for someone of his quasi–Ivy League gentility."

When Sam Lawrence heard that Yates was considering a move to Boston, he was guardedly encouraging: "You know several people here and life in the Boston-Cambridge area is far more pleasant and agreeable than Manhattan. And not as distracting or as expensive. I've always found it so, as does Dan Wakefield, Tim O'Brien, etc." Actually Yates didn't know all that many people in Boston other than Lawrence himself; he'd been gratified to learn that good writers such as Wakefield admired his work, but in fact he'd never been exposed to that circle.* Dubus lived in nearby Haverhill, and Yates's old student DeWitt Henry was in the city, but that was about it. And lest Yates get the idea that Lawrence would exert himself socially, the latter made a not-so-subtle point of suggesting that Yates get in touch with Joan Norris—the nice publicist who'd paid him that visit in the hospital—if he did decide to move to Boston after his release from Northport. "[She] would be glad to show you around if I'm not here," he wrote, adding that he'd be traveling for the next two months except for a brief time in September. Without a doubt Lawrence wanted his disaster-prone friend to find a more congenial place to live and work, but not at his own expense.

By late August Yates and what remained of his worldly possessions were installed at the Sheraton Commander near Harvard Square. "I was a bit taken aback by Dick's abrupt arrival," said Joan Norris, whom Yates called his "welcoming committee of one." He was already in town when he finally got in touch with her, and Norris was struck by the extent to which he seemed dependent on an almost total stranger. Worried that she'd given him the "wrong idea," she nonetheless did her best to get Yates situated: She helped him find an apartment and buy a few pieces of furniture; she showed him the more notable sights. Within a week or so Yates moved into a two-room brownstone apartment at 473 Beacon Street and learned the neighborhood well enough to fend for himself. But he continued to rely on Norris for companionship, despite the fact that she shrank politely from his caresses and always, always declined his invitation to spend the night.

Sam Lawrence did his part with an elegant dinner party at Locke-Ober's, where Yates inscribed freshly minted copies of *The Easter Parade* and finally met Wakefield, O'Brien, and others. Lawrence made the usual

*Despite a close encounter (at the Blue Mill circa 1961) with Wakefield, whose friend Sarel Eimerl had admired Yates's way with women. See above.

display of ordering fine wines and toasting Yates with due ceremony. As a publisher he was good about that sort of thing.

With one infamous exception, reviews for *The Easter Parade* were the best of Yates's career, though in later years he was reluctant to accept praise for it. He suspected it was "too skimpy" to compete with his first novel, and besides he'd "dashed it off in eleven months" because he "needed the money." Nothing that came so easy could be very good in Yates's eyes. When a friend tried to compliment him on the novel's "consistent symbolism" (for example, when Pookie paints the hand mirror with lipstick or Emily is rescued by her nephew the priest), Yates was almost aggressively dismissive—as he put it, the book was "autobiography" rather than "allegory": "Emily fucking Grimes is *me*," he laughed. "I mean it was all there lying around. Peter. My poor pretentious mother." He did give himself credit for one thing, however: "I'm the one who *saw* it."*

During the summer of 1976, though, as advance copies circulated among friends and fellow writers, the word got out that Yates (then a mental patient at the Northport VA) had written a masterpiece. "Ask me about *The Easter Parade*," Vonnegut remarked to random people, "and I'll tell you to ask me about *Madame Bovary*." When Grace Paley came to Brown for a reading, she and her host Verlin Cassill compared notes on what made the novel—never mind its craft—so deeply moving: "[W]e murmured together about how very, very, very *sad* you tell the story," Cassill wrote Yates, "and certainly that's it, though it might be said in more flowery critical terms." Because of the novel's excellence Yates even seemed on the brink of grasping his two great ambitions—publication in *The New Yorker* and front-page notice by the *New York Times Book Review*. "You write so damn well!" exclaimed Michael Arlen, a staff writer for the former. "How bloody difficult it is to write a good novel, and how few writers manage it! Well, congratulations: and I hope it brings

---

*Yates was of course a master at *selecting* life material for maximum effect, though at least one part of *The Easter Parade* that he didn't "see" in this sense was the ending, when Emily is taken in by her kindly nephew Peter. In fact Yates never visited any of Ruth's children after her death, though he did call Peter to apologize for writing such a "hurtful" book. It was the last time they spoke.

you some good money. Damn well should." So now Yates had a wild
admirer on the inside. As for that other business, alas, the scheduled front-
page review of *The Easter Parade* was thwarted by a newspaper strike,
ending up on page 4.

It was still a fine review. A. G. Mojtabai called the novel a "wrenching
tale," and singled out the author's subtle but resonant use of symbolism
(perhaps to Yates's chagrin)—as when Emily realizes her sister couldn't
possibly know how to find Pookie's building at Central Islip when she herself is locked up there: "The image of mother and daughter locked into
separate stone buildings in some vast impersonal construction is never
underlined by the author," Mojtabai noted; "it is nothing spectacular, but
its strength is considerable and cumulative." Ross Feld in the *New Republic* praised the bravery of Yates's "depressing" vision: "In four novels now,
he's gone his way, and with each one he's becoming more unusual and
valuable." Feld thought the modest scope of *The Easter Parade* was deceptive, that in fact it was "paradigmatic" of a vanishing genre—"the urban
WASP novel"—a field all but ceded to Yates by the likes of O'Hara,
Cheever, and Updike, who'd ceased to particularize the bewildered "dis-
enfranchisement" of the middle class: "Few writers now use so much
unflinching care, skill, and discipline to lay out a vision of dogged existence in life's despite," Feld concluded. A few reviewers had qualms with
what they considered a rather narrow, brutal determinism, but could
hardly deny the book's overall power. "[Yates's] characters seldom have a
chance to enhance their lot by moral or emotional choice," wrote Richard
Todd in the *Atlantic*. "But the details of their suffering are exact, indisputable and moving."

Yates's old friend Anatole Broyard begged to differ. "These [characters]
bow down to the imperatives not of life, but of the author's sense of craftsmanship," he sneered in the daily *Times*. "Craft, in *The Easter Parade,*
resembles a kind of etiquette, which keeps the characters inside the con-
fines of predetermined form." A promising salvo, this, for what might
have proved an adept hatchet job, but the rest reads like the sloppy home-
work of a peevish schoolboy. To support his thesis, Broyard ticked off a
number of random examples in which plausible characterization is
allegedly sacrificed to some petty consideration of craft. "Would any

normal . . . father say that to his thrilled little daughters?" Broyard wondered about Walter Grimes's remark that he's "only a copy-desk man."
"Or does he say it because the author enjoys its dying fall?" With unwitting humor (humorous to a biographer), Broyard also expressed petulant
incredulity over a scene that Yates described almost exactly from life—
that is, Emily's last meeting with the alcoholic, toothless Sarah: "Can we
believe that her conventional husband and her grown sons would have
allowed her to appear this way? Or is she again being sacrificed to a 'good
scene'?" And though Broyard concluded his diatribe by accusing contemporary novelists (as if Yates were representative of their worst tendencies)
of being "unwilling or unable to meet their people on their messy terms,"
he'd earlier sniped at the "pointless incongruity" (i.e., "messiness"?) of
Yates's characterizations.

Those who wish Yates ill (for whatever reason) are mostly constrained
to a single line of attack where *The Easter Parade* is concerned: that it's
too perfect, *too* pat, that its merciless craftsmanship works like a kind of
infernal machine to grind its characters down. "Neither of the Grimes sisters would have a happy life," the narrator announces at the outset, "and
looking back it always seemed that the trouble began with their parents'
divorce." Immediately the reader is swept up in the current of the story—
before one can balk at the dark warning of that opening sentence—and
just over two hundred pages and fifty nightmarish years later one suddenly
arrives full circle at the ironic counterpoint of that final line: "Would you
like to come on in and meet the family?" Ah, the family.

If one likes uplift—believes in the family, believes that people tend to
learn from their mistakes and so forth—then clearly *The Easter Parade*
will be a bitter read. But a feat of empty craftsmanship it is not. Life goes
wrong for the Grimes sisters not because of some implausible contrivance
on the part of a sinister narrator, but rather because "they can't help being
the people they are"—Yates's explicit vision of tragedy. Emily fancies herself "a stickler for accuracy" and is determined to avoid her mother's fol-
lies and pass through life without illusions—but illusions (of love or God
or self-worth or whatever) are simply the way people make sense of inex-
plicable suffering, and by trying to comprehend things at face value Emily
comprehends nothing ("I see") and ends up alone. Least of all can she

comprehend Emily Grimes, and hence her male companions tend to be reflections of her own tenuous self-image, and just as unwittingly false. While Emily strives to be an intellectual at Columbia, she ends up with the flabby philosopher manqué Andrew Crawford, who absurdly affects the "demeanor of an athlete at rest." Due for a spell of carnality after Crawford's impotence, she spends a number of luxurious nights with the virile Lars Ericson, who proves to be a narcissistic bisexual given to striking poses à la Michelangelo's *David*. As for Emily's own poses and self-deceptions, the most ruinous by far is that of being essentially independent despite her "unfathomable dread of being alone." The results are evident in Emily's forced behavior toward Howard Dunninger, her last bulwark against total isolation. Dunninger—who works for a company that makes synthetic fibers, no less—is a sturdy burgher who can offer, if not love, the sort of security Emily desperately needs. But her bewildered self-doubt is such that she often hesitates to make an intimate gesture, lest the man think her too demanding or needy. Thus the affair is circumscribed by a number of nice calculations on Emily's part, as she labors to become the precise kind of companion that a prosaic fellow such as Dunninger might want. "As she often told him—and she knew it might have been wiser not to tell him at all—she had never enjoyed herself so much with anyone."

Might it all have worked out differently? Perhaps, if Yates had been the kind of writer Broyard accuses him of being, and thus willing to contrive a particular outcome by making his characters behave implausibly. But of course the opposite is true: Emily and Sarah "can't help being the people they are," and so Emily clings to a mirage of independence rather than saving her sister and perhaps herself ("I don't *want* her dragging down my life"), while Sarah, in turn, doesn't really want to be saved—her marriage is "sacred," after all, and has given her the only real sense of love and security she's ever known. "Most people do the best they can," says Emily's nephew Peter. "When terrible things happen, there usually isn't anyone to blame." The idea runs like a gray thread throughout Yates's work: It's bleakly true in a way, but it's insufficient, and it's meant to be.

As the Flaubertian writer who is "omnipresent and invisible" in his own work, Yates reveals the pattern of his characters' mistakes without manipulating their fates; he's off paring his nails, so to speak, while the characters behave as they must. Some readers express exasperation over the fecklessness of Yates's people, but how would anyone appear from a wholly objective vantage? However we might "rush around trying to do [our] best" (Yates's phrase), a certain degree of squalor awaits us all— loneliness, error, death—and reminders of this are woven artfully into every page of *The Easter Parade*. Sarah is marked for disaster by the "fine little blue-white scar" on her eyelid ("like the hesitant stroke of a pencil"); the main street of St. Charles is dominated by a sign announcing BLOOD AND SAND WORMS; Pookie strives for "flair" but can't put her lipstick on straight and dribbles spaghetti sauce on her chin, and after all her name is *Grimes*. Perhaps the most poignant symbol is the eponymous "Easter Parade" photograph of Tony and Sarah—"smiling at each other like the very soul of romance in the April sunshine"—which Emily finds "hanging awry" after Sarah's funeral, "as if from some heavy blow that had shuddered the wall."

Groping to explain the greatness of *The Easter Parade*, Cassill had it right: It arises from the "very, very, very *sad*" way Yates tells the story, and of course this too is a function of craft. Even the novel's summary narration serves the larger purpose of emphasizing the characters' helplessness, as if things are happening *to* them, suddenly, but with terrible logic. Part Two begins, "For a few years after she divorced Andrew Crawford"—a splendid elliptical leap from the previous line ("I hate your body"); what follows is a bit of deft exposition about Emily's jobs in the meantime, her two abortions, a representative scene of her struggling to make sense of it all (ABORTION: A WOMAN'S VIEW), and finally her grateful return to the everyday routine of work and parties. "Then suddenly it was 1955, and she was thirty years old." All in two pages.

The Easter Parade was one of five novels nominated for that year's National Book Critics' Circle Award (John Gardner's *October Light* won, which must have galled Yates), a *New York Times* Editors' Choice Book of the Year, as well as one of fifty "notable books" selected by the American Library Association. Delacorte sold more than twelve thousand in hardback and the Book-of-the-Month Club sold a colossal (for Yates) 112,000. The breadth of its appeal was such that Saul Bellow declared it one of the "top three novels of the year," which may help to explain why Yates himself thought so little of it.

For Yates there was no more resting between books (if he could help it). In later years his son-in-law would chide him—"If I were you I'd take off for Bermuda"—but the only rewarding escape anymore was writing. As Bob Lacy noted, "Henri Troyat, the biographer, says of Chekhov that by the time he reached forty 'life had become an excuse for writing.' For the Dick Yates I knew, life was *always* an excuse for writing. He didn't have much of a knack for living." Yates would not have demurred, and his life in Boston was almost entirely built around his work; whenever he deviated from his narrow routine, disaster had a way of pouncing.

In a later essay ("A Salute to Mister Yates"), Dubus evoked his friend's spartan apartment on Beacon Street as a kind of objective correlative for Yates's total devotion to his craft: "It was . . . a place that should be left intact when Dick moved, a place young writers should go to, and sit in, and ask themselves whether or not their commitment to writing had enough heart to live, thirty years later, as Dick's did: with time his only luxury, and absolute honesty one of his few rewards." Perhaps, but given the way Dubus described this humble shrine, it's hard to imagine any earnest young apprentice being much daunted by it. He mentioned the L-shaped tables that served as Yates's desk, covered with a tidy assortment of piles: the legal pads he used for first drafts, a typed manuscript for revision, and galley proofs of other writers' books; on the shorter table was a manual typewriter and many sharpened pencils. Yates confined himself almost entirely to the room in which he worked; Dubus "never saw him enter" the tiny spare bedroom where Gina slept during her visits. Next to his desk was a sofa where guests would sit, while Yates sat opposite on his narrow bed ("always made," Dubus pointed out). The rest of his furniture consisted of a bookshelf and a derelict, unplugged TV that the writer Penelope Mortimer had left Yates when she went back to England. (Yates neither watched TV nor went to the movies.) The only decoration on the walls were some of Gina's drawings; there was a large bay window over-looking an alley. The refrigerator was stocked with three items: instant coffee, beer, and yogurt, the last of which Yates ate for breakfast (yogurt was one of the "great discoveries" of his later life: tastes good, goes down easy). Yates himself was quite content with the place.

The words *squalid* and *depressing* appear nowhere in Dubus's essay, though they almost invariably come up when other friends attempt to do justice to that same apartment. "It was so bare and awful," said Peggy Rambach, Dubus's third wife. "It stank of cigarette smoke, the blue velvet curtains had turned brown with dust, the walls were gray with nicotine. I once wrote a poem about a child's picture on Dick's empty wall; it was a very affecting sight." "Dick was the least bourgeois person I ever met," said Mark Costello, referring to Yates's disdain for material frippery, which even the most hardened bohemians might have found excessive. As for that particular apartment, Costello summed it up as "fucking *grim*." There were only one or two wan lights, and particularly at night the place was so gloomy that hardly anyone but Yates could bear it for very long. Robin Metz remembers staring at the circle of crushed cockroaches around Yates's swivel desk chair: "I reflected that his life had constricted to this little space, full of dead roaches, around his writing. That was all that was left: his whole life."

Not entirely. Yates's "clean, well-lighted place" in Boston was the Crossroads Irish Pub on the corner of Beacon and Massachusetts Avenue, about a hundred yards from his apartment. Except for special occasions, Yates ate almost every lunch and dinner there for eleven years. Usually he sat alone in a particular booth opposite the bar in front, smoking and star-ing into space; sometimes he'd mutter to himself between coughing jags. The employees affected not to notice. The owner of the place was a kindly, barrel-shaped Boston Irishman named Michael Brodigan, whose experi-ence with quirky, solitary bachelors was extensive. For a while he had no idea that Yates was a writer, much less a rather celebrated one, but it was pretty much all the same to both men: Brodigan would give Yates a friendly greeting and linger if encouraged, though generally Yates pre-ferred to be left alone with his thoughts. In the afternoon he'd go home and nap, then write for a few more hours and return to the Crossroads around seven. By ten o'clock, usually, he'd drunk enough Michelob to face his dark apartment and get some sleep.

Yates was not one to insist on special treatment—if his usual booth was taken, he'd gloomily proceed to the next—but he was clearly a man who wanted looking after, and the waitresses at the Crossroads did their best. At times when he was drinking liquor he liked his Jim Beam served in a particular skinny four-ounce glass with water on the side, but there was only one such glass on the premises; Yates was noticeably crestfallen when it wasn't available. Soon it was set aside as "Dick's glass." Yates also enjoyed horseradish with the Sunday special—a prime rib sandwich—so a jar was kept behind the bar for the one person who asked for it; when a waitress discovered it empty one Sunday, she ducked across the street to the Marlborough Market in her apron. All of which was part of a larger campaign to cheer the poor man up. At his worst Yates gave the impression of being a uniquely despondent street person: beard matted, raincoat and suit rumpled and stained, muttering and hacking and half mad. (One might add that his button-down shirts were generally clean and pressed no matter what; taking these to the dry cleaner was part of an instinctive routine.) "What're *you* so happy about?" he'd grumble at his waitresses' show of compensatory perkiness; then he'd try to muster a polite smile before putting his head back in his hands and resuming his funk. After he'd gone for his afternoon nap, waitresses would prepare the booth for his return a few hours later, wiping down both sides thoroughly to get all the ashes scattered by his explosive coughing.

One of the few companions who continued to meet Yates over the years was Andre Dubus, who every so often made a point of driving (or being driven) down from Haverhill to drink with his friend at the Crossroads. Dubus's love and admiration for Yates was absolute, though neither man was given to soul-baring intimacies (unless coated in masculine bluster à la "that loneliness shit"), and their talks tended to skim along the well-worn surface of writing and books. Sometimes Dubus would coax his friend to Fenway for a Red Sox game, but Yates was immune to such ancillary enthusiasms and mostly they stayed at the Crossroads. Brodigan noted that the only times he really saw Yates "rowdy"—animated in a happy way—was in Dubus's company (or, later, Dan Wakefield's).

Though he cultivated a certain degree of austerity, Yates hated being so alone in the world. Above all he longed for female companionship, and as one of the greatest living writers in America he was not without opportunity. Any number of women admired his work and wanted to meet him, and generally Yates made a good first impression: modest, courteous, quietly amusing—a gentleman. He also drank too much, got incensed at the least provocation, obliviously raised his voice in public, knocked things over, coughed incessantly, and caused searing embarrassment to himself and others. It didn't require an unusual degree of insight to realize that he couldn't help himself, and most women were willing to be patient up to a point—an inevitable point when, drained, they'd withdraw to a safe (if sympathetic) distance.

Penelope Mortimer was one of these. Writer-in-residence at Boston University when Yates came to the city, she'd admired *The Easter Parade* and found the author a kindred spirit of sorts: Both chain-smoked, both were fed up with teaching (Mortimer, like Yates, emphasized the transience of her duties by keeping her office stripped of adornment or personal effects), and both had tales to tell of long blocked spells that occasionally rendered life all but hopeless. At fifty-eight Mortimer was more mature than Yates usually liked, but she was also handsome and formidable and a wonderful writer. Yates referred to her as a *personage*.

But it wasn't long before she was finding reasons to avoid him: "I'm not calling back just now because I'm sunk and no good for you," she wrote, and gave the rather lame excuse—"this may seem very trivial"—that she'd failed in her latest attempt to quit smoking and was depressed about it. "Richard I'm sorry to be such a near-dead loss at the moment. That's a real apology, not one of yours which are all needless." Yates scribbled a draft of his response on the back of this note, which helps put the matter into more definite perspective:

> My apologies *aren't* "needless"—this last batch was to have been for my
> dreary outburst at your mention of Edward Albee's name. I'll probably get

over that sort of thing some day, but nobody should be expected to wait. I'm very, very sorry you're so low. . . . Please bear in mind that you're a lovely . . . gifted girl, and that I'd rather be [illegible: looks like "quietly" or "quickly"] carried out of your house than welcomed into almost any other I know. Love, Dick

That last statement strongly suggests Yates had already been physically removed from Mortimer's apartment—whether kicking and screaming or calmly supine, one cannot know.* What might be surmised from certain other epistolary remarks, though, was that Yates had a fascination with the novelty (c. 1976–77) of Mortimer's answering machine, and tended to leave rambling and probably sodden messages, particularly when she refused to see him. Also, Mortimer was fiercely opinionated but unwilling, it seems, to weather outbursts from Yates as a result of that fact. "While *Revolutionary Road* is a lot better than a lot of Updike," she wrote him, "it's a lot like a lot of Updike too (don't be MAD at me)." In general she was going through her own bad patch at the time, and while she evidently cared for Yates and empathized only too well with his malaise (she left him her TV after all), such was not the stuff of romance: "Two scared people don't make one brave one, have you noticed?" she wrote.

Around then too he met a middle-aged divorcée named Lynn Meyer at a cocktail party given by Vonnegut's ex-wife. Meyer had read *Revolutionary Road* when it was first published, and was thrilled to meet the "exceptionally courteous" author, to whom she gushed about how much the book had meant to people of their generation. Since she figured Yates was "too shy" to ask for her phone number (emphatic praise of his work tended to make Yates pleased but uncomfortable), she called and invited him to another party a few days later. "It was terrible," she recalled. "Neither of us knew many people there, and everyone was dressed in these Christmas-colored clothes. It was Martha Stewart's worst nightmare."

---

*Mortimer died in 1999, and details of her friendship with Yates are derived from a handful of letters and the scant testimony of a few witnesses.

But Yates gracefully endured, and afterward made Meyer laugh by deconstructing the "smug, rich, dumb" people at the party.

During the month or so that they dated, Yates didn't appear to be drinking much. He offered to keep a bottle of Scotch in his apartment for Meyer's sake, and assured her it wouldn't tempt him. And while he often corrected her with the same acuity he'd brought to his critique of the "dumb" nouveau riche, he was generally tactful about it, as if it were simply a matter of mutual interest. When she mentioned a visit to the "beauty parlor," Yates replied, "You don't say 'beauty parlor.' That's the wrong class. You say 'hairdresser.'" Also they talked about Meyer's children, both in prep school at the time. Yates was intrigued by the general subject of prep schools, but made it clear he'd rather not meet Meyer's children and bitterly remarked on his mother's "creepy" tendency to expose her boyfriends to him as a child.

The two rarely met other people, and as a change of pace they'd planned to drive to the writer George Garrett's house in Maine for a weekend in January. When they met for dinner that Thursday, though, Yates was jumpy and irritable and coughing more than usual: He explained that, as a result of going off his medication, he'd had a seizure the night before and passed out in a snowdrift.* Though he tried to make light of the incident, he was plainly traumatized both mentally and physically; still, he insisted they stick to their weekend plans, and promised to get plenty of rest before their departure two days later.

That Saturday a big snowstorm struck, and Mcyer called Yates to cancel the trip. But Yates wanted to talk about something else. Earlier Meyer had mentioned a friend who, when drunk, rode a horse into her house yelling, "The British are coming! The British are coming!"; Meyer had thought it curious how such people became "situational alcoholics"—that is, given to regular benders but otherwise somewhat abstemious. Yates had

---

*Again, Yates preferred to be viewed as a man who suffered from a "chemical imbalance" rather than an alcoholic. When lucid, Yates almost always took his medication; if he didn't, it meant he was drunk or deranged or both, and the primary reason he passed out in the snowdrift was almost certainly drink, not drug withdrawal.

seemed a touch defensive when the subject first came up, but now he was downright obsessed by it: "Why are you so critical of her?" he snapped on the phone. "I think it's refreshing! I think it's a wonderful gesture!" He went on and on and wouldn't be persuaded to drop it. Finally Meyer told him she was coming over.

She found Yates in very bad shape. "He was drinking and smoking about ten cigarettes at once," she remembered. "He'd light one, forget about it, and light another. I thought he was going to set himself on fire again." Yates hadn't eaten (or slept) since their dinner on Thursday, and Meyer coaxed him out of his apartment to get some food. He never stopped talking for a moment—a "grandiose and strange" monologue about the various people who'd betrayed and abandoned him over the years; when Meyer tried to distract him with happier subjects, he'd become angry (*Why are we talking about this?*"). At last she called her psychiatrist for advice, and was told to stay with Yates until he got exhausted. At the moment it seemed a remote contingency. Yates would begin to lie down, then jump back up and start pacing again, or try to write, all the while lighting cigarettes one after the other and talking, talking. Meyer began to worry that she herself would be the one to get exhausted and wake up in flames.

As night fell, Meyer began to panic. She couldn't hold out much longer, nor could she leave Yates alone like this. "Don't tell my daughters!" he said over and over. The only two people Yates would allow her to call in the Boston area were Mortimer and Dubus, but Meyer couldn't get hold of either. Her psychiatrist advised her to take him "somewhere safe"— that is, the hospital—but Yates frowned on the idea. For hours they went back and forth about it, and finally he relented. "I drove him to the walk-in clinic at Massachusetts General," said Meyer, "which was run by a couple of four-year-olds. They refused to care for him because he had no insurance. I told them he was a famous writer with plenty of money, but it cut no ice." Eventually the suggestion was made that Yates be taken to the Bedford VA, but the ambulance was long in coming and meanwhile the exhausted Meyer was enjoined to stay with the patient. By then Yates was coming down at last, mumbling dazed apologies as the terrible awareness began to dawn.

When it was over Meyer was on the edge of collapse herself, and arranged to visit friends in Florida to recuperate. Before she left town, though, she wanted to make sure somebody was looking after Yates. She called Sam Lawrence—whom she knew slightly through her ex-husband—and left a detailed message as to Yates's whereabouts and condition. She called Vonnegut, and listened as the black humorist regaled her with other Yatesian adventures ("like it was all a big lark"). She called George Garrett to cancel their visit. The upshot of Meyer's laudable concern was that the story of the snowdrift and its aftermath became a cornerstone of Yates's legend. "I was impressed by the way he persevered," said the writer Madison Smartt Bell (who eventually heard the story from Garrett). "After burning down his apartment and falling into that snowdrift, I figured, you know, he'd survived both fire and ice."

After that, Yates became more of a pariah than ever—particularly in Boston, where he was derided in polite literary circles as a drunken joke. "I used to regard Dick as a test by which to judge others," said Bill Keough, an old Iowa friend whom Yates occasionally visited in West Townsend. "If someone was an ambitious shit, he wouldn't care about Dick, because his books didn't sell and people thought him odd, a loser. But if you cared about writing, you cared about Dick too." Very few people in Boston, it seemed, cared about writing, and it soon became apparent to Yates that most people knew the worst *wherever* they happened to live. Shortly after his release from the Bedford VA, he got a long-distance call from his old girlfriend Carolyn Gaiser, who advised him to quit drinking. "I was afraid he'd fly into one of his rages," Gaiser recalled, "but he thanked me for my concern and said he wasn't ready to do anything that drastic. It was pretty clear he wasn't eager to stay on the phone."

As for Lynn Meyer, she returned to Boston in February and had lunch with Yates, who was chastened and gentlemanly as ever. When she mentioned that she'd gotten engaged in Florida, he offered warm congratulations and even came to Meyer's farewell party a few months later and met her new husband. Around that time, too, a party was given for Penelope Mortimer before her return to England. John Updike attended with his new wife, but he and Yates appear not to have spoken. In fact Yates mostly sat alone nursing his drink while the others danced (the guest of honor had particularly wanted dancing). Mortimer's final note to Yates was sent from London in June. "*Please* will you understand how important you are and how necessary both as a writer and a person. . . . I'm sorry if I didn't live up to expectations, but it's a zone I find hard to live in. I'm delighted and honored (American) to know you and to go on knowing you."

Yates found comfort where he could, but in most cases he accepted the defection of random women with a kind of desolate equanimity. As he sat in the Crossroads smoking and muttering, it was mostly Martha on his mind, or so he'd tell others when the need to confide became overwhelming. The last few ghastly years had made him miss her more than ever—if such were possible—and as late as 1977 he continued to put off divorce in hope of her return. Martha, meanwhile, had moved to Marin County, California, in order to put as many miles as possible between her and Yates. "He couldn't grasp that she'd had it with him," said Yates's soon-to-be psychiatrist. "He never could see what a burden he put on other people." Yates blamed himself for the breakup, but the suddenness of it (as he saw it) continued to puzzle him; he could only figure that she'd been taken in by "the Libbers" and what he called "the artsy-fartsy crowd." "Imagine going to California to make gew-gaws!" he'd say, which was how he'd refer to Martha's dabbling in art. In moments of particular bitterness he'd point out that he always thought her photography and whatnot was a sham, and wondered why anyone would swap taking care of a real artist for making "gew-gaws." As for what he imagined to be her motives for moving to Marin County, they were the same attributed to Sarah Davenport in *Young Hearts Crying*: "Marin County . . . had now become well known as a lively and inviting sanctuary for recently divorced young women, many of them mothers—and for swinging, stomping, surprisingly nice young men." She also taught at a Montessori school there.

Yates called to speak to Gina every Sunday morning, and when Martha answered the phone he'd often try to keep her on the line with solicitous inquiries about one thing and another. She'd respond politely, but if he got too personal or began to wax sentimental she'd cut him off, and Yates would be hurt. Finally, when the exasperated woman informed him she was seeking no-fault divorce in California, Yates wrote a letter expressing a forlorn perplexity toward her refusal to talk things over, begging her to explain once and for all her reasons for leaving him. This she did. "I have gotten the impression you would rather believe your own version of things than hear mine," she wrote. "I *resent* your request that I be 'gentle and considerate of my words.' I did that for far too many years at the expense of honesty." And so, with what must have struck the hurting man as brutal candor (rather than a remarkably temperate elision of specific malfeasances on his part), Martha explained the gist of her grievances:

> You're the one who wrote *Revolutionary Road.* You know the torments people go through trying to live out roles, exacting demands from loved ones, secretly longing to be free. But underneath it all I think you don't believe in freedom. It too is a farce in your view. But I always did guiltily long to be free. . . . Your statement that 'most women of your age can be presumed to have found, by now, about as much of themselves as there ever was to find' is *ridiculous* to me. . . . There were many times when I allowed your way of thinking and of seeing things to impose a type of censorship on mine. . . .
>
> I'm afraid that if I don't emphasize how difficult you were to live with, how exhausting it was trying to please you, understand you, and finally how huge was my resentment at having given myself away for so many years, you will miss the point entirely. So here is that emphasis.

Emphasis or no, Yates went on talking about "Libbers" and "gew-gaws," and a year later he'd vent his bitterness in the story "A Natural Girl," which depicts a more benign version of Yates being callously dumped by a simulacrum of Martha. But at some level he knew better, all the more so over time. As Michael Davenport reflects about his young wife, "Sarah was too nice a girl ever to be charged with 'torturing' a man; he had always known that. Still, she had never been the kind of girl who would collaborate in allowing her future to fall apart, and that was something he'd always known about her, too."

The divorce was finalized that spring, which momentarily seemed to improve Martha's mood where her ex-husband was concerned. When he wrote asking her, in effect, to remember the good times and all the ways he'd tried to make her happy—enumerating a number of specific material gifts—Martha replied in a way that suggested he wasn't far wrong in assuming she'd been influenced by certain modish ideas. "Does an apple tree give skirts, does a rosebush give shoes, does the sky give watches?" she wrote, imploring Yates to meditate more on things unseen. Specifically she urged him to get psychoanalyzed: "You've always had *so* many voices, but no one to help you interpret them. This would be called dream therapy, or Jungian therapy—ask among your friends. Accept the obvious gifts of your own psyche."

Whether because of Martha's well-meaning advice, or simply because he needed someone to talk to (even a psychiatrist), Yates subsequently arranged to meet for weekly psychotherapy sessions with the thirty-four-year-old Winthrop Burr at the VA outpatient clinic in Boston. "The nicest thing about me is my stories," he announced at the outset. In a manner that was generally brusque and detached—he was skeptical as ever that airing his pain to a stranger would serve any useful purpose—Yates spoke of his agonizing loneliness since the breakup of his marriage. He mentioned a few people who begrudged him little bits of their time, but really he had no close friends. Also he lived in constant fear of humiliation: People treated him as a "skid-row figure" because, Yates supposed, he coughed and smoked and looked unwell. (That he was often drunk wasn't emphasized as a factor.) For example, he'd gotten into a number of fights with cabbies who were rude to him; Yates would start yelling and they'd make him get out. Once he tried to meet Sam Lawrence for a drink at the Parker House hotel, but employees wouldn't let him in the door. Tracing the cause of his alienation and its manifold effects, Yates would speak of his mother with a scathing, obsessive hatred that sometimes brought him to the brink of tears.

"There was a lot to admire in Yates," said Burr. "He evoked feelings of protectiveness in others." Over the years Yates was occasionally gracious in acknowledging the young psychiatrist's help, though often he was quite the opposite. In retrospect Burr regrets taking him as a patient: "You don't do psychodynamic therapy with people who are drinking. It doesn't help them, and it might make them worse [because] it stirs up emotions that make them *want* to drink." In the beginning, though, Burr wasn't aware of the extent of his patient's drinking, as Yates was at pains to conceal it; but in due course Burr came to believe that Yates's increasingly frequent breakdowns, indeed any number of woes, were all but entirely caused by alcohol.

Meanwhile a happy incongruity between Yates's life and work continued to obtain. As he intensely reflected on his childhood, both for Burr's benefit and that of *A Good School,* he felt more and more compelled to write about that seminal episode when his mother had been commissioned to sculpt FDR (as well as a cluster of other memories from that time, such as her drunkenly getting into bed with him and puking on his pillow). At first Yates considered working the material into his novel somewhere, but finally decided to put the book aside for a month or so and write a separate, self-contained account. It was a breakthrough for Yates, whose every attempt to write short fiction over the past fifteen years (more than twenty, really, with the single exception of "Builders") had come to naught. "I was so pleased with the way ["Oh, Joseph, I'm So Tired"] turned out," he told an interviewer, "that I thought I might try to write six others when *A Good School* was over and make a book of them." Writing stories would also enable him to renew his campaign to breach the walls of *The New Yorker.*

In April, Yates accepted a two-week Visiting Writer stint at Columbia, though in general he was more reluctant than ever to enter a classroom: As always, he was inclined to husband his time and energy for writing, but also the prospect of ridicule and failure had become far more threatening. The Amherst debacle haunted him, and then of course he was morbidly conscious of the way people stared at him on a daily basis, as if he were a curious and disturbing spectacle. "How do I look?" he asked Crossroads owner Michael Brodigan after his ejection from the Parker House. "Is something *wrong* with me?" Even a chance to visit his friend Geoff Clark at Roger Williams was more than he could face at the time: "Thanks for the invitation," he wrote, "but I'll shy away. Every time I meet one of your classes I make a horse's ass of myself, and that tendency would be rampantly worse if I were given a chance to 'explain' *The Easter Parade* to a roomful of girls."

Much more welcome was the chance to resume his mentorly role on a private level with his semi-estranged daughter Monica, who'd switched her college major from chemistry to English—a rather momentous decision. In recent years she'd become vexed by an awareness that *she* was the one most like her father, with all that seemed to portend of potential instability, and hence the pursuit of a science degree had been one way of dodging her fate. Besides, neither parent had ever made much of Yates's writing, which Monica had come to perceive as so much self-indulgent escapism; throughout her childhood she'd told friends he was a "college professor," which sounded better. Then a fellow student turned out to be an ardent admirer of *Revolutionary Road*—indeed, seemed starstruck at the prospect of meeting the author. And Monica's first creative-writing teacher at the University of Massachusetts was none other than George Cuomo—whose career Yates had helped launch as editor of *Stories for the Sixties*—and Cuomo made it clear that Yates had a very considerable reputation. Only then did Monica read her father's entire oeuvre and realize how good he was, which inspired her to be a writer too. "I'm so incredibly lucky to have you!" she wrote him. "As soon as I finish [a story] I really like, I'll bring it to you—we can talk about everything. . . ."

And so it came to pass, and for the most part it was good for both. For the next decade or so, among the first things Yates would mention in almost any conversation was the fact that his daughter was a writer, too. It bolstered his self-respect to know that, at least in one sense, he was a good role model; he gave extensive, tactful critiques of her stories ("He figured things out," she said, "and he was *always* right"), and recommended her best work to Monica McCall, who accepted her namesake as a client. Candidly, though, Yates's misgivings were at least as great as his pride: He considered writing fiction "the hardest and loneliest profession in the world," and knew only too well the kind of dismal toll such a life could take. And then, truth be known (though he was careful not to labor this point in mixed company), Yates didn't think women were cut out to be serious artists, since such a difficult business interfered with their main function as caregivers. He regarded a handful of female writers as first-rate—Jane Austen, George Eliot, Alice Munro, Gina Berriault, perhaps one or two others—and thought the rest would be better off focusing their energy elsewhere. "Dad thought the best, most fulfilling thing for a woman was to get married and have a family," said Monica. But meanwhile, in lieu of such a blessed turn of events, he wished her well.

Among his daughters Monica became his closest confidante, the one who understood him best and vice versa, but Gina was his heart. Affectionate, pretty, utterly nonjudgmental where her father was concerned, she was the great solace of his later years; those who knew Yates at his sickest and saddest were struck by the way he'd light up—his color quite literally returning—at the mention of her name: "She was the one he had a crush on," was how one friend put it. From the beginning they had a breezy rapport. "What's that over your head but not the ceiling?" he'd say to the giggling toddler over the phone. "*Sky.*" "What's that under your feet but not the floor?" "*Ground.*" Along with the sweetness of Gina's nature, another reason the relationship never soured was distance, which necessarily limited their contact to brief visits two or three times a year. At such intervals Yates was careful to be on his best behavior. "I was told at a very early age that Dad had a drinking problem," said Gina. "I remember him always having a beer in hand at his apartments and always ordering lots of drinks at restaurants. However, I don't remember him as ever acting particularly disorderly, slurring, or having boozy breath or anything like that." Her earliest memory of Yates was his visit to California in the summer of 1977, when she was five. In his motel room they made up a game called "mow the meadow": Yates covered his eyes while Gina went around the room with a carton of cigarettes (a make-believe lawn mower) saying "Mow, mow, mow,"—until Yates opened his eyes and exclaimed, "Oh, what pretty flowers!" "He seemed to enjoy the game as much as I did and had unlimited patience," Gina recalled, "repeating the same silly thing over and over without getting bored. We both remembered 'mow the meadow' with fondness over the years." Meanwhile Yates would discuss the girl's mother only in the most glowing terms, romanticizing her to the point of rendering her all but unrecognizable—e.g., "Your mother was always very athletic"—which, as Gina points out, simply wasn't the case.

Friends noticed how Yates continued to pursue Martha, as it were, in the form of other young women of similar body type—"a dancer's body," as Robin Metz described it: "lithe, flat-chested, willowy." Very little is known about a number of these women apart from their first names and whatever else can be gleaned from the odd letter among Yates's papers.* Some were students or aspiring writers who admired his work; some were simply impressionable young women at loose ends who were flattered by the attention of a semi-celebrity. For a short while in the fall of 1977, for example, Yates was attached to a woman named Bonnie—a waitress who fancied herself a painter and wrote such remarks as, "I am planning to make a cutely decorated box in which I am going to drop neatly lettered clichés about my life—THE REAL STUFF—for example . . . 'If you will it, it's not a dream' (Henry Winkler, 'The Fonz') because this is all that is keeping me going, keeping me painting everyday." Bonnie had a girlfriend named Tommie, whom Yates also briefly pursued until she moved that spring to New Orleans, whence she wrote him a note commending his "gentle passion."

Yates's cohort in this occasional Arcadia was Andre Dubus, who expected "salvation not mere pussy" from very young women and kept an apt Fitzgerald quote (from a letter to his daughter) tacked on his wall: "You've heard me say before that I think the faces of most American women over thirty are relief maps of petulant and bewildered unhappiness." Yates would not have disagreed, and in fact was oft given to the rueful reflection that Martha had gone wrong—"got ideas in her head"— around the age of thirty. This, then, was another respect in which he and Dubus were an abiding, if sometimes rivalrous, comfort to each other. Peggy Rambach was a sophomore at Tufts in October 1977, when she met her future husband at the *Boston Globe* book fair; later that day she found herself spliced between him and Yates at a seafood restaurant. "I was nineteen years old," she recalled, "and both of them were putting the moves on me. It was later a joke between them—that Andre had won me.

---

*Yates, a great maker of lists, wrote a chronological memo which gives, year by year, his age, any books of his published, milestone events (e.g., Gina's birth), and the first name of whatever woman or women he was involved with at the time. For example: "52–53 [age] 1978–79 Mary. Laura. Dolly."

At the time I guess I was dazzled. Here were two well-known writers paying so much attention to me."

But in Yates's case they were never dazzled for long, though many remained fond of him. "For fifteen years," noted the writer Mary Robison, "I was just a lot of disappointment to Dick. Oh, but I loved him. How could I not? He was understanding and knowing and kind." Robison was in her twenties when she met Yates, and apart from the matter of her considerable talent, she eminently filled the bill in terms of his preferred "body type" and other aesthetic requirements. "There are many things that I should thank you for," she wrote him after leaving Boston to take a teaching position in Ohio. "I love you, Dick, for what you are, and what you were for me, and the things you did that were nice. Nice." Among the things he did for her (so he told friends) was help with her writing—those celebrated stories about bleak middle-class lives that placed her at the forefront of so-called minimalism, the general trend back to realistic fiction in the seventies and eighties that was partly influenced by Richard Yates. As Robison's reputation grew with a run of stories in *The New Yorker,* Yates would sometimes grumble about how he'd been "used"—but all the while he kept a photo of Robison on his desk, and whenever the two met in Boston or various writers' conferences he was known to make hopeful passes at her. Finally, in 1986, she wrote him a note from Bennington that expressed a paradigm of the sentiments Yates aroused in women who appreciated his finer points but simply couldn't bear him for long: "I've loved you for a decade," she wrote, but added that she was "guaranteed" to disappoint him and asked that he not let her "lead [him] on" anymore. "We both know I can't be with you, Dick."

To some extent Yates blamed the brevity of these attachments on a persistent problem—toward the end of the seventies, he was less and less able to function sexually. "It bothered him a lot," said Winthrop Burr, "and he was quite demanding that something be done about it." Naturally Burr suggested he stop (or drastically reduce) drinking and smoking, but Yates angrily rejected the idea. Burr then referred him to a urologist, who couldn't find much the matter, which only compounded Yates's frustration. All Burr could do was advise and readvise that alcohol and tobacco were indeed major factors. The choice was clear: Either abstain from both or settle for a life of "gentle passion."

"Oh, Joseph, I'm So Tired" was rejected by *The New Yorker*, which offered the editorial gloss that it was "soft-edged and idealized" (a phrase that often sprang to Yates's bitter lips in years to come); it was then published in the February 1978 issue of the *Atlantic*. Its appearance occasioned a number of admiring letters, among them a note from Seymour Krim: "It's this combination of memoir/fiction, rooted in American history, . . . which permits the story to go beyond its characters and makes them representatives of a time as well as themselves." This appeared to be the consensus view, as the story went on to win a National Magazine Award as well as inclusion in that year's O. Henry volume. More importantly it spurred Yates on to a spate of story writing: By April two stories were in "various stages of partial first draft," another was "barely emerging in notes-and-outline form," and still another was "floating around out there in the blue." At the time Yates was planning a total of five long stories for a collection titled *Five Kinds of Dismay*. "The trouble with all this," he wrote a friend, "is that Delacorte doesn't want to mess with it— or at least, if they decide they do, it'll be in a very disgruntled and half-hearted way."

For the moment, though, Yates could afford to call his own shots somewhat. "*A Good School* is magnificent and your strongest book to date," Sam Lawrence gushed in February. "The way you've managed to create an entire world with such incredible economy impresses me more than I can say." Others agreed that Yates's technical mastery was impressive as ever, but what especially struck many were aspects of what Krim called "the mellow Yates": "[*A Good School*] somehow turns a corner," Krim noted, and the writer Hannah Green likewise found the performance "so moving and so perfect" that her letter to Lawrence turned into an almost flustered panegyric: "[Yates is] brilliant, a consummate artist, and it's his *feeling* that is so right, sensitive, refined, strong, firm, RIGHT!" *Feeling*, indeed, seemed the key: Not only had Yates continued to grow as a writer in terms of craft, but also philosophically, salvaging from the ruins of his life a greater degree of compassion for suffering humankind. "I'm moved by a blessed irony that we've all watched slowly unfolding," Cassill wrote Lawrence.

> You know, all his life Dick has wanted to be as good a writer as Fitzgerald— and now, by grace of the irony they both should appreciate, he stands out as a better one. . . . Dick buttresses [his] moral imagination with a craftsmanship that Fitzgerald only displayed sporadically, even in his best things. . . . I'm as moved to tears by thinking about Dick and his long, lonely haul as by his fine new book. How he's kept the faith.

Lawrence's faith as a publisher, meanwhile, was greater than ever: On the strength of such an ecstatic advance response, as well as a preview excerpt to be run in the June 25 issue of the *New York Times Book Review* ("The best free advertising we could hope for"), he ordered an optimistic first printing of fifty thousand copies.

It was a drastic miscalculation, of course, though reviews offered the usual bit of moral recompense. Christopher Lehmann-Haupt, in the daily *Times,* called the novel "thoroughly charming" and noted that while Yates "skirts the edge of sentimentality . . . he steers clear of that, too, and what we end up with is both funny and touching, both likable and ludicrous." Julian Moynahan's lengthy treatment in the Sunday *Times* examined the deceptive complexity of Yates's narrative voice, inasmuch as it prepares the reader for a first-person memoir in the foreword only to revert to fictional omniscience throughout the main narrative; what promises to be merely personal, then, is in fact "a first-class work of the imagination marked by an interest in real history, by a sophisticated awareness of the ambiguous relation between any fiction and its 'real-life' sources, and by a recognition that no authors, including the Joyces, Flauberts, Jane Austens and Henry Millers, have ever been able to write themselves completely out." Even *The New Yorker* tossed the author a sop in its "Briefly Noted" section ("a graceful and articulate narrative"), while Yates's old student Jonathan Penner used the occasion to make a thorough case in the *New Republic* for the larger importance of Yates's work: "In an age embarrassed by story-telling, half-persuaded by chic critics that fiction should repel innocent belief, [Yates] tells stories we believe. In a time when experiment with language is more highly valued than skill with it, he experiments no more than fish do with swimming."

There were a few demurrals. John Skow in *Time* called Yates "a good but doleful writer" and conceded nothing of the novel's relatively hopeful outlook: "Staring unflinchingly at bad nerves and loneliness is admirable, but fearing to look at any other sort of human condition is not." Nicholas Guild of the *Washington Post* found the novel "well-written and entertaining," but added that the balance between "boy plots" and "adult plots" amounted almost to a clash of genres and that the tidy resolution of each was hackneyed and artificial. And finally Thomas R. Edward observed in the *New York Review of Books* that the novel's "principal events seem more suited to television drama than to serious fiction."

Impressed by "the mellow Yates" of *A Good School,* some readers were inclined to overrate it somewhat (not least Sam Lawrence, who doubtless hoped the more upbeat mood would lead to greater sales). The skillful observation and deft pacing of the novel moved Jerome Klinkowitz, an astute critic of Yates's work, to rank it as his best: "If writing were baseball, this would by Richard Yates's perfect game." But this is perhaps going too far. *A Good School* is an expert performance within its narrow range of substance and length, and serves most notably to indicate that Yates was evolving in interesting ways.

As Moynahan pointed out, the dimensions of the book's autobiographical material are broadened by the omniscient narrator (an approach that would culminate in the elaborately shifting viewpoints of *Cold Spring Harbor*), which has the effect of enhancing the protagonist's coming-of-age story with contrapuntal sketches of his fellow misfits, old and young, at Dorset Academy. Like Bill Grove, almost all the characters tend to be afflicted in some way—whether overtly in the case of the polio-stricken Jack Draper's "funny little hands" and "funny little feet," or Terry Flynn's "elegantly stiff" little finger (a nice objective correlative for his latent homosexuality, as it stands primly erect while he "frown[s] soberly over the task" of masturbating Grove), or psychologically in the case of the aptly named Van Loon (he of the lingering bowel movements) or Haskell, who has a full-blown mental breakdown. As for Grove himself, he is a kind of amalgam of maladjustment, and through the eyes of "Frenchy" La Prade we observe him in all his blue-nailed inadequacy: "The kid was a mess. . . . He seemed in danger of stumbling over his own legs as he made his way to a chair, and he sat so awkwardly as to suggest it might be impossible for his body to find composure. What an advertisement for Dorset Academy!" An advertisement indeed, since Dorset Academy is a veritable haven for aberration posing as a pretentious brand of "individualism"—a "school for the sons of the gentry" that appears to have been "conceived in the studios of Walt Disney."

But Yates is not simply making cheap fun of such a place and its people, as witnessed by what novelist Stewart O'Nan called the "complex, generous voice" of Yates's first-person frame narrator: "His voice here is so inviting in his patience and forthrightness," O'Nan wrote, "his willingness to both expose his deepest pain and forgive everyone (even himself) for their shortcomings . . . that naturally other writers have tried to emulate it—Richard Ford most notably in his story 'Communist' and myself in my first novel *Snow Angels*." Tellingly, one of the most unsympathetic characters at the outset of the novel, Steve MacKenzie—the Dorset bully who derides Bill Grove as a "puddle of piss"—comes off best at the end, when the narrator recalls meeting him circa 1955 and being given a bit of kindly, pertinent advice: "Listen, though: don't look back too much, okay? You can drive yourself crazy that way." MacKenzie, then, has grown up to become a decent if unremarkable fellow, as have the rest of Grove's misfit schoolmates in their own pardonable fashion. A few (it is noted) have died in the war—a fate that loomed over every member of Grove's class, and lent poignancy and a touch of grandeur to their incidental foibles. But finally, the one person who should have meant the most to the narrator and meant so little—his father—haunts him now, and the novel's final lines (wherein Grove imagines what he might have said to the man to make amends) linger in the mind like that "pure ribbon of sound" heard fleetingly from some ghost station a thousand miles away:

> I will probably always ask my father such questions in the privacy of my heart, seeking his love as I failed and failed to seek it when it mattered; but all

that—as he used to suggest on being pressed to sing "Danny Boy," taking a backward step, making a little negative wave of the hand, smiling and frowning at the same time—all that is in the past.

A Good School is indeed a "thoroughly charming" novel that in a number of writerly ways transcends its genre; superficially, though, it's liable to strike the general reader as just another coming-of-age story about preppies, and as such it was largely ignored. "I want to reassure you that we will work things out," Lawrence wrote the anxious Yates, when sales stalled around the usual ten thousand copies. "I'm committed to your work and to you as an author till death do us part and I'm not about to let either of us down." It was true, and in the meantime Lawrence was building what he hoped would prove a lucrative backlist, while both men nibbled the tidbits of occasional recognition. For *A Good School* the pickings were rather slim: The *Times* listed it in their annual roundup as one of the notable books of 1978, and it was nominated for the St. Botolph's Award for best novel by a New England writer—won, however, by Yates's old nemesis Maureen Howard, whom he'd made cry some seventeen years before.

A curious postscript were the odd ghosts *A Good School* flushed out of the author's past. "Since reading your book," wrote Yates's old tormenter Richard Edward Thomas ("Ret") Hunter, "I have looked a number of times in the mirror at my 'animal rooting mouth.' " Hunter reported that he was now a lonely and somewhat impoverished widower living in Miami ("If I had been after truffles [that is, with his rooting mouth], I'd now be rich," he wryly remarked), and Yates was so contrite about his unkind description of Hunter that he wrote the man a long mollifying letter. He was also contacted by a woman named Mary Nickerson, who identified herself as a friend of Bick Wright's widow, Ann: "She knows that I also read your books, she and Bick having put all their friends on to you. . . . Ann said she'd wondered if you would like to hear what did happen to Bick." Yates was intrigued, and accepted an invitation to dine at Nickerson's home in Brookline with her and Ann Wright Jones. That night he learned that his rebellious, sardonic, mawkish friend Bick had become an English teacher after quitting the seminary, and for all the man's absurdities (most of which had remained intact over the years) he was a dedicated, inspiring teacher with whom adolescents felt an immediate rapport. He'd died in Houston of a brain tumor at the age of thirty-nine. To the end he remained bitter about the whole privileged ethos of his unhappy childhood.

Yates wanted to hear more, and subsequently invited the widow to meet him at the Crossroads, where he pumped her with questions and begged her to send him a copy of the Avon yearbook (which she did). As Ann Wright Jones remembered the occasion, "I got the impression that Bick's tragedy applied even more to [Yates]—he could never pull out of the past, his family, and apply his perceptiveness to the larger world. At least Bick found some release in his teaching, by relating to children."

CHAPTER SIXTEEN

Young Hearts Crying: 1979-1984

Oh, Joseph, I'm So Tired" particularly impressed a twenty-five-year-old Yale graduate named Laura,* who was on the editorial staff of the *Atlantic*. "Since then I've read all the novels, each one unique, wise, and heartbreakingly fine," she wrote an editor at Pocket Books, whom she hoped to persuade to reissue Yates's work in paperback. "I'm outraged that *Eleven Kinds of Loneliness,* a collection that, along with *Revolutionary Road,* ought to be read by every student of twentieth-century American literature, languishes in a grim (and expensive) hardcover edition published by a reprint house (Greenwood Press)."

Almost a year would pass between the publication of "Joseph" and Yates's first actual meeting with the young *Atlantic* editor, but meanwhile she became known among friends and associates as a relentless advocate of his work—a fan, in short. "I'm the one who's been stalking you," she finally introduced herself in so many words (at a party she made a point of attending because she knew Yates would be there). By then she'd sat in the audience at two of his readings but shyly refrained from approaching him on both occasions; as she later explained to his daughter Monica, she had low self-esteem at the time—the "girl with glasses" syndrome. She was, however, an attractive young woman ("prettier than she thinks" was how Yates put it), and also possessed the proverbial good personality: She was smart, well-mannered, and capable of making Yates laugh. For many years he'd go on quoting witty things she'd told him. After their first night

---

*The woman declined to be interviewed, and clearly preferred that her full name not be given.

together, she wrote him about certain of her misgivings: "[I worried] your friend Mary [Robison] . . . would come back from Ohio with her New Year's resolution . . . to live with you and love with you in a nice apartment in Boston . . . and write touching stories about being almost happy in *The New Yorker*." He'd explained the photograph on his desk.

Yates was twice her age but seemed older, wheezing and frail, and the fact that he was able to hang on to her, if only for a while, attests to a powerful lingering charm. At his best he was nothing if not "understanding and knowing and kind" (as Mary Robison pointed out), all the more so in the presence of pretty young women. But in the case of Laura—the last significant romance of Yates's life—perhaps the best explanation is a basic human tendency to idealize artists because of their work. As Peggy Rambach observed, "Dick's writing was so sensitive, so tender toward children, that Laura figured he'd be that person." He was and he wasn't, but in any case she pursued the man who was. As a courting gesture—lest she get a "sweet send-off" at the outset—she mailed him the complete lyrics to one of his favorite old tunes, "Mountain Greenery": "Whatever happens," she wrote, "it's a great song and I'd love to hear you sing it and, non sequiturally speaking, I love you." And he seemed to love her too, though as Monica Yates remarked, "The physical aspect was hard to fathom."

For a while, though, he seemed rejuvenated—relative, that is, to the morose disheveled old man who smoked and muttered at the Crossroads. While in Arkansas for a reading that February, he was the life of several parties—not only the drunkest but the most ebullient guest. "Dick was bombed, but he was *on*," remembered a married woman with the improbable name of Booghie, with whom he shamelessly flirted. "Do you remember me—Booghie?" she wrote him afterward. "We sat on the couch and you promised to love me forever, and give me big bucks, and kisses all over and we sang songs, and I fell in love. . . . It was the high point of my winter."

Yates even found pretexts for introducing Laura to his daughters— without, however, quite violating his old taboo against exposing them to girlfriends as such. Monica was in her last year of college and considering a career in publishing, so it simply made sense for Yates to invite her to Boston in order to meet a nice, smart "friend" of his who could advise her about the profession. Also, Monica had recently published a story in the *Boston Globe,* whereupon Dubus wrote her a kind letter to the effect that she should "stick to her guns" and keep working on her stories rather than be pressured into writing a novel ("I got the impression," said Monica, "that he was justifying his own career mostly"). As Yates assumed she'd want to meet Dubus too, he proposed that the five of them—Andre and Peggy, he and Laura, and Monica who was about the same age as the other two women—get together for dinner. Monica agreed, but reluctantly: She'd read between the lines *re* Laura's true status and found the prospect of being in the midst of older men and their daughterly girlfriends "creepy"; besides, she was a "mess" at the time—unhappy, high-strung—and didn't relish having to deal with her father in person, knowing he'd be drunk. And so he was, though his well-spoken young "friend" made a good impression; as for Dubus, he was almost as drunk as Yates. Monica was appalled: "Both he and Dad were *very* boisterous. Andre kept telling these tedious anecdotes about going into bars and charming the locals: '*So I walked in and pretty soon the whole place was eating out my hands!*' etcetera. Again and again the waiter warned him and Dad to lower their voices. An *awful* night." Laura herself seemed to enjoy such outings and contribute to the general hilarity, though they soon palled in Peggy Rambach's case: "I was *very* bored during Andre's meetings with Dick. I was the woman and hence ignored. My mind would wander, I'd daydream, concentrate on the length of Dick's cigarette ash and so on. It reminds me of how Dick once inscribed a book to us: 'To Andre with all my respect . . . '—and this and that, on and on, then *finally*—'and to Peggy, who is a lovely girl.' "

Though arguably there was no connection, Monica Yates had a psychotic episode shortly after that meeting with Dubus et al. Like her sister a decade before, she'd taken an hallucinogenic drug (mushrooms) and hadn't come down; like her father she thought she was Christ; like both she had a history of depression. "I was anorexic early in college—five foot nine, 107 pounds—then during my last year I got fat," she said. "I was very upset about this, and I was messing up in a lot of other ways, too—losing close friends, my boyfriend, that sort of thing." After a week in the Northampton mental hospital, her mother arranged for her to be transferred to Grasslands in Westchester, where she stayed for six weeks. At the time she was diagnosed as schizophrenic and given the drug Haldol, though an outpatient psychiatrist decided it was an isolated incident and took her off medication. When it was all over, Monica went to Durango, Colorado, where Martha and Gina had recently moved; she found work in a nursing home, though mostly she "holed up" and wondered what had happened to her and worried about the future. Her father worried too—"Join the club," he'd told her—though his main advice was just to get on with her life and try not to think about it. She thought about it anyway ("Dad didn't do *enough* of that," she said; "the crazier he got, the more he'd deny it"), and perhaps as a further reaction against fate, she became deeply religious. This, however, worked no better than being a chemistry major. During a lonely solo bicycle trip that took her through the Bible Belt, she called her father: "Dad, I don't want to go to heaven if these people are the ones who'll be there!" "Well of *course*, baby," he replied. "Everyone knows *that*."

Meanwhile Sharon Yates's life had grown increasingly tranquil in her father's absence. Two years before, she'd met her future husband Richard Levine, a shy man who'd felt daunted in the presence of his girlfriend's rather celebrated, saturnine father. "Every time Jimmy Carter tells another lie," Yates dourly quipped on meeting Levine, "he grows another tooth." That night at dinner, Levine grew uneasy as the silence expanded at their table; he'd expected Yates to be a lively raconteur, but the man sat leaning to one side with his face set. As it happened, he and Sharon were eavesdropping on a nearby table—a mutual habit when together—and every so often they'd remark caustically on what they overheard. That was in 1977, and on July 21, 1979, Sharon and Levine eloped. Yates was disgusted at first—he'd wanted to walk his daughter down the aisle and give her away—but he soon got over it. A little later they visited him in Boston, and after dinner he took them back to his crepuscular apartment and opened a bottle of champagne.

. . .

Yates's story collection proceeded apace, though he'd had to change the title *Five Kinds of Dismay* because he now planned *six* stories rather than five, and one of them hadn't struck him as particularly dismaying. He'd suggested *Aspects of Home* to Sam Lawrence, who found it "too academic"; Yates altered it to the less Forsterian *Broken Homes*. "Nobody's eyes light up much on hearing my tentative title," he wrote. "The idea, see, is that all the stories will touch in some way on fucked-up families." A somewhat younger author who also favored such themes—indeed was indebted to Yates in a number of ways and modest enough to admit it—visited Boston that summer. "I wanted to tell you again how pleased I was to meet you and to be able to spend a few hours with you," Raymond Carver wrote. "You've been one of my heroes since I first read *Revolutionary Road* and was just stopped dead in my tracks with admiration." Carver had presented Yates with a copy of his first collection, *Will You Please Be Quiet, Please?*, and now enclosed a second, *Furious Seasons,* with the diffident caveat that Yates read only *four* of the stories therein (he listed them). "Don't take any of this, please, as an obligation of any sort," he added. It's unknown whether the two ever met again.

Meanwhile Yates was in financial trouble. In the fall he accepted a one-semester appointment at Harvard Extension teaching two classes—fiction and expository writing (the latter a subject he hadn't taught since his New School days)—but was still unable to pay nine hundred dollars in back taxes to the state of Massachusetts. When they threatened to seize his property (one pauses to wonder what Yates had to fear from such a threat), he called his friend Joe Mohbat in Brooklyn. Usually when he called to talk to the Mohbats, the lonely Yates would immediately apologize for taking up their time ("I know you have better things to do"), but this was different. As Mohbat remembered, "He took a while getting around to it, but he sounded pretty desperate. He insisted I draft a note and charge interest and so on. I wouldn't be surprised if he went without meals to pay me back; it ate him up to ask for money." Yates's first install-ment on the loan was somewhat delayed when the check became buried amid the chaos of his desk—"where, as you'll see," he wrote Mohbat, "it picked up a few traces of roach shit"—but Yates was nonetheless grateful for what he considered the rather ambiguous favor of "[saving his] ram-shackle life."

At that point poverty was a lesser sorrow. Though Yates and Laura were still somewhat together after several months, the end was near. The usual problems applied, though in certain ways the two remained compat-ible despite Yates's lapses; by then, however, he needed more than just an "emotional nurse" (the function he ascribed to past girlfriends and wives), he needed someone to care for him physically—a lot to ask of anybody, much less a charming young woman with her life ahead of her. Such was his infirmity that Geoff Clark was "horrified" when he saw Yates that fall in Rhode Island, noting how Laura was obliged to "guide him about": "[A]fter a quick beer in the union before his reading, Dick, requiring assistance, took minutes—hours, it seemed—to climb the union stairs, stopping periodically on a step, clinging to the railing as he breathed heav-ily, agonizingly, gathering himself for the next step." During his readings, too, Yates was often derailed by coughing and what Clark described as "lip-smacking pauses that broke the rhythm."* As for what it was like sharing a bedroom with Yates—the couple spent a night at Clark's house during the visit, and through the wall he heard Yates "hacking, coughing, muttering, groaning, pacing" all night long.

"I think this may be my last foray into the magic world of young girls," he wrote Mohbat that same month. "Got to face facts, and I'll soon be 54, which everybody knows is the time for carpet slippers and companionship with some pleasant lady whose brains have been utterly scrambled since her third husband walked out in 1965. *That's* what's great about young girls, apart from their vastly superior flesh: their brains haven't yet had time to be scrambled by the world." Yates tried to be philosophical about things, but he was heartbroken and dreaded the loneliness that lay ahead. When the young woman calmly declined a belated proposal of marriage, Yates tried to win her back—or simply forestall the inevitable—with his prose. Probably he spent at least a week polishing the seven typed pages of

---

*Many observed how the older Yates tended to smack his lips and roll his tongue around the inside of his mouth—a common side-effect of lithium and other such medications.

comic *pensées* and vignettes that make up "Notes Toward an Understanding of Laura M—,"* an effort reminiscent of those strenuously witty letters he had written Barbara Beury twenty years earlier, though even more wistful and funny and sad. "Talk of marriage brings on an intellectual power-failure in most contemporary girls," he wrote.

> Their circuits go out one after another, and they must fill silence and darkness with commitment and relationship and identity and sharing and coping and space and meaningful . . . and this-level and that-level and feelings and feelings and feelings and feelings—this spastic paralysis can go on for hours until somebody manages to change the fuse; only then do things come back to life and allow a girl to say "love" again.
>
> So I am forever grateful that Laura M— is an extraordinary girl. Her circuits never go out. Her "no" and her "too old" may hurt like whips, but they are words a man can trust.

One can fill in a lot of blanks based on these pages; suffice to say, the basic trajectory of the romance seems to have been pretty much the same as all the others in Yates's life, if perhaps mitigated by a bit more humor and mutual appreciation than usual. "When Laura said she didn't like my story I shouted ugly stuff for about two hours and made her cry," he wrote. "Since that night, I have been unable to discuss my work with Laura at all except in postures of arrogance or apology." That Yates would have found other reasons to shout at her (and surely did) is beyond doubt, but once she saw fit to criticize his work, however innocently, the die was cast. Indeed, most of Yates's "Notes" seem the product of his creative brooding on that subject, as when he imagined Laura considering one of his stories for the *Atlantic*:

> She reads it through with an open mind, blinking now and then at the soft-edged and idealized parts; then she prepares an inter-office memo to Richard Todd [an editor at the magazine].
> Dick: (And Laura, bless her heart, hasn't yet gotten over a sweet, secret

---

*The woman's last name, given in the actual title, is omitted.

thrill at calling Mr. Todd by his first name) This new R. Yates story leaves much, I think, to be desired. . . .

A few days later she receives Todd's reply:

Laura: I couldn't agree more. Soft-edged, idealized and boring, boring, boring. . . . Reject this piece. Trash it. Wipe it out. We will, I think, be doing the wretched man a favor. . . .

The diamond-bright precision of Todd's intelligence is just the tonic Laura needs to help her compose her letter to me, which reads like this:

Dear Richard Yates: Like most of your previous thirty-four submissions, this one came close. . . .

I'm afraid I can't meet you for a drink on Friday, as promised; something has come up. Try me later in the month, okay?

Kisses, L. . . .

. . .

Whenever I say ugly stuff in restaurants, Laura goes into the ladies' room and cries. This helps her to put me in perspective. . . . I make frequent use of mens' rooms, too, in various bleak and melancholy ways, but Laura doesn't known anything about that. . . .

. . .

This is a multiple-choice question. If Laura is the nicest girl I have ever known . . . then how come I shout ugly stuff at her all the time?

A. Because I want to disappoint her and drive her away like the harsh and terrible old man I am afraid of becoming.

B. Because I am like Doctor Jack-O'-Lantern in having to show I don't need anybody's kindness while dying for it.

C. Because I drink too much beer.

The best answer wavers somewhere between *B* and *C*, though the ramifications of *C* are everywhere in evidence, and help to explain another item:

I am pretty sure Laura thought pushing me over the hedge was funny, but she didn't laugh at the time because that would have spoiled her sense of outrage. In much the same way, she seldom allows outrage to spoil her sense of what's

funny, even on being teased about such matters as vegetarianism and cultivated body hair.

Fair to assume that Laura pushed (and Yates fell) because he was exasperatingly drunk again, and then the fact that she cultivated body hair and
vegetarianism would seem to push the whole opposites-attract principle
beyond the generational pale. Other problems apparently included her
admiration for the brilliance of David Milch (who'd taught her at Yale),
her frequent fraternizing with friends her own age ("this madcap shuttling
between Somerville and Harvard and Jamaica Plain"), and the fact that,
finally, she'd begun to avoid Yates entirely except for the odd weekday
lunch. "I love Laura M—," the "Notes" sadly conclude. "I will love Laura
M—until the day I push aside my Jello and scratch at the window of my
oxygen tent for the last time."

A month or so later, Laura took a job with Random House and moved
to New York. "She's offered ample assurance that we'll still be 'friends,'
but I've never really believed in stuff like that," Yates wrote the Arkansas
woman named Booghie that December. "Still, I've been familiar with
loneliness before, many times, and know I'll survive it. If I can't exactly
welcome it like an old comrade, at least it's no worse than putting up
with some tiresome old acquaintance of mine." In the meantime he wondered if he might address his present correspondent as Margaret:
"Because while 'Booge' is certainly a cute and kicky name—Don't get me
wrong—I think I'd prefer the idea of a lovely, forever unattainable girl
named Margaret, down there in Arkansas, to whom I can write letters
once in a while—on the hopeful assumption that she might once in a
while write back." But he must have decided that Arkansas was too far
away, or that a married woman named Booghie really was too unattainable, or that confessing his loneliness to a relative stranger was unseemly,
or perhaps the letter got lost amid the roach droppings and other refuse.
In any case it was never sent.

Yates had a horror of being pitied (at least by non-intimates), and as his
health declined and the sadness of his life became obvious, he took more

frequent refuge in a gruff, though by no means humorless, persona. "Ahh, mind your own goddamn business!" he'd snap, coughing, when solicitous strangers would advise him to quit smoking. "You guys ever going to start wearing grownup clothes?" he said to Dubus and Jim Crumley, indicating their cowboy boots and jeans. In such a mood he particularly relished the chance to squelch anything smacking of pretension or phoniness. "I just love your work, Mr. Yates," said a critic from the *Boston Globe*. "And I can see why Flaubert is such an influence. Really, there's no great novel that *isn't* about adultery." Yates looked the man up and down, then laughed in his face: "You're out of your mind!" At the same time Yates became all the more sympathetic toward what he perceived as real suffering. The writer John Casey had gotten on Yates's bad side some fifteen years before in Iowa (by seeming overprivileged and picking on Bob Lehrman), but when the two met in 1980 at their mutual friend Bill Keough's house, Yates was strikingly kind. "Yates really likes you," Keough told Casey afterward, and it occurred to the latter that he'd endeared himself by having had the "worst year of [his] life": "My dog and father had died, my wife had left me, and my best friend had just killed himself. I'd been kicked to shit, and now I was a real human being in Dick's eyes." When Casey went on to win the National Book Award, Yates wrote him a warm letter of congratulation.

Early that summer Dan Wakefield returned to Boston after three years in Los Angeles, and immediately got in touch with Yates. "I was in terrible condition, drinking way too much," said Wakefield, "and I knew Dick would be a good person to drink with." That he was, though a proper venue was crucial. Yates became paranoid in upscale establishments such as the Hampshire House, and would argue with waiters who'd slighted him in some way, real or imagined, whereupon he'd be cut off at the bar. It was largely a self-fulfilling prophecy: Because he felt scrutinized he drank more to lessen his anxiety, which naturally resulted in scrutiny-provoking behavior. One night at the Newbury Steak House he lit his beard on fire and sat flapping his hands at his face.

After that, he and Wakefield stuck to the Crossroads, where their Friday night "ritual dinner" was the only regular event on Yates's social calendar.

"He was a wonderful source of solace, encouragement, and literary friendship and support," Wakefield noted. "I loved hearing him put down the 'phonies' and the overrated novels whose style was not really up to snuff . . . as he waved his long, bony finger and smiled knowingly above his beard." Lest one get the impression Yates had mellowed with age—full of benign, finger-wagging wisdom about the perennial rise and fall of literary pretenders—rest assured the reality was a good deal more raucous. *"What a crock of shit!"* was the constant punch line when Yates discussed writers he despised. "Wakefield," he'd rasp, "every seven or eight years a book comes out by *some fucking phony* and gets reviewed on the front page of the *Times* and everybody *loves* it and it's not worth *shit*." The current paradigm was John Irving's *The World According to Garp*—"What a crock of shit!"—or anything by Joseph Heller or Saul Bellow (the friends agreed with Tom Wolfe's definition of hell: A bus ride across America with nothing to read but *Mr. Sammler's Planet*). After six months of such boozy commiseration, Wakefield startled his friend one night by ordering a Diet Coke; while Yates sat stunned and indignant, Wakefield sheepishly admitted that he'd decided to go on the wagon. "A Diet Coke!" Yates roared every time thereafter. "Yeah, and then he's gonna go home and play with his paper dolls!"

Wakefield remembers Yates as a "charming, witty man" whose ugly side only surfaced when he was very drunk or disturbed or both, but the ugly side was all Martha saw after the divorce. On the phone he was usually fine: They'd talk briefly about Gina, and only seldom would he try to lure her into more intimate territory. "But in person," said Martha, "he *invariably* became nasty; seeing me triggered bad feelings in Dick." In the fall he visited Gina in Durango, and the three went out to dinner together. It may have been that Yates resented Martha's insinuating herself into these outings in a vaguely custodial role; in any event he began tipsily baiting her with an off-color story that struck her as inappropriate in the presence of the eight-year-old Gina. The more she warned Yates to stop, the more smirkingly nasty he became, until finally she threw a quiche at him. Affecting high delight, he laughed as they were ejected from the restaurant. In the parking lot Martha asked Gina if she were coming home with her, but the child loyally refused to leave her father. ("I *really* tried to avoid being involved in Dick's visits after that," said Martha.) Gina vividly remembers how Yates, distrait, drank so much beer at breakfast the next day that their waitress politely insisted he have coffee before ordering more.

One night Wakefield got a call from Yates, who said he was sick and had run out of food. Wakefield brought a bag of groceries to Yates's apartment, which "reminded [him] of something out of Dostoyevsky": It was almost completely dark inside (Yates hadn't ventured out in a long time, apparently, and the lightbulb had expired), except for the blue glow of the stove burners, which were turned up against the cold. When Yates called his friend a second time, he was frantic and incoherent. Rather panicked himself, Wakefield called Monica Yates and told her something was terribly wrong with her father, but she didn't seem particularly shaken. "Here he goes again," she said, and tried to reassure the man ("Don't get too upset; it happens a lot"). She suggested he take Yates to the nearest emergency room, where they'd arrange to transfer him to the VA.

The frequency of Yates's breakdowns increased as he became more solitary and miserable. Again and again he'd drink too much and stop eating, subsisting on coffee, cigarettes, and alcohol until he became ill and disoriented. At first Wakefield was a little startled that Yates's daughters didn't seem more concerned, though by then they'd learned the hard way that it didn't pay to meddle. "Ahh, Wakefield's just a damn busybody!" Yates would snap, if Sharon or Monica admitted over the phone that his friend was worried about him (hence the call). Except in states of desperate paranoia or physical distress, Yates would refrain from contacting people and simply lie low in his apartment brooding over some particular delusion. If one of his daughters happened to get him on the phone, he'd interrogate her in a coy, tentative way: "So . . . do you think I did something *terrible* to Gina?" (when in most cases he hadn't seen the girl in months)—whereupon they'd usually call an ambulance or get in touch with Winthrop Burr ("Dad's on the blink again"), who'd authorize hospitalization on the legal grounds that Yates was unable to care for himself. Within a few days— sober, medicated, and somewhat lucid again—Yates would be up in arms with whoever had hospitalized him. "He'd call me *stupid* and say I was missing the point," Burr remembered. "That I harped on his drinking when that wasn't the problem. 'Useless,' 'worthless' . . .. I heard that a lot." Generally Yates would discharge himself at the first opportunity—one nurse reported seeing him leave (or try to) "with tubes hanging out of every orifice"—and angrily vow that he'd *never* go back, that he *refused* to "sit around watching TV and eating ice cream with a bunch of crazies."

Deeply humiliated afterward, Yates seemed to blame others for having seen him at his worst, and the more one tried to help, the more culpable one became. "How did you know? Who told you? Who called the doctor?" he'd grill his daughters after his latest breakdown. He was never contrite, certainly never grateful, and inevitably even the kindest people learned to keep their distance. Joan Norris had remained fond of Yates over the years, but beyond a point she refused to meet him unless Wakefield went with her. "What the hell did you get me up to Boston for, you bitch?" Yates would turn on her. "You're just a groupie!" That he was unwell didn't make such attacks any less stunning. "They were so weird and sudden," said Norris, "like a splash of cold water. There was no trigger, it just happened." Even the tolerant Wakefield began to stay away, though he liked and admired and finally pitied Yates too much to drop him entirely. Yates in turn tended to treat Wakefield with the respect due a fellow writer and dear man, but he would bristle at any suggestion, no matter how meek, that he take better care of himself. "It just got too painful," said Wakefield. "He went on doing the same things over and over."

Around this time Wendy Sears moved back to Boston after several years of marriage in Italy to a monoglot sculptor named Andrea Grassi.* As Yates often made a point of reminding her, he was baffled by the whole Italian sojourn, not to mention the loutish ex-husband, but mostly he just felt touchingly glad to have the pleasure of her company again. Shortly after her return he wrote her a series of love limericks:

---

*For whatever reason she decided to keep the man's name, though to Yates she would always be Wendy Sears (or "Serious"). To avoid confusion I will refer to Wendy Sears Grassi by her maiden name.

The mere presence of sweet Wendy Sears
For the first time in (wow!) fifteen years
Is enough, for a start,
To break a man's heart
And thus make him burst into tears.

The other verses were in a similar vein, reminiscent of the courtly, whimsical Yates of fifteen years before. Indeed, little had changed between the two in most respects. Wendy Sears was somewhat sadder and wiser, to be sure, but essentially the same stoical good sport who'd weathered Yates's rages and exchanged notes with him during tedious meetings at the Justice Department. Though wary of leading Yates on, she'd occasionally meet him for dinner or drinks and agree to be his date for the odd formal function, as when he received the PEN/New England Award for Literary Distinction in late November 1980. "That was one of the better literary parties," Sam Lawrence wrote him the next day. "And an unexpected bonus was seeing you with Wendy Sears again. She hasn't changed one iota."

Sears was inclined to say the same of Yates. "He'd become terribly repetitious," she observed. "He was *stuck*: still wearing the same gray suit, blue shirt and preppy ties, still making the same crabby conversation about the president and politics or whatever. He just didn't pay attention to the changing world—political, social, cultural, nothing. Dick was still back in the fifties." Among others, too, the operative phrase for the later Yates was *out of touch*. Though he was lovingly (or fiercely) eloquent about literary matters, he became dogmatic and rather muddled when conversation took a general turn, and seemed to know little or nothing about basic current events. As such he was bound to be rather tiresome company among nonwriters, tending to lapse into captious correction of a person's grammar, word choice, or social manners. Such punctilios issued a bit incongruously from a man who often couldn't be bothered—as Sears reluctantly noticed—to clean his clothes or beard ("matted with drool and snot"). But still there were glimpses of the old charm, the wit, as if a playful heart were trapped inside this cranky, troubled old man.

...

One aspect of Yates's old-fashioned worldview was a frank, utterly unapologetic homophobia. Some of this went deep indeed, and doubtless had to do with certain conventional insecurities about his "girlishly" round eyes and "bubbly" mouth, to say nothing of his childhood awkwardness and desperate clinging to his mother and sister. Yates was forever at pains to prove his masculinity (even to the point of forbidding a woman to drive)—but apart from all that, he despised what he viewed as the pretension and bad taste of the camp sensibility. He dismissed Knowles's *A Separate Peace* as "a homosexual novel in disguise" ("the emotions are a little too 'purple' for regular boys"), and thought gay literature in toto was overrated due to a specious impression of originality evoked by a nonheterosexual ethos. Be that as it may, the bottom line was simply this: Effeminate gay men drove Yates up the wall, much like his hardboiled counterpart Michael Davenport in *Young Hearts Crying*:

> Oh, shit [he reflects *re* his newborn son]; and there were still other possibilities too dreadful to contemplate. What if, in response to things that struck him as funny, your son took to saying "I love it" or "Oh, how delicious"? What if he wanted to walk around the kitchen with one hand on his hip, telling his mother about the marvelous time he'd had with his friends last night at a really nice new place in town called the Art Deco?

When Monica McCall retired in 1980, Mitch Douglas took over her clients, and Yates found himself contractually bound to an agent who was very evidently gay and given to indignant demands that Yates shape up and turn in his books on time. While Yates didn't like lesbians either, he'd always made a sovereign exception in the case of Monica McCall: She was a "lady," and there was nothing remotely butch or outré about her; she revered his talent and cared for him as a human being; above all she never nagged him about deadlines or discussed his vagaries in general. She'd looked after him in every sense (more so than Yates might have realized) and was all but seamlessly unpatronizing about it; Yates remarked that she'd "saved [his] life" after Martha left him. Following a series of strokes, though, McCall moved to Canada (where she died in 1982), and Yates was that much more alone in the world. Now when he called his agent to ask for money, he was often given a "snitty" lecture by a man whose first (and somewhat abiding) impression of Yates was *qua* lunatic. Yates hated Mitch Douglas.

Their association got off on the wrong foot twice: first at Bellevue in 1974, and again when Douglas adopted Yates as a client six years later. But first a pertinent digression: As Yates continued to produce the long, exquisitely wrought stories for his second collection, *The New Yorker* continued to reject them one after another. At first these rejections were cordial as ever ("this one came close," "keep trying us," and so on), though Yates was not at all mollified anymore. "All I want is a story in the goddamned *New Yorker*!" he'd rage when discussing the ups and downs of his career; also he'd started referring to staple writers for the magazine with an almost reflexive opprobrium—particularly "John fucking Cheever" and "John fucking Updike" (or "Precious John"). One of Monica McCall's last attempted transactions on his behalf was to offer "Trying Out for the Race" to *The New Yorker* in late 1979. "I don't know if you usually write covering letters," Yates wrote her, "but I'd greatly appreciate your doing so in this case: you might find some way to remind [fiction editor] Roger Angell that his magazine has been shamelessly teasing me with 'encouragement' for thirty years or more." Such teasing was about to end forever, though not in a way Yates or any other writer of his stature might have expected. For the moment, though, Angell continued to tease, rejecting "Trying Out for the Race" with a fair degree of tact: "This is written with admirable care and sensitivity, but these lives don't seem worth the trouble he has given them. I also have some difficulty in understanding why this is all happening in the 1930s. . . . [Yates] has many admirers here, and I still hope we will publish him some day." McCall made a practice of copying such (relatively) "nice" rejection letters to Yates, while the more perfunctory or even brutal kind she'd usually paraphrase or keep to herself.

It's worth bearing in mind that, by then, any number of Yates's former colleagues and students had at least one credit in *The New Yorker*, and even his daughter Monica had received a long, detailed letter of encouragement from the same editor (Fran Kiernan) who'd called one of Yates's best stories "soft-edged and idealized." What made it even worse, perhaps, was that Yates *knew* these later stories were among his finest work. When "Regards at Home" was published in the August 1980 issue of the *Atlantic* (having been rejected by *The New Yorker*), Sam Lawrence wrote that it was "magnificent, as fine and perceptive a work as anything being written today"—and a few months later, when Lawrence received the finished manuscript of all seven stories, he found it "simply marvelous": "Congratulations a thousand fold and my profound thanks. It's always been a privilege to be your publisher and now more than ever."

Oddly enough, one of Lawrence's two favorite stories, "Saying Goodbye to Sally," left Roger Angell not only cold but faintly hostile: He called the characters "false and hollow," though he allowed that the unwholesome Beverly Hills milieu was perhaps to blame. No such extenuation, however, was granted in the case of "A Natural Girl": "Mr. Yates is extremely skillful and readable" (at least two conciliatory adjectives were pro forma in all these letters), "but I can't quite believe this dialogue or those lives or, worst of all, such a mean-spirited view of things. . . . Some writers do see the world this way but I think Mr. Yates is just trying it all on for effect." Hard words: "[M]ean-spirited" stories were clearly not to Angell's taste, but the fact that he wasn't even willing to concede the *sincerity* of Yates's attitude ("trying it all on for effect") seemed rather mean-spirited in itself. And by the time Angell had finished the story "Liars in Love," three days later, he seemed to dislike Yates on any number of levels: "This didn't come close. I think he is a confident, accomplished writer, but it seems clearer and clearer to me that his kind of fiction is not what we're looking for. I mean this without offense, and I wonder if it wouldn't save a lot of time and disappointment if you and he could come to that same conclusion."

"I know these rejections will disappoint you," Mitch Douglas wrote Yates, "but I hope not too much so." He enclosed the notes from Angell, adding that he'd tried to remonstrate with the man over the phone, but found him "very stiff and stodgy."

In fact Yates was very, *very* disappointed. It was the end of one of his fondest dreams, and he was in no condition to appreciate the almost artistic inevitability of it all—to wit, that the subtext of all those *New Yorker* rejections over the decades had floated to the surface at last, slowly but suddenly clarified like a darkroom photograph, in the blunt antipathy of Angell's notes: Though Yates was skillful, readable, confident, accomplished and whatever else, his vision of life was *repulsive*. Thus spake *The New Yorker.**

In the years that followed, in the Crossroads or the consulting room of Winthrop Burr, Yates would often hold forth on the subject of his two foremost (extant) bêtes noires: Mitch Douglas and *The New Yorker*. Also, for the benefit of the odd visitor to Beacon Street, Yates would occasionally grope through his papers, find Angell's letters, and read them aloud in a shaky voice—perhaps in the hope of being reassured, once more, that the man and his institution were wrong. Another turn of the screw was the fact that his daughter Monica had recently moved to Manhattan and found a job—as a library assistant at *The New Yorker*. Yates was displeased.

During the early months of 1981, Yates stayed busy but also allowed himself a bit of diversion. With *Liars in Love* (as the book was now called) off his hands, he wrote an engaging essay for the *New York Times Book Review* titled "Some Very Good Masters," which distilled the high points of twenty years' worth of lectures and rumination about his two favorite novels, *Gatsby* and *Madame Bovary*. He closed on a deprecatory, somewhat elegiac note that seemed to indicate a growing concern with his own mortality and literary legacy:

> Time is everything. I am 55 now, and my first grandchild is expected in June. It has been many years since I was a young man, let alone an apprentice writer. But the eager, fearful, self-hectoring spirit is slow to fade. With my 8th book just begun—and with deep regret for the desolate wastes of time that

---

* "Liars in Love"—the story that repelled Angell the most—would seem the favorite of at least one celebrated Yates admirer, Richard Ford, who selected it for *The Granta Book of the American Short Story*.

have kept it from being my 10th or 12th—I feel I haven't really started yet. And I suppose this rather ludicrous condition will persist, for better or worse, until my time runs out.

Yates spent the early summer weeks at Yaddo working on his new novel, but in June he took a break to attend the birth of his grandchild, Sonia, in Brooklyn. He brought flowers to Sharon in the hospital, and took his son-in-law out for a drink toasting the baby. At the time Richard Levine's natural father was dying in a rest home, so the young man particularly appreciated Yates's willingness to assume a paternal role; in general Levine idolized Yates as a writer and a man, so much so that he didn't mind (even rather enjoyed) Yates's goading him to express himself as precisely as possible. "Dick drew me into labor over finding just the right word for some topics of our conversation," Levine noted; "because just a good word was never enough for Dick Yates, whether he was in the company of writers or not." Such was Levine's admiration that he was startled by Yates's confession, that same afternoon, that he felt a sense of failure as a father.

Meanwhile Yates compensated for the bleak regimentation of his life in Boston by getting the most out of larky junkets like out-of-town readings and writers' conferences. Always topmost among his priorities was finding female company, and all things considered he didn't do half badly. Sponsors and fellow writers tended to fuss over Yates at such events, which had the effect of transforming him (figuratively) from a feeble old man into a great writer going ungently into that good night. His friend Ed Kessler, then on the faculty at American University, invited Yates to Washington that summer to give a reading. The two hadn't seen each other in fifteen years or more, and Kessler extended himself to show Yates a good time, putting him up in a fine hotel and throwing a dinner party in his honor. Yates was tipsy at his own reading, and subsequently disappeared with a student admirer; by the time he showed up at the party chez Kessler, dinner was over and his host was vexed. "How do you keep these walls so *white*?" Yates blearily inquired after a long dressing-down. Later Kessler discovered that his guest had run up a sizable bill at the hotel bar, and this was borne in mind when Yates wrote asking for a job.

Also that summer he attended the Wesleyan Writers' Conference, where he encountered such friends as George Garrett and Grace Schulman. Garrett and Madison Smartt Bell drove down for a weekend from the Stone Coast Conference in Maine, and the two arrived in the midst of a late-night, open-ended faculty-student reading ("the precursor of poetry slams," Bell noted). The audience was visibly restless by then, and Yates more visibly than most—seated unsteadily between two young women on the floor. "Yates would make a groping pass at the woman on his left," said Bell, "and she'd politely rebuff him. Then he'd listen to a bit of the reading and commence a growling muttering. Then he'd make a move on the woman on his right. This went on for a while. Finally he had a huge coughing fit, as if he were about to die, and that pretty much ended the reading." Yates pulled himself together for his reunion with Schulman, an effort that seemed to make him cranky ("I thought you had to be here *Thursday*," he snapped); for the most part, though, he managed to sublimate his bitterness into a kind of somber, formal politeness. The two brought each other up-to-date, more or less, but the old rapport was gone and they avoided much talk of the past. After their meeting Yates seemed to let himself go, missing most of his conferences while he staggered about campus in a grass-stained seersucker suit, his pants held up by a piece of rope. "He looks like an Ivy League wino," someone remarked.

And yet, for all that, Yates didn't entirely lose his dignity, and as Garrett pointed out, "The students loved him." Then as ever, Yates treated young writers without condescension of any kind, and his ill health tended to evoke compassion and make his wolfish behavior (such as it was) seem more comical than predatory. Above all he showed a kindly interest in their work, whether he came to conferences or not. In the months after Wesleyan, Yates called up his students one by one (usually late at night) and announced that he'd finally read their manuscripts and was ready to discuss them. One of these students was the writer Elizabeth Cox, whose first novel Yates scrutinized over the course of a year. " 'What does your character *really* say here, in this moment?' Yates asked me again and again," Cox recalled.

And I had to answer right away, at our lunch table or wherever we were. He didn't let any insincere or dishonest remark go unchallenged. . . . Knowing Yates was an exhilarating experience in straight talk. Never had I been with someone who spoke so directly and expected such reciprocal honesty, and it changed me. As a writer, I learned to want only what was true in every moment. As a teacher of writing, I came to believe that challenging another writer in this manner is a sign of real respect.

Another reason Yates's dissolute conduct was easily forgiven, particularly that summer, was the impression he gave of being under a strain that had little to do with loneliness or ill health. As it happened the imminent publication of *Liars in Love* was a prospect Yates dreaded: For almost four years, well after his original advance had run out, he'd exhausted himself chiseling draft after draft, only to have the stories dismissed as "mean-spirited" by *The New Yorker*; moreover, in many respects the book was even more obviously autobiographical than, say, *A Special Providence*. The thought of being perceived as perversely "mean-spirited" on the subject of his own family, his mother and wives and so forth, was almost too much to bear. "I'm lying on the floor in a pool of blood," he told Loree Rackstraw in late-August, when she called after he failed to show up for dinner at her Boston hotel. The "pool of blood" was the result of biting his tongue during an alcoholic seizure, though he didn't go into all that with Rackstraw. "The ambulance is coming—gotta go," he said, and hung up. Many years before, in Iowa, Rackstraw had always called Cassill in moments of Yatesian emergency, and she did so now. This time the man sighed with a mixture of humor and sad exasperation. "I don't watch out for Dick anymore," he said.

The dreaded issues of mean-spiritedness and autobiography did indeed come up in the reviews of *Liars in Love,* but in most cases they were mitigated by praise. Such ambivalence was expressed in the *Atlantic* by James Atlas, who, after an appreciative overview of Yates's career, noted his great reservation: "Too much brutal dialogue, too much mean-spirited circumstance, wears a reader down. Yates is the bleakest writer I know." But Atlas concluded his review with a high compliment: "Yates accomplished what Fitzgerald did at his best: an evocation of life's unbearable poignance, the way it has of nurturing hope and denying it, often in the same instant." Similarly Robert Wilson in the *Washington Post* faulted Yates for "showing too little sympathy for the characters," which Wilson thought diminished the impact of their little or large defeats; but Wilson, too, seemed equivocal in his misgivings ("one of [Yates's] strengths is that he doesn't flinch"), and the stories were otherwise so compelling that he ranked them "with the finest realistic fiction being written."

A number of reviewers arrived at that assessment with hardly any qualms at all. "It is good to report that realism in short fiction is alive and well," began Robert Harris's rave in the *Saturday Review*, and ended, "At a time when much short fiction busies itself with surfaces, it is something of a wonder to find stories that cut to the bone." A late review in *America* asserted "the simple truth of the matter: Yates is one of our best practicing fiction writers," while Dan Wakefield pitched in with a paean in the *Los Angeles Herald-Examiner*, calling his friend "a contemporary master in full command of his fictional power."

The two reviewers who mattered most, though, saw fit to point a glaring spotlight at the autobiographical nature of the material. In his well-meaning notice for the daily *New York Times*, Christopher Lehmann-Haupt described the stories as "wonderfully crafted": "[E]very detail of this collection stays alive and fresh in one's memory." Having applauded the stories' impressive "variety," though, Lehmann-Haupt marveled that such a diversity of setting, incident, and meaning had been milked from what seemed "a single actual experience." He illustrated the point by demonstrating how the stories might be "collapsed into a single history—the career, autobiographical perhaps, of a boy who has been emotionally seduced by his mother ('Oh, Joseph, I'm So Tired'), who grows ashamed of his consequent dependence on her and in compensation begins to lash out at females ('Trying Out for the Race')"—and so on, touching each story in turn, a long paragraph that must have made Yates wince. Two weeks later, though, he might have felt nostalgic for Lehmann-Haupt's benignity on the subject. Robert Towers opened his review in the Sunday *Times* with a tribute to *Eleven Kinds of Loneliness* as "almost the New York equivalent of 'Dubliners'" whose characters "might have been picked almost at random from the fat telephone book of the Borough of Queens." But this turned out to be a premise for the relative disparagement of Yates's other work: "Scrupulous in its realism, honorable in its refusal to evade embarrassment or failure, the longer fiction seems less able than the short to escape the prison of an (apparently) autobiographical self into the freely imagined lives of others. . . . It is as if Yates were under some enchantment that compelled him to keep circling the same half-acre of pain." Towers went on to say other damning and complimentary things, but the "half-acre of pain" remark stuck in Yates's mind—such that in bad moments he was haunted (even more so than before) by a sense of his own limitations and perhaps ludicrous repetitions.

There were other times, fortunately, when he knew better. "All I write about is family," Elizabeth Cox told him. "That's all there is to write about," Yates replied. Lehmann-Haupt had a point: What is particularly impressive about *Liars in Love* is the extent to which Yates *transcended* the apparent "prison" of his autobiographical personae. "Mostly, we authors repeat ourselves," said Fitzgerald. "We learn our trade, well or less well, and we tell our two or three stories . . . as long as people will listen." Fitzgerald's basic story—the ecstasy and disillusion of his romance with Zelda—exerted such force on his imagination that, at his best, he was able to refine the matter into a kind of universal idealism, one aspect of which was the American dream. Whether Yates ever achieved the peculiar magic of *Gatsby* is doubtful (who did?), but arguably he was able to extend his own "two or three stories" in more interesting ways over the long run.

"I keep wishing"—Towers wrote—"that Yates would stand back from all his sad young men and characterize them with the empathy and objectivity (as opposed to facile introspection) that he can bring to bear on a Queens barroom buddy or a London prostitute." Facile introspection? This suggests that there is something solipsistic—or "boringly self-conscious" as Towers puts it—about Yates's protagonists, that the reader is trapped within the "prison" of a single viewpoint. However, with the exception of two stories in *Liars in Love* ("Joseph" and "Regards at Home") and two in *Eleven Kinds of Loneliness* ("Builders" and "A Wrestler with Sharks") and finally the frame narrative of *A Good School*, Yates *always* wrote in the omniscient third person—the point of which was to show *all* characters, not simply his "sad young men," from the inside (empathy) as well as the out (objectivity). There is no egregious emphasis, much less a "facile" one, on the inner life of the Yatesian "Me" character, and such glimpses that are given tend to be ironic, as when the first-person narrator of "Regards" ponders the effect of his girlfriend's desertion:

> So it was over; and for a little while, taking a tragic view of my situation, I thought I would probably die. . . . But I was still expected to hammer out United Press copy eight hours a day, and to ride the subway and pay attention to where the hell I was walking on the street, and it doesn't take long to discover that you have to be alive to do things like that.

Typically the Yates-like protagonist is depicted with the same objectivity as the rest of the characters—or rather depicted with the pitiless *subjectivity* of another character's point of view. Thus David Clark's bored wife in "A Natural Girl" tunes out the man's dull treatise on "position papers" and considers rearranging the furniture, and later watches him "hold his elaborate head in his hands" ("elaborate" because of his modish Jane Fonda haircut) after one of his pathetic outbursts. And meanwhile he in turn wonders what *she* is thinking—alas, the reader already knows, and sees the awful moment coming when she suddenly (to his mind) lowers the boom.

What Towers applauds as the less autobiographical "objectivity" of *Eleven Kinds of Loneliness* is, to some extent, a stylized characterization imposed by the brevity of magazine-length fiction. Precisely because Yates wanted to evoke greater *empathy* for his characters he allowed himself the luxury of novella-size canvases in *Liars in Love*. If a story like "Saying Goodbye to Sally," for example, had been written in five rather than fifteen thousand words, the character of Sally Baldwin might have been reduced to a comic grotesque along the lines of her promiscuous friend

Jill—in which case, perhaps, we'd be left with only her most salient features, such as her bloated upper lip when she drinks, or her weakness for "fudgy little showbusiness" phrases like "a very gutsy lady." As is, we see that side of her in abundance, but we also see the dignity she never quite relinquishes ("You're making fun of me, Jack, and I think you're going to find that's not a very good idea"), as well as the essential perceptiveness that enables her to recognize Fields as a "counterfeit Scott Fitzgerald," as well as the fact that she herself has led "sort of an idle, aimless life." When such a person returns to her loneliness at the end of the story, and Jack to his, it isn't a matter of distasteful people meeting a "mean-spirited" fate, but rather the inevitable end to which those particular individuals are liable to come.

As in *A Good School* and elsewhere, Yates extended his autobiographical territory with an omniscient perspective, but even in his rare first-person stories the lives of characters other than the narrator are "freely imagined," and the effect is anything but mean-spirited or boring. Given what we know of Yates's tormented feelings toward his mother, his attempt to comprehend (in "Joseph") her own fruitless striving and humiliation, from the distance of almost fifty unhappy years, becomes all the more moving. "I can picture how she looked riding the long, slow train back to New York that afternoon," the narrator muses.

Her adventure with Franklin D. Roosevelt had come to nothing. There would be no photographs or interviews or feature articles, no thrilling moments of newsreel coverage; strangers would never know of how she'd come from a small Ohio town, or of how she'd nurtured her talent through the brave, difficult, one-woman journey that had brought her to the attention of the world. It wasn't fair. . . .

She was forty-one, an age when even romantics must admit that youth is gone, and she had nothing to show for the years but a studio crowded with green plaster statues that nobody would buy. She believed in the aristocracy, but there was no reason to suppose the aristocracy would ever believe in her.

At a time when most realistic writers were cultivating "objectivity" with a vengeance—depicting characters who seemed devoid of will or identifying features one way or the other—Yates insisted on substance, roundness, such that his people create their own disasters rather than blundering into them along a path of random circumstance. "And where are the windows? Where does the light come in?"—as ever, in the implication that we're human, we fail, but in our common humanity we belong to one another for better or worse, whether as families or in some ineffable way suggested by the "sound of the city" that Billy's sister describes in "Joseph": "Because you see there are millions and millions of people in New York— more people than you can possibly imagine, ever . . . and because there are so many of them, all those little sounds add up and come together in a kind of hum. But it's so faint—so very, very faint—that you can't hear it unless you listen very carefully for a long time." In the face of so many millions struggling against anonymity, or just to retain dignity, Helen's "brave, difficult, one-woman journey" is bound for obscurity. But then a kind of mystical kinship is evoked, as well as forgiveness, and doom, in the story's final line: "[O]ur mother was ours; we were hers; and we lived with that knowledge as we lay listening for the faint, faint sound of millions." Perhaps Yates achieved the peculiar magic of *Gatsby* after all.

"*Liars in Love* is one of the most highly praised books of the season and I hope you are as pleased as we are," Sam Lawrence wrote in mid-November, a month after publication. "We've sold over 6500 copies to date which is good for a collection of stories." "Good" is one way of putting it; on the other hand such a highly praised book might have sold better, and meanwhile Yates still had to find some way of making alimony and child-support payments, to say nothing of his own mean subsistence. As for the *d'estime* part of the success he was supposed to be having, it was an elusive phenomenon at best. That winter he was invited to give a reading at the University of Massachusetts (Boston), but not a single person showed up. He sat in the silent lecture hall while his two sponsors gazed at their watches; finally Yates suggested they adjourn to a bar. He didn't seem particularly surprised.

Not a moment too soon, he was offered a visiting professorship for the spring 1982 semester in the prestigious creative-writing program at Boston University. The director, Leslie Epstein, wasn't even aware that Yates had any teaching credentials, but such was his admiration that he was willing to take a chance. Twenty years earlier he'd been in Verona, Italy, when a friend had loaned him the newly published *Revolutionary Road,* which Epstein stayed up all night reading. "There aren't many books that make you remember where you were when you read them," said Epstein, whose flattering letter served as the model for Davenport's "clear and definite offer of employment" from BU in *Young Hearts Crying*: "Apart from the business at hand, let me say that I have always considered [*Revolutionary Road*] to be among the finest [novels] written in this country since the Second World War."

Yates was more skittish than ever about subjecting himself to the scrutiny and possible disdain (or pity) of clever young people. For moral support he called a fellow World War II veteran named Bob Doherty, who'd been in his workshop at the Wesleyan conference; Yates explained that he wanted someone his own age in the class and implored Doherty to participate free of charge (an offer the man accepted). When Yates appeared at a party given by faculty member Jayne Anne Phillips, whom he'd met through Sam Lawrence a few years before, his anxiety was contagious. In a mumble he complimented a student on some chili the young man had brought, and when the latter replied, "Oh, it's just a mix," the two lapsed into a flustered silence. Phillips, who was fond of Yates, began to worry lest he show the effect of all the bourbon he was drinking, and asked Epstein to take him home. On his way out Yates handed her his cup, and she noticed a number of cigarette butts floating inside.

Yates began to relax a few minutes into his first class. "I want to write porn movies," said his student John Walter when it was his turn to explain who he was and what he was doing there. Yates welcomed the levity. His group of a dozen students was not only quirky and unpretentious, but talented, and several went on to have considerable careers—Melanie Rae Thon, Julia Johnson, Jennifer Moses, and the would-be pornographer John Walter, who became a playwright.

They adored Yates. "Dick was depressed and very frail, but dignified," said his student Natalie Baturka. "He elicited awe from us. Unlike Jayne Anne and Leslie, who were young and trying to prove themselves, Dick seemed not to give a fuck what others thought of him, but he was also fragile and insecure. In class, though, he had an air of effortless authority." The paradox of Yates's self-assurance and terrible vulnerability—noted by many—occurred to Melanie Rae Thon one day when he called to praise a story of hers. "He was the finest reader I've ever known," she said. "He'd read through a story and see everything you intended there, and give you a vision of what your story could be if you had the patience to bring it to fruition." Unqualified praise from such a reader was a rare, exalting experience, and Thon was feeling pleased with herself when suddenly Yates's voice became small and shy: "Do you ever read *my* work . . . ?"

He was less inclined than ever to mediate wrangling in his workshop; while his students "beat the shit out of each other," as Baturka put it, Yates would listen placidly and later buy the class a pitcher of beer at a campus bar. "Dad's gonna make it all better," he'd say, and presently a spirit of relative amity would prevail. Half his students were romantically involved with one another, which added a certain piquancy to the atmosphere. For his part Yates didn't hesitate to admit that he liked having attractive women in his class, though he often wondered, wistfully, why they didn't wear *dresses* more often. His "courtly macho thing" (as his female students put it) was accepted with good humor and even rather cherished—coming from such a woebegone man, the effect was more endearing than not. "Dick seemed a little scary at first," student Jon Garelick recalled. "Here was this big bent guy with a gray beard and all. But he was totally friendly and charming. Jayne Anne Phillips told us, 'He's *Dick*, not Mr. Yates,' and after that we always called him Dick. 'I'm going to meet Dick for a drink,' or 'Let's go see how Dick's doing.'" When they saw how Dick was living on Beacon Street, they were appalled. John Walter organized a work party, and while Yates sipped beer at the Crossroads, students painted his apartment and sanded the floor on their hands and knees.

Yates's life at BU was a little less lonely, as admiring students adapted themselves to the Kantian regularity of his schedule. If they wanted to talk about a manuscript, or simply "see how Dick's doing," he was always in his booth at the Crossroads (facing the door) between certain hours of the day. Natalie Baturka lived a block away on Beacon Street and met Yates for dinner almost every night that semester. They made an interesting pair. At age twenty-one Baturka was perhaps the youngest student in Yates's graduate class, and by her own account something of a naïf at the time. "Dick was the one who taught me how to drink hard liquor. Meanwhile he made me feel like the most talented, interesting, pretty woman in the world. I didn't see myself that way; I never said a *word* in his class." The two would sit for hours drinking, smoking, and talking (or not), until Yates was ready to leave around ten or eleven; if he was in particularly bad shape, Baturka would walk him all the way to the door of his second-floor apartment and make sure he got into bed. "He'd always make an obligatory pass and ask me to stay the night," she recalled. "Somehow it didn't bother you—it was like he was trying to be polite, as if he thought you expected it." And then, too, there was the ample compulsion of loneliness. "It was hard for women to be friends with Dick without intimacy coming up," said Jayne Anne Phillips, who was taken aback one night when he suddenly kissed her after dinner. Her startled look didn't escape his notice, and the next day he sent Phillips a "very touching and well-worded" note of apology.

At the end of the semester Yates gave a party at his apartment, which Walter and others retidied for the occasion. It was a modest success. Yates exerted himself as host, buying a case of beer at the Marlborough Market and, true to form, refusing the aid of female students as—weaving and wheezing—he carried it down Beacon Street. His guests nibbled politely at hors d'oeuvres (liverwurst on saltines) and a few asked Yates to inscribe copies of his books. "What's *this*?" Yates asked Garelick, annoyed by a discount sticker on the cover of *Liars in Love,* and more so when the young man admitted he hadn't finished the book yet. "Well, there are some people who've read the whole thing," Yates grumbled. Perhaps to redeem himself, Garelick remarked knowingly on the "erotic charge" between the brother and sister in "A Compassionate Leave"; Yates rolled his head along the back of his chair: "Ohh! Ohh!" he groaned over and over.

That summer Yates and Dubus gave a reading together at the Stone Coast Conference in Gorham, Maine. "It was a big hit," George Garrett remembered. "For years people were still talking about it: '*Were you there?*' The rapport between Yates and Dubus was very evident. They bantered for about two hours, and finally Dubus said, 'Maybe we should do this more often.' "

Yates's "minders" at the conference were Ken Rosen and Madison Smartt Bell, both of whom conceded the "stunning" reading Yates gave with Dubus; both, too, wondered at the disparity between Yates's warmth and dignity on stage and cranky drunken fecklessness off it. "God*damn* it, Rosen, you're the biggest namby-pamby I ever met!" he roared when his host sighed a little too audibly at one of Yates's indiscretions. He'd flown to the conference on a one-way ticket, broke, assuming his honorarium would cover his return. The day after his reading, though, the check wasn't ready, so while Rosen taught class and scrambled around trying to expedite payment, Bell kept an eye on their guest. Zealous campus police had already made it known that they took a dim view of Yates's conspicuous drinking, and that afternoon there was a row when he was barred from bringing beer into the student cafeteria. ("The school employees worked for the state," said Bell, "and weren't beholden to students or faculty; they comported themselves like surly postal workers or zookeepers.") Finally, to Bell's relief, Rosen showed up waving an honorarium check and drove Yates to the airport.

Getting him on the plane was another matter. "I was mesmerized by Yates's gruff disregard of ordinary notions of time and space," Rosen mused. "He said something like, 'Well, my plane leaves at 4:30 and it's 4:25 now, so let's have another drink.' " They missed the 4:30 flight, then another, and finally Rosen had to drive Yates back to campus for the night. "I was grading papers in the dorm," Bell remembered, "and I heard a commotion in the hall—and here comes Yates up the stairs, one arm draped over Rosen on one side and Rosen's twelve-year-old daughter Ingrid on the other. Then, at the top of the stairs, Yates flung them off with a kind of James Brown move and yelled, 'Rosen, I'm sick and tired of your OH MY GODS! Fuck you and your OH MY GODS!' " Once Yates was safely back in his room for the night, Rosen took Bell aside: "I think I dropped the ball here," he sighed, and explained what had happened at the airport. He asked Bell to drive Yates to an early morning flight, and when Bell began to protest Rosen assured him that Yates was a "soldier" and would be up and ready to go by dawn. "Just make sure of two things," he said: "get his room key off him, and make sure he has his ticket." Around 6:30 the next morning, natty in his seersucker suit, Yates irascibly flashed his Delta envelope when Bell asked him about it; ten miles later, at the airport, Yates discovered that the envelope was empty except for a receipt. "That's when I lost my twenty-four-year-old temper," Bell recalled. He phoned Rosen, who found the ticket secreted in his own jacket, and together the two men watched Yates board a plane at last.

His teaching duties over and his students dispersed, Yates's life became strictly divided between working and drinking. Even when sober he wandered his half-block of Beacon Street like a lanky oblivious Banquo, head down and muttering. One day there was a fire on the third floor of the Crossroads, and the intersection of Beacon and Massachusetts was a chaos of firetrucks, police cars, swishing hoses, and popping glass. Restaurant employees spotted Yates on the yonder side of the melee and watched, bemused, as he proceeded through the crowd, past the cordon, over the hoses, and into the restaurant. "Dick," said Michael Brodigan, "we're closed." "Why?" Yates asked.

More than ever he was dependent on the place for any remaining congress with the world. His regular waitress throughout the eighties was a cheerful young woman named Jennifer Hetzel, a BU student who eventually wrote her master's thesis on the Crossroads ("Communication in the Restaurant Business"). "He's got emphysema," Hetzel would snap at customers who looked askance at the hacking, besotted old man in the front booth. For his part Yates enjoyed certain ritualistic exchanges with the waitress about her studies and her father's arthritis. ("You're waiting on

Richard Yates?" said her father, director of the University of Pittsburgh Press. "At the *Crossroads?*") When Hetzel got around to reading some of her customer's work she was "astonished": "I couldn't believe this guy who came in and got drunk every day would go home and write this stuff." Afterward she always bought two copies of his books (one for her father) and asked Yates to inscribe them, a request that made him agitated: "What d'you want me to write?" he'd complain, staring into space for an hour or so before coming up with something suitably personal. "For Jennifer, whose dessert may create a national sensation, or may not, but who in any case will always be a lovely girl." (Hetzel sold her own desserts out of the Crossroads.) "For Jennifer, who is living evidence that the world of PR might still be saved." (Yates had been furious when Hetzel, an English major, had decided to pursue her master's in public relations.) Hetzel always drew a little man with a belly button on Yates's checks, but one busy night she omitted the crucial detail. *"Where's the belly button?"* he demanded, with genuine pique.

Around this time Yates had a seizure in the foyer of the Crossroads. After the ambulance had come and gone, Brodigan went to retrieve some of Yates's things and bring them to the hospital. "Oh God, that apartment . . . ," he said afterward, looking haunted. From that point on, whenever Yates would disappear for a few days, someone from the restaurant would go check on him. "We missed you," Hetzel would say after one of his absences, though she knew not to ask questions. It always impressed her, and others, how intervals of relative sobriety and recuperation improved Yates's appearance: His color would return and he'd be sprucer, less vacant looking. Thus he appeared to Hetzel after his death: "I cried when my father told me about it," she said, "then I started dreaming about him. Dick was the sort who worked his way into your heart. He needed help, and we'd wanted to help him get through the day."

During these lost years Yates's greatest source of grief and regret was his estrangement from his older daughters. They still spoke on the phone, but face-to-face meetings were rare and tended to go awry. Gina remembers a number of dinners with her father and Monica that ended in fights between the two, the little girl sitting meekly between them until Monica bolted to her feet and stormed out of the restaurant. "He had this Victorian paterfamilias idea that he'd be the benevolent Dad and I'd be the cheerful, doting little girl," said Monica. "But you can't be a doting daughter to a guy who falls apart like that. You *have* to be strong. After a fight, Dad would say, 'Oh, I just wanted us to be like *this*,' and I'd say 'It *can't* be like that, because I'm not like that and you're not like that.'" What made the impasse more painful was that he and Monica were best friends when Yates was sane and sober. On Sunday mornings they'd talk on the phone for two or three hours at a time, and there was nothing they couldn't discuss freely: "I loved his take on things," she said. "He always *got* it, he always said the right thing." And he always disappointed her in the end. Monica was the one others called when Yates had a breakdown, and by her mid-twenties she was not only jaded but fed up. "I sensed a sort of prurient relish on the part of the callers: 'You can't *believe* what's happened,' they'd say, as if they wanted to test my reaction to it." She was tired, too, of the terrible fights afterward, which often began with Yates berating her for getting involved, then losing all control ("Oh fuck you, baby!") when she defended herself. As ever, too, he'd refuse to admit that there was anything much the matter with him. "What'd I do that seemed so '*crazy*'?" he'd say over and over. Everyone else was to blame.

As for Sharon, she'd found refuge in a family of her own, and cultivated a kind of benign distance from her father. The fact that she wasn't particularly literary left them without much common ground, even less so when Yates turned out to have remarkably little interest in his grandchild. "Oh yes, dear," he'd sigh absently when Sharon talked about Sonia. His indifference toward such subjects as potty training and nursery schools was perhaps understandable, though it was a bit puzzling that such a doting father would become such an apathetic grandfather. It bothered Yates a bit, too. "Am I a monster?" he asked Vonnegut. "Nah," said the latter. "They're not your kids. That's just how it is." Still, Yates hadn't entirely lost his knack for being charming with little girls, and would draw Sonia out on the phone with ingenuous, particular questions about whatever she wanted to prattle about. And he still deferred, usually, to a child's interests in mixed company. "Sonia, you should let Grandpa finish his story first," the girl's parents would admonish her when she interrupted one of his anecdotes. "Ahh, who wants to hear about that anyway?" Yates would say, dropping the subject. Whatever his good intentions, though, Yates's rare visits seldom passed without mishap. While at the Levines' house in 1983, he promptly drank a case of beer and had a seizure. Later, when his daughters visited him in the psychiatric ward, Monica remarked that his toenails needed clipping. "Yeah," Yates intoned, calmly dotty. "You're just going to clip my nails like a prostitute."

One way that Yates tacitly acknowledged his failings, and tried to make amends, was through his generosity with money. "He'd give it to you when he got it and you'd never hear about it again," said Monica. Even his ex-wives were happy to admit this point in his favor. Sheila, despite an otherwise withering appraisal of Yates, gives him due credit for never missing a child-support payment. And later, when the grown-up Monica was working in New York at underpaid editorial jobs, Yates sent her two hundred dollars a month for three years. Everything else, after his own food and rent were covered (and sometimes when they weren't), went to Gina. In later years Yates tended to run through advances before his books were finished and then try to wrestle more out of Sam Lawrence, who was galled by the knowledge of where the money was liable to go. When Martha and Gina moved to Denver in 1983, Yates paid extra for the girl to attend private school, and one friend noted the paradox of Yates's buying her an elaborate antique dollhouse while he, Yates, lived in two wretched rooms. And that wasn't all: "By God, I'm sending her to Harvard if it's the last thing I do!" was a constant refrain.

But then Gina made him happy, and she wasn't fazed in the least by the roaches and dustballs of Beacon Street. She learned early, too, while listening to Monica's literary discussions with her father ("All this bleakness is just *bunk*, Dad! Life isn't that bad!" "Fine fine, baby, throw *all* my books out the window!"), that it might be best to avoid the whole subject of writing, his career, etc., and for the most part she always did. Their Sunday phone chats were determinedly light-hearted and all about her— school, what she'd eaten for breakfast, what she was wearing or looking at or planning to do that day. If Gina seemed inattentive or lazy, Yates would tell her with mock severity to sit up and put her feet on the floor; other than that there was little or no friction. During his lifetime Gina never learned of his mental illness (she thought the pills were for emphysema), nor did he burden her—as he did Monica—with the more desperate details of his daily affairs. "I have loved your father for many years," Dubus told Gina when they stayed at his house in Haverhill. Dubus was the only friend she ever met during her visits to Boston, and Dubus was grateful for the girl's existence. "Andre was always worrying about Dick," said Dubus's first wife Pat. "That he would get sick, lonely, and die. They loved each other."

Others worried too, however distantly. Dubus used to say he could always tell how Yates was doing based on the overall mood of his latest book, and even strangers could sense that all was not well. "I'm writing to tell you that I think you're the best living writer in America," read a fan letter from this time. "Evidently, you've had a hard life and might not be that comfortable or happy, but your work is superb." Gloria Vanderbilt felt the same—about the work anyway. In the spring of 1983 she sat next to Vonnegut at a cocktail party and asked if he'd ever heard of a writer named Richard Yates: "I think he's wonderful," she said. "I adored *The Easter Parade*." Vonnegut replied that in fact Yates was a friend, and informed her that he lived in Boston and would probably appreciate hearing from her. "On impulse [I] hoped to meet you in Boston," she wrote Yates, after a failed attempt to arrange an impromptu luncheon at the Ritz. "I wanted to tell you that because of *you* light comes not only through chinks and cracks but you flood my window with light. I love you and thank you." Yates wrote back suggesting they get together the next time he came to New York, if she wasn't "repelled by the idea," and she assured him that "repelled" was hardly the word: "Scared, perhaps, a little. You know so much about women." Wendy Sears cringed when a giddy Yates told her of his imminent rendezvous with Vanderbilt—"I thought 'My *God*, what will happen when she actually meets him?' "—but apparently it came off without a hitch: Vanderbilt wrote afterward that she "could have talked on and on" to Yates, and even phoned him that Thanksgiving and put a number of her friends and fellow admirers on the line. The problem, perhaps, was their *second* meeting. When Yates was almost destitute a couple of years later, Sears wrote an urgent letter to Vanderbilt about the plight of her favorite author. Within a few days the famous heiress phoned Sears and explained, coldly, that she didn't have that kind of money.

By 1984 Yates's relationship with Dr. Winthrop Burr had deteriorated. During their early years together Yates would sometimes acknowledge that the sessions were a comfort—that they "made him less afraid of himself," as Burr put it—but when the psychiatrist began to emphasize alcoholism as a major factor, Yates grew more and more hostile. Finally, after one enforced hospitalization too many, Yates became so enraged during a session that Burr walked out on him: "He was shouting so loud you could hear him down the hall," said Burr, "calling me stupid, saying I lacked imagination, that my whole profession was corrupt and had fed off him all these years—used him as a guinea pig, done him no good." Later Yates came to the clinic, drunk, and confronted Burr with an ambulance bill. Since his last hospitalization hadn't been necessary in the first place, said Yates, he insisted that Burr pay. Burr pointed out that Yates was drunk (he denied it) and asked him to leave. After that there were no more psychotherapy sessions. Yates still came in for medication refills, and was civil but laconic when Burr asked how he was doing. A short while later Burr left the VA, but offered to take Yates on as a private patient at a reduced fee; Yates declined, though he did write Burr a gracious, rather apologetic letter thanking him for all his help. "Take care of those two beautiful girls," he closed, referring to a portrait in Burr's office of his young son and daughter. Burr continued to contact his successor at the VA and inquire about Yates's condition, but the woman wasn't able to tell him much.

Yates became increasingly cantankerous toward an unimaginative world that had used him ill. "Ahh that's ridiculous!" he'd snap at any remark that didn't jibe with his calcified worldview. For old times' sake Wendy Sears was willing to invite Yates over for *very* special occasions— his fifty-eighth birthday, say—but it was an ordeal to be suffered strictly out of the goodness of one's heart. Any remonstrance, no matter how diffident, over Yates's slovenly ash spilling or aggressive opinionating was apt to spark a tantrum; it was better to let things go and watch the clock. Meanwhile Yates's ambivalence toward such "well-bred" women as Sears and her cohorts became even more pointed, as he detected bad taste and pretension at every turn. One such woman's cluttered, bohemian digs in Cambridge were, to Yates, an "absurd" attempt to deny her birthright, and when Sears and another Brahmin girlfriend worked as caterers' maids, Yates refused to accept that they needed the money. "Oh how madcap," he declared sarcastically.

Happily his literary fame was showing signs of resurgence. The year before, *Revolutionary Road* had been reissued as a Delta paperback, which attracted a long, laudatory notice by Michiko Kakutani in the daily *Times*: "More than two decades after its original publication, it remains a remarkable and deeply troubling book—a book that creates an indelible portrait of lost promises and mortgaged hopes in the suburbs of America." Yates's readership, such as it was, seemed primed for the publication of *Young Hearts Crying* in the fall, and already Yates was not only under way with his next novel, but eager to get started on the one after that. "It's nice that Barrett Prettyman (or whoever it was) suggested publishing a collection of my Bobby Kennedy speeches," Yates wrote Sam Lawrence in June,

> but I've got a better idea: a novel about that period, with Bobby serving as one of the characters and even Jack having a walk-on part. Wendy Sears will be prominently featured, as will a haggard fellow who begrudges every hour spent at speechwriting because it's denying him his life's work; and there'll be a large, mostly funny supporting cast. . . . I've been collecting notes and sketches for it over the past several years; I know how it's going to begin and develop and where it will go from there. I'm planning to call it *Uncertain Times* unless a snappier title comes along.

Lawrence saw nothing ominously uncharacteristic about such an overt, political roman à clef—on the contrary, he thought the idea "infinitely better" than any book of speeches. Unfortunately he wasn't Yates's publisher anymore: A few months back he'd become a casualty of budget cuts and had moved his imprint to Dutton; as a result Yates's next two novels, both under contract to Delacorte, would be published as "Seymour Lawrence" books in name alone. But the Kennedy novel struck Lawrence as a possible commercial breakthrough for Yates, and he wanted to be part of it: "The people at Dutton, from the President on down, are your fans," he wrote. "I wish we could sign a contract right now."

Yates was almost solvent for the first time in years. That August he and three others (Peter Taylor, Stanley Kunitz, and William Meredith) were awarded NEA Senior Fellowships worth twenty-five thousand dollars each—"to support and honor creative writers who have received the highest critical acclaim, but whose work may not be widely known outside the literary field." As Frank Conroy explained on behalf of the Endowment, Yates had been selected by three separate panels of distinguished writers to receive the honor: "That's great," Yates replied (in a voice Conroy described as sounding "like it was coming from the back of a cement mixer which was also making cement while he spoke"); "when do I get the check?" Daunted as ever by the fearful prospect of facing an award reception alone, a bashful Yates asked "Wendy Serious" to be his "girl" again; she declined, of course, though she was willing to attend the reception with him. The evening was blessedly uneventful: Yates mingled a bit stiffly for a while, then stuck close to Sears and only snapped at her once (when she expressed a fondness for the work of John Irving). The high point came when Frank Conroy tipsily serenaded Yates on the piano, though the latter was eager to leave all the same.

As the October publication of his sixth novel approached, Yates's ship appeared to be coming in at last. "I think *Young Hearts Crying* is the finest thing you've done," Sam Lawrence wrote. "The writing is flawless, the dialogue rings absolutely true, and the characters come immediately to life and stay that way. It's a broader canvas than *Revolutionary Road* (to which it will no doubt be compared). There are stark agonizing moments and virtuoso passages of comic relief. I'm proud to have my name on the title page." As with Yates's first novel—to which *Young Hearts Crying* would indeed be compared—an advance excerpt was published in *Esquire,* which described Yates as "one of America's least famous great writers." It was remarkable redemption for a man who, eleven years and five books before, had threatened to shoot the magazine's fiction editor.

Delacorte held a publication party for Yates in the White and Gold Suites at the Plaza Hotel. Once again he asked Wendy Sears to be his date, but when she wanted to bring a friend, Rosie Johnson, Yates sourly disinvited her from the more intimate dinner for family and friends in the Oak Room afterward. The whole occasion had spurred an even worse state of angst than usual: The early reviews of *Young Hearts Crying* had been mixed, and his old friend Anatole Broyard was slated to weigh in with a full-page notice in the *New York Times Book Review* (Herbert Mitgang had interviewed Yates for the inset profile); meanwhile fellow writers such as Dubus, Crumley, Conroy, Thomas McGuane, Robert Stone, and Ann Beattie, to name a few, were on hand at the Plaza to pay homage to a man they viewed as a master. On arrival Sharon and Monica Yates observed that their father was drunk but ambulatory, and both sought more sober people to talk to—Jill Krementz, Hilma Wolitzer, and Yates's old student Richard Price. The guest of honor bore up through dinner, more or less, though his daughters continued to watch his drinking with dismay. As they were leaving, Yates began to quarrel with the Delacorte rep over the *suite*, not *room*, they'd promised him that night at the Plaza.

In *Young Hearts Crying* the writer Carl Traynor is noted as saying that he "wanted to publish fifteen books before he died, and to have no more than three of them—'or four, tops'—be the kind of books that would have to be apologized for." Yates set the same goal for himself and fell short in both respects, one of them fortunate: He published nine books but only felt obliged (usually) to apologize for *two* of them.* Of the latter one was *A Special Providence* and the other was *Young Hearts Crying*.

---

*Sometime in the late eighties Yates made a list of these fifteen books, including the nine he'd already published: Number ten was to be *Uncertain Times*, while number eleven was *The World on Fire*, based on Yates's experiences promoting the UNIVAC for Remington Rand (as already noted, he wrote a 1989 film treatment with the same title, about which more below). The entries for numbers twelve and thirteen are blank, as Yates was saving his other two gestating ideas for last, perhaps because of the valedictory resonance of their titles: *A Cheer for Realized Men* (14) and *Dying on the Riviera* (15).

Even reviewers who were well disposed to Yates tended to find most of the characters flat and unsympathetic, while the (male) protagonist was thought to be downright repulsive. "I got so terribly tired of the weakness of Michael Davenport," wrote Christopher Lehmann-Haupt in the daily *Times,* for whom the novel was "beguilingly vivid yet ultimately tiresome." Jonathan Yardley of the *Washington Post* denounced Davenport as "monumentally inept and boorish," and that was far from all. Noting the similarity to Yates's "deservedly celebrated first novel," Yardley embarked on the wholesale demolition of *Young Hearts Crying* via comparison: "Where the first novel was artful, this latest is awkward; where the first was subtle, this latest is obvious; where the first was sympathetic, this latest is disdainful." The reviewer took particular exception to Yates's "clumsily constructed" plot, what with its two long sections devoted to Lucy and Michael Davenport respectively, while the other all but disappears from the story. "Yates has written some very good books," Yardley concluded, "but *Young Hearts Crying* isn't one of them." Brian Stonehill of the *Los Angeles Times,* however, found the book's structure one of its finest features, as it "unroll[s] itself seamlessly, inevitably, with the ineluctability of a three-act tragedy, but without classic tragedy's effort to raise its characters above our own level." And finally, *Time* magazine's Jay Cocks wrote the sort of encomium that—one hopes, anyway—gave Yates at least a measure of comfort: "*Young Hearts Crying* could stand as a definitive portrait of a man and woman, maturing in the 1940s, who spend the next three decades trying to get a grip on dwindling dreams that will not die and who have to settle down and, finally, settle. . . . [Yates] is just the writer that Michael Davenport always wanted to be."

Yates was at the Crossroads when he read Broyard's long review (suggestively titled "Two-Fisted Self-Pity") on page three of the Sunday *Times,* and his waitress Jennifer Hetzel noticed that he seemed upset. "Everything okay?" she asked. "*Who's going to pay my daughter's goddamn tuition?*" Yates exploded, indicating Broyard's handiwork. Hetzel was struck not only by the vehemence of the outburst—Yates, though often in a grouchy mood, tended to be quiet and polite—but also by the fact that he'd gone so far as to allude to his writing and/or private life, something he almost never did. "He was *that upset*," she recalled. And no wonder. Broyard's review was not just an attack on *Young Hearts Crying*, but a skillful and malicious attempt to erase much of Yates's reputation with a single definitive stroke. "At a time when a wider public is gaining access to Richard Yates's work," a reader protested in a subsequent letter to the *Times*, "it is sad to see a critic of Anatole Broyard's influence decide not only to lambast Mr. Yates's recent novel, . . . but to go for the jugular too by excoriating the man's earlier writing. . . . It is disheartening that [Yates's] long overdue success has brought in the sharks." And this, of course, from a general reader who presumably had no way of knowing that Broyard and Yates were once boon companions, or that Yates had never spoken of his friend's work except with kindness and admiration. Not that such considerations were ever known to interfere with Broyard's brand of "critical objectivity"—indeed the performance might even be called Broyardian. As Dan Wakefield (and others) noted, "Broyard would actually request books by writers he disliked or resented for the express purpose of junking them." But more on that in due course.

To be fair, one doesn't doubt that Broyard genuinely disliked Yates's novel and for roughly the right reasons: "*Young Hearts Crying* fails . . . because Michael Davenport is not an interesting or appealing man." By the time one arrives at that assessment toward the end of the review—such is the suave assuasiveness of Broyard's style—one can scarcely fail to agree that Yates has written a novel all but entirely concerned with a sentimental, self-pitying, bigoted idiot:

In Mr. Yates's attack on phoniness, there is something of the evangelist and of Archie Bunker too. His men are exasperatingly anti-intellectual, almost phobic about large ideas. They're apologetic even about liking literature. . . . [Davenport] almost always adds an expletive or an obscenity, like a beer chaser, to his esthetic pronouncements. . . . Mr. Yates's men enjoy sex, drinking and talking: they *suffer* art. When Michael Davenport meets a new woman, he immediately thinks of her in bed. . . . He calls his women "baby." Carl Traynor, a novelist . . . , also calls women baby. . . . Though Michael

Davenport is a published poet, we never see a single line of any of his poems, and this is odd and unconvincing. He doesn't talk like a poet, . . . and we wonder where he keeps his poetry hidden about his personality.

And so on. As a further example of absurd "macho" posturing in the book, Broyard made light of Davenport's refusal to accept Lucy's millions because it might threaten his "manhood"; ditto the scenes in which Davenport punches party guests in the stomach.

Broyard's observation that both Davenport and Carl Traynor call their women "baby" is crafty on a number of levels, insofar as it leaves the impression that Yates's men are not only a little cretinous but also, taken together, simply cardboard cutouts of the same basic personality—to wit, Yates himself, whose tendency to call women "baby" Broyard knew well. And the fact was, of course, that in the cases of Davenport and Traynor the author *was* duplicating himself, and this points to a legitimate flaw in the novel's conception. Yates's material for *Young Hearts Crying* was wholly autobiographical, and yet he wanted to avoid another obvious alter ego as protagonist (and thereby another "half-acre of pain" review), so he borrowed the intriguing résumé of a man he hardly knew, Peter Kane Dufault, and hence the poetry, Golden Gloves, Harvard, and wealthy wife. But needless to say Michael Davenport remains essentially Yates—or rather how Yates fancied himself, perhaps, had he been a war hero and boxer as well as a writer, not to say devoid of any redeeming, sui-generis qualities such as a sense of humor and excess talent. The resulting composite is a kind of lurching Frankenstein monster of a character who (as Broyard deftly implied) incorporates all of its creator's most conventional, unlikable traits: Yates, like Davenport, was all too apt to refer to the Mahopac-Tonapac estate as a "fruit farm" because "one of America's most celebrated faggot actors" happened to live there; Yates, too, was probably "nettled" (and sometimes enraged) by the perceived phoniness of the cast-off military regalia favored by Bob Parker–Tom Nelson; and doubtless Yates dearly *wished* at times he could fell with a single blow people who made pseudo-intellectual comments at parties ("We're the second Lost Generation") as well as people who played at being artists of one sort or another. To find what's missing in Michael Davenport, one turns to the more substantial "Me character," Carl Traynor, tucked away into a subplot of the novel: "There were times when she'd find [Traynor] so lost in his nervous pacing and chain-smoking, talking too fast and absently pulling at the crotch of his pants the way little boys do, that she couldn't believe he had written the book she admired so completely." Michael Davenport was perhaps too self-consciously masculine to pluck at his crotch in front of women, "absently" or not, but the boyishly anxious Yates (and hence Traynor) could hardly have helped it. And while Davenport can arguably be dismissed as a boorish dolt and little else, Traynor is too human to be merely ridiculous: "But there were other times . . . when [Traynor] was calm and wise and funny and always knew how to please her." Yates was like that, too; as for the wooden Davenport, his one memorable witticism is that people tend to say "I can explain everything" in the movies.

Another flaw that tended to reinforce the others was, simply enough, the novel's length. This is *not* to accuse Yates of clumsy construction as Yardley would have it; if *Young Hearts Crying* is clumsy, then so too is practically any sprawling novel—*Ulysses, Anna Karenina, Valley of the Dolls*—in which certain characters dominate the plot at long intervals while others are shunted offstage, and what of it? No, the problem in Yates's case is pretty much length per se—a determination to be comprehensive, ambitious, to avoid "skimpiness" at all costs, the better to duplicate the *scope* of a famous first novel. Ironically, in that author profile entombed in Broyard's minefield, Yates conceded a pertinent point or two in his own favor: "I make fewer mistakes now, technically. . . . I know when a character can be introduced without a lot of background detail. And I know when a chapter can be hurried along. Generally, I've acquired a better sense of pace." Quite so, particularly in regard to his three previous novels, but *Young Hearts Crying* lacks that kind of elegant compression and all that inheres in it—understatement, irony, off-center silences. Instead the Davenports talk and talk and repeat the same mistakes and suffer the same embarrassments, all at detailed length, which serves finally to emphasize the fact that, alas, both Michael and Lucy are *very* tiresome people.

Is it a bad novel? It is not. Yates didn't write (or publish anyway) bad novels, and a work of fiction is not to be condemned outright on the basis of unlikable characters. The book is always readable and interesting, full of "agonizing moments and virtuoso passages of comic relief" as Sam Lawrence put it: When Davenport yanks the nails out of the carpet to play with Nelson's toy soldiers, or oafishly trades punches at parties, or endures that long bout of impotence with Mary Fontana, most readers are bound to experience a certain pang of recognition whether they like Davenport or not. Moreover such scenes—indeed almost every scene and image in the novel—work to contribute something to our sense of the characters' awkwardness, the awful gulf between who they are and who they wish to be.

In fact the book's virtues are all representative of Yates's best work; Broyard, however, proceeded by exhaustively attacking the novel's biggest flaw—weak characters—and then suggested that *this* was the most typical Yatesian feature, which brought him cunningly to the real business at hand:

> Several critics have praised Mr. Yates's "precision" and his style. . . . A devil's advocate might say that his characters are so simple and unambiguous that they can be "precisely" described. So far as style is concerned, there doesn't seem to be any, and perhaps this is by design, an emblem of Mr. Yates's realism, his refusal to embellish or distort his characters with authorial eloquence.
>
> The main question in Mr. Yates's work is whether we are being asked to see around, or beyond, the characters to some kind of symbolism—or to take them literally. Are we supposed to forgive their shortcomings and their failures as God does, or are they being offered up as intrinsically interesting, without extenuation? Is his perspective metaphysical or entomological? His characters seem shrunk by realism, robbed of invention and reduced to bleak and repetitive rituals.

Defending Yates against the larger charges of what Cassill called (in a sympathetic letter to Yates) the "Anatole assassination" is tempting but redundant at this point. "What happens to a *writer* who says *you* have no style . . . ?" Cassill wrote with wondering indignation, a sentiment that will be shared by Yates's admirers and rejected, perhaps, by his detractors. The same applies to Broyard's insinuation that Yates's characters, *as a rule,* are so shrunken and flat that no enlightened reader could possibly find them intrinsically (or "entomologically") interesting. If one is apt to hold that opinion of the Wheelers, Helen and John Givings, Alice Prentice, John Wilder, the Grimeses, Bill Grove, Gloria Drake, et al., to say nothing of Sobel, Sergeant Reece, Vincent Sabella, Ken Platt, Christine Phillips, Sally Baldwin, et al., then one is probably neither a reader of Yates nor of the present book. (Most of Yates's characters, suffice to say, serve both an "entomological" *and* "metaphysical" purpose—as Yates intended—but one has already gone into all that.)

Truth be known, Broyard was something of a Yates character himself, and as such merits a certain amount of entomological inspection. "You made it and he did not," Cassill wrote Yates. "Back in the time I knew Anatole he was among the white hopes, deservedly so for the merit of the few things he published in the fifties. After that . . . well, only the competent malice of what he has written as a reviewer." Broyard made a minor name for himself as an author of short fiction—most of it parts of a novel he never finished—at a time when, rather like Yates, he was supporting himself by writing direct-mail advertising. When he and Yates became friends, they were on precisely the same level: near-contemporaries who'd published some promising stories and were struggling to complete novels while teaching for beggar's wages at the New School. Then Yates published two brilliant books in two years and was offered fifteen thousand dollars to adapt Styron's novel for the movies. "I hope you're being corrupted by now," Broyard wrote his friend while the latter was in Hollywood. "*I'm* not, I'm so busy reading manuscripts and running to class. . . . We console ourselves with the delusion of grandeur that someday they'll [Broyard's stories] be collected.—And yours were. . . . Someday I may want to get corrupted too." As it happened, Broyard's fiction would never be published in book form, though the corruption part panned out after a fashion: Reviewing for the *Times* gave him financial security as he started a family, as well as an alibi for not writing fiction and a bully pulpit for settling old scores. His friendship with Gordon Lish ended when Broyard maliciously attacked the first novel of one of Lish's favorite new discoveries. As Lish recalled, "Anatole actually admitted to me that he was getting his own back because I was publishing all these first novelists, while he was struggling to produce a novel of his own. Anatole didn't *want* to be a reviewer. He was quite determined to punish people."

By the time Broyard left Manhattan in 1963, his friend Yates was already showing signs of becoming a full-time drunk, and one imagines Broyard thinking kindly of him in the long years of literary silence that followed. Then rather abruptly Yates began publishing one acclaimed book after another, and the level of bile rose accordingly as Broyard saw fit to review three of them. *Young Hearts Crying*, with its theme of youthful manqué promise ending in bitterness and regret, must have been especially provoking (quite apart from its aesthetic defects): "[A]n insufficient talent is the cruelest of all temptations," Broyard noted, with perhaps unwitting irony, in reference to the Davenports.

"Anatole died as he lived, with a hatchet in his hand," Sam Lawrence wrote Yates in 1990.

> A few weeks before he died he publicly destroyed the reputation and life work of Leonard Michaels in the *NY Sunday Times*. For nearly 20 years, Anatole was under contract to us for a novel, first at the Atlantic Monthly Press, then Delacorte, and he would introduce me as his "publisher." I never had the heart to deny it. He couldn't bring himself to complete a sustained work, either fiction or his memoir (which I read in part and which mostly concerned his seducing women in the Village).*

. . .

The reception of *Young Hearts Crying*, capped by the humiliation of being ridiculed for the benefit of millions of *Times* readers, sent Yates into a tailspin from which, in some respects, he never quite recovered. Perhaps the most damaging effect of Broyard's review was that it made Yates genuinely doubt his value as a writer—though, to be sure, he recognized

---

*Published posthumously as *Kafka Was All the Rage*.

certain nonliterary motives on the reviewer's part. One night at the Cross-roads, he told Wakefield that Broyard had once coveted a girlfriend of his (Barbara Beury?); Yates quipped that Broyard's reviewer bio at the end of "Two-Fisted Self-Pity" should read, *Anatole Broyard wanted to fuck Richard Yates's girlfriend in the early sixties.* The more he and Wakefield considered the matter, the more incensed (and drunk) they became, until finally they decided to get on a train *that night* and go "beat the shit out of Anatole"; but reason was presently restored to its throne. At other times Yates would agonize over the relative justice of Broyard's remarks—he'd always held the highest regard for the man's intelligence and taste, after all. And whenever someone would try to compliment him for *Young Hearts Crying,* Yates would wince and say it was "soap opera" that he'd only written to fulfill a contract.

Another blow fell in the form of a brief, waggish essay titled "A Clef" by his old friend Bob Parker. "One day around Christmas . . . ," it began, "I found a new book by Richard Yates in a bookstore in Connecticut.

I always keep track of his books because he and I used to be friends. The photo on the book jacket showed him looking sullen and hurt. My mother once surprised me by saying he was handsome.

As I looked through the book, a novel called *Young Hearts Crying,* some words jumped out at me: "painter," "toy soldiers," "Putnam County." I concentrated on the text for a moment, then with a flush I realized that I was a character in the book, "Tom Nelson." I bought *Young Hearts Crying* and read it in one evening, growing more uneasy as each chapter unfolded. Tom Nelson was insufferable. I went to bed feeling angry and embarrassed. I hoped none of my friends would read the book.

I tried to reason with myself. When I paint a portrait, it's the irregularities and crooked places in a face that interest me. I supposed it was the same with Yates, but I was hurt anyway. . . .

It was clear from the start of the book that the hero, a writer called "Davenport," is Yates, although Yates does a far better job of disguising himself than he does me. Many of our old friends from Putnam County are there as well—the painter Tony Vevers ("Paul Maitland"), Ed Sherin ("Ralph Morin") and Will Geer ("Ben Duane") from the theater, and the writer Bob Riche ("Bill Brock"). . . .

When Davenport meets Nelson, he observes that Nelson "wasn't even dressed right, instead of a suit coat he wore an Army tanker's jacket. . . ." Davenport, a war hero, immediately ascertains that Nelson is not entitled to his tanker's jacket. I remember that jacket; in fact, I think I still have it somewhere. Yates, who had no more business owning a tanker's jacket than I did, gave it to me. . . .

I don't know what Davenport would make of New York City today, thirty years after I started wearing Army jackets. There, on every street, are men dressed as fighter pilots with helmets, goggles and silk scarves; Eighth Army desert rats; Bosnian sharpshooters; Zouaves; Turcos; and Wehrmacht Feldwebels. I imagine Davenport staggering across town quivering with suppressed rage, hoping he can get to the station and away from all that khaki before yet another nervous breakdown lands him in Bellevue.

When you read a roman à clef and find yourself depicted as one of the great idiots of your generation, you do have to wonder if this is the author's jaundiced, self-serving perception or the opinion of everyone who knows you. As soon as I had finished the book, I dialed another friend from the old days in Putnam County, Peter Kane Dufault, the poet.

"I just read Richard Yates's new book, *Young Hearts Crying*," I told him.

"Never heard of it."

"Well, I appear in it as a painter called 'Nelson.' "

"Who is Richard Yates? Did I ever know him?"

"He used to stand around at parties of mine, looking sad and wondering what William Styron and William Humphrey were doing."

"Oh yes . . ."

. . . "There's one chapter where he has Davenport punch Tony Vevers at a party, only he calls Vevers 'Paul Maitland.' "

"Wait. . . . *I* punched Tony Vevers!"

"Yeah, and he also has himself going to Harvard."

"I didn't know him there," Peter said.

"Well, he didn't go. In fact, he never finished high school. There's more—

he makes himself into a boxing champion and a poet. He marries a rich wife."

"He's describing me," said Peter. . . .

Parker wrote the piece "in a fit of anger" the day after he finished *Young Hearts Crying*, and promptly mailed copies to Yates and the journal *Grand Street*.* From the former he got no response. It's possible that at some point Yates was able to look back on Parker's effort as witty and not so bad humored under the circumstances, but at the time it was water down a drowning man's throat. The last thing Yates wanted the public to know was that his fictional people were harsh caricatures of former friends, or that he'd filched the glamorous details of another man's life to bedizen an essentially autobiographical persona (one that had a tendency to land in Bellevue, no less); or that he himself was perceived as a boozy climber who mooned over the doings of Styron and so on. And whether the piece was published or not, the mere fact that Yates's old Putnam County friends were aware of how he'd portrayed them, and very hurt and angry about it, was enough to prey on his mind.

One night Yates's old friend from the Kennedy days, Barrett Prettyman, called to catch up and congratulate him on *Young Hearts Crying*. As Prettyman noted in a subsequent letter to Yates, it was "a very strange telephone conversation." Yates seemed not only drunk and bewildered but peculiarly angry at Prettyman himself: When the latter mentioned that he'd recently married a younger woman, Yates denounced him (with no apparent irony) as a dirty old man. "Despite this unpleasantness, which concerns and puzzles me," Prettyman wrote, "I very much hope that you continue to be successful and to turn out such beautiful work."

A godawful year and a half later, in mid-1986, Yates's general shame and distress had subsided enough for him to muster an apology: "As you probably know," he wrote Prettyman,

---

*Again, *Grand Street* accepted the essay and set it in type, but never published it.

I've had periodic spells of certifiable insanity for many years, and on the day of your phone call I was trying, unsuccessfully, to recover from the humiliating reviews of my last book. Not long after that I did go crazy, and had to be taken once again into the VA madhouse that has sort of become my second home here in Boston. . . .

Of all the unkind and unpleasant things I said to you, the one that rankles my memory most was trying to make crude fun of you for having a youthful new wife. That was dumb as well as nasty; and besides, I'm nobody to talk: I married a lovely twenty-year-old when I was forty, and would give anything to have her back with me now. . . . I will feel a *little* less like an asshole about all this if you can somehow let me know we're back on good terms.

Prettyman promptly did so—but again, all that came later.

CHAPTER SEVENTEEN

No Pain Whatsoever: 1985-1988

In the mid-eighties Yates's former acquaintances would sometimes see a gaunt, stupefied, ragged old man staggering around the streets of Boston; an incredulous second look would confirm that the wretch was none other than Richard Yates. The usual impulse was to hurry away before one was recognized by this poor ghost, though of course there was no danger of that. When not in the hospital or seated at his desk, Yates spent his days in an alcoholic fog.

Underlying his other woes, Yates was almost broke again. *Young Hearts Crying* had made a brief appearance at the bottom of the *Boston Globe* best-seller list and was an alternate selection of the Book-of-the-Month Club, but still hadn't sold more than ten thousand copies in hardcover. Delacorte had been losing money on Yates for years, and was less and less willing to extend advances to cover the time he needed to finish his books. By the spring of 1985 the situation was desperate: Yates's work-in-progress, *Cold Spring Harbor,* was little more than half done and his advance money was about to run out; nor was Yates in any condition to resort to his old recourse, teaching, even if such jobs had been available to him.

For some time DeWitt Henry had intended to publish, under the auspices of *Ploughshares,* Yates's screenplay adaptation of *Lie Down in Darkness*; almost ten years before, Yates had wryly dug this relic out of his trunk, brushed away the vermin turds, and handed it over to Henry. The idea was that publication might renew interest in producing the film, a hope that Yates had never quite relinquished in times of particular fiscal anxiety. Finally, in May 1985, publication was at hand: *William Styron's*

"Lie Down in Darkness": A Screenplay was to be launched with a gala reading by Yates and Styron at the BU Armory, an event that would be attended by a number of Boston's cultural nobs. Yates was excited about it, though not in any positive sense.

Around this time Dubus got a raving phone call from Yates—the CIA had given him rat poison and he'd been kicked out of the Crossroads, etc. Dubus called DeWitt Henry and Henry called Michael Brodigan, who confirmed that, yes, Yates had become unruly and been told to leave the restaurant two days before. When he hadn't come back or answered his phone, Brodigan had called Monica Yates, who was likewise unable to reach her father. Another two days passed, and then Henry learned from his *Ploughshares* cofounder, Peter O'Malley, that the Cambridge police had arrested Yates in Harvard Square for public drunkenness and transferred him to a drying-out facility.

Yates resurfaced shortly before the Styron reading on May 11, and Henry arranged to meet him at the Crossroads. One look at Yates and Henry realized that alcohol was only part of the problem, something he'd suspected (without knowing for sure) ever since reading *Disturbing the Peace.* "His short-tempered, fragmented ravings reminded me of King Lear," said Henry, who walked Yates back to his apartment and urged him to get some sleep. The next day Henry got a call from Dan Wakefield: Yates was locked in his apartment and needed their help. When they arrived, in a heavy rain, Yates buzzed them into the building and shoved a key under his door. "The room was a mess," Henry recalled, "clothes, money, and papers strewn around, spilled ashtrays, bottles and beer cans. . . . Dick sat hunched on his couch, shakily smoking, while Dan and I sat facing him in folding chairs. Dick turned on me: 'Get high school outta here! What are you looking at? Those eyes!' He pointed at my rubbers: 'My mother taught me to take off my rubbers in the house!' " Wakefield got the number of Yates's VA psychiatrist, who arranged for the police to dispatch a squad car. "You're calling the cops!" Yates yelled over and over, but began to calm down somewhat when the police arrived and coaxed him to gather his things for the hospital, a familiar enough ritual by then.

A few days later an apologetic Yates called Henry and asked him to bring a carton of cigarettes to the VA. Henry felt as he were being "taken into Bluebeard's castle" as he passed through security stations en route to the twelfth floor, Ward C, for mental patients and detoxing alcoholics. "Dick had always seen me as 'high school,' 'Mr. Big Eyes,'" said Henry, "a protégé whose good opinion he wanted to keep. But this broke the ice between us about his mental illness." He found Yates in bed, where he'd been working on *Cold Spring Harbor* using the swinging food table as a desk. As they walked down the hall to an open lounge, Yates greeted a number of other patients and greedily broke out the cigarettes. Henry had brought several copies of the published screenplay for Yates to sign; once Styron had signed them too, they'd be sold as hundred-dollar collectors' items to help *Ploughshares* recoup its investment.

That night at the armory, Henry announced to the crowd that Yates was "in the hospital with pneumonia" and conveyed his apologies; Robert Brustein, director of the Loeb Drama Center at Harvard, agreed at the last minute to read Yates's part of the program. In his opening remarks, Henry noted Yates's affinity with the other writer on the dais, William Styron: "Both would probably agree with George Eliot's definition of tragedy. . . . 'If we had a keen vision and feeling of all ordinary human life, it would be like hearing the grass grow and the squirrel's heartbeat, and we should die of that roar which lies on the other side of silence.' . . . Both masters have shown us courage and spirit by functioning on the edge of that other side of silence." After Brustein read from the screenplay, Styron thanked the crowd for observing such a "worthy occasion: celebrating Richard Yates"; he then read the first chapter of *Revolutionary Road,* which he called an "exceptional" and "definitive" novel.

Yates was soon released from the hospital, whereupon he moved to a tiny apartment above the Crossroads. Thus his life shrank a half block more. Now he hardly had to go outside at all if he didn't want to—though the flight of stairs, taken twice a day, was more than enough exercise for such a decrepit man. Still, Yates was satisfied with the new arrangement: The nightly hubbub from below was a companionable noise, and the aroma of cigarettes and beer was, to Yates, a delightful nosegay. Shortly after he moved in, he attended a christening party at the home of his new landlord, Mike Brodigan. Yates sat in the corner vacantly sipping whiskey, smiling vaguely when spoken to.

Around midsummer Yates's latest advance—actually an advance for the book *after* the unfinished *Cold Spring Harbor,* since by then he was a full book behind on his contract—ran out, and Delacorte held fast against further payments until the present novel was delivered. At such desperate moments in the past, Monica McCall had not only commiserated with Yates—weathering his panicky phone calls with motherly patience and signing her notes with "Love"—but she'd also found ways of putting money in his pocket until the crisis had passed. Mitch Douglas did his best: He, too, loaned Yates money, and only a few years ago he'd compelled Sam Lawrence to increase his advances to Yates by confronting him with a firm offer from another publisher. All the while, though, Douglas was given to hectoring Yates about meeting his contractual obligations, and it was clear to both men that neither was very dear to the other. Douglas had come to dread that doleful voice on the phone—carefully polite, but with an edge of hysteria ("like a quiver on the launching pad"): "Hi, it's Dick Yates, I need money." And their chats would go downhill from there.

That summer Douglas seemed genuinely alarmed by his client's deterioration, and as a last resort he had a make-or-break discussion with Delacorte's editor in chief, Jackie Farber. Perhaps out of an understandable sense of urgency or exasperation, Douglas permitted himself to be far more candid than Yates (or Monica McCall for that matter) would have been likely to condone. Douglas explained that the stress of meeting deadlines before his money ran out was "depleting [Yates] mentally and physically," and pointed out that Yates's increasingly frequent breakdowns were landing him in the hospital again and again. He said that a number of publishers were willing to pay Yates for the prestige of his name, to which Farber rejoined by wondering if they were also willing to reimburse Delacorte for the unearned advances Yates had accumulated over the years. She further asserted that it was a little unseemly of Douglas to negotiate by making her feel guilty about Yates's personal distress. The next day Douglas recapitulated his basic position in writing—"[I]f you are going to hold on to an author, then you have to be willing to accept whatever problems must come with a package"—and went on to suggest that pathetic references to Yates were fairly unavoidable at this point: "[C]an you imagine how I feel," he wrote,

> as it happened yesterday, when Richard Yates tells me that [he] has lost 15 pounds and looks like a concentration camp victim because he has had to survive the past few weeks on two eggs mixed in a glass of milk, and that he was going to have to go back in the hospital simply to have food to eat. . . . I can't feel very good as an agent or as a human being when I have indications that there are publishers out there who are willing to pay Yates the kind of advances he needs to meeting financial obligations and put food in his mouth.

Farber must have been touched in spite of herself, as she insisted on taking Yates to lunch and trying to work out their differences in person. Douglas went along ("my heart in my mouth"): "Within twenty minutes," he recalled, "Dick had downed four drinks and spilt a fifth on the tablecloth, and then burnt a hole in it." There were no more lunches after that, and Douglas proceeded to negotiate a contract with Atheneum for *Uncertain Times.* Meanwhile Yates became more bitterly determined than ever to end his association with Douglas, for reasons that were only incidentally professional.

The moment arose when Monica Yates submitted a novel, *Looking Good,* based on her experience as a nurse at an Avon Old Farms camp for overweight children. Monica herself didn't have a very high opinion of this effort—"*No,* it's terrible," she'd tell her father when he asked to see it—but thought at the time that, if nothing else, it might have commercial possibilities. Besides, it was becoming more and more embarrassing to identify herself at New York parties as "a writer," and a published novel would at least validate the claim somewhat. But already she was backing away from a literary career, and when Douglas agreed to represent the work ("a terrific read"), she implored him not to let her know about any rejections; like her father, she had a tendency to take things hard. "I will respect your wishes about not telling you about rejections," Douglas replied, "but that worries me. Rejection is a big part of this business. . . . If you can't deal with the rejection factor—perhaps you should be doing something other than writing?? I love you and think you are very gifted— but I want you to be happy and part of the business is dealing with the business on its own terms." With this note he enclosed the standard one-page agency agreement, which "irrevocably" tied her to ICM as agent for the work in question. Monica refused to sign it. Such an agreement, after all, was even then causing her father a lot of grief.

Monica was more relieved than not when Douglas regretted that he couldn't represent her if she wouldn't sign, but when Yates heard of the matter he was furious, or affected to be. *"Nobody talks to my little girl like that!"* he raged at Douglas in the course of firing him over the phone. ("One of the most welcome communications I ever had in my life," said Douglas.) Such was Yates's disdain that he was willing to terminate Douglas's services even though the man would continue to receive commission on Yates's future work. Still, he had few regrets about firing Douglas at whatever cost: Apart from his less rational antipathies, he viewed the agent as an indiscreet man who lacked a proper appreciation for his work.* "Since breaking off with you on the phone that day," he wrote Douglas, "I have only become more certain, rather than less, that it was the right decision. I'm very glad too that you will continue to receive your share of whatever income the novel *Uncertain Times* may bring. I won't forget the many examples of your patience with me over the years, and hope we can remain on decent and businesslike terms." It would be hard to say which man was more relieved to be rid of the other.

Yates was drinking too much to be anything but a burden, and his company was simply unbearable most of the time. His daughter Monica adored him, but at a distance: He was the one person who seemed to understand her perfectly, and their long animated phone conversations were a solace to both in these later years. Moreover, Monica's appreciation for her father's work continued to grow over time, and she was

---

*"I know that you have not been tremendously pleased with the quality of [Yates's] last two books," Douglas wrote Jackie Farber, "and frankly I don't see the situation getting any better." One of the two books was *Liars in Love*.

forever thrusting his books on acquaintances. One of these was her ex-boyfriend Larry David, a comedian and future cocreator of the TV show *Seinfeld*.* He and Monica had remained good friends after their break-up, and such was David's admiration for her father that Monica invited him to meet Yates over dinner. When David began to demur ("I didn't want to meet him or anybody"), Monica pleaded: Her father was bound to drink too much, and she dreaded being alone with him. Reluctantly David relented. When he arrived at the Algonquin on the night in question, Monica was late, and David found himself face-to-face with the writer he admired so much. The latter was gruffly civil, though he seemed to take a dim view of David's teetotaling. The younger man tried to break the ice with a funny story about how he'd pretended to be suicidal to get out of Vietnam, and showed Yates the tragic face he used to pull while marching with the national guard. Yates pointed out that he himself was a veteran of World War II. Eventually Monica turned up. Over dinner her father remained mostly sober, though he had at least one awful coughing fit and his wheezy muttering was all but unintelligible to David, who relied on Monica to translate. In general Yates was not amused by David, deploring his lack of courtliness toward Monica, though the couple were only friends. As for David, he was thoroughly intimidated, and when it came time to leave the restaurant he found himself in a bind: It had begun snowing outside, and David's expensive suede jacket would almost certainly be ruined; he was tempted to turn it inside out, but the lining was garish and liable to be denounced by Yates. As David recalled, "Should I risk a rebuff from a great writer? I decided to eat [i.e., absorb the cost of] the jacket. It was never the same." The loud lining may or may not have provoked Yates, but the *Seinfeld* episode based on this meeting most certainly did (as we shall see).

Usually the repercussions of Yates's rare forays into the world were far from comical. When he combined a visit to Gina with a writers' conference at the University of Denver, he almost managed to undo fourteen years' worth of (relatively) good behavior with his daughter. His old

*Larry David used Monica as a partial model for the character Elaine Benes in the series.

friend Seymour Epstein was on the Denver faculty, and Yates got up for their meeting with a heedless drinking spree. At a conference luncheon, Yates took the hostess aside and said "Look, I'm an alcoholic. When I sit down to eat, I need a glass of bourbon beside me at all times. Is that understood?" By the time he arrived at Martha's door the next day, he was haggard and trembling with hangover. And for once not even Gina could cheer him up—indeed, nothing she said was right. "Why d'you say that? What d'you mean?" Yates snapped at her, over and over. On the brink of tears but determined as ever to please, Gina tried to explain that she was paying him a *compliment*—that she was proud to have such a famous writer for a dad. Yates looked more pained than ever. "You don't understand," he said, "you don't *get* it." Then, at urgent tortuous length, he tried to explain that *fame* wasn't important, he didn't want to be loved for that; but his speech began to fail as if he were lapsing into aphasia. He'd stutter and stop in mid-sentence, then make a frustrated face and start over. "Listen, I'm not sick, I'm just tired," he told the concierge, as he kept stuttering and stopping while trying (for whatever reason) to change his room. When Gina woke up next morning, Yates was sitting on the other bed staring at her; then he took a step toward the bathroom and collapsed. The terrified girl ran screaming into the hall and flagged down an employee, who called an ambulance. "It's okay, we just had a little seizure here," a medic said as they loaded Yates onto the gurney.

When Epstein heard that his friend had been taken to Porter Hospital, he called Martha to apologize: Knowing Yates's history as well as he did, he should have watched him better; in the meantime was there anything Epstein could do? "Look," said Martha, "I don't want to go *near* the man, or vice versa." But Gina urged her to reconsider, and Yates was finally allowed to recuperate on the couch for a couple days. It was not a happy reunion for either him or Martha. "Thanks for the 'hospitality,'" Yates said with bleak sarcasm as he took leave of his ex-wife. Toward Gina he was frantically apologetic: He suffered from a medical condition called epilepsy, he explained, urging the girl to ask her teacher about it. A few days later, Gina's teacher took her out of class to discuss the matter; Yates had called the woman and insisted she do so.

Back in Boston he lost himself in work—"busy in the best sense," he reported to Prettyman: "sane and working every day: tired every night." One day that spring (1986) a young admirer named Don Lee spotted Yates on a bench in the Prudential Center. Yates was on his way to the post office to mail *Cold Spring Harbor* to his publisher and had to stop every few yards to get his wind back. He sat pensively weighing the manuscript in his hand. "It's a small novel," he sighed. "So was *The Great Gatsby*," said Lee. Yates affected to cheer up: "That's right," he said. "That's right."

Yates regarded *Cold Spring Harbor* as another "plateau performance"—a modest, craftsmanlike effort that "may help take the edge off some of the terrible things that were said about *Young Hearts Crying*." He didn't seem to worry much about personal exposure either, having somewhat disguised himself as the adolescent Phil Drake, while his mother made her fourth appearance in the novels as the feckless hysteric Gloria. As with Pookie in *The Easter Parade*, Yates not only "stripped" Gloria of his mother's artistic pretense, he actually seemed to milk her repugnant features all the more, perhaps in order to reinvent the character or, as he put it, simply to get his mother "right." In that respect he felt he'd succeeded at last, and this was a matter of no small satisfaction. "You are one hell of a good writer," wrote Vonnegut, to whom the book was dedicated, "and the best reporter I know of big messages in small gestures and events. Your most striking contribution to American literature, though, . . . is your harrowingly honest inventory of the meager resources available to middle-class mediocrities."

That was about as good a way as any to summarize Yates's achievement, and most critics agreed that *Cold Spring Harbor* succeeded along just those lines—in the smallness of the "gestures and events" as well as the polished, unflinching portrayal thereof. "Reading this meticulously crafted novel, one wonders why the author has made matters so difficult for himself," wrote Elaine Kendall of the *Los Angeles Times*, bluntly describing the plot as having to do with "pitiful losers" who "slide passively into poverty, alcoholism, blindness and lunacy"—an unpromising synopsis, but hardly inaccurate. "Against all odds," Kendall continued, "Yates has managed to show that chronic misery can be as much an art form as acute agony." Howard Frank Mosher, writing in the *Washington Post,* also felt obliged to win back the faint-hearted after a grinding recital of the novel's plot: "If all this sounds terribly bleak, I should quickly point out that *Cold Spring Harbor* is so consistently well-written, just, unsentimental and sympathetic that the intertwined lives of the Shepherds and Drakes are every bit as fascinating as they are grim." Most revealing was the dialectic between the daily and Sunday reviews in the *New York Times,* by Michiko Kakutani and Lowry Pei respectively, which reminded one yet again of what Stewart O'Nan called "the tricky heart of Yates's fiction": that is, the question of whether his "pitiful losers" are so much "literary cannon fodder" (Broyard's phrase), or rather the product of Yates's objective yet compassionate view of average, suffering humanity. "Mr. Yates writes of these characters with sympathy so clear-hearted that it often feels like nostalgia for his own youth," Kakutani observed, "and yet he is also thoroughly uncompromising in revealing their capacity for self-delusion, their bewilderment in the face of failure." Lowry Pei, however, thought Yates had stumbled in walking his usual tightrope between sympathy and brutal detachment: "Mr. Yates's narrative voice often sounds like that of a misanthropic anthropologist, making it difficult if not impossible to feel sympathy with the characters' dreams. The frequent, and occasionally unclear, shifts in the narrator's attention from one character's viewpoint to the next . . . intensify this feeling."

Thirty years before, in his revision notes for his first novel, Yates pondered what he viewed as the single biggest flaw in his work—sentimentality, the fact that his protagonists Frank and April were "too nice": "See and show both of these people from the outside, in the round, and from the inside too. Be 'simultaneously enchanted and repelled by their inexhaustible variety.' *Think* about them, and the hell with the reader's sympathies. Make them *love and hate* each other the way real people do." Yates seized on this approach—showing his characters from the outside and in—as the key to making otherwise unexceptional people interesting, and nowhere in his fiction is the omniscient view more flexible, even to the point of apparent vacillation, than in *Cold Spring Harbor.* Rather tellingly, Pei echoed Yates's (and hence Fitzgerald's) own words when he called the effect "an uneasy combination of acceptance and revulsion"—

that is, an unfocused viewpoint, as if the author himself didn't quite know what he thought of these characters and wished to have it both ways.

In fact Yates wanted to have it many ways, every conceivable way, just as long as the basic integrity of a character remains intact—a fixed entity viewed from a variety of angles. Thus, over cocktails with the elder Shepherds, Gloria watches her beloved daughter with a gelid eye as the latter burbles to her in-laws that she's "never been happier": "It reminded [Gloria] of Curtis Drake at his most vapid; but then, Rachel had always been her father's child." This is unkind, though it aptly reflects Gloria's jealousy toward her daughter's happiness and closeness with the Shepherds (and Curtis Drake), while at the same time being a fairly just observation— Rachel *is* vapid. Rachel, in turn, is loyal enough to Gloria not to discuss the latter's "rotten tomato smell" with her brother, but she's also determined to be a better mother to her own child than Gloria was to her. In short, both mother and daughter "*love and hate* each other the way real people do," an ambivalence that particularly applies to families. In the same way Yates manages to make the loutish Evan Shepherd a somewhat interesting, somewhat sympathetic character. Evan's extreme limitations lead him from one dreary disappointment to the next, but he goes on doing his little best withal: He refrains from outright rudeness toward the egregious Gloria, and is a doting if doltish father to his young daughter; but then, too, he hits his wife and calls her "soft as shit," and in the eyes of his brother-in-law he's a "dumb bastard": "This asshole was going to spend the rest of his life on the factory floor with all the other slobs, and it would serve him right." And that's true too, as Gloucester says in *Lear*.

But Pei has a point of sorts: The narrator's essential attitude toward Gloria Drake would seem mostly one of revulsion, period, such that the reader is unlikely to feel anything but gratified by her eventual comeuppance. Indeed there seems something a little gleeful—even "misanthropic"—in the narrator's tabulation of Gloria's defects, most of them expressed in grossly physical terms: Her attempt at a "girlish and disarming" laugh serves only to "call attention to how loose and ill-defined her lips [are]" and thus makes her look "like a shuddering clown"; her hair is a "blend of faded yellow and light gray, as if dyed by many years of drifting cigarette smoke"; she has a "frail, slack little figure"; she talks "until veins the size of earthworms [stand] out in her temples . . . until white beads of spit" gather at the corners of her mouth; to "pantomime 'worry' she [makes] as if to put her hand on her heart, but instead [cups and clasps] her pendulous left breast, as if she were feeling herself up"—and so on, and *on*. It's a bit much, and barely ameliorated by Charles Shepherd's gallant observation that it's wrong to make fun of a lonely woman, in this case Gloria, as if all lonely women are doomed to become cackling, malodorous clowns. On the other hand, such people *do* exist in some form or another, and one can only reiterate that Yates viewed Gloria as the best likeness of Dookie he ever managed: a triumph. And if she fails to win the reader's sympathies? As Yates was careful to remind himself, "the hell with the reader's sympathies."

Which, in a nutshell, may explain why *Cold Spring Harbor* didn't sell and why, for that matter, Yates's books keep going out of print. To repeat the obvious, most people don't like reading about, much less identifying with, mediocre people who evade the truth until it rolls over them. And yet most of us face such a reckoning sooner or later, and few of us are really the brave stoical mavericks or handsome heedless romantics out of Hemingway and Fitzgerald, who *do* stay in print. If Yates seemed to vacillate between "acceptance and revulsion" toward his people—with a decided emphasis on the latter in the case of Gloria Drake and certain others—it was at least in pursuit of an honest synthesis.

Cold Spring Harbor is a good minor novel, not one of Yates's best or worst, but utterly representative. As such it wasn't likely to attract new readers or alienate old ones (what few were left), and this was perhaps as it should be. Impoverished, broken in health, often drunk and demented, Yates deviated not a whit from the true north of his artistic conscience; *Cold Spring Harbor,* then, was a suitable last transcendence, though to Yates it was simply a matter of nine books down and six to go.

The delivery date for *Uncertain Times* was November 1987, and Yates felt fairly confident he could manage it: Though certain scenes were already proving "stubborn and difficult," the basic plot was blocked out, and most of the book—the early parts anyway—had been "a pleasure to write." Meanwhile he also produced an essay on the subject of Cassill's 1961 novel *Clem Anderson,* which Yates described as "the best novel I know of on the subject of writing, or on the condition of being a writer" (the very theme Yates himself was then grappling with); "and that alone seems marvelous because so many other novelists have found only embarrassment in the same material."

Yates's appreciation appeared in both *Ploughshares* and the volume *Rediscoveries II,* and was instrumental in persuading Pushcart Press to reissue Cassill's novel a few years later, an edition for which the essay served as introduction. Yates's effort was in homage to a man who'd provided enormous moral and professional support over the years, in light of which Yates was only a little disgruntled—but distinctly so—when he noticed that, in the new edition, "special thanks" were offered to David Madden, Peggy Bach, and DeWitt Henry, but not himself. In fact the essay had been a strain for Yates, and not simply because he took little pleasure in writing criticism. "Spent most of the day trying to wade through Verlin Cassill's endless, endless novel and haven't finished the damn thing yet," Yates had noted a quarter century earlier, when *Clem Anderson* was first published.

He's still a very good writer but oh Jesus how the book does go on and on. There are pieces of very bad writing in it too, both through carelessness and artiness, and I'm not sure but that there's something essentially weak in the overall idea of the thing. Haven't been able to say what yet, though, except that his central character becomes a terrible bore after a while instead of the "genius" he is supposed to be. . . .

Either Yates's later praise of the book was a little disingenuous—a true measure of the deep gratitude he felt for past favors—or he'd changed his mind over time; perhaps a bit of both. In any case he never mentioned his hurt feelings to Cassill.

For longer and longer intervals Yates brooded away the hours downstairs at the Crossroads, almost always alone. On bad days especially (bad writing, bad health) he seemed to agonize over the lasting value of his work—this at a time when he knew his reputation was already fading. Often a stranger's compliment would leave him incredulous, and any mention of his lesser novels pained him deeply. Don Lee, then an M.F.A. student at Emerson, visited Yates occasionally at the Crossroads, and one day saw him intently scribbling on a napkin. Embarrassed when Lee asked him about it, Yates reluctantly revealed that he'd listed the titles of his own books (a frequent occupation by then). "Nine books," said Yates. "Nine's not so bad, is it?"

Yates appreciated company—any company—though conviviality took precious energy he was careful to hoard for his work. He rarely wrote or received letters anymore, and most of his friends had fallen out of touch one by one. No matter how ravaged and feeble he became, though, the sight of a pretty woman acted on Yates like a galvanic elixir, and his standards remained as ambitious as ever. At an Emerson College party he turned to Wakefield and wheezed, "Look at that one! I'm gonna put the moves on her!" The girl was perhaps nineteen, and sure enough Yates hobbled over, for better or worse. Around this time, too, Robin Metz came to Boston and was sad to find his old friend so sickly and forlorn; at their second meeting, though, Metz brought a former student who'd moved to the area, one Sue Doe, and Yates seemed to drop twenty years in an instant. But whether he was able to accept it or not, Yates's lothario days were over. Once he called Wendy Sears and asked her to come to his apartment and help him make his bed; while she arranged the dank grayish sheets as best she could, Yates excitedly told her that he had a date that night with an attractive young woman—the first in a long, long while—and hoped to make love to her after a fashion. A few days later Sears asked how it went, and Yates sadly admitted the woman had stood him up.

Most of the time he understood the reasons for his loneliness all too well. On the rare occasion that some random admirer sought him out, Yates would often avoid drinking in order to make a better impression. Ten years before, at the behest of their mutual friend Seymour Krim, a man named Raymond Abbott had arranged to meet Yates while in Boston, and had ended up driving him to the airport; when Abbott called again in 1986, Yates eagerly invited him to the Crossroads, though he hadn't the faintest idea who the man was. "To Ray," he inscribed *Cold Spring*

Harbor, "In regret for having been smashed on the way to the airport that time." During their second meeting Yates sipped club soda and chain-smoked; after several hours of halting conversation, Abbott tried to say good-bye. "Do you have to go just yet, Ray?" Yates asked again and again. "Can't you stay a bit longer?" His loneliness was so painfully obvious that Yates was obliged to explain, in so many words, that most people had given him up as a drunk; when Abbott asked about women, Yates just shrugged and shook his head. That year another admirer, Martin Jukovsky, spent a single "strange and somewhat distressing afternoon" with Yates. "He kept up a brilliant stream of conversation," Jukovsky recalled, "but his voice had a tremble. He would often drift into old woes, such as regrets about his marriage; when this happened, he would seem ready to break into tears, his voice would get this odd, weepy sound, though he never actually cried." Yates also spoke obsessively about being trapped in a "rotten contract" with a "wretched literary agent," and begged the bewildered man for advice. As with Abbott, he drank nothing stronger than club soda.

Every so often the awfulness would overwhelm Yates, and he'd go from soda to beer to bourbon and back to the hospital. His health was such that any kind of sustained drinking was all but guaranteed to cause a break-down. That winter Wendy Sears called to check on Yates, who gagged and gurgled on the phone for some fifteen minutes before finally hacking out, "*Help me.*" Sears was afraid of what she'd find in Yates's apartment, and called around until DeWitt Henry agreed to investigate. He and Brodigan found Yates unconscious in a room spattered with blood and garbage. When Sears visited Yates a few days later at the VA, he seemed in a daze of pain and didn't speak; she thought he was dying. The next week Yates called with the cheery news that he was back home and feeling much better. He'd been taken off lithium and given Tegretol, which (it was hoped) would do double duty in controlling his seizures and manic episodes. But none of it was any good, of course, if Yates wouldn't stop drinking.

It had been a bad year all around. That summer Yates's beloved friend Andre Dubus was hit by a car and permanently crippled; in September his left leg was amputated at the knee. There would be no more hilarious, comforting get-togethers at the Crossroads or Yates's apartment. Mean-while Yates did what he could. Amid the mixed literary company of John

Irving, Jayne Anne Phillips, Updike, Vonnegut, and others, Yates participated in a benefit reading that February at the Charles Hotel in Cambridge
to raise money for Dubus's medical expenses. While Dubus smiled at him
from a portable hospital bed in the back of the ballroom, Yates kicked off
the event with his story "Trying Out for the Race," which he described as
"a little tarnished, but it'll have to do." When he finished—"charm[ing]
the audience with a quiet, dreamy tale," according to the Boston Globe—
he introduced the next reader, Vonnegut, who (Yates said) had promised
to be "just as long and just as lugubrious."

Nothing much happened to Yates for another five months, when his
second grandchild Emily was born July 17, 1987. Yates took a shuttle
flight to New York and left the same day, lingering long enough to deliver
a bouquet of flowers to Sharon and, once again, take his son-in-law out
for a celebratory drink. As Yates was leaving the hospital he heard a familiar voice— "Hi, Dick!"—and there was his first wife Sheila, whom he
hadn't laid eyes on in twenty years. Startled, he dropped something to the
floor but was too feeble to bend over and pick it up; Sheila handed it to
him. "He was so weak and done in," she remembered. "His life was over.
And we had nothing to say to each other." Later Yates called Sharon and
expressed his amazement: "My God, she's an old lady! She let her hair go
white!"

By the end of the summer it was clear that Uncertain Times wouldn't be
finished by November or anywhere close. Nor was there any question of
renegotiating his contract: Yates had no agent, no capacity for handling
such matters on his own, and no semi-tractable publisher such as Sam
Lawrence. By a somewhat happy coincidence, his friend DeWitt Henry was
then acting chair of the creative writing program at Emerson, and was able
to provide Yates a one-semester appointment teaching undergraduates;
after that he was on his own. By then Yates was viewed in Boston (and
beyond) as an unemployable drunk, but if he managed to acquit himself at
Emerson he might regain a measure of credibility. That was the idea anyway, and in fact Yates rose to the occasion rather nicely: He met all his
classes and even recommended a student's work for the "Discovery" issue
of Ploughshares, writing an introduction to the accepted story.

But it was shaping up to be a cold winter. With his advance gone and the semester almost over, Yates was facing total destitution, and even the better-case scenarios were grim: The Emerson job had served to remind him that he had neither the energy nor the desire to teach anymore, yet the alternatives were nil, and he'd have to count himself fortunate if anyone was willing to hire him at all; meanwhile he was forced to borrow money from Vonnegut, whose affable eagerness to help didn't make the request any less excruciating. Only three years before he'd been an NEA Senior Fellow, America's "least famous great writer" according to *Esquire,* and all his books (but one) were back in print for the first time in years; now, at age sixty-one, he'd be lucky to keep a roof over his head. On the other hand, it was more than a little miraculous that he was even alive.

And then a number of things happened to remind Yates that, as he put it, "the world [wasn't] really at [his] throat after all." Dubus, Vonnegut, and others got the word out that Yates was in trouble, and benefactors soon began to appear. For years Dubus and George Starbuck had been urging Don Hendrie at the University of Alabama to hire Yates, his old teacher, for the prestigious (and lucrative) Coal Royalty Endowed Chair in Writing. Clearly the time was now, but the earliest Hendrie could schedule Yates was the fall 1988 semester; it was possible, though, that an interim stipend could be worked out if Yates was willing to read student manuscripts and visit the odd class. The thought of living in the Deep South ("fucking *Dixie*") was anathema to Yates for any number of reasons, but this time he couldn't see a way around it. By December he'd arranged to forward his mail to the Alabama English Department, but then a most improbable savior intervened.

Yates's old nemesis David Milch was now in Los Angeles as producer of the hit TV series *Hill Street Blues*. Looking back, Milch can't recall who told him of Yates's predicament; in any case Milch was in a position to help and didn't hesitate to do so, though he realized he'd have to make it seem like a legitimate job offer lest his proud old teacher refuse. He invited Yates to write treatments for TV pilots, and assured him he'd have plenty of time left over to finish his novel—anyway they'd work out the details later, and meanwhile Yates was welcome to stay in Milch's guest house for as long as he liked. Yates was in no position to question such generosity. As for Milch, he wonders if he was fully conscious of his own motives at the time. "As Katherine Anne Porter once said," he remarked, " 'I never heard of a perfect synonym, or an unmixed motive.' "

CHAPTER EIGHTEEN

A Cheer for Realized Men: 1988-1992

By February, Yates had moved into Milch's guest house and was hard at work on some treatments proposed by his benefactor: One idea concerned two families with lots of foster children, a kind of postmodern *Brady Bunch* meets *Eight Is Enough*; another was about a group of young newspaper reporters living in a communal house in Washington, D.C. Yates despised the work ("There were a lot of jokes on the word 'treatment,'" his daughter Monica recalls), but Milch was covering his room, board, and child-support payments—as well as dispensing plenty of "walking-around money" as he called it—so Yates bent himself to the task of contriving joys and sorrows related to the business of communal living. "I remember Milch well," Vonnegut wrote Yates, "since he took a strong dislike to me, which, you will agree, I'm sure, makes about as much sense as hating hot fudge sundaes or Helen Hayes." Vonnegut wryly observed that *Hill Street Blues* was "a very important work of art," but applauded the fact that Milch had "thrown lucrative work in the direction of good writers who would like to make some real money for a change."

Yates was miserable. He desperately wanted to believe that he was doing something worthwhile for Milch—at any rate he was determined to persuade Milch of that fact—but something in the latter's manner belied any such hope. "How we doin' today, Sport?" Milch would greet him of a morning, clapping him on the shoulder. ("That little shit! He called me 'Sport'!" Yates raged wonderingly to a friend.) At other times, though, the two would sit and talk about writing, at seeming ease with each other; Gina Yates, who knew how damaging the arrangement was to her father's ego, nevertheless got the distinct impression that Yates and Milch were friends. And really Milch *was* fond of Yates—perhaps more so than he'd anticipated—but at the same time he harbored "a real undisclosed anger" for having been bullied and rejected all those years before at Iowa: "It was kind of an ongoing humiliation for Dick to be the recipient of generosity," said Milch. "Thank God I wasn't aware of it consciously, but in retrospect all those elements fed into it. This was payback for 'Wouldn't you like to be David Milch?' "

After tactfully rejecting a number of treatments, Milch suggested that TV work wasn't Yates's line and encouraged him to go back to his novel. Yates was crestfallen. He proposed that part of his debt to Milch—which would eventually climb to $36,000—could serve as an option on *Uncertain Times,* and he constantly assured Milch that he'd pay back the rest of it one way or the other. Whatever he proposed was fine with Milch ("Fine, fine"), but the whole situation was far from fine with Yates: "He chafed and chafed and chafed that this young snotnose was supporting him," said Monica. "He was *always* growling about the $36,000 he owed Milch: '*I'll get him that goddamn $36,000!*' It wasn't an issue to Milch, but Dad wouldn't drop it." Meanwhile Yates's cigarette fumes were forever wafting about chez Milch, an otherwise smoke-free environment where children lived besides. "Well, if there's no real work for me out here," Yates stiffly told his host one day, "I guess I'll go home and tie up some loose ends." Milch said that was fine.

After a long despondent bender in Boston, Yates reappeared in Los Angeles looking as if he were on the verge of death. His hands trembled, he couldn't catch his breath, he seemed in pain all the time. He was frantic to finish his novel, but equally to do whatever he could to earn his keep with Milch. Milch was appalled: He urged Yates to concentrate on his health and novel, in that order, and let the rest go; they formalized a financial arrangement and found an apartment for Yates in west Los Angeles. Naturally Yates insisted on something spartan, and he got it: a furnished one-bedroom in a motel-like complex built around a shabby courtyard. On the orange shag carpet Yates set up a card table for his manual Royal, then nailed three portraits of his daughters to the wall and that was that.

The apartment—as noted by a reporter who later interviewed Yates there—"was the kind of place people hole up when they're on the lam from the law."

Other than Milch, Yates's only companion during these months was a three-hundred-pound recovering heroin addict named Larry, who was dying of AIDS. Milch had put the man up in an apartment near Yates's, and in return Larry cooked breakfast for Milch's children and served as Yates's chauffeur. "Larry and Dick formed the most unlikely duo," Milch remarked with twinkling understatement. "They were the best thing in each of their lives. Driving Dick around gave Larry something to do during the day, and gave Dick something to bitch about." The poignant Larry seemed to provoke Yates in a number of ways: The car always stank of his cigars (though he was careful to put them out as soon as Yates got in), and he insisted on taking Yates to intolerable movies; also, he was morbidly devoted to David Milch and Narcotics Anonymous, and Yates thought it was all a bunch of hokum—both Larry's ease with accepting charity and his faith in twelve-step programs. Mainly Yates was exasperated by the hopelessness of the man: When he wasn't placidly resigned to whatever remained of his life, he tended to dwell on the guilt he felt for being a bad father during his addict days. "You're a *hive* of regret!" Yates would explode. "Dick resented everything about Larry, but in fact adored him," said Milch. "He'd gather all his strength to berate Larry's taste in movies or whatever, then he'd be tired and go to sleep, and Larry could go home. That's why Larry was such a gift to Dick: Dick's ranting was just background music to Larry, who understood it for what it was."

Yates's rancor spared no one; indeed, at times, it seemed the only thing keeping him alive. Once he'd gotten over his initial gratitude, he became particularly abusive toward Milch, as if he were baiting the man to cast him into the outer darkness. As Milch recalled, "A necessary precondition for any conversation with Dick was to spend five or ten minutes on the extent to which I'd abused my gifts and abdicated my responsibilities as a writer. By then he was out of breath so we couldn't talk about anything else." In the end Milch was no more offended by such bluster than Larry—if anything it was simply painful to witness, as when Yates would insist on showing Milch bits of manuscript to prove his novel really existed. But no matter how pitiful Yates occasionally seemed, he commanded respect and hence forgiveness; he was struggling to keep his dignity, and he refused to give up.

One day he asked Milch to meet him for dinner at the Bicycle Café on Wilshire. (The place was around the corner from Yates's apartment, and soon became his Crossroads and Blue Mill in Los Angeles.) "After the usual diatribe about my having embraced everything philistine and inauthentic in American culture," Milch remembered, "we settled down to business. It was hard for Dick to ask for anything: You had to figure out what he wanted, offer it to him, then be lambasted for a while for having offered it." Yates embarked on an elaborate preamble about how "full of shit" Hollywood parties were, how Milch's parties were liable to be worse than most ("I'd never been to a Hollywood party," said Milch, "but I was trying to agree with him in principle"), full of "fucking Hollywood phonies" and so forth. Then Yates segued to the topic of his sixteen-year-old daughter Gina, who was coming out for a visit; he hadn't seen her in a long time, etc. "Dick, I have an idea," said Milch, getting the picture. "Why don't we have a party?" Yates consented, and seemed pleased with the result: The other guests made much of him, and Gina seemed to enjoy herself and plainly adored her father. At some point the tipsy Yates, expansive with happiness, made to embrace Gina and caught his thumb in her hoop earring, tearing the lobe. As the blood gushed from her ear, Yates became abject, and Gina forgot her own distress and fell to consoling him. "It was so sad," said Milch, "and yet a perfect moment from one of Dick's stories: the best of intentions, but some fundamental inauthenticity or incapacity with devastating results . . . and yet something transcendently beautiful in the failure of the moment."

What Monica Yates called her "last hurrah as a writer" was a 1988 stay at the MacDowell Colony, where she tried to revise her novel into something more literary, or anyway less embarrassing; in her cabin she noticed her father's name on the roster of previous occupants, an ambiguous portent at best. Back in New York she was earning good wages as a part-time word-processor at Skadden Arps law firm, but Yates perceived her life as lonely and bleak. "I'm *not* Emily Grimes," Monica would protest. "This *isn't* depressing." Then one night in September, as luck would have it, her building burned down and her novel with it. Monica watched from the street as everything she owned went up in smoke; she didn't even have a toothbrush. She wondered if this was some kind of sign.

Yates wasn't inclined to put it that way, though he thought it might be a nice opportunity for both of them: He needed company in Los Angeles; she needed a place to stay and time to think; he'd sleep on the couch and she could have the bedroom all to herself. Monica was tempted—any change seemed good at that point—though she did have one predictable reservation. "I *like* to drink," Yates had always balked in the past. "I enjoy it. It's the one thing I really enjoy." Monica had suggested he find something else. "Like what?" he asked. "Nature and exercise?" His last alcoholic collapse in Boston had coincided with Monica's time at Mac-Dowell, and over the phone she'd angrily insisted that he *finally* make the connection between drinking, drugs, and breakdowns. Yates professed to see her point and afterward seemed to limit himself to the occasional beer, but Monica demanded total abstinence before she'd move to Los Angeles. In the end Yates agreed: By then he was tired enough of hangovers, break-downs, contretemps of all sorts—and loneliness—to give full-time sobri-ety a try.

As Larry drove them in from the airport, Yates mentioned in passing that there was "a little bit of a cockroach problem" at his apartment. This proved to be an impressive understatement: Yates's kitchen had been all but annexed by the pests; one cabinet in particular, where a rotten potato forlornly reposed, was "a moving sheet of cockroaches." Monica spent her entire first night in Los Angeles smashing, spraying, and finally scrubbing away the sticky brown residue of the slaughter—though for weeks afterward, every morning, dead and dying roaches would appear on the floor with fresh abundance. Monica came to think of her father's housekeeping as "tidy, but not clean": Though he seemed oblivious to the ashes that covered the place like volcanic soot, to vermin of all sorts, to the gray slime left by the black sponge he sometimes ran over counters, to the stench emanating from a broken disposal unit, he nonetheless kept his manuscripts in neat piles, made up his couch each morning, and was nettled by his daughter's inclination to leave newspapers strewn any which way.

Other than that, they got along remarkably well. Though Yates missed alcohol every waking hour of the day, he kept his promise and stayed sober. The change in his temperament was astounding: Once again he became the doting, playful father whom Monica had known and adored as a child, with the difference that now they could live as companionable adults. Every morning they read and loudly discussed the *New York Times*. "People around here must think we *hate* each other," they'd say, laughing at their own raised voices and merry *fuck you*'s. One night they went out with Larry David (who'd come to Los Angeles to work on the *Seinfeld* pilot), as well as actor-comedian Richard Lewis and a starlet he was dating at the time. Afterward a tearful Monica lamented that her life was going nowhere—she was holed-up in a one-bedroom apartment with her father, while Lewis's starlet lived in a penthouse. "Ah baby," said Yates. "Cheer up. At least we're not as bad as Woody Herman and his daughter"—whereupon he showed her a story in the *Times* about how the jazz great and his middle-aged daughter had washed up on a Los Angeles lawn, evicted with all their worldly goods.

Amid this idyll Monica persisted in her childhood tendency to badger Yates about his bad habits—"baiting the lion in his lair," she called it. Taped to the wall was a piece of paper titled "Things to Do," and in Yates's column she'd written such items as "Quit smoking"; "Stop saying 'fuck'"; "Improve posture." Yates, in turn, chided his daughter's lack of discipline as a writer: "You read too much, you exercise too much, you do everything but write," he told her. The truth was, whatever wan literary impulse abided in Monica was being killed by the daunting example of her father's absolute commitment. Despite mortal illness and constant fatigue, he wrote for hours every day; even a letter to the electric company was polished into lapidary perfection. "I thought *ugh*, I can't do that," said Monica. When Yates would remonstrate with her on the subject, she'd sometimes accuse him of wanting her to be like him, to which Yates would reply *No*, he truly thought writing was the only fulfilling thing for her—apart from being a wife and mother. "He was very sincere about it," said Monica, "and he was partly right: I had that sort of temperament, but not enough talent or drive. Still, it made me happy to hear him say that, since it made me see that he himself *was* fulfilled by his writing. He thought it a great, worthy life—the *only* life."

The most disquieting aspect of living with Yates was to witness at close range the morbidities of failing health. Every morning he'd hawk and retch in a desperate effort to clear his lungs; as his emphysema worsened, the wet bronchial cough of twenty years earlier gave way to a ragged hacking, the mucus drying up and the alveoli collapsing. Even more disturbing were symptoms akin to those of mental illness. Not long after Monica's arrival, Yates was hospitalized with pneumonia, prior to which he seemed to be slipping into dementia—in one case obsessing about a check to Martha he'd already sent. "Gotta get her that check, baby," he panted over and over as Monica tried to calm him. Not until later, when she became a nurse, did Monica realize that her father had been suffering from the effects of hypoxia—lack of oxygen to the brain and other tissues. At the time, however, such behavior was an ominous reminder of past lapses.

Though he had every intention of finishing *Uncertain Times* and, with any luck, a few other books, Yates began to accept at least the possibility that he might die soon—out of print, forgotten, and broke. The old mirage of a big movie deal seemed the only hope of providing an inheritance for his daughters (he still wanted to send Gina to Harvard), and in his final years this became a fixed idea of sorts. In 1988 a Denver-based filmmaker named Donna Dewey optioned *Cold Spring Harbor* and hired Yates's old friend Bill Harrison (of *Rollerball* fame) to write the screenplay. Harrison decided that the apparent protagonist, Evan Shepherd, was too unsympathetic to build a story around, and decided instead to focus on Phil Drake—that is, Phil's bike riding around Long Island with the affluent loser "Flash" Ferris. Harrison proposed to call this adaptation *Bicycle Summer,* and further proposed not to reveal the details to Yates until it was too late for him to howl in protest. Over dinner at Tutto Bene in November, Yates sipped seltzer and pressed Harrison about his screenplay—questions Harrison artfully dodged, both then and during Yates's subsequent phone calls. Finally Harrison and Dewey submitted the script to Jack Clayton, director of the 1974 remake of *Gatsby,* who seemed interested. Alas, the movie was never made, though for Yates it would have been a bittersweet experience at best.

"There's just no whore in that man at all," Dubus once remarked of Yates. Despite his sheepish claims to the contrary, Yates could never deliberately write "soap opera" or be party to it (if he could help it), at least where his serious work was concerned; indeed, he felt hideous anguish when it was cheapened in even the most incidental way. Just before leaving Boston, he'd finally acquired a new agent—a young man named Ned Leavitt, who also handled Dan Wakefield. About a year later Leavitt arranged for Random House to reissue *Revolutionary Road, Eleven Kinds of Loneliness,* and *The Easter Parade* as part of their popular Vintage Contemporaries line, a deal that promised to revitalize Yates's career somewhat. This happy prospect was diminished, however, when Yates saw the cover art, which so enraged him that he was tempted to stop the presses with legal action. "Why has surrealism been chosen as the cover style for these novels, when I can find it on no other Vintage books?" he wrote in a memo to Leavitt, which he copied to his lawyer friend Prettyman. The proposed cover for *Revolutionary Road* depicted a small suburban house and church within a floating glass jar, against which was propped a ladder; Yates thought this inexplicably evoked Sylvia Plath's *Bell Jar,* that the ladder was a "mixed metaphor," and that the church was "wholly inappropriate." He demanded that the "three offending images" be removed and the house lowered to the ground. As for the cover of *The Easter Parade* (two hanging dresses with folded human arms): "The picture is gruesome, to no purpose. Does it mean to suggest identical twins who have only coat-hanger hooks where their heads ought to be? I am entirely baffled and believe readers will be, too." With little change, though, the covers were allowed to stand.*

Meanwhile Yates was casting about for some way to achieve financial

---

*All three covers were illustrated by Theo Rudnak, who in fact offered alternative—but equally surreal—art for *Revolutionary Road* and *The Easter Parade:* The first depicted the back of a man in a business suit, both in and out of a jail cell (the bars come down on either side of him à la an M. C. Escher effect), gazing out the window at a suburban scene; the second depicted dangling chromium styluses in female shape. Yates was presumably appalled.

independence, and toward that end he suspended work on his novel in early 1989 to write a twenty-two-page "proposal for a screenplay" titled *The World on Fire.* The treatments for Milch had been hateful labor, but the well-crafted and funny *World on Fire* reads like a pleasant exercise in nostalgia, if a somewhat mercenary and left-handed one. "This will be a story of the early 1950's in America," it begins, "when electronic computers were still an infant technology with a great if barely discernible future." The protagonist is a twenty-eight-year-old salesman for Remington Rand named Harold Clark, whose go-getting ingenuity wins him a transfer from Wichita to New York, where he's expected to promote the "cumbersome, intricate and expensive" UNIVAC by developing applications "sexy" enough to stir the public imagination. Harold is hindered in this venture by a bland, unimaginative boss named Ed Grundy, whose staff is comprised of "cool, languid snobs who have long made a virtue of despising their work." Harold's brainchild is to use the UNIVAC to predict the outcome, on national TV, of the 1952 presidential election; he railroads the idea past an envious sales staff and doubtful engineers, whereupon an "avalanche of publicity" ensues: "If machines relieve mankind of thought as a burden, will we then be free for more creative lives?" the media wonders. "Will the computer revolution bring a new Age of Enlightenment?"

Yates used his insider's knowledge of the UNIVAC and its various controversies to good effect, and bolstered it all with a subplot addressing his favorite theme of mediocre people—women in particular—who wistfully pursue "creative" lives. Harold's bored wife Elaine falls in with a circle of women who "allow themselves long and adventurous days in Manhattan," trying to "find themselves" via "psychotherapy and its numbing jargon" as well as painting, acting, dancing, and writing classes. Elaine enrolls in a lecture course at the New School called "Strategies of Indirection in the Novel" taught by a witty rake, Thurston Picard, who naturally seduces her. Picard surprises Elaine by finding her husband's work interesting—computers, he says, may prove "a way of transcending reality"—but on the night of the election, everything goes wrong for Harold. The UNIVAC (with its "two separate, cable-linked components . . . each the size of a room") all but crowds out the broadcasting equipment at the television network, and then delivers results that are not only late but grossly inaccurate. Harold's disgrace is mirrored by that of another modest visionary, Yates's hero Adlai Stevenson, while the fatuous Eisenhower "is shown waving both arms, displaying the wide empty grin that will come to personify the United States for the next eight years." It would seem a typical Yates ending, but this was for the movies, after all. Thus, when Professor Picard pointedly tells his students that the UNIVAC fiasco reminds him of "Flaubert's great image of the carp on the kitchen table," Elaine leaves the class in disgust and goes back to her sacked husband, who is far too plucky to be daunted long by this setback. The movie ends with the couple popping champagne on the road back to Wichita, as the song "Side by Side" comes up on the soundtrack.

The proposal was shopped around the major studios, whose representatives tended to pass on the story but commend the writing; Ruth Pomerance and Scott Rudin at Columbia told Yates's agent they were "huge fans and would like to develop something with him"—but nothing came of this, or of *The World on Fire*. In the latter case it was perhaps for the best, since the story's pivotal event is fundamentally inaccurate: In fact the UNIVAC made history by predicting Eisenhower's 1952 landslide based on less than 1 percent of the vote. Yates was puzzled when he couldn't find newspaper accounts to verify his own version, though probably he didn't research the matter very thoroughly. In later years he was intimidated by librarians (and cabbies and waiters and doormen) who were liable to look askance at his wheezing disheveled helplessness; a couple of years before, after one abortive attempt to research *Uncertain Times* at a Boston library, he'd asked the young Don Lee to go in his stead and find part of a speech he'd written in an old microfilmed issue of *Time* magazine.

Yates was heartily sick of living off Milch. A university placement service had shopped his résumé all over the country, but apart from a few nibbles, "nobody would touch him" as Monica Yates put it. Finally he called the director of the USC Masters of Professional Writing program, James Ragan, and laid it on the line: His daughter had come to live with him, Yates said, and he "want[ed] to give her stability"; he'd take anything the man could give him. As it happened Ragan had nothing, but such was his admiration for Yates—mixed with pity, perhaps—that he offered a half course for the spring 1989 semester, paid out of Ragan's own budget, with a full course to follow if all went well. That was the end of the Milch money.

For a while Yates rallied, endearing himself to students and faculty alike with his grim,, almost miraculous resolve to overcome his decrepitude. He was so determined to wean himself from Milch that, rather than rely on Larry for transportation, he attempted (once) to take a bus to campus—a "disaster," Yates reported. Before long a protective network of students had formed to drive him to class or the grocery store or wherever he wanted to go. He also befriended Ragan, who often invited Yates to his home and let him smoke as much as he wanted. One night the two were having dinner at the faculty center, when Ragan noticed that Yates's face had turned blueish and blankly helpless. Ragan administered an inexpert Heimlich, but only a bit of food came up; by the time the ambulance arrived Yates looked about to expire. Ragan followed him to the emergency room and anxiously awaited the verdict: "I thought Dick had met the same fate as Tennessee Williams," he recalled, "and on *my* watch." After half an hour or so, Yates emerged smiling and insisted on teaching his class that night. As they taxied back to campus, Yates remarked, "I kept thinking of Tennessee Williams"—and Ragan laughed. Yates gave him a bitter look: "What the hell are you laughing about? Williams choked to *death*!"

Sheer desperation was the only thing that kept Yates going. He was tired, anxious, and broke, in no condition either to teach or write at anything like his old level, yet the only alternative was death. His students' work was mostly bad, and Yates couldn't think of anything to say about it; he began to take double doses of tranquilizers just to get through his classes, and soon his mind began to slip. He became more obsessed than ever by his debt to Milch, and amid a spell of increasingly odd behavior he wrote the man a note and hand-delivered it to his wife, who looked it over and smiled—a good sign, Yates thought. (When asked about this, Milch quoted Robert Penn Warren: " 'Some foolishness a man is due to forget.' ") Monica was horrified by the change in her father: He began to giggle and stare at her; he stopped sleeping and talked incessantly. "How am I 'not right'?" he demanded. "What's wrong with me? What d'you mean I'm *crazy*? What's *crazy* about this?" One night she woke up and found him standing in her room wearing a raincoat, frantically pushing a vacuum cleaner and saying he couldn't work it—what could he do—? Monica left the apartment and checked into a Holiday Inn ("I had to get some sleep"), but next morning she returned and insisted they go to the hospital. At length Yates seemed to agree, but once they arrived he pretended that nothing was wrong, and responded with fluent disdain to such questions as "What year is it?" and "Who's the president?" Faced with the prospect of taking the deranged man home, Monica began to cry, and Yates went berserk: "What're you gonna do, *cry* now? *What's your problem?*" he yelled over and over. The doctors assumed that he was a danger to others and hustled him off to the locked psychiatric ward for a mandatory thirty days. Monica found him "drooling and bleary-eyed" when she visited, and was so unnerved by the whole business that she began seeing a VA therapist herself. Within a week or so, she said a sad good-bye to her father and moved to a place of her own in Venice Beach.

On his release in April, Yates was gratified to learn that Ragan had gladly kept his job open for however long it took to recover from his latest bout of "pneumonia." Meanwhile Yates called Don Hendrie at the University of Alabama and expressed his strong desire to occupy the Strode House as soon as possible. The best Hendrie could do was fall 1990, but at least it gave Yates something to look forward to.

Around this time his old friend Barrett Prettyman paid a visit, and found Yates pleasant, if somewhat chastened and faded. Yates hit it off with Prettyman's companion, Noreen McGuire, and after a fairly jolly brunch he put his arm around her as they walked back to the car—affectionately, but also because he needed support. Along the way Yates bent down to pat a dog and almost toppled over. He seemed frustrated by his frailty and spoke openly of dying: He wasn't so much afraid as he was sad—he still had a number of projects to finish, and wanted to be closer to his daughters. Back at his apartment, his friends noticed that he kept his front door unlocked, and Yates explained that he didn't have keys as he'd only lose them. Wasn't he afraid of thieves? "Nah, if they break in, they won't steal this," said Yates, indicating his manuscript and rickety manual typewriter. Indeed, there was little else to steal.

That summer the Vintage reprints of Yates's three best books were published amid a small flurry of acclaim. David Streitfeld interviewed him for the short-lived celebrity magazine *Fame,* while Elizabeth Venant wrote a long feature article for the Sunday *Los Angeles Times.* Both reporters seemed aghast to find Yates in such straitened circumstances, and a common indignant theme of their stories ("The Great Unknown" and "A Fresh Twist in the Road") was the bewildering extent to which a writer of Yates's stature had been forgotten, the awful toll such neglect had taken. "It's a pretty bad time," Yates admitted to Streitfeld, in a voice the latter described as "thick and furry, steeped in tobacco and Jim Beam." In both interviews Yates made a point of mentioning that he was on the wagon— he took it for granted they'd heard he was a drunk—though he was hardly self-congratulatory about it. "I was more affable when I was drinking," he told Venant. "Now I'm sort of shrunk into myself from the effort to keep from drinking." Whatever the subject, Yates responded with the same flat, almost drab candor, refusing to glamorize either his life or work, past or present. "I've been in and out of bughouses, yes," he said, when Streitfeld wondered about the recurrence of madness in his fiction, and for the same reason Venant inquired about his childhood: "Most people looking back believe their childhood was more poignant than anyone else's," Yates replied. "So I won't compete for the poignancy prize. My parents were decent people. My childhood was OK."

In September, Yates's old friend Seymour Krim, ill with heart disease and related problems, took his own life with the help of instructions from the Hemlock Society. A week before, he'd mailed a last wave of postcards to friends, explaining that he'd been sick and expressing his affection one last time before "checking out." In recent years, whenever he went to New York, Yates had visited Krim, and was well aware of the man's deteriorating health. Despite their past disputes on the subject, Yates wasn't at all disposed to characterize his friend's suicide as "self-indulgent"; he thought it a commendable end to an intolerable situation. "Seymour Krim was a champion," Yates wrote for the memorial service at the Village Gate. "[He] gave so much of his energy helping other writers, in any number of crucial ways, that nobody will ever know how many of us are indebted to him . . . but we have one proud and honorable thing in common: Seymour Krim was a friend of ours." One year later Yates would have the satisfaction of outliving a very different kind of friend, Anatole Broyard.

A year that began with poverty and madness was ending on a decidedly upbeat note. Ever since moving his list to Houghton-Mifflin, Sam Lawrence had been negotiating to buy out Yates's contract for *Uncertain Times,* and in December he was finally able to offer his friend a two-book deal providing a fresh advance and thirty-three monthly payments. Elizabeth Venant of the *Los Angeles Times* paid Yates a "return visit" at the end of 1989, and cheerfully reported the "lucky break" that would enable him to quit teaching for several months and devote all his time to finishing his novel. "*Uncertain Times* is scheduled for publication in the spring," Venant concluded, "and perhaps for Yates, times will be uncertain no more."

Indeed, it was shaping up to be a banner year. Also that December, Yates received a flattering letter from a woman in New York named Susan Braudy, who'd just optioned *The Easter Parade,* which she planned to adapt herself for television. A novelist and former Warner Brothers vice president, Braudy was well connected in the industry and had an uncommon degree of enthusiasm for the project at hand (which in retrospect she calls "a labor of love and desperation"). As she wrote Yates, "The book was first given to me by Paul Schrader who wrote *Taxi Driver,* the movie, among other things. He told me what a major work it was, advised me to stay home from work for a day to read it and have a full cry which I did." Then a few years later Braudy was watching Woody Allen's *Hannah and Her Sisters* when she noticed Yates's novel mentioned in one scene: "That's my favorite book!" she blurted out in the theater. She was so enthused that she wrote Woody Allen a letter praising both the movie and his taste in fiction; Allen replied that he knew little about Yates but loved his "clean prose and way of telling a story." That same year, in fact, Allen had remarked in the *New York Times* that he loved books about the "problems and strengths of women," and therefore "couldn't wait to get

[his] hands on . . . the Richard Yates novel, *The Easter Parade*." Finally, in 1989, Braudy wrote Allen again to let him know she'd optioned the book and would appreciate any help or advice; Allen replied with a gracious note that Braudy enclosed for Yates's perusal: "I'm delighted to hear you are planning to dramatize 'Easter Parade,' " Allen wrote in part. "I called [actress] Dianne Wiest and told her about it and you can feel free to call her. . . . She hasn't read the book, but I told her how wonderful it is and that you were serious about a high quality presentation of it." Yates was elated by Woody Allen's interest, and promptly followed-up with a call to Bruce Ricker, a lawyer and independent filmmaker whom Yates had met through Krim. Ricker happened to be acquainted with Wiest, and wrote her that "Woody Allen [had] highly recommend[ed]" her for a part in *The Easter Parade*, a copy of which he enclosed. Susan Braudy had already done as much, and may have been a bit piqued by Yates's unsolicited initiative; in any case she eventually got in touch with her favorite author by phone—the beginning of a very curious chapter in both their lives.

For the rest of his time in Los Angeles, Yates hardly left his apartment except for weekly dinners with Monica. Free until August to do nothing but write, he hoped to finish his novel and perhaps get started on the next. But willpower alone wasn't enough anymore, and every day the work got harder. Meanwhile his manner was becoming odd again, and his daughter simply couldn't bear it. "What do you mean my *voice* sounds funny?" he'd ask when she refused to meet him for dinner, and sometimes he'd try to make a joke about it: "You think FDR's daughter would refuse to have dinner with him because *his* voice sounded funny?" Monica found such humor "forced and strange," and the more Yates worked to put her at ease the worse he seemed. "I kept asking the VA shrink to *do* something," she recalled, "make him right again the way Burr had always been able to. But it wasn't his mind or the meds this time, it was hypoxia, and the doctors should have known that even if they weren't pulmonologists."

In his daughter's absence Yates found solace where he could. "Dick was losing touch with reality toward the end," said Milch. "And one did what one could just to sit and hold his hand. And there was a bit of grace that came to him and me in that—no illusions or retributions involved. But then that haunted look would come back in his eyes and it would be time to go."

As he was wheeled off the plane in Birmingham, one of the few signs of life Yates showed was a flicker of embarrassment as alarmed graduate students hustled him out to a car and drove to the hospital, where a pulmonologist determined that Yates could no longer endure air travel, or for that matter the ordinary demands of daily life, without oxygen tanks. "Is he going to die?" a frantic Monica asked the doctor over the phone. "How long does he have?" The doctor ("a prick") replied that he had no idea. As for Yates, he was sounding like a new man now that more oxygen was getting to his brain.

Apart from a slight acquaintance with Don Hendrie, the program director, the only people Yates knew in Tuscaloosa were George and Kathy Starbuck, the first of whom was badly debilitated by Parkinson's disease. Yates had dinner with the couple once a week, and was often compelled to summon Kathy to the hospital to deal with paperwork and other problems. Now with two invalids on her hands, the woman's good humor would occasionally flag. Once, after yet another call in the dead of night, she brought along a young friend named Mary to boost her morale and serve as a buffer of sorts; both women arrived to find Yates "damn near dead" on a gurney. After Mary left the room, Yates feebly beckoned to Starbuck. "*God*," he gasped, "she's got great legs!"

Hendrie's assistant Tony Earley, a graduate student, was designated the "Yates Coordinator"—a job requiring tact, compassion, patience, and resourcefulness, in no particular order.* Yates's embarrassment at his own helplessness could often flare into anger, and as Earley put it, "One was at pains not to let Dick know how much trouble he was." When Yates was first installed in the Strode House, Earley was mortified to find the place infested with fleas—and it was his fault! He'd let a friend with a pet wolf

---

*Earley went on to a distinguished career: Author of the novel *Jim the Boy* and other works, he was chosen by *Granta* in 1996 (along with Yates's former student Melanie Rae Thon) as one of twenty "Best Young American Novelists." Another of Yates's caretaker-students at Alabama, Tim Parrish, has published an acclaimed story collection, *Red Stick Men*.

sleep there just before Yates's arrival. Happily the new writer-in-residence seemed oblivious to the pests popping all around him like black sparks, and Earley arranged for an exterminator to come while Yates was out teaching. A more immediate problem was how to get Yates upstairs so he could use the bathroom; Earley had a stair-chair put in, and promptly got a "vicious call" from the university physical plant about hiring an outside contractor. Then, when the chair broke down, Earley rushed over and tried to fix it himself; finally the original mechanic had to return, and Earley was berated again for fiddling with the thing. Most intriguing were the weekly logistics of getting Yates to his classroom a hundred yards away: Since Yates wouldn't accept deliberate assistance, and couldn't walk the distance without collapsing, Earley had to arrange for a member of the "Yates Task Force" to appear at the Strode House "by chance" and offer Yates a lift. "There was a constant discreet flurry around Dick to keep him going," said Earley, "since he was dead-set against any fuss. We laughed at the predicaments we'd find ourselves in while helping Dick, but we were awed by the man himself, by his courage and resilience." Yates was resilient enough to regard the indignities of his life with occasional humor: Lankily settling himself onto the stair-chair and grinding slowly upstairs to relieve himself, Yates would rest his cheek against a fist and with his free hand pretend to shoot himself in the head.

An abiding feature of Yates's legend at Alabama is the way he "trashed the Strode House" with his constant smoking—by the time he departed, the furniture was scored with burn marks, the carpet was grayish with ground-in ashes, the curtains sagged with assimilated nicotine. For Yates it seemed a point of pride to keep smoking, and to hell with oxygen tanks. (Another aspect of Earley's duties, so the joke went, was to be ready at any time to douse Yates when he burst into flames.) Yates's coughing fits were so violent and extended that one scarcely expected the man to survive them; after ten minutes or so, he'd at last subside with a deep shuddery sigh and light another cigarette. For an ashtray he used a large salad bowl that didn't have to be emptied so often; he also used it as a receptacle for the profusion of Kleenex required for a cold he suffered more or less constantly. A graduate student, Tim Parrish, once stopped by the Strode House to give Yates a lift, and the latter flicked his butt into the bowl and began to shuffle away. A wad of Kleenex ignited with an emphatic finger of flame. This posed a problem for Parrish: If he rushed to extinguish the fire himself, Yates would be humiliated and hence furious. Meanwhile smoke was billowing out of the bowl. "Uh, Dick, are you sure that cigarette is out?" Yates turned around. "Oh fuck!" he roared. *"Fuck!"*

A wheelchair was kept in the building where Yates taught, but he still had to walk a few yards from the car, and the effort would leave him gasping with exhaustion; wherever he went, then, he liked to arrive early so he could get his wind back and finish coughing without being ogled. As the chair writer, Yates was required to give at least one public reading—a well-attended event which his handlers had been dreading. Earley asked if he wanted a chair on stage and a clip-on microphone, but Yates refused. He insisted on climbing the stairs to the podium and standing, by his own power, and he wanted the wheelchair stashed out of sight before anyone arrived. When the time came, Earley and the others could hardly bear to watch. "Dick climbed the stairs and didn't even hold the podium," Earley recalled. "It was magnificent: he read in a deep, strong voice with a lot of feeling. Then he went back to the front row." After the last well-wisher had departed—but not before—Yates doubled over in his chair.

One benefit of his infirmity was that he could indulge his gruffness as a teacher; whatever he said was at the expense of precious air, and he wasn't expected to waste himself on idle blandishment. Thus in his literature course Yates luxuriated in his own dogma, and those who begged to differ "were screwed" as one student put it. The second half of *Lord Jim*, Yates declared, was little more than a boy's adventure story; Conrad should have allowed Jim to fail, and cut the whole "phony redemption" business. When one student modestly opined that he thought the novel "worked as a whole," Yates dogged the youth for months, in class and out, determined to make him admit his error. It was in workshops, though, where Yates showed the full extent of his mettle. After three decades of discussing student work, he'd become purified into a grim ghost of the man who, in his docile salad days, used to "appease every difference of opinion in the room." No more. Yates advised one student with a "good ear for dialogue" to cultivate deafness, and in the margin of another student's admittedly "terrible" story, Yates scribbled (re one character's disparagement of another), "That's the understatement of the fucking century!"

The odd wrathful critique depended somewhat on Yates's mood—a sick man is apt to be crabby—but he'd later agonize over the wounds he'd inflicted. In a copy of *The Easter Parade* owned by the author of the "terrible" story, Yates wrote, "To Bill, with heartfelt apologies for an episode he has been gracious enough to forget." And then there was the sequel to the burning salad bowl. "Dick was agitated that night and his blood was up," said Parrish, who drove Yates to Allen Wier's workshop after they'd put the fire out. The first story under discussion was a bit of "Magical Beautyshop Realism," as Tony Earley described it, about a spooky barber who gives bad haircuts and strange advice. Yates hated the story, denouncing its heavy-handed whimsy in no uncertain terms. The author sat biting her lip and trying not to cry; the rest of the class was too stunned to speak. Finally—to break the silence, and perhaps because he was dating the author—Earley offered a few words in the story's defense. Yates regarded him sadly: "Tony, Tony, Tony . . ." Earley's own story "Aliceville" was next, and he was somewhat hopeful since Yates had liked his previous effort, "My Father's Heart." " 'My Father's Heart' was like good sex," Yates began. " 'Aliceville' is like masturbation." Yates later apologized to Earley, though probably not to the woman who wrote the barbershop story.

By 1990 the zeitgeist of the American campus, even in the South, was sufficiently altered for Yates to seem either a quaint midcentury relic or a throwback, depending on how you looked at it. Most students were amused by his somewhat archaic Ivy League uniform of tweeds, flannels, and desert boots, his hair that seemed to stay short whether he cut it or not, his careful manners, his cultivated distance from a changing world. Yates loved to talk about the old days—radio programs, McCarthyism, the movies of his youth—and once when Earley admitted he didn't know a particular Hoagy Carmichael tune, Yates sang it to him verse after verse. ("The most extraordinary thing that ever happened to me in the literary community," said Earley.) Young women, alas, tended to be less amused by Yates. "I wish I had a little girl to make potatoes for *me*," he said with wistful gallantry at a potluck dinner, while the subject of this pleasantry lapsed into wondering silence along with the rest of the guests. Worse were the women who actually stood up for themselves and their sex. "What's *that* got to do with anything?" a student's wife snapped at Yates—who'd just observed, neutrally enough, that a new addition to the English faculty "[wasn't] very pretty."

Yates didn't get it. "Earley, get over here," he'd say, after some courtly bon mot had gone mysteriously awry. "What the hell's the problem? What'd I *say*?" Any attempt to explain would only vex him further, and soon such women began to seem foreign as Martians to Yates, who treated them with a kind of wary restraint. The truth was, what Yates had always regarded as courtesy seemed creepy and affected to certain of his female students, who made a point of avoiding him; if he hadn't been so pitifully frail, it would have been worse. The situation pained Yates deeply. He'd regale his young male companions with tales of the old *Revolutionary Road* days when he could get almost any girl he wanted—a girl who goddammit *looked* like a girl too, in a proper *dress*—but now he wasn't even regarded as a sexual being anymore. To Dan Childress, who later became Yates's main caretaker, he confessed a poignant recurring dream of running, sprinting—*virility*—though he hadn't been able to run or much else in many years.

Nor could Yates have known that the beloved authors he'd always taught—Flaubert, Fitzgerald, Hemingway, Conrad, Ford, et al.—were now viewed as a veritable rogues gallery of dead white males. At the beginning of the semester he broke out his hoary assortment of marked-up paperbacks, the same that had stood him in good stead since his Iowa days, and read aloud the beloved bits of dialogue, objective correlatives, character details, and whatnot. When the students requested a bit more open discussion, the haggard Yates was only too happy to oblige; he noticed, however, that three or four students rarely spoke and indeed seemed to be boycotting the books in question. It might have been when somebody pointed out the absence of women or "people of color" among the assigned authors that a bemused Yates called one student "a pantywaist"—and perhaps the lunar silence that followed was what persuaded him, finally, that he'd better relent a little. He asked the students to suggest a book that *they* wanted to read. All but unanimously they picked Toni Morrison's *Beloved,* which Yates professed to like all right.

. . .

Toward the end of Yates's semester as chair writer—on December 20, 1990, to be exact—he and a few others gathered at Tim Parrish's house to watch the *Seinfeld* episode based on Yates's dinner with Larry David five years before. Monica had watched the show's taping and thought her father might get a kick out of it. The Yates character—a great but neglected writer called "Alton Benes," also Elaine's father—was played by an imposing stone-faced actor named Lawrence Tierney, known for his gruff gangster roles. In this episode, titled "The Jacket," Elaine begs her friends Jerry and George to have dinner with her and her father: "I need a buffer," she says. The evening is a disaster. Elaine is late, and Jerry and George are forced to make conversation with the dour Benes, who greets them with a coughing fit and scowls at their nonalcoholic beverages. "Which one's the funny guy?" he asks, and when George indicates Jerry, Benes fixes him with a baleful look and says, "We had a funny guy with us in Korea. Tail gunner. They blew his brains out all over the Pacific." Jerry escapes to the bathroom, and George unctuously remarks that he really enjoyed Benes's novel *Fair Game*. "Drivel!" says Benes. "Well, maybe *some* parts," George concedes uncomfortably, and Benes snaps *"What parts?"*—after which George pleads a phone call and joins Jerry in the bathroom, where the desperate men discuss their predicament ("How could she leave us alone with this lunatic?"). At last Elaine arrives, and as the four prepare to go to dinner, Jerry turns his expensive new suede jacket inside out so it won't be ruined by the snow. Elaine's father sees the jacket's candy-striped lining and stops Jerry at the door: "You're not walking down the street with me and my daughter dressed like that," he growls. "That's for damn sure." The terrified Jerry reverses the lining, and the jacket is ruined.

When the show was over, Yates sat smacking his lips. "Well," he said. "What'd you think?" Sensing Yates's chagrin throughout, the others had tried not to laugh, and now they could see how "scalded" he looked. "Well," somebody broke the silence, "it was *kind* of funny, Dick." *"I'd like to kill that son of a bitch!"* Yates erupted, and shambled out of the room. Later, speaking to Monica about it, he picked over details they'd gotten "wrong": Benes had worn a broad-brimmed hat, said Yates, while he himself had never worn a hat in his life (perhaps he'd forgotten the "much-handled brown fedora" he'd affected as a young UP reporter); he'd fought in WWII, *not* Korea; and Monica never told stories in the present-tense à la Elaine. And so on. "I'm not *that* scary," he said at last.*

That month Yates moved out of the Strode House and stayed with the Parrishes for a week or so until he found a place of his own. He'd decided to remain in Tuscaloosa for at least as long as it took to finish his novel: The cost of living was low, and the university had arranged for him to receive a modest stipend for reading manuscripts and working with students privately—though perhaps the main reason, as Earley put it, was "because he'd made friends there who looked out for him and were kind to him." Still, it made Yates queasy to be the object of kindness, as it churned up a lot of bitterness over being poor and relatively forgotten—a charity case, in short. While at Parrish's house he talked obsessively about Vonnegut: a nice guy and good writer, he said, though he (Yates) was at *least* as good, and look at the difference in their lives! At one point he fretfully lit a cigarette while a fresh one burned in the ashtray. "Oh *shit*," he said when his host reminded him. "Goddamn it. Listen, Parrish: I used to smoke five fucking packs a day, and it was *great*. . . ."

Yates's last apartment was a small two-bedroom duplex on Alaca Place. He installed an L-shaped desk in the spare bedroom, bought a few other derelict scraps of furniture from the Salvation Army, and arranged his daughters' photos on the wall. The other bit of decoration was a quote from Adlai Stevenson that he taped over his desk (he was considering it as an epigraph to *Uncertain Times*): "Americans have always assumed, subconsciously, that every story will have a happy ending." Mark Costello, who succeeded Yates as the fiction chair writer, remarked with amazement that the dark little bungalow was "even *more* grim than Boston": "It

---

*Monica suspects her father was more pleased than not by the *Seinfeld* episode and only waxed indignant in front of the graduate students because he felt it was expected of him: "I was just so relieved at Larry's choices," said Monica. "He could have focused on the physical infirmity, the frailness, the runny nose, the drinking—all the things I dreaded when people met Dad during those Boston years. But what he saw was gruffness, the inherent power of Dad's opinions and intelligence, the humor of his old-time masculinity."

was as if Dick's indifference to his surroundings was catching up with him. I had to remind myself that Dick didn't care, because otherwise the place depressed me. I couldn't stay there. I had to get out."

Yates's health had improved over the past few months: What with oxygen and steady care, his color was better and he seemed a bit stronger. The ordeal of looking after him, though, had been of such Sisyphean proportions that one wondered what would become of him in the absence of a coordinated, pluralistic effort. What anyone in Yates's condition needed, at the very least, was a full-time nurse: There were oxygen tanks to replace, meals to provide (for a man who often neglected to eat), and the constant possibility he'd get sick and require immediate medical attention. Graduate students such as Earley, Parrish, and J.R. Jones continued to invite Yates over and visit from time to time, while Ron Sielenski and Shelley Hippler (his "research assistants" as chair writer)* cleaned his apartment and ran the odd errand; but Yates's main caretaker was a rough-hewn student/car-mechanic named Dan Childress. "Dan was closest to Dick in temperament," Tim Parrish observed. "Both became isolated from women and other people, and both were conflicted about their writing. It was a real kinship. Dick was a hero to Dan—he loved the man and took good care of him."

Among Childress's self-assumed duties was to check the oxygen level of Yates's tanks, since Yates himself almost never remembered to do so; when the time came, Childress would drive to a strip mall in the suburb of Northport and pick up replacement tanks at the medical supply store. No matter how vigilant he tried to be, though, there were days when he'd find Yates blue-lipped and gasping, too disoriented to speak or even listen unless the young man looked him straight in the eye and yelled his words in order to "get them in there." Again and again he took Yates back to the hospital, and to this day Childress bitterly maintains that "the VA killed him": "They treated everyone like shit. The waits, even with an appointment, were *hours* long." One day Yates ran out of oxygen by the time

---

*Later husband and wife. Shelley Hippler had a reputation for toughness—more than equal to the task of "handling" Yates: "She'd get annoyed as shit at some of the [chauvinistic] things he said," Dan Childress noted, "but she knew he meant well."

Childress wheeled him into the examination room, and when Yates began to hiss at an orderly for help, the man said, "You need to calm down. You won't get anything until you act right." Yates continued to gasp and flail in a furious panic, while the man pointedly ignored him; finally Childress spotted an oxygen tank mounted on the wall and helped himself. "Shut the fuck up, Dick," he said soothingly as he fitted the mask over his face.

Yates had never cooked for himself and wasn't about to start now, and rather than go to the exhausting bother of leaving his apartment for lunch or dinner, he'd often dispense with eating. Childress reminded him that he could get a free lunch at the nearby senior center, but Yates refused. Finally Childress arranged for a friend named John Dobson, who delivered pizzas at night, to become a "fictitious box-lunch driver"—that is, to deliver daily lunches to Yates as if it were part of Dobson's regular job or grad-student duties. The meals came from a lunch counter called Mama Jewel's, which specialized in fatty Southern dishes that were cheap but tasty—a meat and three vegetables for less than four dollars. Yates never questioned or complained about the arrangement.

He wanted more independence, though, and finally asked Childress to get him a car ("the cheapest you can find"). For seven hundred dollars the young man found a rusty reddish Mazda of early-seventies vintage that was in good mechanical shape, though rather too small for its owner's sprawling frame. As a driver Yates soon became a familiar sight in Tuscaloosa: a gaunt whiskered old man hunched over the wheel of his tiny car, a cigarette smoldering in one fist while the other clasped an oxygen mask to his face—"a bomb on wheels" as one student put it. The car had a cranky shift box and no power steering, and when Yates's strength failed he'd pop over curbs and drift into the wrong lane and always, always park awry (lane-parked in a parallel space or vice versa) at the Quik Snak, where he took to eating breakfast most mornings. Childress, who kept the car in running order, considered disabling it before Yates killed himself— though already the locals seemed to be adjusting, automatically making way whenever the telltale Mazda came tooling into their ken. As ever, too, strangers rallied to help Yates: Now that he was drinking beer again (why not?) he'd drive to a particular convenience store where the clerks would carry a case of Heineken out to his car—or else wave him away, whereupon

Yates would realize it was *Sunday*, the goddamn blue laws, and he'd have
to borrow beer from Childress or one of the others. Whatever his errand,
Yates was always exhausted by the time he got back to Alaca Place, sitting
forlornly in his car for an hour or so before he could muster the strength
to stagger back to his house.

It had been a long time since Yates was part of the lively social atmosphere of a small-town academic community, and now that he was no
longer chair writer he tried to make the most of it. Among the seven professors and sixty graduate students in the writing program, there were as
many as four gatherings a week—readings, receptions, raucous parties—
where Yates was treated as the venerable fixture he was. For Yates it was an
alternative to drinking alone on Alaca Place, though he didn't seem to
enjoy himself much. At student parties, particularly, the breathless man
could hardly hear himself speak over the blaring music (the Ramones and
such, whose appeal baffled Yates), nor could he participate in the drunken
croquet games on the lawn. Mostly he sat watching with a vaguely pleased-
but-puzzled look, and would wince with the effort of hearing the odd solicitous remark. When the Starbucks came to a party, as rarely happened,
Yates would be overjoyed at the sight of people his own age. Still, he liked
to think he *belonged* among the younger set, and when Parrish failed to
invite him to a big Halloween party Yates was hurt. "Look, if you don't
want me to come to your house, just say so!" he huffed, as Parrish tried to
explain that such a party was apt to get, well, pretty out of control. In the
end Yates showed up in his usual tweed and khakis, and when he spotted
Tony Earley he began mournfully shaking his head: "Oh—my—*God* . . ."
Twin Peaks was big at the time, and Earley had come to the party as the
corpse of Laura Palmer, wearing a wig, lingerie, and clear plastic wrapping. "I don't get it," Yates said whenever someone tried to explain.

He preferred smaller gatherings, and since he didn't own a TV he was
often invited to people's houses to watch something of particular interest.
Yates was delighted by a documentary about RFK's standoff with George
Wallace in 1963, and excitedly pointed and coughed at the screen whenever he recognized one of his old Justice Department colleagues. When he
asked J. R. Jones if he'd ever heard of an actor named Joe Pesci—who held
the option to *Disturbing the Peace*—Jones invited him over to watch

Raging Bull; Yates found the movie excellent, and wondered who this guy "Martin Scorsese" was. For the most part, though, Yates's hatred of the movies remained intact to the end. Childress was at least as passionate a buff as Larry in Los Angeles, and like Larry he tried coaxing Yates into watching with him. Finally Yates thought of a movie he'd always wanted to see, Kubrick's *Lolita*, but after the first twenty minutes he told Childress to turn it off. A travesty, he said.

All this, of course, was but a fleeting distraction from Yates's ultimate concern. "Why aren't you *writing*?" he'd hector Childress and the others—or, if a given story was already written (and set in type), "Why aren't you *revising* this? You should be *constantly* revising!" Nothing was finished in Yates's eyes, not even his own best work: "How could I *improve* it?" he'd fire back, rather than accept a simple compliment, or else he'd point to some flaw that he himself had discovered post facto, to his everlasting chagrin (e.g., the same meal served twice in *Revolutionary Road*). Such zeal had the same effect on Childress as on Monica two years before—he began to realize that if *this* was what a true vocation involved, then perhaps he should consider something else. In fact five years had passed since Childress had written the one story he was somewhat proud of, and Yates was forever harassing him to improve it. And "harassing" was pretty much the mot juste. Yates appeared to be entering a manic phase when Parrish sought his advice about a bleak story titled "Exterminator," about a man whose common-law wife leaves him to go live in a trailer with another man who beats her. "Now this scene here," Yates panted, getting louder and louder, "it needs *squalor. More squalor!*" "What you're saying, Dick, is that it needs 'squalor'?" "SQUALOR!" ("I realized he was exactly right," said Parrish. "He'd put his finger on it.")

Yates had mellowed as a parent, at least, particularly toward his beloved Gina. Whatever she did was all right by him, even if it meant relinquishing his dream of sending her to Harvard (after a pleasant summer vacation in Vancouver, she decided to go to the University of British Columbia). She was the last pretty girl in Yates's life, and he acted toward her like a kind of platonic suitor—funny and affectionate and quietly wise. He always enclosed a loving note with his checks ("I would rather spend an hour on the phone with you than be elected by a landslide"), and approved of her future husband Chad in absentia because, he said, she'd become a warmer person for knowing him. The transformative effects of love were such that Yates didn't even object to the tattoo (a flower) Gina showed him on the back of her leg; indeed he seemed to startle himself by finding it "cute," laughing that if his older daughters had done as much he'd have "hit the ceiling." When Gina came to Tuscaloosa, Yates rebuffed Childress's offer to show her around. "Nah, you're a dangerous man," he said, though the outing was to be chaperoned by Childress's jealous girlfriend. The fact was, Yates wanted Gina all to himself, and for two weeks they happily chatted about whatever came to mind (except writing): love, sex, marriage, the way Gina liked to smoke pot when she listened to music. Yates faintly deplored the latter, and pointed out that cows piss in the fields where the stuff is grown. "Later on," Gina recalled, "during a pause in a totally different conversation, Dad says, 'You know who else lives in those marijuana fields?' And I said, 'Who?' *Marijuana rats,'* he said sternly. 'Those little bastards *live* to piss!' "

"I loved and hated Richard Yates," said Susan Braudy, "as I believe he did me. I miss talking to him very much." More than his daughters or even Dan Childress, Braudy became the most fixed presence in Yates's life during his last two years in Alabama—though many miles apart, the two spoke on the phone almost every day, including the day Yates died. Originally Braudy had called to discuss her screenplay of *The Easter Parade,* in the hope of drawing Yates out about the "nuts and bolts" of what was "probably [her] favorite novel in the world." Yates shrunk from the subject. "Sure, sure," he said finally. "*The Easter Parade* probably *is* about the failure of love." Soon they found other things to talk about, and Braudy saw a more appealing side to the man. He was forthright but not maudlin about the grim facts of his life, and gruffly opinionated about Braudy's. When she mentioned that she wanted to refurbish an old church in the country, Yates insisted the idea was gauche. But he was also hard on himself, and inclined to be contrite when he sensed that he'd gone too far and hurt Braudy's feelings. This was easily done, as Braudy was nothing if not tenderhearted, to the point of being sorely distressed by the sadness of Yates's life and determined to do something about it. It was Braudy who got in touch with Childress and arranged to pay for the "fictitious box-lunch driver," and sometimes she'd send money straight to Yates; once, after she'd given him five hundred dollars, he casually admitted that he'd sent it to Gina so she could buy a car.

Yates often made it known that his fondest desire was to return to New York—he had no intention of "nodding out in Dixie"—but as things were, he couldn't even afford to visit. Braudy's affection for her favorite writer was buoyed by a preoccupation with certain Jewish ethical impera-tives, namely *Honor elders*, so she decided to bring Yates to New York and honor him one way or another. It wouldn't do, though, simply to buy him a plane ticket and put him up for a few days: It was one thing for such a proud man to accept the odd check out of the blue, another to let a woman explicitly offer him charity. Besides, Braudy wasn't rich, despite whatever Yates had surmised to the contrary because of her generosity and Central Park South address (he was under the impression she was a "dowager" à la Gloria Vanderbilt). She decided, then, to organize a read-ing and pay Yates an honorarium, raised with donations of a thousand to fifteen hundred dollars apiece from a few well-heeled admirers, starting with Woody Allen. "Ms. Braudy found that many writers shared Mr. Allen's take on Mr. Yates and has now organized a group of them to bring the novelist to New York for a tribute," read an item in the *New York Observer* for April 15, 1991. "Mr. [Paul] Schrader, Richard Price, and Kurt Vonnegut are among the literary stars who've contributed money to fly Mr. Yates in from his home in Tuscaloosa, Alabama. He is scheduled to read at the Donnell Library on April 11 at 6 P.M., with a reception to fol-low at the Gotham Book Mart on West 47th Street."

Yates planned to arrive the day before his reading—as it happened, his daughter Monica's thirty-fourth birthday. She'd recently moved back to New York prior to starting nursing school at Columbia in the fall,* and when she learned of her father's visit she was plunged into a funk. She dreaded seeing him so deathly ill, not to mention drinking again, and

---

*Nursing school had ended Monica's writing career for good. "The day I got accepted at Colum-bia," she said, "I thought *Fuck this, I'm free!*—and dropped the entire manuscript of my reworked novel down the garbage chute."

figured the reading would be a failure and he'd be sad. She spent the day gloomily riding her bicycle until, as a kind of despondent "madcap stunt," she rode it down a flight of stairs and gave herself a black eye and a swollen, badly bruised chin.

Meanwhile air travel had taken its usual toll on Yates. "He was a total mess," said Braudy. "Thinner than any living person should be, and too weak to walk from the plane to a cab." The appalled woman called for a wheelchair, while Yates muttered dazedly that he'd be all right as soon as he got to the Algonquin, where he'd arranged to have oxygen tanks waiting in his room. Before they arrived, though, Yates seemed to perk up a bit. "You're no dowager," he said to Braudy in the cab, staring at her intently. "You're a young girl." Braudy was hardly a "girl" except by Yates's quaint reckoning, though she was very pretty and her relations with Yates had shifted the moment his head cleared enough to get a good look at her. But eros alone wasn't enough to resurrect such a wasted man, and by the time they got to the Algonquin—where the oxygen tanks wouldn't work—he seemed on the verge of total, perhaps permanent collapse. Nonetheless he insisted on meeting Monica and his old student Richard Price as planned, so Braudy assisted him into the dining room; by the time the others arrived, Yates had put his head on the table and begun panting for air. "Not drunk," he gasped to Monica. "Not drunk, baby." Then he noticed his daughter's grossly swollen face. "What can I say?" he managed to quip. "I love the big lug."

While Yates tried to pull himself together, his companions exchanged glances. "No, Dick," said Price, as Yates croaked at the waiter for menus, "I think we'd better get you upstairs." In the room they called the house doctor, and soon Yates was bound for New York Hospital in an ambulance. Braudy, Price, and Monica followed in a cab. After Yates had been taken into the emergency room and given oxygen and fluids, Braudy returned to his side and he groggily resumed pitching woo. "I'm falling in love with you," he said with a faint smile. As Braudy recalled, "He was half dead, but coming on to me! And I'm a complete wreck!" Finally, around four in the morning, Yates was admitted as a patient. In the meantime Braudy and Monica sat talking outside the ER cubicle, and the latter reflected that this was a hell of a way to spend her birthday.

Sharon Yates remembers her father looking "very jaunty" in his hospital bed, and Braudy confirms that he was "in fine fettle." Yates was impressed by how much nicer the hospital was than his usual VAs, and of course it always pleased him to cheat death with a certain stylish insouciance. It was fine to be back in New York and in love again. His agent Ned Leavitt visited and noticed something distinctly in the air between Yates and Braudy, at least on Yates's part, and Monica noticed the same with exasperation. Meanwhile a steady stream of visitors came to pay their last respects, or so it seemed at the time. Richard Price visited every day, and Monica brought the writer Elizabeth Cullinan, whom Yates found impressively pretty despite the fact that she was almost his own age. Monica also invited her father's old Boston girlfriend Laura, who sat by his bed for a long time and made him laugh.

Everybody agreed that the reading at the Donnell Library and the reception afterward were "Yatesian occasions." A reporter from the *New York Times* abruptly departed when he learned that Yates himself wasn't among those present. Braudy had made an audiotape of Yates in the hospital, wheezing his way through one of his stories, and this was played for a bemused audience of seventy-five or so. Paul Schrader and the journalist Harvey Shapiro read from *The Easter Parade,* after which the crowd adjourned by foot to the Gotham Book Mart for a reception hosted by Braudy and the actor Patrick O'Neal, who still owned the rights to *Revolutionary Road* and still planned to make a movie of it written and directed by himself. The bookstore was soon divided between a defiant group of smokers and those who reviled them, until a number of guests repaired to the hospital to visit Yates, who received them bravely.

Four days later, after Braudy had paid the hospital bill with fifteen hundred dollars of honorarium money, she and Yates returned to the airport. As she wheeled him out to the ambulance, his suitcase slipped off his lap and cracked open on the street. Braudy chased down and repacked his effects, then sat with him during the ambulance ride. Yates began to light a cigarette, and when Braudy snapped it out of his hand he tried to kiss her. This went on for the rest of the ride. "Finally I'm wheeling him to his gate at the airport," said Braudy, "and he begs me to come live with him in Alabama. After that I felt very obligated and spoke to him almost every day."

Having been feted in his hospital bed, Yates wanted more than ever to go on living long enough to return to New York, where clearly he had a number of admirers as well as a lovely "girl" to pursue. He even quit smoking on his return to Alabama: In light of his recent collapse, the bravado of a four-pack-a-day habit began to seem a bit silly; besides, the way people stared at him when he lit up with oxygen tanks made him feel freakish. To Yates's mild surprise—and awful regret—he found that stopping cold after fifty years was remarkably easy.

Getting back to New York was a different story. The only affordable housing in Manhattan seemed to be WestBeth, the low-rent artists' tenement on the Hudson that Yates had briefly considered fifteen years earlier, after the fire that sent him to Boston. As ever there was a long waiting list, but Braudy had a friend on the tenants' board, Hugh Seidman, who thought an exception might be made in Yates's case based on his distinction and ill health. Seidman arranged an exploratory meeting with the board, and Monica came to plead her father's case—a humiliating experience, as it turned out. The board was mostly made up of artists and dancers who'd never heard of Yates and were unwilling to make an exception in any case, and Monica resented having to "play the role of begging daughter." Above all she felt sad that things had come to this.

Meanwhile Yates was a few months away from depleting his latest advance—that is, an advance on "Book II" of his two-book contract with Sam Lawrence—and his progress on *Uncertain Times* was slower and more problematic than ever. Sometimes he'd call up friends and ask their opinion of certain passages, a temptation he'd always resisted in the past and proof of just how doubtful he'd become. "He couldn't seem to finish it, didn't want to let it go," said Bob Lacy, whose opinion Yates sought. He was mortified by the prospect of asking Lawrence for more money, but as he told Prettyman that summer, he'd be completely broke by December and needed at least $2,000 a month to live; the two men discussed whether Prettyman (a mutual friend) should "drop a hint" to Lawrence, but in the end Yates decided he should handle it on his own. As Ned Leavitt recalled,

"It was an odd situation: As agent, I didn't have anything to offer Lawrence, who had a faint hope (but not much) that he'd finally get *Uncertain Times,* and definitely doubted he'd ever see 'Book II.' Dick's health was just too precarious by then." Still, Lawrence had always maintained that "*someday* Dick's books will sell," and he'd kept the faith too long to give up now; at any rate their old friendship made it impossible to refuse. In September, then, the contract was amended yet again to provide nine more payments of $2,300 a month.

That summer Yates's ex-wife Martha remarried in Bisbee, Arizona, where she'd gone to think things over after several years as an art therapist. "She's gone and married an electrician," Yates dolefully announced. Until then he'd never quite given up hope that maybe someday Martha would come to her senses and take him back; as he'd quickly admit to any acquaintance, he still "carried a torch" for his ex-wife. But he gracefully let go of that dream when the time came: "Congratulations," he wrote Martha. "I am very glad for your new happiness. With best wishes always, Dick." After that, his old ardor assumed a more paternal form. "Oh, those poor kids!" he exclaimed when Gina told him about the hardscrabble, odd-job life Martha and her husband were leading in arty Bisbee. "What are they *eating* on!"

He continued to implore Susan Braudy to visit, if not keep house with him, and she didn't have the heart to refuse outright; indeed, Yates anticipated her arrival for many months and spoke of little else. He told Prettyman that he was worried about his "performance"—it had been a long time—and while he thought the emotional Braudy was "a little crazy," he was very excited about seeing her all the same. When Mark Costello came to Alabama that fall, he proved every bit as lovelorn as Yates; Tony Earley called the two "poster children for depressed writers." Costello was involved with a former Iowa student who'd gone on to a rather distinguished career, but Yates warned him that two writers didn't make a good match. (Then he'd inquire: "*How* many stories you say she's had in *The New Yorker? . . . Six?* Goddamn it!") As for his own infatuation with Braudy—also a writer, though Yates hardly considered her as such—he told Costello again and again of her impending visit, of his moving to New York to be with her and so on, but beneath it all was a belying melancholy. "We both spent a lot of time together in expectation of women who wouldn't come," said Costello. "Dick was too physically infirm for that sort of thing, and he knew it." Knowing it was one thing, accepting it another. Such was the candor of his talks with Braudy, his lonely need to tell her everything, that one day he excitedly confided that a young waitress seemed attracted to him; he planned to comb his hair and take her to a movie. When Braudy asked about it later, though, Yates sighed and said he'd gone back to the diner and realized it was nothing.

Yates had fewer manic spells now that he was drinking less, and those he had tended to burn out quickly for want of energy. At first his friends in Alabama didn't know what to make of Yates's mania—he didn't discuss his illness—only that it came and went, and seemed to leave him no worse for wear. Once he called Tim Parrish and sounded as if his "head [was] exploding": "It was a brilliant and terrifying stream of consciousness," Parrish remembered, "and I sensed there was some overarching theme that I wasn't capable of grasping. Dick was referencing events on the senate floor in the fifties, quoting speeches verbatim. It gave me a sense of what a trial it was to be Richard Yates." Every so often Yates would "veer into paranoid speculations" about this or that person, and Parrish would try to calm him ("Oh, I don't think that's true, Dick"). Another time an alarmed Dan Childress called Costello and reported that he'd found Yates "totally whacked"; to this day Costello is puzzled by the episode. "I went to Dick's house and he was drunker than I'd ever seen him, but there were no bottles around. There was no booze in the place at all." This time the "overarching theme" of Yates's spiel had to do with an official tour of Germany that Vonnegut had made with Nobel laureate Heinrich Böll (which had actually taken place during a PEN conference in the seventies): Yates said that Vonnegut was chosen for the junket because he was German and a WWII veteran and of course *famous*. . . . "Costello—goddamn it—Murphy—" he panted, pausing now and then to catch his breath (he called Costello *Murphy* after the latter's fictional alter ego); finally he closed his eyes and fell asleep. Two days later he was fine again.

Lucid or not, Yates's lack of fame didn't bother him nearly so much as his lack of money, especially now that time was running out. He'd regularly call his friend Bruce Ricker to discuss possible movie deals, and impress on the lawyer his urgent desire to provide some kind of inheritance for his daughters. Yates realized the best bet for a feature-length adaptation of his work was *Revolutionary Road,* and he was desperate to wrest the property away from Patrick O'Neal, who owned it outright. O'Neal had written a screenplay of the novel that he still hoped to produce and direct someday, but Yates thought the script godawful and was tired of the man's stalling. O'Neal wouldn't budge: "It's in the stars," he'd tell Ned Leavitt with a mellow sense of assurance. Such "new agey" pronouncements, said Leavitt, "used to send Dick through the roof."

A far more "tortured" situation, as Leavitt put it, developed over Braudy's adaptation of *The Easter Parade.* Calder Willingham, the author of a number of novels and successful screenplays (e.g., *Paths of Glory* and *One-Eyed Jacks*), was a great Yates fan and common friend of Seymour Krim. For a long time he'd wanted to adapt *The Easter Parade,* but his hands were tied as long as Braudy held the option. Yates demanded to see Braudy's screenplay, and after a bitter argument she finally sent it to him; later, when she asked his opinion, he said he'd decided not to read it after all. This was by way of sparing her feelings. He'd read it and immediately directed Leavitt not to renew the woman's option under any circumstances. But Braudy would not go quietly: She'd invested a lot of time and emotion in the project, to say nothing of money, and legally she was within her rights. "I feel like taking a gun and shooting you!" she told Leavitt, who lapsed into stunned silence. Even Yates was impressed: "You've scared everybody to death," he told her. But still he insisted she relinquish her option; he calmly explained that the project would be more "viable" if Willingham wrote the screenplay. When Yates spoke of the matter to Leavitt, though, he reverted to an "operatic" rage: He was *sick* of the woman, he said, and wanted to be rid of her once and for all. "But he kept letting her back into his life," Leavitt mused, "even though he didn't like her screenplay. He seemed to make a distinction between her as a writer and a person, and basically he was a sweet-natured man, even when he was pissed off. After he'd rail against Braudy or Patrick O'Neal, I'd remind him of their positions and he'd back off. In fact he felt sympathy for Braudy." And vice versa. "For my birthday he drew me a cartoon of this dilapidated person holding a heart," she recalled. "I don't know, looking back, how I had the fortitude to deal with the situation."

For the first half of 1992 Yates all but disappeared from public view as he made a last sustained effort to finish *Uncertain Times*. Sam Lawrence hoped to publish the book in the fall, and Rust Hills bought a long excerpt for *Esquire* and encouraged the author by calling the pages "vintage Yates."* According to Childress, Yates was keeping "long writing hours" despite his condition, and was irritated by unexpected interruptions. To the last, though, Yates expressed a tormented ambivalence toward his work in progress: On some days he'd seem pleased and say the end was in sight, then he'd say the whole thing was a mess and he'd have to do it over. Nor was the book's relative merit the only issue: In 1991 Styron had published *Darkness Visible,* a memoir of his struggle with clinical depression; Yates was appalled, considering it unseemly for a writer to air his personal life in nonfictional form (this despite his admiration for Fitzgerald's *Crack-Up* essays). But *Uncertain Times* was itself a curious amalgam of fact and fiction, with a protagonist who resembled Yates almost as baldly as "Kennedy" did Kennedy, and what it revealed about the author's life was at least as embarrassing as anything Styron had openly confessed about his. So there was that. Finally Yates showed his manuscript to "some foolish person," as his daughter Monica recalled, "who read it and said it wasn't any good." Yates soon lost heart after that, and besides he was simply too oxygen deprived to continue. His last manuscript note is dated August 28, 1992.

At the time of his death, the novel was perhaps two-thirds finished: about 250 pages of narrative in various stages of revision. The first 100 pages are typed and polished, with only the occasional word struck out or

---

*Esquire never published the excerpt, though Hills had returned a ninety-page edited typescript to Yates with a note on the first page: "These are passages extracted to make a narrative from the unfinished novel, *Uncertain Times,* by Richard Yates. [Signed] Rust Hills." Yates kept the excerpted segment with the rest of his manuscript. On the last page Hills had written the word "END," and this was probably the bottom page of the manuscript Allen Wier found after Yates's death.

changed. The next 100 pages are much rougher—mostly typed, but heavily revised with drastic deletions and emendations, marginal notes, and many inserted holograph pages. The last fifty pages are fairly chaotic: A few of these are typed and heavily revised; the rest are written in a rapid, hard-to-decipher scrawl. Also, there are about 70 pages of additional material: notes, fragments of scenes and dialogue, lists and outlines. Yates's own dating suggests that the first, relatively fluent 150 pages or so were written before 1989—after that, his failing stamina is poignantly evident on the page: "FIX" is scrawled again and again in the margin, as well as a number of fretful glosses such as, "She wouldn't *say* that." As he got bogged down in the slow agony of revision—many pages are frantically scored with deletions, minute insertions, and finally struck out altogether—the frustrated Yates began to abandon unfinished, unsatisfactory sections ("FIX") in order to get on with his story, writing several scenes out of sequence. Some of these later pages seem to have been written as rapidly as possible, with hardly any correction, as if Yates were in a race with that day's tiny store of concentration. By the end he appeared to be writing in minute spurts of a few lines a day, and was so oxygen deprived that he sometimes referred to the same character by different names from one sentence to the next—hence "Bill" becomes "Jim" and then "Bill" again; "Arnold" becomes "Henry," and so on.

The novel opens on New Year's Day 1963, as Bill Grove happily anticipates the "avalanche of money" he'll receive as soon as his screenplay (based on an acclaimed novel by the more famous Paul Cameron, a "good if not close" friend) is made into a movie starring Henry Fonda and Natalie Wood. Grove hopes that such a stroke of success will help reverse certain morbid trends in his life—two mental breakdowns in the past three years, a squalid basement apartment in the Village, and a drunken slatternly girlfriend named Nora Harrigan. By February, however, everything has gone wrong: The movie is red-lighted when its stars pull out, and meanwhile Grove's second novel ("about some young guys in the army in Europe during the last few months of the war") has become all but impossible to write, such that Grove worries he's "ready to go off again." For a few months he tries halfheartedly to return to public-relations work, until one night—while he and Nora lugubriously discuss her "toe-jam"—Paul

Cameron calls to report that he's recommended Grove as speechwriter for Bobby Kennedy. Grove is skeptical ("I'm not even sure I *like* the fucking Kennedys"), but hardly in a position to refuse. After an interview with the great man in Washington, and a trial speechwriting assignment that (to his surprise) he enjoys, Grove is hired.

For a while he does well at the job: His first few speeches (transcribed almost in full for the reader) are so well received that he's asked to submit a draft for the president's civil rights address on national television. Almost from the start, though, Grove finds himself at odds with the "true believers" whose idealism blinds them to the Kennedys' essential speciousness; also there's a constant dissonance between Grove's feckless, messy private life and the clean-living, go-getting atmosphere of public service. Grove transplants the squalor of his Barrow Street cellar to his "office" at the Justice Department—a dusty, cluttered file room he appropriates in order to be alone with his thoughts and cigarettes. Meanwhile, too, a pending FBI background check threatens to reveal that Grove's been hospitalized twice as a mental patient and has an ongoing drinking problem. Grove tries to adjust somewhat to his new circumstances by purging the drunken, depressing Nora in favor of a genteel virgin named Holly Parsons; also he moves into the suburban Washington home of an old army buddy, Frank Marr, whose conventional middle-class family offers a stark and somewhat stabilizing alternative to Grove's raffish bachelor lifestyle.

So it goes for the first 150 pages, more or less, and so far so good. The pace is brisk (though arguably *one* transcribed speech would suffice), the prose clean, and best of all a nice ironic balance is struck between Grove's private and public lives—a crucial dialectic that begins when Grove's "toe-jam" remarks coincide with his being summoned to public service by the glamorous Paul Cameron. Nor does Yates indulge in any easy satire of the Kennedys as merely "figments of the public imagination," as the cynical Nora Harrigan describes them. Rather, in typical Yatesian fashion, Grove remains "simultaneously enchanted and repelled" by the world he encounters at the Justice Department: "You're getting a rare concentration of intelligence and decency in there," Warren Pickering (the Prettyman surrogate) aptly observes. "Lot of plain courage, too, because some of these guys've risked their necks down South once or twice and they will again." This is true, but on the other hand such idealism has its dark or dull side, exemplified by RFK's press secretary Jim Thurman—a fatuous, humorless Babbitt who speaks of the "real Americans" in the Midwest and reads nothing but "an occasional detective story or Western to help him kill time on airplanes." As for Kennedy himself, he's evoked as boyish and well-meaning and slightly out of his depth: "part of his shirttail bulge[s] loose on one side" as he interviews Grove, and he speaks with a lot of halting, inarticulate *ah*'s as he tries to marshal his thoughts. But then, too, he's egocentric and calculating, often lapsing into a gum-chewing, people-ignoring trance between public performances, and cursing himself for having neglected to shake hands with motorcycle cops while the cameras roll.

When Grove begins to lose interest in his speechwriting duties, and the focus shifts to his private life, the novel goes off the rails. There is less dramatized conflict between the world of action and that of the skeptical introspective writer, and more introspection per se. Grove broods a lot over his stalled novel, for instance, which entails a precise rehashing of certain aspects of *A Special Providence* as well as the actual experiences that inspired it. But mostly the plot becomes dominated by the ups and downs (mostly downs) of Grove's affair with the wholly uninteresting Holly Parsons. ("I never had a feeling Dick had any idea who I really was," said Wendy Sears, who was bemused when Yates told her he was putting her in a novel. "He always talked about his *own* ideas, his *own* point of view on things. I was just a vessel for him.") Parsons, a blandly good-natured "classy" girl, serves as witness and sounding board for Grove's various inadequacies: his impotence, sexual and otherwise; his precarious mental health; his tendency to fly into drunken rages at the slightest provocation. Again, when all this is balanced with the can-do ethos of Kennedy-era idealism, rather than a "classy" abstraction such as Holly Parsons, it makes some kind of narrative sense; otherwise it's so much ranting in a vacuum. Yates himself couldn't seem to figure out where he was going with all this, apart from contriving one humiliation after another for his alter ego: Hence Grove spends a night in jail after yelling at Holly in public, but afterward seems to "redeem" himself when (according to Yates's notes) he "discovers he can get laid"—though Holly implicitly diminishes this feat by calling it a simple act of friendship on her part; Grove again gets laid at the MacDowell Colony with a different woman, who also punctures his ego by asking, "How well do you *really* know Paul Cameron?"; and finally Grove's novel is rejected by his agent— the apparent climax of *Uncertain Times*.

Given better health and alertness, could Yates have pulled it all together and made it work? Possibly, though it would have taken at least as much "brain-scrambling" effort as *Revolutionary Road*—the same exhausting, extended struggle to reconcile exquisite ambiguities in his own mind in order to convey them in art: "If the suburbs *are* to blame," Yates wrote in a 1956 memo to himself, "—and they are to no greater extent than the 'artist' illusion—remember that—it must be implied by cumulative effect rather than slammed home in every chapter. . . . *I must never let the meanings escape both me and the reader through my efforts to hold his interest* [italics added]." Reading *Uncertain Times*, one gets the impression that Yates couldn't quite determine the *meaning* of Grove's disaffection with public service, and was all too aware that in writing more and more about himself (that is, Grove), he was holding nobody's interest but his own. "'Solipsism,'" Yates wrote in his notes: "'a theory holding that the self can know nothing but its own modifications and that the self is the only existing thing' . . . Holly P. uses this word in criticizing Grove." Thus Yates tried to explain to himself the fundamental conflict between Grove's self-absorption and the relatively unreflective nature of political idealism—and thus, too, he tried to explain why, perhaps, he'd come to dwell so entirely on Grove and *his* times, rather than those of the greater world.

No doubt Yates found himself more interesting than the public figures who populate the earlier, more readable, but ultimately underwhelming chapters of *Uncertain Times*. Because Yates could only animate such characters as Kennedy, Burke Marshall, Edwin Guthman, et al., in terms of their public personae, the final effect reads like nothing so much as highly competent political fiction—"It isn't *felt*," as Yates would tell his students. Meanwhile the story of Grove's various demons *was* felt, but it didn't quite mesh with the rest of the material and was also uncomfortably confessional in the context of an historically accurate roman à clef.

Such was the quandary Yates couldn't resolve, though he (almost) died trying.

The last time Monica Yates visited her father was in May 1992, about six months before his death. She couldn't help but suspect she was seeing him for the last time: He "looked like a scarecrow" and was so feeble he could hardly walk to the bathroom without sitting down every few steps; he shuffled and stumbled from one piece of furniture to the next. Sometimes the surgical tubing that connected him to the humming tanks in the bedroom would snarl, and his lips would turn blue. For the most part he was able to laugh off the worst of his infirmity. One night the two went to dinner with George Starbuck, who was then in the final stages of Parkinson's; the man's speech was labored and he made constant "pill-rolling" motions with his hands, but he was still a bit stronger than Yates. "Oh *God,* baby—" gasped the latter, faced with stairs at the restaurant, "we can't *do* this!" Somehow, with Monica's strenuous help, the dying men managed the ascent, and seemed pleased but hardly able to eat or speak from the strain. It was a relatively mellow visit for Monica, though her father could still be provoked; his reading was now limited to the *New York Times* and works of political history, about which he cultivated a kind of cranky punditry. "How can you *say* that?" he demanded of Monica in a restaurant, when she remarked that Nixon "wasn't so bad."

As time ran out, though, and he began to let go of things, Yates subsided into a larger peace. When Gina visited in August, she found her father "enlightened and very accepting": He liked to say he was "in the bright winter of life," that his only wish was to go back to New York before he "checked out"; as for his novel, he doubted more and more that he had the energy to finish it. Nor could he muster the strength or desire to venture out much. Childress had moved to Arizona that summer, and the only people who visited regularly were Ron Sielenski and Shelley Hippler, who continued to tidy his house and make sure he was okay. But mostly Yates preferred to be alone—he knew how mortal he looked, and simply wanted to drink beer and think about the past. When he got tipsy and nostalgic enough, he'd call up old friends to say, in effect, good-bye, though he was sometimes hard to understand because of emphysema or beer or both. The last time Yates spoke to Loree Rackstraw he could hardly finish a sentence without gasping. "He ended the conversation by saying, 'We had some good times in Iowa City, didn't we?' It was heartbreaking."

Writing had kept Yates alive all these years. He'd always promised Monica not to die until he finished his novel, but one day he admitted he'd given it up. "You know, I'm just tired," he explained. "Don't want to live much longer." If he felt sorry for himself at all, it was in that particular respect—he'd never write again—but such a mood was touched with a kind of exaltation when he considered the transcendence of his life's work. A month before he died, he called Bob Lacy and asked the man if he'd like to know what he, Yates, had done the night before; Lacy said he would. "Get this," Yates wheezed. "I got smashed last night, and then you know what I did? I sat here on this couch in my lousy apartment reading the first chapter of *Revolutionary Road* out loud to myself and crying like a baby. . . . Tears running down my cheeks. Can you believe that?" Another time Susan Braudy begged him to read her the last page of *Gatsby*; he'd always said it was his favorite piece of prose, the very passage that had made him so determined to write ("If there wasn't a Fitzgerald, I don't think I would have become a writer"). "Dropping the telephone to make an unpleasant rolling clatter as he opened a can of beer," Braudy remembered, "he started to read in the most matter-of-fact and loving way." Yates got as far as the following lines:

> He had come a long way to this blue lawn, and his dream must have seemed so close that he could hardly fail to grasp it. He did not know that it was already behind him, somewhere back in that vast obscurity beyond the city, where the dark fields of the republic rolled on under the night.

There was a long silence. "Sorry, sweetheart," said Yates, "I better hang up. I'm crying like a damn fool."

One of the last people to see Yates alive was Scott Bradfield, author of the novel *The History of Luminous Motion*. Three weeks before Yates's death, Bradfield had arranged an interview for the London *Independent*. "Richard Yates was America's finest post-war novelist and short story writer," the article began, "but he was a surprisingly difficult man to contact." Bradfield had tried tracking Yates down through his latest publisher, Vintage, whose people knew nothing of his whereabouts and seemed indifferent to promoting the author of a few three-year-old paperback reprints. "I've been ill, you see," said Yates, when Bradfield finally managed to get him on the phone, "and I may go into the VA hospital shortly, but I'd really like to do this, I really would." A couple days later Bradfield drove all the way from Chicago to Tuscaloosa, and spent a few hours chatting with Yates in his living room. Though "extremely cordial," Yates seemed disinclined to discuss his work much, and would bridle mildly at what he called "slick" questions. "You're giving me too much at once," he said, or "I'm just not smart enough to answer big questions about things like 'themes' and 'purposes' in my work." He was especially exasperated by the "slick" tag *realist*: "All fiction is filled with technique," he said. "It's ridiculous to suggest one technique is any more realistic than any other." Again and again Yates tried to steer the discussion away from himself, even if it meant interviewing the interviewer: Where did Bradfield get that T-shirt? Where was he born? What did he want to do next?

"Finally we broke for lunch," Bradfield wrote, "and there was something dimly Yatesian about how the rest of the afternoon developed—a constant slippage between intentions and effects." When Yates discovered that his favorite steak house was already closing, he drove them to the Red Lobster franchise restaurant, where he was faintly disappointed to find that their only steak was a New York cut—much too big. Bradfield urged him to order it ("This is on *The Independent*. Let's break the suckers"), but Yates scrupulously refused: "[a] waste," he said, and ordered the chicken. Exhausted when they returned to Alaca Place, Yates nonetheless offered his guest a last beer and took cordial leave of him. " 'It was very, well, enjoyable,' he said, showing the sort of care with which he has selected virtually every single word of his published prose. Not a 'great' afternoon. Not even 'exciting' or 'funny' or 'wonderful.' But 'enjoyable,' yes. It was very, well, enjoyable." When the article ran on November 21, Yates was already dead, and Bradfield appended a suitable envoi: "I can live with the uncomprehending publishers, the dumb reviews of his work, the dull place he ended up in, even the second-rate restaurant and the slow, awkward circuit around the driveway we made three or four times before Yates could find the exit on to the main road. . . . [But] I wish he'd ordered the goddamn steak."

"Keep this," Yates had scribbled next to a sentence typed on a piece of looseleaf and attached to the manuscript of *Uncertain Times*: "This book is dedicated to men and women of the United States Veterans' Administration, past and present, in gratitude for their courtesy and kindness no less than for their excellent medical care."

It's more accurate to say that writing *and* VA hospitals had kept Yates alive over the years, so that he gladly accepted their occasional slipshod treatment, even to the bitter end. For years VA doctors had put off operating on Yates's inguinal hernia, which had become more and more painful as his coughing got worse and he had to drag tanks around. The hernia was forever popping out like a sausage link, but it took several grueling trips to Birmingham before the doctors finally deemed it "emergency" enough to operate. By that time Yates was almost dead anyway—but then, he'd always wanted to die in a hospital where people would clean him up. "Sam, I'm dying," he gasped to his publisher a few days before the trip. "I can't work anymore. I can't do anything."

When Gina called from Mexico that Sunday, Yates cheerfully assured her it was only a routine procedure. They were about to say good-bye when the phone cut out, a common occurrence. "In the past," Gina remembered,

> we had agreed that if we got cut off before saying goodbye, we would just leave it until the following week. Even so, I was inexplicably compelled to ask the [concierge] to call back. After about half an hour he got through. Dad said, "You didn't have to call back—we were finished!" And I said, "I know, I just wanted to say goodbye and I love you!" He said he loved me too, and we hung up.

Monica considered hiring a private nurse (or coming down herself) to tend her father following the operation, but in the end she simply couldn't afford it—besides, as Yates blithely insisted, it was no big deal. After surgery on Thursday, November 5, he told Monica the wound wasn't closing properly and they might have to operate again; a little later he left a message on her machine: "Don't worry, baby, they put this mesh thing in, and it's going to be okay."

Probably his last conversation, Friday night, was with Susan Braudy. He sounded unwell, and when she pressed him about it, he admitted—his voice dropping a little sheepishly—that he was in a lot of pain. "Ask the nurse for painkillers!" said Braudy, and Yates promised he would. He left the phone off the hook when he tried to hang up, and Braudy continued to listen as a nurse asked Yates if he needed anything. "No," she heard him say, "I'm fine."

At around three in the morning Yates apparently had a coughing fit that caused him to vomit. No nurse was around (though arguably a person in Yates's condition should have been recuperating in the ICU), and he struggled to get out of bed. The next morning they found him on the floor, dead of suffocation.

Epilogue

Yates used to ruminate gloomily about the kind of obituary he'd get—
"two inches in the *Times*," he'd say, "*at best*, and the only book
they'll mention is *Revolutionary Road*." One likes to think he would have
been pleased that he was at least somewhat mistaken, since in fact the
Times's lead obituary for Monday, November 9, was Yates's; and while
it's true that his first and most famous novel was the only one discussed at
length, the other titles were duly listed and collectively described as being
"about self-deception, disappointment, and grief." The rest of his career
was limned from Yonkers to Avon to the army to Remington Rand, from
speechwriting to teaching and two broken marriages. Sam Lawrence got
in a plug for *Uncertain Times*, though he added that he wasn't sure yet
whether the manuscript was in "publishable form." Yates was dubbed in
the headline a "Chronicler of Disappointed Lives." Fair enough.

Monica was the first to be notified of her father's death, and for a long
time she felt "complete desolation and brokenheartedness": "I didn't
know how I was going to keep going without him. Who else would
respond to me like that? No one else would really see me the way he did,
and think I was so interesting, and *get* what I was saying when I said it."
Monica had become so attached to her father that, as his health failed, she
begged him to reassure her that *some* sort of afterlife existed so they could
be reunited. But Yates wasn't having any of that: "Nah baby," he'd say,
"just blackness!" Gina was still in Mexico when her father died; she called
him that Sunday as usual, hoping he'd already be home after his "routine
procedure." Fearing the worst when he didn't answer, she called her

mother, who'd just gotten the news from Sharon. "Gina burst into tears," Martha recalled. "Destroyed." Outside the family, the person who probably took Yates's death the hardest was Andre Dubus, who seemed not only devastated but angry when he called his first wife Pat. "Dick *let* himself die," he sobbed.

Two weeks later Monica and Sharon went to Tuscaloosa to pack up their father's things and decide what to do about the body, which was being kept in cold storage at a local funeral home. There were a few complications. Yates was entitled to a free burial at the VA cemetery in Alabama, but his daughters agreed he wouldn't have liked that, so they arranged to pay for cremation; at the last moment, though, the funeral home director discovered that a *third* daughter existed—in Mexico—and refused to proceed without her signature. Monica and Sharon joked about stowing the body in Yates's old Mazda and shipping it home, but as it happened there was no extra charge for a few more weeks of refrigeration. Meanwhile they had to clear out the bungalow on Alaca Place. Allen Wier and some graduate students had already cleaned up the worst of it, including the loose change strewn about the floor, which they'd left for the daughters in a tidy plastic bag. Yates's remaining effects were as follows: an air-conditioner and typewriter, which were stashed in the Mazda and trucked back to Brooklyn; some books and unpacked boxes of letters ("I should throw this shit out," Yates had said in May *re* his life's store of letters, but Monica talked him out of it); a spavined old sofa, table, and bed; some soiled sheets in the back of the closet which Yates had lacked the energy to clean. The books and letters were mailed home, the rest abandoned. On the plane back to New York, Monica and Sharon sat putting the loose change into rolls. "Our inheritance!" they laughed. "The family fortune!"

On December 16, 1992, Sam Lawrence and Kurt Vonnegut hosted a memorial service for Yates at the Century Club in Manhattan. In his eulogy Vonnegut spoke of the "forced march" he'd made through all nine of Yates's books before preparing his remarks: "Not only did I fail to detect so much as an injudiciously applied semicolon; I did not find even one paragraph which, if it were read to you today, would not wow you with its power, intelligence, and clarity." He remembered how his old friend Yates had always "yearned to live as F. Scott Fitzgerald lived when Fitzgerald was rich and famous and young, to jump into the Plaza fountain with his clothes on and his pockets stuffed with paper money"; but even though Yates was "a more careful writer than Fitzgerald, and one who was even more cunningly observant," he could never escape the middle-class life he wrote about so well. Finally Vonnegut looked back on the early days of their friendship at the Writers' Workshop in Iowa City. "One of our colleagues was Nelson Algren," he concluded, "another world-class story-teller and outsider who died broke, but who was more famous than Yates because he had made love to Simone de Beauvoir. These things matter."

Vonnegut read tributes by Dubus and Loree Rackstraw, then a number of illustrious people—Yates's "good if not close" friends—read from his work: Styron, Frank Conroy, Barrett Prettyman, David Milch, Dan Wakefield, and Robert Stone. Richard Price and Richard Levine gave reminiscences, as did Yates's short-lived girlfriend from the mid-seventies, Carolyn Gaiser, who startled the crowd (*"Who is that?"*) with a wittily impious evocation of Yates as, essentially, a lonely alcoholic given to "monumental" tantrums. The last item on the program was a long "requiem" by Sam Lawrence, read by his son Nick because of the former's stammer. Among other things Lawrence remembered his boozy Harvard Club dinners with Yates in their youth, and dwelled at curious length on facts and figures relating to their various contracts. All in all, though, it was a fair and heartfelt summation of Yates's career. "He drank too much, he smoked too much, he was accident-prone, he led an itinerant life, but as a writer he was all in place," said Lawrence. "He wrote the best dialogue since John O'Hara, who also lacked the so-called advantages of Harvard and Yale. And like O'Hara he was a master of realism, totally attuned to the nuances of American behavior and speech." Lawrence ended, "You know what I think he would have said to all this? 'C'mon, Sam, knock it off. Let's have a drink.'"

And so they did. While a jazz pianist played the standards Yates had loved so well, an odd assortment of long-lost friends and family ate, drank, and caught up. Yates's nephews Peter and Fred Rodgers were there, as was his niece Ruth ("Dodo"), who spoke bitterly about her alcoholic mother. Grace Schulman was there; at one point guests had been asked to stand and share memories of Yates, and she mentioned the advice he'd given her as an apprentice poet ("Write with balls, Grace!") as well as the way he'd insisted on fining her and Jerry a dime for saying "unkind words about absent people." Wendy Sears was there, and read aloud a letter the lonely Yates had written from Hollywood in 1965, all about how cheered he'd been by a Father's Day poem from the eight-year-old Monica. Bob Riche was there, despite having written a 1990 novel whose protagonist Bill Brock (named after Riche's oafish persona in *Young Hearts Crying*) reflects thus on his old friend "Pritch Bates": "[He] managed to squeeze out a half-dozen largely ignored lifeless novels in which with increasing bitterness he blamed his mother, his father, his sister, his ex-wives and whatever former friends he once had for the miserable mess he has since made of his life."* And Bob Parker was there, though he was a bit unsettled to learn that Monica ("I'm surprised to see *you*!") was bitterly aware of his 1985 lampoon, "A Clef": "So big deal Bob Parker," she wrote him afterward,

you had a few asshole qualities and Dad focused on those and brought them to life [i.e., in *Young Hearts Crying*]. . . . I hope in the end you see the compliment he paid you, deeming you artist enough to face that, the way he always did. When you read one of Dad's books you cringe at all the characters' foibles and feel uncomfortable and exposed. That is why his books aren't popular—only people who are made happy enough by great art for it to outweigh the discomfort can enjoy them. . . . Far from despising you he admired and wondered about you and considered you an authentic artist. He also considered your life luckier than his, and your nature safer.

---

*He sent the novel (*What Are We Doing in Latin America?*) "for old times' sake" to Yates, who replied graciously: "Reading about 'Pritchard Bates' did inflict an acute little cut, but it was mercifully brief and therefore hardly comparable to my own more extended and clumsy swiping at 'Bill Brock' in a failed '84 novel that I'll always regret having written." Yates sent a glowing blurb to the publisher in behalf of Riche's book.

"Don't be sorry for coming to the funeral," Monica added in the margin. "Sharon and I were happy to see you in spite of ourselves—we both agreed it was kind and admirable of you to have made a point of being there."

Andre Dubus hosted another, somewhat smaller memorial service at Harvard's Lamont Library on February 3, Yates's sixty-seventh birthday. Notably absent on both occasions was Yates's daughter Gina—in Arizona at the time. "I knew it would be a literary event," she explained, "and that whole side of Dad's life was separate from our relationship."

Four months after Yates's death, Sam Lawrence came to the "painful conclusion" that *Uncertain Times* wasn't "complete enough to publish": "There are, of course, wonderful things in it and how we wish your father could have finished it and made it the novel he envisioned," he wrote Monica. "But to publish it in its present state would serve neither the loyal Yates fans and readers nor his own memory. As you well know, your father was a perfectionist and I doubt if he would have wanted this manuscript published or possibly even read in its unfinished state." Lawrence had decided not to pursue collection of the large unearned advance, in deference to "an author [he] loved and admired." Ten months later—just over a year after Yates's death—Lawrence himself died of a heart attack. Yates was not listed by the *Times* as one of the "many important writers" Lawrence had introduced to the public, though Richard Brautigan and J. P. Donleavy were.

In his will Yates left everything to his daughters in equal shares, and named Monica his executor. He died deep in debt, and remained so even after Lawrence forgave the advances. There was David Milch's "walking-around money," which perhaps bothered Yates's shade (*"I'll get him that goddamn $36,000!"*) if not Milch, but the federal government wasn't so easily appeased. Again and again Monica was contacted about her father's unpaid income tax, until finally even the IRS realized that collection was hopeless. "It was a big hole," said Monica, "and we turned our backs on it all and felt bad."

Yates's first wife Sheila, however, inherited her mother's shrewdness about money, and lives comfortably on her investments after retiring as a schoolteacher. Monica once mentioned to her father that Sheila had managed to save one hundred thousand dollars: "Why doesn't she give *you* a thousand, baby?" said Yates. "Then she'd have *ninety-nine* thousand fucking dollars saved!" Eventually Sheila came through in her own way. When Monica was engaged to a surgeon named Brian Shapiro in 1995, her mother paid for a modest wedding in Scarsdale. At the reception Sharon asked Harvey Shapiro (no relation to Monica's husband) to go introduce himself to Sheila. "Hi," he said. "I'm Harvey Shapiro. I knew your husband." Sheila gave him a hard stare and walked away without a word.

Sheila's brother Charlie is alive and spry. For the last decade or so he's worked as a ward clerk at the last VA hospital where he was a patient. He's often floated from ward to ward, as he has a tendency to rearrange the nurses' station wherever he goes: "They set it up to talk on the *phone,*" he says emphatically, "not to *work*!" The only people he sees are family, and during holidays he hovers about the kitchen bouncing on the balls of his feet à la John Givings.

Martha Speer moved to Hancock, Michigan, after her second marriage ended in 1993.

As for Monica, she went on to lead the sort of life that her father had always thought would be most fulfilling for her: She is now a housewife and mother to three boys and a girl.

As young women both Sharon and Monica suffered a single "isolated psychotic episode," never to recur; Gina's turn came in 1998. She and her husband had been traveling almost five months out of every year, and after a bout of dysentery in Southeast Asia, Gina began to experience a euphoric sense of omniscience. For a while she thought she was a witch with psychic powers, and just before a long blackout she fancied herself the Goddess of the North Pole (emergency room medics were on hand, so she thought at the time, to verify this). A little later her father appeared to her, and Gina asked him what the secret to being a great writer was. "Is that all you want to know?" he smiled ("as if to imply that there were more important things in life," said Gina). "All right. If you really want to know, then I'll tell you." Very deliberately he spoke the words: "It's all in that last . . . final . . . hesitation. But if you don't want to end up like me, you have to *reverse* it." Gina lay in bed intoning, over and over, *Reverse that final hesitation.* . . . When she related Yates's cryptic advice to her half-sister Monica, the latter burst out laughing: "I was really hoping there'd be something in there we could *use!*" she said. "What are we supposed to do with that?"

Yates's ashes, still in their original shipping box, reside in the basement of Sharon's house in Brooklyn. She and Monica can't decide what to do with them; they've considered scattering them in Washington Square or, better still, over all of Manhattan from a plane. Their exasperated mother tells them to take the box down the street to Green-Wood Cemetery, where no less than Peter Cooper and Louis Comfort Tiffany are buried. But Sharon's gotten used to having the ashes in her basement; recently, when Yates finally got a story in *The New Yorker,* she gave the shipping box a little shake: "Way to go, Dad!"

"To write so well and then to be forgotten is a terrifying legacy," Stewart O'Nan wrote in his 1999 essay, "The Lost World of Richard Yates"— O'Nan went on to predict, however, "Eventually the books will make it back in print, just as Faulkner's and Fitzgerald's did, and Yates will take his place in the American canon." In the years after Yates's death, as his books dropped out of print and his reputation seemed headed for almost total oblivion, a number of devotees (mostly writers themselves) continued to press Yates's work on a new generation of readers—to preserve what Robin Metz called "the tradition continuum from Flaubert to Fitzgerald to Yates"—to enact a "cultural-literary secret handshake," as Richard Ford would have it. Yates's former students have felt the apostolic burden most keenly. DeWitt Henry calls Yates "one of the few good voices in [his] head," and he tries to impart that voice to his own students: "I hear his vigilant hectoring always, for genuine clarity, genuine feeling, the right word, the exact English sentence, the eloquent detail, the rigorous dramatization of story. Don't evade. Don't cheat." Another student, Edwin Weihe, remembers the loving way Yates found "small truths" in his students' stories, "the descriptions of things, like a hanger snapping when you jerked a coat from it." Many years later Weihe encountered Yates again, and asked if his old teacher remembered him. "Yes, of course," the latter replied, "the snapping hanger." "Richard Yates," said Weihe— echoing Ford, echoing others—"was the place you went back to."

The resurrection of Richard Yates began in earnest with Random House's 2000 edition of *Revolutionary Road,* with an introduction by Ford that was also published in the *New York Times Book Review.* Ford described the novel as a "cultish standard," especially among writers "who have kept its reputation burnished by praising it, teaching it, some-times unwittingly emulating its apparent effortlessness, its complete acces-sibility, its luminous particularity, its deep seriousness toward us human beings, about whom it conjures shocking insights and appraisals." This edition has continued to sell briskly, such that one might venture to hope that *Revolutionary Road* is now installed in the so-called canon, whatever that is. The novel was listed by the Harvard Book Store as one of the "100 Favorite Titles" among college students, and the Dalkey Archive Press named it one of their thirty "Most Influential Novels of the 20th Cen-tury." When a new edition was published in the UK in 2001, Paul Con-nolly of *The Times* noted that "finally the British reading public will be given the opportunity to discover America's finest forgotten author." Also that year—a banner year in what one is emboldened to call the Yates Revival—Holt published *The Collected Stories of Richard Yates,* which actually made best-seller lists in Washington, Boston, San Francisco, and elsewhere. New editions of *The Easter Parade, A Good School,* and *A Special Providence* have followed, and soon perhaps Yates's entire oeuvre will be back in print—to stay.

One imagines Yates pleased, if not particularly happy. Like his own characters, he couldn't help being who he was; if he'd lived to see his fame increase, no doubt he'd fret over his imperfections all the more, and resume the lonely struggle to do better ("this crazy, obsessive business of trying to be a good writer"), while he endured his nonwriting life as best he could—which is to say, not very well. "Henry James spoke of the 'obstinate finality of human being,'" said David Milch, "and Dick was that. He was an aching example of what an artist is, and what being an artist *doesn't* solve in our human predicament."

Perhaps, but imagine a Richard Yates to whom it never occurred to write a word, and *there* would be a picture of misery, rather than one of redemptive heroism. And happiness too—yes—that, too, after a fashion. "I remember how much you laughed," said Andre Dubus in memoriam, "how easy it was to make you laugh, how much of your laughter was at yourself.

It's your mornings I imagine, Dick; you never complained to me about your body, so I imagine you waking to a room, a world, that seemed to have enough air for everyone but you, and gathering yourself, putting on those gentleman's clothes you wore, and bringing your great heart and your pure writer's conscience to the desk, the legal pad, the pencil. You just kept doing it, morning after morning, and you inspired me, you gave me courage, taking your morning stand against your flesh and circumstance, writing your prose that was like a blade, a cloud, a flame, a breath.

So you rest, old friend. I'll always love you. And about all those words you wrote in all your books on my shelf, I'll say as you used to about a book or story you loved: They're swell, Dick, they're really swell; it's a sweetheart of a life's work, it's a sweetheart.

Notes

The following abbreviations appear in these notes:

BU-MM   Mugar Memorial Library, Boston University, Monica McCall
          Collection

BU-RY   Mugar Memorial Library, Boston University, Richard Yates
          Collection

CSH   *Cold Spring Harbor*

CSRY   *The Collected Stories of Richard Yates*

DP   *Disturbing the Peace*

EP   *The Easter Parade*

GS   *A Good School*

RR   *Revolutionary Road*

RY   Richard Yates

SP   *A Special Providence*

UM-SL   J. D. Williams Library, University of Mississippi, Seymour
          Lawrence Collection

YHC   *Young Hearts Crying*

Most of the letters to Richard Yates cited below are from his personal papers, and I'm deeply grateful for permission to quote from them. With the signal exception of Yates's letters to Sheila in 1953 (copies of which were found among his papers), letters from Yates are in the hands of the recipients unless otherwise noted. Quotations are only cited when the source is not explicitly given in the text. Interview subjects are cited initially, and thereafter only when needed for the sake of clarity;

otherwise the reader may assume that uncited quotations are from personal interviews.

Prologue

1. "a touch of emphysema": Int. Monica Yates Shapiro.
1. "Can you believe it?": Int. Tom Goldwasser.
2. "Getting out of here": Elizabeth Venant, "A Fresh Twist in the Road," *Los Angeles Times,* July 9, 1989, section 6, page 8.
2. "The Host of Yates fans": Don Hendrie Jr. to RY, April 27, 1989.
3. "We were touched": Int. Tony Earley.
3. "The implication": Int. Allen Wier.
5. "Not much for one": Quoted in Steve Featherstone, "November 7, 1992," *Black Warrior Review* 21, no. 1 (Fall/Winter 1994), 157–158.

Chapter One *The Caliche Road: 1926–1939*

7. "My little legs": Int. Grace Schulman.
7. "I must've had the most": Ms. of "A Natural Girl," BU-RY.
8. she later spelled *Darke*: Ruth Yates misspelled the name of her home county on her application for a Social Security number, April 21, 1943.
9. "He says I am the best clerk": Amos Maurer to Fannie Walden, July 29, 1873, papers of Rev. Peter Rodgers.
9. "I should like to have seen": F. Walden to A. Maurer, August 3, 1873, ibid.
9. "[He] was buried": F. Walden to A. Maurer, October 10, 1873, ibid.
9. "I know thine's no worldly heart": A. Maurer to F. Walden, October 16, 1873, ibid.
10. "Uncle Dick never liked": Ruth Rodgers to Peter Rodgers, May 21, 1964, ibid.
11. For Ruth Maurer Yates's misdated entry see *Who's Who of American Women,* 2nd ed. (Chicago: Marquis, 1962), 1091.
11. "[S]he had probably grown up": *CSRY,* 184.
11. "I know," he replied: Int. Peter Rodgers. The Reverend Mr. Rodgers was kind enough to share his considerable genealogical research on the Cleveland and Bradford lines of the Yates family.
12. Details of Horatio Yates's career are derived from his obituaries in the *Auburn Citizen* and the *Auburn Daily Advertiser,* April 4, 1912.
12. Such a life was conducive: Warden Gershom Powers is quoted in John N. Miskell, "Offering Hope: The Connection between Auburn Theological Seminary and Auburn State Prison," unpublished manuscript, papers of John N. Miskell.
12. Details of Kemmler's friendship with Chaplain Yates are derived from the *Auburn-Cayuga Patriot,* August 5, 1890; for the description of Kemmler's electrocution, I'm indebted to Ted Conover's account in his book, *Newjack: Guarding Sing Sing* (New York: Random House, 2000), 187–188.

14. "[H]e came upon his father": "Lament for a Tenor," *Cosmopolitan,* February 1954, 50–57.
14. "Dook knew right away": Sheila Yates to RY, July 22, 1953.
15. "I didn't give a shit": Int. Seymour Epstein.
16. "because [he] could scarcely": *CSRY,* 179.
17. As he explained in a 1972: DeWitt Henry and Geoffrey Clark, "An Interview with Richard Yates," *Ploughshares* 1, no. 3 (Winter 1972), 69. Hereafter cited as *Ploughshares.*
18. she even pretended: Int. Peter Rodgers.
18. "broaden his horizons": Letter to author from Barbara Beury McCallum.
19. "confused and unpleasant": *SP,* 123.
20. Her family hadn't approved: Ruth Rodgers to Peter Rodgers, May 21, 1964, Rodgers papers.
20. "Elsa was very sensible": Int. Sheila Yates.
20. "Dook's fantastic schemes": Sheila Yates to RY, June 15, 1953.
20. "hysterical odyssey": *SP,* 10.
21. "the only new boy": Ibid.
22. she smelled bad: E-mail to author from Gina Yates.
22. "cruel, bullying voices": Int. Frances Doel.
23. "I wasn't a bookish child": "Some Very Good Masters," *New York Times Book Review,* April 19, 1981, 3.
24. Dookie and "Cush" became friends: Ruth Rodgers to Peter Rodgers, undated letter, Rodgers papers.
24. "they would get together and trash things": Int. Stephen Benedict.
24. "Richard, we are growing old": Elisabeth Cushman to RY, May 8, 1945.
25. "liked to use words like 'simpatico' ": *SP,* 138.
25. "a sad-eyed, seven-year-old philosopher": *CSRY, 195.*
25. "Yates felt enraged": Int. Dr. Winthrop A. Burr.
26. "the most stable": *CSH,* 46.
26. "They were comrades": Int. Martha Speer.
27. As a teenager she joined: Int. Peter Rodgers.
28. BUST GIVEN ROOSEVELT: *New York Times,* April 16, 1933, section 2, page 3.
28. "had a wife in England": *SP,* 143.
29. "the question of whether or not": Ibid., 157.
30. lest he seem a sissy: Int. Nancy Cushman Dibner.
30. Background about the Vanderlip estate in Scarborough, as well as Cheever's time there, is found in Susan Cheever, *Home Before Dark* (New York: Pocket Books, 1985), and *The Letters of John Cheever,* ed. Benjamin Cheever (New York: Simon & Schuster, 1988).
31. "He used to speak of it": Int. Sharon Yates Levine.
31. Yates submitted a blank sheet: Int. Nancy Cushman Dibner.

31. "He doodled on everything": *Richard Yates: An American Writer* (New York: Seymour Lawrence, 1993), 17. Hereafter cited as *RYAW*.

32. "I remember how you used to delight us": Mary Jo McClusky Sup to RY, March 7, 1977.

32. "The only noise I hear all day": RY to Stephen Benedict, April 2, 1940.

32. "We energetically rehearsed": *RYAW*, 18.

33. "Dookie hired a Mr. Bostelman": Int. Nancy Cushman Dibner.

33. Russell Benedict . . . started a weekly newspaper: Int. Russell Benedict.

33. "Had dinner tonight with an old boyhood": RY to Barbara Beury, February 15, 1961.

36. "I guess I sort of love her": Quoted in Geoffrey Clark, "The Best I Can Wish You," *Northeast Corridor* 1, no. 2 (1994), 34.

Chapter Two *A Good School: 1939–1944*

37. "We're celeberaties": RY to Stephen Benedict, March 7, 1940.

37. " 'blow-by-slug' description": RY to Benedict, February 13, 1940.

38. "just like a big kaht": RY to Benedict, September 16, 1939.

38. "I really wrote you the verra nite": RY to Benedict, November 14, 1939.

38. "It will be peachy": RY to Benedict, March 7, 1940.

39. "My school is peachy (oh-so)": RY to Benedict, October 24, 1939.

40. "Aubrey Beardsley mouth": Int. Murray Moulding.

40. "You might be inerested": RY to Benedict, December 5, 1939.

40. "Me and another guy who swings": RY to Benedict, October 24, 1939.

40. "You're invited to a peachy joint": RY to Benedict, c. June, 1940.

40. "Bud Hoyt is getting": RY to Benedict, July 6, 1940.

41. "You can still come": RY to Benedict, July 28, 1940.

42. Background on the Rodgers family, Ruth's courtship with Fred, and life on "Genius Row" is mostly derived from my interviews with Ruth's sister-in-law, Louise Rodgers.

43. "Oh, I believe in humanity": *EP*, 74.

44. "and I only passed History": "Ten Americans to Watch," *Pageant*, February 1963, 43.

44. "Such 'movie-haunted' stories": "Some Very Good Masters," 3.

45. "conceived in the studios": *GS*, 5.

45. Background on Theodate Pope Riddle and Avon Old Farms: Brooks Enemy, *Theodate Pope Riddle and the Founding of Avon Old Farms* (Avon, Conn.: Avon Old Farms School, 1973); Clarence Derrick, "Recollections of Avon Old Farms School 1935–1941," unpublished manuscript, papers of Daniel Gates; Gordon Ramsey, *Aspiration and Perseverance: The History of Avon Old Farms School* (Avon, Conn.: Avon Old Farms School, 1984).

46. "in aging they would warp and sag": *GS*, 5.

47. "Given good-enough clothes": *YHC*, 347.
48. " 'FRANKLIN SIMON!' the students yelled": Int. Lothar Candels.
49. "That's me, all right": Int. Harry Flynn.
49. "What a flood of memories": Mason Beekley to RY, December 11, 1978.
49. "almost unalloyed in its misery": *SP*, 12.
49. "the pain implicit": Quoted in *Writer's Choice,* ed. Rust Hills (New York: David McKay Co., 1974).
50. "held together by safety pins": Int. Seymour Epstein.
50. "Thin, haggard, disheveled": Int. David Bigelow.
50. "Dick was obviously poorer": Int. Hugh Pratt.
50. "He was fragile": Int. Jim Stewart.
51. " 'Sue the bastard' ": Richard E. T. Hunter to RY, February 19, 1979.
51. Yates was not actually masturbated: Int. Irv. Jennings.
52. "wondering how he was going to live": *GS*, 27.
52. Details relating to the wedding of Ruth Yates and Fred Rodgers are derived from my interviews with Louise Rodgers.
54. "mutual admiration society": Int. Lothar Candels.
55. "I suppose you know Ruth is married": RY to S. Benedict, August 24, 1942.
55. "Re-reading the Cold Spring Harbor letter": Letter to author from Stephen Benedict.
56. "All I do is rush around": RY to S. Benedict, August 24, 1942.
58. Yates was at Van Nordan's bedside: Int. Sheila Yates.
58. A mutual friend described Pratt: Int. David Bigelow.
59. "Dick ran everything": Letter to author from Gilman Ordway.
59. Information about Ernest "Bick" Wright is derived from my interviews with his widow, Ann Wright Jones, and his friend Don Nickerson.
61. Family lore has it: Int. Fred Rodgers Jr.
62. "Emily fucking Grimes is *me*": *RYAW*, 21.
63. "All I'm really qualified to remember": *GS*, 177.
63. "Cigarettes were a great help": *Uncertain Times* ms., hereafter cited as *UT*.
64. "learning how to behave in college": *GS*, 94.
64. "quite good": Int. David Bigelow.
66. "struggling artist": Int. Hugh Pratt.
67. This account of summer 1943 is mostly based on pages 13–16 of *A Special Providence,* whose essential accuracy has been corroborated by letters and interviews. Dookie's employment at the Optima Optical Company is noted on her Social Security application, likewise RY's employment at the *New York Sun,* which he later also mentioned in *Pageant* magazine (February 1963), 43.
70. "I think you're pretty good": Elizabeth Nowell Perkins to RY, November 7, 1943.
72. It was a bad Christmas: Int. Ann Barker.

Chapter Three *The Canal: 1944–1947*

75. "People don't recover": Quoted in David Streitfeld, "The Great Unknown," *Fame*, Summer 1990, 30.

75. "Do you like girls?": E-mail to author from Gina Yates.

76. "[They] tend to sort in large groups": Quoted in Kay Redfield Jamison, *Touched with Fire: Manic-Depressive Illness and the Artistic Temperament* (New York: Free Press, 1993), 107.

77. "mild and pampered": *SP*, 29.

77. "Dick was hilarious": Int. Pat Dubus.

78. "Dick cultivated an anti-intellectual manner": Int. DeWitt Henry.

78. Basic information about Yates's military service is taken from his honorable discharge, dated June 19, 1946.

80. "He took pride in delivering": *SP*, 86.

80. "I mean after this Horbourg business": Ibid., 89.

81. A doctor . . . poked him in the chest: Int. Sheila Yates.

81. peculiar stench of the pneumonia ward: Int. Dan Childress.

81. "shut off [his] mind": *UT*.

82. Knorr had been the B.A.R. man: Int. Janis Knorr.

82. Yates . . . would occasionally claim . . . B.A.R. man: Int. Franklin Russell and Edward Hoagland.

82. "more goddamn trouble": *CSRY*, 375.

83. "out of badly made shoes and boots": Seymour Krim to RY, September 24, 1978. In the letter Krim paraphrases Yates's remark to this effect.

84. Dookie and Elisabeth Cushman's boozy celebration of VE-day is recounted in Cushman's letter to RY, May 8, 1945.

84. "seriously afraid something had happened to [him]": Ernest B. Wright to RY, May 31, 1945.

85. "enjoy good food, women": Davis Pratt to RY, May 17, 1945.

85. "Your knowledge . . . mayhap": Hugh Pratt to RY, June 2, 1946.

86. "one of the brethren": H. W. Harwood to RY, February 22, 1946.

86. "Connie says . . . plaything": "Joan" [last name unknown] to RY, February 2, 1946.

87. "He was full of . . . joie de vivre": Int. Tony Vevers.

87. "Yates, please tell me": "F. G." [?] to RY, March 9, 1946.

87. "You don't sound very keen": "Joan" to RY, February 18, 1946.

88. Details of Yates's morose homecoming to High Hedges are derived from my interviews with Louise Rodgers and Fred Rodgers Jr.

89. Yates's postwar stint at the radical *York Gazette and Daily* were mentioned in interviews with two people otherwise unknown to each other, Ken Rosen and Natalie Baturka.

90. "At twenty, fresh out of the Army": "Some Very Good Masters," 3.

90. "dumb, arrogant thing to do": *Pageant,* February 1963, 43.

90. "God, you can't mean that!": Quoted in Clark, "The Best I Can Wish You," 30–31.

90. "Wishing I'd Gone Myself": RY to Peter Najarian, September 24, 1960.

91. it just wasn't "real journalism": Int. Monica Yates Shapiro.

91. RY's postwar freelancing escapades with Russell Benedict are based on my interviews with the latter.

91. "No, I didn't know": Virginia Shafer Cox to RY, July 8, 1961.

92. "Bick was right about that, too": Int. Ann Wright Jones.

93. "I am sorry to hear": "Joan" to RY, November 15, 1946.

94. " 'back on [her] feet' in no time": *CSRY,* 298.

94. According to records provided by Pen and Brush, Ruth Yates was named "Resident Sculptor" in June 1944.

95. "oddly satisfying": *CSRY,* 299.

95. "utterly defeated": Ibid.

Chapter Four *Liars in Love: 1947–1951*

96. Russell Benedict . . . beginning to pall: RY had suggested as much in a letter to Sheila Yates, June 29, 1953.

96. "young, poor, bright": Sheila Yates to RY, c. June 1953. Sheila was clearly expressing an ideal coveted by both her and RY.

96. "trying to figure out": *CSRY,* 300–301.

96. *plerb* ("a synonym for . . ."): from the 1944 *Winged Beaver* yearbook. Macaulay's role in introducing RY to Sheila was mentioned by the latter.

97. For background on Sheila's father, Charles Bryant, I'm greatly indebted to Gavin Lambert, *Nazimova* (New York: Alfred A. Knopf, 1997).

98. Marjorie would go on . . . John Birch: Int. Sharon Yates Levine.

99. "very good at acting the actress": Int. Ann Barker.

100. "the movies had proved": *CSRY,* 301.

100. "terribly good-looking": Int. Doris Bialek.

101. "half-phoney art talk": RY to Sheila Yates, July 1, 1953.

101. found the two in bed together: The friend was Jerry Cain, and the anecdote was supplied by a May 17, 1953 letter from Sheila to RY: "Do you know why [Cain] was so cool to me when we first knew them? Well, it seems they thought I was some loose Village girl you'd got mixed up with who was ruining your life and sleeping around for laughs."

102. "[Y]ou had [my writing] figured": RY to Sheila Yates, June 8, 1953.

103. "I borrowed three hundred dollars": *CSRY,* 304.

103. Blanchard "Jerry" Cain: E-mail to author from Robin Cain.

104. Cain would later remark: Ibid.

105. "Hansel and Gretel cottage": Int. David Bigelow.
105. "Unusual free-lance opportunity": Sheila Yates confirmed that Yates did indeed ghostwrite for a cabbie as described in "Builders."
106. The editors of *Harper's*: Letters from the magazine to RY, December 7, 1949, and January 3, 1950.
106. "in meekness and urgency": *CSRY*, 304.
107. "sweating out the ax": Ibid., 161.
107. "right in the middle": Ibid., 168.
107. winding up toy kittens: Robin Cain confirmed that Yates actually held such a job.
107. "badly printed": *CSRY*, 72.
108. "unabashed worshiper": Robert Lacy, "Remembering Richard Yates," *North Stone Review* 12 (1995), 215.
109. "formal introduction to the craft": "Some Very Good Masters," 3.
109. "to Fitzgerald and Lardner": "Authors Comment on Living Author They Most Admire," *New York Times Book Review*, December 4, 1977, 3.
109. "the essence of aplomb": Letter to author from Natalie Bowen.
112 . Yates attempted suicide: Int. Sheila Yates.
112 . "big, ambitious, tragic novel": *CSRY*, 169.
112. "Mr. Yates may understand": RY to Barbara Beury, October 24, 1960.
113. "[A]ll I knew then": *CSRY*, 317.
114. "I think death was on": Ms. of "Regards at Home," BU-RY.
114. "Harvard, Yale, and Princeton": *RYAW*, 61.
114. "without whose work": "Some Very Good Masters," 21.
115. "that cat belongs": Int. John Kowalsky.
115. "grass widow": Int. Ann Barker.
115. "wait-and-see basis": RY to Sheila Yates, May 10, 1953.
116. "you're the only person": Sheila Yates to RY, August 11, 1953.
116. "anywhere in the world": *CSRY*, 317. Letters to RY from the Veterans Administration confirm the exact monthly sum of $207.
116. "steer clear of the conventional": RY to Stephen Benedict, March 8, 1951.
116. "Our only plans": RY to Stephen Benedict, March 25, 1951.
116. "cramped farewell . . . I had luck": *CSRY*, 318–19.

Chapter Five *The Getaway: 1951–1953*

118. "walked himself weak": *RR*, 132.
118. "[grind] out short stories": RY to Stephen Benedict, April 10, 1953.
118. "that awful feeling": Sheila Yates to RY, April 7, 1953.
122. "[Pinner's] old broken espadrilles": RY to Sheila Yates, May 10, 1953.
122. "Yates is without question a writer": Monica McCall to Charles Bryant, January 15, 1952.

122. Background on Monica McCall: Int. Mitch Douglas, Robert Gottlieb, and Richard Frede; also McCall's Social Security SS-5 form.

123. "please call [him] Dick": McCall to RY, February 1, 1952.

124. McCall responded . . . critique: McCall to RY, March 6, 1952.

125. "At its best and sunniest": E-mail to author from Stephen Benedict.

125. "semi-separation in Cannes": Sheila Yates to RY, January 17, 1962.

125. "Yates has a lot of talent": this and other rejections were quoted in McCall's letter to RY dated April 4, 1952.

126. "perfectly handled": Quoted in McCall to RY, October 22, 1952.

126. "Why does he have to write": Quoted in McCall to RY, c. September, 1952.

126. "What a good story": McCall to RY, April 24, 1952.

126. "[T]he playboy setting": Quoted in McCall to RY, c. September, 1952.

126. "The cruelty which forms": Quoted in McCall to RY, February 1, 1955.

126. "let-down": Quoted in McCall to RY, July 15, 1957.

126. "Hope you . . . will let us": Quoted in McCall to RY, February 20, 1958.

127. "Rust Hills did have the grace": McCall to RY, May 15, 1958.

127. "too pat": Quoted in McCall to RY, May 28, 1958.

127. "for fairly obvious": Quoted in McCall to RY, May 21, 1958.

127. "I'm a jazz snob": Int. Vance Bourjaily.

128. "It is a good story": McCall to RY, April 4, 1952.

129. "Close, but no cigar": Quoted in McCall to RY, September 16, 1952.

129. "You are progressing well": McCall to RY, July 1, 1952.

129. "swell story": McCall to RY, July 8, 1952.

129. "an esoteric little": Quoted in McCall to RY, September 16, 1952.

130. "[they] should be more acted out": McCall to RY, August 18, 1952.

130. "readable and amusing": Quoted in Rosalie Becker to RY, July 28, 1953.

130. "on the basis . . . God's sake": RY to Sheila Yates, c. August 1953.

132. "suffers from a confusion": Quoted in McCall to RY, October 1, 1952.

132. play games like: Int. Sharon Yates Levine.

132. "snarky and sick": Sheila Yates to RY, July 22, 1953.

132. "perfect . . . outside aspects": Sheila Yates to RY, August 11, 1953.

133. "quarreling had belonged": CSRY, 240.

133. "Number 15 off the production": RY to Stephen Benedict, April 10, 1953.

133. "Oh the new one": McCall to RY, September 16, 1952.

133. "by the narrowest margin": Quoted in McCall to RY, October 15, 1952.

133. ATLANTIC BUYING JODY: McCall to RY, October 21, 1952.

134. "Sweet of you": McCall to RY, October 27, 1952.

134. "That was one grand": Frances Phillips to RY, January 30, 1953.

134. "I should like . . . opportunity": Jacques Chambrun to RY, January 28, 1953.

134. "I want to tell . . . Jody": Seymour Lawrence to RY, February 6, 1953.

134. "Stand in the stream": from the class notes of RY's student, Loree Wilson Rackstraw.

135. "You've done it with 'Jody' ": J. S. Dorsey to RY, c. February 1953.

135. "sensitive . . . basic trainee's": Lt. Col. Roger Little to RY, July 26, 1965.

136. "prick with ears!": Int. Sharon Yates Levine.

136. "If he were free": Sheila Yates to RY, April 7, 1953.

137. "Bryant family emergency": RY to Stephen Benedict, April 10, 1953.

137. "Talk about missing": RY to Sheila Yates, March 26, 1953.

138. "Dear Rich . . . I felt so sad": Sheila Yates to RY, April 2, 1953.

138. "Sheila and Ruth and Sheila's mother": Elsa Maurer to RY, May 3, 1953.

138. "knick-knacky and scatter-ruggy": Sheila Yates to RY, April 7, 1953.

138. "Charlie's hate is making him sick": Sheila Yates to RY, c. April 1953.

139. "far, far too American": Dorothy Daly to RY, April 17, 1953.

139. "[she] showed . . . Sweetheart": Sheila Yates to RY, April 12, 1953.

139. "I know nothing . . . pictures": McCall to Sheila Yates, April 23, 1953.

139. "[M]ost of my ideas": RY to Stephen Benedict, April 10, 1953.

139. "trying to explain . . . sentimentality": RY to Sheila Yates, May 10, 1953.

139. "Oh that is a wonderful story!": McCall to RY, May 18, 1953.

139. "ever seems to talk about": RY to Sheila Yates, July 1, 1953.

140. "[I]t'll be nice . . . to share": RY to Sheila Yates, March 31, 1953.

141. "In the past three months": RY to Sheila Yates, June 23, 1953.

141. "a beautiful sunlit garden": Sheila Yates to RY, April 7, 1953.

141. "completely recessed": Sheila Yates to RY, April 12, 1953.

142. "Haf a chicherette, gramer": Sheila Yates to RY, April 7, 1953.

142. " 'innumerable things' he didn't write": Sheila Yates to RY, April 20, 1953.

142. "a far cry from the drab": RY to Sheila Yates, May 5, 1953.

143. "decidedly not queer": RY to Sheila Yates, May 10, 1953.

143. "seem[ed] to spend . . . money": RY to Sheila Yates, May 21, 1953.

143. "Here's this month's alimony": RY to Sheila Yates, May 5, 1953.

143. "I sort of forgot": Sheila Yates to RY, c. May 1953.

144. "Charlie's offer of the $165": RY to Sheila Yates, May 10, 1953.

145. "Everything you say about us" Sheila Yates to RY, May 17, 1953.

145. "income just over the horizon": Sheila Yates to RY, late May, 1953.

145. "pray that the time comes soon": Elsa Maurer to RY, May 3, 1953.

145. "pretty childish attitude": RY to Sheila Yates, May 30, 1953.

146. "wasteland": Sheila Yates to RY, May 17, 1953.

146. "The Levittown houses": Sheila Yates to RY, late May 1953.

146. "creative slump": RY to Sheila Yates, May 21, 1953.

146. "completely aimless, pointless": RY to Sheila Yates, June 16, 1953.

146. "bitter astringency of tone": Jean Malcolm to RY, June 11, 1953.

146. "[didn't] have room . . . boy": Quoted in McCall to RY, June 12, 1953.

146. coronation . . . "terrific show": RY to Sheila Yates, June 8, 1953.

146. "grubby, homely Village type": RY to Sheila Yates, June 16, 1953.
147. "about a million . . . biddies": RY to Sheila Yates, June 8, 1953.
147. "wolloping good party": RY to Sheila Yates, June 23, 1953.
147. "there mightn't be anyone": Sheila Yates to RY, June 29, 1953.
147. "We're never going to get rich": RY to Sheila Yates, May 30, 1953.
148. "If you had a job": Sheila Yates to RY, June 4, 1953.
148. "violent opposition": RY to Sheila Yates, June 8, 1953.
148. "demand[ing] restitution . . . rights": RY to Sheila Yates, June 23, 1953.
149. "rush around trying to do their best": *Ploughshares*, 69.
150. "stay of execution": Sheila Yates to RY, June 19, 1953.
150. "I am praying": Sheila Yates to RY, June 29, 1953.
150. "She'd never stimulate me": Sheila Yates to RY, June 1, 1953.
150. "If I do come home before August": RY to Sheila Yates, June 8, 1953.
150. "[kick] up an awful row": Sheila Yates to RY, June 29, 1953.
150. "feed [Mussy] lots of ice cream": RY to Sheila Yates, July 9, 1953.
150. "For a while . . . zenith": Ms. of "The Game of Ambush," BU-RY.
151. "pretty good B-plus": RY to Sheila Yates, June 16, 1953.
151. "[I]t's *technically* as good": RY to Sheila Yates, June 23, 1953.
151. "as good or perhaps better": Sheila Yates to RY, July 9, 1953.
151. "It came to me in a flash": RY to Sheila Yates, July 9, 1953.
152. Sheila changed "('pretty good')": Sheila Yates to RY, July 1, 1953.
152. "I remember thinking . . . cliché": Sheila Yates to RY, mid-July 1953.
152. "I love the story": McCall to RY, July 14, 1953.
152. "stubborn as a mule": RY to Sheila Yates, July 24, 1953.
152. "funny and nice letter": Rosalie Becker to RY, July 28, 1953.
152. "continue[d] to be interested": Quoted in McCall to RY, August 27, 1953.
152. "drearier and drearier": RY to Sheila Yates, July 1, 1953.
153. COSMOPOLITAN BUYING: McCall to RY, July 14, 1953.
153. "How much money . . . *stand*?": RY to Sheila Yates, July 17, 1953.
154. "[McCall] has left me . . . jam": RY to Sheila Yates, July 24, 1953.
155. "what an odd view": Sheila Yates to RY, August 11, 1953.
156. "Absence . . . grow fonder": RY to Sheila Yates, August 17, 1953.
156. "quaint and Villagy": Sheila Yates to RY, August 9, 1953.
156. "it might be a bit awkward": RY to Sheila Yates, early September.
156. "all about meats": RY to Sheila Yates, August 21, 1953.
156. "with some temerity": Sheila Yates to RY, August 20, 1953.
156. "The main illustration": RY to Sheila Yates, early August, 1953.
157. "quite tasteful": Sheila Yates to RY, August 11, 1953.
157. "So I looked into cat-baskets": RY to Sheila Yates, August 21, 1953.
157. "a coloring book with *water*": Sheila Yates to RY, August 20, 1953.
157. "best-looking kind of suit": RY to Sheila Yates, early August 1953.
157. "[they'd] been . . . 1066": RY to Sheila Yates, August 12, 1953.

158. "I don't think . . . depressed": RY to Sheila Yates, early September.

158. the food was "wonderful": RY to Sheila Yates, September 12, 1953.

Chapter Six *A Cry of Prisoners: 1953–1959*

159. Andy Borno (the physical model . . .): Int. Robert Riche. Riche, who also wrote freelance PR for Remington Rand, was very helpful in explaining the nature of Yates's assignments.

159. "All this . . . boring stuff": *Contemporary Authors,* vol. 10, ed. Deborah A. Straube, New Revision Series (Detroit: Gale, 1981), 535.

161. "no different than I ever was": Riche to RY, March 21, 1991.

161. there was no flirtation: Int. Pamela Vevers.

162. "You know . . . mother works?": Int. Seymour Epstein.

162. Background on Dookie and the City Center: Jean Dalrymple, *From the Last Row* (Clifton, N. J.: James T. White and Co., 1975); "City Center Adds an Art Gallery," *New York Times,* September 15, 1953; "Art Gallery Opens in City Center Corridor," *New York Times,* September 30, 1953; Int. Louise Rodgers.

164. Twice a week . . . WGSM: Int. Fred Rodgers Jr.

165. "crack *The New Yorker*": Ruth Rodgers to Peter Rodgers, undated, Rodgers papers.

165. "a mellow sort of man": Int. Ruth Rodgers Ward.

166. "we would order . . . Jack Daniel's": *RYAW*, 55.

166. "a big deal for me": RY to DeWitt Henry, November 21, 1972.

166. "The first time I met Sam Lawrence": Joseph Kanon was quoted thus in Lawrence's obituary in the *New York Times,* January 7, 1994, A22.

166. Background on Lawrence: Int. DeWitt Henry, Merloyd Lawrence, and Dan Wakefield.

167. "The psychology . . . true": Lawrence to McCall, February 10, 1954.

167. "frankly stumped": McCall to RY, December 23, 1954.

167. "a little masterpiece": McCall to RY, September 24, 1954.

167. "The B.A.R. Man . . . New Yorker": McCall to RY, November 1, 1954.

167. "a beauty as usual": McCall to RY, December 6, 1954.

168. "Oh Bob, . . . better-looking": Int. Robert Riche.

170. "get the hell out": Int. Ann Barker.

170. "engineering square": Int. John Kowalsky.

170. "Stop this clownlike behavior": Int. Sharon Yates Levine.

171. "In Connecticut you . . . cops": Ibid.

172. "I hate the thought": Sheila Yates to RY, April 14, 1962.

174. "He kissed her . . . a little uncertain": Ms. of "The End of the Great Depression," BU-RY.

174. "get so involved . . . daydreams": Quoted in McCall to RY, January 3, 1955.

174. "The Walter Mitty scenes . . . clichés": Quoted in McCall to RY, November 15, 1957.

175. "Are you aware—you must be": Richard Mitchell to RY, undated. RY's response was written on the back of Mitchell's letter, and may not have been sent.

176. "I never thought of that": Int. Tim Parrish.

176. "that absolutely supreme . . . editor": McCall to RY, March 22, 1955.

176. "Like all publishers": McCall to RY, April 14, 1955.

177. "daily watching the mails": McCall to RY, October 21, 1955.

177. "I hope your silence": McCall to RY, January 10, 1956.

177. "real ability and . . . worth": Quoted in McCall to RY, May 8, 1956.

177. "I thought of the girl dying": *Ploughshares*, 66.

177. "*Very* much impressed": Lawrence to McCall, May 31, 1956.

177. "as a vote of our confidence": Lawrence to McCall, June 8, 1956.

178. "one of the many imitators": *RYAW*, 56.

178. "narrative competence": Quoted in McCall to RY, August 8, 1956.

178. "Most of my first drafts": *Ploughshares*, 68.

180. "Who's got my arm . . . ?": Int. Sharon Yates Levine.

181. "felt like a million dollars": RY to Booghie Salassie, December 29, 1979 (unmailed).

181. "your best [work has] . . . writer": Lawrence to RY, April 25, 1957.

181. "gotten away . . . women-hating": Quoted in McCall to RY, July 15, 1957.

181. "encouragingly": McCall to RY, September 9, 1959.

184. "I used to get a headache behind my eyes": Int. Robert Andrew Parker.

184. Background on the stomach-punching episode: Int. Tony and Elspeth Vevers, Peter Kane DuFault, Robert Parker, and Robert Riche.

185. "They seemed to connect": Int. Dot Parker.

185. singing a ribald ditty: Int. Robert Riche.

186. "Ever since I first met you": Sheila Yates to RY, c. January 1962.

186. Conrad Jones affair: "Bright Young Men in America," *Esquire*, September 1958.

186. "Greetings! I feel a little pale": Conrad Jones to Robert Parker, September 8, 1958, papers of Robert Andrew Parker.

186. "I surely do say 'yes'": Parker to Jones, undated. This letter and the ones that follow, though signed by Parker, were all but entirely written by Yates. Parker was kind enough to send me both the typed, polished versions of these letters, as well as holograph drafts (lovingly preserved) in Yates's handwriting.

188. "Margaret Truman" . . . "druggist's daughter": E-mail to author from Robert Riche.

188. precise ugly grimace: Int. Tony Vevers.

189. "kept cracking each other up": RY's memories of his first meetings with R. V. Cassill are contained in "Appreciation," *December* 23, nos. 1–2 (1981), 41–44.
190. "a happy and peaceful solution": McCall to RY, March 7, 1958.
190. "I have absolute faith": Lawrence to RY, April 30, 1958.
190. "I fully appreciate your longtime": McCall to Lawrence, May 13, 1958.
190. Reviews of *Short Story 1*: William Peden, *New York Times Review,* October 26, 1958; Granville Hicks, *Saturday Review of Literature,* September 13, 1958; R. H. Glauber, *New York Herald Tribune,* January 18, 1959; Kenneth Millar, *San Francisco Chronicle,* October 19, 1958.
191. "I can't remember when": Gina Berriault to RY, October 8, 1958.
191. "Richard Yates is my guardian angel": *RYAW,* 19.
193. "It seems to me now . . . Frank's idea . . . psychoanalyzed": Sheila Yates to RY, c. July 1962.
194. "needless expense" of divorce: RY to Barbara Beury, September 9, 1960.
194. "other commitments": RY to Paul Engle, c. August 1959.

Chapter Seven *A Glutton for Punishment: 1959–1961*
195. "thirty-three years ago": Peter Najarian, *The Great American Loneliness* (San Francisco: Blue Crane, 1999).
196. "My New School class": RY to Barbara Beury, September 30, 1960.
197. "If you were teaching": Int. Sidney Offit.
197. "Emphasis is on the craft and art": Yates's course description in the *New School Bulletin,* Fall 1960.
197. "He didn't seem into teaching": Int. Peter Najarian.
198. "a nineteen-year-old . . . delinquent": RY to R. V. Cassill, May 5, 1960.
198. "Theodore Schwertheim": RY to Peter Najarian, undated.
199. "You are worth a thousand": Najarian to RY, September 2, 1960.
199. "I've had a real ball": RY to Cassill, May 5, 1960.
199. "There was something broken": Int. Betty Rollin.
200. "I thought I was witnessing": Int. Gail Richards Tirana.
200. "It was exhausting": Int. Warren Owens.
201. "I felt we deserved . . . contempt": Susan Grossman to RY, c. March 1961.
201. "Baked Alaska!" . . . *A Star Is Born*: Int. Warren Owens.
201. "some of the finest autobiographical fiction": *Ploughshares,* 71.
201. "the greatest cocksman": Int. Anne Bernays.
202. "Dick was forthright . . . Broyard was the opposite": Int. R. V. Cassill.
202. "one of the most fruitful": Lawrence to RY, October 2, 1959.
203. "[T]his option was very important": Charles Scribner Jr. to RY, October 22, 1959.
203. "every sentence right": *RYAW,* 56.

203. "Although you may not learn": Lawrence to RY, March 30, 1960.

204. "Congratulations on your Bread Loaf": Lawrence to RY, June 22, 1960.

205. "funny evening": Lawrence to RY, July 8, 1960.

205. "[I]'s practically impossible": Lawrence to RY, July 12, 1960.

205. "Owing to its autobiographical": RY's undated Guggenheim statement, BU-MM.

205. "a work of history and not": Lawrence to RY, July 12, 1960.

206. "We have a terrific novel": Int. Dan Wakefield.

206. RY's various titles for *Revolutionary Road* are among his notes at BU. Robin Metz was the friend to whom RY mentioned his favorite, *The Bullshit Artist.*

206. "He used to stand around": Robert Parker, "A Clef," unpublished ms., papers of Robert Parker.

206. Kay Cassill remembers . . . "awe": Int. Kay Cassill.

207. "A deft, ironic, beautiful novel": Styron's comment was used by Little, Brown in promotion of the first edition, and appeared as a cover blurb on most later editions of the novel.

207. "grubby little writing for hire": *YHC,* 168.

207. "I smoke too much": Styron is quoted in Streitfeld, "Book Report," *Washington Post,* December 27, 1992, X15.

207. "Dick was always lubricating": Int. William Styron.

207. "He's a great guy": RY to DeWitt Henry, January 20, 1972.

207. met the poet Marianne Moore: Int. Robert Parker.

208. *"Booo, Dartmouth!":* Int. Robert Riche.

209. "drunken and frantic": RY to Barbara Beury, September 23, 1960.

209. "Dreadnought Dick": Int. John A. Williams.

209. "I well remember": John Williams to RY, November 5, 1970.

209. "And speaking of incredible": RY to Barbara Beury, September 30, 1960.

210. "premature ejaculation": RY to Grace and Jerry Schulman, May 18, 1962.

210. Yates's "Lost Soul quality": Int. Edward Kessler.

210. hallucination? "Because that's": RY to Beury, December 22, 1960.

211. "A massive lethargy": RY to Cassill, May 5, 1960.

211. The NIMH study on manic-depressive disorder is discussed in Jamison, *Touched with Fire.*

212. "Zelda and F. Scott FitzYates": Int. Barbara Beury McCallum.

212. "drunk and self-absorbed": RY to Beury, September 30, 1960.

212. "The worst possible way": RY to Beury, September 9, 1960.

213. *"Tell this dumb son of a bitch":* Int. Seymour Epstein.

214. "real beds, chrome-and-leatherette": *DP,* 55.

214. "I have given the Bellevue authorities": RY to Beury, September 9, 1960.

214. "Bellevue was an epiphany": Int. Grace Schulman.

215. "Yates was always the smart one": Int. Dr. Winthrop A. Burr.

215. "For God's sake, take it easy": RY to Najarian, September 24, 1960.

216. "beautiful" . . . "very well-written": RY to Beury, September 9, 1960.

217. "I wish you wouldn't 'worry' ": RY to Beury, September 23, 1960; Beury's side of the exchange is surmised from RY's reply.

217. "I think it's a very swell": RY to Beury, September 30, 1960.

219. "This excellent novel is a powerful": Kazin's edited blurb appeared on the first edition of *RR*; the whole quote was included in Little, Brown promotional material found among RY's papers.

219. "After Little Brown got that letter": RY to Beury, September 23, 1960.

219. "delighted to work with [Yates]": Saul David to McCall, October 27, 1960.

219. "never read a more brilliant": Quoted in RY to Beury, November 11, 1960.

220. "The Presentation today": RY to Beury, November 21, 1960.

221. "very nice and un-awesome": RY to Beury, September 30, 1960.

221. "a gruesome failure": RY to Beury, November 11, 1960.

221. "[Anatole] has expressed": Ibid.

222. "The whole three days": RY to Beury, October 24, 1960.

222. "formal divorce talk": RY to Beury, September 23, 1960.

223. "The only nice thing": RY to Beury, November 11, 1960.

224. "big Celebrity Interview": RY to Beury, December 22, 1960.

224. "shocking": Gingrich to McCall, January 22, 1961.

225. "You are free to remarry": Leonard Golditch to RY, February 9, 1961.

225. "Got my final divorce": RY to Beury, c. February 15, 1961.

226. "Dick would hand you a tumbler": Int. Alan Cheuse.

226. "For God's sake": RY to Edward Kessler, March 6, 1961.

226. "Maureen seemed like a tough": Int. Edward Kessler.

227. "I was fascinated": Updike's blurb for *RR* was included in Little, Brown promotional material found among RY's papers.

227. "Here is more than fine writing": Lawrence mailed RY a copy of Tennessee Williams's remarks on February 27, 1961; Williams's blurb has appeared on most subsequent editions of *RR*.

227. "Oh yes," he responded: *Contemporary Authors* interview, 1981.

227. Reviews of *Revolutionary Road*: J.C. Pine, *Library Journal*, February 1, 1961; R.D. Spector, *New York Herald Tribune*, March 5, 1961; W.E. Preece, *Chicago Tribune*, March 5, 1961; Martin Levin, *New York Times Book Review*, March 5, 1961; Orville Prescott, *New York Times*, March 10, 1961; "Briefly Noted," *The New Yorker*, April 1, 1961; David Boroff, *Saturday Review of Literature*, March 25, 1961; Jeremy Larner, *New Republic*, May 22, 1961; Dorothy Parker, *Esquire*, June 1961; F.J. Warnke, *Yale Review*, June 1961; Theodore Solotaroff, *Commentary*, July 1961.

229. "remains one of the few novels": James Atlas, "A Sure Narrative Voice," *Atlantic,* November 1981, 84–85.

230. "a cultish standard": Richard Ford, "American Beauty (Circa 1955)," *New York Times Book Review,* April 9, 2000, 16.

230. "strikes too close to home": Fred Chappell, essay on *RR,* in *Rediscoveries,* ed. David Madden (New York: Crown, 1971), 247.

234. "Doesn't it sound like a real name?": Int. Robin Metz.

235. "You threaten the intellectuals": Andrew Sinats to RY, March 16, 1961.

235. "If this was indeed": Donn C. McInturff to RY, April 5, 1962.

235. "Not knowing where else": Thalia Gorham Kelly to RY, May 30, 1961.

236. "very healthy indeed": Lawrence to RY, March 7, 1961.

236. "We are over 9,000": Lawrence to RY, April 4, 1961.

236. "I cannot recall . . . launched": Lawrence to RY, May 1, 1961.

236. "the lousy way the book": RY to DeWitt Henry, November 21, 1972.

237. "[I]n my more arrogant or petulant": *Ploughshares,* 74.

Chapter Eight *The World on Fire: 1961–1962*

238. "re-read Fitzgerald's 'Crack Up' ": RY to Beury, c. January 1961.

239. "The idea of the writer": Int. David Milch.

239. "Dick was both melancholy": Int. James Whitehead.

239. "How's the *schoolteaching*": Int. Robert Riche.

240. "When Emma dies, I die": Int. Grace Schulman.

242. "It takes many amateur writers": *Contemporary Authors,* 1981.

242. "*Don't worry* if it comes slowly": RY to the Schulmans, April 16, 1962.

243. "[I] still feel like a turd": RY to the Schulmans, April 2. 1962.

243. "PAY NO ATTENTION": RY to Grace Schulman, April 28, 1966.

243. "I always thought Dick was incorruptible": *RYAW,* 48.

244. "Best regards to Cyrilly": RY to the Schulmans, April 16, 1962.

245. "I got turned down for that job": RY to Beury, May 4, 1961.

245. "knowing you both": RY to the Schulmans, November 23, 1971.

246. "It was the nicest thing": Int. Natalie Bowen.

249. "Before the meal was over": Dan Wakefield to RY, July 2, 1976.

249. "You make . . . uncomfortable": Susan Grossman to RY, March 17, 1961.

249. "You'd be bored": Quoted in Grossman to RY, late March 1961.

249. "incurable keeps-player": RY to Beury, September 9, 1960.

249. "*How dare that crook*": Int. Natalie Bowen.

252. "Forgot to tell you that my mother": RY to Beury, May 4, 1961.

252. "I guess I was a bit of a bastard": RY to Beury, mid-February, 1961.

253. "Even if you end up marrying": RY to Beury, June 26, 1961.

255. "This confident, good-looking": *RYAW,* 39.

255. "soulmate drinker": Int. Franklin Russell.

255. "Outrageous!" he shouted: Ibid.

255. "Beverly *who*?": E-mail to author from Robert Riche.

256. Yates felt certain that his "effeminate": Int. Natalie Bowen.

256. "experimental warm-up": *Ploughshares,* 70.

256. "[about] a 'colorful' character": Rust Hills to McCall, May 24, 1961.

257. "Jerome Weidman writes three": *Saturday Review of Literature,* July 1, 1961, 14.

257. "No culture has placed": Yates's course description in the New School Bulletin, Spring 1961.

257. "Had a dreary class": RY to Beury, April 26, 1961.

258. "a considerable amount of dough": RY to Beury, June 26, 1961.

259. "[They] are talking . . . 'wait and see' ": RY to Beury, July 23, 1961.

260. "physically stronger but mentally": RY to Beury, November 26, 1961.

260. "I am not, as you so neatly": Ruth Rodgers to RY, c. October 1961.

260. "It was Bob Jones": Ruth Rodgers to RY, c. September 1961.

261. painted lipstick on her reflection: For the real-life basis of this memorable scene in *The Easter Parade,* see *RYAW,* 22.

261. "The deaths of parents": Quoted in *American Voices,* ed. Sally Arteseros (New York: Doubleday, 1992), 1.

261. "I sweated blood": *Ploughshares,* 67.

262. "[W]e don't mark our bottles": Rella Lossy to RY, September 9, 1961.

262. "He had . . . spoiled child": Int. Julia Child.

262. "Dick never praised simply": Int. Miller Williams.

262. "I can't tell you how impressed": Lawrence to RY, September 8, 1961.

262. Broyard . . . avoided Yates as . . . drunk: Int. Alexandra Broyard.

262. "lively if somewhat confused": RY to Miller Williams, January 20, 1962.

263. "endless sophomoric discussions": RY to Beury, November 26, 1961.

263. "Christ, Dick, you're no cad": Beury to RY, January 23, 1962.

264. "a perfect gentleman": Int. Sandra Walcott Eckhardt.

264. "On the first day of class": Int. Lee Jacobus.

265. "hole-in-corner deal": Sheila Yates to RY, c. January 1962.

265. "I have learned what it is": Sheila Yates to RY, January 17, 1962.

265. "a hell of a lot of trouble": Sheila Yates to RY, April 14, 1962.

265. "rather exaggerated emptiness": RY to Beury, November 26, 1961.

266. "the two terrible traps": *Ploughshares,* 70.

266. "special type of writer": Int. John Frankenheimer.

266. "The Movie Deal that seemed": RY to Beury, November 26, 1961.

266. "no whiff of a contract": RY to Miller Williams, January 20, 1961.

267. "Mr. Yates, how can I make sure": Charles Leap to RY, January 2, 1961.

267. "the book was a shattering": Lawrence to RY, January 30, 1962.

267. Yates . . . Wallant . . . commiserate: Int. Lee Jacobus.

267. Background of the 1962 NBA controversy: Gay Talese, "Critics Hear Tale of Novel's Prize," *New York Times*, March 15, 1962.

267. "a beautiful writer": *Ploughshares*, 77.

267. "a pathetic lush": Letter to author from Carolyn Gaiser.

268. "Want it? *Want* it?": Clark, "The Best I Can Wish You," 36.

268. "Just to save you anxiety": Int. Grace Schulman.

268. "I spent the first week": RY to the Schulmans, April 2, 1962.

269. "Do you think Hollywood": Sheila Yates to RY, c. March 1962.

270. "Baby, this is Crazyville": RY to Kessler, April 23, 1962.

270. "the drug I've been needling": Jerry Schulman to RY, April 5, 1962.

270. "He's probably some semi-literate": RY to Schulmans, April 16, 1962.

270. Reviews of *Eleven Kinds of Loneliness*: Peter Buitenhuis, *New York Times Book Review*, March 25, 1962; Richard Sullivan, *Chicago Tribune*, April 1, 1962; Hollis Alpert, *Saturday Review of Literature*, April 21, 1962; J.C. Pine, *Library Journal*, April 15, 1962.

271. A translated version of Cabau's review of *EKL* in the French weekly *Express* was mailed to RY on October 24, 1963, by Monica McCall: "You are now a pet of the French critics," she wrote.

272. "stands at the pinnacle": Jonathan Penner, *New Republic*, November 4, 1978.

273. "the mere mention of its title": Robert Towers, *New York Times Book Review*, November 1, 1981, 3.

274. "he believes this light to be a lie": *CSRY*, XX.

274. "economics of publishing": Lawrence to McCall, April 16, 1962.

275. "They're there, and now all": Lawrence to RY, April 24, 1962.

275. "a kind of literary snow-blindness": *Stories for the Sixties*, ed. RY (New York: Bantam, 1963), vii.

275. "quite impressed": Rust Hills to RY, April 17, 1962.

276. "Maybe the little bastard": RY to the Schulmans, May 18, 1962.

276. "It was almost as if he knew": *Ploughshares*, 75.

276. "At the rate Yates is going": Malcolm Stuart to McCall, May 25, 1962, BU-MM.

276. "discovering endless problems": RY to the Schulmans, May 18, 1962.

276. "Don't think I'm neglecting": RY to Robert Parker, May 13, 1962.

278. The birthplace and maiden name of Catherine Downing are found on her Social Security SS-5 form; other details about Downing were cobbled together from epistolary evidence in RY's papers as well as interviews with Frances Doel and others.

279. "You didn't leave anything": Int. Monica Yates Shapiro.

279. "a whole new avalanche": *UT*.

279. "Good novels—let's say great novels": *Ploughshares*, 72.

280. "delivering great globs": *William Styron's "Lie Down in Darkness": A Screenplay* (Watertown, Mass: Ploughshares, 1985).
281. "At a distance in time": Sheila Yates to RY, April 14, 1962.
281. "old, reliable tranquility": Sheila Yates to RY, c. March 1962.
281. "I will never—and I mean": Sheila Yates to RY, April 14, 1962.
282. "I should, damn it, have known": John Ciardi to RY, September 10, 1962.
283. "ugly fucking battle-ax": Int. Grace Schulman.
283. "You can take my word": Ciardi to RY, September 13, 1962.
283. "After it's over I wince": Quoted in Jamison, *Touched with Fire*, 32.
284. predicted he'd kill himself: Marilyn Renzelman to RY, February 20, 1963.
284. "Any hope that we can work": Sheila Yates to RY, June 10, 1963.

Chapter Nine *Uncertain Times: 1962–1964*
286. "revolutionized the treatment": *New York Times,* February 14, 1983, D10.
287. "This is what keeps your old daddy": Int. Geoffrey Clark.
287. Frankenheimer had assured: Frankenheimer to RY, October 2, 1962.
287. "ninety-eight per cent sure": Cassill to RY, October 9, 1962.
288. "Miss Wood's agent decided": RY to Miller Williams, March 14, 1964.
288. "Frankenheimer's mills": Styron to RY, March 14, 1963.
289. "I'm working hard as hell": RY to Cassill, February 7, 1963.
289. "spasm of writing": *UT.*
291. Background on Ruth's marriage: Int. Fred and Peter Rodgers, Ruth Rodgers Ward, Sheila Yates.
292. "mentally ill, incompetent": Cassill to RY, April 3, 1963.
292. The meeting was a fiasco: "Kennedy and Baldwin: The Gulf," *Newsweek,* June 3, 1963, 19.
293. "turn them into words with a snap": *RYAW,* 43.
293. Prettyman called . . . Styron: Int. E. Barrett Prettyman Jr., Styron.
293. "I don't even know if I *like*": *UT.*
293. "short, clipped sentences": Ibid.
293. "We're living in very uncertain": Venant, "A Fresh Twist in the Road," sec. 6, p. 8.
294. "School is out, girls": *UT.*
295. "more of an honorarium kind of thing": *UT.*
295. "I couldn't resist": RY to Miller Williams, March 14, 1964.
295. "Dick composed the most memorable": *RYAW,* 43.
295. "He used RFK as a ventriloquist's": Int. Kurt Vonnegut.
296. "Dick was respectful": Int. Jack Rosenthal.
296. "Sorry I've been so elusive": *UT*; Int. Wendy Sears Grassi.
296. "The FBI wheels": Sheila Yates to RY, June 10, 1963.
298. "a fine-looking young man": *UT.*

299. "hunched and impassioned": Ibid.
299. "Dick, I recall feeling": John A. Williams to RY, November 5, 1970.
299. "If my questioning you": RY to Williams, c. early 1971.
300. "There! I wrote that!": Int. Janis Knorr.
300. "White people of whatever kind": *Robert F. Kennedy: Collected Speeches,* ed. Edwin O. Guthman and C. Richard Allen (New York: Viking Penguin, 1993), 98–100.
301. "a little heavy in the leg.": The phrase was used to describe Sears's fictional alter ego Holly Parsons in *UT.*
302. "it hurt to listen": Int. Joseph Mohbat.
305. as a matter of principle it rankled: Int. Noreen McGuire.
305. "When I'm writing, I'm *writing*": Int. Jack Rosenthal.
306. a stock anecdote in Yates's repertoire: Int. E. Barrett Prettyman Jr., Carolyn Gaiser.
307. "After searching for months": "Periscope," *Newsweek,* September 16, 1963, 16.
307. Was this Richard Yates the *writer*: Int. Dan Wakefield.
309. "suave, expensive and quiet restaurant": RY to DeWitt Henry, November 21, 1972.
310. Yates shook hands . . . ran out of cigarettes: Int. Wendy Sears Grassi, Joseph Mohbat.
310. "and just about that time the president": RY to Miller Williams, March 14, 1964.
311. "Richard Yates, the novelist . . . did not like": Arthur M. Schlesinger Jr., *Robert Kennedy and His Times* (Boston: Houghton-Mifflin, 1978), 876.
311. "Never look for political ideas": *UT* notes.
313. "glad it happened": Wendy Sears recounts this exchange in her letter to RY, c. June 1964.
313. "this makes [my husband]": Ruth Rodgers to RY, August 14, 1964.
315. "There are of course a number of elements": McCall to RY, January 30, 1964.
316. "I'm working like a bastard": RY to Miller Williams, March 14, 1964.
317. A representative artifact: "QWERTYUIOP$\frac{1}{2}$," *Esquire,* October 1966, 98.
317. during a boozy night with Styron: Styron to RY, January 12, 1965.
318. "you work all day and carouse": Lawrence to RY, March 3, 1964.
318. "Yates was pleasant enough": Int. Richard Frede.
318. Charlie was now working: Sheila Yates to RY, July 15, 1964.
318. "I'll put a dime": Grace Schulman to RY, July 15, 1964.
318. "rich, waspy": Int. Monica Yates Shapiro.
319. "The damn place [MacDowell]": RY to the Schulmans, August 8, 1964.
319. "Brendan Behan drank": Wendy Sears to RY, August 18, 1964.
320. "There's a good writer who goes": Int. Sharon Yates Levine.

Chapter Ten *A New Yorker Discovers the Middle West: 1964–1966*

321. Background on the Iowa Writers Workshop: *Seems Like Old Times: Iowa Writers Workshop Golden Jubilee*, ed. Ed Dinger (Iowa City: 1986), hereafter cited as *SLOT*; *The Workshop: Seven Decades of the Iowa Writers Workshop*, ed. Tom Grimes (New York: Hyperion, 1999), hereafter cited as *Workshop*; John Hess, "Where Have All the Writers Gone? To Iowa City, That's Where," *Holiday* (June 1970), 60–68.

321. "The business of teaching": Venant, "A Fresh Twist in the Road."

322. "I must admit I'm a little leery": RY to Cassill, February 7, 1963.

322. "few places interesting to eat": Cassill to RY, February 25, 1964.

322. His car . . . caught fire: Tom Gatten, *Workshop*, 731.

322. "I found myself talking": Int. William Kittredge.

322. "Turn at the sign": Int. Loree Wilson Rackstraw.

322. cartoon of a sad daddy: Int. Monica Yates Shapiro.

322. "I think we all wanted": Lacy, "Remembering Richard Yates," 211.

323. "What's this . . . *club tie?*": Int. Robin Metz.

324. "sublime, rugged presence": Luke Wallin, *SLOT*, 66.

326. "rhetorical style . . . 'Flowering Judas'": Int. Loree Wilson Rackstraw.

326. "I'm going to the Airliner": Int. James Crumley.

326. "Now that is fucking good writing!": Int. Murray Moulding.

326. "Now, if that's Daisy talking": Int. Robert Lacy.

327. trashing of *All the King's Men*: Int. James Crumley.

327. "Oh c'mon, you don't really mean that!": Int. Geoffrey Clark.

327. "smelly and shy": Int. Dan Childress.

328. "Yates had no doubt": Robert Lehrman, *Workshop*, 746.

329. Mark Dintenfass was startled: Int. Mark Dintenfass, Robert Lehrman.

329. "Dick demonstrated the keenest": Clark, "The Best I Can Wish You," 29.

330. "They're rushing you": Int. John Casey.

330. "I hope this won't . . . sore": RY to DeWitt Henry, May 13, 1968.

330. "I simply can't imagine": RY to DeWitt Henry, November 21, 1972.

330. "Hm, did you really": Int. William Keough.

331. "*You motherfuckers*": Int. William Kittredge.

331. "Milch was a slasher": Int. Robin Metz.

332. "*That* many writers": Int. Seymour Epstein.

332. "Andre wanted . . . tough guy": Int. Peggy Rambach.

333. "Most of the clowns here": RY to Miller Williams, October 3, 1964.

333. "Getting a letter from Richard Yates": Dubus to RY, July 1, 1970.

333. "Richard Yates is one of our great writers": Andre Dubus, "A Salute to Mister Yates, *Black Warrior Review* 15, no. 2 (Spring 1989), 160.

334. "God, how we loved that song!": Lacy, "Remembering Richard Yates," 217.

335. "If that goddamned movie": Int. Geoffrey Clark.

335. "hug [him] to pieces": Wendy Sears to RY, October 26, 1964.

335. "Steve Salinger sneaked in": Jonathan Penner, *Workshop*, 724.

335. "I don't think I'm at all cut out": RY to McCall, November 1, 1964, BU-MM.

335. "Dick saw more in me": Int. Lyn Lacy.

337. "He talked of prospects": RY to DeWitt Henry, November 21, 1972.

337. "I resigned from Knopf": Lawrence to RY, November 7, 1964.

338. "Sam's attitude . . . deplorable": McCall to RY, November 19, 1964.

338. "I know apologies are a bore": RY to the Schulmans, January 10, 1965.

338. "people don't stop caring": Grace Schulman to RY, March 4, 1965.

339. "lonesome as hell": RY to the Schulmans, February 28, 1965.

339. "a crash program": RY to the Schulmans, January 10, 1965.

339. "[T]he 'teaching' routine": RY to the Schulmans, February 28, 1965.

339. "tinkered and brooded and fussed": *Ploughshares*, 74.

340. "Verlin Cassill's verdict": RY to the Schulmans, February 28, 1965.

341. "What will *you* do?": Int. Robin Metz.

341. "a cherry when I got married": Dubus to RY, February 2, 1967.

342. "I've wanted to publish you": Robert Gottlieb to RY, February 15, 1965.

342. "Was Sam ever useful": McCall to RY, March 22, 1965.

343. "mustn't worry": McCall to RY, March 4, 1965.

343. "making notes and . . . spooky": RY to the Schulmans, February 28, 1965.

344. "If calling me when . . . panic": McCall to RY, May 7, 1965.

345. Yates scribbled on his bill: found among RY's papers.

345. "ridiculous amounts of money": RY to Schulmans, July 11, 1965.

345. "Hitler's car": Int. Frances Doel. As a patriotic vet, RY deplored his having bought the Führer's infamous "people's car."

345. "grubby white edifice": *DP*, 210.

345. "the Goddamn movies": Int. Frances Doel.

346. "Guess what, hey": RY to Wendy Sears, July 2, 1965, BU-RY.

346. "[W]hatever kind of place": RY to Schulmans, July 11, 1965.

346. "[Corman] turns out to be": Ibid.

346. "I poke around trying": RY to Robert and Dot Parker, July 24, 1965.

347. "funny Hollywood story": RY to Schulmans, July 11, 1965.

348. "friendly but reserved": Int. Roger Corman.

348. "There's really not much": Catherine Downing to RY, September 12, 1975.

350. "West Hollywood Sheriff's Office": Discarded draft of *DP*, BU-RY.

350. Bill Reardon, who caught a flight: Int. Sharon Yates Levine.

351. "In the bughouse": Int. Frances Doel.

351. "We have had a wonderful": Sheila Yates to RY, August 22, 1965.

351. "the right thing": Bowen to RY, September 13, 1965.

351. "spread any unfortunate": Marc Jaffe to RY, August 30, 1965.

352. "The fact of talent": Rust Hills to RY, August 27, 1965.
352. "he is *not* my doctor": RY to McCall, October 6, 1965, BU-MM.
352. "the kind of place . . . suicide": Int. Frances Doel.
352. "People found it very warm": Rust Hills to RY, August 27, 1965.
353. "There are several good things": RY to Cassill, January 18, 1966.
353. "fine well-focused script": Dubus to RY, February 10, 1966.
353. "This is your third breakdown": Sheila Yates to RY, September 29, 1965.
354. "He's a very, very touchy": RY to DeWitt Henry, July 24, 1972.
354. "never seen such a change": RY to Cassill, March 23, 1966.
354. "I'm John Gregory Dunne": Letter to author from Carolyn Gaiser.
354. "you are one of the very few": Joan Didion to RY, September 13, 1970.
356. hourly tormented . . . Portis: Int. Murray Moulding.
356. "Haven't done any more wrestling": RY to Cassill, January 18, 1966.
356. "Is just 'functioning' ": Quoted in Dubus to RY, February 25, 1966.
356. "I'm feeling pretty jaunty": RY to Cassill, March 23, 1966.
356. "Not an unhappy experience": Marc Jaffe to RY, June 1, 1966.
356. "[Yates] has been in Hollywood": Cassill to Carolyn Kizer, c. May 1966.
357. "take the curse off": RY to Cassill, January 18, 1966.
358. "Is this some kind of AA thing?": Int. Jerry Schulman.
358. "The purpose of this letter": Craige ——— to RY, May 28, 1966.
358. "[The story] is all tricked out": RY to Cassill, January 18, 1966.
358. Wolper . . . fired Yates: RY wrote to Frances Doel (September 7, 1966), "It's [i.e., a $10,000 grant] the same amount I lost in being fired from the Remagen Bridge flick." The details of RY's dismissal are unknown.
359. "I wouldn't want to try it": *Contemporary Authors*, 1981, 536.
359. "We are delighted": Bourjaily to RY, June 7, 1966.
360. "Still hate [Hollywood]": RY to Cassill, March 23, 1966.
361. "Forgive me . . . but I called": Frances Doel to RY, July 15, 1966.
361. " brilliant," an "emotional genius": Carole ——— to RY, c. June 1970.

Chapter Eleven *A Natural Girl: 1966–1968*
364. "Dick's helplessness": Int. Mark Costello.
364. "get [his] brains . . . focus": RY to Frances Doel, September 7, 1966.
365. "If we stick together": Ruth Rodgers to RY, September 15, 1966.
365. "bowled over": Int. Martha Speer.
366. "I'm sorry your friend": Martha Speer to RY, September, 1966.
367. "traumatic and cowardly": Carole ——— to RY, c. June 1970.
368. "I was afraid to face": Martha Speer to RY, November 2, 1976.
368. "As an occasional palindromist": Roger Angell to RY, October 3, 1966.
369. "one of the best books": Vonnegut wrote this blurb for the 1971 Dell reprint of *RR*, and it has appeared on perhaps every edition since.

369. "a very unpopular lecture": Int. Kurt Vonnegut.

371. "From Coover I learned": Kittredge, *SLOT*, 66.

371. "Well, I'm just a dumb guy": Int. Mark Dintenfass.

371. "a seething mix": Robert Lehrman, *Workshop*, 745.

372. "faggots" and worse: Int. Robert Lehrman.

372. "in the past four or five": RY to Cassill, April 2, 1967.

373. "Good work to you": Dubus to RY, February 28, 1967.

373. "Dick, guess what we're doing?": Int. Joseph Mohbat.

373. "We would be prepared": Lawrence to RY, September 16, 1966.

374. "I do know that the pressures": McCall to RY, April 5, 1967.

374. "repay the outstanding": Lawrence to RY, January 6, 1968.

374. "In the end I told Sam": RY to DeWitt Henry, November 21, 1972.

374. "lugubrious" . . . "roaring drunk": Int. Gordon Lish.

375. "clear impression": Int. Peter Davidson.

375. "The Workshop . . . incestuous": Int. William Murray.

376. *"Where's the pencil pusher?"*: Ibid.

376. "[He was] clearly upset": Robert Lehrman, *Workshop*, 746.

377. "I thought 'this is life' ": Martha Speer to RY, November 2, 1976.

377. "No chance of finishing": RY to Cassill, April 2, 1967.

378. "I hope you're not sorry": Sheila Yates to RY, July 9, 1967.

379. "about the sex lives of graduate": RY to Dewitt Henry, May 13, 1968.

379. "I have so many daughters": Int. Grace Schulman.

379. "She's twenty years younger": RY to Cassill, January 7, 1968.

380. "We wanted . . . happier life": Lehrman, *Workshop*, 746.

Chapter Twelve *A Special Providence: 1968–1969*

382. "chummy, bubbly, tolerant": Int. Martha Speer.

383. "wiped out with admiration": RY to E. B. Prettyman, February 23, 1968.

385. "Straight ahead: don't look right": Int. Martha Speer.

386. "sick, in shock": Int. Fred Rodgers Jr.

386. "Your brother killed": Int. Louise Rodgers.

386. "more hopeful now": RY to Prettyman, May 9, 1968.

387. "hideous loss": RY to Prettyman, August 4, 1968.

387. "that scares the shit": RY to Cassill, December 1, 1968.

388. "[The novel] may not . . . good": RY to Prettyman, February 20, 1969.

389. "idle, boozy": RY to Robert Lehrman, June 10, 1969.

389. *"very* high on [his] book": McCall to RY, June 11, 1969.

390. "moving and sensitive": McCall enclosed Rosenthal's letter with hers of September 4, 1969.

391. "because it is much harder": Carole ———— to RY, c. June 1970.

392. "What kind of *guy* . . . Bennington?": Int. William Keough.

392. "With time on my hands": Sharon Yates to RY, December 7, 1968.
394. "dropping [his] pants in Macy's": Int. Dr. Winthrop A. Burr.
394. "I imagine you are now": Vonnegut to RY, September 24, 1969.
394. "It is a beautiful book": Joan Didion to RY, October 14, 1969.
395. HOPE YOU SAW: Styron to RY, October 27, 1969.
395. "I remember how many times": Dubus to RY, November 12, 1969.
395. "What do Alice Prentice's dreams": Robin Metz to RY, November 25, 1969.
395. "a lot of people . . . much of it": RY to Prettyman, December 14, 1969.
395. Reviews of *A Special Providence*: Joyce Carol Oates, *The Nation*, November 10, 1969; John Thompson, *Harper's*, November 1969; Elizabeth Dalton, *New York Times Book Review*, December 14, 1969.
396. "the true enemies of the novel": Quoted in Ronald Baugham, "Richard Yates," *Dictionary of Literary Biography Yearbook* (Detroit: Gale, 1992), 301.
397. "the two terrible traps": *Ploughshares,* 70.
398. considered omitting it: *RYAW,* 59.
400. "better and easier": RY to Prettyman, December 14, 1969.
400. "Let's see": Clark, "The Best I Can Wish You," 34.

Chapter Thirteen *Fun with a Stranger: 1970–1974*

401. "But you must not brood": McCall to RY, January 21, 1970.
401. "most desirous of establishing": Howard Gotlieb to RY, April 14, 1970.
401. "the added disadvantage": *Ploughshares,* 74.
401. "I've sort of decided": RY to DeWitt Henry, December 13, 1967.
402. "require the same kind": *Contemporary Authors,* 1981, 534.
402. "had it in for him.": Int. Jack Leggett.
402. "slinking around with a secret": Int. Martha Speer.
404. "Martha seemed a nurse": Int. William Harrison.
404. "A problem has come up": William Murray to RY, June 15, 1970.
405. "80% of the writing faculty": Hayes B. Jacobs to RY, July 6, 1970.
405. "progressively, irredeemably crazy": *Ploughshares,* 73.
406. "Hollywood writers": Int. Jayne Anne Phillips.
407. "I recall trying to say": RY to John A. Williams, October 26, 1970.
407. "the 'book' might be in the form": Ibid.
407. "the mediocre . . . soldiers": Williams to RY, November 5, 1970.
408. "about the hideous whim": RY to Williams, early 1971.
408. "Do you know . . . out of print": Clark, "The Best I Can Wish You," 40.
408. "All the time I praise": Vonnegut to RY, September 14, 1970.
408. "deep" into his new novel: RY to DeWitt Henry, May 7, 1971.
409. "There's a great deal of interest": Bruce Cutler to RY, June 22, 1971.
410. "dream up an original": McCall to RY, October 27, 1971.

410. "break [his] heart": Quoted in McCall to RY, November 9, 1971.

410. "in something of a muddle": RY to the Schulmans, November 23, 1971.

411. "Say, Geoff, tell me": Clark, "The Best I Can Wish You," 33.

411. "I felt like a teenybopper": Int. Ellen Wilbur.

412. "I seem to recall . . . clown": RY to Geoffrey Clark, April 9, 1972.

412. "fragmentary, diffuse": DeWitt Henry to RY, April 12, 1972.

412. "chances [were] very good": David Milch to RY, June 27, 1972.

413. "must be beautiful": Gina Berriault to the Yateses, July 14, 1972.

413. "Believe it or not": RY to DeWitt Henry, July 24, 1972.

414. "A popular writer, a writer": from Henry's transcription of original interview, found among RY's papers.

416. "cogent and back-to-work": Int. DeWitt Henry.

416. "in all its carefully-edited": RY to DeWitt Henry, November 21, 1972.

416. "I've just finished reading": Lawrence to RY, November 13, 1972.

416. "So who knows?": RY to DeWitt Henry, November 21, 1972.

417. "devilishly hard": Hayes Jacobs to RY, February 13, 1973.

417. Various drafts of RY's résumé were found among his papers.

418. "a lot of commitment": Arthur Roth to RY, January 30, 1973.

418. Yates's review of The Morning After: *New York Times Books Review*, January 28, 1973, 6.

419. "putting the story through": McCall to RY, February 20, 1973.

419. "Dick—I'm doing . . . trust me": Gordon Lish to RY, February 22, 1973.

419. "Your performance was an appalling": Lish to RY, February 28, 1973.

421. "I am your daughter": Monica Yates to RY, March 5, 1973.

421. Martha prepared a list of symptoms: found among RY's papers.

423. "Those monthly payments": *RYAW, 59.*

423. "How much do you need": Int. Dan Wakefield.

423. "at his best he's a solid": RY to Geoffrey Clark, October 26, 1978.

424. Yates would mimic him: Int. Sharon Yates Levine.

425. "become . . . whiskey-head": RY to Geoffrey Clark, July 22, 1973.

426. "Three thousand articles": E-mail to author from John P. Lowens.

427. "taking his enormous success": RY to Geoffrey Clark, July 22, 1973.

428. "What's most important . . . right": Lawrence to RY, February 7, 1974.

428. "lovable Irish alcoholic": *RYAW, 29.*

430. "Trouble with me and my friends": Dubus to RY, July 12, 1976.

430. "Women have been oblique": Martha Speer to RY, November 2, 1976.

Chapter Fourteen *Disturbing the Peace: 1974–1976*

433. "that loneliness shit": Dubus to RY, June 18, 1974.

433. "It always made me pleased": Loree Rackstraw to RY, February 11, 1975.

434. "PERSONAL RECORD": found among RY's papers.

436. "Whatever you do": Int. Mitch Douglas.

436. "Yates was absolutely nonfunctional": Int. Dr. George Hecht.

437. "What little I've accomplished": *The Letters of F. Scott Fitzgerald,* ed. Andrew Turnbull (New York: Dell, 1963), 96.

437. "the desolate wastes": "Some Very Good Masters," 21.

438. "It may be an old one": Lawrence to RY, September 14, 1974.

439. "I think about you often": Martha Speer to RY, September 10, 1974.

439. "[M]y mind just wants things": Martha Speer to RY, November 20, 1974.

439. "Jesus Christ," he'd gasp: Int. Carolyn Gaiser.

439. "We should approach": Ted Maass to Lawrence, January 24, 1975.

440. "You and I were the only": Int. Marjorie Owens.

440. "call girls, dope addicts": Quoted in Natalie Bowen to RY, February 22, 1965. As a matter of odd coincidence, Bowen dated Krim briefly in the mid-sixties.

441. "Oh, I just give everybody an A": E-mail to author from Geoffrey Clark.

441. "Oh, bullshit!" he sneered: John Gilgun to RY, February 25, 1972.

441. *"Where's my mail?!"*: Int. Carolyn Gaiser.

442. "envious but scornful": Letter to author from Loree Rackstraw.

442. "My mother . . . Dutch Act": Krim to RY, November 7, 1975.

442. "Richard Yates has regained": Quoted in Lawrence to RY, June 7, 1975, UM-SL.

442. "the best novel [he'd] read": George Garrett to RY, August 30, 1975.

443. "I think it's okay": RY to Geoffrey Clark, August 26, 1975.

443. "Things I regret": RY to Joseph and Nancy Mohbat, September 15, 1975.

443. Reviews of *Disturbing the Peace*: Gene Lyons, *New York Times Book Review,* October 5, 1975; Anatole Broyard, *New York Times,* September 9, 1975; William Pritchard, *Hudson Review,* Spring 1976; Peter S. Prescott, *Newsweek,* September 15, 1975.

447. "that literary work . . . achievement": Dwight MacDonald to RY, February 20, 1976.

447. "Oh, what the hell . . . $2,000": *RYAW,* 30.

448. "in the home stretch": RY to Geoffrey Clark, December 8, 1975.

448. "about that second-rate": Int. Carolyn Gaiser.

448. "The tenants were on rent-strike": Int. John P. Lowens.

450. "This is *not* a rush book!": Delacorte office memorandum from Lucy Hebard to John Carter, found among RY's papers.

451. "pay and pay and pay": Fitzgerald to Hemingway, September 9, 1929, *Letters of FSF,* 333.

452. "As I fled down the street": *RYAW,* 30.

453. "whiskery old bullshit artist": Clark, "The Best I Can Wish You," 30.

453. "When do I see the head honcho?": Int. William Pritchard.

454. "Went . . . sweaty business": RY to Geoffrey Clark, April 26, 1976.
455. "tepid" . . . "climbing all over": Ibid.
455. "Three guesses how": Streitfeld, "The Great Unknown," 28.
455. Details of RY's fire are mostly derived from interviews with his daughters.
456. Russell soaked the manuscript: Int. Franklin Russell.
456. "Aren't you celebrating": Int. Sharon Yates Levine.
457. "You look fabulous in green": Int. Joan Norris.
458. "I'm looking for a girl": Int. Galen Williams.
459. asked Ruth to pick up a broom: Int. Ann McGovern.
460. "ennobling brotherhood": Arthur Roth to RY, September 21, 1976.
460. "My father spent years in Northport": Ibid.
461. "The abandonment of Yates, tied": E-mail to author from Franklin Russell.
461. "the most intensely dramatic": Arthur Roth to RY, September 21, 1976.
461. "I was surprised and disappointed": Grace Schulman to Arthur Roth, August 18, 1976, papers of G. Schulman.

Chapter Fifteen *Out with the Old: 1976–1978*

463. "ugly and humiliating": Quoted in Arthur Roth to RY, September 21, 1976.
463. "You know several people": Lawrence to RY, August 7, 1976, UM-SL.
465. "dashed it off in eleven months": *RYAW,* 21.
465. "Ask me about *The Easter Parade*": Quoted in Galen Williams to RY, July 6, 1976.
465. "we murmured together": Cassill to RY, July 17, 1976.
465. "You write so damn well!": Michael Arlen to RY, September 23, 1976.
466. Reviews of *The Easter Parade*: A.G. Mojtabai, *New York Times Book Review,* September 19, 1976; Ross Feld, *New Republic,* October 9, 1976; Richard Todd, *Atlantic,* October 1976; Anatole Broyard, *New York Times,* September 7, 1976.
470. "If I were you . . . Bermuda": Int. Richard Levine.
470. "Henri Troyat, the biographer": Lacy, "Remembering Richard Yates," 212.
471. yogurt . . . "great discoveries": Int. Sharon Yates Levine.
472. "Dick's glass": Int. Jennifer Hetzel Genest.
473. only times . . . "rowdy": Int. Michael Brodigan.
473. Yates referred to her as a *personage*: Int. DeWitt Henry.
473. "I'm not calling back just now": Penelope Mortimer to RY, undated.
474. Yates had a fascination . . . answering machine: "Please call any time if you feel like it, either to talk to me or the machine (you're good at that)," Mortimer to RY, January 20, 1977.
474. "it's a lot like a lot of Updike": Mortimer to RY, undated.

474. "Two scared people": Ibid.

474. "exceptionally courteous" author: Int. Lynn Meyer.

477. "I was impressed . . . persevered": Int. Madison Smartt Bell.

478. a party was given for Penelope Mortimer: Int. Sayre Sheldon.

478. "*Please* will you understand": Mortimer to RY, c. June 1977.

478. "He couldn't grasp": Int. Dr. Winthrop A. Burr.

478. "Imagine going to California": Int. William Keough.

479. "I have gotten the impression": Martha Speer to RY, November 2, 1976.

480. "Does an apple tree give skirts": Martha Speer to RY, April 20, 1977.

481. "I was so pleased": *Contemporary Authors,* 1981, 535.

481. "Thanks for the invitation": RY to Geoffrey Clark, November 7, 1977.

482. "As soon as I finish [a story]": Monica Yates to RY, undated.

483. "She was the one . . . crush on": Int. Susan Braudy.

483. "What's that over your head": Int. Carolyn Gaiser.

483. "I was told at a very early age": E-mail to author from Gina Yates.

484. "I am planning to make": Bonnie Lucas to RY, December 13, 1977.

484. "gentle passion": Tommie Cotter to RY, June 5, 1978.

484. "salvation not mere pussy": Dubus to RY, February 25, 1974.

484. "You've heard me say": Quoted in Dubus to RY, August 22, 1973.

485. "For fifteen years": *RYAW,* 45.

485. "There are many things . . . thank you": Mary Robison to RY, undated.

485. he'd been "used": Int. Robin Metz.

485. "I've loved you for a decade": Robison to RY, July 20, 1986.

486. "soft-edged and idealized": Int. Monica Yates Shapiro.

486. "It's this combination": Krim to RY, January 17, 1978.

486. "various stages of partial": RY to Geoffrey Clark, April 16, 1978.

486. "*A Good School* is magnificent": Lawrence to RY, February 19, 1978, UM-SL.

486. "the mellow Yates": Krim to RY, September 24, 1978.

486. "so moving and so perfect": Hannah Green to Seymour Lawrence, October 15, 1978.

486. "I'm moved by a blessed irony": Cassill to Lawrence, undated.

487. "The best free advertising": Lawrence to RY, June 11, 1978, UM-SL.

487. Reviews of *A Good School:* Christopher Lehmann-Haupt, *New York Times,* December 8, 1978; Julian Moynahan, *New York Times Book Review,* November 12, 1978; "Briefly Noted," *The New Yorker,* September 4, 1978; Jonathan Penner, *New Republic,* November 4, 1978; John Skow, *Time,* August 21, 1978; Nicholas Guild, *Washington Post,* September 10, 1978; Thomas R. Edward, *New York Review of Books,* November 23, 1978.

488. "If writing were baseball": Jerome Klinkowitz, *The New American Novel of*

Manners: The Fiction of Richard Yates, Dan Wakefield, and Thomas McGuane (Athens: University of Georgia Press, 1986).

489. "complex, generous voice": Stewart O'Nan, "The Lost World of Richard Yates," *Boston Review*, October/November 1999, 45.

490. "I want to reassure you": Lawrence to RY, December 17, 1978, UM-SL.

490. "Since reading your book": Richard E. T. Hunter to RY, February 19, 1979.

490. wrote . . . mollifying letter: E-mail to author from Geoffrey Clark.

490. "She knows that I also read": Mary Nickerson to RY, undated.

490. accepted an invitation: Int. Mary Nickerson, Ann Wright Jones.

Chapter Sixteen *Young Hearts Crying: 1979–1984*

492. "Since then I've read all the novels": Laura ⸺ to Margaret Blackstone, June 20, 1979.

492. "I'm the one . . . stalking you": Int. Monica Yates Shapiro.

493. "[I worried] your friend Mary": Laura ⸺ to RY, undated.

493. "Dick was bombed": Int. Booghie Salassi.

496. "too academic": Lawrence to RY, March 5, 1979, UM-SL.

496. "Nobody's eyes light up": RY to Booghie Salassi, December 29, 1979 (unmailed).

496. "I wanted to tell you": Raymond Carver to RY, September 17, 1979.

497. "a few traces of roach shit": RY to Joseph Mohbat, September 23, 1979.

497. "horrified" . . . "guide him about": Clark, "The Best I Can Wish You," 36.

497. "I think this . . . last foray": RY to Joseph Mohbat, September 23, 1979.

498. "Notes Toward an Understanding of Laura M—": found among RY's papers.

500. "She's offered ample assurance": RY to Booghie Salassi, December 29, 1979 (unmailed).

501. "Ahh, mind your own": Int. Geoffrey Clark.

501. "You guys . . . grownup clothes?": Int. James Crumley.

501. "I just love your work": Int. John Casey.

501. "He was a wonderful source of solace": *RYAW*, 53.

504. one nurse reported seeing: Int. Ivan Gold.

505. "The mere presence of sweet": papers of Wendy Sears Grassi.

505. "That was . . . literary parties": Lawrence to RY, November 25, 1980, UM-SL.

506. "a homosexual novel in disguise": RY to Geoffrey Clark, October 26, 1978.

507. often given a "snitty" lecture: Int. Monica Yates Shapiro.

507. "All I want . . . goddamned *New Yorker*!": Int. William Keough.

507. "John fucking Cheever": E-mail to author from Joseph Mohbat.

507. "I don't know if you usually": RY to McCall, September 7, 1979, ICM files.

507. "This is written with admirable": Quoted in McCall to RY, September 25, 1979.

508. "magnificent . . . perceptive": Lawrence to RY, December 30, 1980, UM-SL.

508. "false and hollow": Roger Angell to Mitch Douglas, February 23, 1981.

508. "This didn't come close": Angell to Douglas, February 26, 1981.

508. "I know these rejections": Douglas to RY, March 6, 1981.

509. find Angell's letters . . . shaky voice: Int. Robin Metz.

510. "Dick drew me into labor": *RYAW*, 37.

511. "Ivy League wino": Int. George Garrett.

511. "What does your character": Elizabeth Cox, "Meet Richard Yates," *Pif* (www.pifmagazine.com), February 4, 2001.

512. "I don't watch out for Dick": Int. Loree Rackstraw.

512. Reviews of *Liars in Love*: James Atlas, *Atlantic*, November 1981; Robert Wilson, *Washington Post*, November 29, 1981; Robert Harris, *Saturday Review of Literature*, November 1981; Peter LaSalle, *America*, January 30, 1982; Christopher Lehmann-Haupt, *New York Times*, October 15, 1981; Robert Towers, *New York Times Book Review*, November 1, 1981.

517. "*Liars in Love* . . . highly praised books": Lawrence to RY, November 16, 1981, UM-SL.

517. He sat in the silent lecture hall: Int. Shaun O'Connell, Chet Frederick.

518. "There aren't many books": Int. Leslie Epstein.

518. "Oh, it's just a mix": Int. Jon Garelick.

518. "I want to write porn movies": Int. Natalie Baturka.

519. "He was the finest reader": Int. Melanie Rae Thon.

521. "God*damn* it, Rosen": Int. Ken Rosen.

524. "Am I a monster?": Int. Richard Levine.

525. "By God, I'm sending her to Harvard": Int. Dan Wakefield.

526. "I think he's wonderful": Int. Kurt Vonnegut.

526. "On impulse [I] hoped": Gloria Vanderbilt to RY, June 8, 1983.

526. "Scared, perhaps, a little": Vanderbilt to RY, June 27, 1983.

526. "could have talked on and on": Vanderbilt to RY, November 28, 1983.

527. "Ahh that's ridiculous!": Int. Wendy Sears Grassi.

528. "More than two decades . . . publication": Michiko Kakutani, *New York Times*, April 25, 1983, C15.

528. "It's nice that Barrett Prettyman": RY to Lawrence, June 30, 1984, UM-SL.

529. "The people at Dutton": Lawrence to RY, August 30, 1984, UM-SL.

529. "That's great," Yates replied: *RYAW*, 25.

529. "I think *Young Hearts Crying*": Lawrence to RY, August 30, 1984, UM-SL.

530. "one of America's least famous": "The Right Thing," *Esquire*, August 1984.

531. Reviews of *Young Hearts Crying*: Christopher Lehmann-Haupt, *New York Times*, October 15, 1984; Jonathan Yardley, *Washington Post*, October 7, 1984; Brian Stonehill, *Los Angeles Times*, November 18, 1984; Jay Cocks, *Time*, October 15, 1984; Anatole Broyard, *New York Times Book Review*, October 28, 1984.

532. "At a time when a wider public": Letter to *The New York Times Book Review,* January 6, 1985.

535. "Anatole assassination": Cassill to RY, November 2, 1984.

536. "I hope you're being corrupted": Broyard to RY, April 12, 1962.

537. "Anatole died as he lived": Lawrence to RY, October 16, 1990, UM-SL.

538. "One day around Christmas": "A Clef," papers of Robert Parker.

540. "a very strange telephone conversation": Prettyman to RY, February 12, 1985.

540. "As you probably know": RY to Prettyman, May 15, 1986.

Chapter Seventeen *No Pain Whatsoever: 1985–1988*

543. "His short-tempered, fragmented ravings": DeWitt Henry, *Arrivals,* unpublished ms., papers of DeWitt Henry.

544. That night at the armory: DeWitt Henry kindly provided me with an audiotape of this event.

545. "depleting [Yates] mentally": Mitch Douglas to Jackie Farber, August 21, 1985, ICM files.

546. "I will respect your wishes": Douglas to Monica Yates, January 13, 1986, ICM files.

547. "Since breaking off with you": RY to Douglas, March 13, 1986, ICM files.

548. "I didn't want to meet him or anybody": Int. Larry David.

549. "Look, I'm an alcoholic": Int. Seymour Epstein.

550. "busy in the best sense": RY to Prettyman, July 21, 1986.

550. "It's a small novel": *RYAW,* 36.

550. "may help take the edge": RY to Prettyman, July 21, 1986.

550. "You are one hell of a good writer": Vonnegut to RY, June 14, 1986.

550. Reviews of *Cold Spring Harbor*: Elaine Kendall, *Los Angeles Times,* September 19, 1986; Howard Frank Mosher, *Washington Post,* September 28, 1986; Michiko Kakutani, *New York Times,* September 27, 1986; Lowry Pei, *New York Times Book Review,* October 5, 1986.

551. "See and show both of these people": "Notes on *The Getaway/Revolutionary Road,*" BU-RY.

553. "stubborn and difficult": RY to Prettyman, July 21, 1986.

553. "the best novel I know . . . writing": "R.V. Cassill's *Clem Anderson,*" *Ploughshares* 14, nos. 2–3 (1988), 189.

554. "Spent most of the day": RY to Barbara Beury, May 17, 1961.

555. "Nine's not so bad, is it?": *RYAW,* 36.

556. "Do you have to go": Raymond Abbott, "Richard Yates," unpublished ms., papers of Raymond Abbott.

556. "He kept up a brilliant": Martin Jukovsky, "Richard Yates—A Meeting," www.channell.com/users/martyj/yates.html.

557. "charm[ing] the audience": "The Friends of Andre Dubus," *Boston Globe*, February 20, 1987.

558. "the world . . . throat": RY to Prettyman, July 21, 1986.

Chapter Eighteen *A Cheer for Realized Men: 1988–1992*

560. postmodern *Brady Bunch*: The two treatment ideas given in the text are to the best of Monica Yates Shapiro's recollection.

560. "I remember Milch well": Vonnegut to RY, July 13, 1988.

560. "That little shit!": Int. Robin Metz.

562. "was the kind of place . . . law": Streitfeld, "Book Report," X15.

565. "Things to Do": Streitfeld, "The Great Unknown," 30.

567. "There's just no whore": Ibid., 28.

567. "Why has surrealism been chosen": Memo from RY to Ned Leavitt, papers of E. Barrett Prettyman Jr.

568. "proposal for a screenplay": found among RY's papers.

569. "huge fans and would like to develop": from William Morris Agency memo to Irene Webb, May 24, 1989.

569. asked the young Don Lee: Int. Don Lee.

569. "want[ed] to give her stability": Int. James Ragan.

570. a "disaster": Int. Noreen McGuire.

572. "Seymour Krim was a champion": RY to Bruce Ricker, September 9, 1989, papers of Bruce Ricker.

573. "return visit": Venant, "*View* staff pays a return visit," *Los Angeles Times*, December 31, 1989.

573. "a labor of love": Int. Susan Braudy.

573. "The book was first given": Susan Braudy to RY, c. December 1989.

574. "I'm delighted . . . 'Easter Parade' ": Woody Allen to Braudy, December 4, 1989.

574. "Woody Allen [had] highly": Bruce Ricker to Dianne Wiest, January 11, 1990.

575. "damn near dead": Int. Kathy Starbuck.

576. "trashed the Strode House": E-mail to author from J. R. Jones.

577. those who begged to differ "were screwed": Int. Dan Childress.

578. "That's the understatement": Quoted in Featherstone, "November 7, 1992," 150.

578. "I wish I had a little girl": Int. Tony Earley.

579. "What's *that* got to do": E-mail to author from J. R. Jones.

579. called one student "a pantywaist": Int. Nikki Schmidt.

580. the *Seinfeld* episode: Larry David kindly provided me with a videotape of this episode.

580. "scalded": Int. J. R. Jones.

580. *"I'd like to kill that son of a bitch!"*: Int. Tim Parrish.

583. "a bomb on wheels": Quoted in Featherstone, "November 7, 1992," 161.

586. "I loved and hated Richard Yates": *RYAW*, 21.

587. The details of RY's adventure in New York were mostly provided by Susan Braudy, RY's daughters, Ned Leavitt, and one or two others.

590. "He couldn't seem to finish it": Lacy, "Remembering Richard Yates," 218.

590. "drop a hint": from Prettyman's personal diary, July 18, 1991.

591. "She's gone and married an electrician": Int. Mark Costello.

591. "Congratulations," he wrote: RY drafted his reply in holograph on Martha's announcement, dated July 11, 1991.

591. He told Prettyman . . . "performance": Prettyman's diary, July 18, 1991.

593. "I feel like taking a gun": Int. Susan Braudy.

594. "vintage Yates": Quoted in Lacy, "Remembering RY," 219.

594. Yates was appalled: Int. Tony Earley.

594. The manuscript of *Uncertain Times* is now part of the Richard Yates Collection at Boston University. An excerpt from the novel was published in *Open City* 3 (1995), 35–71.

600. "He ended the conversation": Letter to author from Loree Rackstraw.

600. "I got smashed last night": Lacy, "Remembering Richard Yates," 220.

600. "Dropping the telephone": *RYAW*, 22.

600. "Richard Yates . . . finest post-war novelist": Scott Bradfield, "Follow the Long and Revolutionary Road," *The Independent*, November 21, 1992, 31.

602. "Sam, I'm dying": *RYAW*, 61.

Epilogue

605. "two inches in the *Times*": E-mail to author from John P. Lowens; Robert Lehrman, *Workshop*, 746.

606. "Dick *let* himself die": Int. Pat Dubus.

606. "forced march": *RYAW*, 13–15.

607. Gaiser . . . startled the crowd: Int. Grace Schulman.

607. "He drank too much": *RYAW*, 61.

608. "[He] managed to squeeze out": Robert Riche, *What Are We Doing in Latin America?* (Sag Harbor, NY: Permanent Press, 1990), 75.

608. "Reading about 'Pritchard Bates' ": RY to Riche, March 3, 1991.

608. "So big deal Bob Parker": Monica Yates to Robert Parker, undated, Parker papers.

609. "painful conclusion": Lawrence to Monica Yates, March 8, 1993.

609. "many important writers": Seymour Lawrence's obituary appeared in the *New York Times*, January 7, 1994, A22.

611. "one of the few good voices": *RYAW*, 31.

611. "the descriptions of things, like a hanger": Edwin Weihe, *Workshop*, 743.

612. "finally the British reading public": Paul Connolly, *The Times* (London), January 27, 2001.

613. "I remember how much you laughed": *RYAW*, 27.

Index

Note: *Titles by Richard Yates are listed in their alphabetical place. Women are listed by their maiden names.*